MW00451845

Lotus Notes
& Domino
Essential Reference

The New Riders Professional Library

Lotus Notes & Domino Essential Reference

Tim Bankes and Dave Hatter

New Riders

201 West 103rd Street, Indianapolis, IN 46290

Lotus Notes & Domino Essential Reference

Tim Bankes and Dave Hatter

Copyright © 1999 by New Riders Publishing

All rights reserved. No part of this book shall be reproduced, stored in a retrieval system, or transmitted by any means, electronic, mechanical, photocopying, recording, or otherwise, without written permission from the publisher. No patent liability is assumed with respect to the use of the information contained herein. Although every precaution has been taken in the preparation of this book, the publisher and author(s) assume no responsibility for errors or omissions. Neither is any liability assumed for damages resulting from the use of the information contained herein.

International Standard Book Number: 0-7357-0007-9

Library of Congress Catalog Card Number: 98-88582

Printed in the United States of America

First Printing: *June, 1999*

01   00   99   3   2   1

Trademarks

All terms mentioned in this book that are known to be trademarks or service marks have been appropriately capitalized. New Riders cannot attest to the accuracy of this information. Use of a term in this book should not be regarded as affecting the validity of any trademark or service mark.

Warning and Disclaimer

Every effort has been made to make this book as complete and as accurate as possible, but no warranty or fitness is implied. The information provided is on an "as is" basis. The authors and the publisher shall have neither liability nor responsibility to any person or entity with respect to any loss or damages arising from the information contained in this book.

Publisher
David Dwyer

Executive Editor
Laurie Petrycki

Development Editor
Jim Chalex

Technical Editors
Lakshmi Annavajhala
Robert Perron
Graham Stalley

Managing Editor
Sarah Kearns

Project Editor
Caroline Wise

Copy Editor
Gayle Johnson

Indexer
Larry Sweazy

Proofreader
Debra Neel

Graphic Conversion Technician
Benjamin Hart

Layout Technician
Cheryl Lynch

About the Authors

Tim Bankes is a partner and principal information systems consultant with Definiti, Inc., a Lotus Premium Business Partner and Microsoft Solutions Provider located in Cincinnati, Ohio. He contributed as a coauthor to *Special Edition Using Lotus Notes and Domino 4.6* (Que, 1998). He has been working with Lotus Notes since version 3.0 and specializes in the design, development, and deployment of comprehensive groupware/workflow solutions. His primary responsibilities include working with clients to redesign and automate business processes and serving as the technical lead of multiple sales force/enterprise management systems.

Bankes is a Certified Lotus Professional as a Principal Application Developer and System Administrator. He holds a B.B.A. in Information Systems, a B.B.A. in Management, and a certificate in International Business from the University of Cincinnati.

If you have questions, comments, or snide remarks, Bankes can be reached at tbankes@definiti.com or timothy@one.net.

Dave Hatter is a principal consultant at Definiti (http://www.definiti.com), a Lotus Premium Business Partner in Cincinnati specializing in Internet, intranet, and extranet solutions. He has nearly 10 years of programming experience and has been working with Lotus Notes/Domino for nearly five years. He is a Certified Lotus Professional Principal Application Developer, a Certified Lotus Professional Principal System Administrator, and a Microsoft Certified Product Specialist. He holds a B.S. in Information Systems from Northern Kentucky University. Hatter has coauthored five other books: *Special Edition Using Lotus Notes 4.0, Special Edition Using Lotus Notes and Domino 4.5, Using Lotus Notes 4.5, Windows NT Server Security Handbook,* and *Lotus Notes and Domino Server 4.6 Unleashed,* all from Macmillan Computer Publishing. Additionally, he has served as a technical editor for the following books: *Sams Teach Yourself Lotus Notes 4.5 in 14 Days, Lotus Notes and Domino 4.5 Developer's Guide, Lotus Notes and Domino Server 4.6 Unleashed,* and *Sams Teach Yourself Lotus Notes 4.6 in 24 Hours,* all from Sams Publishing.

Hatter stays active in his community in a number of ways. He is a city councilman and Webmaster for the city of Fort Wright, Kentucky (http://www.fortwright.com). He is a member of the Telecommunications Board of Northern Kentucky, the 4th District Republican Party Advisory Committee, and the Kenton County Republican Party Executive Committee. He is the Webmaster for the KCRP Web site (http://www.kcrp.org) and the American Legion. He is an instructor of various computer classes through NKU's Community Education program (http://www.nku.edu/~commed). He occasionally writes technology-related articles for several local newspapers. Additionally, he is a regular guest on WKRC's (http://www.wkrc.com) 12 News Saturday program and Intermedia Cable's Northern Kentucky Magazine show. Hatter can be reached via e-mail at dhatter@definiti.com or dhatter@one.net. Alternatively, you can visit his Web page at http://w3.one.net/~dhatter.

About the Reviewers

These reviewers contributed their considerable practical, hands-on expertise to the entire development process for Lotus Notes and Domino. As the book was being written, these individuals reviewed all the material for technical content, organization, and usability.

Lakshmi Annavajhala is a technical writer with Lotus in Westford, Mass. She has been documenting LotusScript classes for Lotus Notes and Domino for two years.

Robert Perron is a documentation architect with Lotus in Cambridge, Mass. He has developed documentation for Lotus Notes and Domino for over five years, with a primary concentration on programmability. He developed the documentation for the LotusScript and Java Notes classes, and he coauthored *60 Minute Guide to LotusScript 3: Programming for Notes 4.*

Graham Stalley has over twenty years of experience as a software developer. He is currently the Senior Notes developer at Boston Financial, a large real estate investment company based in Boston, MA. Graham is president and owner of Virtually Nowhere, a company that provides free resources to Notes developers through the NotesDesign web site, located at http://www.NotesDesign.com. He may be reached at the web site, or via e-mail: Graham@VirtuallyNowhere.com.

Contents

Acknowledgments

Tim Bankes

To my parents, Richard and Judy, who have taught me more than I could ever put into words in a book. The gratitude I have for their love and guidance is often understated, but never forgotten, and is appreciated more than I could ever dream to express.

To my siblings, Liz, Belinda, and Julie, for their eternal love, understanding, and encouragement. They are a constant reminder of what love is and what it means to be part of a loving family.

To Jake and Leah, just for being. I love you both.

To Molly, for being patient and supportive, knowing that eventually this book would be completed. Thanks for understanding when understanding wasn't easy.

To Jim Chalex and Laurie Petrycki. I could never overstate the role they played in conceiving, designing, and completing this book and keeping us on schedule. Thanks for making this a reality. You two are the greatest!

To all my friends at Definiti, and to friends elsewhere for their support.

And to Dave, my coauthor, for making this possible. Without him, none of the pages that follow would exist.

Dave Hatter

This book is dedicated first and foremost to the world's greatest wife and mother, Leslee Hatter, without whose indefatigable patience and support I would never have finished it. Also, to the world's greatest sons, Samuel and Wyatt Hatter, who are the two greatest joys of my life.

I want to thank several other key people who have been instrumental in my life: my father, Jack Hatter, who instilled in me a strong work ethic and took care of me for nine long years as a single parent; my grandfather, George Young, who was my hero, and who is sorely missed; my "second mom," Rose Wezel, who was always there for me when I needed something; and many other family members and friends too numerous to mention. I love you all very much and could not have done it without you!

Additionally, Jim Chalex and Laurie Petrycki at New Riders deserve tremendous thanks, because it was their hard work and perseverance that brought this book to fruition.

Finally, I thank God for giving me the knowledge, ability, and stamina to do this book. It is proof that with God, all things are possible!

Tell Us What You Think!

As the reader of this book, you are our most important critic and commentator. We value your opinion and want to know what we're doing right, what we could do better, what areas you'd like to see us publish in, and any other words of wisdom you're willing to pass our way.

As Executive Editor at New Riders, I welcome your comments. You can fax, email, or write me directly to let me know what you did or didn't like about this book—as well as what we can do to make our books stronger.

Please note that I cannot help you with technical problems related to the topic of this book, and that due to the high volume of mail I receive, I might not be able to reply to every message.

When you write, please be sure to include this book's title and author, as well as your name and phone or fax number. I will carefully review your comments and share them with the author and editors who worked on the book.

Fax: 317-581-4663
Email: newriders@mcp.com
Mail: Laurie Petrycki
              Executive Editor
              New Riders Publishing
              201 West 103rd Street
              Indianapolis, IN 46290 USA

Introduction

This book is primarily designed to serve as an easy-to-use reference that will provide fast answers to common questions about developing Domino applications using LotusScript and/or Java through version 5.0. It is *not* an exhaustive, step-by-step guide on how to develop Notes/Domino applications. We have written it with the experienced developer in mind.

It is broken down into two major sections. The first covers the Domino Object Model as accessed through LotusScript, and the second covers Java. Within each section, you will find all the accessible classes listed in alphabetical order.

Using This Book

In this book, we have employed a consistent flow of information in which the highest "unit" is the specific class under LotusScript or Java and the lowest "unit" is the particular property, method, or event. Therefore, each class can be seen as a separate entity or chapter, and should be thought of as such. The following list details, in order, the way in which we have organized the information within each class:

- ▶ **Class name and version(s)** it is supported under.

- ▶ **Class description.**

- ▶ A partial **object hierarchy** shows the current class in relation to other classes. A single line denotes a normal relationship, and a double line indicates that the class is inherited. Classes in italic are front-end classes. Classes preceded or followed by an ellipsis (…) signify that there are multiple ways to get or set the class.

- ▶ A **jump table** is provided to aid your search. It includes the page numbers for all the relevant properties, methods, and events.

- ▶ **Syntax.** Multiple examples are given, but this section isn't always exhaustive. We usually show the *most common* ways to access the current class.

- ▶ **Parameters.** All the parameters for the current class are listed. For each parameter, you see whether it is required, the data type, and its description. If there are no parameters for the current class, this section is omitted.

- ▶ **Properties.** All the properties for the current class are listed. Properties are listed in alphabetical order and contain the following information, in this order: the property name; Read, Write, or Read/Write; the data type; the syntax (the current property appears in bold); the description; and an example. Not all properties have examples.

- ▶ **Methods.** All the methods for the current class are listed. Methods are listed in alphabetical order and contain the following information in this order: the method name, the syntax (the current method appears in bold), the parameters (including the parameter name, whether it's required or optional, the data type, and the description), the description, and an example. Not all methods have parameters and/or examples.

  Note that some methods in Part II (Java) have multiple syntaxes for one method, with parameters that can be used with these various syntaxes some or all of the time. To avoid confusion, we simply listed all the syntaxes and all the parameters in the order that they can be used (not alphabetically, in some cases).

▶ **Events.** All the events for the current class are listed. Events are listed in alphabetical order and contain information similar to that of a property section.

▶ **Remarks.** This section has general, overarching information pertaining to the usage of the current class.

▶ **Example.** Incorporates many of the aforementioned elements into an example.

Conventions and Typographical Features

The following conventions and abbreviations are used to maximize space and save you time.

Cross-references are used within text to refer you to another class, method, property, or event when we have deemed it useful. (This is not to imply that *all* the classes and so on are referenced in this way.) The cross-reference looks like this (▶ 217) and follows the particular class, property, method, or event.

Version icons appear in the margin when a specific property, method, or event was added *after* the initial release of the class.

Code continuation characters (➡) are inserted into code when a line should not be broken, but we simply ran out of room on the page.

Margin notes help you find a specific property, method, or event quickly as you flip through the book. They have been placed on the outside edges of the page to maximize visibility.

Running heads at the top of the page display the page number and the current property, method, event, or section.

The **data types** used in this book and their abbreviations are listed in the following table:

Data Type	Abbreviation
Array	()
Boolean	T/F
Currency	@
Double	#
Integer	%
Long	&
Object	O.Ref
Single	!
String	$
Variant	?

Some uncommon data types aren't listed here because they are exceptions to the norm and are self-explanatory.

The following typographical conventions are also used:

Convention	Usage
Italic	A class or object. In Part II (Java), objects are listed in their long format for clarity (such as *lotus.domino.ClassName*).
Bold	In syntax, bold shows the current element being described.
`ALL CAPS AND MONOSPACE TEXT`	Designates a constant value in Part I (LotusScript).
`monospace text`	Shows any number of syntactical elements, including Java constants, methods, events, LotusScript properties, and LotusScript code.
File | Open	Menu selections are separated by a vertical bar.

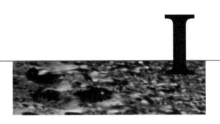

Lotus Notes Front-End Classes

Lotus Notes Back-End Classes

The *Button* object represents clickable design elements that are either buttons, actions, or hotspots. These design elements must be created and stored as design elements within the form, view, navigator, or action bar of the Notes database or within a rich text field of a *NotesDocument* (▸ 127).

LotusScript Syntax

Currently, this object can't be created or modified with LotusScript.

Button Events

Click

Click(Source as Button)

Source	R	O.Ref.

The button, action, or hotspot.

This event is triggered when the button, action, or hotspot is selected. Refer to the Example section for an example of this event.

ObjectExecute

ObjectExecute(Source as Button, Data as Variant)

Source	R	O.Ref.

The button, action, or hotspot.

Data	R	Variant

The handle to the OLE2 dispatch/Automation interface.

This event is triggered by an OLE2 server that is FX/Notesflow-enabled.

Remarks

Buttons, actions, and hotspots are stored within forms, actions are stored within views, buttons and hotspots are stored within navigators, and actions are stored within action bars. The ability to create a *Button* with LotusScript or Java currently isn't supported by Domino/Lotus Notes. Therefore, it doesn't have any properties or methods, although scripts can be used to take action with the firing of events.

Although the *Button* class has no properties or methods and can't be created using LotusScript, this doesn't mean that these objects can't be dynamically created within Domino/Lotus Notes. Therefore, these objects must be either previously created by the database designer and stored with the design of the database and its respective design elements (such as form, view, navigator, or action bar), or created within an open Notes document (in an open Notes document with the UI exposed) and saved within a rich text field of a *NotesDocument* object. However, when stored within a rich text field of a Notes document, the *Button* class is not accessible with LotusScript or Java.

Example

The following example (which would be located in the Click event of this class)
locates a document displayed in the DocumentByUNID view within the
Generic database. Once the document is located, it is opened in the front-end
user interface in edit mode.

```
Dim ns As New NotesSession
Dim nws As New NotesUIWorkspace
Dim ndb As NotesDatabase
Dim nvw As NotesView
Dim uidoc As NotesUIDocument
Dim ndoc As NotesDocument
Dim ndoccurrent As NotesDocument
Dim strDbName As String
Dim strDbType As String
Dim strFName As String
Dim strFpath As String
Dim strServer As String
strDbName ="Generic."
strDbType=Right$(ns.CurrentDatabase.Filepath,3)
strFpath = ns.Currentdatabase.FilePath
strFName=Left$(strFpath,Len(strFpath)-(Len(strFpath)))
strServer = ns.CurrentDatabase.Server
Set ndb = ns.GetDatabase(strServer, strFname & strDbName & strDbtype)
Set ndoccurrent = nws.CurrentDocument.Document
Set nvw = ndb.GetView( "DocumentByUNID" )
Set ndoc =nvw.GetDocumentByKey(Left(currentdoc.tDocumentID(0),15),False)
Set nuid = nws.EditDocument(True, ndoc)
```

The *Field* object represents a field on a form. This should not be confused with a *NotesItem* object stored within a *NotesDocument* (▸ 127). These design elements must be created and stored as design elements within the form design of the Notes database.

LotusScript Syntax

Currently, this object can't be created or modified with LotusScript.

Field Events

Entering

Entering(Source as Field)

Source	R	O.Ref.

The field.

This event is triggered when the cursor's focus is placed on a field on the form, as when the user enters the field in edit mode or the cursor is sent to the field from another design element.

The following example tests the value of the kwStatus field. If the status is currently Active, a message is displayed in the status bar and the cursor is sent to the tContactNumber field, thereby making this file noneditable.

```
Dim nws As New NotesUIWorkspace
If nws.CurrentDocument.IsNewDoc Then
    Call nws.CurrentDocument.SelectAll
Elseif nws.CurrentDocument.Document.kwStatus(0) = "Active" then
    Print "This field can not be edited on active contacts."
    Call nws.CurrentDocument.GotoField("tContactNumber")
End If
```

Exiting

Exiting(Source as Field)

Source	R	O.Ref.

The field.

This event is triggered when the cursor's focus leaves a field on the form, as when the user exits the field in edit mode.

The following example sets the test contained within the field to its proper case value. In other words, the first letter is capitalized. This example could be used in a field that stores a Last Name value.

```
Dim nws As New NotesUIWorkspace
Dim strfld As String
Dim strnewfld As String
strfld = nws.CurrentDocument.Document.tContactLastName(0)
If strfld <> "" Then
    strnewfld = Ucase$( Left$(strfld, 1)) & Right$( strfld ,
    ➡Len(strfld) - 1 )
    nws.CurrentDocument.Document.tContactLastName = strnewfld
End If
```

Remarks

The ability to create a *Field* with script currently isn't supported by Domino/
Lotus Notes. Therefore, it doesn't have any properties or methods through
LotusScript that can be used to take action with the firing of the Entering or
Exiting events. The Entering or Exiting events of the Notes *Field* are commonly
used to check or validate the contents of a field prior to allowing the user to
move to another field or take a subsequent action. For example, the Exiting
event might check the value of the field the user is exiting to ensure that it
falls within a predetermined range or is not invalid. If this event was not used,
another form event would have to be triggered, or the entire form might have
to be refreshed to check one or all values on the form. Using these events allows
the developer to check only specific value(s) after they have been modified.

Another use of the Exiting event might be to toggle certain variables and flags
that hide certain design elements, prompt the user, modify other field values,
force the cursor to exit a field so it can't be edited by the user, and so on. If you
use this event to toggle variables that display or hide other design elements, you
will have to call RefreshHideFormulas and possibly the Refresh method of the
NotesUIDocument class (▶ 36). However, one caveat for using these events
is the order in which they fire. When exiting one field and entering another,
the Entering event of the new field that is acquiring focus will fire prior to the
Exiting event of the field the cursor is leaving. This is important to know so the
form's functionality and usability aren't affected by the unusual firing order of
these events.

Example

The following example could be placed in an editable text field (named tSSN) that
stores a social security number. This code automatically formats the field even if
the user hasn't properly formatted the social security number and prompts the
user if an incorrect number of digits have been entered.

```
Dim nws As New NotesUIWorkspace
Dim strFld As String
Dim intErrorflag As Integer
Dim sreNewfld As String
strFld = Trim$(nws.CurrentDocument.FieldGetText("tSSN"))
If strFld <> "" Then
    If (Len(strFld) = 9) And Isnumeric(strFld) Then
        strNewfld=Left$(strFld,3) & "-"& Mid$(strFld,4,2) & "-"&
        ➥Mid$(strFld,6,4)
        intErrorflag = 2
    Else
        If Len(strFld) <> 11 Then
            intErrorflag = 1
        Elseif Mid$(strFld ,4 , 1) <> "-" Then
            intErrorflag = 1
```

continued >>

continued >>

```
                   Elseif Mid$(strFld ,7 , 1) <> "-" Then
                       intErrorflag = 1
                   Elseif Not Isnumeric(Left$(strFld, 3)) Then
                       intErrorflag = 1
                   Elseif Not Isnumeric(Mid$(strFld, 5, 2)) Then
                       intErrorflag = 1
                   Elseif Not Isnumeric(Mid$(strFld, 8, 4)) Then
                       intErrorflag = 1
                   End If
               End If
           End If
           If intErrorflag = 1 Then
               Msgbox "The proper format for the SSN is: XXX-XX-XXXX" & Chr$(13) & _
               "Correct the format or leave the field empty." & Chr$(13) & _
               "For example: 123-45-6789",      32, "Social Security Number Invalid"
               Call nws.CurrentDocument.GotoField("tSSN")
           Elseif intErrorflag = 2 Then
               Call nws.CurrentDocument.FieldSettext( "tSSN", strNewfld )
           End If
```

4.0 4.1x 4.5x 4.6x 5.0 Navigator

The *Navigator* object represents clickable design elements that are navigator buttons, hotspots, or other navigator clickable objects. These design elements must be created and stored as design elements within the navigator of the Notes database.

LotusScript Syntax

Currently, this object can't be created or modified with LotusScript.

Navigator Events

Click

Click **Click**(Source as Navigator)

Source	R	O.Ref.

The button or hotspot.

This event is triggered when the button or hotspot is selected.

Remarks

The *Navigator* class has no properties or methods, and the ability to create this object with LotusScript or Java is not supported by Domino/Lotus Notes. Therefore, these objects must be previously created by the database designer and stored with the design of the database and its respective navigator.

Example

The following example could be used when developing a multi-database Web application. This code determines the current database location (within the Domino data directory) and uses it to build a valid URL to open a new form. This code replaces all backslashes in the file path with forward slashes and calls the URLOpen function to launch the specified page.

```
Dim ns As New NotesSession
Dim nws As New NotesUIWorkspace
Dim ndb As NotesDatabase
Dim strDbpath As String
Dim strUrl As String
Set ndb = ns.CurrentDatabase
strDbpath = ndb.filepath
Do While Instr(strDbpath,"\")
    strBbpath = Left$(strDbpath, Instr(strDbpath,"\")-1) + "/" + _
    Right$(strDbpath,Len(strDbpath)-Instr(strDbpath,"\"))
Loop
strUrl = "http://webserver/" & strDbpath & "/Main?OpenForm"
Call nws.URLOpen( strUrl )
```

NotesUIDatabase

4.5x   4.6x   5.0

This class represents the *NotesDatabase* object that is currently open in the *NotesUIWorkspace* object. Although several *NotesDatabases* can be opened in other windows, this class represents the *NotesDatabase* that currently has focus.

```
NotesUIDatabase
  ├─ NotesDocumentCollection
  │    └─ NotesDocument
  │         └ . . .
  └─ NotesDatabase
       ├─ NotesACL
       │    └─ NotesACLEntry
       ├─ NotesAgent
       ├─ NotesDocument
       │    └ . . .
       ├─ NotesDocumentCollection
       │    └─ NotesDocument
       ├─ NotesForm
       ├─ NotesOutline
       │    └─ NotesOutlineEntry
       ├─ NotesReplication
       └─ NotesView
            └ . . .
```

LotusScript Syntax

The *NotesUIDatabase* is a front-end object class that can't be created dynamically through script. In order to let you access this object's properties, methods, and events, this object will automatically dimension the *NotesUIDatabase* object in the respective *NotesUIDatabase* event as Source.

NotesUIDatabase Properties

Database   R   O.Ref.

Database

To get: Set ndbNotesDatabase = nuidbNotesUIDatabase.**Database**

Returns a handle on the back-end *NotesDatabase* object of the currently open *NotesUIDatabase* object.

Documents   R   O.Ref.

Documents

To get: Set ndcNotesDocumentCollection = nuidbNotesUIDatabase.**Documents**

Returns a handle on the *NotesDocumentCollection* that the current *NotesUIDatabase* object is running on.

NotesUIDatabase Methods

5.0 OpenNavigator

OpenNavigator

Call nuidbNotesUIDatabase.**OpenNavigator**(strNavigatorName, intFullwindow)

strNavigatorName   Required   %
The name or alias of the navigator to open.

intFullwindow   Optional   T/F
Determines whether the navigator should be displayed full-screen or in the navigator pane with a Notes view. TRUE displays the navigator full-screen. FALSE displays the navigator in the adjustable navigator frame.

This method of the *NotesUIDatabase* class will open the specified navigator and give it focus within the user interface. Because of the nature of the *NotesUIDatabase* class, this method can be used only within one of the *NotesUIDatabase* class events because this is the only way to get a handle on the *NotesUIDatabase* object (automatically dimensioned as Source). Nevertheless, this method enables the developer to programmatically open a navigator (with focus) or to control which navigator is opened (if placed in the PostOpen event of the *NotesUIDatabase*). An example of this is shown in the PostOpen event at the end of this class entry (▶ 16).

OpenView

OpenView

Call nuidbNotesUIDatabase.**OpenView**(strViewname, strKey, intNewinstance)

strViewname   Required $
The name or alias of the view to open.

5.0   strKey   Optional $

The string name of the document value located in the first sorted column to automatically highlight when the view is opened.

5.0   intNewInstance   Optional   T/F

Specifies whether you want the view opened in a new window, regardless of whether a window for that database is already open. TRUE opens the view in a new window. FALSE opens the view without opening a new window.

This method of the *NotesUIDatabase* class opens the specified view and gives it focus within the user interface. Because of the nature of the *NotesUIDatabase* class, this method can be used only within one of the *NotesUIDatabase* class events because this is the only way to get a handle on the *NotesUIDatabase* object (automatically dimensioned as Source). Nevertheless, this method enables the developer to programmatically open a view (with focus) or control which view is opened (if placed in the PostOpen event of the *NotesUIDatabase*). If the view is sorted, Notes will scroll and automatically highlight the document whose value is displayed in the first sorted column in the strViewname. If this strKey isn't specified, no specific document will be highlighted, and the view will open based on the view's design specifications.

When specifying a key, if there are multiple sorted columns in the view, only the first sorted column is used to locate the key document. An example of this is shown in the PostOpen event at the end this chapter.

NotesUIDatabase Events

PostDocumentDelete

PostDocumentDelete(Source as NotesUIDatabase)   PostDocument
Delete

Source   R   O.Ref.

The current database (where this script is located).

This event is triggered immediately after one or more documents are flagged for deletion—by using the deletion button or by flagging documents programmatically, or if a document is cleared or cut from the database. Ironically, although this event is supposed to be triggered after the document has been deleted, this is not always the case. The user access rights are not challenged until after this event is triggered. Therefore, users who are not authorized to delete documents will successfully execute this event even though Notes won't let them actually delete the document! Because of this, you will need to halt the user within the QueryDocumentDelete event or test the user's access programmatically prior to executing the script.

The following example informs users when their actions will be reflected on the server, depending on their current location. This could be helpful for new users or users who rarely delete documents. You will notice that the *NotesUIDatabase* object is already dimensioned as Source and can be accessed directly. Keep in mind that when you create code in this event, the first and last line of this script will be generated automatically.

```
Sub Postdocumentdelete(Source As Notesuidatabase)
    If source.Database.Server = "" Then
        Messagebox "The " & Source.Documents.Count & _
        " marked document(s) will be deleted next replication"
    Else
        Messagebox "The " & Source.Documents.Count & _
        " marked document(s) deleted from " & source.Database.Server
    End If
End Sub
```

5.0 PostDragDrop

PostDragDrop(Source as NotesUIDatabase, EntryName, Continue)

Source	R	O.Ref.

The current database (where this script is located). This parameter is already dimensioned within the event.

EntryName	R	Variant

The name of the object (folder) that the current document was dropped into. This parameter is already dimensioned within the event.

Continue	R/W	T/F

A Boolean value that determines whether to allow the drag and drop to successfully complete. TRUE or -1 allows the drag and drop. FALSE or 0 prevents it. This parameter defaults to TRUE.

This event is triggered after a document is selected and dragged into a folder. The following code snippet informs the user that he has successfully dropped a document into a folder. Keep in mind that when you create code in this event, the first and last line of this script will be generated automatically.

```
Sub Postdragdrop(Source As Notesuiview)
    Dim ns As New NotesSession
    Dim strMessage As String
    strMessage$ = "Thank you " & ns.CommonUserName & _
    ".  This document(s) has been added to the folder."
    Msgbox strMessage$, 32, "Drag and Drop complete..."
End Sub
```

PostOpen

PostOpen(Source as NotesUIDatabase)

Source	R	O.Ref.

The current database (where this script is located). This parameter is already dimensioned within the event.

This event is triggered after the user has been authenticated and it has been determined that he has sufficient access control rights to access the database, and the database has been opened in the user interface (in the front end). However, both the QueryOpen method of *NotesUIView* (▶ 45) and the PostOpen method of *NotesUIView* (▶ 44) are triggered before the PostOpen event of the *NotesUIDatabase* is triggered.

The following example could be placed in the PostOpen event of the mail template file (.ntf) on an organization's mail server. It reminds the users on the first day of each month when they open the database to purge unnecessary messages. While in reality this example would be impractical, it does show how this functionality could be used. Keep in mind that when you create code in this event, the first and last line of this script will be generated automatically.

```
Sub Postopen(Source As Notesuidatabase)
    Dim intCurrentDay As Integer
    intCurrentDay = Day(Today)
    If intCurrentDay = 1 Then
        Msgbox "Please purge old E-Mail messages.", 32, "Reminder..."
    End If
End Sub
```

QueryClose

QueryClose(Source as NotesUIDatabase, Continue as Variant)

Source   R   O.Ref.

The current database (where this script is located). This parameter is already dimensioned within the event.

Continue   R/W   T/F

Indicates whether this event should allow the database to be closed. TRUE allows the database to close. FALSE keeps it from closing.

QueryClose is triggered before the database is closed. This event can be used to perform housekeeping routines or to validate specific parameters prior to allowing the database to successfully close.

The following example demonstrates one such functional use of this event. This code checks to see if there are any unprocessed documents in the database when the user is closing the database. In addition, it informs the user that there are unprocessed documents. It then prompts the user to either keep the database open so that the documents can be acted upon, or allow the database to close, regardless. Keep in mind that when you create code in this event, the first and last line of this script will be generated automatically.

```
Sub Queryclose(Source As Notesuidatabase, Continue As Variant)
    Dim ndbCurrent As NotesDatabase
    Dim ndcCollection As NotesDocumentCollection
    Set ndbCurrent = source.Database
    Set ndcCollection = ndbCurrent.UnprocessedDocuments
    If ndcCollection.Count > 0 Then
        Msgbox "You have " & Str$(ndcCollection.Count) & " unprocessed docs"
    End If
End Sub
```

QueryDocumentDelete

QueryDocumentDelete(Source as NotesUIDatabase, Continue as Variant)

Source   R   O.Ref.

The current database (where this script is located). This parameter is already dimensioned within the event.

Continue   R/W   T/F

Indicates whether this event should let the document be deleted. TRUE allows the database to close. FALSE keeps it from closing.

This event is triggered before a document (or a collection of selected documents) is flagged for deletion or cleared/cut from a *Notes View*.

The following example demonstrates one practical use of this event. This code checks to see whether the user who is flagging the document for deletion is the same person who created the document. If the current user is not the author, the system prompts the user, warning him that he is deleting a document created by another user. This code could be modified to not allow deletions (by setting Continue to FALSE) or to take some other action based on this scenario. Keep in mind that when you create code in this event, the first and last line of this script will be generated automatically.

```
Sub Querydocumentdelete(Source As Notesuidatabase, Continue As Variant)
    Dim ns As New NotesSession
    Dim ndocCurrent As NotesDocument
    Dim strAuthor As String
    Dim strCurrentUser As String
    strCurrentUser = ns.UserName
    Dim ndccollection As NotesDocumentCollection
    Set ndccollection = source.Documents
    Set ndocCurrent = ndccollection.GetFirstDocument
    strAuthor = ndocCurrent.Authors(0)
    If strAuthor <> strCurrentUser$ Then
        If Msgbox("You're not the author, are you sure?",36) <> 6 Then
            Print "The document will not be deleted."
            Continue = False
        End If
    End If
End Sub
```

QueryDocumentUnDelete

QueryDocument
UnDelete

QueryDocumentUnDelete(Source as NotesUIDatabase, Continue as Variant)

Source   R   O.Ref.
The current database (where this script is located). This parameter is already
dimensioned within the event.

Continue   R/W   T/F
Indicates whether this event should allow the document to be deleted. TRUE allows the
database to close. FALSE keeps it from closing.

This event is triggered before the deletion flag is removed from a document (or a
collection of selected documents).

5.0 QueryDragandDrop

Query
DragandDrop

QueryDragandDrop(Source as NotesUIDatabase, EntryName, Continue)

Source   R   O.Ref.
The current database (where this script is located). This parameter is already
dimensioned within the event.

EntryName   R   Variant
The name of the object (folder) that the current document was dropped into. This
parameter is already dimensioned within the event.

Continue   R/W   T/F
This value determines whether to allow the drag and drop to successfully complete. TRUE
or -1 allows the drag and drop. FALSE or 0 prevents it. This parameter defaults to TRUE.

This event is triggered immediately before documents are dropped into a folder.

Remarks

When you're accessing the properties, methods, and events of the *NotesUIDatabase* object, a handle to the *NotesUIDatabase* is already dimensioned as source. In addition, the code (and syntax) that is used in this event to establish the event and its required default parameters is created for you.

In addition, there are certain scenarios when some of the events won't fire, although you would think that they are occurring logically. For example, the PostOpen event will fire when the database is being opened from a database link or a view link. However, if a document is opened in this database from another database using a document link, the PostOpen event won't fire. This event will also fire if this database is being opened programmatically using the Notes Macro language or LotusScript as long as the database is being opened and rendered to the user interface. Finally, the PostOpen event will fire only once as long as the database is open in one of the currently active windows, even if the windows are open in the background.

Example

The following example shows how you can use the OpenNavigator and OpenView method with the PostOpen event of the *NotesUIDatabase* to control which navigator and view are opened to the user—depending on the user's access control to the database. If the user has manager access, an administration navigator and the respective default administration view are opened. If the user is a designer, the database is opened to the default view and view navigation, without using a customized navigator. For all other users, the database is opened with the common navigator and view. This functionality can be used to give the user access to sensitive information, incorporating filtered relevancy of enterprise information to the user. This is especially helpful since elements stored in the *NotesNavigator* object can't use hide-when functions.

```
Sub Postopen(Source As Notesuidatabase)
    Dim ns As New NotesSession
    Dim ndb As NotesDatabase
    Dim nacl As NotesACL
    Dim naclEnter As NotesACLEntry
    Set ndb = source.Database
    Set nacl = ndb.ACL
    Set nacleEntry = acl.GetEntry( ns.UserName )
    Print nacleEntry.Level
    If nacleEntry.Level = ACLLEVEL_MANAGER Then
        Call source.OpenView("ManagerView")
        Call source.OpenNavigator("ManagerNavigator", True)
    Elseif nacleEntry.Level = ACLLEVEL_DESIGNER Then
        Call source.OpenView("DesignerView")
        'We will use the Notes default navigator here...
    Else
        Call source.OpenView("StandardView")
        Call source.OpenNavigator("StandardNavigator", True)
    End If
End Sub
```

NotesUIDocument

4.0 4.1x 4.5x 4.6x 5.0

The *NotesUIDocument* class represents the *NotesDocument* that is currently open and being displayed in the user interface. While several *NotesDocuments* can be opened in other windows, this class represents the *NotesDocument* that currently has focus and is, therefore, the *NotesUIDocument*.

NotesUIWorkspace
└ NotesUIDocument

continued >>

LotusScript Syntax

You can establish a handle on the *NotesUIDocument* object by either referencing an existing *NotesDocument* object or creating a new *NotesDocument* object (▶ 127). You can access an existing *NotesDocument* by using one of the following methods:

Reference the `CurrentDocument` property of the *NotesUIWorkspace* (▶ 48).

Reference the `EditDocument` method of the *NotesUIWorkspace* (▶ 52).

Use one of the *NotesUIDocument* events, referencing the `source` parameter automatically dimensioned within the event, thus establishing a handle on the current *NotesUIDocument* object being used. (You'll read more about this later in this chapter.)

Create a new *NotesDocument* by using the `ComposeDocument` method of the *NotesUIWorkspace* (▶ 49).

NotesUIDocument Properties

AutoReload   R/W   T/F

```
To set: nuidNotesUIDocument.AutoReload = intReload
To get: intReload = nuidNotesUIDocument.AutoReload
```
AutoReload

This property indicates whether the current front-end *NotesUIDocument* should automatically be refreshed when changes are made to the back-end *NotesDocument*. In other words, if the *NotesUIDocument* object was created by referencing an existing *NotesDocument* and that *NotesDocument* is modified (potentially by a button on the form), this property indicates whether these changes are immediately rendered to the user and the *NotesUIDocument* object in memory. `TRUE` indicates that the document should automatically be reloaded when the back-end document is modified. `FALSE` indicates that it should not. However, this property applies only when the handle on the back-end *NotesDocument* was accessed via the `Document` property of the *NotesUIDocument*. If the handle to the *NotesDocument* was established using the `Document` property, changes will immediately appear to the user interface and in memory. This property is useful when the *NotesDocument* handle was established using other methods (such as locating the document in a *NotesDocumentCollection* or by using `GetDocumentByKey` or `GetDocumentByUNID`). Although this ensures that the user and the *NotesUIDocument* object are accessing up-to-date information, this setting has a negative impact on performance and should be enabled only when necessary. However, the current *NotesUIDocument* can also be reloaded by calling the `Reload` method, also contained by the *NotesUIDocument* (▶ 36).

Because of the robust properties of *NotesRichTextItems*, this property doesn't apply to the contents of the *NotesRichTextItem*. In other words, modifications made to *NotesRichTextItems* on the back-end *NotesDocument* can't be reloaded and rendered to the user interface, even if the `Reload` method is called. Therefore, the document must be closed and reopened in order for the modifications to *NotesRichTextItems* to be recognized. Similarly, if the respective *NotesDocument* is modified by another user or an agent, the document must be closed and reopened. The important distinction here is that when a *NotesDocument* is opened by a user, he is essentially looking at a snapshot of the back-end data.

Any changes that are made to the current *NotesUIDocument* are not immediately modified on the server or file system until the document is saved or submitted. Once the document is saved, the server verifies against replication or save conflicts and takes any necessary action. However, only if the user modifies the back-end *NotesDocument* through its respective *NotesUIDocument* is he allowed to update the back-end data.

CurrentField   R $

CurrentField   To get: strFieldname = nuidNotesUIDocument.**CurrentField**

This property returns the name of the field that has focus in the user interface (the field that the cursor is in). Logically, this field returns NULL if the none of the fields has focus or if the *NotesUIDocument* is not currently in edit mode.

DialogBoxCanceled   R   T/F

DialogBox   To get: intDbCanceled = nuidNotesUIDocument.**DialogBoxCanceled**
Canceled

This property indicates whether the user has clicked Cancel on the previously called dialog box. TRUE indicates that the user clicked Cancel in the dialog box, and FALSE indicates that he clicked OK. A dialog box can be created using the @Dialogbox function of the Lotus Notes formula language. This method is applicable only when it's used in the QueryClose event of the *NotesUIDocument* of the dialog box, described later in this chapter (▶ 38). This is important, because when dialog boxes are called, the information changed within the dialog box may or may not affect the field values contained in the parent *NotesUIDocument* that called the dialog box. It is often necessary to recognize whether the user canceled the dialog box or clicked OK. Prior to the existence of this property, the developer was required to write to a profile document or to the .ini file in order to trap this event.

Document   R   O.Ref.

Document   To get: Set ndocNotesDocument = nuidNotesUIDocument.**Document**

This property returns a handle to the back-end *NotesDocument* currently being rendered to the front-end *NotesUIDocument*. If the back-end document is accessed using this method, any modifications are immediately made in memory and displayed to the user interface. If the *NotesDocument* handle was established using other methods (such as locating the document in a *NotesDocumentCollection* or by using GetDocumentByKey or GetDocumentByUNID), the current *NotesUIDocument* can also be reloaded by calling the Reload method, also contained by the *NotesUIDocument* (▶ 36).

Because of the robust properties of *NotesRichTextItems,* modifications made to the back-end *NotesDocument* are not displayed to the front-end *NotesUIDocument.* Similarly, the *NotesUIDocument* can't be reloaded and rendered to the user interface, even if the Reload method is called. Therefore, the document must be closed and reopened in order for the modifications to the *NotesRichTextItems* to be recognized.

The following example uses the Document property in conjunction with the extended syntax to move the current document to a folder based on a field value stored on the form. This code is placed in the QuerySave event of the *NotesUIDocument* to categorize documents based on their status. This example would be well-suited for a sales tracking/automation tool.

```
Sub Querysave(Source As Notesuidocument, Continue As Variant)
If Not source.IsNewDoc Then
    Select Case source.Document.Status(0)
    Case "Hot Suspects"
        Call source.Document.PutInFolder("Hot Suspects")
```

```
      Case "In Negotiation"
         Call source.Document.PutInFolder("In Negotiation")
      Case "Active"
         Call source.Document.PutInFolder("Active")
      Case "Lead"
         Call source.Document.PutInFolder("Lead")
      Case "Prospect"
         Call source.Document.PutInFolder("Prospect")
      Case "Suspect"
         Call source.Document.PutInFolder("Suspect")
      Case Else
         Call source.Document.PutInFolder("n/a")
      End Select
   End If
   End Sub
```

EditMode   R/W   T/F

```
To set: nuidNotesUIDocument.EditMode = intEditmode
To get: intEditMode = nuidNotesUIDocument.EditMode
```
EditMode

This property indicates whether the current document is in edit mode or read mode. This is TRUE if the document is in edit mode. FALSE indicates that the document is in read mode.

A common use of this method is to determine the current mode of the *NotesUIDocument* so that the appropriate action can be taken. This code tests the document's current mode. If the document isn't in edit mode, it is placed in edit mode. Then it modifies the contents of the tmessage field on the form.

```
Dim nws As New NotesUIWorkspace
Dim nuidoc As NotesUIDocument
Set nuidoc = nws.CurrentDocument
If Not nuidoc.EditMode Then
   nuidoc.EditMode = True
End If
nuidoc.Document.tMessage = "Document is ready to be edited..."
Call nuidoc.GotoField("tMessage")
```

FieldHelp   R/W   T/F

```
To set: nuidNotesUIDocument.FieldHelp = intFieldhelp
To get: intFieldhelp = nuidNotesUIDocument.FieldHelp
```
FieldHelp

This property indicates whether the field help display has been enabled. TRUE indicates that the field help has been enabled. FALSE indicates that it has been disabled. Because field help is required only when the document is being edited, this property can be modified only when the document is in edit mode. The user can override this property manually using the pull-down menu options from the Notes client.

HiddenChars   R/W   T/F

```
To set: nuidNotesUIDocument.HiddenChars = intHiddenChars
To get: intHiddenChars = nuidNotesUIDocument.HiddenChars
```
HiddenChars

This property indicates whether the hidden characters located in a rich text field in the current document should be displayed. TRUE displays the hidden characters. FALSE hides the hidden characters from the user. Hidden characters are comprised of carriage returns, newline characters, tabs, and so on. This property can be set only when the current document is in edit mode. The user can override this property manually using the pull-down menu options from the Notes client.

HorzScrollBar   R/W   T/F

HorzScrollBar   To set: nuidNotesUIDocument.**HorzScrollBar** = intHorzbar
To get: intHorzbar = nuidNotesUIDocument.**HorzScrollBar**

This property indicates whether the horizontal scroll bar should automatically be displayed at the bottom of the screen. TRUE displays the horizontal scroll bar; FALSE suppresses it. The user can override this property manually using the pull-down menu options from the Notes client.

In some applications you might want to suppress the horizontal scroll bar and the field help when a form is opened if they aren't being used. The following code could be placed in the form's PostOpen event to ensure that these two options are suppressed when the documents are opened.

```
Sub Queryopen(Source As Notesuidocument, Mode As Integer, Isnewdoc As
➥Variant, Continue As Variant)
    Source.HorzScrollBar = False
    Source.FieldHelp = False
End Sub
```

InPreviewPane   R   T/F

InPreviewPane   To get: intInPreviewpane = nuidNotesUIDocument.**InPreviewPane**

This property indicates whether the current document is being accessed from the preview pane. TRUE indicates that the document is being accessed using the preview pane from within a *NotesView*. FALSE indicates that the document was explicitly opened and is being rendered in the user interface as the *NotesUIDocument*. This might be useful when you want to hide or reveal certain buttons, text, or objects if the document is being previewed.

IsNewDoc   R   T/F

IsNewDoc   To get: intIsnewdoc = nuidNotesUIDocument.**IsNewDoc**

This property indicates whether the document is a newly created document that hasn't yet been saved. TRUE indicates that the document hasn't yet been saved. FALSE indicates that it has already been saved. Once the document is saved, it is no longer considered a new document, even if it was created previously and the window hasn't yet been closed.

The following example tests to see if the current *NotesDocument* being saved is a new document. If it is, and the user is currently working off the server, a unique number between one and one million is generated. This code doesn't include error checking to ensure that the number hasn't been generated for another document. This would have to be done before this code could be used in a real-world scenario.

```
Sub Querysave(Source As Notesuidocument, Continue As Variant)
    Dim ns As New NotesSession
    If source.document.strTitle(0) = "" Then
        Msgbox ¦You must enter a value for the "Title" prior to saving¦
        Continue = False
        Exit Sub
    End If
    If source.IsNewDoc Then
        If ns.CurrentDatabase.Server <> "" Then
            Msgbox "You must be connected to the server to generate number."
        Else
            Randomize
            source.Document.intUniqueNumber = Int(Rnd() * 1000000)
        End If
    End If
End Sub
```

PreviewDocLink   R/W   T/F

```
To set: nuidNotesUIDocument.PreviewDocLink = intPrevdoclink
To get: intPrevdoclink = nuidNotesUIDocument.PreviewDocLink
```
PreviewDocLink

This property indicates whether the preview pane is being displayed for the current document link (doclink). TRUE indicates that the doclink's preview pane is being displayed. FALSE indicates that it isn't being displayed. Keep in mind that if this property is set to TRUE and no doclink exists for the current document, the preview pane will display a message saying that the user should click on a doclink. The user can override this property manually using the pull-down menu options from the Notes client.

PreviewParentDoc   R/W   T/F

```
To set: nuidNotesUIDocument.PreviewParentDoc = intPreview
To get: intPreview = nuidNotesUIDocument.PreviewParentDoc
```
PreviewParent Doc

This property indicates that the preview pane is being displayed for the document link (doclink) of the parent document. TRUE indicates that the parent document's preview pane is being displayed. FALSE indicates that it is not being displayed. The user can override this property manually using the pull-down menu options from the Notes client.

Ruler   R/W   T/F

```
To set: nuidNotesUIDocument.Ruler = intRuler
To get: intRuler = nuidNotesUIDocument.Ruler
```
Ruler

This property indicates whether the ruler should be displayed at the top of the document. TRUE indicates that it should be displayed. FALSE indicates that it should not. This property can be set only when the document is in edit mode. The user can override this property manually using the pull-down menu options from the Notes client.

WindowTitle   R $

```
To get: strWindowTitle = nuidNotesUIDocument.WindowTitle
```
WindowTitle

This property represents the title being displayed in the title bar of the current window.

NotesUIDocument Methods

Categorize

```
Call nuidNotesUIDocument.Categorize(strName)
```
Categorize

strName   Optional $

The name of the category.

This method categorizes a document with the strName passed as a parameter. If no value is passed for the strName, the user is prompted to select a category from the Categorize dialog box. This method is available only for documents that have already been saved. It displays the error message Cannot categorize unsaved document when called from new documents. This can be tested using the IsNewDoc property of the *NotesUIDocument* (▶ 26).

Clear

```
Call nuidNotesUIDocument.Clear
```
Clear

This method deletes from the document the text, graphic, or object that is currently selected in an editable field. Because the item(s) to be deleted must be selected before this method is called, the document must be in edit mode. This method is synonymous with pressing the Delete key. In other words, the information is not copied to the clipboard. If you want the information to be copied to the clipboard, use the `Cut` method of the *NotesUIDocument* (▶ 28).

Close

Close   `Call nuidNotesUIDocument.`**`Close`**

This method closes the *NotesUIDocument* as if the user selected File | Close or clicked on the close window tab for the current window. In addition, if the document has been edited, the user will be prompted to save changes before the window is closed.

CollapseAllSections

CollapseAll   `Call nuidNotesUIDocument.`**`CollapseAllSections`**
Sections
This method collapses all the sections in the current document. All the sections in the document are collapsed regardless of whether they are part of the form design or are contained in rich text fields. In addition, all the sections will collapse regardless of their respective expand/collapse settings.

Copy

Copy   `Call nuidNotesUIDocument.`**`Copy`**

This method copies the currently selected text, graphics, or other object to the clipboard. Any data that previously existed on the clipboard is overwritten.

CreateObject

CreateObject   `To set: variant = nuidNotesUIDocument.`**`CreateObject`** `= (strName, strType,`
➥`strFilepath)`

strName	Optional	$
The name of the object.		
strType	Optional	$
The type of object to create using the OLE registry.		
strFilepath	Optional	$
The path and filename of the source document used to create the object.		

The method returns a handle to an OLE object. This method creates an OLE object in the rich text field that currently has focus, so the document must be in edit mode and the cursor must be located in a rich text field. When calling this method, either `strType` or `strFilepath` can be specified, but not both. If you pass the `strFilepath` parameter, the object is created in the rich text field, but a handle on the object is not established. Therefore, you must explicitly call the `GetObject` method of the *NotesUIDocument* in order to establish a handle on the object in memory (▶ 33). If no parameters are passed when calling this method, the user is prompted with the Create Object dialog box. This method isn't currently supported under OS/2, UNIX, or Macintosh.

Cut

Cut   `Call nuidNotesUIDocument.`**`Cut`**

This method cuts the current selection (text, graphics, or another object) from the document and places its contents on the clipboard. The document must be in edit mode. Any previous data on the clipboard is overwritten.

DeleteDocument

`Call nuidNotesUIDocument.`**`DeleteDocument`**

This method closes the current document (if open) and marks it for deletion. This method is similar to highlighting the document in a *NotesUIView* and pressing the Delete key. The document isn't actually deleted when this method is called; it is only flagged for deletion. The actual deletion stub is created when the view is refreshed or the *NotesDatabase* is closed. Once this method has been called, the corresponding *NotesUIDocument* object is no longer available. (Attempting to access the *NotesUIDocument* creates an error that reads `NotesUIDocumentWnd is no longer valid`.) If the current *NotesDocument* has already been marked for deletion, no action is taken, and the document remains marked for deletion (it doesn't toggle the deletion mark as it would from a *NotesUIView*). If this method is called from within a document that is currently being edited, the error `Document command is not available` is displayed.

DeselectAll

`Call nuidNotesUIDocument.`**`DeselectAll`**

This method deselects any existing selections in the current document. If nothing in the current document is selected, the `Document command is not available` error is generated.

ExpandAllSections

`Call nuidNotesUIDocument.`**`ExpandAllSections`**

This method expands all the sections in the current document. All the sections in the document are expanded, regardless of whether they are part of the form design or contained in rich text fields. In addition, all the sections will expand, regardless of their respective expand/collapse settings.

FieldAppendText

`Call nuidNotesUIDocument.`**`FieldAppendText`**`(strFieldname, strText)`

| strFieldname | Required | $ |

The name of the field to append the text to. Use an empty string (`""`) to append text to the current field.

| strText | Required | $ |

The value appended to the text field.

This method appends a text string to a field on the specified *NotesDocument*. The existing field values are preserved since the additional text is appended to the end of the field, after the last character. In order to call this method, the field being modified must be editable, and the document must be in edit mode, or an error is generated that reads `You must be in edit mode to change the value of a field`. If the `strFieldname` doesn't already exist in the *NotesDocument,* an error is generated that says `Cannot locate field definition for fieldname$`.

FieldClear

`Call nuidNotesUIDocument.`**`FieldClear`**`(strFieldname)`

| strFieldname | Optional | $ |

The name of the field to clear.

This method clears the contents of the specified field in the *NotesUIDocument*. If no `strFieldname` is specified, the current field contents are cleared. The field must be editable, and the document must be in edit mode, or an error is generated.

FieldContains

```
intFieldcontains = nuidNotesUIDocument.FieldContains(strFieldname,
➥strTextvalue)
```

strFieldname	Optional	$

The name of the field to check (search). Use an empty string (" ") to check the current field.

strTextvalue	Optional	$

The string value to check (search) for.

This method checks (or searches) for the existence of a string value in a field on the currently open document. If the strTextvalue is located in the strFieldname, this method returns TRUE; otherwise, FALSE is returned. This method doesn't perform a full-text search against the field, but it essentially accomplishes the same function by attempting to locate a specified string within the field value.

FieldGetText

```
strTextvalue = nuidNotesUIDocument.FieldGetText(strFieldname)
```

strFieldname	Optional	$

The field whose contents are retrieved. If an empty string is passed (" "), the contents of the current field are returned.

This method returns the string contents of the specified field. If the values contained in the specified field are not of type STRING, they are automatically converted to STRING when the method is executed. This method will run if the document is in either read or edit mode. If the field being examined is a multivalue field, all of its contents are returned as a text string, separated by the field's multivalue separator for display purposes.

FieldSetText

```
Call nuidNotesUIDocument.FieldSetText(strFieldname, strTextvalue)
```

strFieldname	Required	$

The name of the field whose contents are to be modified. Use an empty string (" ") to modify the current field.

strTextvalue	Required	$

The string value to assign to the field.

This method sets the value of the specified field on the document. Any existing value contained in the field is overwritten. If the value type is not text, it is automatically converted to its appropriate data type when the document is saved. The specified field must be editable, and the document must be in edit mode, or an error is generated that says You must be in edit mode to change the value of a field.

FindFreeTimeDialog

```
intRetVal = nuidNotesUIDocument.FindFreeTimeDialog(strReqPeopleItems,
➥strOptPeopleItems, strReqRoomsItems, strOptRoomItems,
➥strReqResourceItems, strOptResourceItems, strRemovedPeopleItems,
➥strStartDateItem, strEndDateItem)
```

strReqPeopleItems	Required	$

The name of the field that contains the names of required people to use in the meeting free time search.

strOptPeopleItems   Required $

The name of the field that contains the names of people to use in the meeting free time search whose attendance is optional.

strReqRoomsItems   Required $

The name of the field that contains the names of required rooms to use in the meeting free time search.

strOptRoomItems   Required $

The name of the field that contains the names of optional rooms to use in the meeting free time search.

strReqResourceItems   Required $

The name of the field that contains the names of required resources to use in the meeting free time search.

strOptResourceItems   Required $

The name of the field that contains the names of optional resources to use in the meeting free time search.

strRemovedPeopleItems   Required $

The name of the field that contains the names of people to remove from the attendance list.

strStartDateItem   Required $

The name of the field that contains the meeting's start time.

strEndDateItem   Required $

The name of the field that contains the meeting's end time. This value must be later than `strStartDateItem`.

This method displays the Find Free Time dialog box and returns TRUE if the user clicks OK or FALSE if the user clicks Cancel. Although all the parameters are required, they don't all need to have a value. You can use NULL ("") for parameters that aren't required for your free time search.

5.0 FindFreeTimeDialogEx

```
intRetVal = nuidNotesUIDocument.FindFreeTimeDialogEx(strReqPeopleItems,
➥strOptPeopleItems, strReqRoomsItems,
➥strOptRoomItems,strReqResourceItems, strOptResourceItems,
➥strRemovedPeopleItems,strStartDateItem, strEndDateItem)
```

FindFreeTime
DialogEx

---

strReqPeopleItems   Required $

The name of the field that contains the names of required people to use in the meeting free time search.

strOptPeopleItems   Required $

The name of the field that contains the names of people to use in the meeting free time search whose attendance is optional.

strReqRoomsItems   Required $

The name of the field that contains the names of required rooms to use in the meeting free time search.

strOptRoomItems   Required $

The name of the field that contains the names of optional rooms to use in the meeting free time search.

strReqResourceItems   Required $

The name of the field that contains the names of required resources to use in the meeting free time search.

strOptResourceItems   Required $

The name of the field that contains the names of optional resources to use in the meeting free time search.

strRemovedPeopleItems   Required $

The name of the field that contains the names of people to remove from the attendance list.

strStartDateItem   Required $

The name of the field that contains the meeting's start time.

strEndDateItem   Required $

The name of the field that contains the meeting's end time. This value must be later than `strStartDateItem`.

This method displays the Find Free Time dialog box and returns `TRUE` if the user clicks OK or `FALSE` if the user clicks Cancel. Although all the parameters are required, they don't all need to have a value. You can use `NULL` (`""`) for parameters that aren't required for your free time search.

This method works like the `FindFreeTimeDialog` method, except that all the parameters are string arrays (except for `strStartDateItem` and `strEndDateItem`).

5.0 FindString

FindString

```
Call NotesUIDocument.FindString(strText, intWholeword, intBackwards,
  ➡intCaseSensitive, intWildCards, intAccentSensitive, intSearchDocument,
  ➡intFindNext, intWrapAround, intIgnoreDiacritics)
```

---

strText   Required $

The text string to locate.

intWholeword   Optional   T/F

Determines whether the search should match on the entire word.

intBackwards   Optional   T/F

Determines whether the search should search backward. Otherwise, the search will search forward (the default).

intCaseSensitive   Optional   T/F

Determines whether the search should be case-sensitive.

IntWildCards   Optional   T/F

Determines whether wildcards should be used in the search.

intAccentSensitive   Optional   T/F

Determines whether the search should be accent-sensitive.

intSearchDocument   Optional   T/F

Determines whether the search should search the document contents.

intFindNext   Optional   T/F

Determines whether the search should find the next match.

intWrapAround   Optional   T/F
Determines whether the search should use word wrap-arounds.

intIgnoreDiacritics   Optional   T/F
Determines whether the search should utilize or ignore diacritics.

This method finds the specified text in the current user interface, such as when a
NotesView is being displayed and the user types text or selects Edit | Find/Replace...
or Edit | Find Next....

Forward

```
Call nuidNotesUIDocument.Forward
```
Forward

This method forwards the current document as the body of a new mail memo.
Essentially, a new memo is created, and the contents of the body are prepopulated
with the current document. The memo can still be modified as a normal mail memo
(assigning the addressees, adding content, and so on). This method will work if the
current document is in read or edit mode. Any changes to the current document must
be saved in order to be included when the document is forwarded.

GetObject

```
Set varhandle = nuidNotesUIDocument.GetObject(strName)
```
GetObject

This method returns a handle (as a variant) to the OLE object specified by the
`strName` parameter. If the object specified is not found, the method returns nothing.
To create an object, you can also use the `CreateObject` method of *NotesUIDocument*
(▶ 28) in order to establish a handle on the object in memory. This method isn't
currently supported under OS/2, UNIX, or Macintosh.

5.0 GetSelectedText

```
strtext = nuidNotesUIDocument.getSelectedText(strFieldname)
```
GetSelectedText

strFieldname   Optional $
The name of the field that contains the selected text.

This method returns the string value of the text that is currently selected or highlighted in the user interface.

GotoBottom

```
Call nuidNotesUIDocument.GotoBottom
```
GotoBottom

This method places the focus in the user interface on the last object in the current form.
Specifically, the cursor is placed in the last editable field or the last button on a document. Because the focus of the cursor on the current document is being manipulated,
this method works only if the current document is in edit mode.

GotoField

```
Call nuidNotesUIDocument.GotoField(strFieldname)
```
GotoField

strFieldname   Optional $
The name of the field on which to place focus.

This method places the focus in the user interface in an editable field specified in the
`strFieldname` parameter. Because the focus of the cursor on the current document is
being manipulated, this method works only if the current document is in edit mode. A
handy use of this method is within the `PostOpen` of the *NotesUIDocument* to position
the cursor in a specific field, possibly based on certain field values or other criteria.

GotoNextField

`Call nuidNotesUIDocument.`**`GotoNextField`**

This method places the focus in the user interface on the next editable field on the current document. The position of the next field is determined by tab order (if required—as in layout regions) or by the physical layout of the field. In the latter case, the next field is located by searching to the right of the current field and then below the current field. Because the focus of the cursor on the current document is being manipulated, this method works only if the current document is in edit mode.

GotoPrevField

`Call nuidNotesUIDocument.`**`GotoPrevField`**

This method places the focus in the user interface on the previous editable field on the current document. The position of the previous field is determined by tab order (if required—as in layout regions) or by the physical layout of the field. In the latter case, the previous field is located by searching to the left of the current field and then above the current field. Because the focus of the cursor on the current document is being manipulated, this method works only if the current document is in edit mode.

GotoTop

`Call nuidNotesUIDocument.`**`GotoTop`**

This method places the focus in the user interface on the first object in the current form. Specifically, the cursor is placed in the first editable field or the first button on a document. Because the focus of the cursor on the current document is being manipulated, this method works only if the current document is in edit mode.

5.0 Import

`Call nuidNotesUIDocument.`**`Import`**`(strFilter, strFilename)`

strFilter	Optional	$
The type of filter to use for the import.		

strFilename	Optional	$
The name of the file to import.		

This method imports a file into a rich text field contained in the current form. If no filter is specified when calling this method, the Open File dialog box will prompt the user to select from the currently selected filters. Prior to calling this method, the focus of the cursor must be in a rich text field. If the cursor is not located in a rich text field, an error is generated that reads `Document command is not available`. Therefore, you might need to place the focus of the cursor in a rich text field prior to calling this method. This method is available only when the document is in edit mode.

InsertText

`Call nuidNotesUIDocument.`**`InsertText`**`(strTextvalue)`

strTextvalue	Required	$
The string to insert into the current field.		

This method inserts a text value into the field that currently has focus in the *NotesUIDocument* (where the cursor is currently waiting). This method is available only when the document is in edit mode.

NavBarSetText

```
Call nuidNotesUIDocument.NavBarSetText(strUrltext, strWindowtitle)
```

strUrltext	Required	$

The URL text string.

strWindowtitle	Required	$

The window title.

This method sets text for the URL navigation bar when using an Internet Explorer browser.

NavBarSpinnerStart

```
Call nuidNotesUIDocument.NavBarSpinnerStart
```

This method starts the URL navigation spinner when you're using the Internet Explorer browser.

NavBarSpinnerStop

```
Call nuidNotesUIDocument.NavBarSpinnerStop
```

This method stops the URL navigation spinner when you're using the Internet Explorer browser.

Paste

```
Call nuidNotesUIDocument.Paste
```

This method pastes the contents of the clipboard into the cursor's current position. The cursor must be located in a field and the document must be in edit mode for this method to work.

Print

```
Call nuidNotesUIDocument.Print(intNumcopies, intFrompage, intTopage,
➥intDraft)
```

intNumcopies	Optional	%

The number of copies to print. Setting this value to 0 will print one copy. If this parameter is omitted, the File Print dialog box is displayed.

intFrompage	Optional	%

The page on which to begin printing. If this parameter is omitted or set to 0, the printing will begin on page 1.

intTopage	Optional	%

The page on which to stop printing. If this parameter is omitted or set to 0, the printing will stop on the last page of the document.

intDraft	Optional	%

Determines whether the document is printed in draft mode. TRUE prints the document in draft mode. FALSE does not.

This method either prints the current document or calls the File Print dialog box. If one or more of the available parameters are specified when calling this method, the document output is sent directly to the printer. If no parameters are specified or the first parameter is omitted, this method will call the File Print dialog box. Therefore, it isn't necessary to pass any parameters when calling this method.

Refresh

`Call nuidNotesUIDocument.Refresh(intIncludeRichTextItems)`

intIncludeRichTextItems   Optional   T/F

Determines whether *NotesRichTextItems* should be refreshed.

This method refreshes the current document and recalculates the computed fields on the document. This method is valid only when the document is in edit mode. Prior to Notes 5, calling this method didn't update any *NotesRichTextItems* that existed on the form. The only way to update their displayed values in the user interface was to close and then reopen the *NotesDocument*. Now, if you set this parameter to TRUE, all the *NotesRichTextItems* will be refreshed when this method is called. However, this is an expensive operation. Many form designs require calling the `Refresh` method to recalculate standard *NotesItems* fields. Therefore, set `intIncludeRichTextItems` to TRUE only when it is necessary to refresh the rich text fields.

RefreshHideFormulas

`Call nuidNotesUIDocument.`**`RefreshHideFormulas`**

This method recalculates the hide-when formulas on the current document's form. Keep in mind that because calling this method has a negative impact on performance, you should call it only when necessary.

Reload

`Call nuidNotesUIDocument.`**`Reload`**

This method reloads, or refreshes, the current *NotesUIDocument* with any changes that have been made to the corresponding back-end document. Calling this method updates the values displayed in the workspace and the *NotesDocument* representation in memory. This method is available only when the document is in edit mode.

Because of the robust properties of *NotesRichTextItems,* the `Reload` method doesn't apply. In other words, modifications made to *NotesRichTextItems* on the back-end *NotesDocument* can't be reloaded and rendered to the user interface, even if the `Reload` method is called. Therefore, the `Reload` method must be called while setting `intIncludeRichTextItems` to TRUE, or the *NotesDocument* must be closed and reopened in order for the modifications to *NotesRichTextItems* to be recognized. Similarly, if the respective *NotesDocument* is modified by another user or an agent, the document must be closed and reopened. The important distinction here is that when a *NotesDocument* is opened by a user, he is essentially looking at a snapshot of the back-end data. Any changes that are made to the current *NotesUIDocument* are not immediately modified on the server or file system until the document is saved or submitted. Once the document is saved, the server verifies against replication or save conflicts and takes any necessary action. However, only if the user modifies the back-end *NotesDocument* through its respective *NotesUIDocument* is he allowed to update the back-end data.

Save

`Call nuidNotesUIDocument.`**`Save`**

This method updates or saves the current document to disk if the current document is in edit mode.

SaveNewVersion

`Call nuidNotesUIDocument.`**`SaveNewVersion`**

This method saves a copy of the current document to disk as a new version, or copy.

In order to use this method, the form used to create the document must have enabled one of the three following versioning options: new versions become responses, prior versions become responses, new versions become siblings.

Using this method utilizes the response document hierarchy used with *NotesDocuments*. In order to use this method, the form used to display this document must be set to create versions manually. If the form used to save the document is set to save new versions automatically, this method is not necessary. Also, if the form has the version option set to none, calling this method will generate a `Document command is unavailable` error.

SelectAll

```
Call nuidNotesUIDocument.SelectAll
```
SelectAll

This method selects the contents of the current field if the document is in edit mode. If the document is in read mode, the entire contents of the current document are selected.

Send

```
Call nuidNotesUIDocument.Send
```
Send

This method sends an e-mail of the currentdocument. In order for this method to complete successfully, the document must have a SendTo field containing the recipients of the e-mail. Other optional fields that can be included (but that are not required) include CopyTo, BlindCopyTo, DeliveryPriority, DeliveryReport, and ReturnReceipt.

5.0 SpellCheck

```
Call nuidNotesUIDocument.SpellCheck
```
SpellCheck

This method opens the Spell Check dialog box and checks the contents of the document for misspellings.

NotesUIDocument Events

PostModeChange

PostModeChange(Source as NotesUIDocument)
PostMode Change

Source	R	O.Ref.

The current document rendered through the user interface (read-only).

This event is triggered after the document changes from read mode to edit mode or from edit mode to read mode and before focus is granted to the user. You can use the `EditMode` property of the *NotesUIDocument*, automatically dimensioned here as `Source`, to determine the current mode.

PostOpen

PostOpen(Source as NotesUIDocument)
PostOpen

Source	R	O.Ref.

The current document rendered through the user interface (read-only).

This event is triggered after the document has been opened but before focus is granted to the user.

PostRecalc

PostRecalc(Source as NotesUIDocument)

Source	R	O.Ref.

The current document rendered through the user interface (read-only).

This event is triggered after the document has been recalculated and all the formulas on the document's form have been executed and have passed validation.

5.0 PostSave

PostSave(Source as NotesUIDocument)

Source	R	O.Ref.

The current document rendered through the user interface (read-only).

This event is triggered after the document has been saved.

QueryClose

QueryClose(Source as NotesUIDocument, Continue as Variant)

Source	R	O.Ref.

The current document rendered through the user interface (read-only).

Continue	R/W	T/F

Indicates whether the current document should be allowed to close or remain open. TRUE allows the document to be closed. FALSE forces the document to remain open.

This event is triggered just before the document is closed.

QueryModeChange

QueryModeChange(Source as NotesUIDocument, Continue as Variant)

Source	R	O.Ref.

The current document rendered through the user interface (read-only).

Continue	R/W	T/F

Indicates whether the current document should be allowed to switch modes. TRUE allows the document to switch modes. FALSE forces the document to remain in the current mode.

This event is triggered just before the document switches from read mode to edit mode or from edit mode to read mode.

QueryOpen

QueryOpen(Source as NotesUIDocument, Mode as Integer, ➥IsNewDoc as Variant, Continue as Variant)

Source	R	O.Ref.

The current document rendered through the user interface (read-only).

Mode	R	%

Indicates the current mode of the document when opened. 0 indicates read mode. 1 indicates edit mode.

IsNewDoc	R	T/F

Indicates whether the document is new. TRUE indicates that the user is creating a new document. FALSE indicates that the user is opening an existing document.

Continue   R/W   T/F

Indicates whether the document should open successfully. TRUE allows the document to open. FALSE keeps the document from opening.

This event is triggered before the current document opens.

QuerySave

QuerySave(Source as NotesUIDocument, Continue as Variant)   QuerySave

Source   R   O.Ref.

The current document rendered through the user interface (read-only).

Continue   R/W   T/F

Indicates whether the document should be saved successfully. TRUE allows the document to be saved. FALSE keeps the document from being saved.

This event is triggered before the current document is saved.

Remarks

The "LotusScript Syntax" section mentioned that the *NotesUIDocument* can be accessed by referencing an existing *NotesDocument*.

However, another possible scenario for creating a new *NotesUIDocument* is to create a new *NotesDocument* back-end class and immediately open that new document to the front-end *NotesUIDocument* using the ComposeDocument method of the *NotesUIWorkspace* (▶ 49). The following code shows how that might be accomplished using dynamic variables.

```
Dim ns As New NotesSession
Dim nws As New NotesUIWorkspace
Dim nuidoc As NotesUIDocument
Dim strFileName As String
strFileName=Left$(ns.Currentdatabase.FilePath,Len
➡(ns.Currentdatabase.filepath)-(Len(ns.currentdatabase.Filename)))
Set nuidoc=nws.ComposeDocument(ns.CurrentDatabase.Server, strFileName &
➡"OppMgr.nsf", "Opportunity")
```

Example

The following LotusScript example uses FieldSetText and FieldGetText to read the phone number value of a field located on the current *NotesUIDocument*. It also attempts to format the value entered by the user with proper formatting.

```
Dim nws As New NotesUIWorkspace
Dim nuidoc As notesUIDocument
Dim strFieldname As String
Set nuidoc = nws.CurrentDocument
strFieldname = nuidoc.FieldGetText("strPhoneNumber")
If strFieldname <> "" Then
    If Isnumeric(strFieldname) Then
        If Fraction(Cdbl (strFieldname)) = 0 Then
```

continued >>

continued >>

```
If (Len(strFieldname) = 10) Then
    strNewFieldname = Left$(strFieldname, 3) & "-" &
    ➥Mid$(strFieldname, 4, 3) & "-" &
    ➥Mid$(strFieldname, 7, 4)
Else
    If strFieldname = "0" Then
        strNewFieldname = ""
    Elseif (Len(strFieldname) = 7) Then
        strNewFieldname = Left$(strFieldname, 3) & "-" &
        ➥Mid$(strFieldname, 4, 4)
    Elseif (Len(strFieldname) = 8) Then
        strNewFieldname = Left$(strFieldname, 1) & "-" &
        ➥Mid$(strFieldname, 2, 3) & "-" &
        ➥Mid$(strFieldname, 5, 4)
    Elseif (Len(strFieldname) = 11) Then
        strNewFieldname = Left$(strFieldname, 1) & "-" &
        ➥Mid$(strFieldname, 2, 3) & "-" &
        ➥Mid$(strFieldname, 5, 3) & "-" &
        ➥Mid$(strFieldname, 8, 4)
    Else
        strNewFieldname = strFieldname
    End If
End If
Else
    strNewFieldname = strFieldname
End If
Else
    strNewFieldname = strFieldname
End If
Else
    strNewFieldname = ""
End If
Call nuidoc.FieldSettext("strPhoneNumber", strNewFieldname)
```

NotesUIView

The *NotesUIView* class allows you to access the view that is currently open in the *NotesWorkspace*.

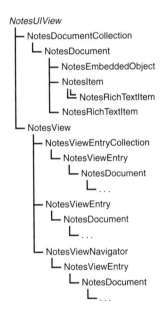

NotesUIView
— NotesDocumentCollection
  └ NotesDocument
    ├ NotesEmbeddedObject
    ├ NotesItem
    │ └└ NotesRichTextItem
    └ NotesRichTextItem
— NotesView
  ├ NotesViewEntryCollection
  │ └ NotesViewEntry
  │   └ NotesDocument
  │   └ …
  ├ NotesViewEntry
  │ └ NotesDocument
  │   └ …
  └ NotesViewNavigator
     └ NotesViewEntry
        └ NotesDocument
           └ …

LotusScript Syntax

Accessing a *NotesUIView* object is a little different from accessing most objects in Notes. You can access it only by scripting the events that Notes views expose— such as `QueryOpen`, `PostOpen`, and `QueryClose`.

NotesUIView Properties

5.0 CalendarDateTime	R		?

CalendarDate Time

`To Get: vDate = nuivNotesUIView.`**`CalendarDateTime`**

Returns the date and time (as a variant of type date) of the current region of a calendar-style view.

5.0 CaretCategory	R		?

CaretCategory

`varCategory = nuivNotesUIView.`**`CaretCategory`**

Returns the categories in which the current document appears in the current view. Used primarily for categorized views.

Documents	R		O.Ref.

Documents

`To get: Set ndcDocuments = nuivnotesUIView.`**`Documents`**

Returns a *NotesDocumentCollection* (▶ 149) containing the documents being acted upon by an event in a *NotesView* (▶ 279). Accessing the `Documents` property from the `QueryOpen`, `PostOpen`, `QueryClose`, and `QueryRecalc` events will always be empty because these events don't apply to documents—they apply to the view itself.

View	R		O.Ref.

View

`To get: Set nvwCurView = nuivnotesUIView.`**`View`**

Returns a *NotesView* (▶ 279) object containing the currently open view.

ViewName	R		$

ViewName

`strName = nuivnotesuiview.`**`ViewName`**

Returns the name of the current view as a string.

NotesUIView Methods

5.0 Print

Print

`Call nuivCurview.`**`Print`**`(intCopies, intFrom, intTo, intDraft, intPageSep,`
`↪strFormOverride, intPrintView, varStartDate, varEndDate)`

intCopies	Optional	%

Specifies the number of copies you want to make.

intFrom	Optional	%

Specifies the starting page of the print range. Specify `0` to print all selected documents.

intTo   Optional   %

Specifies the ending page of the print range. Specify 0 to print all selected documents.

intDraft   Optional   T/F

Indicates whether draft mode should be used for printing. Specify TRUE to print in draft mode and FALSE to print in normal mode.

intPageSep   Optional   %

Specifies whether a page separator should be used.

strFormOverride   Optional $

If specified, prints documents using the named form rather than the form that was last used to save the documents.

intPrintView   Optional   %

Specifies whether the current view should be printed rather than the currently selected documents (which is the default action).

varStartDate   Optional   ?

Specifies a starting date to use to filter the documents that are printed.

varEndDate   Optional   ?

Specifies an ending date to use to filter the documents that are printed.

This method allows you to programmatically print the current view or selected documents and provides excellent control over the printing process.

The following example demonstrates asking the user if they want to print the current view when it's closed.

```
Sub Queryclose(Source As Notesuiview, Continue As Variant)
    'This code prompts the user to print the current view when it's closed
    If Msgbox("Would you like to print the view?", 32+4,"Print current
    ➥ view?")=6 Then
        Call Source.Print(1,0,0,0,False,"",True)
    End If
End Sub
```

SelectDocument

```
Call nuivCurView.SelectDocument(ndocDocToSelect)
```
SelectDocument

ndocDocToSelect   Required   O.Ref.

A handle on the document that is to be selected.

This method allows you to select a document in the current view.

NotesUIView Events

PostDragDrop
PostDragDrop

```
PostDragDrop(nuivSource as NotesUIView)
```

niuvSource   O.Ref.

A *NotesUIView* object representing the view that is currently open on the workspace.

This event fires immediately after any DragDrop event is fired and is valid only for calendar views.

PostOpen

PostOpen(nuivSource as NotesUIView)

nuivSource	O.Ref.

A *NotesUIView* object representing the view that is currently open on the workspace.

This event fires immediately after the current view is opened.

PostPaste

PostPaste(nuivSource as NotesUIView)

nuivSource	O.Ref.

A *NotesUIView* object representing the view that is currently open on the workspace.

This event fires immediately after a document is pasted into the current view.

QueryAddToFolder

QueryAddToFolder(nuivSource as NotesUIView, strTarget as string, ➥intContinue as integer)

nuivSource	O.Ref.

A *NotesUIView* object representing the view that is currently open on the workspace.

strTarget	$

The name of the folder that the document is being moved to.

intContinue	T/F

This parameter is used to indicate whether QueryAddToFolder should proceed. Setting intContinue to FALSE cancels the operation, and the document(s) won't be added to the folder.

This event fires immediately before a document is moved to a folder.

QueryClose

QueryClose(nuivSource as NotesUIView, intContinue as integer)

nuivSource	O.Ref.

A *NotesUIView* object representing the view that is currently open on the workspace.

intContinue	T/F

This parameter is used to indicate whether QueryClose should proceed. Setting intContinue to FALSE cancels the operation.

This event fires immediately before the current view is closed.

QueryDragDrop

QueryDragDrop(nuivSource as NotesUIView, intContinue as integer)

nuivSource	O.Ref.

A *NotesUIView* object representing the view that is currently open on the workspace.

intContinue	T/F

This parameter is used to indicate whether QueryDragDrop should proceed. Setting intContinue to FALSE cancels the operation.

This event fires immediately before any DragDrop event and is valid only for calendar views.

QueryOpen

```
QueryOpen(nuivSource as NotesUIView, intContinue as integer)
```

nuivSource   O.Ref.
A *NotesUIView* object representing the view that is currently open on the workspace.

intContinue   T/F
This parameter is used to indicate whether QueryOpen should proceed. Setting intContinue to FALSE cancels the operation.

This event fires immediately before the current view is opened.

QueryOpenDocument

```
QueryOpenDocument(nuivSource as NotesUIView, intContinue as integer)
```

nuivSource   O.Ref.
A *NotesUIView* object representing the view that is currently open on the workspace.

intContinue   T/F
This parameter is used to indicate whether QueryOpenDocument should proceed. Setting intContinue to FALSE cancels the operation.

This event fires immediately before a document in the current view is opened.

QueryPaste

```
QueryPaste(nuivSource as NotesUIView, intContinue as integer)
```

nuivSource   O.Ref.
A *NotesUIView* object representing the view that is currently open on the workspace.

intContinue   T/F
This parameter is used to indicate whether QueryPaste should proceed. Setting intContinue to FALSE cancels the operation.

This event fires immediately before a document is pasted into the current view.

QueryRecalc

```
QueryRecalc(nuivSource as NotesUIView, intContinue as integer)
```

nuivSource   O.Ref.
A *NotesUIView* object representing the view that is currently open on the workspace.

intContinue   T/F
This parameter is used to indicate whether QueryRecalc should proceed. Setting intContinue to FALSE cancels the operation.

This event fires immediately before the current view is refreshed.

RegionDoubleClick

```
RegionDoubleClick(nuivSource as NotesUIView)
```

nuivSource   O.Ref.
A *NotesUIView* object representing the view that is currently open on the workspace.

This event fires immediately after the user double-clicks a cell in a calendar view. This event is valid only for calendar views.

Remarks

NotesUIView is a very handy class when you want to position the selection bar on a specific document in a view, and also when you're working with calendar-style views. Keep in mind that as a front-end class, *NotesUIView* is not available when you use Web clients with a Domino server.

Example

The following example demonstrates printing only "open" documents from the QueryClose event of a view.

```
QueryClose(Source As Notesuiview, Continue As Variant)
  Dim ndocCurDoc As NotesDocument
  Set ndocCurDoc = Source.Documents.GetFirstDocument
  Do While Not ndocCurDoc is Nothing
    If Not ndocCurDoc.Status(0) = "Closed"  Then
      Call source.SelectDocument( ndocCurDoc)
      Call Source.Print(1,0,0,0,0,"",0)
    End If
    Set ndocCurDoc = Source.Documents.GetNextDocument(ndocCurDoc)
  Loop
End Sub
```

NotesUIWorkspace

4.0 4.1x 4.5x 4.6x 5.0

The *NotesUIWorkspace* object is one of the most useful and frequently used objects in the Notes/Domino toolbox. It allows you to access other front-end objects in the current workspace window—that is, objects that are available in the user interface.

NotesUIWorkspace
└ NotesUIDocument
   └ NotesDocument
      ├ NotesEmbeddedObject
      ├ NotesItem
      │ └ NotesRichTextItem
      └ NotesRichTextItem

LotusScript Syntax

```
Dim workspace As New NotesUIWorkspace
```

The only way to instantiate a new *NotesUIWorkspace* object is to use the New keyword.

NotesUIWorkspace Properties

CurrentCalendarDateTime   R   ?

CurrentCalendar
DateTime

To get: vardate = nwsNotesUIWorkspace.**CurrentCalendarDateTime**

Returns a variant of type date (7) that represents the currently selected region of a calendar-style view.

CurrentDatabase   R   O.Ref.

Current
Database

To get: nuidbCDb = nwsNotesUIWorkspace.**CurrentDatabase**

Returns a *NotesUIDatabase* object (▶ 13) representing the current database.

CurrentDocument   R   O.Ref.

Current
Document

To get: Set nuidCurDoc = nwsNotesUIWorkspace.**CurrentDocument**

Returns a *NotesUIDocument* for the document that is currently open in the Notes workspace. If no document is currently open, this property returns the constant Nothing. The following example uses extended class syntax to reference the *CurrentDocument* object and call the FieldSetText method.

```
Dim nwsWs As New NotesUIWorkspace
Dim intSalesMultiplier As Integer, intMinimumQuota As Integer
If Not nwsWs.CurrentDocument Is Nothing Then
    If Cdbl(nwsWs.CurrentDocument.FieldGetText("SalesQuota"))=0 Then
        Call nwsWs.CurrentDocument.FieldSetText("SalesQuota",
        ➥Cstr(intSalesMultiplier * intMinimumQuota))
    End If
Else
    Msgbox "There is no document currently selected on the workspace.",
    ➥64, "Selection Error"
End If
```

CurrentView   R   O.Ref.

CurrentView

To get: setnuivCurView = nwsNotesUIWorkspace.**CurrentView**

Returns a *NotesUIView* object (▶ 41) representing the view that is currently open in the workspace.

NotesUIWorkspace Methods

AddDatabase

AddDatabase

```
Call nwsnotesUIWorkspace.AddDatabase(strServer, strDbFile)
```

---

strServer   Optional $

Specifies on which server the database can be found. If it's set to an empty string (" ")
or omitted, the local workstation is assumed.

strDbFile   Optional $

Specifies the full path and filename of the database to add. Keep in mind that this
doesn't assume that the default Notes\Data directory is part of the path, as is the case
when you're using the formula language.

The `AddDatabase` method allows you to add a database's icon to a user's workspace.
The following example briefly demonstrates the use of this method.

```
Dim nwsWs As New NotesUIWorkspace
Dim nsSession As New NotesSession
Dim ndirDirectory As NotesDbDirectory
Dim ndbCurDb As NotesDatabase
Dim intCount as Integer
Set ndirDirectory = nsSession.GetDbDirectory("Gonzo/Definiti")
Set ndbCurDb = ndirDirectory.GetFirstDatabase(DATABASE)
While Not(ndbCurDb Is Nothing)
    intCount=intCount+1
    Call nwsWs.Adddatabase(ndbcurDb.Server, ndbcurDb.FilePath)
    Set ndbCurDb = Directory.GetNextDatabase
Wend
Msgbox Trim$(Str$(intCount)) & " databases were added to your
➥workspace.", 64 ,"Summary"
```

CheckAlarms

```
Call nwsnotesUIWorkspace.CheckAlarms()
```
CheckAlarms

This method causes the Alarm agent to scan a user's mail file for alarms.

ComposeDocument

```
Set nuidnotesUIDocument = nwsnotesUIWorkspace.ComposeDocument(strServer,
➥strFile, strForm, dblWindowWidth, dblWindowHeight)
```
Compose
Document

---

strServer   Optional $

Specifies the server where the database you want to create a document in resides. If
strServer is set to an empty string (" ") or omitted, a local copy will be used.

strFile   Optional $

Specifies the full path and filename of the database in which you want to compose a
document. If this parameter and the strServer parameter are set to an empty string
(" ") or omitted, the current database object will be used. Keep in mind that this
doesn't assume that the default Notes\Data directory is part of the path, as when
you're using the formula language.

strForm   Optional $

Indicates which form to use when composing the document. If it's omitted or set to
an empty string (" "), the user will be prompted with the *Create Other* dialog box,
which lets him choose a form in the specified database.

dblWindowWidth   Optional   #

Specifies in inches how wide the window containing the form will be. If omitted, the
width will be the current window width.

dblWindowHeight   Optional   #

Specifies in inches how high the window containing the form will be. If omitted, the height will be the current window height. The `dblWindowWidth` and `dblWindowHeight` parameters will have no effect in MDI mode when the window is maximized on the desktop. Regardless, the window will be centered in the enclosing window (MDI mode) or desktop (SDI mode).

The `ComposeDocument` method allows you to create a new *NotesDocument* in the database using a form that you specify as the third parameter. Consider the following example.

```
Dim nwsWs As New NotesUIWorkspace
Dim strDbPath As String
Dim ndbQDb As NotesDatabase
Dim nvwQView As NotesView
Dim ndocQdoc As NotesDocument
Dim nuidUIDoc As NotesUiDocument
Set nuidUIDoc=nwsWs.CurrentDocument
strDbPath=Left$(nuidUIDoc.Document.ParentDatabase.FilePath,
➡(Len(nuidUIDoc.Document.ParentDatabase.FilePath)-Len
➡(nuidUIDoc.Document.ParentDatabase.FileName)))
Set ndbQDb= New NotesDatabase(nuidUIDoc.Document.ParentDatabase.Server,
➡strDbPath & "keys.nsf")
Set nvwQView=ndbQDb.GetView("Keys")
Set ndocQDoc=Qview.GetDocumentByKey("SalesQuota")
If nuidUIDoc.Document.SalesTotal(0)<ndocQDoc.SalesQuota(0) Then
    Set nuidUIDoc=nwsWs.ComposeDocument("","","ExceptionReport")
End If
```

DialogBox

```
intReturn = nwsnotesUIWorkspace.DialogBox(strForm, intAutoHorzFit,
➡intAutoVertFit, intNoCancel, intNoNewFields, intNoFieldUpdate,
➡intReadOnly, strTitle, ndocNotesDocument, intSizeToTable,
➡intNoOkCancel)
```

---

strForm   Optional $

Used to pass the name of the form or subform used when displaying a document in a dialog box.

intAutoHorzFit   Optional   T/F

When set to TRUE and the underlying form or subform uses a layout region, the layout region will be horizontally scrolled to fit in the dialog box. If FALSE or omitted, the layout will not be scrolled. This parameter is necessary only when layout regions are displayed in the form or subform. If you set this parameter to TRUE, you should set `intAutoVertFit` to TRUE as well.

intAutoVertFit   Optional   T/F

Set to TRUE to cause the layout region to be scrolled vertically to fit in the dialog box. If FALSE or omitted, the layout won't be scrolled. This parameter is necessary only when layout regions are displayed in the form or subform. If you're setting this parameter to TRUE, you should set `intAutoHorzFit` to TRUE as well.

intNoCancel   Optional   T/F

Controls the appearance of the Cancel button in the dialog box. If set to TRUE, no Cancel button will be displayed. If FALSE or omitted, the Cancel button will be displayed.

intNoNewFields   Optional   T/F

Determines whether new fields in the dialog box will be passed back to the underlying document. Setting this parameter to TRUE keeps any fields that are present in the dialog box but not on the underlying document from being passed back to the underlying document. If FALSE or omitted, the fields will be passed back from the underlying document.

intNoFieldUpdate   Optional   T/F

Determines whether edits in the dialog box will be passed back to the underlying document. TRUE keeps edits in the dialog box from being passed to the underlying document. If FALSE or omitted, all edits are passed back to the underlying document.

intReadOnly   Optional   T/F

Determines whether edits will be allowed in the dialog box. If TRUE, edits are not allowed. If FALSE or omitted, edits are allowed. Setting this parameter to TRUE causes intNoCancel to be set to TRUE as well.

strTitle   Optional $

When specified, this is used as the window title of the dialog box.

ndocNotesDocument   Optional   O.Ref.

Using this parameter causes any valid Notes document to be opened rather than the currently selected or open document.

intSizeToTable   Optional   T/F

Specify TRUE for this parameter to scale a table to fit correctly into a dialog box.

intNoOkCancel   Optional   T/F

Specify TRUE for this parameter to cause the dialog box to exclude the OK and Cancel buttons. Omitting this parameter or passing FALSE (the default) causes the dialog box to display OK and Cancel buttons.

This method launches a dialog box that displays data from a Notes document using the form design element or subform design element that you specify. This method returns an integer value. If the intReturn value is TRUE, the user clicked the OK button. If intReturn is FALSE, the user clicked the Cancel button. Consider the following example.

```
Public Sub GetHelp(strKey, strTopic)
Dim nwsWs As NotesUIWorkspace
Dim ndbHelpDb As NotesDatabase
Dim nvwHelpView As NotesView
Dim ndocHelpDoc As NotesDocument
Dim strFilePath as String
strFilePath=Left$(nwsWs.CurrentDocument.Document.ParentDatabase.
➥FilePath,(Len(nwsWs.CurrentDocument.Document.ParentDatabase.
➥FilePath)-Len(nwsWs.CurrentDocument.Document.ParentDatabase.
➥FileName)))
Set ndbHelpDb=New NotesDatabase(nwsWs.CurrentDocument.Document.
➥ParentDatabase.Server, strFilePath & "help.nsf")
If (Not ndbHelpDb Is Nothing And ndbHelpDb.IsOpen) Then
    Set nvwHelpView=ndbHelpDb.GetView("(helpbykey)")
    Set ndocHelpDoc=nvwHelpView.GetDocumentbyKey(strKey)
        If ndocHelpDoc Is Nothing Then
            Msgbox "No help was found for " & strKey, 16, "No Help Found"
            Exit Sub
        Else
```

continued >>

continued >>

```
                        Call nwsWs.DialogBox("Help", TRUE, TRUE, FALSE, TRUE, TRUE,
                        ➡FALSE, "Help For " & strTopic, HelpDoc)
                End If
        Else
            Msgbox "Could not access the help database, please contact your
            ➡administrator", 16, "System Error"
        End If
        End Sub
```

EditDocument

EditDocument

```
set nuidNotesUIDocument = nwsnotesUIWorkspace.EditDocument(intMode,
➡ndocDocument, intReadOnly, strdocAnchor)
```

---

intMode   Optional   T/F

Set to TRUE (the default) to open the specified document in edit mode. The current user must have a minimum of author access to the document.

ndocDocument   Required   O. Ref.

The target document you want to open.

intReadOnly   R   T/F

Works in conjunction with intMode. When intMode is FALSE and intReadOnly is TRUE, the document is opened in read-only mode, and the user is prevented from switching to edit mode later. If intReadOnly is FALSE or omitted, the user will be able to toggle between read and edit mode if he has at least author access.

strdocAnchor   O $

This parameter enables you to open a document to the specified anchor/location in the document.

The EditDocument method is used to open an existing document in either read or edit mode. It returns a *NotesUIDocument* object. Consider the following example.

```
Dim nsS as New NotesSession
Dim nwsWs As New NotesUIworkspace
Dim ndbLDb As NotesDatabase
Dim nvwLview As Notesview
Dim ndocLdoc As NotesDocument
Set ndbLDb=S.GetDatabase(nsS.CurrentDatabase.Server, "contacts.nsf")
If Not ndbLDb Is Nothing And ndbLDb.IsOpen Then
    Set nvwLview=ndbLDb.GetView("people")
    Set ndocLdoc=nvwLview.GetDocumentByKey(nwsWs.CurrentDocument.Document.
    ➡CustomerKey(0))
    If ndocLdoc Is Nothing Then
        Msgbox "No customer records were found for: " &
        ➡nwsWs.CurrentDocument.Document.CustomerKey(0), 64 ,
        ➡"Customer Not Found"
    Else.nuidCurDoc=nwsWs.EditDocument(TRUE, ndocLDoc, FALSE)
    End If
Else
    Msgbox "Could not open database: " & "contacts.nsf, please contact
    ➡your administrator.", 16, "Error"
 End If
```

EditProfile

EditProfile

```
Call nwsnotesUIWorkspace.EditProfile(strProfilename, strUsername)
```

---

strProfilename   Required $

The name or alias of the profile document you want to retrieve.

strUsername   Optional $

An optional string parameter used as a key to retrieve profile documents stored with a user name. Only one profile document with a specific name can be stored in the same database at a time for each user. If this parameter isn't used, only one profile document of this name is created for the entire database. However, the user must have designer access to create a profile document without using the `strUserName` parameter.

The `EditProfile` method can be used to create a new profile document or access an existing one. This method has no return value. Consider the following example.

```
Dim nsSession As New NotesSession
Dim nwsWs As New NotesUIWorkspace
Dim nuidProfile As NotesUIDocument
Set nuidProfile=nwsWs.EditProfile("HitCount", nsSession.CommonUserName)
```

EnableAlarms

```
intReturn = nwsNotesUIWorkspace.EnableAlarms(intEnable)
```

EnableAlarms

The `EnableAlarms` method takes one Boolean parameter that, when set to TRUE, starts the agent that checks a user's calendar for alarms. This method returns a Boolean value.

New

```
Dim nwsWS as New NotesUIWorkspace
```

Used to instantiate a new *NotesUIWorkspace* object.

5.0 Folder

```
varFolder = nwsNotesUIWorkspace.Folder(strFolderName, intMove)
```

Folder

strFolderName   Optional $
Specifies the name of the folder in which to place the current document. If this parameter isn't specified, the Move to Folder dialog is displayed.

intMove   Optional   T/F
A Boolean that specifies whether the document should be moved to the target folder. If the `strFolder` parameter is empty (" "), this parameter is ignored.

This method allows you to move the current document to the specified folder or launches the Move to Folder dialog, allowing the user to interactively select a folder.

5.0 GetListofTunes

```
varTunesList=nwsNotesUIWorkspace.GetListofTunes()
```

GetListofTunes

This method takes no parameters. It returns an array of strings containing the names of the system sounds on your machine.

OpenDatabase

```
Call nwsNotesUIWorkspace.OpenDatabase(strServer, strFile, strView,
➥strKey, intNew, intTemp)
```

OpenDatabase

strServer   Required $
Specifies the server on which the database resides.

strFile   Required $
Specifies the full path and name of the database to open. Keep in mind that this doesn't assume that the default Notes\Data directory is part of the path, as when you're using the formula language.

strView	Optional	$

Indicates which view to display when the database is opened.

strKey	Optional	$

Used to position the selection bar on a document matching the key.

intNew	Optional	T/F

Causes the view to be opened in its own window, even if the database has an open window. When set to FALSE (the default), a new window will be opened only when the database has no open windows.

intTemp	Optional	T/F

Temporarily opens the database without adding it to the workspace when set to TRUE. Omitting this parameter or setting it to FALSE causes the database icon to be added to the user's workspace.

This method is used to open a *NotesDatabase* to a view specified in the strView parameter. Consider the following example.

```
Dim nsSession As New NotesSession
Dim nwsWs As New NotesUIWorkspace
Dim strKey As String
strKey=Inputbox("Find User", "Enter the name of the user to find", "")
If strKey$ <> "" Then
    Call nwsWs.OpenDatabase(nsSession.CurrentDatabase.Server,
    ➥"contacts.nsf", "people", strKey, TRUE, FALSE)
End If
```

5.0 OpenFileDialog

OpenFileDialog

```
varFiles = nwsNotesUIWorkspace.OpenFileDialog(intMult, strTitle,
➥strFilters, strInitDir, strInitFile)
```

---

intMult	Optional	T/F

TRUE indicates that multiple files may be selected. FALSE indicates a single file selection.

strTitle	Optional	$

If specified, this string serves as a title for the file dialog box.

strFilters	Optional	$

If specified, this string is used to limit the types of files displayed in the dialog box. An example is "Text Files¦*.txt¦", which would display only text files.

strInitDir	Optional	$

If specified, this string indicates which directory should initially be displayed.

strInitFile	Optional	$

If specified, this parameter indicates which file should initially be selected.

This very useful and long-awaited method allows you to eschew the Windows API and call the standard Windows file dialog. It returns an array of strings containing the names of the selected files if OK is clicked or EMPTY if Cancel is clicked. EMPTY is an internal constant value used by LotusScript (read only) to represent variants that have no value (i.e. when they are created). It is automatically converted to a string value ("") when used in string operations and automatically converted to a 0 when used in numeric operations. You can also test the existence of a variant value by using the IsEmpty function of LotusScript.

5.0 OpenFrameset

```
Call nwsNotesUIWorkspace.OpenFrameset(strFrameset)
```

strFrameset	R	$

A string specifying the name of the frameset to open.

This method lets you open a frameset in the current target frame.

5.0 OpenPage

```
Call nwsNotesUIWorkspace.OpenPage(strPage)
```

strPage	R	$

A string specifying the name of the page to open.

This method lets you open a page in the current target frame.

5.0 PickListCollection

```
Set ndc=nwsNotesUIWorkspace.PickListCollection(intType, intMult,
➥strServer, strDbFileName, strView, strTitle, strPrompt, strCategory)
```

intType	Optional	%

This parameter determines the type of view to display. Currently, this parameter is restricted to the constant `PICKLIST_CUSTOM`.

intMult	Optional	T/F

This parameter, when set to `TRUE`, allows multiple document selections. Otherwise, only a single document may be selected.

strServer	Optional	$

A string value specifying on which server the database resides.

strDbFileName	Optional	$

A string specifying the name of the database to use.

strView	Optional	$

A string containing the name of the view to use.

strTitle	Optional	$

A string specifying a title to use dialog.

strPrompt	Optional	$

A string specifying the prompt to display inside the dialog.

strCategory	Optional	$

If specified, this string parameter indicates which category should be selected in the view. Needless to say, the view must be categories for this parameter to have any effect.

This method is functionally equivalent to the @PickList function in the Notes formula language. It lets you create a modal dialog containing a *NotesView*. The selected document (or documents if `intMult` is set to `TRUE`) is returned as a *NotesDocumentCollection* if OK is clicked. If Cancel is clicked, `Nothing` is returned. At the present time, the `intType` parameter can only be set to `PICKLIST_CUSTOM`, which then requires that all optional parameters (meaning all parameters in this case) must be supplied.

5.0 PickListStrings

PickListStrings   `varSelections = nwsNotesUIWorkspace.`**`PickListStrings`** `(intType, intMult,`
`➥strServer, strDbFileName, strView, strTitle, strPrompt, intColumn)`

intType   Optional   %

This parameter determines the type of dialog to display. The first three constants in the following list—`PICKLIST_NAMES`, `PICKLIST_ROOMS`, and `PICKLIST_RESOURCES`—launch predefined dialogs showing people from the NAB or Rooms or Resources from the Resources database. `PICKLIST_CUSTOM` parameter allows you to define any view to display. It's very similar to the `PickListCollection` method, except that the selected documents have the indicated column returned as an array of strings. If the `PICKLIST_CUSTOM` option is selected, all of the following parameters must be specified. Otherwise, specify only the `intType` parameter.

Option	Description
PICKLIST_NAMES	Launches the names dialog.
PICKLIST_ROOMS	Launches the rooms dialog.
PICKLIST_RESOURCES	Launches the resources dialog.
PICKLIST_CUSTOM	Launches the names dialog.

intMult   Optional   T/F

This parameter, when set to `TRUE`, allows multiple document selections. Otherwise, only a single document may be selected.

strServer   Optional $

A string value specifying on which server the database resides.

strDbFileName   Optional $

A string specifying the name of the database to use.

strView   Optional $

A string containing the name of the view to use.

strTitle   Optional $

A string specifying a title to use for the dialog.

strPrompt   Optional $

A string specifying the prompt to display inside the dialog.

intColumn   Optional   %

If specified, this integer indicates which column you want returned in the array of strings.

This method is similar to the @PickList function in the Notes formula language. It lets you create a modal dialog containing a *Notes View*. The selected document (or documents if `intMult` is set to `TRUE`) is returned as an array of strings if OK is clicked. If Cancel is clicked, `Nothing` will be returned. At the present time, the `intType` parameter can only be set to `PICKLIST_CUSTOM`, which then requires that all optional parameters (meaning all parameters in this case) must be supplied.

5.0 PlayTune

PlayTune   `Call nwsNotesUIWorkspace.`**`PlayTune`**`(strTuneName)`

strTuneName   Required $

A string specifying the name and path of a sound file to play.

This method causes the specified sound file to be played.

5.0 Prompt

Prompt

varSelections=nwsNotesUIWorkspace.**Prompt**(intType, strTitle, strPrompt, ➡varDefault, varValues)

intType   Optional   %

This parameter determines the type of prompt to display. It can be one of the following constants:

Constant	Description
PROMPT_OK	The prompt has an OK button only.
PROMPT_YESNO	The prompt has Yes and No buttons.
PROMPT_YESNOCANCEL	The prompt has Yes, No, and Cancel buttons.
PROMPT_OKCANCELEDIT	The prompt has OK and Cancel buttons and a single editable text field.
PROMPT_OKCANCELLIST	The prompt has OK and Cancel buttons and a single select list of values.
PROMPT_OKCANCELCOMBO	The prompt has OK and Cancel buttons and a drop-down list.
PROMPT_OKCANCELEDITCOMBO	The prompt has OK and Cancel buttons and a drop-down editable list.
PROMPT_OKCANCELLISTMULT	The prompt has OK and Cancel buttons and a multi-select list of choices.
PROMPT_PASSWORD	The prompt has OK and Cancel buttons and a single, hashed, editable field.

strTitle   Optional $

A string specifying a title to use for the dialog.

strPrompt   Optional $

A string specifying the prompt to display inside the dialog.

varDefault   Optional $

If specified, this parameter is used as the default value for the prompt. This parameter can be either a string, string array, a variant of type string, or variant array of type string.

varValues   Optional $

If specified, this parameter sets the values displayed in the prompt's listbox. This parameter can be either a string, string array, a variant of type string, or variant array of type string.

This method is functionally equivalent to the @Prompt function. It creates and returns a value based on what the user does in the dialog box. If the user clicks OK, a variant containing a string array is returned. Otherwise, **EMPTY** is returned.

5.0 RefreshParentNote

Call nwsNotesUIWorkspace.**RefreshParentNote**()

RefreshParent Note

This method takes no parameters. When called in a dialog box, it causes the underlying document to be updated based on values entered in the dialog box. Additionally, the dialog box is closed without the need to click the OK or Cancel button. This method is most useful in the **QueryClose** event of a dialog box.

5.0 ReloadWindow

`Call nwsNotesUIWorkspace.`**`ReloadWindow`**

Calling this method reloads the contents of the current window.

5.0 SaveFileDialog

`varFiles = nwsNotesUIWorkspace.`**`SaveFileDialog`**`(intMult, strTitle,`
➥`strFilters, strInitDir, strInitFile)`

intMult	Optional	T/F

TRUE indicates that multiple files may be selected. FALSE indicates a single file selection.

strTitle	Optional	$

If specified, this string serves as a title for the filedialog box.

strFilters	Optional	$

If specified, this string is used to limit the types of files displayed in the dialog box. An example is Text Files¦*.txt¦, which would display only text files.

strInitDir	Optional	$

If specified, this string indicates which directory should initially be displayed.

strInitFile	Optional	$

If specified, this parameter indicates which file should initially be selected.

Displays the File Save dialog box. If a filename (or files if intMult is TRUE) is selected or entered and the OK button is clicked, this method returns a string array containing the name(s) of the selected files. If Cancel is clicked, EMPTY will be returned.

5.0 SetCurrentLocation

`Call nwsNotesUIWorkspace.`**`SetCurrentLocation`**`(strLocationName)`

strLocationName	Optional	$

If supplied, this string indicates which location to make current. If a location name is not specified, the *Change Location* dialog box is displayed.

This method allows you to programmatically set a location on the current workstation.

5.0 SetTargetFrame

`Call nwsNotesUIWorkspace.`**`SetTargetFrame`**`(strTarget)`

strTarget	Required	$

A string specifying the name of the frame that a document, view, frameset, or page should open into.

This allows you to target a specific frame when opening a document, view, frameset, or page.

URLOpen

`Call nwsNotesUIWorkspace.`**`URLOpen`**`(strURLtoOpen, intRefresh, intURLList,`
➥`strCharset, strUsername, strWebpassword, strProxyusername,`
➥`strProxywebpassword, intNotesretriever)`

strURLtoOpen	Optional	$

The URL of the Web site you want to visit. If this parameter is omitted, the Open URL dialog box is displayed.

intRefresh   Optional   %

Dictates how the page will be fetched. If set to **0** (the default), the page is fetched from the host only if it doesn't exist in the Notes Web Navigator database. When set to 1, the page is fetched from its Internet host each time. When set to 2, the page is loaded from the host only if it has been modified since it was stored in the Web Navigator database.

intURLList   Optional   %

If the current Web page contains links to other Web pages, this parameter indicates if the Web Navigator should save URL links to other Web pages in a reserved Notes field named "URLLinks1". If **TRUE**, the new field is created containing all the URL links to the other Web pages. Additional new fields are created and the numeric value of the field name is incremented when the size of the current field reaches 64K. Therefore, when the "URLLinks1" field grows to 64K, a new field is automatically created named "URLLinks2", and so on. The values stored in these fields can then be used by agents to open all the Web pages specified by the URL links.

strCharset   Optional $

Used to tell the Web Navigator which **MIME** character set to use when processing the Web page.

strUsername   Optional $

Used to pass a user name to an Internet host for authentication.

strWebpassword   Optional $

Used to pass a password to an Internet host for authentication.

strProxyusername   Optional $

Used to supply a user name to a proxy server if a user name is needed for authentication.

strProxywebpassword   Optional $

Used to supply a password to a proxy server if authentication is required.

intNotesretriever   Optional   T/F

Specifies which browser to use when opening the URL. If present or set to **TRUE**, the Notes browser is used. If omitted or set to **FALSE**, the Notes browser is used.

This very useful method makes it easy to open any known resource on the Internet, an intranet or extranet simply by supplying a URL.

UseLSX

```
Call nwsNotesUIworkspace.UseLSX(strLibraryName)
```
UseLSX

strLibraryName   R $

Contains the full path to the lsx file you want to call (or it can be prepended with an asterisk). The scope of the loaded extensions remains contained in the calling module and the modules it calls.

This method allows you to load a LotusScript extension file containing public definitions that you can call from your LotusScript applications.

ViewRefresh

```
Call nwsNotesUIworkspace.ViewRefresh
```
ViewRefresh

When called, this method refreshes the current view so that it displays the most current data. If a document is open in the current window, the underlying view will be refreshed when the window is refreshed.

Remarks

The *NotesUIWorkspace* class is at the top of the front-end classes hierarchy and has no events. Because it's a front-end class, it is not accessible from background agents, agents called through an API, or agents called by the *NotesAgent* Run method. Additionally, it can't be used with Java.

Example

The following example demonstrates sending databases via e-mail to mobile users and adding them to their workspace from a button in the mail message. The following code would run from a button's click event.

```
Sub Click(Source As Button)
    ' This code assumes that becuase you are mailing the files as
    ' attachments, you don't need to test for the existence of an RTF
    ' field (Body) and that you know the names of the attachments.
    On Error Goto Errhandler
    Dim nwsWs As New NotesUIWorkspace
    Dim nsS As New NotesSession
    Dim aDbNames(1) As String
    aDbNames(0)="CMGR.NSF"
    aDbNames(1)="SYSTEM.NSF"
    Dim varDataPath As Variant
    varDataPath=nsS.GetEnvironmentString("Directory",True)
    ' get the default data directory for the current Notes client
    Dim neoFile1 As NotesEmbeddedObject
    Dim neoFile2 As NotesEmbeddedObject
    Set neoFile1 = nwsWs.CurrentDocument.Document.GetAttachment
➥(aDbNames(0))   ' get handle to attachment
    Set neoFile2 = nwsWs.CurrentDocument.Document.GetAttachment
➥(aDbNames(1))    ' get handle to attachment
    Call neoFile1.ExtractFile(varDataPath(0))   ' detach file1 into
                                                ' default notes data
                                                ' directory
    Call neoFile2.ExtractFile(varDataPath(0))   ' detach file2 into
                                                ' default notes data
                                                ' directory
    If Msgbox("Would you like to delete the attached files now?", 36,
➥"Delete Attachments") =6 Then
        Call noeFile1.Remove
        Call noeFile2.Remove
    End If
    For intI=0 To 1
        Call nwsWs.AddDatabase("" , aDbNames(intI))   ' add each
                                                      ' database to the
                                                      ' workspace
    Next
    If Msgbox("The new databases have been successfully added.  Would
➥you like to open the Contact Manager now?", 36,
➥"Open Contact Manager") =6 Then
```

```
            Call nwsWs.OpenDatabase("", aDbNames(0), "","",True,False)
                ' open the contact manager database
        End If

        Exit Sub

ErrHandler:
        Msgbox "An error"  & Error$ & " (" &Trim$(Str$(Err)) & ") has
        ➡occured detaching attached files, please contact your
        ➡administrator.", 16, "Error"
        Exit Sub
End Sub
```

NotesACL

The *NotesACL* object represents the Access Control List (ACL) of the parent *NotesDatabase* object. The ACL is one of the layers of security (at the database level) provided by Domino/Lotus Notes. The ACL contains lists of users, servers, and groups of users and servers that grant or restrict access to the database.

```
NotesSession
  └ NotesDatabase
      └ NotesACL
```

OR

```
NotesSession
  └ NotesDbDirectory
      └ NotesDatabase
          └ NotesACL
```

OR

```
NotesUIDatabase
  └ NotesDatabase
      └ NotesACL
```

LotusScript Syntax

```
Dim NotesACL as NotesACL
Set NotesACL = ndbNotesDatabase.ACL
```

The Notes robust security model allows for the access or restriction of data and information at various levels, ranging from the server level to the field level. However, the ACL set at the database level is most often used and modified by developers and administrators. The *NotesACL* and *NotesACLEntry* objects are used within all Notes databases. The *NotesACL* object is accessed through the ACL property of *NotesDatabase*. By declaring and getting a handle on the *NotesACL* object, you can access and modify the ACL settings for the respective *NotesDatabase*.

Once you have created or modified a *NotesACL* object in a *NotesDatabase,* you must call the Save method of *NotesACL* to save changes before closing the *NotesDatabase* object.

You can also access and modify database ACL settings without establishing a handle on the *NotesACL* object by accessing the ACL settings directly from *NotesDatabase* by using the methods of the *NotesDatabase* class (▶ 89) to query (QueryAccess), grant (GrantAccess), or revoke (RevokeAccess) access to a person, group, or server. However, in order to use these methods of the *NotesDatabase* object, you must know the name of the person, group, or server.

NotesACL Properties

5.0 InternetLevel   R/W   %

Internet
Level

```
To get: intLevel = naclNotesACL.InternetLevel
To set: naclNotesACL.InternetLevel = intLevel
```

Indicates the maximum access allowed to Web users who have authenticated with the Domino server using their respective Internet name and password. Therefore, you can limit the access allowed to a particular database for Web users who have equal or higher access when using a native Notes client. When working with Notes databases from a Notes client in the Notes user interface, you modify this property from the Database Access Control (select File | Database | Access Control...) in the Advanced section by using the drop-down list titled Maximum Internet name & password access. Here are the integer values associated with each ACL level:

ACL Constant Integer Values

Constant	Integer Value	Description
ACLLEVEL_NOACCESS	0	No access: Can't access the database.
ACLLEVEL_DEPOSITOR	1	Depositor: Can only create documents. Can't edit, delete, or read documents (even documents created by the depositor).
ACLLEVEL_READER	2	Reader: Can read documents but can't create, edit, or delete documents.

Constant	Integer Value	Description
ACLLEVEL_AUTHOR	3	Author: Can create and read documents. The author can optionally edit and delete his or her own documents.
ACLLEVEL_EDITOR	4	Editor: Can create, edit, read, and optionally delete all documents.
ACLLEVEL_DESIGNER	5	Designer: Has the same document access as the editor and can also create, edit, and delete design elements.
ACLLEVEL_MANAGER	6	Manager: Has complete access to documents (delete is optional), access to the database design, and access to modify the Database Access Control.

The following example determines the InternetLevel setting for the current database and displays the interpreted level within a message box:

```
Dim ns As New NotesSession
Dim ndb As NotesDatabase
Dim nacl As NotesACL
Dim strLevel As String
Set ndb = ns.CurrentDatabase
If Not ( ndb.IsOpen ) Then
    Call ndb.Open( "", "" )
End If
Set nacl = ndb.ACL
Select Case nacl.InternetLevel
Case 0
    strLevel = "No Access"
Case 1
    strLevel = "Depositor"
Case 2
    strLevel = "Reader"
Case 3
    strLevel = "Author"
Case 4
    strLevel = "Editor"
Case 5
    strLevel = "Designer"
Case 6
    strLevel = "Manager"
End Select
Msgbox "The internet level is: " & strLevel & ".", 32, "Internet Level"
```

Parent   R   O.Ref.   Parent

```
Set: ndbNotesDatabase = naclNotesACL.Parent
```

Returns a handle on the *NotesDatabase* object (▶ 89) of the database to which this ACL entry pertains.

Roles   R   ()   Roles

```
To get: aRoles = naclNotesACL.Roles
```

Returns a string array of all the roles that are defined in the respective Access Control List. Each element within the array represents the name of a role. If only one role is defined for this ACL entry, an array is still returned with only one element.

The role name for Notes versions after release 2 is surrounded by square brackets (such as [Admin]). Release 2 role names are surrounded by parentheses (such as (Admin)).

```
Dim ns As New NotesSession
Dim ndbNAB As NotesDatabase
Dim nacl As NotesACL
Dim varACLRoles As Variant
Dim strRoles As String
Dim intLoop As Integer
Set ndbNAB =New NotesDatabase(ns.currentdatabase.Server,"names.nsf")
If Not ( ndbNAB.IsOpen ) Then
   Call ndbNAB.Open( "", "" )
End If
Set nacl = ndbNAB.ACL
varACLRoles = nacl.Roles
For intLoop = 0 To Ubound(varACLRoles)
   strRoles = strRoles & Chr$(13) & varACLRoles(intLoop)
Next
Msgbox "The available roles are: " & strRoles, 32, "User Roles..."
```

UniformAccess	R/W	T/F

Uniform Access

```
To get: intUniform = naclNotesACL.UniformAccess
To set: naclNotesACL.UniformAccess = intUniform
```

Indicates whether uniform access has been set for the respective *NotesDatabase*. (TRUE means that uniform access is set, and FALSE means that it is not set.) If this property is set to TRUE, all replica copies that are created from this database and that replicate with this database must use a consistent ACL among one another. In other words, they must have identical entries for all their ACL entries. Otherwise, when the databases authenticate with one another, replication will not be allowed. When you're working with Notes databases from a client in the Notes user interface, this property would be enabled/disabled from the Database Access Control (select File | Database | Access Control...) in the Advanced section by using the checkbox titled Enforce a consistent Access Control List across all replicas of this database.

Be careful when using this property. If this property has been enabled, be sure that any changes made to the database access control are made only on the Administration Server for this database. Otherwise, if changes are made on the nonadministration server or a local copy, replication for this database will be permanently disabled with other replica copies. This is a powerful, but potentially hazardous, security feature.

NotesACL Methods

AddRole

AddRole

```
Call naclNotesACL.AddRole(strName)
```

strName	Required	$

The name of the new role.

This method adds a new role to the ACL entry of the respective *NotesACL* object. The value passed for strName should never include parentheses or brackets since they are automatically added to the string value. Changes made with this method are not permanent until the Save method of the *NotesACL* class is called.

The following example displays the existing roles for the current database and then prompts the user to add more roles. If you want to, you can add more roles by using an input box.

```
Dim ns As New NotesSession
Dim ndb As NotesDatabase
Dim nacl As NotesACL
Dim varACLRoles As Variant
Dim strRoles As String
Dim intLoop As Integer
Dim strNewRole As String
Set ndb = ns.CurrentDatabase
If Not ( ndb.IsOpen ) Then
    Call ndb.Open( "", "" )
End If
Set nacl = ndb.ACL
varACLRoles = nacl.Roles
For intLoop = 0 To Ubound(varACLRoles)
    strRoles = strRoles & Chr$(13) & varACLRoles(intLoop)
Next
If Msgbox("Roles:" & strRoles & Chr$(13) & "Add another?",36) = 6 Then
    strNewRole = Inputbox$("Enter the name of the new role.", "Add Role")
    If strNewRole <> "" Then
        Call nacl.AddRole(strNewRole)
        Call nacl.Save
    End If
End If
```

CreateACLEntry

```
Set nacleNotesACLEntry = naclNotesACL.CreateACLEntry(strName, intLevel)
```
Create ACL Entry

strName   Required $

The name of the person, group, or server for the new ACL entry.

intLevel   Required   %

The access level to assign to the person, group, or server defined in the strName. Here are the constants for this parameter:

Constant Value	Access Level
ACLLEVEL_NOACCESS	No access
ACLLEVEL_DEPOSITOR	Depositor access
ACLLEVEL_READER	Reader access
ACLLEVEL_AUTHOR	Author access
ACLLEVEL_EDITOR	Editor access
ACLLEVEL_DESIGNER	Designer access
ACLLEVEL_MANAGER	Manager access

The value returned from this method is the newly created *NotesACLEntry* (▶ 71). You must save any newly created *ACLEntries* to disk by calling the Save method of *NotesACL,* or they will be discarded.

DeleteRole

```
Call naclNotesACL.DeleteRole(strName)
```
DeleteRole

strName   Required $

The name of the role you want to remove.

This method will delete a role from the currently selected Database *NotesACL* entry
(▶ 71). Any newly deleted roles are not permanently removed from *NotesACL* until
the Save method of *NotesACL* is called. If the role specified doesn't exist in the
selected *NotesACL*, Notes will return the Role name not found error.

The following example displays the existing roles and prompts the user to delete a
role. This code was used as the click event of a hotspot button.

```
Sub Click(Source As Button)
On Error Goto ProcessError
Dim ns As New NotesSession
Dim ndb As NotesDatabase
Dim nacl As NotesACL
Dim varACLRoles As Variant
Dim strRoles As String
Dim intLoop As Integer
Dim strDeleteRole As String
Set ndb = ns.CurrentDatabase
If Not ( ndb.IsOpen ) Then
    Call ndb.Open( "", "" )
End If
Set nacl = ndb.ACL
varACLRoles = nacl.Roles
For intLoop = 0 To Ubound(varACLRoles)
    strRoles = strRoles & Chr$(13) & varACLRoles(intLoop)
Next
If Msgbox("Roles: " & strRoles & Chr$(13) & "Delete role?",36) = 6 Then
    strDeleteRole = Inputbox$("Name of the role to delete.","Delete")
    If strDeleteRole <> "" Then
        Call nacl.DeleteRole(strDeleteRole)
        Call nacl.Save
    End If
End If
Exit Sub
ProcessError:
Msgbox ¦Can't delete "¦ & strDeleteRole & ¦" role, it does not exist.¦
Exit Sub
End Sub
```

GetEntry

GetEntry   `Set nacleNotesACLEntry = naclNotesACL.GetEntry(strName)`

---

strName   Required $

The string name of the ACL entry you are looking for.

This method returns a handle to the *NotesACLEntry* object (▶ 71) that matches the
value passed in strName. The type of ACL entry can be a person, group, or server.
However, this method looks only for names explicitly defined in the database ACL.
It doesn't search within groups (whose values are defined in the Name and Address
Book) for a particular name specified in strName. If this functionality is required, use
the QueryAccess method specified in the *NotesDatabase* class. This value is not case-
sensitive. If the *NotesACLEntry* is not found, this method returns Nothing.

GetFirstEntry

GetFirst   `Set nacleNotesACLEntry = naclNotesACL.GetFirstEntry`
Entry

This method returns a handle on the *NotesACLEntry* (▶ 71) that is listed first in the Database ACL. For an example using this method, refer to the `GetNextEntry` method of the *NotesACL* class.

GetNextEntry

```
Set nacleNotesACLEntry =naclNotesACL.GetNextEntry(NotesACLEntry)
```
GetNextEntry

NotesACLEntry   **Required**   O.Ref.

The current *ACLEntry* for the respective database.

This method returns a handle on the next *NotesACLEntry* (▶ 71) listed in the Database ACL. If there are no more entries in the *NotesACL*, this method will return `Nothing`.

The following example displays all the *NotesACLEntries* for the current *NotesDatabase*.

```
Dim ns As New NotesSession
Dim ndb As NotesDatabase
Dim nacl As NotesACL
Dim nacle As NotesACLEntry
Dim strMessage As String
Dim intLoop As Integer
Set ndb = ns.CurrentDatabase
If Not ( ndb.IsOpen ) Then
    Call ndb.Open( "", "" )
End If
Set nacl = ndb.ACL
Set nacle = nacl.GetFirstEntry
Do While Not (nacle Is Nothing)
    strMessage = strMessage & Chr$(13) & nacle.Name
    Set nacle = nacl.GetNextEntry(nacle)
Loop
Msgbox"The ACL Entries are: " & strMessage, 32, "ACL Entries..."
```

RenameRole

```
Call naclNotesACL.RenameRole( strOldname, strNewname)
```
RenameRole

strOldname   **Required** $

The current name of the role.

strNewname   **Required** $

The new name to assign the current role.

This method will change the name of a role defined in the *NotesACL*. All entries located in the ACL that had the old role defined in them will get the new role assigned to them instead.

Save

```
Call naclNotesACL.Save
```
Save

This method saves any changes that have been made to the Database ACL. You must save the changes that you have made to the database before closing the database, or they will be discarded.

Remarks

Keep in mind that the script performing these operations (whether developed in LotusScript or Java) must still adhere to the Notes security model. Therefore, the program or user who is running the script must have Manager access to the database in order to modify the ACL. If this script is being run on the server by an agent, the script might be using the access control level of the person who last modified the agent, since the person who last modifies the agent signs that agent and thus becomes its owner. When the agent is designed, it is an option to have the agent run as the current user or as the user who last saved the agent.

Example

The following script will read all the *NotesACLEntries* and roles for the current database and display their values using a message box.

```
Dim ns As New NotesSession
Dim ndb As NotesDatabase
Dim nacl As NotesACL
Dim nacle As NotesACLEntry
Dim varACLRoles As Variant
Dim strRoles As String
Dim strACLEntries As String
Dim intLoop As Integer
Set ndb = ns.CurrentDatabase
Set nacl = ndb.ACL
If nacl.UniformAccess Then
    Msgbox "Uniform access is set, don't modify the ACL", 16, "Warning"
    Exit Sub
Else
    varACLRoles = nacl.Roles
    For intLoop = 0 To Ubound(varACLRoles)
        strRoles = strRoles & Chr$(13) & varACLRoles(intLoop)
    Next
    Set nacle = nacl.GetFirstEntry
    Do While Not (nacle Is Nothing)
        strACLEntries = strACLEntries & Chr$(13) & nacle.Name
        Set nacle = nacl.GetNextEntry(nacle)
    Loop
    Msgbox "ACL Entries:" & strACLEntries & Chr$(13) & "Roles: " &
    ➥strRoles
End If
```

NotesACLEntry

4.0 4.1x 4.5x 4.6x 5.0

This object represents an entry in the Domino/Lotus Notes Access Control List (ACL). The user type for this entry can be either a person, server, or group of type person, server, or mixed. The ACL is one of the layers of security (at the database level) provided by Domino/Lotus Notes.

NotesSession
  └ NotesDatabase
      └ NotesACL
          └ NotesACLEntry

OR

NotesSession
  └ NotesDbDirectory
      └ NotesDatabase
          └ NotesACL
              └ NotesACLEntry

OR

NotesUIDatabase
  └ NotesDatabase
      └ NotesACL
          └ NotesACLEntry

LotusScript Syntax

```
Dim NotesACLEntry As New NotesACLEntry(NotesACL,strName,intLevel)
```

or

```
Set NotesACLEntry = New NotesACLEntry(NotesACL,strName,intLevel)
```

If you want to create a new *NotesACLEntry* from scratch, you can use the New keyword with the Dim or Set statement, as shown in the preceding examples.

Once you have created a *NotesACLEntry* object in a *NotesACL,* you must call the Save method of the *NotesACL* (▶ 69) to save to disk the changes made to the ACL.

LotusScript Parameters

NotesACL	Required	O.Ref.

A *NotesACL* object that represents the Access Control List (ACL) that you are modifying or creating.

strName	Required	$

A string value that represents the name you want to give the new *NotesACLEntry* or the name of the *NotesACLEntry* that you want to modify. This value will be a name of a person type, group type, or server type.

intLevel	Required	%

The access control level to assign to the new person, group, or server. This value is actually a constant that must be one of the values listed in the following table:

Constant Value	Assigned Access
ACLLEVEL_NOACCESS	No access
ACLLEVEL_DEPOSITOR	Depositor
ACLLEVEL_READER	Reader
ACLLEVEL_AUTHOR	Author
ACLLEVEL_EDITOR	Editor
ACLLEVEL_DESIGNER	Designer
ACLLEVEL_MANAGER	Manager

NotesACLEntry Properties

CanCreateDocuments	R/W	T/F

CanCreate Documents

```
To get: intCreateDoc = nacleNotesACLEntry.CanCreateDocuments
To set: nacleNotesACLEntry.CanCreateDocuments = intCreateDoc
```

This property indicates whether the current entry has access to create new documents in the database. (TRUE indicates that the entry member(s) can create new documents. FALSE indicates that they can't.) This property affects only entries that are set at Author access to the database. It has no effect on all other entry levels, since their ability to create documents is already determined by their respective ACL entry.

Specifically, this setting is automatically set to TRUE for entries that are Manager, Designer, Editor, and Depositor and that can't be revoked. Similarly, this setting is automatically set to FALSE for entries that are Reader, Depositor, or No Access and that can't be modified. For entries that are set at Author access, this property will default to TRUE.

You must call the Save method of the *NotesACL* object in order to save the changes to disk and make the modifications take effect. Otherwise, the modifications are lost when the script is complete.

5.0 CanCreateLsorJavaAgent   R/W   T/F

```
To get: intCreateagt = nacleNotesACLEntry.CanCreateLsorJavaAgent
To set: nacleNotesACLEntry.CanCreateLsorJavaAgent = intCreateagt
```

CanCreateLsor JavaAgent

This property indicates whether the current entry has access to create LotusScript/Java agents in the database. (TRUE indicates that the entry member(s) can create LotusScript/Java agents. FALSE indicates that they can't.) This property doesn't affect Manager entry levels, because their ability to create documents is already determined by their respective ACL. In other words, Managers are automatically allowed to create LotusScript and Java agents, and this access can't be revoked. ACL entries that are set to Designer, Editor, Author, and Reader can be modified by this property. (For these entries, the default value for this property is FALSE.) Entries set to Depositor or No Access are automatically set to FALSE and can't be modified.

You must call the Save method of the *NotesACL* object in order to save the changes to disk and make the modifications take effect. Otherwise, the modifications are lost when the script is complete.

CanCreatePersonalAgent   R/W   T/F

```
To get: intCreatepers = nacleNotesACLEntry.CanCreatePersonalAgent
To set: nacleNotesACLEntry.CanCreatePersonalAgent = intCreatepers
```

CanCreate PersonalAgent

This property indicates whether the current entry has access to create personal agents in the database. (TRUE indicates that the entry member(s) can create personal agents. FALSE indicates that they can't.) This property doesn't affect Manager and Designer entry levels, because their ability to create personal agents is already determined by their respective ACL. In other words, they are automatically allowed to create personal agents, and this access can't be revoked. ACL entries that are set to Editor, Author, and Reader can be modified by this property. (For these entries, the default value for this property is FALSE.) Entries set to Depositor or No Access are automatically set to FALSE and can't be modified.

You must call the Save method of the *NotesACL* object in order to save the changes to disk and make the modifications take effect. Otherwise, the modifications are lost when the script is complete.

CanCreatePersonalFolder   R/W   T/F

```
To get: intCreatefld = nacleNotesACLEntry.CanCreatePersonalFolder
To set: nacleNotesACLEntry.CanCreatePersonalFolder = intCreatefld
```

CanCreate PersonalFolder

This property indicates whether the current entry has access to create personal folders in the database. (TRUE indicates that the entry member(s) can create personal folders. FALSE indicates that they can't.) This property doesn't affect Manager and Designer entry levels, because their ability to create personal folders is already determined by their respective ACL. In other words, they are automatically enabled to create personal folders, and this access can't be revoked. ACL entries that are set to Editor, Author, and Reader can be modified by this property. (For these entries, the default value for this property is FALSE.)

Entries set to Depositor or No Access are automatically set to FALSE and can't be modified.

You must call the Save method of the *NotesACL* object in order to save the changes to disk and make the modifications take effect. Otherwise, the modifications are lost when the script is complete.

The following example tests to see if the current user has rights to create a personal folder in the current database. If the user has sufficient rights to create personal folders, he can proceed with the current script. If he doesn't have sufficient access, he is informed that he isn't allowed to perform this request, and the script is abandoned. Keep in mind that although this property can be modified to enable or retract the rights for the current ACL entry, some *NotesACLEntries* rights are predetermined as a result of their respective *NotesACL* access level. For example, this property for a user with Depositor access will default to FALSE and can't be modified with this property. Likewise, a user with Manager access will automatically be granted rights to create personal folders, and this right can't be revoked. In these cases, the property becomes Read Only.

```
Dim ns As New NotesSession
Dim ndb As NotesDatabase
Dim nacl As NotesACL
Dim nacle As NotesACLEntry
Set ndb = ns.CurrentDatabase
Set nacl = ndb.ACL
Set nacle = nacl.GetEntry( ns.username)
If Not(nacle.CanCreatePersonalFolder) Then
    Msgbox "You're not allowed to create Personal Folders.", 64
    Exit Sub
Else
    'Continue with script since user has sufficient access!
End If
```

5.0 CanCreateSharedFolder   R/W   T/F

CanCreate
SharedFolder

```
To get: intCreatefdr = nacleNotesACLEntry.CanCreateSharedFolder
To set: nacleNotesACLEntry.CanCreateSharedFolder = intCreatefdr
```

This property indicates whether the current entry has access to create shared folders in the database. (TRUE indicates that the entry member(s) can create shared folders. FALSE indicates that they can't.) This property doesn't affect Manager and Designer entry levels, because their ability to create shared folders is already determined by their respective ACL. In other words, they are automatically enabled to create personal folders, and this access can't be revoked. ACL entries that are set to Editor can be modified by this property. (For these entries, the default value for this property is set to FALSE.) Entries set to Author, and Reader, Depositor, or No Access are automatically set to FALSE and can't be modified.

You must call the Save method of the *NotesACL* object in order to save the changes to disk and make the modifications take effect. Otherwise, the modifications are lost when the script is complete.

CanDeleteDocuments   R/W   T/F

CanDelete
Documents

```
To get: intDelete = nacleNotesACLEntry.CanDeleteDocuments
To set: nacleNotesACLEntry.CanDeleteDocuments = intDelete
```

This property indicates whether the current entry has access to delete *NotesDocuments* in the database. (TRUE indicates that the entry member(s) can delete documents. FALSE indicates that they can't.) This property doesn't affect Reader, Depositor, or No Access entry levels, because their ability to delete documents is already determined by their respective ACL.

In other words, they are automatically set to FALSE and therefore aren't allowed to delete documents. This access can't be modified. All other ACL entries that are set to Author access or higher can be modified by this property. For entries that are set at Author access, this property will default to TRUE.

You must call the Save method of the *NotesACL* object in order to save the changes to disk and make the modifications take effect. Otherwise, the modifications are lost when the script is complete.

5.0 IsAdminReaderAuthor   R/W   T/F   AdminReader
                                                                                Author
```
To get: intAdmin= nacleNotesACLEntry.IsAdminReaderAuthor
To set: nacleNotesACLEntry.IsAdminReaderAuthor = intAdmin
```

This property indicates whether the current entry is designated as the Administration Server for the current *NotesDatabase* object with rights to modify reader/author fields. (TRUE indicates that the entry member(s) are designated as the adminstrator reader/author. FALSE indicates that they aren't.)

You must call the Save method of the *NotesACL* object in order to save the changes to disk and make the modifications take effect. Otherwise, the modifications are lost when the script is complete.

5.0 IsAdminServer   R/W   T/F
```
To get: intAdmin = nacleNotesACLEntry.IsAdminServer                            IsAdminServer
To set: nacleNotesACLEntry.IsAdminServer = intAdmin
```

This property indicates whether the current entry is designated as the Administration Server for the current *NotesDatabase* object. (TRUE indicates that the entry member(s) can delete documents. FALSE indicates that they can't.) When working within the user interface of the Domino/Lotus Notes client, select File | Database | Access Control.... Then select the Advanced section. This setting is located under the Administration Server. However, be careful! This property can be set to any *NotesACLEntry,* even if the entry isn't a server user type and doesn't have manager access. In other words, you could assign an entry that has an access level of No Access with an unspecified user type as the Administration Server. This property is FALSE by default.

You must call the Save method of the *NotesACL* object in order to save the changes to disk and make the modifications take effect. Otherwise, the modifications are lost when the script is complete.

5.0 IsGroup   R/W   T/F   IsGroup
```
To get: intGroup = nacleNotesACLEntry.IsGroup
To set: nacleNotesACLEntry.IsGroup = intGroup
```

This property indicates whether the current entry is designated as a group user type. (TRUE indicates that the entry member(s) are a group user type. FALSE indicates that they aren't.) Setting this property to FALSE will result in the User Type being set to Unspecified. This property works in tandem with the IsServer and IsPerson properties. By default, setting IsGroup to TRUE will cause the user type of the current entry to be set to Mixed Group. However, if the IsServer property is set to TRUE, this setting will be set to Server Group. Similarly, if the IsPerson setting is set to TRUE, this property will be set to Person Group. This property is FALSE by default.

You must call the Save method of the *NotesACL* object in order to save the changes to disk and make the modifications take effect. Otherwise, the modifications are lost when the script is complete.

The following example steps through all the ACL entries for the current database and tells whether they are a person, server, or group.

```
Dim ns As New NotesSession
Dim ndb As NotesDatabase
Dim nacl As NotesACL
Dim nacle As NotesACLEntry
Dim strMsg As String
Set ndb = ns.CurrentDatabase
Set nacl = ndb.ACL
Set nacle = nacl.GetFirstEntry
Do While Not (nacle Is Nothing)
    If nacle.IsGroup Then
        strMsg = "The " & nacle.Name & " is a group" & _
        " with access set to " & nacle.Level
        Msgbox strMsg, 32, "Group Entry..."
    Elseif nacle.IsPerson Then
        strMsg = "The " & nacle.Name & " is a person" & _
        " with access set to " & nacle.Level
        Msgbox strMsg, 32, "Person Entry..."
    Elseif nacle.IsServer Then
        strMsg = "The " & nacle.Name & " is a server" & _
        " with access set to: " & nacle.Level & _
        " and IsAdminserver set to: " & nacle.Isadminserver
        Msgbox strMsg, 32, "Server Entry..."
    End If
    Set nacle = nacl.GetNextEntry(nacle)
Loop
```

5.0 IsPerson   R/W   T/F

IsPerson
```
To get: intPerson = nacleNotesACLEntry.IsPerson
To set: nacleNotesACLEntry.IsPerson = intPerson
```

This property indicates whether the current entry is designated as a person user type. (TRUE indicates that the entry member(s) are a person user type. FALSE indicates that they aren't.) Setting this property to FALSE will result in the User Type being set to Unspecified. This property works in conjunction with the IsGroup property. By default, setting IsPerson to TRUE will cause the user type of the current entry to be set to Person. However, if the IsGroup property is set to TRUE, this setting will be set to Person Group. This property is FALSE by default.

You must call the **Save** method of the *NotesACL* object in order to save the changes to disk and make the modifications take effect. Otherwise, the modifications are lost when the script is complete.

IsPublicReader   R/W   T/F

IsPublicReader
```
To get: intPubReader = nacleNotesACLEntry.IsPublicReader
To set: nacleNotesACLEntry.IsPublicReader = intPubReader
```

This property indicates whether the current entry is a public reader of the database. (TRUE indicates that the entry member(s) are a public reader. FALSE indicates that they aren't.) This property is FALSE by default.

IsPublicWriter   R/W   T/F

IsPublicWriter
```
To get: intpubwriter = nacleNotesACLEntry.IsPublicWriter
To set: nacleNotesACLEntry.IsPublicWriter = intpubwriter
```

This property indicates whether the current entry is a public writer of the database. (TRUE indicates that the entry member(s) are a public writer. FALSE indicates that they aren't.) This property is FALSE by default.

5.0 IsServer   R/W   T/F

```
To get: intServer = nacleNotesACLEntry.IsServer
To set: nacleNotesACLEntry.IsServer = intServer
```
IsServer

This property indicates whether the current entry is designated as a server user type. (TRUE indicates that the entry member(s) are a server user type. FALSE indicates that they aren't.) Setting this property to FALSE will result in the User Type being set to Unspecified. This property works in conjunction with the IsGroup property. By default, setting IsServer to TRUE will cause the user type of the current entry to be set to Server. However, if the IsGroup property is set to TRUE, this setting will be set to Server Group. This property is FALSE by default.

You must call the Save method of the *NotesACL* object in order to save the changes to disk and make the modifications take effect. Otherwise, the modifications are lost when the script is complete.

Level   R/W   %

```
To get: intLevel = nacleNotesACLEntry.Level
To set: nacleNotesACLEntry.Level = intLevel
```
Level

This property indicates the access level of the current entry.

The value returned for this property is a constant of type integer. Here are the values that can be returned:

Constant Value	Assigned Access
ACLLEVEL_NOACCESS	No access
ACLLEVEL_DEPOSITOR	Depositor
ACLLEVEL_READER	Reader
ACLLEVEL_AUTHOR	Author
ACLLEVEL_EDITOR	Editor
ACLLEVEL_DESIGNER	Designer
ACLLEVEL_MANAGER	Manager

For an example that uses this property, refer to the IsGroup property of the *NotesACLEntry* class (▶ 75).

Name   R/W $

```
To get: strName = nacleNotesACLEntry.Name
To set: nacleNotesACLEntry.Name = strName
```
Name

The string value representing the name of the current entry.

Changing the entry's name doesn't affect the other attributes of *NotesACLEntry*, such as the ACL level and whether the entry is a person, server, and so on. For an example that uses this property, refer to the Roles property of the *NotesACLEntry* class (▶ 77).

Parent   R   O.Ref.

```
To get: Set naclNotesACL = nacleNotesACLEntry.Parent
```
Parent

This property returns a handle to the *NotesACL* object that contains the current *NotesACLEntry*.

Roles   R   ()

```
To get: aRoles = nacleNotesACLEntry.Roles
```
Roles

This property returns a string array of the roles that are enabled for a specified entry. Each element contained within this array represents the role name surrounded by brackets.

The following code snippet steps through all the entries in the current database's *NotesACLEntries*. For each entry, a list of all the roles enabled for that entry is built and displayed to the user in a message box.

```
Dim ns As New NotesSession
Dim ndb As NotesDatabase
Dim nacl As NotesACL
Dim nacle As NotesACLEntry
Dim strRoleslist As String
Dim intLoop As Integer
Set ndb = ns.CurrentDatabase
Set nacl = ndb.ACL
Set nacle = nacl.GetFirstEntry
Do While Not (nacle Is Nothing)
    For intLoop = 0 To Ubound(nacle.Roles)
        strRolesList = strRoleslist & Chr$(13) & nacle.Roles(intLoop)
    Next
    Msgbox strRoleslist, 32, "Roles for " & nacle.Name
    Set nacle = nacl.GetNextEntry(nacle)
    strRoleslist = ""
Loop
```

UserType	R/W	%

UserType

```
To set: nacleNotesACLEntry.UserType = intUserType
To get: intUserType = nacleNotesACLEntry.UserType
```

This property indicates the type of the *NotesACLEntry*. Along with the need to have a logical segmentation of the various users, groups and servers, each entry's respective type also has ramifications on how the security model is enforced. Therefore, it is important that the proper UserType be specified to insure that the access rights granted/restricted to each user, group, and/or server responds in the anticipated manner.

Here are the values that can be assigned or returned: Unspecified, Person, Server, MixedGroup, PersonGroup, ServerGroup.

NotesACLEntry Methods

DisableRole

DisableRole

```
Call nacleNotesACLEntry.DisableRole(strName)
```

strName	Required	$

The name of the role to disable.

This method disables the specified role for the current *NotesACLEntry*. If the specified role has already been disabled for the current *NotesACLEntry*, this method will do nothing. If the specified role does not exist for the current *NotesACLEntry*, this method will return a Role name not found error. Refer to the IsRoleEnabled method of the *NotesACLEntry* class (▶ 79) for an example using this method.

EnableRole

EnableRole

```
Call nacleNotesACLEntry.EnableRole(strName)
```

strName	Required	$

The name of the role to enable.

This method enables the specified role for the current *NotesACLEntry*. If the specified role has already been enabled for the current *NotesACLEntry,* this method will do nothing. If the specified role does not exist for the current *NotesACLEntry,* this method will return a `Role name not found` error. Refer to the `IsRoleEnabled` method of the *NotesACLEntry* class (▶ 79) for an example using this method.

IsRoleEnabled

```
intEnabled = nacleNotesACLEntry.IsRoleEnabled(strName)
```
IsRoleEnabled

strName   **Required**   **T/F**

The name of the role.

This method indicates whether the specified role is enabled for the current *NotesACLEntry* object. (`TRUE` indicates that the role is enabled for the entry. `FALSE` indicates that it is not.)

The following example checks all the *NotesACLEntries* to see if the `NewsEditor` role is enabled. If the role is enabled, the user is prompted to disable it. If the role is disabled, the user is prompted to enable it.

```
Dim ns As New NotesSession
Dim ndb As NotesDatabase
Dim nacl As NotesACL
Dim nacle As NotesACLEntry
Dim varACLRoles As Variant
Dim intFlag As Integer
Dim strMsg As String
Set ndb = ns.CurrentDatabase
Set nacl = ndb.ACL
Set nacle = nacl.GetFirstEntry
Do While Not (nacle Is Nothing)
    intFlag = nacle.IsRoleEnabled("NewsEditor")
    If intFlag Then
        strMsg = "The NewsEditor role is enabled for " & nacle.Name & _
        ".  Would you like to disable it?"
        If Msgbox(strMsg, 36, "NewsEditor role...") = 6 Then
            Call nacle.DisableRole("NewsEditor")
        End If
    Else
        strMsg = "The NewsEditor role is disabled for " & nacle.Name & _
        ".  Would you like to enable it?"
        If Msgbox(strMsg, 36, "NewsEditor role...") = 6 Then
            Call nacle.EnableRole("NewsEditor")
        End If
    End If
    Set nacle = nacl.GetNextEntry(nacle)
Loop
Call nacl.Save
```

New

```
Dim nacleNotesACLEntry As New NotesACLEntry (NotesACL,strName,intLevel)
```
New

or

```
Set nacleNotesACLEntry = New NotesACLEntry(NotesACL, strName,intLevel)
```

This method creates a new *NotesACLEntry* object and returns a handle to the new object. Once you have created a *NotesACLEntry* object in *NotesACL,* you must call the `Save` method of the *NotesACL* (▶ 69) to save to disk the changes made to the ACL.

This method creates a new *NotesACLEntry* object and returns a handle to the new object. The description and syntax of this method are described in the "LotusScript Syntax" section near the beginning of this chapter (▶ 72).

Remove

`Call nacleNotesACLEntry.`**`Remove`**

This method removes an entry from the Access Control List.

Remarks

Using the parent class *NotesACL,* you can access an existing *NotesACLEntry* in one of three ways. If you know the name of the *ACLEntry,* you can use the `GetEntry` method of the *NotesACL* object. Similarly, you can use the `GetFirstEntry` or the `GetNextEntry` of *NotesACL* to step through the entries of the *NotesACL* object. When manipulating databases' Access Control Lists, be careful not to accidentally remove yourself, any manager or designer groups, or servers when manipulating the *NotesACLEntry* and *NotesACL* objects, especially when testing and debugging your code.

Example

The following example shows a practical use of the *NotesACLEntry* class. This code, which could be saved in an agent and then run against all new or existing databases, will update the access control of the specified database to a standard format. After tweaking this example, you could use this code to make the maintenance of the access control settings simpler to administer. "ACME" represents the name of the organization or company for this specific server. When working with databases that reside on servers that might be accessible by other servers, domains, and companies, it is a good practice not to use generic ACL entry names such as LocalDomainServers or Designers, because they will have different meanings with other servers or organizations. It's almost always more efficient and secure to be as specific as possible when naming groups, especially with issues related to security. The following example adds the following groups to the ACL of the currently selected database object with the following settings:

NotesACLEntry Name	Entry Type	Access Level
ACMEServers	Server Group	Manager access
ACMEAdminServer	Server	Manager access as Admin server
OtherServers	Server Group	Editor access
ACMEManagers	Person Group	Manager access
ACMEAdmin	Person Group	Editor access
ACMEDesigners	Person Group	Designer access
ACMEUsers	Person Group	Author access
Terminations	Mixed Group	No access

In addition, this example removes the default database access control entries for LocalDomainServers and OtherDomainServers if they exist.

```
Dim ns As New NotesSession
Dim ndb As NotesDatabase
```

```
Dim nacl As NotesACL
Dim nacleACME As NotesACLEntry
Dim nacleadminserver As NotesACLEntry
Dim nacleotherserver As NotesACLEntry
Dim naclemanager As NotesACLEntry
Dim nacleadmin As NotesACLEntry
Dim nacledesigner As NotesACLEntry
Dim nacleuser As NotesACLEntry
Dim nacletermination As NotesACLEntry
Dim nacle As NotesACLEntry
Set ndb = ns.CurrentDatabase
If Not ( ndb.IsOpen ) Then
    Call ndb.Open( "", "" )
End If
Set nacl = ndb.ACL
'Add new entries into current database access control
Set nacleACME = New NotesACLEntry(nacl,"ACMEServers",ACLLEVEL_MANAGER)
nacleACME.IsGroup = True
nacleACME.IsServer = True
Set nacleadminserver = New NotesACLEntry(nacl,"ACMEAdminServer",
➥ACLLEVEL_MANAGER)
nacleadminserver.IsServer = True
nacleadminserver.Isadminserver = True
Set nacleotherserver = New NotesACLEntry(nacl,"OtherServers",
➥ACLLEVEL_EDITOR)
nacleotherserver.IsGroup = True
nacleotherserver.IsServer = True
Set naclemanager = New NotesACLEntry(nacl,"ACMEManagers",
➥ACLLEVEL_MANAGER)
naclemanager.IsGroup = True
naclemanager.IsPerson = True
Set nacleadmin = New NotesACLEntry(nacl,"ACMEAdmin",ACLLEVEL_EDITOR)
nacleadmin.IsGroup = True
nacleadmin.IsPerson = True
nacleadmin.Cancreatepersonalagent = True
nacleadmin.Cancreatepersonalfolder = True
nacleadmin.Cancreatesharedfolder = True
Set nacledesigner = New NotesACLEntry(nacl,"ACMEDesigners",
➥ACLLEVEL_DESIGNER)
nacledesigner.IsGroup = True
nacledesigner.IsPerson = True
nacledesigner.Cancreatelsorjavaagent = True
Set nacleuser = New NotesACLEntry(nacl,"ACMEUsers",ACLLEVEL_AUTHOR)
nacleuser.IsGroup = True
nacleuser.IsPerson = True
nacleuser.Cancreatepersonalagent = True
nacleuser.Cancreatepersonalfolder = True
Set nacletermination = New NotesACLEntry(nacl,"Terminations",
➥ACLLEVEL_NOACCESS)
nacletermination.Isgroup = True
'Now clean up the default database ACL entries
Set nacle = nacl.GetEntry( "LocalDomainServers")
If Not ( nacle Is Nothing ) Then
    Call nacle.remove
End If
Set nacle = nacl.GetEntry( "OtherDomainServers")
If Not ( nacle Is Nothing ) Then
    Call nacle.remove
End If
Call nacl.Save
```

4.0 4.1x 4.5x 4.6x 5.0 NotesAgent

The *NotesAgent* class allows you to access existing public, personal, and Notes 3 macro agents in a *NotesDatabase*. You can't create new agents with this class.

NotesSession
    └ NotesAgent

OR

. . .
    └ NotesDatabase
        └ NotesAgent

LotusScript Syntax

```
Dim Agent as NotesAgent
```

To access an agent object, you have two basic choices: You can either use the CurrentAgent property of *NotesSession* to access the currently running agent (if there is one), or you can use the Agents property of *NotesDatabase* to iterate through a collection of all the agents in a database. Unfortunately, there is no method that allows you to access an agent directly by name.

NotesAgent Properties

Comment   R $

Comment   To Get: strComment = nagtnotesAgent.**Comment**

Returns a text string containing a comment describing the agent, as entered by the agent's programmer.

CommonOwner   R $

CommonOwner   To get: strCommonOwner = nagtnotesAgent.**CommonOwner**

Returns the common name of the last person to edit and save the agent.

5.0 HasRunSinceModified   R   T/F

HasRunSince   To get: intHasRunSinceModified = nagtnotesAgent.**HasRunSinceModified**
Modified
Indicates whether the agent has run since created or last modified.

Isenabled   R/W   T/F

Isenabled   To set: nagtnotesAgent.**IsEnabled** = intEnabled
To get: intEnabled = nagtnotesAgent.**IsEnabled**

Indicates whether the agent is enabled. (This is TRUE if the agent is enabled and FALSE if it is not.) Because this property is designed for scheduled agents, setting it for agents that are hidden or run from the menu will have no effect. If you make a change to this property, you must call the Save method on NotesAgent.

5.0 IsNotesAgent   R   T/F

IsNotesAgent   To get: intNotesAgent = nagtnotesAgent.**IsNotesAgent**

Indicates whether the agent can run when called from a *Notes* client.

IsPublic   R   T/F

IsPublic   To get: intPublic = nagtnotesAgent.**IsPublic**

Indicates whether the agent is public (stored in the database and accessible to all the database's users) or personal (stored in the owner's desktop.dsk file). This property returns TRUE if the agent is a public agent and FALSE otherwise.

5.0 IsWebAgent   R   T/F

IsWebAgent   To get: intWebAgent = nagtnotesAgent.**IsWebAgent**

Indicates whether the agent can run when called from a browser.

LastRun   R   ?

```
To get: varLastRunDate = nagtnotesAgent.Lastrun
```
LastRun

This property returns a variant of type date (7), indicating the time and date the agent was last executed. If a particular agent has never been run, Lastrun will return the infamous 12/30/1899.

Name   R $

```
To get: strAgentName = nagtnotesAgent.Name
```
Name

This property returns the name of the agent as a string value.

```
        Dim nsSession As New NotesSession
        Dim strAgentName As String
        strAgentName="Empty Trash"
' loop through all agents in the current database
        Forall agent In nsSession.CurrentDatabase.Agents
            If agent.name=strAgentName Then
' check to see if the agent has been run since the database was
' last modified
                If agent.Lastrun<nsSession.CurrentDatabase.LastModified
                ➥Then
                    agent.IsEnabled=True ' enable the agent
                    Call agent.save ' save the agent to disk
                End If
            End If
        End Forall
```

Owner   R $

```
To get: strOwner = nagtnotesAgent.Owner
```
Owner

Returns the hierarchical name of the person who last saved the agent.

Parent   R   O. Ref.

```
To get: ndbNotesDatabase = nagtnotesAgent.Parent
```
Parent

Returns a NotesDatabase object that represents the database containing the agent.

```
Dim nsSession As New NotesSession
Dim nagtAgent As NotesAgent
Dim ndbCDb As NotesDatabase
Set nagtAgent=nsSession.CurrentAgent
Set ndbCDb=nagtAgent.Parent
Msgbox "The parent database of this agent is: " &_
ndbCDb.FileName & " (" & ndbCDb.Title & " )" , 64, "Information"
```

Query   R $

```
To get: strQuery = nagtnotesAgent.Query
```
Query

Returns the query string used by the agent to select documents if the Add Search button is used to add a query. If this feature is not used, this property will return an empty string (" ").

ServerName   R/W $

```
To get: strServer = nagtnotesAgent.ServerName
To set: nagtnotesAgent.ServerName = strServer
```
ServerName

This property returns the name of the server on which the agent runs. The exact value returned varies, depending on whether the agent is scheduled. If the agent is scheduled, `ServerName` returns the name of the server on which the agent runs. For unscheduled agents in a database on a server, it returns the name of the parent database. For unscheduled agents in a local database, it returns the common user name. If you want the agent to run on any server, set this property to `"*"`.

```
Dim nsSession As New NotesSession
Dim nagtAgent As NotesAgent
Set nagtAgent=nsSession.CurrentAgent
nagtAgent.ServerName="*"
Call nagtAgent.Save
```

5.0 Target   R   %

Target   `To get: intTarget = nagtnotesAgent.Target`

Indicates which documents the agent acts on. Valid values are as follows: `TARGET_ALL_DOCS, TARGET_NEW_DOCS, TARGET_NEW_OR_MODIFIED_DOCS, TARGET_SELECTED_DOCS, TARGET_ALL_DOCS_IN_VIEW, TARGET_UNREAD_DOCS_IN_VIEW, TARGET_PROMPT_USER, TARGET_UI_SELECTABLE_OBJECT, TARGET_NONE.`

5.0 Trigger   R   %

Trigger   `To get: intTrigger = nagtnotesAgent.Trigger`

Indicates when the agent runs. Valid values are as follows: `TRIGGER_NONE, TRIGGER_SCHEDULED, TRIGGER_NEW_MAIL, TRIGGER_DOC_PASTED, TRIGGER_MANUAL, TRIGGER_DOC_UPDATE, TRIGGER_BEFORE_NEW_MAIL.`

NotesAgent Methods

Remove

Remove   `Call nagtAgent.Remove`

This method takes no parameters and is used to permanently delete an agent from the database.

Run

Run   `Call nagtAgent.Run`

This method takes no parameters and is used to execute an agent. There are a few caveats to note when using the `Run` method to execute an agent. First, agents can't be run from themselves (recursively). Second, front-end classes can't be used in agents run in this manner (for example, *NotesUIWorkspace* can't be used). Finally, no user interaction is possible, including the debugger.

5.0 RunOnServer

RunOnServer   `Call nagtAgent.RunOnServer`

This method runs the agent on the parent database, which must be remote.

4.6 Save

Save   `Call nagtAgent.Save`

This method was introduced in version 4.6 and is used to save the agent when the `Isenabled` or `ServerName` properties are changed via code.

Remarks

It's very important to remember to call the Save method whenever you make changes to an agent using its properties, or the changes won't be written to disk.

Example

```
Dim nsSession As New NotesSession
Dim ndbMailDb As NotesDatabase
Dim ndtLastRunThreshold As New NotesDateTime("Today")
Dim ndtLastRunDate As NotesDateTime
Set nvwPeopleView=S.CurrentDatabase.GetView("People")
Set ndocPerson = nvwPeopleView.GetFirstDocument
Dim lngDiff As Long
Dim strAgentName as string
Call ndtLastRunThreshold.AdjustMonth(-1)
strAgentName="Periodic Archive"
Do While Not ndocPerson Is Nothing
     Set ndbMailDb=nsSession.GetDatabase
     ➥(nsSession.CurrentDatabase.Server,
     ➥ndocPerson.MailFile(0))
     If Not ndbMailDb Is Nothing And ndbMailDb.IsOpen Then
          Forall agent In ndbMailDb.Agents
               If agent.Name=strAgentName Then
                    ndtLastRunDate.LsLocalTime=agent.LastRun
                    lngDiff=ndtLastRunDate.TimeDifference
                    ➥(ndtLastRunThreshold)
                    If 2592000/lngDiff > 1 Then ' # of seconds
                    ➥in 30 ' days/by time difference
                         agent.IsEnabled=True
                         Call agent.Save
                    End If
               End If
          End Forall
     Else
          Msgbox "Could not open " & ndocPerson.MailFile(0) , 16,
          ➥"Error"
     End If
     Set ndocPerson=nvwPeopleView.GetNextDocument
Loop
```

NotesDatabase

4.0 4.1x 4.5x 4.6x 5.0

The *NotesDatabase* class is one of the most powerful and fundamental of all the Notes classes, because the *NotesDatabase* (Notes Storage Facility) is the primary means of storing data in Notes/Domino. Mastering its many properties and methods is essential to becoming a proficient Notes/Domino developer.

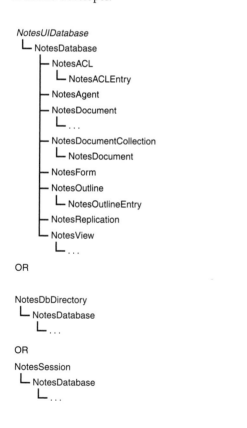

continued >>

LotusScript Syntax

```
Dim NotesDatabase As New NotesDatabase(strServer, strFileName)
```

or

```
Set NotesDatabase = New NotesDatabase(strServer, strFileName)
```

You have a plethora of choices when it comes to accessing a *NotesDatabase* object. Any of the following options will work:

You can use the `Create` method to create a new database from scratch.

If you want to create a new database based on an existing one, try `CreateCopy`, `CreateFromTemplate`, or `CreateReplica`.

To access an existing database when its server and filename are known, you can use either the `New` method or the `GetDatabase` method of *NotesSession* (▶ 263).

To access the database in which a script is currently running, without indicating a server or filename, use the `CurrentDatabase` property of *NotesSession* (▶ 265).

To open an existing database when the server and `ReplicaID` are known, use the `OpenByReplicaID` method.

If you know a database's server but not its filename, try the *NotesDbDirectory* class (▶ 123).

To determine which databases are address books and open them, use the `AddressBooks` property of *NotesSession* (▶ 264).

If you want to open the current user's mail database, use the `OpenMail` method.

If you have any of the following objects—*NotesView, NotesDocument, NotesDocumentCollection, NotesACL, NotesViewEntry,* or *NotesViewEntryCollection*—try the `Parent` or `ParentDatabase` property.

LotusScript Parameters

strServer	Required	$

A string value that contains the name of the server on which a database resides. Use an empty string (`""`) to indicate that the database resides on a local machine.

strFileName	Required	$

A string value that contains the path and filename of a Notes database within the Notes data directory. If the database isn't in the Notes data directory, you must use a full path to the file in this parameter.

NotesDatabase Properties

ACL	R	O.Ref.

```
To Get: setnACLCurACL = ndbNotesDatabase.ACL
```

ACL

Returns a NotesACL object (▶ 63) containing the database's Access Control List.

Agents	R	?

Agents

To get: varAgents = ndbNotesDatabase.**Agents**

Returns an array of *NotesAgent* objects (▶ 83). If this property is accessed on a workstation, the array will contain both public agents and personal agents that belong to the current user. If this property runs on a server, the array will contain only public agents.

AllDocuments	R	O.Ref.

AllDocuments

To get: setndcAllDocuments = ndbNotesDatabase.**AllDocuments**

This property returns an unsorted *NotesDocumentCollection* (▶ 149) that contains all the documents in the database. Use this property only if you really want to access all the documents in a database, because this might return a huge collection. If you're interested in accessing a subset of documents in the database, explore the GetAllDocumentsByKey method of *NotesView* (▶ 289), the Search (▶ 108) or FTSearch (▶ 100) methods of *NotesDatabase,* or the GetAllEntriesByKey method of *NotesViewEntry.* The following example illustrates using this property.

```
Dim S As New NotesSession
Dim ndcCollection As NotesDocumentCollection
Set ndcCollection=S.CurrentDatabase.AllDocuments
Call ndcCollection.StampAll("CreatedBy" ,"Samuel Hatter" )
Call ndcCollection.UpdateAll
```

Categories	R/W	?

Categories

To get: varCategories = ndbNotesDatabase.**Categories**
To set: ndbNotesDatabase.**Categories** = varCategories

Contains the categories under which a database appears in the Notes Database Library. If this property contains multiple categories, they are separated by commas or semicolons.

Created	R	?

Created

To get: varCreatedDate = ndbNotesDatabase.**Created**

This property returns a variant of type DATE (7) indicating the time and date the database was created.

CurrentAccessLevel	R	%

Current Access Level

To get: intCurAccess = ndbNotesDatabase.**CurrentAccessLevel**

Returns the current user's access level as an integer between 0 (no access) and 6 (manager access). Keep in mind that this property returns the access level of the current user on a workstation but returns the access level of the script owner (the person who last saved the script) on a server. Each of these integers can be represented as one of the following constants:

Constant	Description
ACLLEVEL_NOACCESS	No access
ACLLEVEL_DEPOSITOR	Depositor access
ACLLEVEL_READER	Reader access
ACLLEVEL_AUTHOR	Author access
ACLLEVEL_EDITOR	Editor access
ACLLEVEL_DESIGNER	Designer access
ACLLEVEL_MANAGER	Manager access

DelayUpdates   R/W   T/F

```
To get: intDelayUpdates = ndbNotesDatabase.DelayUpates
To set: ndbNotesDatabase.DelayUpdates = intDelayUpdates
```

This property indicates whether write operations to the database are processed immediately or are batched for better performance. When set to FALSE (the default), database
updates are posted immediately, causing script execution to stop until the write operation completes. Conversely, when set to TRUE, updates are cached and posted later, and
the script continues to execute. Keep in mind that although performance is boosted,
data can be lost if the server crashes. This property affects both save and remove operations on documents.

DesignTemplateName   R $

```
To get: strTemplateName = ndbNotesDatabase.DesignTemplateName
```

If a database inherits its design from a template, this property returns the template's
name. Otherwise, this property returns an empty string (""). If a database inherits only
specific design elements (such as a view or navigator) rather than its entire design, this
property returns an empty string ("").

```
Dim S as New NotesSession
MsgBox "The Current Design Template is: " &
➥S.CurrentDatabase.DesignTemplateName,64, "Information..."
```

FileName   R $

```
To get: strFileName = ndbNotesDatabase.FileName
```

Returns the actual filename and extension of a database without the path.

The following example demonstrates building a generic routine that uses server properties of *NotesDatabase,* including Server, FilePath, and FileName to return the location of the current database. This would make a useful addition to a script library,
especially if you tend to build multidatabase applications and store all the databases in
the same directory (which is a good practice).

```
Public Function ResolveCurrentLocation(ndbCur As NotesDatabase) As Variant
' This is a generic routine that will return the current
' server and filepath
Dim aLocation(1) As String
Dim strFilePath As String
strFilePath=Left$(ndbCur.FilePath, (Len(ndbCur.FilePath)-
➥Len(ndbCur.FileName)))
aLocation(0)=ndbCur.Server
aLocation(1)=strFilePath
ResolveCurrentLocation=aLocation
End Function
```

FilePath   R $

```
To get: strFilePath = ndbNotesDatabase.FilePath
```

Returns the actual filename and extension of a database, as well as its path. Databases
on a workstation return the complete path (such as C:\Notes\data\definiti\cmgr.nsf),
and databases on a server return a path relative to the Notes data directory (such as
definiti\cmgr.nsf).

5.0 FolderRefsEnabled   R/W   T/F

```
To get: intFldrRefs = ndbNotesDatabase.FolderRefsEnabled
To set: ndbNotesDatabase.FolderRefsEnabled = intFldrRefs
```

This property can be used to indicate whether folder references are enabled for a particular database. If set to TRUE, this determines which folder a document is in. Before attempting to test a document's folder references, be sure to test this property. Additionally, each database that uses folder references must have the `FolderRef`.

Forms	R/W	()

Forms

To get: varAllForms = ndbNotesDatabase.**Forms**

This property returns an array of all the *NotesForm* (▶ 167) objects in the database.

5.0 IsDirectoryCatalog	R	T/F

IsDirectory Catalog

To get: intIsDirCatalog = ndbNotesDatabase.**IsDirectoryCatalog**

Use this property to determine whether a database is a Directory Catalog database, otherwise known as a Lightweight NAB. This property returns FALSE for any databases that aren't accessed through the `AddressBooks` property of *NotesSession* (▶ 264) and that are explicitly opened (the `IsOpen` property returns TRUE; see the description of `IsOpen`).

IsFTIndexed	R	T/F

IsFTIndexed

To get: intIsIndexed = ndbNotesDatabase.**IsFTIndexed**

This property indicates whether a database has a full-text index. It returns TRUE if an index exists and FALSE otherwise.

IsMultiDbSearch	R/W	T/F

IsMultiDb Seach

To get: intMultiDbSearch = ndbNotesDatabase.**IsMultiDbSearch**

This property returns TRUE if a database is part of a multidatabase search index and FALSE otherwise.

IsOpen	R	T/F

IsOpen

To get: intIsOpen = ndbNotesDatabase.**IsOpen**

Indicates whether a database has been opened. If the database is open, this property returns TRUE. Otherwise, it returns FALSE.

IsPrivateAddressBook	R	T/F

IsPrivate AddressBook

To get: intPrivNAB = ndbNotesDatabase.**IsPrivateAddressBook**

For any database accessed through the `AddressBooks` property of *NotesSession* (▶ 264) that is a Personal Address Book, this property returns TRUE. For any other database, including Personal Address Books *not* accessed through the `AddressBooks` property of *NotesSession,* this property returns FALSE.

IsPublicAddressBook	R	T/F

IsPublic AddressBook

To get: intPubNAB = ndbNotesDatabase.**IsPublicAddressBook**

For any database accessed through the `AddressBooks` property of *NotesSession* (▶ 264) that is a Public Address Book, this property returns TRUE. For any other database, including Public Address Books *not* accessed through the `AddressBooks` property of *NotesSession,* this property returns FALSE.

LastFTIndexed	R	?

LastFTIndexed

To get: varLastIndexDate = ndbNotesDatabase.**LastFTIndexed**

Returns as a variant of type DATE the date and time the database was last full-text indexed. If the database has no index, this property returns the popular 12/30/1899.

LastModified	R	?

```
To get: varModDate = ndbNotesDatabase.LastModified
```

Returns as a variant of type DATE the date and time the database was last modified.

Managers	R	()

```
To get: varManagers = NotesDatabase.Managers
```

This property returns an array containing the names of people, servers, and groups who have been granted manager access to a database.

The following example demonstrates using this property to mail the managers of the database to request higher access. This might be an agent called by an action button.

```
Dim S As New NotesSession
Dim ndocMail As NotesDocument
Set ndocMail=S.CurrentDatabase.CreateDocument
Dim nrtBody As New NotesRichTextItem(ndocMail, "Body")
ndocMail.Subject="Please review my access level..."
Call nrtBody.AppendText("I believe I have insufficient access to the
➥following database:")
Call nrtBody.AddNewLine(2)
Call nrtBody.AppendText("Title: " & S.CurrentDatabase.Title)
Call nrtBody.AddNewLine(1)
Call nrtBody.AppendText("FileInfo: " & S.CurrentDatabase.Filepath &
➥" on " &  S.CurrentDatabase.Server)
Call nrtBody.AddNewLine(1)
Call nrtBody.AppendText("RepID: " & S.CurrentDatabase.ReplicaID)
Call nrtBody.AddNewLine(1)
Call nrtBody.AppendText("Please review my access to this database.")
Call ndocMail.Send(False, S.CurrentDatabase.Managers)
```

5.0 MaxSize	R	&

```
To get: lngMaxSize = ndbNotesDatabase.MaxSize
```

This property returns the maximum allowable size of a database as set when the database was created.

5.0 MaxSizeV5	R	#

```
To get: dblMaxR5Size = ndbnotesDatabase.MaxSizeV5
```

Returns the maximum allowable size for a Release 5 database.

Parent	R	O.Ref.

```
To get: setnsSession = ndbNotesDatabase.Parent
```

This property returns a *NotesSession* object (▶ 263) representing the current *NotesSession*.

PercentUsed	R	#

```
To get: dblUsed = ndbNotesDatabase.PercentUsed
```

This property returns the amount of space utilized in a database to store real data as a double. Consider the following example.

```
Dim S As New NotesSession
If S.CurrentDatabase.PercentUsed <90 Then
  Call S.CurrentDatabase.Compact
End If
```

ReplicaID	R	$

ReplicaID   `To get: strRepID = ndbNotesDatabase.`**`ReplicaID`**

This property returns a database's replica ID (which is a 16-digit alphanumeric string).

5.0	ReplicationInfo	R	O.Ref.

ReplicationInfo   `To get: setnrRepInfo = ndbNotesDatabase.`**`ReplicationInfo`**

Each Notes database contains one *NotesReplication* object (▶ 227), and you can use this property to access it.

Server	R	$

Server   `To get: strServer = ndbNotesDatabase.`**`Server`**

This property returns the name of the server on which the database resides. If the database is on a workstation, this property returns an empty string ("").

Size	R	#

Size   `To get: dblSize = ndbNotesDatabase.`**`Size`**

This property returns the size of the database in bytes as a double.

SizeQuota	R/W	?

SizeQuota   `To get: lngQuota = ndbNotesDatabase.`**`SizeQuota`**
`To set: ndbNotesDatabase.`**`SizeQuota`**` = lngQuota`

This property contains the size quota for a database (which is the amount of disk space that the database is allowed to occupy). Not all databases have a quota; this property returns **0** for such databases. If a script (meaning its owner) has administrative access to a server, it can change this property, but in mostcases, this property will be read-only.

TemplateName	R	$

TemplateName   `To get: strTplName = ndbNotesDatabase.`**`TemplateName`**

This property returns an empty string ("") if the database is not a template. Otherwise, it returns the value entered for the template name.

Title	R/W	$

Title   `To get: strTitle = ndbNotesDatabase.`**`Title`**
`To set: ndbNotesDatabase.`**`Title`**` = strTitle`

This property contains the database's title (as displayed on the database icon). You can't change the title of a database in which this property is being accessed.

UnprocessedDocuments	R	O.Ref.

Unprocessed   `To get: setndcUnprocessed = ndbNotesDatabase.`**`UnprocessedDocuments`**
Documents

This incredibly useful property is valid only for agents or view action scripts. It can be used only on *NotesDatabase* objects obtained from the `CurrentDatabase` property of the *NotesSession* object (▶ 265). It returns a *NotesDocumentCollection* object (▶ 149) containing the documents in a database that the current agent or view action considers to be "unprocessed." When accessed outside an agent or view action, the returned collection will contain zero documents. If called from a *NotesDatabase* object that was not accessed from the `CurrentDatabase` property, this method raises an error.

Keep in mind that if you're using agents that run on new and modified documents, newly received mail documents, pasted documents, or newly modified documents, you must use the `UpdateProcessedDoc` method of *NotesSession* (▶ 273) to mark each document in the collection as "processed." This prevents each document in the collection from being processed more than once—unless it's modified, mailed, or pasted again.

By not calling this method for each document, the agent will process the same documents each time it runs. You should note that UpdateProcessedDoc marks a document as processed only for the specific agent in which it is called.

If you're using the UnprocessedDocuments property in a view action, it returns the same documents as a database that runs on selected documents.

The following table illustrates exactly what to expect when accessing this property:

Task (what agent is set to run on)	Outcome is a Document Collection that meets the following requirements
All documents in database	Search criteria specified in Database Builder met.
All new and modified documents since last run	Not previously processed by this database with the UpdateProcessedDoc method.
Newly created or modified	Search criteria specified in Database Builder met.
All unread documents in view	In view and unread. Search criteria specified in Database Builder met.
All documents in view	In view and unread. Search criteria specified in Database Builder met.
Selected documents/View action	Selected in view. Search criteria specified in Database Builder met.
Run once	The current document.
New mail documents	Just mailed to database. Search criteria specified in Database Builder met.
Newly modified documents	Documents just modified. Search criteria specified in Database Builder met.
Pasted document	Documents just pasted into the database. Search criteria specified in Database Builder met.

Views   R   ()

```
To get: varViews = ndbNotesDatabase.Views
```
Views

This property returns an array containing all the *NotesView* objects (▶ 279) in a database.

NotesDatabase Methods

Compact

```
LngSizediff = ndbNotesDatabase.Compact
```
Compact

This method takes no parameters and returns, as a long, the amount of space freed up after compacting.

Create

```
Call ndbNotesDatabase.Create(strServer, strFilename, intOpenFlag,
intMaxSize)
```
Create

strServer   Required $

The name of the server on which you want to create the database. You can pass an empty string ("") to create the database on the current machine.

strFilename   Required $

The filename to use for the new database.

intOpenFlag   Required   T/F

Use this parameter to open the database when it's created. When this is set to TRUE, the database is opened. Otherwise, this parameter is FALSE. To open the database later, you can use the Open or OpenIfModified methods.

intMaxSize   Optional   %

The maximum allowable size of a database.

This method allows you to create new *NotesDatabase* objects. Both the strServer and strFileName parameters can contain an empty string if you have already instantiated the *NotesDatabase* object with a server and filename.

CreateCopy

CreateCopy

```
Set ndbNotesDatabase = ndbNotesDatabase.CreateCopy(strServer, strFileName,
➥intMaxSize)
```

strServer   Required $

The name of the server where the new copy of the database will reside. Pass an empty string ("") to create the new copy on the current machine.

strFileName   Required $

The filename you want to assign to the new copy.

intMaxSize   Optional   %

The maximum allowable size of a database.

This method creates a new copy (not a replica) of the current database, which is returned as a *NotesDatabase* object. Keep in mind that if an existing database on the server specified in strServer has the same name as that specified in strFileName, an error will be reported. Also, the ACL will be copied to the new database.

CreateDocument

CreateDocument

```
Set ndbNotesDocument = ndbNotesDatabase.CreateDocument
```

This method takes no parameters and returns a new *NotesDocument* object (▶ 127). You can use this method with OLE automation to create a new document without using the New method. Remember to call the save method of *NotesDocument* to save the new document to disk.

CreateFromTemplate

CreateFrom
Template

```
Set ndbNotesDatabase = ndbNotesDatabase.CreateFromTemplate(strServer,
➥strFileName, intInherit, intMaxSize)
```

strServer   Required $

The name of the server where the new copy of the database will reside. Pass an empty string ("") to create the new copy on the current machine.

strFileName   Required $

The filename you want to assign to the new copy.

intInherit   Required   T/F

If you want the new database to inherit its design from the current database, set this parameter to TRUE. Otherwise, set it to FALSE.

intMaxSize   Optional   %

The maximum allowable size of a database.

Use this method to create a new database from an existing one. The new database will contain all the design elements and documents of the source database. It returns a *NotesDatabase* object representing the new database.

CreateOutline

```
Set noeNotesOutline = ndbNotesDatabase.CreateOutline(strName,
➥intDefaultOutline)
```
CreateOnline

strName	Required	$

The name of the new outline.

intDefaultOutline	Optional	T/F

Specify TRUE to create the new outline with the default entries.

This method allows you to create a new outline in the current database.

CreateReplica

```
Set ndbNotesDatabase = ndbNotesDatabase.CreateReplica(strServer, strFileName)
```
CreateReplica

strServer	Required	$

The name of the server where the new copy of the database will reside. Pass an empty string ("") to create the new copy on the current machine.

strFileName	Required	$

The filename you want to assign to the new copy.

This method returns a *NotesDatabase* object representing a new replica copy of the current database. The ACL of the current database is copied to the new replica. As with the `CreateCopy` method, if an existing database on the server specified in `strServer` has the same name as that specified in `strFileName`, an error will be reported. Also, the ACL will be copied to the new database.

EnableFolder

```
Call ndbNotesDatabase.EnableFolder(strFolderName)
```
EnableFolder

strFolderName	Required	$

The name of the folder to enable.

This method provides a way to enable folders.

5.0 FTDomainSearch

```
Set docNotesDocument = ndbNotesDatabase.FTDomainSearch(strQuery, intMaxDocs,
➥strEntryForm, intSortOptions, intOtherOptions, intStart, intCount)
```
FTDomainSearch

strQuery	Required	$

The query you want to execute.

intMaxDocs	Required	%

Indicates the maximum number of documents you want returned when the query is executed. You can set this parameter to 0 to get all documents matching the query.

strEntryForm	Required	$

The name of the search form in the domain catalog.

intSortOptions	Optional	%

Indicates which of three sorting options you want to use. You should use one of the following constants:

Constant	Description
FT_SCORES	Sorts results by relevance score. This is the default.
FT_DATE_DES	Sorts results by document creation date in descending order.
FT_DATE_ASC	Sorts results by document creation date in ascending order.

intOtherOptions   Optional   %

Indicates additional search options. You can use one of the following constants:
FT_STEMS, FT_DATABASE, FT_FILESYSTEM, or FT_FUZZY.

intStart   Optional   %

The first page to return.

intCount   Optional   %

The number of pages to return.

This very powerful method executes a full-text search of all the documents in a domain.
It returns a *NotesDocument* (▶ 127) containing a list of formatted documents that match
the query. In order to use this method, you must first set up a Domain Catalog.

FTSearch

FTSearch

```
Set ndcNotesDocumentCollection = ndbNotesDatabase.FTSearch(strQuery,
➡intMaxDocs, intSortOptions, intOtheroptions)
```

strQuery   Required $

The query you want to execute.

intMaxDocs   Required   %

Indicates the maximum number of documents you want returned when the query is
executed. You can set this parameter to 0 to get all documents matching the query.

intSortOptions   Optional   %

Indicates which of three sorting options you want to use. You should use one of the
following constants:

Constant	Description
FT_SCORES	Sorts results by relevance score. This is the default.
FT_DATE_DES	Sorts results by document creation date in descending order.
FT_DATE_ASC	Sorts results by document creation date in ascending order.

intOtherOptions   Optional   %

Indicates additional search options. You can use one of the following constants:
FT_STEMS, FT_DATABASE, FT_FILESYSTEM, or FT_FUZZY.

This method searches all the documents in a database and returns a
NotesDocumentCollection (▶ 149) containing all the documents that match the full-text
query. The documents are sorted based on the intSortOptions parameter. If no sort
options are specified, the documents are returned sorted by their relevance score. If the
results are sorted by date, no relevance scores are returned. It's important to note that
although this method will work if the database isn't full-text indexed, it will work
much more slowly.

If you don't want to search against all the documents in the database, you can use the
FTSearch method in *NotesView* (▶ 287) to search only the documents contained in a
particular view. You can also use the FTSearch method in *NotesDocumentCollection*.

The following example demonstrates building a generic full-text search function.

```
Public Function ExecuteSearch(strQuery As String, intmaxDocs As Integer)
➥As NotesDocumentCollection
Dim S As New NotesSession
If Not S.CurrentDatabase.IsFTIndexed Then
  If S.CurrentDatabase.Server="" Then
    Call S.CurrentDatabase.UpdateFTIndex(True)
  Else
  If Msgbox("This database is NOT full-text indexed! You can still perform
➥a full-text search but it will be slower... Do you want to search
➥anyway?", 32+4, "Db Not FTIndexed")=7 Then
      Exit Function
    End If
  End If
End If
Set ExecuteSearch=S.CurrentDatabase.FTSearch(strQuery, intMaxDocs)
End Function
```

GetAgent

```
Set nagtNotesAgent = ndbNotesDatabase.GetAgent(strAgentName)
```
GetAgent

strAgentName	Required	$

The name of the agent you want to retrieve.

This method returns a *NotesAgent* object (▶ 83) representing the named agent.

GetDocumentByID

```
Set ndocNotesDocument = ndbNotesDatabase.GetDocumentByID(strNoteID)
```
GetDocument
—ByID

strNoteID	Required	$

The NoteID of a document.

This method returns a *NotesDocument* object (▶ 127) representing the document whose NoteID matches the value specified in strNoteID. Consider the following example.

```
Dim S As New NotesSession
Dim ndocDocument As NotesDocument
Set ndocDocument=S.CurrentDatabase.getDocumentById("57CA")
' other code here
```

GetDocumentByUNID

```
Set ndocNotesDocument = ndbNotesDatabase.GetDocumentByUNID(strNoteUNID)
```
GetDocument
—ByUNID

strNoteUNID	Required	$

The Universal ID of a document.

This method returns a *NotesDocument* object (▶ 127) representing the document whose Universal ID matches the value specified in strUNID. Consider the following example.

```
Dim S As New NotesSession
Dim ndocDocument As NotesDocument
Set ndocDocument=S.CurrentDatabase.getDocumentByUNID
➥("B46F3758FF0ZB05A7852565F60044A3E5")
' other code here
```

GetDocumentByURL

```
Set ndocNotesDocument = ndbNotesDatabase.GetDocumentByURL(strURL,
➥intReload, intUrllist, strCharset, strWebusername , strWebpassword,
➥strProxywebusername, strProxywebpassword, intReturnimmediately)
```

strURL	Required	$

The URL of the page you want to retrieve. You can enter up to 15KB.

intReload	Optional	%

This parameter determines how the page should be retrieved. Set this parameter to 0 (the default) to load the page from its host only if it doesn't already exist in the Web Navigator. Specify 1 to reload the page from its host and 2 to reload the page only if the version on the host has been modified.

intUrllist	Optional	%

This parameter allows you to specify whether you want to save links in the retrieved page into a field called URLLinksn in the Notes document. (The Web Navigator creates a new URLLinksn field each time the field size reaches 64KB.) Set this parameter to TRUE to indicate that you want to use this feature.

Specify 1 (TRUE) if you want to save the URLs in the URLLinksn field(s). Specify 0 (FALSE) or omit this parameter if you don't want to save the URLs in the URLLinksn field(s). If you save the URLs, you can use them in agents. For example, you could create an agent that opens Web pages in the Web Navigator database and then loads all the Web pages saved in each of the URLLinksn field(s).

strCharset	Optional	$

Specifies the MIME character set (such as ISO-8859-1 for U.S.) that you want to use when the Web Navigator processes the Web page. This parameter should be specified only when the Web Navigator is unable to determine the page's correct MIME character set.

strWebusername	Optional	$

If a host requires authentication, you can use this parameter to pass it a username.

strWebpassword	Optional	$

If a host requires authentication, you can use this parameter to pass it a password.

strProxywebusername	Optional	$

Use this parameter to specify a username to proxy servers that require authentication.

strProxywebpassword	Optional	$

Use this parameter to specify a password to proxy servers that require authentication.

intReturnimmediately	Optional	%

This parameter indicates whether the script should continue without waiting for the retrieval process to complete. Specify TRUE for immediate return or FALSE (the default) to wait. Remember that if you specify TRUE, this method will not return a *NotesDocument* object representing the page referenced by the supplied URL.

This method creates a document in the Web Navigator database and returns a *NotesDocument* object for it (unless the intReturnImmediately parameter is set to FALSE). It works with both the Server Web Navigator and Personal Web Navigator databases.

```
Dim S As New NotesSession
Dim ndocDocument As NotesDocument
```

```
Set ndocDocument=S.CurrentDatabase.getDocumentByURL
➡(http://www.definiti.com, 1)
' other code here
```

GetForm

```
Set nfrmNotesForm = ndbNotesDatabase.GetForm(strName)
```
GetForm

strName   Required $

The name or alias of the form you want to access.

This method returns a *NotesForm* object (▶ 167) representing the form specified in the
strName parameter.

GetOutline

```
Set noeNotesOutline = ndbNotesDatabase.GetOutline(strName)
```
GetOutline

strName   Required $

The name of the outline you want to access.

This method allows you to access existing outline objects.

GetProfileDocCollection

```
Set ndcNotesDocumentCollection = ndbNotesDatabase.GetProfileDocCollection
➡(strName)
```
GetProfile
DocCollection

strName   Required $

The name of the collection to retrieve.

This method returns a collection of profile documents.

GetProfileDocument

```
Set ndocNotesDocument = ndbNotesDatabase.GetProfileDocument(strProfilename,
➡strUsername)
```
GetProfile
Document

strProfilename   Required $

The name or alias of the profile document you want to create or access.

strUsername   Optional $

The user name or key of the profile document you want to retrieve or create.

If no profile document matches the specified parameters, this method creates a new
profile document with the name and user name specified by strProfilename and
strUsername. Otherwise, a *NotesDocument* object (▶ 127) representing the matching
profile document will be returned. Consider the following example.

```
Dim S As New NotesSession
Dim ndocDocument As NotesDocument
Set ndocDocument=S.CurrentDatabase.getProfileDocument("DataStore",
➡S.UserName)
' other code here
```

GetURLHeaderInfo

```
strHeader = NotesDatabase.GetURLHeaderInfo(strURL, strHeadername,
➡strWebusername, strWebpassword, strProxywebusername,
➡strProxywebpassword)
```
GetURL
HeaderInfo

strURL	Required	$

The URL of the page you want to retrieve. You can enter up to 15KB.

strHeadername	Required	$

Specifies a header string for the URL header you want to retrieve. For more information on acceptable header strings, check the HTTP specification (http://www.w3.org/).

strWebusername	Optional	$

If a host requires authentication, you can use this parameter to pass it a username.

strWebpassword	Optional	$

If a host requires authentication, you can use this parameter to pass it a password.

strProxywebusername	Optional	$

Use this parameter to specify a username to proxy servers that require authentication.

strProxywebpassword	Optional	$

Use this parameter to specify a password to proxy servers that require authentication.

This method returns as a string the requested header value. If an empty string (" ") is returned, either the specified URL wasn't found, or the requested header value wasn't found in the header of the specified URL.

GetView

GetView

```
Set nvwNotesView = ndbNotesDatabase.GetView(strViewName)
```

strViewName	Required	$

This parameter specifies the name or alias of the view or folder that you want to access. Be sure to use either the entire name of the view or folder (including backslashes for cascading views and folders), or an alias, but not both.

If you call this method on a local database, it returns public and personal views and folders. For server-based databases, it returns only public views and folders.

This method returns a *NotesView* object (▶ 279) representing the view or folder specified by the **strViewName** parameter.

GrantAccess

GrantAccess

```
Call ndbNotesDatabase.GrantAccess(strName, intLevel)
```

strName	Required	$

Use this parameter to indicate the name of the server, person, or group whose access level you want to set.

intLevel	Required	%

Indicates the level of access you want to grant. The following table lists the acceptable constants for this parameter:

Constant	Description
ACLLEVEL_NOACCESS	No access
ACLLEVEL_DEPOSITOR	Depositor access
ACLLEVEL_READER	Reader access
ACLLEVEL_AUTHOR	Author access
ACLLEVEL_EDITOR	Editor access
ACLLEVEL_DESIGNER	Designer access
ACLLEVEL_MANAGER	Manager access

This method allows you to set the appropriate access level for any server, person, or group in the database ACL. If the server, person, or group specified in strName exists in the ACL, it is updated with the access level specified by intLevel. Otherwise, the name is added to the ACL with the specified level. When this method is called, it sets ACL roles to their default values.

New

```
Dim ndbNotesDatabase As New NotesDatabase(strServer, strFileName)
```
New
```
Set ndbNotesDatabase = New NotesDatabase(strServer, strFileName)
```

strServer   Required $
The name of the server where the database resides. If the database exists on the local machine, use an empty string (" ").

strFileName   Required $
The actual filename of the database you want to access.

This method returns a *NotesDatabase* object representing the database located at the server and filename specified. If possible, it opens the database. Remember that this method (unlike the behavior of the New method in other classes) does *not* create a new database on disk. Use one of the three aforementioned Create methods (namely, Create, CreateCopy, or CreateReplica) to create a new database.

Open

```
intflag = ndbNotesDatabase.Open(strServer, strFileName)
```
Open

strServer   Required $
Specifies the name of the server where the database is located. If the database is local (the current machine), specify an empty string (" ").

strFileName   Required $
Specifies the actual filename of the database you want to open. If the *NotesDatabase* object has already been instantiated, use an empty string (" ").

This method allows you to open a database so that a script can access its methods and properties. It returns TRUE if the specified database was found and opened successfully. FALSE is returned if the specified database couldn't be opened. In order to use this method, the calling script must have at least reader access to the database.

There are two basic ways to use this method. The first is to open a database that has already been instantiated. In this case, simply pass an empty string (" ") for both parameters. The second way is to open an existing database that hasn't been instantiated, in which case you must specify a server name and filename.

OpenByReplicaID

```
intFlag = ndbNotesDatabase.OpenByReplicaID(strServer, strRepID)
```
OpenByReplicaID

strServer   Required $
This parameter indicates the name of the server where the database is located. If the database is local (the current machine), specify an empty string (" ").

strRepID   Required $
Specifies the replica ID of the database you want to open.

This method uses a database's replica ID to attempt to open the database. If successful, this method returns TRUE. Otherwise, it returns FALSE. Consider the following example.

```
Dim S As New NotesSession
Dim ndb As New NotesDatabase("","")
intflag = ndb.OpenByReplicaID( "", "8525664B:005100C1")
```

OpenIfModified

OpenIfModified

```
intFlag = ndbNotesDatabase.OpenIfModified(strServer, strDbfile,
➥ndtNotesDateTime)
```

strServer   Required $

This parameter indicates the name of the server where the database is located. If the database is local (the current machine), specify an empty string ("").

strDbfile   Required $

Specifies the filename of the database you want to open.

ndtNotesDateTime   Required   O.Ref.

A *NotesDateTime* object (▶ 115) representing a cutoff date. If any documents in the database have been modified since the specified date, the database is opened. If no documents have been modified, the database is not opened.

This method allows you to conditionally open a database based on whether documents in it have been changed. It returns TRUE if the named database was opened successfully and FALSE otherwise.

OpenMail

OpenMail

```
Call ndbNotesDatabase.OpenMail
```

This method takes no parameters and attempts to locate the current user's mail database and open it. If this method is called by a script running on a workstation, it determines the user's mail file by looking in the NOTES.INI (or Notes Preferences) file. If called on a server, the agent determines the script owner's mail server and mail file by examining the Public Address Book on the server. Remember that scripts running on a server can't access other servers, so when this method is called on a server, it must attempt to access a mail file on the same server, or an error will be generated.

OpenURLDb

OpenURLDb

```
intFlag = ndbNotesDatabase.OpenURLDb
```

This method attempts to open the Web Navigator database. It returns TRUE if successful or FALSE otherwise.

OpenWithFailover

OpenWithFailover

```
intFlag = ndbNotesDatabase.OpenWithFailover(strServer, strFileName)
```

strServer   Required $

The name of the primary server in the cluster on which the database resides.

strFileName   Required $

The actual filename of the database to open.

This method allows you to take advantage of Domino clustering and open a database on a server in the cluster. It returns TRUE if the database is successfully opened and FALSE otherwise. If the database can't be opened on the specified server, this method automatically looks for a replica in the cluster. If a replica is located, that database is opened, and the Server property reflects the server on which the database was found.

QueryAccess

```
intLevel = ndbNotesDatabase.QueryAccess(strName)
```
QueryAccess

strName   Required $

This parameter specifies the name of the person, group, or server for which you want to know the access level.

This method searches a database's ACL for the value specified in the strName parameter. It returns a constant that represents the access level for that name, as shown in the following table:

Constant	Description
ACLLEVEL_NOACCESS	No access
ACLLEVEL_DEPOSITOR	Depositor access
ACLLEVEL_READER	Reader access
ACLLEVEL_AUTHOR	Author access
ACLLEVEL_EDITOR	Editor access
ACLLEVEL_DESIGNER	Designer access
ACLLEVEL_MANAGER	Manager access

The following paragraphs define how this method derives the access level:

If the specified name is explicitly listed in the ACL and is also a member of a group or groups listed in the ACL, the highest access level is returned.

If the specified name is a group member, the access level of the group is returned.

If the specified name is a member of several groups in the ACL, the highest access level granted to any of the groups is returned.

If the specified name is not a member of any group, the default access level is returned.

It's important to remember that this method uses the Primary Address Book on the machine where the script is being executed. On a workstation, it uses the Personal Address Book. On a server, the Public Address Book on that server is used.

Remove

```
Call ndbNotesDatabase.Remove
```
Remove

This method takes no parameters. It permanently deletes a database from the disk drive.

Replicate

```
intFlag = ndbNotesDatabase.Replicate(strServerName)
```
Replicate

strServerName   Required $

Specifies the name of the server to replicate with. If there is more than one replica of the database on the specified server, they will all replicate.

This method provides the ability to automate the replication process. It returns TRUE if the replication completes successfully and FALSE if any errors are generated. Consider the following simple example.

```
Dim S As New NotesSession
S.CurrentDatabase.Replicate("Gonzo/Definiti")
```

RevokeAccess

```
Call ndbNotesDatabase.RevokeAccess(strName)
```

strName   Required $

This parameter is used to specify the name of the server, person, or group whose access you are revoking.

This method allows you to remove a server, person, or group from a database's ACL, effectively granting the revokee default access to the database. Bear in mind that this is not the same as assigning No Access with the `GrantAccess` method, which will totally lock a server, person, or group out of the database. If this method can't find the server, person, or group specified in `strName`, an error is generated.

Search

```
Set ndcNotesDocumentCollection = ndbNotesDatabase.Search(strFormula,
➥ndtNotesDateTime, intMaxDocs)
```

strFormula   Required $

This parameter is used to pass a @function formula defining the selection criteria.

ndtNotesDateTime   Required   O.Ref.

This parameter is a *NotesDateTime* object (▶ 115) that is to be used as a cutoff date so that only documents created or modified after the cutoff date are searched.

intMaxDocs   Required   %

This parameter specifies the number of documents that should be returned in the collection. You can pass **0** to indicate that you want all matching documents.

This method returns an unsorted *NotesDocumentCollection* containing all the documents that match the selection criteria. This method is always substantially slower than performing a full-text search and should be avoided when a full-text search can be performed.

UnprocessedFTSearch

```
Set ndcNotesDocumentCollection = ndbNotesDatabase.UnprocessedFTSearch
➥(strQuery, intMaxDocs, intSortOptions, intOtherOptions)
```

strQuery   Required $

The query you want to execute.

intMaxDocs   Required   %

Indicates the maximum number of documents you want returned when the query is executed. You can set this parameter to **0** to get all documents matching the query.

intSortOptions   Optional   %

Indicates which of three sorting options you want to use. You should use one of the following constants:

Constant	Description
FT_SCORES	Sorts results by relevance score. This is the default.
FT_DATE_DES	Sorts results by document creation date in descending order.
FT_DATE_ASC	Sorts results by document creation date in ascending order.

intOtherOptions   Optional   %

Indicates additional search options. You can use one of the following constants: `FT_STEMS`, `FT_DATABASE`, `FT_FILESYSTEM`, or `FT_FUZZY`.

This method is valid only for agents or view action scripts. It can be used only on *NotesDatabase* objects obtained from the `CurrentDatabase` property in *NotesSession* (▶ 265). It returns a *NotesDocumentCollection* object (▶ 149) containing the documents in a database that the current agent or view action considers to be "unprocessed." When accessed outside an agent or view action, the returned collection will contain zero documents. If called from a *NotesDatabase* object that was not accessed from the `CurrentDatabase` property, this method will raise an error.

Keep in mind that if you're using agents that run on new and modified documents, newly received mail documents, pasted documents, or newly modified documents, you must use the `UpdateProcessedDoc` method of *NotesSession* (▶ 273) to mark each document in the collection as "processed." This prevents each document in the collection from being processed more than once, unless it's modified, mailed, or pasted again. By not calling this method for each document, the agent will process the same documents each time it runs. You should note that `UpdateProcessedDoc` marks a document as processed only for the specific agent in which it is called.

If you're using the `UnprocessedDocuments` property in a view action, it returns the same documents as a database that runs on selected documents.

The following table illustrates exactly what to expect when accessing this property:

Task (what agent is set to run on)	Outcome is a Document Collection that meets the following requirements
All documents in database	Search criteria specified in Agent Builder met.
All new and modified documents since last run	Not previously processed by this agent with the `UpdateProcessedDoc` method.
Newly created or modified	Search criteria specified in Agent Builder met.
All unread documents in view	In view and unread. Search criteria specified in Agent Builder met.
All documents in view	In view and unread. Search criteria specified in Agent Builder met.
Selected documents/View action	Selected in view. Search criteria specified in Agent Builder met.
Run once	The current document.
New mail documents	Just mailed to database. Search criteria specified in Agent Builder met.
Newly modified documents	Documents just modified. Search criteria specified in Agent Builder met.
Pasted document	Documents just pasted into the database. Search criteria specified in Agent Builder met.

If these conditions are met, this method performs a full-text search against the documents that are considered by the agent or view action script to be unprocessed and returns the results as a sorted document collection.

UnprocessedSearch

```
Set ndcNotesDocumentCollection = ndbNotesDatabase.UnprocessedSearch
➥(strFormula, ndtNotesDateTime, intMaxDocs)
```

Unprocessed Search

strFormula   Required $

This parameter is used to pass a @function formula defining the selection criteria.

ndtNotesDateTime   Required   O.Ref.

This parameter is a *NotesDateTime* object (▶ 115) to be used as a cutoff date so that only documents created or modified after the cutoff date are searched.

intMaxDocs   Required   %

This parameter specifies the number of documents that should be returned in the collection. You can pass 0 to indicate that you want all matching documents.

This method returns an unsorted *NotesDocumentCollection* containing all the documents that match the selection criteria. This method is always substantially slower than performing a full-text search and should be avoided when a full-text search can be performed.

This method is valid only for agents or view action scripts. It can be used only on *NotesDatabase* objects obtained from the CurrentDatabase property in *NotesSession*. It returns a *NotesDocumentCollection* object containing the documents in a database that the current agent or view action considers to be "unprocessed." When accessed outside an agent or view action, the returned collection contains zero documents. If called from a *NotesDatabase* object that wasn't accessed from the CurrentDatabase property, this method raises an error.

Keep in mind that if you're using agents that run on new and modified documents, newly received mail documents, pasted documents, or newly modified documents, you must use the UpdateProcessedDoc method of *NotesSession* (▶ 273) to mark each document in the collection as "processed." This prevents each document in the collection from being processed more than once, unless it's modified, mailed, or pasted again. By not calling this method for each document, the agent will process the same documents each time it runs. You should note that UpdateProcessedDoc marks a document as processed only for the specific agent in which it is called.

If you're using the UnprocessedDocuments property in a view action, it returns the same documents as a database that runs on selected documents.

The following table illustrates exactly what to expect when accessing this property:

Task (what agent is set to run on)	Outcome is a Document Collection that meets the following requirements
All documents in database	Search criteria specified in Agent Builder met.
All new and modified documents since last run	Not previously processed by this agent with the UpdateProcessedDoc method.
Newly created or modified	Search criteria specified in Agent Builder met.
All unread documents in view	In view and unread. Search criteria specified in Agent Builder met.
All documents in view	In view and unread. Search criteria specified in Agent Builder met.
Selected documents/View action	Selected in view. Search criteria specified in Agent Builder met.
Run once	The current document.
New mail documents	Just mailed to database. Search criteria specified in Agent Builder met.
Newly modified documents	Documents just modified. Search criteria specified in Agent Builder met.
Pasted document	Documents just pasted into the database. Search criteria specified in Agent Builder met.

If these conditions are met, the method performs a search against the documents that are considered by the agent or view action script to be unprocessed and returns the results as a sorted document collection.

UpdateFTIndex

```
Call ndbNotesDatabase.UpdateFTIndex(intCreateFlag)
```

intCreateFlag   Required   T/F

If no index exists, specifying TRUE will create a new index (this is valid only in local databases). Otherwise, an existing index will be updated. If the database is not local, specify FALSE.

This method allows you to programmatically create (local databases only) or update full-text indexes.

Remarks

Keep the following things in mind when working with the *NotesDatabase* class:

In most cases, you must explicitly open a database before most of its properties can be accessed with LotusScript.

The IsOpen property can be tested to determine whether the database is open. If it isn't, it can be opened by calling the Open or OpenIfModified methods.

In order to open a database, you or your script (script owner) must have a minimum of reader access.

Any script running on a server can't access a database on another server. This will generate an error if it is attempted. Likewise, if a script doesn't have the appropriate access to perform a function, it will be denied.

If a *NotesDatabase* object is accessed through a *NotesDbDirectory* object, it is not considered open. *NotesDatabase* objects accessed through the AddressBooks property in *NotesSession* are not open. However, the following properties are available on the closed database: FileName, FilePath, IsOpen, IsPrivateAddressBook, IsPublicAddressBook, Parent, and Server.

NotesDatabase objects instantiated using the New method are not open unless the database exists at the strServer and strFileName specified. The following properties are available on the closed database: FileName, FilePath, IsOpen, Parent, and Server.

Example

The following example checks to see whether the current user is in the ACL of the current database and whether he has at least author access. If so, he is given editor access. If the user doesn't have at least author access, he is granted editor access.

```
Dim S As New NotesSession
Dim naclCur As NotesAcl
Dim naclEntry As NotesACLEntry
Dim intFound As Integer
Set naclCur=S.CurrentDatabase.ACL
Set naclEntry=naclCur.GetFirstEntry
```
continued >>

continued >>

```
Do While Not naclEntry Is Nothing
  If S.UserName=naclEntry.Name Then
    If naclEntry.Level<=ACLLEVEL_AUTHOR Then
      naclEntry.Level=ACLLEVEL_EDITOR
    End If
    Exit Sub
  End If
Loop
Call S.CurrentDatabase.GrantAccess( S.UserName, ACLLEVEL_EDITOR )
```

NotesDateRange

4.5x 4.6x 5.0

The *NotesDateRange* class provides a
mechanism to work with a range of dates
and times.

NotesSession
  └ NotesDateRange
      └ NotesDateTime

LotusScript Syntax

```
Set NotesDateRange = notesSession.CreateDateRange()
```

To create a new *NotesDateRange* object, you must use the `CreateDateTime` method of *NotesSession* (▶ 268).

NotesDateRange Properties

StartDateTime	R/W	O. Ref.

StartDateTime

```
To Get: ndtNotesDateTime = notesDateRange.StartDateTime
To Set: ndrNotesDateRange.StartDateTime = ndtnotesDateTime
```

A *NotesDateTime* (▶ 115) object that is used to set the starting date and time of a *NotesDateRange*.

EndDateTime	R/W	O. Ref.

EndDateTime

```
To Get: ndtNotesDateTime = notesDateRange.EndDateTime
To Set: ndrNotesDateRange.EndDateTime = ndtnotesDateTime
```

A *NotesDateTime* (▶ 115) object that is used to set the ending date and time of a *NotesDateRange*.

Text	R/W	$

Text

```
To set: ndrNotesDateRange.Text = strDateRange
To get: strDateRange=ndrNotesDateRange.Text
```

The text value of a *NotesDateRange*.

Example

```
Dim nsSession As New NotesSession
Dim ndrDateRange As NotesDateRange
Dim ndtStartTime As New NotesDateTime(Date$ & " " & Time$)
Call ndtStartTime.AdjustHour(8)
Dim ndtEndTime As New NotesDateTime(ndtStartTime.LSLocalTime)
Call ndtStartTime.AdjustHour(-8)
Set ndrDateRange = nsSession.CreateDateRange()
Set ndrDateRange.StartDateTime = ndtStartTime
Set ndrDateRange.EndDateTime = ndtEndTime
Msgbox ndrdateRange.Text, 64,"Current Time Range"
```

NotesDateTime

4.0   4.1x   4.5x   4.6x   5.0

The *NotesDateTime* object allows you to easily manipulate time and date values in LotusScript.

NotesSession
   └─ NotesDateTime

OR

NotesSession
   └─ NotesDateRange
       └─ NotesDateTime

LotusScript Syntax

```
Dim NotesDateTime As New NotesDateTime(strDatetime)
```

or

```
Set NotesDateTime = New NotesDateTime(strDatetime)
```

There are two ways to create a *NotesDateTime* object. To create a new *NotesDateTime* object from scratch, you can either use the New keyword with the Dim or Set statements, as shown in the syntax, or you can use the CreateDateTime method of the *NotesSession* class (▶ 268) to create a new *NotesDateTime* object.

LotusScript Parameters

strDatetime	Required	$

A string value that representing the time and date to use.

NotesDateTime Properties

DateOnly	R/W	$

DateOnly
```
To set: ndtNotesDateTime.DateOnly = strDate
To get: strDate = ndtNotesDateTime.DateOnly
```

Returns the date portion of a *NotesDateTime* in the local time zone. If you set this property, it will change the date represented by the object, which also affects the GMTTime, LSLocalTime, and LSGMTTime properties.

GMTTime	R	$

GMTTime
```
To get: strGMT = ndtNotesDateTime.GMTTime
```

Returns a string containing the date-time converted to Greenwich Mean Time, which is time zone 0.

IsDST	R	T/F

IsDST
```
To get: intDST = ndtNotesDateTime.IsDST
```

Indicates whether the date-time is using daylight saving time (TRUE if it is, FALSE if it isn't).

5.0 IsValidDate	R	T/F

IsValidDate
```
To get: intValidDate = ndtNotesDateTime.IsValidDate
```

Indicates whether the string used to create the *NotesDateTime* object is valid. An invalid string sets *NotesDateTime* to a wildcard value.

LocalTime	R/W	$

LocalTime
```
To set: ndtNotesDateTime.LocalTime = strLocalTime
To get: strLocalTime = ndtNotesDateTime.LocalTime
```

Contains the date-time of the local time zone. If you set this property, it will change the date represented by the object, which also affects the DateOnly, GMTTime, LSLocalTime, LSGMTTime, and TimeOnly properties.

```
Dim nsSession As New NotesSession
Dim ndtDateTime As NotesDateTime
Set ndtDateTime=nsSession.CreateDateTime("Today")
' Set local time using Date$ and Time$ function
ndtDateTime.LocalTime=Date$ & " " & Time$
Msgbox ndtDateTime.LocalTime, 64 ,"Testing"
```

LSGMTTime   R   ?

```
To get: varGMT = ndtNotesDateTime.LSGMTTime
```
LSGMTTime

A variant (type 7) that contains the date-time converted to Greenwich Mean Time.

LSLocalTime   R/W   ?

```
To set: ndtNotesDateTime.LSLocalTime = varDateTime
To get: varDateTime = ndtNotesDateTime.LSLocalTime
```
LSLocalTime

A variant (type 7) that contains the date-time in the local time zone. If you set this property, it will affect the DateOnly, GMTTime, LSGMTTime, and TimeOnly properties.

TimeOnly   R $

```
To get: strTime = ndtNotesDateTime.TimeOnly
```
TimeOnly

Contains the time portion of a date-time in the local time zone.

TimeZone   R   %

```
To get: intTimeZone = ndtNotesDateTime.TimeZone
```
TimeZone

Represents the time zone of a date-time. May be positive or negative.

ZoneTime   R $

```
To get: strZoneTime = ndtNotesDateTime.ZoneTime
```
ZoneTime

A string representation of the time adjusted for the TimeZone and IsDST properties. When a *NotesDateTime* object is created, the ZoneTime property is the same as LocalTime. Once the ConvertToZone method is called, changes to TimeZone and IsDST are reflected in ZoneTime, but LocalTime stays the same.

NotesDateTime Methods

AdjustDay

```
Call ndtNotesDateTime.AdjustDay(intNumberofDays, intLocalZone)
```
AdjustDay

intNumberofDays   Required   %
Number of days to increment or decrement the *NotesDateTime* object.

intLocalZone   Optional   T/F
If the adjustment to the date-time crosses the boundary for daylight saving time purposes, you can set this parameter to TRUE. Setting this parameter to FALSE or omitting it will not adjust for daylight saving time. By adjusting the number of days so that the date-time moves into or out of daylight saving time, the time component is incremented or decremented by one hour.

```
Dim nsSession As New NotesSession
Dim nwsWs As New NotesUIWorkspace
Dim nuidUIDoc As NotesUIDocument
Set nuidUIDoc=nwsWs.CurrentDocument
Dim ndtReservationDate As New NotesDateTime(nuidUIDoc.Document.
➥ReservationDate(0))
If Weekday(ndtReservationDate.LocalTime) =1  Then
  If Msgbox("Your reservation falls on a Sunday, would you like to
  ➥move it to Monday?", 32+4, "Move Reservation")=6 Then
    Call ndtReservationDate.AdjustDay(1) ' push reservation forward
                                         ' to Monday
  End If
Elseif Weekday(ndtReservationDateTime.LocalTime)=7 Then
  If Msgbox("Your reservation falls on a Saturday, would you like to
  ➥move it to Monday?", 32+4, "Move Reservation")=6 Then
    Call ndtReservationDate.AdjustDay(2) ' push reservation forward
                                         ' to Monday
  End If
End If
```

AdjustHour

AdjustHour   `Call ndtNotesDateTime.`**`AdjustHour`**`(intNumberofHours, intLocalZone)`

intNumberofHours   Required   %

The number of hours to increment or decrement the NotesDateTime object. This value can be positive or negative.

intLocalZone   Optional   T/F

If the adjustment to the date-time crosses the boundary for daylight saving time purposes, you can set this parameter to TRUE. Setting this parameter to FALSE or omitting it will not adjust for daylight saving time. By adjusting the number of days so that the date-time moves into or out of daylight saving time, the time component is incremented or decremented by one hour.

A *NotesDateTime* object that contains only a date component will not be changed by this method. If you increment (or decrement) the *NotesDateTime* object by enough hours to move into a new day, the date component will be adjusted accordingly.

AdjustMinute

AdjustMinute   `Call ndtNotesDateTime.`**`AdjustMinute`**`(intNumberofMinutes, intLocalZone)`

intNumberofMinutes   Required   %

The number of minutes to increment or decrement the NotesDateTime object. This value can be positive or negative.

intLocalZone   Optional   T/F

If the adjustment to the date-time crosses the boundary for daylight saving time purposes, you can set this parameter to TRUE. Setting this parameter to FALSE or omitting it will not adjust for daylight saving time. By adjusting the number of days so that the date-time moves into or out of daylight saving time, the time component is incremented or decremented by one hour.

A *NotesDateTime* object, which contains only a date component, will not be changed by this method. If you increment (or decrement) the *NotesDateTime* object by enough minutes to move into a new day, the date component will be adjusted accordingly.

AdjustMonth

```
Call ndtNotesDateTime.AdjustMonth(intNumberofMonths, intLocalZone)
```

intNumberofMonths   Required   %

The number of months to increment or decrement the date-time. This value can be positive or negative.

intLocalZone   Optional   T/F

If the adjustment to the date-time crosses the boundary for daylight saving time purposes, you can set this parameter to TRUE. Setting this parameter to FALSE or omitting it will not adjust for daylight saving time. By adjusting the number of days so that the date-time moves into or out of daylight saving time, the time component is incremented or decremented by one hour.

If you increment (or decrement) the *NotesDateTime* object by enough minutes to move into a new year, the date component will be adjusted accordingly.

AdjustSecond

```
Call ndtNotesDateTime.AdjustSecond(intNumberofSeconds, intLocalZone)
```

intNumberofSeconds   Required   %

The number of seconds to increment or decrement the *NotesDateTime* object. This value can be positive or negative.

intLocalZone   Optional   T/F

If the adjustment to the date-time crosses the boundary for daylight saving time purposes, you can set this parameter to TRUE. Setting this parameter to FALSE or omitting it will not adjust for daylight saving time. By adjusting the number of days so that the date-time moves into or out of daylight saving time, the time component is incremented or decremented by one hour.

A *NotesDateTime* object that contains only a date component will not be changed by this method. If you increment (or decrement) the *NotesDateTime* object by enough seconds to move into a new day, the date component will be adjusted accordingly.

AdjustYear

```
Call ndtNotesDateTime.AdjustYear(intNumberofYears, intLocalZone)
```

intNumberofYears   Required   %

The number of years to increment or decrement the *NotesDateTime* object. This value can be positive or negative.

intLocalZone   Optional   T/F

If the adjustment to the date-time crosses the boundary for daylight saving time purposes, you can set this parameter to TRUE. Setting this parameter to FALSE or omitting it will not adjust for daylight saving time. By adjusting the number of days so that the date-time moves into or out of daylight saving time, the time component is incremented or decremented by one hour.

```
' A simple Y2K compliance test
Dim nsSession As New NotesSession
Dim ndtDateTime As NotesDateTime
Set ndtDateTime=nsSession.CreateDateTime("Today")
Call ndtDateTime.AdjustYear(1)
```

continued >>

continued >>
```
Msgbox Format$(ndtDateTime.LocalTime, "mm/dd/yyyy"),64,"Testing Y2k
  ➥Compliance"
```

5.0 ConvertToZone

ConvertToZone
```
Call ndtNotesDateTime.ConvertToZone(intTimeZone, intIsDST)
```

---

intZone   Required   %

Changes the `TimeZone` property.

intDST   Required   T/F

This method allows you to change the `IsDST` property. Affects `ZoneTime` but not
`LocalTime` and `GMTTime`.

New

New   Used to create a new *NotesDateTime* object (▶ 115).

SetAnyDate

SetAnyDate
```
Call ndtNotesDateTime.SetAnyDate
```

This method takes no parameters and sets the date portion of a *NotesDateTime* object
to a wildcard date.

SetAnyTime

SetAnyTime
```
Call ndtNotesDateTime.SetAnyTime
```

This method takes no parameters and sets the time portion of a *NotesDateTime* object
to a wildcard time.

SetNow

SetNow
```
Call ndtNotesDateTime.SetNow
```

This method takes no parameters and sets a *NotesDateTime* object to the current
system date and time.

TimeDifference

Time
Difference
```
intTimeDiff&= ndtNotesDateTime.TimeDifference(ndtNotesDateTime)
```

This method calculates the difference between two *NotesDateTime* objects and returns
the value in seconds as a long.

5.0 TimeDifferenceDouble

TimeDifference
Double
```
DoubleTimeDiff#= ndtNotesDateTime.TimeDifference(ndtNotesDateTime)
```

This method calculates the difference between two *NotesDateTime* objects and returns
the value in seconds as a double.

Remarks

Keep in mind that *NotesDateTime* objects contain both a time zone and
hundredths of a second, whereas LotusScript date-time variants contain only a
date and time. There is no time zone information, and the precision of the time
is in seconds. If you need this additional precision, or if you're looking for an
easy way to compare and manipulate time values, use the *NotesDateTime* object.

Example

The following agent demonstrates using the *NotesDateTime* class to test the "age" of documents and archive documents that have "expired."

```
Dim nsSession As New NotesSession
Dim ndbLDb As NotesDatabase
Dim nvwLView As NotesView
Dim ndocLDoc As NotesDocument
Dim ndbADb As NotesDatabase
Dim ndocADoc As NotesDocument
Dim ndocTDoc As NotesDocument
Dim ndocCurrDoc As NotesDocument
Dim lngDiff As Long, lngResult As Long, lngMonths As Long
' Get handle to archive database
Set ndbABD=nsSession.GetDatabase(nsSession.CurrentDatabase.Server,
➥"archive.nsf")
' Get handle to system database
Set ndbLDb=nsSession.GetDatabase(nsSession.CurrentDatabase.Server,
➥"control.nsf")
Set nvwLView=ndbLDb.GetView("KeyLookup")
' Get doc in system db that contains the expiration threshold
Set ndocLDoc=nvwLView.GetDocumentByKey("Expiration")
Dim ndtArchiveThreshold As New NotesDateTime("Today")
Dim ndtToday As New NotesDateTime("Today")
'Set archive date by adjusting month by threshold
Call ndtArchiveThreshold.AdjustMonth(Cint(ndocLDoc.KeyValue(0)))
' Get first document in Unprocessed documents collection
Set ndocCurrDoc=nsSession.CurrentDatabase.UnProcessedDocuments.
➥GetFirstDocument
' Loop through all documents in Unprocessed collection
For intI = 1 To nsSession.CurrentDatabase.UnProcessedDocuments.Count
    ' Calculate the time difference in seconds
    lngDiff = ndtToday.TimeDifference(ndtArchiveThreshold)
    lngMonths=2592000*Clng(ndocLDoc.KeyValue(0))
    ' See if the threshold in the control database has been reached or
    ' surpassed.
    If lngDiff/lngMonths  >=1 Then
        Set ndocADoc=ndbADb.CreateDocument  ' create document in archive
                                            ' database
        Call ndocCurrDoc.CopyAllItems(ndocADoc, True)
        Set ndocTDoc=ndocCurrDoc
        Set ndocCurrDoc=nsSession.CurrentDatabase.UnProcessedDocuments.
        ➥GetnthDocument(intI%)
        Call ndocTDoc.Remove(True)
    Else
        Set ndocCurrDoc=nsSession.CurrentDatabase.UnProcessedDocuments.
        ➥GetnthDocument(intI%)
    End If
    Next
End Sub
```

NotesDbDirectory

4.0 4.1x 4.5x 4.6x 5.0

The directories store Notes databases on a specified server or on the local computer. Using this method, you can navigate through all the databases on a particular server or navigate through databases stored locally, as well as open and create new *NotesDatabase* objects.

NotesSession
 └─ NotesDbDirectory
     └─ NotesDatabase
         ├─ NotesACL
         │   └─ NotesACLEntry
         ├─ NotesAgent
         ├─ NotesDocument
         │   └─ . . .
         ├─ NotesDocumentCollection
         │   └─ NotesDocument
         ├─ NotesForm
         ├─ NotesOutline
         │   └─ NotesOutlineEntry
         ├─ NotesReplication
         └─ NotesView
             └─ . . .

LotusScript Syntax

```
Dim NotesDbDirectory As New NotesDbDirectory(strServername)
```

or

```
Set NotesDbDirectory = New NotesDbDirectory(strServername)
```

LotusScript provides two ways to create a *NotesDbDirectory* object. If you want to create a new *NotesDbDirectory* object from scratch, you can either use the New keyword with the Dim or Set statements, as shown in the preceding syntax, or you can use the GetDbDirectory method of the *NotesSession* class (▶ 270) to create a new *NotesDbDirectory* in a *NotesSession*.

LotusScript Parameters

strServername	Required	$

A string value representing the name of the server containing the database files you want to view. Specifying an empty string will open the database directory on the local computer.

NotesDbDirectory Properties

Name	R	$

Name   To get: strServername = ndirNotesDbDirectory.**Name**

Returns the string value of the name of the server you are currently searching. This property will return an empty string value (" ") when searching the local computer.

NotesDbDirectory Methods

GetFirstDatabase

GetFirst   Set ndbNotesDatabase = ndirNotesDbDirectory.**GetFirstDatabase**(intFiletype)
Database

intFiletype	Required	%

The constant type of database file to search.

Database Filetype Constants

Filetype Integer	Indicated Filetype
DATABASE	All Notes databases that have an .nsf, .nsg, .nst, or .nsh extension
TEMPLATE	All Notes database templates that have an .ntf extension
REPLICA_CANDIDATE	All Notes databases or templates in which replication has not been disabled
TEMPLATE_CANDIDATE	All Notes databases and templates

This method returns a handle to the first database located in the *NotesDbDirectory* on the server or local computer of the specified file type. This method does not open the specified database. Instead, it gets a handle on the back-end *NotesDatabase* object. Therefore, the database is not opened to be displayed in the front-end user interface. If you want to open the database with focus to the user interface, apply the `Open` method or the `OpenIfModified` method of the *NotesDatabase* object.

Every time this method is called, a new search is conducted in the *NotesDbDirectory*. In other words, the handle to the existing *NotesDbDirectory* is discarded in memory and reinitialized. This feature is necessary since you might not want the new search to be conducted on the same file type as the previous search. When using LotusScript, refer to the `New` method.

```
Dim ndir As NotesDbDirectory
Dim ndb As NotesDatabase
Set ndir = New NotesDbDirectory("")
Set ndb = ndir.GetFirstDatabase(DATABASE)
Msgbox ndb.Filepath, 32, "First Db Filepath..."
```

GetNextDatabase

```
Set ndbNotesDatabase = ndirNotesDbDirectory.GetNextDatabase
```
GetNext
Database

This method returns a handle to a *NotesDatabase* object located on the server or on a local machine specified in the *NotesDbDirectory*. If there are no more databases in the *NotesDbDirectory*, a NULL value is returned. Similar to the `GetFirstDatabase` method, this method does not open the specified database. Instead, it gets a handle on the back-end *NotesDatabase* object. Therefore, the database is not opened or displayed in the front-end user interface. If you want to open the database with focus to the user interface, apply the `Open` method or the `OpenIfModified` method of the *NotesDatabase* object.

```
Dim ndir As NotesDbDirectory
Dim ndb As NotesDatabase
Set ndir = New NotesDbDirectory("")
Set ndb = ndir.GetFirstDatabase(DATABASE)
Do While Not Isnull(ndb)
    Msgbox ndb.Title, 32, "Current Db Name..."
    Set ndb = ndir.GetNextDatabase
Loop
```

Remarks

When working with the *NotesDbDirectory* class, keep in mind that the directory structure assumes that you are working within the Notes directory structure and the virtual file system maintained by Notes. Therefore, the "root" directory is the directory specified within the notes.ini file for the respective server or the local computer—for example, the line in the .ini file that reads `Directory=C:\notes5\ data`. This is important, because the actual physical file location on the file server is not relevant. Notes, along with the script that is searching the directory structure using the *NotesDbDirectory* methods, searches only for Notes database files within the notes\data directory or directories that might be mapped using .dir files on the server. Therefore, you don't need to be concerned about the actual file path (such as when you're opening a file for I/O operations using the `Open` statement in LotusScript). This method works in the same manner as selecting File | Open.

It is important to remember that the `GetFirstDatabase` and `GetNextDatabase` methods return a handle to the *NotesDatabase* object but don't actually open the Notes database. If it is necessary to open the database to exploit certain methods of the *NotesDatabase,* you must first use the `Open` method of the *NotesDatabase* class (▶ 105).

Example

The following script evaluates the *NotesDbDirectory* and creates two arrays. The first string array will contain all the filenames of all the Notes databases, and the second string array will contain all the Notes templates. Each dynamic array is built as the script reads the Notes directory. Both arrays are then written to fields stored within the current document using the extended syntax.

```
Dim nws As New NotesUIWorkspace
Dim ndir As NotesDbDirectory
Dim ndb As NotesDatabase
Dim adbarray() As String
Dim atplarray() As String
Dim intCount As Integer
Set ndir = New NotesDbDirectory("")
Set ndb = ndir.GetFirstDatabase(DATABASE)
Do While Not (ndb Is Nothing)
    intCount = intCount + 1
    Redim Preserve adbarray(intCount)
    adbarray(intCount) = Str$(intCount) & ". " & ndb.FileName
    Set ndb = ndir.GetNextDatabase
Loop
intCount = 1
Set ndb = ndir.GetFirstDatabase(TEMPLATE)
Do While Not (ndb Is Nothing)
    Redim Preserve atplarray(intCount)
    atplarray(intCount) = Str$(intCount) & ". " & ndb.FileName
    Set ndb = ndir.GetNextDatabase
    intCount = intCount + 1
Loop
nws.CurrentDocument.Document.slDatabaseList = adbarray
nws.CurrentDocument.Document.slTemplateList = atplarray
```

NotesDocument

4.0 4.1x 4.5x 4.6x 5.0

The *NotesDocument* object represents a collection or subset of *NotesDocuments*. *NotesDocument* is the common data-storage mechanism used throughout Domino/Lotus Notes that contains the *NotesItems, NotesRichTextItems,* and any *NotesEmbeddedObjects*.

```
NotesUIDatabase
 └ NotesDocument
      ├ NotesEmbeddedObject
      ├ NotesItem
      │  └└ NotesRichTextItem
      └ NotesRichTextItem

OR

NotesDocumentCollection
 └ NotesDocument
      └ . . .

OR

. . .
 └ NotesView
      └ NotesDocument
           └ . . .

OR

. . .
 └ NotesDatabase
      └ NotesDocument
           └ . . .

OR

NotesSession
 └ NotesNewsletter
      └ NotesDocument
           └ . . .
```

Page   Contents

Syntax

Properties

continued >>

LotusScript Syntax

```
Dim ndoc As New NotesDocument
```

Various methods and properties can be used to establish a handle on an existing *NotesDocument* object. Which method you use depends on what action you want to perform on the *NotesDocument* object. The following paragraphs explain the various methods you can use to access existing *NotesDocuments* and why you would use each.

NotesView. Establish a handle based on the document's position in a *NotesView* object (▶ 279).

Use the FTSearch method to locate all documents that match the search query criteria (▶ 287).

NotesDatabase. Establish a handle based on the document's UNID or NoteID by using the GetDocumentByID (▶ 101) or GetDocumentByUNID (▶ 101) methods.

Establish a handle on all the documents contained in the *NotesDatabase* using the AllDocuments property (▶ 92).

Use the FTSearch method to locate all documents that match the search query criteria (▶ 100).

Use the Search method to locate all documents that match the search criteria determined using the formula language (▶ 108).

Establish a handle on all the documents that haven't been processed by a *NotesAgent* using the UnproccessedDocuments property(▶ 96), UnproccessedFTSearch (▶ 108), or UnprocessedSearch (▶ 109) methods.

NotesDocument. Establish a handle on all the response documents of the current *NotesDocument* using the Responses property (▶ 135).

Establish a handle on the parent document using the ParentDocumentUNID property of the current *NotesDocument* (▶ 134).

To create a new *NotesDocument* object, you can use either the New method of the *NotesDocument* or the CreateDocument method of the *NotesDatabase* object (▶ 98).

If a new document is created using the New method, you must first establish a handle on the *NotesDatabase* in which the document is going to be created. Here is the syntax used when creating a new *NotesDocument:*

```
Dim ndocDocument As New NotesDocument (NotesDatabase)
```

or

```
Set ndocDocument = New NotesDocument (NotesDatabase)
```

LotusScript Parameters

NotesDatabase	Required	O.Ref.

The database that the new document will reside in when it is saved to disk by calling the Save method.

NotesDocument Properties

Authors   R   ()

Authors

To get: strAuthors() = ndocDocument.**Authors**

Represents the usernames (fully distinguished if the name is hierarchical) of everyone who has previously saved the document.

The following example displays the names of all the entries in the `Authors` field.

```
Dim ns As New NotesSession
Dim ndb As NotesDatabase
Dim ndc As NotesDocumentCollection
Dim ndoccurrent As NotesDocument
Dim strnames As String
Set ndb = ns.CurrentDatabase
Set ndc = ndb.AllDocuments
Set ndoccurrent = ndc.GetFirstDocument
Stop
For z = 0 To Ubound(ndoccurrent.Authors)
    strnames = strnames & ndoccurrent.Authors(z) & Chr$(13)
Next
Msgbox strnames, 32, "Author Names"
```

ColumnValues   R   ()

ColumnValues

To get: varColValues() = ndocNotesDocument.**ColumnValues**

If the current handle on the *NotesDocument* was established from a parent *NotesView*, this property stores an array of values, each corresponding to the column values of the current document's parent view. The order of the elements contained in the array logically corresponds to the columns in the respective parent view. In other words, the first element of the array is the value that appears in the first column of the view, the second element of the array is the value that appears in the second column of the view, and so on.

It's important to understand that the value contained in the `ColumnValues` array may or may not match any actual item value contained in the current document. This is because the value contained in the `ColumnValues` array represents the value displayed in the view, which may be altered as a result of the view's column formulas. In addition, because `ColumnValues` is derived from the *NotesView*, if a column value displays a `NULL` value, the respective array element will be `NULL` as well.

If the current *NotesDocument* wasn't accessed using a *NotesView*, this property will return `NULL`.

If it's necessary to retrieve an item value from the document, using this property to access particular items in a *NotesDocument* is more efficient than accessing the *NotesItem* value from the document directly. However, often the required item value isn't displayed in the *NotesView*.

This property ignores the "Responses Only" design feature of the *NotesView* column formulas. It will return a value regardless of the document type.

The following example is similar to performing a @DbLookup when you're developing with the formula langauge. It locates a document based on a specific key and returns the value stored in the second column of the view.

```
Dim ns As New NotesSession
Dim ndb As NotesDatabase
Dim nview As NotesView
```

```
Dim ndoccurrent As NotesDocument
Dim strValue As String
Set ndb = ns.CurrentDatabase
Set nview = ndb.GetView("StandardView")
Set ndoccurrent = nview.GetDocumentbyKey("Acme Inc.", True)
strValue = ndoccurrent.ColumnValues(1)
Msgbox strValue, 32, "Lookup value..."
```

Created   R   Time/Date

```
To get: ndtCreated() = ndocNotesDocument.Created
```
Created

Represents the date that the *NotesDocument* was created. This property returns a variant of type DATE.

EmbeddedObjects   R   O.Ref.

```
To get: nembEmbeddedObjects() = ndocNotesDocument.EmbeddedObjects
```
Embedded
Objects

Represents an array of the OLE/1 and OLE/2 embedded objects that are contained in the *NotesDocument*. This property doesn't contain any file attachments or OLE/1 objects that were created in release 3. If the *NotesForm* used to create the document had an embedded object in its design, that object could be accessed using this property provided it was activated, modified, and saved in the *NotesDocument*. EmbeddedObjects isn't currently supported under OS/2, UNIX, or Macintosh.

EncryptionKeys   R/W $

```
To get: strKeys() = ndocNotesDocument.EncryptionKeys
To set: ndocNotesDocument.EncryptionKeys = strKeys
```
EncryptionKeys

Represents the keys used to encrypt the document. The keys set or returned from this property are used when the Encrypt method is called (▶ 138). When retrieving this value using the get syntax just shown, the value returned is an array of strings. When setting this property, either a single string value or an array of strings can be used. The string value, or each element of the string array, contains the name of the encryption key. Any users who have the encryption key can decrypt the document.

The name of the specified encryption key is stored in the *NotesDocument* in a *NotesRichTextItem* named SecretEncryptionKeys. If the document is encrypted but no encryption keys are specified, the document is encrypted using the current user's public key. Therefore, the document can be decrypted only by that user.

As when modifying other properties of the *NotesDocument,* you must explicitly call the Save method after setting the encryption keys to encrypt the document.

EncryptOnSend   R/W   T/F

```
To get: intEncryptonsend = ndocNotesDocument.EncryptOnSend
To set: ndocNotesDocument.EncryptOnSend = intEncryptonsend
```
EncryptOnSend

Indicates whether the document is to be encrypted when mailed. TRUE indicates that it should be encrypted when mailed. FALSE indicates that it should not be encrypted. This property defaults to FALSE. When the document is mailed, the system attempts to locate the public key for each recipient in the Directory (Public Address Book). Each user whose public key can't be located will still receive the e-mail, but their messages will not be encrypted. The users whose public key was located will receive an encrypted document.

FolderReferences   R   ()

```
To get: strFolderRef() = ndocNotesDocument.FolderReferences
```
FolderReferences

Indicates what folders (as an array of strings) in the current *NotesDatabase* have references to the *NotesDocument*. For this property to have any effect, the *NotesDatabase* must support folder references and have the hidden FolderRef view design. The `FolderRefsEnabled` property of the *NotesDatabase* can be tested to ensure that the current database has folder references enabled (▶ 93).

FTSearchScore   R   %

FTSearchScore   `To get: intScore = ndocNotesDocument.`**`FTSearchScore`**

Returns the full-text search score of the documents that were retrieved as the result of a full-text search. The document's score is based on the search query and the frequency of successful hits for the document—in other words, the number of successful words that were located in the document, any term weights specified for the words, and any proximity characters specified. Because a document can be contained in multiple *NotesDocumentCollections* and *NotesViewEntryCollections,* `FTSearchScore` will reflect the score of the most recent search. If a document is added to a collection, is deleted from a view, or wasn't retrieved as part of a full-text index, `FTSearchScore` will be set to `0`. If the document was retrieved using the `FTSearch` method but the *NotesDatabase* wasn't full-text indexed, the search will still work. However, the value assigned to `FTSearchScore` will be unreliable.

HasEmbedded   R   T/F

HasEmbedded   `To get: intHasEmbedded = ndocNotesDocument.`**`HasEmbedded`**

Indicates whether the document contains one or more *NotesEmbeddedObjects* (embedded objects, database links, view links, document links, and file attachments). `TRUE` indicates that embedded objects are contained in the document. `FALSE` indicates that no embedded objects are recognized. This property has no effect on OS/2, UNIX, or Macintosh operating systems.

IsDeleted   R   T/F

IsDeleted   `To get: intIsDeleted = ndocNotesDocument.`**`IsDeleted`**

Indicates whether the document has been deleted from the *NotesDatabase*. `TRUE` indicates that it has been deleted. `FALSE` indicates that it has not.

IsNewNote   R   T/F

IsNewNote   `To get: intIsNewNote = ndocNotesDocument.`**`IsNewNote`**

Indicates whether the document is a new *NotesDocument*—that is, you haven't yet saved it to disk by calling the `Save` method. `TRUE` indicates that it is a new document. `FALSE` indicates that it is not new and has previously been saved to disk.

The following simple example could be used in the `QuerySave` event of the *NotesUIDocument*. This example tests the value of the field called `kwHotClient`, which is a checkbox located on the current form (which is a company profile document). If this field has been selected, the current document is then copied to the Hot Clients folder automatically.

```
If Not source.IsNewDoc Then
    If source.Document.kwHotClient(0) = "Yes" Then
        Call source.Document.PutInFolder( "Hot Clients" )
    End If
End If
```

IsProfile   R   T/F

IsProfile   `To get: intIsProfile = ndocNotesDocument.`**`IsProfile`**

Indicates whether the document is a profile document—a special type of *NotesDocument* Domino object that stores user-specific information.

The following example iterates through all the documents in the current database, displaying a prompt when each profile document is located. Then it tests to see when the document was last modified or accessed. Any documents that weren't modified today are deleted.

The following example is an administrative function that removes all the profile documents in the current database that weren't modified during the current day. This function is helpful if the information stored in the profile document is relevant only for the current day.

```
Dim ns As New NotesSession
Dim ndb As NotesDatabase
Dim nview As NotesView
Dim ndc As NotesDocumentCollection
Dim ndoccurrent As NotesDocument
Dim strValue As String
Set ndb = ns.CurrentDatabase
Set ndc = ndb.AllDocuments
Set ndoccurrent = ndc.GetFirstDocument
Do While Not ndoccurrent Is Nothing
    If ndoccurrent.IsProfile Then
        If ndoccurrent.LastAccessed <> Today Then
            strValue = ndoccurrent.NameofProfile
            If NotesDocument.Remove( True ) Then
                Print "Profile Document named " & strValue &
                ➥" was removed..."
            Else
                Print "Profile document located but not removed..."
            End If
        End If
    End If
    Set ndoccurrent = ndc.GetNextDocument(ndoccurrent)
Loop
```

IsResponse	R	T/F	

```
To get: intIsResponse = ndocNotesDocument.IsResponse
```
IsResponse

Indicates whether the document is a response document to a parent *NotesDocument*. TRUE indicates that it is a response. FALSE indicates that it is not. Of course, the parent *NotesDocument* can also be a response or main document.

IsSigned	R	T/F	

```
To get: intIsSigned = ndocNotesDocument.IsSigned
```
IsSigned

Indicates whether the document is signed, therefore containing a *NotesItem* object of type SIGNATURE. TRUE indicates that the document contains one or more signatures. FALSE indicates that it does not contain any signatures.

IsUIDocOpen	R	T/F	

```
To get: intIsUIDocOpen = ndocNotesDocument.IsUIDocOpen
```
IsUIDocOpen

Indicates whether the current back-end *NotesDocument* is also opened in the user interface in a front-end *NotesUIDocument*. TRUE indicates that the document is opened in a *NotesUIDocument*. FALSE indicates that it is not.

IsValid	R	T/F	

```
To get: intIsValid = ndocNotesDocument.IsValid
```
IsValid

Indicates whether the document represents a "valid" *NotesDocument* object and not a deletion stub. TRUE indicates that the document is not a deletion stub. FALSE indicates that the document is a deletion stub. This property differs from the IsDeleted property in that IsValid indicates that the document was deleted before a handle to the *NotesDocument* was established. After the document handle has been established, the IsDeleted property can be examined to ensure that the document wasn't deleted while the user or script was processing it.

Items	R	O.Ref.

Items   To get: nitemNotesItems = ndocNotesDocument.**Items**

Represents an array of all the *NotesItems* contained in the *NotesDocument*.

Key	R	$

Key   To get: strKey = ndocNotesDocument.**Key**

If the *NotesDocument* is a profile document, this property indicates the username (or key) used with the profile document.

LastAccessed	R	Time/Date

LastAccessed   To get: varLastAccessed = ndocNotesDocument.**LastAccessed**

Represents the date that the document was last accessed (this includes modifications or reading).

For an example of LotusScript that uses LastAccessed, refer to the IsProfile property (▶ 132).

LastModified	R	Time/Date

LastModified   To get: varLastModified = ndocNotesDocument.**LastModified**

Represents the date that the document was last modified.

NameofProfile	R	$

NameofProfile   To get: strNameofProfile() = ndocNotesDocument.**NameofProfile**

If the *NotesDocument* is a profile document, this property indicates the name of the profile document.

For an example of LotusScript that uses NameofProfile, refer to the IsProfile property (▶ 132).

NoteID	R	$

NoteID   To get: strNoteID = ndocNotesDocument.**NoteID**

Indicates the NoteID of the *NotesDocument*. The NoteID is an eight-character combination of letters and numbers used to uniquely identify the document location in the *NotesDatabase*. Therefore, the NoteID for each document is unique for each database. However, NoteIDs are not consistent across replica copies of the *NotesDatabases*. Each NoteID is the same for the document and is unique to the document until it is deleted.

ParentDatabase	R	O.Ref.

Parent
Database   To get: ndbNotesDatabase = ndocNotesDocument.**ParentDatabase**

Represents the parent *NotesDatabase* that contains the *NotesDocument*.

ParentDocumentUNID	R	$

Parent
DocumentUNID   To get: strParDocUNID = ndocNotesDocument.**ParentDocumentUNID**

If the *NotesDocument* is a response document, this property represents the `UniversalID` (▶ 136) of the document's parent. If the document isn't a response document (and thus doesn't have a parent) this property returns an empty string (`""`).

ParentView   R   O.Ref.

```
To get: nvwNotesView = ndocNotesDocument.ParentView
```
ParentView

If the *NotesDocument* handle was retrieved from a *NotesView*, this property returns the name of the view from which it was retrieved. If the document handle was established from other methods (such as from a *NotesDocumentCollection* or a *NotesDatabase*), this property returns `Nothing`.

Responses   R   O.Ref.

```
To get: ndcNotesDocumentCollection = ndocNotesDocument.Responses
```
Responses

Returns a *NotesDocumentCollection* of the immediate response documents to the current *NotesDocument*. All the entries in the collection are immediate responses (children) only. Therefore, responses to the responses are not included in the collection. If the current *NotesDocument* has no response documents, this property returns an empty collection with a count of `0`.

SaveMessageOnSend   R/W   T/F

```
To get: intSaveMsg = ndocNotesDocument.SaveMessageOnSend
To set: ndocNotesDocument.SaveMessageOnSend = intSaveMsg
```
SaveMessage
OnSend

Indicates whether the document should be saved immediately after it is mailed (by calling the `Send` method of the *NotesDocument*). `TRUE` indicates that the document is saved after being mailed. `FALSE` indicates that it is not. This property will work only when the *NotesDocument* is a new document and hasn't yet been saved. Therefore, subsequent calls to the `Send` method will not resave the document.

SentByAgent   R   T/F

```
To get: intSendByAgent = ndocNotesDocument.SentByAgent
```
SentByAgent

Indicates whether the document was mailed to the current user by LotusScript. `TRUE` indicates that the document was mailed by script. `FALSE` indicates that it was mailed by a person. This property uses a reserved *NotesItem* named `$AssistMail` that is set to `1` if the document is mailed by script. This *NotesItem* is automatically created and saved to the *NotesDocument* when the document is mailed.

Signer   R $

```
To get: strSigner = ndocNotesDocument.Signer
```
Signer

If the document is signed, this property represents the name of the person who created the signature contained in the *NotesDocument*. If the document hasn't been signed, this property returns an empty string (`""`).

SignOnSend   R/W   T/F

```
To get: intSignOnSend = ndocNotesDocument.SignOnSend
To set: ndocNotesDocument = SignOnSend = intSignOnSend
```
SignOnSend

Indicates whether the document is signed when mailed. `TRUE` indicates that the document is signed when mailed. `FALSE` indicates that it is not.

Size   R   &

```
To get: lngSize = ndocNotesDocument.Size
```
Size

Indicates the size in bytes of the *NotesDocument*. The value represented here includes all the items and file attachments that are contained in the document.

UniversalID   R/W $

```
To get: strUniversalID = ndocNotesDocument.UniversalID
To set: ndocNotesDocument.UniversalID = strUniversalID
```

Represents the Universal ID of the *NotesDocument*. The Universal ID is a 32-character combination of hexadecimal digits that uniquely identifies the document. This identification is unique across all replicas of this database (unlike the `NoteID`). In fact, this property is used to determine whether documents in replica *NotesDatabases* are replicas of one another. Therefore, if a document's `UniversalID` is modified, the document then becomes a new document. The hexadecimal digits include the numbers 0 to 9 and the letters A to F. Because each `UniversalId` must be unique within all replicas of the database, you can't set this value to an existing `UniversalID` in the *NotesDatabase*. Attempting to do so generates a runtime error 4000 message.

Verifier   R $

```
To get: strVerifier = ndocNotesDocument.Verifier
```

If the *NotesDocument* is signed, this property represents the name of the certificate that was used to verify the signature contained in the document.

NotesDocument Methods

AppendItemValue

```
Set nitemNotesItem = ndocNotesDocument.AppendItemValue(strItemname,
➥value)
```

strItemname   Required $
The name of the new *NotesItem*.

value   Required   Varies
The value of the new *NotesItem*.

This method creates and returns a handle on a new *NotesItem* in the *NotesDocument* and sets the item's value. The data type of the new *NotesItem* depends on the data type of the `Value` passed in the method call. Here are the possible resulting data types:

Data Type of `value`	Data Type of New *NotesItem*
String	Text item
Array of strings	Text item array
Integer	Number item
Array of integers	Number item array
Variant of type `DATE`	Date-time item
Array of variants of type `DATE`	Date-time item array
NotesDateTime	Date-time item represented by the *NotesDateTime* object
NotesItem	*NotesItem* data type matching the value(s) of the *NotesItem* data type

The new *NotesItem* isn't permanently saved to disk until the `Save` method of the *NotesDocument* is called. Also, if an item already exists in the *NotesDocument* that has the same name as the `strItemName` specified when this method is called, a new *NotesItem* is created in the document. In other words, both *NotesItems* are preserved in the document even though they share the same item name.

NotesItems can also be created for the *NotesDocument* by using extended syntax, which allows you to add and modify *NotesItems* as if they were properties of the *NotesDocument*. This technique is described in the "Remarks" section near the end of this chapter (▶ 145).

ComputeWithForm

```
intflag = ndocNotesDocument.ComputeWithForm(intDoDataTypes,
➥intRaiseError)
```
ComputeWith
Form

intDoDataTypes	Required	T/F

This method is currently ignored.

intRaiseError	Required	T/F

Indicates whether an error should be raised if validation fails.

This method validates the *NotesDocument* by executing all the default field values (if they don't already exist), translation formulas, and validation formulas of the field design elements stored in the specified form. This is similar to refreshing the document when it is opened in the user interface. This method returns TRUE if the validation was successful and no errors were returned, or FALSE if there are errors on the document. The form design elements used for the validation are determined in the following order:

1. The form stored in the document. This is done during the document's creation.

2. The value stored in the *NotesItem* named "Form."

3. The default database form if not *NotesItem*.

Unlike creating *NotesDocuments* using the native Notes client user interface, documents created using LotusScript don't use a form when they are created. Consequently, form-specific default field values, translation formulas, and validation formulas are not used when new documents are created. This method allows *NotesDocuments* that are created as back-end objects to conform to the requirements of *NotesDocuments* that are created as front-end objects in the user interface. Unlike when documents are created in the user interface, documents can still be saved even if not all of the field validation formulas pass.

You should always specify a *NotesItem* named "Form" when creating new *NotesDocuments,* regardless of whether this method is being called. This will ensure that the documents are opened using the correct form.

CopyAllItems

```
Call ndocNotesDocument.CopyAllItems(NotesDocument, intReplace)
```
CopyAllItems

NotesDocument	Required	O.Ref.

The destination *NotesDocument*.

intReplace	Required	T/F

Indicates whether the *NotesItems* in the destination document should be replaced or appended. TRUE replaces the current items. FALSE appends them.

This method copies all the *NotesItems* in the current *NotesDocument* to the destination *NotesDocument*. The actual names of the *NotesItems* and their respective values are unchanged.

CopyItem

```
Set nitemNotesItem = ndocNotesDocument.CopyItem(NotesItem, strNewname)
```
CopyItem

NotesItem	Required	O.Ref.

The *NotesItem* to copy.

strNewname   Required $

The name to assign to the new *NotesItem.* Specify " " to use the existing name.

This method returns a handle on a *NotesItem* that is copied into the current *NotesDocument.* It also assigns it the name specified in the `strNewName` parameter (if specified).

CopyToDatabase

CopyTo
Database
```
Set ndocNotesDocument = ndocNotesDocument.CopyToDatabase(NotesDatabase)
```

NotesDatabase   Required   O.Ref.

The *NotesDatabase* to copy the *NotesDocument* into.

This method copies a *NotesDocument* into the specified *NotesDatabase* and returns a handle on the new *NotesDocument.*

CreateReplyMessage

CreateReply
Message
```
Set ndocNotesDocument = ndocNotesDocument.CreateReplyMessage(intAll)
```

intAll   Required   T/F

Specifies whether the recipient list should contain all the members of the original list. TRUE includes all the original recipients. FALSE includes only the sender of the original memo.

This method creates a new *NotesDocument* as a reply to the current *NotesDocument* and returns a handle to the new reply document. Prior to sending the new document, be sure to specify a value for the "Subject" *NotesItem.* Also, the new document won't get mailed unless the Send method is explicitly called (▶ 144).

CreateRichTextItem

CreateRich
TextItem
```
Set nrtiNotesRichTextItem = ndocNotesDocument.CreateRichTextItem(strName)
```

strName   Required $

The name of the new *NotesRichTextItem.*

This method creates a new *NotesRichTextItem* for the specified *NotesDocument* and returns a handle to the new rich text item. The name of the new rich text item is determined by the `strName` passed as a parameter in the method. This method is OLE-friendly, because it allows for the creation of *NotesRichTextItems* without having to use the New keyword, which OLE-compliant applications don't understand.

Encrypt

Encrypt
```
Call ndocNotesDocument.Encrypt
```

This method encrypts the *NotesDocument* and all the *NotesItems* contained in the document that have the IsEncrypted property set to TRUE. This encryption doesn't take effect until you write the document to disk by calling the Save method.

The keys used to encrypt the document can be either a single string value or an array of strings. The string value (or each element of the string array) contains the name of the encryption key. Any users who have the encryption key can decrypt the document.

The name of the specified encryption key is stored in the *NotesDocument* in a *NotesRichTextItem* named SecretEncryptionKeys. If the document is encrypted but no encryption keys are specified, the document is encrypted using the current user's public key. Therefore, the document can be decrypted by that user only.

If the script calling this method is running on a server, the server must have permission to use the Encrypt method.

GetAttachment

```
Set nembNotesEmbeddedObject = ndocNotesDocument.GetAttachment
➥(strFilename)
```

strFilename   Required $

The name of the file attachment to locate.

This method returns a handle to the *NotesEmbeddedObject* for the specified file attachment. This method locates any file attachments, regardless of whether they are contained in a *NotesRichTextItem*. If the file attachment specified in strFilename isn't located, this method returns Nothing. Also, the Parent property of the *NotesEmbeddedObject* returns Nothing as well because the file attachment wasn't accessed through the *NotesRichTextItem*.

GetFirstItem

```
Set nitemNotesItem = ndocNotesDocument.GetFirstItem(strName)
```

strName   Required $

The name of the *NotesItem* to locate.

This method returns a handle on the first *NotesItem* in the document with the name specified in the strName parameter. If no *NotesItem* named strName is located, this method returns Nothing.

This method doesn't work with *NotesRichTextItems,* even though *NotesRichTextItems* inherit the properties and methods of the *NotesItem.* However, you can still use this method to access *NotesRichTextItems* as long as they are dimensioned as a variant. When the GetFirstItem method is called, the rich text value is created in the variant, which is converted as a type RICHTEXT.

The following example locates an embedded .wav file in the current *NotesDocument* and plays the sound file when a document using this form is opened. This example is platform-specific and uses the winmm DLL. Therefore, this example will only run on Windows 95 or Windows 98.

The following code must be placed in the Declarations section of the *NotesForm:*

```
Declare Function sndPlaySound Lib "winmm.dll" Alias "sndPlaySoundA"
➥(Byval lpszSoundName As String, Byval uFlags As Long) As Long
Const SND_SYNC = &H0          ' play synchronously (default)
Const SND_ASYNC = &H1         ' play asynchronously (default)
Const SND_NODEFAULT = &H2     ' silence not default, if sound not found
```

The following code must be placed in the QueryOpen event of the *NotesForm:*

```
Dim ndoc As NotesDocument
Dim nrti As Variant
Dim strNotesdatapath As String
Dim varExecute As Long
Dim ndir As New NotesDbDirectory("")
Dim ndb As NotesDatabase
Set ndir = New NotesDbDirectory( "" )
Set ndb = ndir.GetFirstDatabase( DATABASE )
Call ndb.Open( "", "" )
strNotesdatapath = Left(ndb.FilePath,Instr(ndb.FilePath,ndb.FileName)
➥- 1)
Set ndb = Nothing
Set ndoc = Source.Document
Set nrti = ndoc.GetFirstItem( "rtWaveFile" )
If ( nrti.Type = RICHTEXT ) Then
```
continued >>

continued >>

```
Forall o In nrti.EmbeddedObjects
  If ( o.Type = EMBED_ATTACHMENT ) Then
    If (Dir(strNotesdatapath + o.Source) = "") Then
      Call o.ExtractFile( strNotesdatapath & o.Source )
    End If
    varExecute = sndPlaySound(strNotesdatapath & o.Source,
    ➥SND_ASYNC Or SND_NODEFAULT)
  End If
End Forall
End If
```

GetItemValue

GetItemValue

```
value() = ndocNotesDocument.GetItemValue(strItemname)
```

strItemname	Required	$

The name of the *NotesItem*.

This method returns the value(s) of the specified *NotesItem* in the *NotesDocument*. If the *NotesItem* has only one element, an array is returned with only one element. This is because an array is always returned for all text, number, and time-date items. If the *NotesItem* has more than one value, an array of elements is returned, where each element corresponds to a value in the *NotesItem*. The data type of the returned value depends on the data type of the *NotesItem*. Here are the possible resulting data types:

Data Type of *NotesItem*	Returned Value Type
Rich text	String (the plain text of the item)
Text or text list (for Names, Authors, and Reader types)	Array of strings
Number or number list	Array of doubles
Date-time or a range of date-time values	Array of variants of type DATE

NotesItems can also be accessed from the *NotesDocument* by using extended syntax, which enables you to locate *NotesItems* as if they were properties of the *NotesDocument*. This technique is described in the "Remarks" section near the end of this chapter (▶ 145).

HasItem

HasItem

```
strHasItem = ndocNotesDocument.HasItem(strItemname)
```

strItemname	Required	T/F

The name of the *NotesItem*.

This method indicates whether the *NotesItem* specified in the strItemName is contained in the *NotesDocument*. TRUE indicates that the *NotesItem* exists in the *NotesDocument*. FALSE indicates that it does not.

MakeResponse

MakeResponse

```
Call ndocNotesDocument.MakeResponse(NotesDocument)
```

NotesDocument	Required	O.Ref.

The *NotesDocument* that will become a response to the initial *NotesDocument*.

This method makes the *NotesDocument* passed as the parameter (in parentheses) a response to the initial *NotesDocument*. Both *NotesDocuments* must be located in the same *NotesDatabase*. In addition, you must explicitly call the Save method (▶ 143) before the *NotesDocument* is permanently set as a response document to the parent document.

PutInFolder

PutInFolder

```
Call ndocNotesDocument.PutInFolder(strFoldername, intCreateonFail)
```

strFoldername   Required $

The name of the folder to add the document to.

IntCreateonFail   Optional   T/F

Determines whether a new folder should be created if the specified folder doesn't already exist. TRUE creates the folder if it doesn't exist. FALSE specifies that the folder should not be created.

This method adds the *NotesDocument* to the folder specified as strFolderName. If the folder doesn't exist, the IntCreateonFail parameter determines whether the folder should be created. If the folder is created, it is created in the current *NotesDatabase*.

If the folder is nested in another folder, specify the complete path to the destination folder, separating the folder names with backslashes (much as you would in the file directory). If any or all of the folders specified in the path do not exist, they will be created if the IntCreateonFail parameter is set to TRUE. Therefore, if this method is called, if the strFolderName is Administration\Projects\Billing, if IntCreateonFail is set to TRUE, and if none of the folders exists, they will all be created automatically. If the script is running locally on the user's workstation, the folder can be a personal folder.

If the document already exists in the destination folder, calling this method does nothing. Also, if the destination folder is a "Shared, Personal on first use" a document must already be added, or this method will generate an error. Once a document has already been added, this method can add documents to the folder.

Remove

Remove

```
intRemove = ndocNotesDocument.Remove(intForce)
```

intForce   Required   T/F

Specified whether the document should be deleted even if another user has modified the document after the current user began accessing it. TRUE forces the deletion. FALSE aborts the deletion.

This method permanently deletes (removes) a *NotesDocument* from the current *NotesDatabase* and returns a Boolean value indicating whether the deletion was successful. TRUE indicates that the deletion was successfully completed. FALSE indicates that the document wasn't deleted because another user modified it. You can't call this method if the handle on the back-end *NotesDocument* was accessed through a front-end *NotesUIDocument*. Therefore, this method can be called only on *NotesDocuments* accessed through the back-end classes.

The following example can be used with a Web-enabled application to remove (delete) the current document from the *NotesDatabase*. This code could be placed in a Notes agent and called from the WebQueryOpen event of a *NotesForm*. This agent reads the value of the *NotesDocument's* unique ID to be deleted from the Query_String item value (passed in the URL) of the current form. It then locates the respective document based on its unique ID. Once the handle on the document is established, the *NotesDocument* is removed, and a new URL address is opened to display a meaningful message to the Web user.

```
Dim ns As New NotesSession
Dim ndocOriginal As notesdocument
Dim ndb As NotesDatabase
Dim strDbpath As String
Dim ndocCurrent As NotesDocument
Dim strAction As String
```

continued >>

continued >>
```
Set ndocCurrent = ns.DocumentContext
Set ndb = ns.currentdatabase
If Instr(ndb.filepath,"\") Then
    strDbpath = Left$(ndb.filepath, Instr(ndb.filepath,"\")-1) + "/" +
    ➥Right$(ndb.filepath,Len(ndb.filepath)-Instr(ndb.filepath,"\"))
Else
    strDbpath = ndb.filepath
End If
strAction = "[/" + strDbpath + "/(WebDocDeleted)?OpenForm] "
'Get the document
OriginalUNID = Mid(ndocCurrent.Query_String(0),
➥Instr(ndocCurrent.Query_String(0), "&")+1, 32)
Set ndocOriginal = ndb.getdocumentbyunid(originalunid)
'Remove the document
ndocOriginal.Remove(True)
'Tell the user
Print strAction
```

RemoveFromFolder

RemoveFrom
Folder

`Call ndocNotesDocument.`**`RemoveFromFolder`**`(strFoldername)`

strFoldername	Required	$

The name of the folder to remove the document from.

This method removes the *NotesDocument* from the folder specified as `strFolderName`. If the *NotesDocument* isn't contained in the folder, or if the folder doesn't exist, this method does nothing.

If the folder is nested in another folder, specify the complete path to the destination folder, separating the folder names with backslashes (much as you would in the file directory). If the script is running locally on the user's workstation, the folder can be a personal folder.

RemoveItem

RemoveItem

`Call ndocNotesDocument.`**`RemoveItem`**`(strItemname)`

strItemname	Required	$

The name of the *NotesItem* to remove from the *NotesDocument*.

This method deletes the *NotesItem* specified in the `strItemName` parameter from the *NotesDocument*. If more than one *NotesItem* in the form has the same name, they are all removed. If `strItemName` is not contained in the *NotesDocument,* this method does nothing. You must explicitly call the `Save` method (▶ 143) in order for the *NotesItem* to be permanently removed from the document. Also, you can remove *NotesItems* from *NotesDocuments* by calling the `Remove` method of the *NotesItem* class (▶ 182).

RenderToRTItem

RenderToRT
Item

`intRenderToRTItem = ndocNotesDocument.`**`RenderToRTItem`**`(NotesRichTextItem)`

NotesRichTextItem	Required	O.Ref.

The *NotesRichTextItem* to store the image in.

This method creates an image of the specified *NotesDocument* and places it into a *NotesRichTextItem.* A Boolean value is returned, indicating whether the method call was successful. `TRUE` indicates that it was successful. `FALSE` indicates that it was not. The image is rendered as a capture of the current *NotesDocument* and *NotesForm,* so all field formulas (default, translation, and validation formulas) and hide-when formulas are executed.

ReplaceItemValue

```
Set nitemNotesItem = ndocNotesDocument.ReplaceItemValue(strItemname,
➥value)
```

strItemname   Required $

The *NotesDocument* to be replaced.

value   Required   Varies

The value of the new *NotesItem*.

This method replaces all the *NotesItems* of the name specified in strItemName with the specified value and returns a handle on a new *NotesItem* in the *NotesDocument*. The data type of the modified *NotesItem* depends on the data type of the value passed in the method call. Here are the possible resulting data types:

Data Type of value	Data Type of New *NotesItem*
String	Text item
Array of strings	Text item array
Integer	Number item
Array of integers	Number item array
Variant of type DATE	Date-time item
Array of variants of type DATE	Date-time item array
NotesDateTime	Date-time item represented by the *NotesDateTime* object
NotesItem	*NotesItem* data type matching the value(s) of the *NotesItem* data type

The modified value of the *NotesItem* doesn't need to be the same type as the previous *NotesItem* value. When using this method to modify the contents of the *NotesItem*, the IsSummary property of the *NotesItem* is set to FALSE, so the new item value won't display in a view or folder. You must set this property to TRUE if you want this item to be able to be displayed in views and folders.

The new *NotesItem* isn't permanently saved to disk until the Save method of the *NotesDocument* is called.

NotesItems can also be created for the *NotesDocument* by using extended syntax, which allows you to modify *NotesItems* as if they were properties of the *NotesDocument*. This technique is described in the "Remarks" section near the end of this chapter.

Save

```
intSave = ndocNotesDocument.Save(intForce, intCreateResponse,
➥intMarkRead)
```

intForce   Required   T/F

Indicates whether the document should be saved even if another user has modified and saved it since it was opened by the current user. TRUE forces the latest version to overwrite the previous version. FALSE causes the method to use the intCreateResponse setting.

intCreateResponse   Required   T/F

If intForce is FALSE, setting this parameter to TRUE forces the current document to become a response document. If FALSE, the save is canceled.

intMarkRead	Optional	T/F

Indicates whether the document should be marked as read. TRUE marks the document as read. FALSE does not.

This method saves to disk any changes made to the current *NotesDocument* and returns a Boolean variable indicating whether the save was successful. TRUE indicates that the save was successful. FALSE indicates that it failed. If intForce is set to TRUE, the intCreateResponse parameter has no effect.

The following example creates a *NotesDocument* in the back end and populates the items on the new *NotesDocument* using values contained in the current *NotesUIDocument*. The new back-end document is then saved, and a meaningful message is printed to the user's status bar. The path to the destination *NotesDatabase* is built dynamically using the current *NotesDatabase* filepath.

```
Dim ns As New NotesSession
Dim nws As New NotesUIWorkspace
Dim ndb As NotesDatabase
Dim nuid As NotesUIDocument
Dim strFilename As String
Set nuidoc = nws.CurrentDocument
strFilename = Left$(ns.Currentdatabase.FilePath,
➥Len(ns.Currentdatabase.filepath)-
➥(Len(ns.currentdatabase.Filename)))
Set ndb = New NotesDatabase( ns.CurrentDatabase.Server, strFilename +
➥"Acme.nsf" )
Dim ndocNew As New NotesDocument( ndb )
With ndocNew
    .Form = "Customer Profile"
    .strFormname = "Customer Profile Form"
    .strParentCompany = nuid.Document.strParentCompany(0)
    .strLocation = nuid.Document.strLocation(0)
    .strCustNumber = nuid.Document.strCustNumber(0)
    .strCustName = nuid.Document.strCustName(0)
    .strTransactionType = nuid.Document.strTransactionType(0)
    .intTransactionNumber = nuid.Document.intTransactionNumber(0)
    .dtTransactionDate = nuid.Document.dtTransactionDate(0)
    .strTransactionDescription =
    ➥nuid.Document.strTransactionDescription(0)
    .strTransactionComments = nuid.Document.strTransactionComments(0)
End With
Call ndocNew.Save(True, False, False)
Print "Document has been saved."
```

Send

Send   `intSend = ndocNotesDocument.`**`Send`**`(intAttachform, strRecipients)`

---

intAttachform	Required	T/F

Indicates whether the form should be stored and sent with the document. TRUE stores the document. FALSE does not.

strRecipients	Optional	$

Specifies the recipients of the document.

This method mails the *NotesDocument* to the recipients specified in the strRecipients parameter. If intAttachform is set to TRUE, the size of the document increases, but this causes the recipient(s) to view the document in its original form design. The recipients can be people, groups, or mail-in databases. If the *NotesDocument* contains a SendTo field, this parameter is ignored. If the document doesn't contain a `SendTo` field, this parameter is required. Also, if the document contains additional `CopyTo` or `BlindCopy` fields, they will be sent the document as well. Other mail-routing-specific *NotesItems* are used as well. For example, Delivery Priority, DeliveryReport, and ReturnReceipt are also used when the document is mailed.

Set the `SaveMessageOnSend` property of the *NotesDocument* to `TRUE` and `intAttachForm` to `TRUE` if you want the document to be saved when it is mailed.

When the document is mailed, Notes automatically creates a *NotesItem* called `$AssistMail` in the document. This allows the `SentByAgent` property to determine whether the document was mailed by script. If the script calling this method is running locally on a user's workstation, the user's name will automatically be assigned to the `From` *NotesItem*. If the script is running as a scheduled agent, the `From` item will contain the name of the person who last signed the agent.

For an example of LotusScript that uses the `Send` method, refer to the "Example" section at the end of this chapter (▶ 146).

Sign

```
Call ndocNotesDocument.Sign                                    Sign
```

This method signs the document with the current user's signature. You must explicitly call the `Save` method to permanently save the signature to disk, or the signature will be discarded when the script completes. If this method is called and the script is running on the server, this method has no effect.

Remarks

When working with the *NotesDocument* object, it is important to remember that you must explicitly call the `Save` method before any of the changes are permanently saved and written to disk. This is true when existing documents are modified, when new documents are created, or when existing documents are deleted from the *NotesDatabase*. Failing to call the `Save` method will cause all the modifications to be ignored when the current script completes. When the `Save` method is called, the document is resaved, even if it was not previously modified in the script.

You can use the *NotesDocumentCollection* to access all *NotesDocuments* or a subset of *NotesDocuments* contained in a *NotesDatabase*. In addition, the *NotesView* can also be used to access *NotesDocuments* based on specific criteria. Accessing *NotesDocuments* using the *NotesView* class can be much more efficient and easier to program, because these *NotesDocuments* are already indexed based on the design specifications of the *NotesView*. Often, when performing actions on multiple *NotesDocuments*, performance can become a major consideration, especially since you're working with nonrelational data. However, when using *NotesViews* to locate specific *NotesDocumentCollections*, the content of the view must be predetermined and can't be built on-the-fly. Often, *NotesDocumentCollections* can be created using a *NotesView* to retrieve a subset of the *NotesDocuments* based on specific criteria (such as the form used to create the document) and then refined programmatically.

Under the hood, a *NotesDocument* can reside in several *NotesDocumentCollections* simultaneously. These collections essentially contain pointers to the actual *NotesDocuments*. Within the lsxbe, the document is a single object, but it can have multiple parent indexes and be located in multiple collections.

Therefore, consider this when working with multiple collections or when deleting or modifying *NotesDocuments* that might be referenced by other collections.

The properties of the *NotesDocument* can be extended to allow for a more efficient way to create *NotesItems* for the current document. Once you have determined the name of the item value (and its value if you're creating or modifying), you can use extended class syntax to manipulate item values or one of the following methods of the *NotesDocument* class:

NotesDocument **Method**	**Result/Action**
GetItemValue	Gets an item's value
ReplaceItemValue	Sets an item's value
AppendItemValue	Creates a new item
HasItem	Checks to see whether the item exists in the document
RemoveItem	Deletes the item from the document

When using extended class syntax to create or modify the *NotesItem,* you are essentially treating the *NotesDocument* as an extended class and using the item name as a property of the *NotesDocument* object. When using extended class syntax, the values assigned can be any LotusScript data type—namely, a scalar data type, an array, or a reference to another *NotesItem* object, *NotesDateTime* object, or *NotesDateRange* object. Unlike the AppendItemValue method, when a new *NotesItem* is created using the extended syntax and a *NotesItem* of the same name already exists in the *NotesDocument,* the item is replaced with the new value. (When you're using the AppendItemValue method, another *NotesItem* is created using the same name.) Also, the AppendItemValue method returns a handle on the *NotesItem* object so that its properties can be modified and its method called is desired. These are not available when using extended syntax.

Using extended class syntax reduces the amount of code that must be written and thus can make the code easier to read. In addition, it can preserve memory because the need to dimension additional *NotesItems* is eliminated. However, using extended class syntax doesn't let you manipulate the value data type or use the intSpecialType. For example, if the new *NotesItem* must be an Authors field type, you can't use extended syntax to create the field (this is a common mistake made by inexperienced developers).

If the current *NotesDocument* is encrypted, the script will attempt to decrypt the *NotesDocument* after it attempts to access one of the document's properties or call one of the document's methods.

Example

The following example could be used as a daily scheduled agent to send the recipient's e-mail notifications about upcoming birthdays and anniversaries stored in a personal information manager or contact database. This example won't run independently because it relies on several other design elements in order to execute (namely, hidden views that display the birthday and anniversary values contained in the documents). However, this does show how automation can be used to push relevant information to the user, incorporating the existing e-mail messaging and the doc-link functionality of Domino/Lotus Notes.

```
Dim ns As New NotesSession
Dim ndb As NotesDatabase
Dim ndocMail As NotesDocument
Dim ndocTodayBD As NotesDocument
Dim ndocTodayAnn As NotesDocument
Dim nrtiBody As NotesRichTextItem
Dim nvwBirthday  As NotesView
Dim nvwAnniversary As NotesView
Dim strCurBDExec As String
Dim strCurAnnExec As String
Dim strCurAcctExec As String
Dim intCount As Integer
Dim varCurDate As Variant
Set ndb = ns.CurrentDatabase
Set nvwBirthday  = ndb.GetView("(LookupByBirthday)")
Set nvwAnniversary = ndb.GetView("(LookupByAnniversary)")
varCurDate = Format(Today, "mm/dd")
Set ndocTodayBD = nvwBirthday .GetDocumentByKey(varCurDate)
Set ndocTodayAnn = nvwAnniversary.GetDocumentByKey(varCurDate)
If Not ndocTodayBD Is Nothing Then
    strCurBDExec = ndocTodayBD.ColumnValues(1)
End If
If Not ndocTodayAnn Is Nothing Then
    strCurAnnExec = ndocTodayAnn.ColumnValues(1)
End If
While Not(ndocTodayBD Is Nothing) And Not(ndocTodayAnn Is Nothing
    If strCurBDExec <= strCurAnnExec Then
        strCurAcctExec = strCurBDExec
    Else
        strCurAcctExec = strCurAnnExec
    End If
    Set ndocMail = New NotesDocument(ndb)
    ndMail.Form = "Memo"
    ndMail.SendTo = strCurAcctExec
    ndMail.Subject = "Fortisma Daily Reminder Message"
    Set nrtiBody = New NotesRichTextItem(ndMail, "Body")
    'Get Today's Birthday documents
    Call nrtiBody.AppendText("Birthdays for " + varCurDate)
    Call nrtiBody.AddNewLine(1)
    intCount = 0
    While (strCurAcctExec = strCurBDExec) And Not(ndocTodayBD Is Nothing)
        intCount = intCount + 1
        Call nrtiBody.AppendText("   " + ndocTodayBD.ColumnValues(2) + "  ")
        Call nrtiBody.AppendDocLink(ndocTodayBD, "Click here to open.")
        Call nrtiBody.AddNewLine(1)
        Set ndocTodayBD = nvwBirthday .GetNextDocument(ndocTodayBD)
        If Not ndocTodayBD Is Nothing Then
            strCurBDExec = ndocTodayBD.ColumnValues(1)
            If varCurDate <> ndocTodayBD.ColumnValues(0) Then
                Set ndocTodayBD = Nothing
                strCurBDExec = ""
            End If
        End If
    Wend
```

continued >>

continued >>

```
            If intCount = 0 Then
                Call nrtiBody.AppendText("       None.")
            End If
            'Get Today's Anniversary documents
            Call nrtiBody.AddNewLine(1)
            Call nrtiBody.AppendText("Anniversaries for " + varCurDate)
            Call nrtiBody.AddNewLine(1)
            intCount = 0
            While (strCurAcctExec =strCurAnnExec) And Not(ndocTodayAnn Is Nothing)
                intCount = intCount + 1
                Call nrtiBody.AppendText("   " + ndocTodayAnn.ColumnValues(2) + " ")
                Call nrtiBody.AppendDocLink(ndocTodayAnn, "Click here to open.")
                Call nrtiBody.AddNewLine(1)
                Set ndocTodayAnn = nvwAnniversary.GetNextDocument(ndocTodayAnn)
                If Not ndocTodayAnn Is Nothing Then
                    strCurAnnExec = ndocTodayAnn.ColumnValues(1)
                    If varCurDate <> ndocTodayAnn.ColumnValues(0) Then
                        Set ndocTodayAnn = Nothing
                        strCurBDExec = ""
                    End If
                End If
            Wend
            If intCount = 0 Then
                Call nrtiBody.AppendText("       None.")
            End If
            'Mail message
            Call ndMail.Send(False)
        Wend
```

NotesDocument Collection

4.0 4.1x 4.5x 4.6x 5.0

The *NotesDocumentCollection* object represents a collection or subset of *NotesDocuments*. This collection of documents can be derived from the front end and back end of a *NotesDatabase* class, the *NotesView* class, or the current *NotesSession* class. Accessing the *NotesDocumentCollection* lets you modify, perform specific actions on, search, and navigate through particular documents based on document content, specific keys, optional sorted order, and so on.

```
NotesSession
  └ NotesDocumentCollection
      └ NotesDocument
          └ ...

OR

NotesUIDatabase
  └ NotesDocumentCollection
      └ NotesDocument
          └ ...

OR

NotesUIView
  └ NotesDocumentCollection
      └ NotesDocument
          └ ...

OR

...
  └ NotesDatabase
      └ NotesDocumentCollection
          └ NotesDocument
              └ ...
```

LotusScript Syntax

```
Dim doccollection As New NotesDocumentCollection
```

There are various methods and properties to establish a handle on a *NotesDocumentCollection* object. The method used depends on which action you want to perform on the *NotesDocuments* contained in the collection and the parent class used to derive the *NotesDocumentCollection* object.

The following methods and properties of the *NotesDatabase* class will create a *NotesDocumentCollection* object. Refer to the *NotesDatabase* class (▶ 89) for details on how to use these properties and methods.

`AllDocuments` property (▶ 92)

`UnprocessedDocuments` property (▶ 96)

`Search` method (▶ 108)

`UnprocessedSearch` method (▶ 109)

`FTSearch` method (▶ 100)

`UnprocessedFTSearch` method (▶ 108)

NotesDocumentCollection Properties

Count	R	%

Count

```
To get: intCount = ndcNotesDocumentCollection.Count
```

Returns an integer value that represents the number of documents in the current *NotesDocumentCollection*.

There are various reasons why you would want to perform an action on a collection of *NotesDocuments*. However, you often need to know how many documents are contained in a collection before any action can be taken. Another common use of this property is to determine the count so that a loop statement can be run on all the documents without stepping through them one at a time. In addition, this document can be used in conjunction with the `UnprocessedDocuments` property of *NotesDatabase* to determine the number of currently selected documents in a view. (For more information on *NotesDatabase*, ▶ 89.) The following code gets a handle on the currently selected documents in the current view and prompts the user if he or she has selected more than one.

```
Sub Click(Source As Button)
Dim nws As New NotesUIWorkspace
Dim ns As New NotesSession
Dim ndc As NotesDocumentCollection
Dim ndoccurrent As NotesDocument
Dim strRecipient As String
Set ndc=ns.Currentdatabase.UnProcessedDocuments
If ndc.Count > 1 Then
    Msgbox "You have selected more than one document, please refine your
    ➥selection to one document and try again.",16,"Error..."
```

```
Elseif ndc.Count < 1 Then
    Msgbox "There are no unprocessed documents in this database.",16,
    ➥"Error..."
    Exit Sub
Else
    Set ndoccurrent = ndc.GetNthDocument(1)
    strRecipient = Inputbox$("Enter the recipient's E-Mail address.",
    ➥"Forwarding a Notes document...")
    If strRecipient <> "" Then
        Call ndoccurrent.Send( True, strRecipient)
    End If
End If
End Sub
```

IsSorted   R   T/F

`To get: intIsSorted = ndcNotesDocumentCollection.IsSorted`   IsSorted

Indicates whether the documents contained in the *NotesDocumentCollection* are sorted. (This is TRUE if the documents are sorted, and FALSE if they are not.) Documents can be sorted only when the collection was built using the full-text search method of a *NotesDatabase*. How a document is sorted is determined by its relevance score (the number of matches found in the current document based on the search criteria). The relevance score is then assigned to each document, with the most relevant document appearing first. The remaining documents are then sorted in descending order.

Parent   R   *O.Ref.*

`To get: ndbnotesDatabase = ndcNotesDocumentCollection.Parent`   Parent

Returns a handle to the parent *NotesDatabase* (▶ 89) that contains the document collection.

Query   R $

`To get: strQuery = ndcNotesDocumentCollection.Query`   Query

This property returns the text value representing the query that was used to build the document collection. This property applies only to document collections that are built using a search method, such as a full-text search. Therefore, collections built without using a search will return a NULL value ("").

NotesDocumentCollection Methods

5.0 AddDocument

`Call ndcNotesDocumentCollection.AddDocument(NotesDocument)`   AddDocument

NotesDocument   Required   *O.Ref.*
The *NotesDocument* to be added.

This method adds a *NotesDocument* entry to the existing collection of documents. In versions of Domino/Lotus Notes prior to 5.0, if you wanted to add a document to the existing collection, you had to discard the current collection and rebuild it based on the new criteria. Of course, then you had to make sure that none of the information being located was being cached.

If the *NotesDocumentCollection* is sorted, the added document is appended to the end of the collection. When the collection is not sorted, the document is inserted into the collection, most likely based on its unique document ID. This makes it difficult to locate the document's current position in the *NotesDocumentCollection*. In fact, the only way to determine its position is to navigate to the previous or next document in the collection and attempt to determine its location relative to the preceding or following document.

This method will automatically check for duplicates prior to inserting or appending the new document into the collection.

Be careful when using this method, because it can have a significant effect on performance. Also, since the document's position is unknown, locating the documents can negatively affect performance.

5.0 DeleteDocument

Delete
Document

`Call ndcNotesDocumentCollection.`**`DeleteDocument`**`(NotesDocument)`

NotesDocument	Required	*O.Ref.*

The *NotesDocument* to be deleted.

This method deletes (removes) a document entry of the document collection. It doesn't actually delete the *NotesDocument* from the database. Instead, it simply removes the document from the current document collection. This method will generate an error if the *NotesDocument* does not exist in the collection or has been removed (from the collection or the database). You can use the `GetDocument` method of the *NotesDocumentCollection* class to test for this (▶ 153).

FTSearch

FTSearch

`Call ndcNotesDocumentCollection.`**`FTSearch`**`(strQuery, intMaxdocs)`

strQuery	Required	$

A string representing the rules for the full-text query. These rules are outlined in a moment.

intMaxdocs	Required	%

The maximum number of *NotesDocuments* to return from the query. Set this parameter to 0 to return all matching documents.

This method performs a full-text search of all the *NotesDocuments* contained in the *NotesDocumentCollection* or refines an existing collection. The result of the full-text search is a collection of documents, which are sorted in descending order of relevance. In other words, the document with the most hits (highest relevance) is first, and the document with the fewest hits (lowest relevance) is last. The actual relevance score is accessible using the `FTSearchScore` property of the *NotesDocument* (refer to the `FTSearchScore` property of the *NotesDocument* (▶ 132).

Fortunately, this method will run even if the *NotesDatabase* is not full-text indexed, although the user will encounter a performance loss. If it's likely that this method will be run more than once (which is usually the case), you can test for an existing full-text index before calling this method using the `IsFTIndexed` method of the *NotesDatabase*. If no full-text index exists, you can create one programmatically using the `UpdateFTIndex` method of the *NotesDatabase*. (Refer to the `IsFTIndexed` (▶ 94) property and `UpdateFTIndex` (▶ 111) method of the *NotesDatabase* class.)

Although this method works on *NotesDocuments* located in the *NotesDocumentCollection,* you can also apply it to the *NotesDatabase* and *NotesView*.

As you would expect when using a legitimate search engine, the rules for defining the search allow for building search criteria using Boolean values and specific operators. The rules for using these operators are listed in the following table.

Search Operators and Rules

Operators	Rules and Description
Plain text	For simple searches, you can enter the word or phrase to search against. It isn't necessary to include quotes, unless you're searching for specific keywords or reserved operators. Placing quotes around the words or phrases ensures that they are treated as literal search criteria and not operators. These rules are similar to typical searching standards. You can always include the text in quotes, regardless, to ensure that whatever text is being searched against is not treated as an operator. When programmatically defining the search criteria within LotusScript, use double quotes so that the quotes are passed as part of the literal search criteria.
Wildcards	Wildcards are supported when you perform searches. Typical to most search engines, they are represented by the ? or * characters. Use the ? to allow for any single character in its respective position and * to match multiple (or no) characters in their respective positions in the word.
Hyphenated words	Used to find pairs of words that are hyphenated as a single word or separated by a space.
Logical operators	Allow you to build more-complex searches (often referred to as "Boolean searches") by using logical operators to further restrict or expand the search algorithm. The allowed operator keywords and their respective symbols (listed in order of precedence) are not or !, and or &, accrue or ,, and or or ¦.
Proximity operators	Allow you to search for words that are close to one another. That is, you can specify if the words are located in proximity to each other by using the operators near, sentence, and paragraph.
Exactcase operator	Allows you to restrict the search to match a specified case.
Termweight operator	Allows you to modify the search's relevance scores by defining the relevance ranking. This is done by specifying a value for n between 0 and 100 representing its relevance score.
Field operators	A powerful capability of the Domino/Lotus Notes search engine. This feature lets you perform a search based on a specific field. The syntax for this search is FIELD *fieldname operator*. *fieldname* is the name of the *NotesItem* that you are performing the operation against. The allowed operators are contains, =, >, and <. Using contains is helpful when you're searching rich text fields. You can't combine operators as in normal programming (such as >=). Therefore, you must build a more-complex search algorithm using the or operator for multiple criteria. You may also need to help define the precedence order of the search using parentheses.

5.0 GetDocument

```
Set ndocNotesDocument = ndcNotesDocumentCollection.GetDocument
➥(NotesDocument)
```
GetDocument

This method returns a handle to the *NotesDocument* entry located in the document collection. Of course, the *NotesDocument* is used as a parameter when calling this method. However, this does allow you to check for the existence of the *NotesDocument* to ensure that it hasn't been removed. If it is indeed no longer present in the collection, this method will return NULL. Otherwise, a handle to the *NotesDocument* entry is again returned.

GetFirstDocument

```
Set ndocNotesDocument = ndcNotesDocumentCollection.GetFirstDocument
```

NotesDocument   Required   O.Ref.

The current document in the *NotesDocumentCollection.*

This method sets the *NotesDocument* to the first document in the collection. If no documents are contained in the *NotesDocumentCollection,* this method returns Nothing.

For an example using the GetFirstDocument method, refer to the GetNextDocument method, also discussed in this chapter (▶ 154).

GetLastDocument

```
Set ndocNotesDocument = ndcNotesDocumentCollection.GetLastDocument
```

This method sets the *NotesDocument* to the last document in the collection. If no documents are contained in the *NotesDocumentCollection,* this method returns Nothing.

GetNextDocument

```
Set ndocNotesDocument = ndcNotesDocumentCollection.GetNextDocument
➡(NotesDocument)
```

NotesDocument   Required   O.Ref.

The current document in the *NotesDocumentCollection.*

This method sets the *NotesDocument* to the next document in the collection, immediately following the current document passed as the parameter. If no more documents are contained in the *NotesDocumentCollection,* this method returns Nothing.

The following example establishes a handle on all the documents in a particular *NotesDatabase* (using the UnprocessedDocuments property of the *NotesDatabase* (▶ 96)). This code was placed in an agent that was run manually from the Actions menu. The *NotesDocumentCollection* can contain both main documents and response documents. This code will rebuild the *NotesDocumentCollection* on-the-fly by removing any documents contained in the collection that are response documents. In larger databases, this would be a costly procedure if run against all the documents in the database. But if run on smaller collections or by scheduled agents, this code could be useful when acting on *NotesDocuments.*

```
Dim ns As New NotesSession
Dim ndb As NotesDatabase
Dim nvw As NotesView
Dim ndc As NotesDocumentCollection
Dim ndoccurrent As NotesDocument
Dim ndocprevious As NotesDocument
Dim intCount As Integer
Set ndb = ns.CurrentDatabase
Set nvw = ndb.Getview("All")
Set ndc  = ndb.UnprocessedDocuments
Set ndoccurrent = ndc.GetFirstDocument
Msgbox "Processing " & Str$(ndc.Count) & " docs..."
Do While Not(ndoccurrent Is Nothing)
    If ndoccurrent.IsResponse Then
    'Need to establish handle on previous doc since we will lose our place
        Set ndocprevious = ndc.GetPrevDocument(ndoccurrent)
        Call ndc.DeleteDocument(ndoccurrent)
        intCount = intCount + 1
        'Document is gone, but let's keep going...
        Set ndoccurrent = ndc.GetNextDocument(ndocprevious)
    Else
        Set ndoccurrent = ndc.GetNextDocument(ndoccurrent)
    End If
```

```
Loop
Msgbox "Finished processing. " & Str$(intCount) & " responses removed."
Msgbox Str$(ndc.Count) & " documents left in collection."
```

GetNthDocument

```
Set ndocNotesDocument = ndcNotesDocumentCollection.GetNthDocument
➥(intCount)
```
GetNth
Document

intCount   Required   %

The position (count) of the *NotesDocument* contained in the collection to return. This value begins at 1 for the first document.

This method returns a handle on a *NotesDocument* based on its relative position in the *NotesDocumentCollection*. If no document is located at the position specified in the *NotesDocumentCollection,* this method returns `Nothing`. This is commonly used when stepping through an entire *NotesDocumentCollection*. For example, you could establish a *NotesDocumentCollection* and then loop through the documents using a `Forall` loop, setting the current *NotesDocument* to the current value of the `Forall` variable. However, this is an inefficient method of traversing through the *NotesDocumentCollection*. A more efficient method is to use the `GetFirstDocument` followed by the `GetNextDocument` to step through the collection.

Another consideration when using this method is how current the index is when you're looking for a specific document in the collection. Specifically, certain entries might have been deleted or modified in such a manner that modifies the *NotesDocumentCollection* index. The position of the *NotesDocument* or entry is stored with the document or entry. Therefore, if there have been many deletions or modifications to the documents contained in the *NotesDocumentCollection,* this operation could be inefficient.

GetPrevDocument

```
Set ndocNotesDocument = ndcNotesDocumentCollection.GetPrevDocument
➥(NotesDocument)
```
GetPrev
Document

NotesDocument   Required   O.Ref.

The current document in the *NotesDocumentCollection*.

This method sets the *NotesDocument* to the previous document in the collection. If no more documents are contained in the *NotesDocumentCollection,* this method returns `Nothing`.

For an example using the `GetPrevDocument` method, refer to the `GetNextDocument` method, also discussed in this chapter (▶ 154).

PutAllInFolder

```
Call ndcNotesDocumentCollection.PutAllInFolder(intFoldername,
➥intCreateonfail)
```
PutAllInFolder

intFoldername   Required $

The name of the folder to place the *NotesDocuments* contained in the *NotesDocumentCollection* into.

intCreateonfail   Optional   T/F

Determines if a new folder should be created if the specified folder does not exist (`TRUE` to create a folder if one does not exist, `FALSE` to not create a new folder).

This method moves the contents of the *NotesDocumentCollection* into the folder specified in the parameter. If the script performing this action is located in the user's local workstation, the folder can be a personal folder. You can place the documents in nested folders (folders contained in other folders) by using backslashes to specify the folder path (similar to specifying directories in the file system). If the document is already located in the specified folder, no action is taken on that document (it's already there!). If the folder doesn't exist, it is automatically created. Similarly, if the path specified doesn't exist, it is automatically created. The method will adhere to the access control settings for the *NotesDatabase* as well (that is, the ability to create personal folders and views and the ability to create shared folders and views).

RemoveAll

RemoveAll

```
Call ndcNotesDocumentCollection.RemoveAll(intForce)
```

intForce	Required	T/F

Specifies whether this method should force the collection to become empty even if documents are modified by other users after they are opened. (**TRUE** forces the collection to become empty, and **FALSE** allows documents to remain after this method is executed.)

This method deletes the documents in the collection from the database. Unlike the `DeleteDocument` method, which simply removes the *NotesDocument* from the *NotesDocumentCollection,* the `RemoveAll` method actually removes the *NotesDocument* from disk. Entries in the collection are also removed when this method is executed. In other words, the *NotesDocumentCollection* is updated to reflect the removed documents. Therefore, if all the documents were removed, the collection will be empty and will have a count of zero.

RemoveAllFromFolder

RemoveAllFrom
Folder

```
Call ndcNotesDocumentCollection.RemoveAllFromFolder
➥(strFoldername)
```

strFoldername	Required	$

The name of the folder to remove the *NotesDocuments* from.

This method removes the contents of the *NotesDocumentCollection* from the folder specified in the parameter. If the script performing this action is located in the user's local workstation, the folder can be a personal folder. You can remove documents in nested folders (folders contained in other folders) by using backslashes to specify the folder path (similar to specifying directories in the file system). If the document isn't located in the specified folder, no action is taken on that document. If the folder doesn't exist, this method does nothing.

StampAll

StampAll

```
Call ndcNotesDocumentCollection.StampAll(strItemname, value)
```

strItemname	Required	$

The name of the *NotesItem* whose value should be modified.

value	Required	Varies

The value to assign to the *NotesItem.*

This method replaces all the *NotesItem* values for all the *NotesDocuments* contained in the collection with the value specified. If the *NotesItem* doesn't yet exist in the *NotesDocument,* it is automatically created. Modifications made to the documents contained in the collection are automatically written to back-end documents and therefore are automatically saved to disk. Consequently, the `Save` method doesn't need to be called because the changes are already written to disk. Similarly, any documents to be modified by the `StampAll` method must have already been saved to disk prior to executing this method. In other words, the documents must already physically exist before this method can modify the document contents.

UpdateAll

`Call ndcNotesDocumentCollection.`**`UpdateAll`**   UpdateAll

This method marks all the *NotesDocuments* contained in the collection as being processed by the current agent. This ensures that the agent runs only on documents that haven't yet been processed by the agent—namely, new or modified documents in the database. (Refer to the `UpdateProcessedDoc` method of the *NotesSession* class (▶ 273) for information on updating processed documents.)

Remarks

In addition to using the *NotesDocumentCollection* to access all documents or a subset of documents contained in a *NotesDatabase,* the *NotesView* can also be used to access documents based on specific criteria. Accessing documents using the *NotesView* class can be much more efficient and easier to program, because these documents are already indexed based on the design specifications of the *NotesView.* Often, when you perform actions on multiple documents, performance can become a major consideration, especially since you are working with a nonrelational database store. However, when you use *NotesView* to locate specific document collections, the content of the view must be predetermined and can't be built on-the-fly. Often, document collections can be created using a *NotesView* to retrieve a subset of the documents based on specific criteria (that is, the form used to create the document) and then refined programmatically.

Nevertheless, the *NotesDocumentCollection* is usually desired when the criteria for the collection is too complex to be met with a *NotesView,* when there is no *NotesView* that contains all the documents that are needed, or when you need to navigate through the hierarchy of the documents (using the documents' parents, children, siblings, and so on).

When you create a *NotesDocumentCollection* using an `FTSearch` method, the *NotesDocuments* contained in the collection are sorted based on the search criteria. When collections are constructed using other methods, they are automatically sorted by the `DocumentUNID`. The `DocumentUNID` is a special text item of the *NotesDocument* that represents that document's unique ID. In document collections, this item is used to sort the collection alphanumerically.

Under the hood, a *NotesDocument* can reside in several *NotesDocumentCollections* simultaneously. These collections essentially contain pointers to the actual *NotesDocuments.* Within the `lsxbe`, the document is a single object, but it can have multiple parent indices and be located in multiple collections. Therefore, consider this when working with multiple collections or when deleting or modifying *NotesDocuments* that might be referenced by other collections.

Example

The following example could be used in an application that moves or copies documents to a particular folder based on certain criteria of the document. The folder could be a "Hot Prospects," "Dead Leads," "Archived," or another folder where personal categorization would be helpful. This code checks the contents of all the documents in the current *NotesDocumentCollection* and moves any documents whose form type is "Prospect" and that have been created on the same day into the "New Leads" folder. The *NotesDocumentCollection* is a collection of all the unprocessed documents in the current database. Processed documents are ignored because they have already been moved, if required.

```
Dim ns As New NotesSession
Dim ndb As NotesDatabase
Dim ndc As NotesDocumentCollection
Dim ndoccurrent As NotesDocument
Dim ndocprevious As NotesDocument
Set ndb = ns.CurrentDatabase
Set ndc  = ndb.UnprocessedDocuments
Set ndoccurrent = ndc.GetFirstDocument
Do While Not(ndoccurrent Is Nothing)
    'Loop for all documents in collection
    If ndoccurrent.Form(0) = "Prospect" Then
        If Format$(ndoccurrent.Created, "Short Date") = Format$(Today,
        ➥"Short Date") Then
            flag = True
        Else
            flag = False
        End If
    Else
        flag = False
    End If
    If flag = False Then
        'Establish secondary handle on document prior to delete
        Set ndocprevious = ndc.GetPrevDocument(ndoccurrent)
        Call ndc.DeleteDocument(ndoccurrent)
        If ndocprevious Is Nothing Then
            Set ndoccurrent = ndc.GetFirstDocument
        Else
            'Get next document using secondary handle
            Set ndoccurrent = ndc.GetNextDocument(ndocprevious)
        End If
    Else
        Set ndoccurrent = ndc.GetNextDocument(ndoccurrent)
    End If
Loop
Call ndc.PutAllInFolder("New Leads")
```

NotesEmbeddedObject

4.0 4.1x 4.5x 4.6x 5.0

The *NotesEmbeddedObject* object contains an array of all the OLE/1 and OLE/2 embedded objects, file attachments, and links to other objects (database links, view links, and document links) that are contained in the *NotesRichTextItem*. At the time this chapter was written, this class wasn't supported for OS/2 and Macintosh clients.

...
```
└ NotesDocument
    └ NotesEmbeddedObject
```

Page	Contents
	Syntax
	Properties
160	Class
160	FileSize
160	FitBelowFields
161	FitToWindow
161	Name
161	Object
161	Parent
161	RunReadOnly
162	Source
162	Type
162	Verbs
	Methods
162	Activate
162	DoVerb
163	ExtractFile
163	Remove
163	**Remarks**
163	**Example**

LotusScript Syntax

In order to create a new *NotesEmbeddedObject,* you must use the `EmbedObject` method of the *NotesRichTextItem* class (▶ 240). This method lets you create a new object, object link, or file attachment. In order to establish a handle on an existing *NotesEmbeddedObject* contained in a rich text field stored in a document, you must use the `GetEmbeddedObject` or `EmbeddedObjects` methods of the *NotesRichTextItem.* Use the `GetEmbeddedObject` method to access an object, object link, or attachment when you know the name of the object and the *NotesRichTextItem* that contains it. Using the `EmbeddedObjects` method lets you access all the objects, object links, or file attachments in the respective rich text item.

In order to establish a handle to an object or object link stored in a document as part of the form design used to create that document, you can use the `EmbeddedObjects` property of the *NotesDocument* class (▶ 131). The *NotesEmbeddedObject* can't be created from scratch using the `New` keyword. It must derive its value from the existing *NotesRichTextItem* or *NotesDocument* class.

NotesEmbeddedObject Properties

Class   R $

Class   To get: strClassname = nembNotesEmbeddedObject.**Class**

This property returns the name of the application that was used to create the embedded object. All objects created and stored with a *NotesRichTextField* or *NotesDocument* have a default object name assigned to them. When the *NotesEmbeddedObject* is a file attachment, this property will return `NULL` (an empty string, `""`). Some default object names and their respective applications are listed in the following table.

Applications and Default Object Names

Application	Class Name
Lotus WordPro	WordPro.Application.9
Lotus Freelance	Freelance.Application.98
Microsoft Word 97	Word.Document.8
Microsoft Excel 97	Excel.Application.8
Microsoft PowerPoint	PowerPoint.Application.8
Lotus Notes	Notes.NotesSession
Visio	Visio.Application.5

FileSize   R   &

FileSize   To get: lngSize = nembNotesEmbeddedObject.**FileSize**

This property returns the size in bytes of the embedded object, object link, or file attachment.

FitBelowFields   R/W   T/F

FitBelowFields   To get: intFitBelowFields = nembNotesEmbeddedObject.**FitBelowFields**
To set: nembNotesEmbeddedObject.**FitBelowFields** = intFitBelowFields

This property indicates whether the *NotesEmbeddedObject* is set to display below the fields on the form. TRUE indicates that it is set to display below the fields. FALSE indicates that it should display where the *NotesEmbeddedObject* was originally placed on the form design layout.

FitToWindow   R/W   T/F

```
To get: intFitToWindow = nembNotesEmbeddedObject.FitToWindow
To set: nembNotesEmbeddedObject.FitToWindow = intFitBelowFields
```
FitToWindow

This property indicates whether the *NotesEmbeddedObject* should display expanded so that the object size occupies the entire window or if the object should display in its native size (or in a size determined by the object parameters). TRUE indicates that the object should display in the entire window. FALSE indicates that it should not.

Name   R $

```
To get: strName = nembNotesEmbeddedObject.Name
```
Name

The name used to reference the embedded object or object link. When the *NotesEmbeddedObject* is a file attachment, this property returns a NULL value (an empty string, ""). In addition, it is possible for the embedded object or object link not to have a name associated with it. Therefore, it will also return a NULL value.

If the embedded object or object link was created using the EmbedObject of the *NotesRichTextItem* object, this property will return the Name parameter that was used when the object was created.

Despite the fact that this property is read-only when you're accessing the object with a script, this property of the object can actually be edited when you're accessing the object through the user interface. The value returned by this property is displayed in the info box of the Object Properties as "*Object Name:*" when you view the object properties.

Object   R   Variant

```
To get: Set varObject = nembNotesEmbeddedObject.Object
```
Object

Once the *NotesEmbeddedObject* has been successfully loaded into memory, this property returns an OLE handle to the embedded object. If the object supports OLE automation, you can programmatically access the object's properties and methods via the established handle.

Because this property is accessing other objects created with foreign applications, there is always a possibility that some functionality might be lost or inaccessible. For example, when establishing a handle on an object link, this property is often unable to return a handle on the embedded object link, because this functionality isn't supported by the OLE-compliant application.

Parent   R   *O.Ref.*

```
To get: nrtiNotesRichTextItem = nembNotesEmbeddedObject.Parent
```
Parent

The name of the *NotesRichTextItem* that contains the *NotesEmbeddedObject*.

RunReadOnly   R/W   T/F

```
To get: intRunReadOnly = nembNotesEmbeddedObject.RunReadOnly
To set: nembNotesEmbeddedObject.RunReadOnly = intRunReadOnly
```
RunReadOnly

This property indicates whether the *NotesEmbeddedObject* should launch in read-only mode. TRUE indicates that it should be launched in read-only mode. FALSE indicates that it should not.

Source	R	$

Source   To get: strSource = nembNotesEmbeddedObject.**Source**

This property returns a different value depending on the type of the *NotesEmbeddedObject.* If the embedded object is an object or object link, this property will return a string name representing the internal name that Domino/Notes uses to refer to the source document. If the embedded object is a file attachment, this property returns the filename of the attachment. Furthermore, if the EmbedObject method was used to embed the object in a *NotesRichTextItem,* this property will return the full path and filename of the file attachment. Otherwise, this property returns only the attachment's filename.

Type	R	%

Type   To get: intType = nembNotesEmbeddedObject.**Type**

This property indicates the type of the *NotesEmbeddedObject*—namely, whether it is an embedded object, object link, or file attachment. Here are the constant values allowed for intType:

intType Constant Values

Constant	Description
EMBED_ATTACHMENT	The object is a file attachment.
EMBED_OBJECT	The object is an embedded object.
EMBED_OBJECTLINK	The object is an object link.

Verbs	R	()

Verbs   To get: strVerbs() = nembNotesEmbeddedObject.**Verbs**

If the *NotesEmbeddedObject* is an OLE/2 embedded object, this property returns the verbs that an object supports. The supported Verbs are returned as an array of strings. In order to invoke a verb on the object, use the DoVerb method (▶ 162).

NotesEmbeddedObject Methods

Activate

Activate   Set objecthandle = nembNotesEmbeddedObject.**Activate**(intshow)

---

intshow	Required	T/F

Determines whether the server application will display the object and server application to the user interface. TRUE displays the object; FALSE hides it.

This method causes the OLE server to load the object and return an OLE handle to the *NotesEmbeddedObject.* If the object or object link does not support OLE automation, this method will return Nothing. This method will return an error if the *NotesEmbeddedObject* is a file attachment.

When establishing an OLE handle for object links, this property will often be unable to return a handle, because this functionality is not supported by the OLE-compliant application.

DoVerb

DoVerb   Variant = nembNotesEmbeddedObject.**DoVerb**(strVerb)

`strVerb`	Required	$

The string name of an object's verb.

This method executes the object verb of the *NotesEmbeddedObject*. While this method returns a variant, because it is executing an action in the OLE object, the return value of the variant is always empty.

ExtractFile

```
Call nembNotesEmbeddedObject.ExtractFile(strFilepath)
```
ExtractFile

`strFilepath`	Required	$

The path and filename of where to store the extracted file on the file system or disk.

This method copies the file attachment to the file system or disk. This method won't work for embedded objects and object links and will raise an error when invoked.

Remove

```
Call nembNotesEmbeddedObject.Remove
```
Remove

This method removes (deletes) the object from the *NotesRichTextItem*. This method doesn't take effect until you save the parent *NotesDocument* object to disk by calling the **Save** method of the *NotesDocument*.

Remarks

In addition to using the **EmbeddedObjects** property of the *NotesRichTextItem,* you can also use the **HasEmbedded** property of the *NotesDocument* object to determine whether the document has any embedded objects in it. This property will not only detect embedded objects in *NotesRichTextItem* fields but will also detect embedded objects that were stored in a document at the time of its creation. This feature is limited to native Lotus Notes, and you must enable it in Lotus Notes form design (however, this will not detect file attachments).

Also, not all of the methods and properties available for both embedded objects and linked objects are available for file attachments. These methods and properties were noted in their descriptions in this chapter.

Example

The following example is somewhat more complicated than most examples, because using embedded objects and the features available in those objects is often more complex. The following example performs some OLE2 automation functions with Microsoft Word 97. Specifically, this example locates and launches a Microsoft Word 97 document and then populates a bookmark by creating a new Word table containing three columns. The columns will be populated with the contents of a Notes view. The first column will contain the date the document was created, the second column will contain the form name of the document, and the third column will contain the subject of the document. There are two parts to this example that will run when placed in a button design element located in a Lotus Notes form.

The form will also need to contain a rich text field called Body that contains an existing Word document. The Name property of this object can use the default name assigned by the OLE server. The final requirement is that the Word document must contain a bookmark called Notesbookmark.

Although this example as it currently reads would not be significantly helpful, it could be modified slightly to create a powerful OLE2 automation engine between Lotus Notes and Microsoft Word 97.

Place the following code in the "Declarations" of the button:

```
Const WDGOTOBOOKMARK = -1
Const WDCELL = 12
Const WDLINE = 5
Const WDSTARTOFRANGECOLUMNNUMBER = 16
Const WDADJUSTNONE = 0
'Declare Globals
Dim db As NotesDatabase
Dim view As NotesView
Dim collection As NotesDocumentCollection
Dim currentdoc As NotesDocument
Dim rtitem As Variant
' Define WordTable class
Class WordTable
' Declare object properties
    Public Error As Integer
' Declare member variables
    OLEHdl As Variant
    objTable As Variant
    thisTable As Variant
' Define constructor
    Public Sub New (varHdl As Variant, Byval strBMName As String, Byval
    ➥lngCols As Long)
        If varHdl.Bookmarks.Exists(strBMName) And (lngCols > 0) Then
            Set OLEHdl = varHdl
            Set thisTable = OLEhdl.Application.Selection
            thisTable.Goto WDGOTOBOOKMARK, , ,strBMName
            Set objTable = OLEhdl.Tables.Add(thisTable.Range,1,lngCols)
            Me.Error = False
        Else
'Bookmark does not exist or cols parameter less than 1
            Me.Error = True
        End If
    End Sub
'Define destructor
    Public Sub Delete
        Set OLEhdl = Nothing
        Set thisTable = Nothing
        Set objTable = Nothing
    End Sub
    Public Sub SetColumnWidth(Byval lngCol As Long, Byval sngWidth As
    ➥Single)
        Dim intInchesToPoints
        intInchesToPoints = 72
        If (lngCol > 0) And (lngCol <= objTable.Columns.Count) And
        ➥(sngWidth >= 0.1) Then
            objTable.Columns(lngCol).SetWidth intInchesToPoints * sngWidth,
            ➥WDADJUSTNONE
        Me.Error = False
```

```
        Else
            Me.Error = True
        End If
    End Sub
    Public Sub SetText(Byval strText As String)
        thisTable.TypeText strText
        Me.Error = False
    End Sub
    Public Sub AddText(Byval strText As String)
        ThisTable.TypeText strText
        thisTable.MoveRight WDCELL
        Me.Error = False
    End Sub
    Public Sub MoveHorz(Byval intDirection As Integer, Byval lngCount As
    ➥Long)
        If (lngCount > 0) Then
            If (intDirection <= 0) Then
                thisTable.MoveLeft WDCELL, lngCount
            Else
                thisTable.MoveRight WDCELL, lngCount
            End If
            Me.Error = False
        Else
            Me.Error = True
        End If
    End Sub
    Public Sub MoveVert(Byval intDirection As Integer, Byval lngCount As
    ➥Long)
        If (lngCount > 0) Then
            If (intDirection <= 0) Then
                thisTable.MoveUp WDLINE, lngCount
            Else
                thisTable.MoveDown WDLINE, lngCount
            End If
            Me.Error = False
        Else
            Me.Error = True
        End If
    End Sub
End Class
```

Place the following code in the "Click" of the button:

```
Dim session As New NotesSession
Dim ws As New NotesUIWorkspace
Dim currentcount As Long
Set doc = ws.CurrentDocument.Document
Set db = Session.CurrentDatabase
Set view = db.GetView("All")
Set rtitem = doc.GetFirstItem( "Body" )
If ( rtitem.Type = RICHTEXT ) Then
    Set objOLE = rtitem.GetEmbeddedObject( "Microsoft Word Document" )
    If ( objOLE Is Nothing ) Then
        Msgbox "Unable to find Microsoft Word Document,", 16, "Unable to
        ➥load Word Document..."
    Else
'Launch Word Object...
        ...Print "One moment, activating Microsoft Word Document.  This
        ➥may take several seconds..."
'Create handle to OLE objects IDispatch interface
```

continued >>

continued>>

```
            Set handle = objOLE.Activate(True)
            If ( handle Is Nothing ) Then
                Msgbox "The embedded object has no OLE automation interface."
            Else
                Set object = objOLE.object
                Print "One moment, populating Microsoft Word Document with
                ➡Lotus Notes Data..."
                Set currentdoc = view.GetFirstDocument
                Set customtable = New WordTable(handle, "NotesBookmark",4)
                If customtable.Error Then
                    Msgbox "Couldn't create table in word document"
                Else
                    customtable.SetText "Number"
                    customtable.MoveHorz +1,1
                    customtable.AddText "Date Created"
                    customtable.AddText "Author"
                    customtable.AddText "Subject"
                    Do While Not (currentdoc Is Nothing)
                        customtable.AddText Str$(currentcount&)
                        customtable.AddText currentdoc.Created
                        customtable.AddText currentdoc.Authors(0)
                        customtable.AddText currentdoc.Subject(0)
                        Set currentdoc = view.GetNextDocument(currentdoc)
                        currentcount& = currentcount& + 1
                    Loop
                    customtable.SetColumnWidth 1,1
                    customtable.SetColumnWidth 2,2
                    customtable.SetColumnWidth 3,2
                    customtable.SetColumnWidth 3,2
                End If
            handle.Save
            End If
        End If
End If
    Msgbox "Finished, the Microsoft document is ready for use.", 32,
    ➡"OLE Automation complete..."
Exit Sub
```

4.5x 4.6x 5.0 NotesForm

The *Form* object represents a form in *NotesDatabase* (▶ 89).

```
. . .
└ NotesDatabase
    └ NotesForm
```

LotusScript Syntax

```
Dim Form as NotesForm
```

Currently, there are only two ways to access a form. You must either iterate through the Forms property of *NotesDatabase* or call the GetForm method of *NotesDatabase*.

NotesForm Properties

Aliases   R   ()

Aliases   To Get: varAliases = nfrmNotesForm.Aliases

Returns an array of strings containing the aliases of a form, if there are any. Use IsEmpty() to test this property if you think it's empty.

Fields   R   ()

Fields   To get: varFields = nfrmNotesForm.Fields

Returns a string array containing the names of all the fields in a form.

```
' This agent builds an array of all fields in a form that end in _e,
' indicating that these are exportable fields.
Dim nsSession As New NotesSession
Dim nfrmForm As NotesForm
Dim intLength as Integer
Dim aExportableFields() As String
Dim intCount As Integer
Set nfrmNotesForm=nsSession.CurrentDatabase.GetForm("Task")
Forall field In nfrmNotesForm.Fields
  If Instr(1, field, "_e") Then
    Redim Preserve aExportableFields(intCount)
    intLength=Len(field)
    aExportableFields(intCount) = Left$(field,(intLength-2))
    intCount=intCount+1'
  End If
End  Forall
If Ubound(ExportableFields)>0 Then
  Call ExportData(ExportableFields)
End If
```

FormUsers   R/W   ()

FormUsers   To set: nfrmNotesForm.FormUsers = varFormUsers
To get: varFormUsers = nfrmNotesForm.FormUsers

This property represents the contents of the $FormUsers field. You can set the $FormUsers field using the Who can create documents with this form option on the Key tab of the form properties info box. When it's set to All Authors and above, anyone with author access or higher can create documents using the form. If users and groups are explicitly named, only the named groups create documents using the form. FormUsers expects and returns an array of strings.

IsSubForm	R	T/F

```
To get: intSubForm = nfrmNotesForm.IsSubForm
```
IsSubForm

Indicates whether a form is or is not a subform. If a form is a subform, this property returns TRUE. Otherwise, it returns FALSE.

Name	R	$

```
To get: strName = nfrmNotesForm.Name
```
Name

This property returns the name of the form.

ProtectReaders	R/W	T/F

```
To get: intProtRead = nfrmNotesForm.ProtectReaders
To set: nfrmNotesForm.ProtectReaders = intProtRead
```
ProtectReaders

This property determines whether replication can update $Readers items. If set to TRUE, replication can update $Readers items. If FALSE, replication can't make changes to $Readers items.

ProtectUsers	R/W	T/F

```
To get: intProtUsers = nfrmNotesForm.ProtectUsers
To set: nfrmNotesForm.ProtectUsers = intProtUsers
```
ProtectUsers

This property determines whether replication can update $FormUser items. If set to TRUE, replication can update $FormUser items. If FALSE, replication can't make changes to $FormUser items.

Readers	R	()

```
To set: nfrmNotesForm.Readers = varFormReaders
To get: varFormReaders = nfrmNotesForm.rReaders
```
Readers

This property represents the contents of the $Readers field. You can set the $Readers field using the Default read access for documents created with this form option on the Key tab of the form properties info box. When set to All Readers and above, anyone with reader access or above can read documents using the form. If users and groups are explicitly named, only the named groups can read documents using the form. Readers expects and returns an array of strings.

NotesForm Methods

Remove

```
Call nfrmNotesForm.Remove
```
Remove

This method takes no parameters and is used to permanently delete a form from the database.

Remarks

The *Form* object can be very useful, especially if you want to present the user with a list of all the fields on a form.

Example

```
' This agent updates the $FormUsers and $Readers items and
' changes the ProtectUser and ProtectReaders properites so that
' replication will not be permitted to update these fields
' for all the "admin" forms in a database. After this agent runs,
' all "Admin" forms can be used for reading, but only users and
' groups named in the NewUsers array can create documents
Dim nsSession As New NotesSession
Dim nfrmForm As NotesForm
Dim aNewUsers(4) As String
Dim strUpdates As String
Dim intCount As Integer
' Load new Users
aNewUsers(0)="Definiti Administrators"
aNewUsers(1)="CMGR Administrators"
aNewUsers(2)="CMGR Editors"
aNewUsers(3)="Samuel Hatter"
aNewUsers(4)="Wyatt Hatter"
Forall form In nsSession.CurrentDatabase.Forms
    If Instr(1, form.name, "Admin") Then
        intCount=intCount+1
        Set nfrmForm=nsSession.CurrentDatabase.GetForm(form.name)
        nfrmForm.FormUsers=NewUsers
        nfrmForm.Readers=""
        nfrmForm.ProtectReaders=True
        nfrmForm.ProtectUsers=True
        strUpdates=strUpdates & nfrmForm.Name & Chr(10)
    End If
End Forall
If intCount>0 Then
    strUpdates=strUpdates & Chr(10) & Chr(10) & Trim$(Str$(intCount)) &
    ➥" forms processed."
    Msgbox "Update Admin Form Security Complete. Updated the following
    ➥forms:" & Chr(10) & Chr(10) & strUpdates, 64, "Agent Infomation"
Else
    Msgbox "Update Admin Form Security Complete. No actions taken.", 64,
    ➥"Agent Infomation"
End If
```

NotesInternational

4.5x 4.6x 5.0

The *NotesInternational* class allows you to access your operating system's current international settings. If any of these settings are changed through the operating system, Domino will immediately recognize the new setting.

NotesSession
  └ NotesInternational

LotusScript Syntax

```
Set NotesInternational = NotesSession.International
```

The only way to access a *NotesInternational* object is through the `International` property of a *NotesSession* object.

NotesInternational Properties

AMString	R	$

To get: strAMString = nintlNotesInternational.**AMString**

Returns the string value used to denote an a.m. time.

CurrencyDigits	R	%

To get: intDigits = nintlNotesInternational.**CurrencyDigits**

Returns the number of decimal places to allow in currency values.

CurrencySymbol	R	$

To get: strCurSymbol = nintlNotesInternational.**CurrencySymbol**

Returns the symbol used to denote that a numeric value is currency.

DateSep	R	$

To get: strDateSep = nintlNotesInternational.**DateSep**

Returns the character used as a delimiter to separate months, days, and years.

DecimalSep	R	$

To get: strDecimalSep = nintlNotesInternational.**DecimalSep**

Returns the character used to denote the decimal place in a numeric value.

IsCurrencySpace	R	T/F

To get: intCurSpace = nintlNotesInternational.**IsCurrencySpace**

Returns TRUE if currency values contain a space between the currency symbol and the number. Returns FALSE if there is no embedded space.

IsCurrencySuffix	R	T/F

To get: intCurSuffix = nintlNotesInternational.**IsCurrencySuffix**

Returns TRUE if the currency symbol follows the number in currency values. Returns FALSE if the currency symbol does not follow the currency value.

IsCurrencyZero	R	T/F

To get: intCurZero = nintlNotesInternational.**IsCurrencyZero**

Returns TRUE if fractions have a 0 before the decimal point in number format. Otherwise, returns FALSE.

IsDateDMY   R   T/F

```
To get: intDateDMY = nintlNotesInternational.IsDateDMY
```

Returns TRUE if the date is formatted day, month, year. Otherwise, returns FALSE.

IsDateMDY   R   T/R

```
To get: intDateMDY = nintlNotesInternational.IsDateMDY
```

Returns TRUE if the date is formatted month, day, year. Otherwise, returns FALSE.

IsDateYMD   R   T/F

```
To get: intDateYMD = nintlNotesInternational.IsDateYMD
```

Returns TRUE if the date is formatted year, month, date. Otherwise, returns FALSE.

IsDST   R   T/F

```
To get: intDST = nintlNotesInternational.IsDST
```

Returns TRUE if the time format reflects daylight saving time. Otherwise, returns FALSE.

Is24HourTime   R   T/F

```
To get: int24HourTime = nintlNotesInternational.IsTime24Hour
```

Returns TRUE if the time values are formatted as military time (which uses a 24-hour clock). Otherwise, returns FALSE.

PMString   R $

```
To get: strPM = nintlNotesInternational.PMString
```

Returns the string value used to denote a p.m. time.

ThousandsSep   R $

```
To get: strKSep = nintlNotesInternational.ThousandsSep
```

Returns a string value containing the character used as a placeholder in numeric values greater than 1,000. The default for English is the comma character (,).

TimeSep   R $

```
To get: strTimeSep = nintlNotesInternational.TimeSep
```

Returns a string value containing the character used as a placeholder in time values. The default for English is the colon character (:).

TimeZone   R   %

```
To get: intTimeZone = nintlNotesInternational.TimeZone
```

Returns an integer representing the time zone.

Today   R $

```
To get: strToday = nintlNotesInternational.Today
```

Returns a string value that means today in the client's language. For example, this property returns "Today" in English.

Tomorrow	R	$

Tomorrow

To get: `strTomorrow = nintlNotesInternational.`**`Tomorrow`**

Returns a string value that means tomorrow in the client's language. For example, this property returns "Tomorrow" in English.

Yesterday	R	$

Yesterday

To get: `strYesterday = nintlNotesInternational.`**`Yesterday`**

Returns a string value that means yesterday in the client's language. For example, this property returns "Yesterday" in English.

Example

```
Function SpaceCurrencyCharacter(strCurrency)
  Dim nsS As New NotesSession
  Dim nintlInternational as NotesInternational
  Dim strCurrencyValue as String
  Dim strCurrencyChar as String
  Dim strTemp as String
  Dim intLength as Integer
  intLength=Len(strCurrency)
  If Not nintlInternational.IsCurrencySpace Then
    strCurrencyChar = Left$(strCurrency,1)
    strTemp=Mid$(strCurrency, 2,((intLength-1))
  End If
  SpaceCurrencyCharacter=strCurrencyChar & " " & strTemp
End Function
```

4.0 4.1x 4.5x 4.6x 5.0 NotesItem

The *NotesItem* object is much like a field in a relational database. It holds a specific piece of data in a document and is the smallest unit of storage (atomic) in a Notes database.

```
...
 L NotesDocument
    L NotesItem
       L NotesRichTextItem
```

LotusScript Syntax

```
Dim NotesItem As New NotesItem(NotesDocument,strName,value
➡[,intSpecialType])
```

or

```
Set NotesItem = New NotesItem(NotesDocument,strName,value
➡[,intSpecialType])
```

LotusScript provides two simple ways to create a *NotesItem* object. If you want to create a new *NotesItem* from scratch, you can use the New keyword with the Dim or Set statement, as just shown, or you can use the AppendItemValue or ReplaceItemValue methods of the *NotesDocument* class (▶ 127) to create a new *NotesItem* in a *NotesDocument*.

The second way is used when you want to create a new *NotesItem* object from an existing *NotesItem* object. In this case, you can use the CopyItemToDocument method of *NotesItem* to copy the item to a different *NotesDocument*. Alternatively, you can use the CopyItem or ReplaceItemValue of the *NotesDocument* object.

Once you have created a *NotesItem* object in a *NotesDocument*, you must call the Save method of the *NotesDocument* to save the data to disk.

LotusScript Parameters

NotesDocument	Required	O.Ref.

A *NotesDocument* object that represents the document in which to create the new *NotesItem*.

strName	Required	$

A string value that contains the name you want to give the new *NotesItem* or the name of the item(s) you want to replace.

Value	Required	%,&,!,#,@,$

The value to assign to the new item. The value's data type determines the type of item that Notes creates. If you're replacing an existing *NotesItem,* the data type doesn't need to match the data type of the original *NotesItem*.

intSpecialtype	Not Required	%

Passing in one of the following constants—NAMES, READERS, or AUTHORS— indicates that a text item should be of type Names, Readers, or Authors. The only way to create a new item of type Name, Readers, or Authors is to use the intSpecialtype% parameter of *NotesItem* in conjunction with passing a string or an array of strings for the value parameter.

LotusScript Item Data Type Values

Value Data Type	*NotesItem* Type
String	Text (if the intSpecialType parameter is used, may be Names, Readers, or Authors)
Array of strings	Text List (if the intSpecialType parameter is used, may be Names, Readers, or Authors)
Integer, long, single, double, or currency	Number

Value Data Type	*NotesItem* Type
Array of integers, longs, singles, doubles, or currencies	Number List
Variant of type Date	Date/Time
Array of variants of type Date	Date/Time range

NotesItem Properties

DateTimeValue   R/W   *NotesDateTime*

```
To get: ndtNotesDateTime = nitmNotesItem.DateTimeValue
To set: nitmNotesItem.DateTimeValue = ndtNotesDateTime
```
DateTimeValue

Returns a *NotesDateTime* object containing the value of the item if the item is of type date-time. For other item types, such as text and numeric, this property returns nothing. Unlike LotusScript date-time variants, Notes date-time items and *NotesDateTime* objects store a time zone and hundredths of a second.

IsAuthors   R/W   T/F

```
To get: intAuthors = nitmNotesItem.IsAuthors
To set: nitmNotesItem.IsAuthors = intAuthors
```
IsAuthors

Indicates whether the *NotesItem* is of type Authors. This is TRUE if the item is of type Authors, and FALSE if it is not.

IsEncrypted   R/W   T/F

```
To get: intEncrypt = nitmNotesItem.IsEncrypted
To set: nitmNotesItem.IsEncrypted = intEncrypt
```
IsEncrypted

Indicates whether the item is encrypted. This is TRUE if the item is enrypted, and FALSE if it is not. Setting this property to TRUE will not cause the item to be encrypted unless and until the encrypt method of the parent *NotesDocument* is called.

IsNames   R/W   T/F

```
To get: intNames = nitmNotesItem.IsNames
To set: nitmNotesItem.IsNames = intNames
```
IsNames

Indicates whether the *NotesItem* is of type Names. This is TRUE if the item is a Names item, and FALSE if it is not.

IsProtected   R/W   T/F

```
To get: intProtected = nitmNotesItem.IsProtected
To set: nitmNotesItem.IsProtected = intProtected
```
IsProtected

Indicates whether the user needs a minimum access level of editor to edit the *NotesItem*. If TRUE, the current user needs at least editor access to modify the item. If FALSE, the current user does not need editor access and therefore can modify the item if he or she has author access or better.

IsReaders   R/W   T/F

```
To get: intReaders = nitmNotesItem.IsReaders
To set: nitmNotesItem.IsReaders = intReaders
```
IsReaders

Indicates whether the *NotesItem* is of type Readers. This is TRUE if the item is of type Readers, and FALSE if it is not.

IsSigned R/W T/F

IsSigned

```
To get: intSigned = nitmNotesItem.IsSigned
To set: nitmNotesItem.IsSigned = intSigned
```

Indicates whether the *NotesItem* has been digitally signed. This is TRUE if the item is signed, and FALSE if it is not.

IsSummary R/W T/F

IsSummary

```
To get: intSummary = nitmNotesItem.IsSummary
To set: nitmNotesItem.IsSummary = intSummary
```

Indicates whether the item can be displayed in a view or folder. This is TRUE if the item is a summary, and FALSE if it is not. When a new *NotesItem* is created using the New keyword or the ReplaceItemValue method in *NotesDocument,* this property defaults to FALSE. Similarly, this property always returns FALSE for *NotesRichTextItem* since rich text can't appear in views. *NotesItems* created with the extended class syntax or by using the AppendItemValue method in *NotesDocument* have this property set to TRUE by default.

LastModified R Variant

LastModified

```
To get: vardate = nitmNotesItem.LastModified
```

Returns a variant of type date of the date and time this document was last modified and saved to disk.

Name R $

Name

```
To get: strItemname = nitmNotesItem.Name
```

Returns the item's name as a string. Multiple items with the same name can exist in one document, and all file attachments have the name $FILE. You can use the GetFirstItem and Items properties of *NotesDocument* to access several items that have the same name.

Parent R O.Ref.

Parent

```
To get: Set ndocNotesDocument = nitmNotesItem.Parent
```

Returns a *NotesDocument* object that refers to the document in which the item exists.

SaveToDisk R/W T/F

SaveToDisk

```
To get: intSaved = nitmNotesItem.SaveToDisk
To set: nitmNotesItem.SaveToDisk = intSaved
```

Indicates whether the *NotesItem* should be saved to disk when its parent document is saved. This is TRUE if the item is saved to disk when the document is saved, and FALSE if the item is not saved to disk when the document is saved. This property defaults to TRUE. If you specify that an existing item should not be saved, it will disappear from disk the next time you save the document.

Text R $

Text

```
To get: strItemtext = nitmNotesItem.Text
```

Returns a string containing the text representation of the item's value. (When you use it with *NotesRichTextItem,* all nontext data is ignored.) If the item contains multiple values, the string value returned will have each item separated by semicolons. If the item's value is larger than 64K, the returned string will be truncated at the 64K mark. When you use this property with HTML items, it returns NULL.

Type   R   %

To get: intItemtype = nitmNotesItem.**Type**   Type

Indicates the datatype of an item. The constants are described in the following table.

Datatype Constants

Datatype	Description
ATTACHMENT	The item contains a file attachment
AUTHORS	An Authors item that limits edit access to those explicitly named
DATETIMES	The item contains a date-time value or a range of date-time values
EMBEDDEDOBJECT	The item contains an embedded object
ERRORITEM	An error occurred while accessing the type
FORMULA	The item contains a Notes formula
HTML	The item contains HTML source text
ICON	The item is an icon
NAMES	The item is of type Names
NOTELINKS	A link to a database, view, or document
NOTESREFS	The item is a reference to the parent document
NUMBERS	The item is a number or number list
OTHEROBJECT	Another object
READERS	A Readers item that limits read access to those explicitly named
RICHTEXT	Rich text
SIGNATURE	The item contains a digital signature
TEXT	The item is a text value or text list
UNAVAILABLE	The item's data type isn't available
UNKNOWN	The item's data type isn't known
USERDATA	User data
USERID	The item contains a User ID name

ValueLength   R   &

To get: lngSize = nitmNotesItem.**ValueLength**   ValueLength

Represents the item's size in bytes.

Values   R/W   Variant

To get: varvalues = nitmNotesItem.**Values**   Values
To set: nitmNotesItem.**Values** = varvalues

Returns the values the item contains, varying data types depending on the item's type
(see the following table). This property returns the same value(s) for an item as the
GetItemValue method in *NotesDocument* (▶ 140). This property always returns an array
for text, number, date-time items, and attachments, even when there is only a single
value in the item. If you know the item contains only a single value, you should access
the first element in the array at the index 0. When working with attachments, you can
use this property to determine the name of the attachment. Then you can use the
returned value with the GetAttachment method in *NotesDocument* to get a handle on
the file attachment.

Item Type Value	Data Type
Rich text	String. The text in the field, rendered into plain text. This is the same value returned by the `FormattedText` method of *NotesRichTextItem*.
Text or text list	Array of strings.
Number or number list	Array of doubles.
Date-time or range of date-time values	Array of doubles.
Attachment	Array of strings. The name of the attachment in element 0.

NotesItem Methods

Abstract

Abstract

```
strAbbreviation = nitmNotesItem.Abstract(lngMaxlength, intDropVowels,
➥intUseDictionary)
```

lngMaxlength   Required   &

The maximum length of the string to return.

intDropVowels   Required   %

Indicates whether vowels should be dropped from the abbreviation. TRUE drops vowels. FALSE retains vowels.

intUseDictionary   Optional   %

Indicates whether the table of abbreviations defined in NOTEABBR.TXT should be used. TRUE uses the abbreviation table. FALSE doesn't use it.

This method returns a text string that contains the abbreviated contents of a text item.

AppendToTextList

AppendToText
List

```
Call nitmNotesItem.AppendToTextList( strNewvalue )
```

strNewvalue   Required $

The string value you want to add to the item.

This very handy method allows you to add a new text element to a multivalue item while preserving the existing values.

The following code appends the Common UserName of the current user to the Modified By item and saves the document to disk.

```
nws.currentdocument.Document
+modified By = S Common username
```

Contains

Contains

```
intFlag = nitmNotesItem.Contains( strValue )
```

strValue	Required	$

The value to search the method for. String, number, or variant of type DATE.

This method can be used to search an item that contains multivalues (a list). The data type of this parameter should match the data type of the item you are trying to search. For example, if you want to search a date-time range to see if a time exists in the range, you must pass it a *NotesDateTime* (▶ 115). Likewise, if you want to search a text list, you must pass it a string value. This method will return a Boolean value indicating whether the value was found in the item. It will be TRUE if the value matches one of the values in the item, and FALSE if the value doesn't match one of the values in the item. If value is a distinguished name, and if the item contains Notes user names, the distinguished name matches the common version of the hierarchical name. You should not use this method to search for a particular character, string, word, or phrase.

The following example checks the contents of the Categories field, which is a multivalue field, to see if one of the values in the field has the string value of "Competitor Products".

```
Dim nws As New NotesUIWorkspace
Dim nDoc As NotesDocument
Dim nItm As NotesItem
Set ndoc = nws.CurrentDocument.Document
If ndoc Is Nothing Then
   Msgbox "Could not retrieve any documents.", 16, "Error."
   Exit Sub
Else
Set nItm = nDoc.GetFirstItem("Categories")
   If nItm.Contains( "Competitor Products" ) Then
      Msgbox "Ready to continue...", 32, "Everything is okay!"
   Else
      Msgbox "This action is not authorized...", 16, "Sorry!"
   End If
End If
```

CopyItemToDocument

```
Set nitmNotesItem= nitmNotesItem.CopyItemToDocument(NotesDocument,
➥strNewname)
```

CopyItemTo
Document

NotesDocument	Required	O.Ref.

The target document object.

strNewname	Required	$

The name of the new item in the target document.

This method provides a simple way to copy an item from a source document to a target document. To use the same name as the original item, simply pass an empty string (""). This method returns a copy of the *NotesItem*.

The following example runs on every document currently selected in a view. It creates a new document of type "Company" in the current database. Then it copies the values of the Company Name and Phone Number into the newly created document from the currently selected document. Finally, it saves the new document to disk.

```
Dim nss As New NotesSession
Dim ndb As NotesDatabase
Dim ndoc As NotesDocument
Dim ndocNew As NotesDocument
Dim nItmName As NotesItem
```

continued >>

continued>>
```
Dim nItmNewName As NotesItem
Dim nItmPhone As NotesItem
Dim nItmNewPhone As NotesItem
Set ndb = nss.Currentdatabase
Set ndoc=ndb.UnprocessedDocuments.GetFirstDocument
If ndoc Is Nothing Then
    Msgbox "Could not retrive any documents.", 16, "Error."
    Exit Sub
End If
Do While Not ndoc Is Nothing
    Set ndocNew = New NotesDocument( ndb )
    ndocNew.Type = "Company"
    Set nItmName =Cdoc.GetFirstItem("CompanyName")
    Set nItmPhone =Cdoc.GetFirstItem("OfficePhone")
    Set nItmNewName =nItmName.CopyItemToDocument(ndocNew,"CompanyName")
    Set nItmNewPhone =nItmPhone.CopyItemToDocument(ndocNew,"OfficePhone")
    Call ndocNew.Save(True,False)
    Set ndoc=ndb.UnprocessedDocuments.GetNextDocument(ndoc)
Loop
```

New

New   Used to create a new *NotesItem* object (▶ 175).

Remove

Remove   `Call nitmNotesItem.`**`Remove`**

This method permanently deletes an item from a document. You must call the `Save` method of the parent *NotesDocument* to write your changes to disk. You can also remove an item from a *NotesDocument* using the `RemoveItem` method in the *NotesDocument* class.

Remarks

When using LotusScript, you don't have to declare the *NotesItem* in order to create, access, or modify the item values and their respective values. Once you have determined the name of the item value (and its value, if you're creating or modifying), you can use the extended class syntax to manipulate item values or one of the following methods of the *NotesDocument* class:

NotesDocument **Method**	**Result/Action**
GetItemValue	Get an item's value
ReplaceItemValue	Set an item's value
AppendItemValue	Create a new item
HasItem	Check to see if the item exists in the document
RemoveItem	Delete the item from the document

When you use the extended class syntax to create or modify the *NotesItem*, you are essentially treating the *NotesDocument* as an extended class and using the item name as a property of the *NotesDocument* object. When you use extended class syntax, the values assigned can be any LotusScript data type—namely, a scalar data type, an array, or a reference to another *NotesItem* object, *NotesDateTime* object, or *NotesDateRange* object.

The extended class syntax is not available for Java. Therefore, the `lotus.notes.document` and `lotus.notes.item` methods must be used to reference item values.

Using the extended class syntax reduces the amount of code that must be written and can make the code easier to read. In addition, it can preserve memory because you eliminate the need to dimension additional *NotesItems*. However, using the extended class syntax prevents you from manipulating the value data type and using the `intSpecialType` parameter.

For example, if you have created a new *NotesDocument* using LotusScript, you will (at a minimum) need to set the form value for this document so that the document will be opened with the proper form in the user interface. The following line of code sets the form item to the value of `"Initialrequest"`:

```
...Document is created and other document and item values
are manipulated
Document.Form = "Initialrequest"
...script completes and document is saved
```

Example

To demonstrate the power and flexibility of the *NotesItem* class, consider the following example. You need to write an agent that will search all documents in a view and determine whether the document contains a multivalue *NotesItem* named `rnReaders`. The item, if it exists, will be of type `Readers` and will require editor access or higher to change. If the item exists, and it has not been modified during the same day that the agent is being run, you need to delete it and re-create it from an array. Additionally, because this is a Readers field, to increase security you don't want it to be displayed in a view or folder.

The following code, placed in the `click` event of a view action, demonstrates one way to accomplish this:

```
Dim nss As New NotesSession
Dim ndb As NotesDatabase
Dim ndoc As NotesDocument
Dim nitmTest As NotesItem
Dim nitmNew As NotesItem
Set ndb = nss.Currentdatabase
Set ndoc = ndb.UnprocessedDocuments.GetFirstDocument
If ndoc Is Nothing Then
    Msgbox "Could not retrieve any documents.", 16, "Error."
    Exit Sub
End If
Do While Not ndoc Is Nothing
    If ndoc.HasItem("rnReaders") Then
        Set nitmTest = ndoc.GetFirstItem("Form")
        If nitmTest.LastModified<>Date$ Then
            Call nitmTest.Remove
            Set nitmNew = New NotesItem(ndoc,"rnReaders",DocReaders,READERS)
            nitmNew.IsProtected=True
            Call ndoc.Save(True,False)
        End If
    End If
    Set ndoc = ndb.UnprocessedDocuments.GetNextDocument(ndoc)
Loop
```

4.x 4.5x 4.6x 5.0 NotesLog

The *NotesLog* class provides extensive logging capabilities, making it easy to record the actions that occur as a script runs, as well as any errors that might occur. You can log errors in any of the following manners: to a Notes database, in a mail memo, to a text file (if the script runs locally), or to an agent log.

NotesSession
  └ NotesLog

LotusScript Syntax

```
Dim NotesLog As New NotesLog(strScriptName)
```

or

```
Set notesLog = New NotesLog(strScriptName)
```

or

```
Set notesLog = Session.CreateLog(strScriptName)
```

As with most Notes classes, there are two basic ways to create a NotesLog object. The first way is to use the New keyword with the Set or Dim keywords, as just shown. Alternatively, you can use the CreateLog method of the *NotesSession* class (▶ 268), which is also shown.

LotusScript Parameters

strScriptName	Required	$

A string value that contains the name that you want to use to identify the code that is being logged. Examples include the name of an agent that is being logged, or the name of a script library that is being executed.

NotesLog Properties

LogActions	R/W	T/F

LogActions

```
To get: intLogAction = nlogNotesLog.LogActions
To set: nlogNotesLog.LogActions = intLogAction
```

This property is used as a toggle to indicate whether a script's actions should be logged. When this is set to TRUE (the default), actions are logged.

LogErrors	R/W	T/F

LogErrors

```
To get: intLogError = nlogNotesLog.LogErrors
To set: nlogNotesLog.LogErrors = intLogError
```

Much like the LogActions property, this property is used as a toggle to indicate whether a script's errors should be logged. When it's set to TRUE (the default), errors are logged.

NumActions	R	%

NumActions

```
To get: intNumActions = nlogNotesLog.NumActions
```

Returns the number of actions that have been logged for the script.

NumErrors	R	%

NumErrors

```
To get: intNumErrors = nlogNotesLog.NumErrors
```

Returns the number of errors that have been logged for the script.

OverwriteFile	R/W	T/F

OverwriteFile

```
To get: intOverwrite = nlognotesLog.OverwriteFile
To set: nlognotesLog.OverwriteFile = intOverwrite
```

If you're logging to a file, this property can be used to indicate that the existing log file should be overwritten or appended. To overwrite an existing log file, be sure to set this property to `TRUE` before calling the `OpenFileLog` method. This property has no effect if you're logging to a mail message, database, or agent.

ProgramName   R/W $

```
To get: strScriptName= notesLog.ProgramName
To set: notesLog.ProgramName = strScriptName
```
ProgramName

This property can be used to determine and/or change the name associated with the script that is being logged. By default, it returns the name that was used when the *NotesLog* object was created.

NotesLog Methods

Close

```
Call NotesLog.Close
```
Close

Calling the `Close` method closes the *NotesLog* object. If you're logging to a mail message, it will be sent when this method is called.

LogAction

```
Call NotesLog.LogAction(strDescription)
```
LogAction

strDescription   Required $
The description of the action performed that you want to write to the log.

This method allows you to describe the action that your script has performed. Its exact functionality will vary, depending on the type of log you're writing.

If you called `OpenNotesLog` to log to a *NotesDatabase,* this method creates a new document in the specified database with an `$ACTION` item containing the description you specified.

When you're logging to a mail memo using `OpenMailLog`, the description is added to a new line in the `BODY` item of the memo, as are the current date and time.

Calling the `OpenFileLog` method causes the description to be written to a new line in the file, along with the value of the `ProgramName` property and the current date and time.

LogError

```
Call notesLog.LogError(intcode, strdescription)
```
LogError

intCode   Required   %
A numeric value representing the error that has occurred.

strDescription   Required $
The description of the error that has occurred.

This method can be used to log errors that occur during the execution of your script. Like the `LogAction` method, the functionality of this method varies, depending on the type of log you're writing.

The `OpenNotesLog` method creates a new document in the specified database and writes the `intCode` and the `strDescription` to the `A$ERRCODE` and the `A$ERRMSG` items, respectively.

When you're logging to a mail memo using `OpenMailLog`, the error code and description are added to a new line in the `BODY` item of the memo, as are the current date and time.

Calling the `OpenFileLog` method causes the error code and the description to be written to a new line in the file, along with the value of the `ProgramName` property and the current date and time.

LogEvent

LogEvent   `Call notesLog.LogEvent(strMessage, strQuename, intType, intSeverity)`

strMessage	Required	$

The message you want to send over the network.

strQuename	Required	$

The name of the queue to use. Passing an empty string (`""`) allows Notes to pick the queue.

intType	Required	%

A constant specifying the type of event being logged. Here are the different types: `EV_ALARM`, `EV_COMM`, `EV_MAIL`, `EV_MISC`, `EV_REPLICA`, `EV_RESOURCE`, `EV_SECURITY`, `EV_SERVER`, `EV_UNKNOWN`, `EV_UPDATE`.

intSeverity	Required	%

Specifies the severity of the event being logged. The different types are as follows: `SEV_FAILURE`, `SEV_FATAL`, `SEV_NORMAL`, `SEV_WARNING1`, `SEV_WARNING2`, `SEV_UNKNOWN`.

This method can be used only with scripts running on a server. It lets you define a Notes event and severity and send it out over the network. If you elect to use this event, it will have no effect on other open logs, and vice versa. For more information on Notes events and severity, refer to the Domino Administration Database.

New

New   Used to create a new *NotesLog* object (▶ 185).

OpenAgentLog

OpenAgentLog   `Call notesLog.OpenAgentLog`

Call this method to store all `LogAction` and `LogError` messages to the agent log of the currently running agent. As you might expect, this method will fail if it isn't called from an agent.

OpenFileLog

OpenFileLog   `Call notesLog.OpenFileLog(strFilePath)`

strFilePath	Required	$

The full path and filename of the log file to use. If the file doesn't exist, it is created. If a directory in the path is nonexistent, an error is generated.

This method opens a file for logging. It will fail if used on a Domino server.

OpenMailLog   R $

OpenMailLog   `Call notesLog.OpenMailLog(varRecipients, strSubject)`

varRecipients	Required	?

A string or array of strings containing the person or people who should receive the log.

strSubject	Required	$

The message to use as the mail memo's subject.

This method opens a new mail memo in the current user's mail database for logging. Calling the `Close` method causes the memo to be mailed to the people or groups named in the `varRecipients` parameter. The mail memo isn't saved in the user's mailbox.

OpenNotesLog

```
Call notesLog.OpenNotesLog(strServer, strDbname)
```
OpenNotesLog

strServer	Required	$

The name of the server where the log database resides. Use an empty string (`""`) to indicate the current machine.

strDbName	Required	$

The path to and name of the log database.

This method opens the specified database and creates one document in the database for each error or action logged. Each "log" document has a `FORM` item set to "Log Entry" and the following items:

OpenNotesLog Items

Item Name	Value
A$PROGNAME	The `ProgramName` property
A$LOGTIME	The date and time an action or error was logged
A$USER	The name of the user running the script when the error or action was logged
A$LOGTYPE	Contains either "Error" or "Action," depending on the type of logging
A$ACTION	The description entered for an action
A$ERRCODE	For errors, the error code
A$ERRMSG	The description entered for an error

While actions and events can be logged to any Notes database, Lotus provides a database template called StdR4AgentLog (`ALOG4.NTF`) that is specifically designed to facilitate action and event logging as well as viewing. Using or customizing this template can save you a lot of work.

Remarks

This class can be especially helpful when you're attempting to debug agents that are being run from a Web browser. You can log any actions and errors to easily see what the agent does during each run.

Example

```
Sub Initialize
    ' This agent uses a view that shows only response docs
    ' to check for orphans
```
continued >>

>>*continued*

```
On Error Goto ErrHandler
Dim nsS As New NotesSession
Dim nvwChildren As NotesView
Dim ndocChild As NotesDocument
Dim ndocParent As NotesDocument
Dim nlLog As NotesLog
Dim intCount As Integer, intProc As Integer

Dim Recipients(6) As String
Recipients(0)="Samuel Hatter"
Recipients(1)="Wyatt Hatter"
Recipients(2)="Leslee Hatter"
Recipients(3)="George Young"
Recipients(4)="Rose Wezel"
Recipients(5)="Jack Hatter"
Set nlLog=nsS.CreateLog(nsS.CurrentAgent.Name)
Call nlLog.OpenMailLog( Recipients, nsS.CurrentAgent.Name &
➥" Log for " & Date$ & "@" & Time$ )

Set nvwChildren=nsS.CurrentDatabase.GetView("(Children)")
Set ndocChild =nvwChildren.GetFirstDocument
Do While Not ndocChild Is Nothing
      intProc=intProc+1
      Set ndocParent=S.CurrentDatabase.GetDocumentByUNID
➥(ndocChild.ParentDocumentUNID)
      If ndocParent Is Nothing Then
            Call nlLog.LogAction("No parent was found for child: " &
➥ndocChild.NoteId)
            ndocChild.Orphan=True
            Call ndocChild.Save(True,False)
            intCount=intCount+1
      End If
      Set ndocChild =nvwChildren.GetNextDocument(ndocChild)
Loop
Call nlLog.LogAction(Trim$(Str$(intProc)) & " children docs
➥processed, " & Trim$(Str$(intCount)) & " orphans found
➥and marked." )
Call nlLog.Close
Exit Sub

ErrHandler:
      Call nlLog.LogError(Err,"Error: " & Error$ & " has occurred on
➥line " & Trim$(Str$(Erl)) & "." )
      Resume Next
End Sub
```

NotesName

The name of the user or server for the current session.

NotesSession
 └ NotesName

Page	Contents
	Syntax
	Properties
192	Abbreviated
192	Addr821
192	Addr822Comment1
192	Addr822Comment2
193	Addr822Comment3
193	Addr822LocalPart
193	Addr822Phrase
193	ADMD
193	Canonical
193	Common
193	Country
193	Generation
194	Given
194	Initials
194	IsHierarchical
194	Keyword
194	Organization
194	OrgUnit1
194	OrgUnit2
194	OrgUnit3
194	OrgUnit4
195	PRMD
195	Surname
	Methods
195	New
195	**Remarks**
195	**Example**

LotusScript Syntax

```
Dim NotesName As New NotesName(strName)
```

or

```
Set NotesName = New NotesName(strName)
```

LotusScript provides two simple ways to create a *NotesName* object. If you want to create a new *NotesName* object from scratch, you can use the New keyword with the Dim or Set statements, as just shown, or you can use the CreateName method of the *NotesSession* class (▶ 268) to create a new *NotesName*.

LotusScript Parameters

strName	Required	$

A string value representing the name of the user or server. This value will be created as a flat name if the name passed is not in the format of an abbreviated or canonical hierarchical name.

NotesName Properties

Abbreviated	R	$

Abbreviated

```
To get: strAbbrev = nnameNotesName.Abbreviated
```

Returns a string representation of the hierarchical name in the abbreviated format. If this property is not defined or is empty, this property will return NULL.

```
Dim ns As New NotesSession
Dim nnUser As New NotesName(ns.UserName)
Print nnUser.Abbreviated
```

Addr821	R	$

Addr821

```
To get: strAddress = nnameNotesName.Addr821
```

Returns a string representation of the internet address of the name for the current *NotesName* in the format based on RFC 821 Address Format Syntax.

Addr822Comment1	R	$

Addr822
Comment1

```
To get: strAddress = nnameNotesName.Addr822Comment1
```

Returns a string representation of Comment1 component of the internet address of the name for the current *NotesName* in the format based on RFC 822 Address Format Syntax.

Addr822Comment2	R	$

Addr822
Comment2

```
To get: strAddress = nnameNotesName.Addr822Comment2
```

Returns a string representation of Comment2 component of the internet address of the name for the current *NotesName* in the format based on RFC 822 Address Format Syntax.

Addr822Comment3   R $

`To get: strAddress = nnameNotesName.`**`Addr822Comment3`**

Returns a string representation of Comment3 component of the internet address of the name for the current *NotesName* in the format based on RFC 822 Address Format Syntax.

Addr822
Comment3

Addr822LocalPart   R $

`To get: strAddress = nnameNotesName.`**`Addr822Localpart`**

Returns a string representation of LocalPart component of the internet address of the name for the current *NotesName* in the format based on RFC 822 Address Format Syntax.

Addr822Local
Part

Addr822Phrase   R $

`To get: strAddress = nnameNotesName.`**`Addr822Phrase`**

Returns a string representation of Phrase component of the internet address of the name for the current *NotesName* in the format based on RFC 822 Address Format Syntax.

Addr822Phrase

ADMD   R $

`To get: strAdmin = nnameNotesName.`**`ADMD`**

The Addr properties return Internet addresses based on RFC 821 Address Format Syntax and RFC 822 Address Format Syntax.

Returns a string representation of the administration management domain name associated with the current *NotesName*.

ADMD

Canonical   R $

`To get: strCanonical = nnameNotesName.`**`Canonical`**

Returns a string representation of the canonical form of the name for the current *NotesName*.

Canonical

Common   R $

`To get: strCommon = nnameNotesName.`**`Common`**

Returns the string representation of the common-name component of a hierarchical name. If the *NotesName* is flat, the entire name is returned. This value is typically denoted as CN by most Lotus Notes documentation and when the Lotus Notes macro language is used for development.

Common

Country   R $

`To get: strCountry = nnameNotesName.`**`Country`**

Returns the string representation of the country component of a hierarchical name. This value is typically denoted as C by most Lotus Notes documentation and when the Lotus Notes macro language is used for development.

Country

Generation   R $

`To get: strGeneration = nnameNotesName.`**`Generation`**

Returns the string representation of the generation component of a *NotesName*. This method returns values such as Sr. and Jr.

Generation

Given	R	$

Given

```
To get: strGiven = nnameNotesName.Given
```

Returns the string representation of the given part of a *NotesName*.

Initials	R	$

Initials

```
To get: strInitials = nnameNotesName.Initials
```

Returns the string representation of the initials part of a *NotesName*.

IsHierarchical	R	T/F

IsHierarchical

```
To get: intHierarchical = nnameNotesName.IsHierarchical
```

Indicates whether the name is hierarchical. This method returns TRUE if the name is hierarchical and FALSE if it is not.

Keyword	R	$

Keyword

```
To get: strKeyword = nnameNotesName.Keyword
```

Returns the string representation of the components of a hierarchical name in order, separated by backslashes, such as country\organization\organizational unit1\ organizational unit2\etc.

Organization	R	$

Organization

```
To get: strOrg = nnameNotesName.Organization
```

Returns the string representation of the organizational component of a hierarchical name. This value is typically denoted as O by most Lotus Notes documentation and when the Lotus Notes macro language is used for development.

OrgUnit1	R	$

OrgUnit1

```
To get: strOU1 = nnameNotesName.OrgUnit1
```

Returns the string representation of the first organizational unit component of a hierarchical name. This value is typically denoted as OU by most Lotus Notes documentation and when the Lotus Notes macro language is used for development.

OrgUnit2	R	$

OrgUnit2

```
To get: strOU2 = nnameNotesName.OrgUnit2
```

Returns the string representation of the second organizational unit component of a hierarchical name. This value is typically denoted as OU by most Lotus Notes documentation and when the Lotus Notes macro language is used for development.

OrgUnit3	R	$

OrgUnit3

```
To get: strOU3 = nnameNotesName.OrgUnit3
```

Returns the string representation of the third organizational unit component of a hierarchical name. This value is typically denoted as OU by most Lotus Notes documentation and when the Lotus Notes macro language is used for development.

OrgUnit4	R	$

OrgUnit4

```
To get: strOU4 = nnameNotesName.OrgUnit4
```

Returns the string representation of the fourth organizational unit component of a hierarchical name. This value is typically denoted as OU by most Lotus Notes documentation and when the Lotus Notes macro language is used for development.

PRMD	R	$	

```
To get: strPrivmgmtdom = nnameNotesName.PRMD
```

Returns the string representation of the private management domain name of the *NotesName*.

Surname	R	$	

```
To get: strSurname = nnameNotesName.Surname
```

Returns the string representation of the surname of the *NotesName*.

NotesName Methods

New

Used to create a new *NotesName* object (▶ *191*).

Remarks

The properties of the *NotesName* class are commonly used to manipulate how a username is displayed to the screen or saved to disk within a document so that it is more meaningful. For example, a field that stores a historical audit trail of everyone who has edited a *NotesDocument* might not need to be stored (or later displayed) in the canonical format. It might be equally meaningful, but more friendly, for it to be stored using the abbreviated or common format. In addition, it might be necessary to extract the property value (that is, the organizational unit or country) programmatically in order to take some action dependent on the current user's respective component value.

Example

The following code displays most of the components described in this section for the current username.

```
Dim ns As New NotesSession
Dim nnUser As New NotesName(ns.UserName)
If nnUser.IsHierarchical Then
    Messagebox nnUser.Canonical, 32, "Canonical name..."
    Messagebox nnUser.Abbreviated, 32, "Abbreviated name..."
End If
Messagebox nnUser.Common, 32, "Common name..."
If nnUser.Country <> "" Then
    Messagebox nnUser.Country, 32, "Country..."
End If
If nnUser.Organization <> "" Then
    Messagebox nnUser.Organization, 32, "Organization..."
End If
If nnUser.OrgUnit1 <> "" Then
```

continued >>

continued >>

```
                Messagebox nnUser.OrgUnit1, 32, "OrgUnit1..."
        End If
        If nnUser.OrgUnit2 <> "" Then
                Messagebox nnUser.OrgUnit2, 32, "OrgUnit2..."
        End If
        If nnUser.OrgUnit3 <> "" Then
                Messagebox nnUser.OrgUnit3, 32, "OrgUnit3..."
        End If
        If nnUser.OrgUnit4 <> "" Then
                Messagebox nnUser.OrgUnit4, 32, "OrgUnit4..."
        End If
        If nnUser.Given <> "" Then
                Messagebox nnUser.Given, 32, "Given..."
        End If
        If nnUser.Surname <> "" Then
                Messagebox nnUsere.Surname, 32, "Surname..."
        End If
        If nnUser.Initials <> "" Then
                Messagebox nnUser.Initials, 32, "Initials..."
        End If
        If nnUser.Generation <> "" Then
                Messagebox nnUser.Generation, 32, "Generation..."
        End If
        If nnUser.ADMD <> "" Then
                Messagebox nnUser.ADMD, 32, "ADMD..."
        End If
        If nnUser.PRMD <> "" Then
                Messagebox nnUser.PRMD, 32, "PRMD..."
        End If
        If nnUser.Keyword <> "" Then
                Messagebox nnUser.Keyword, 32, "Keyword..."
        End If
```

NotesNewsletter

4.0 4.1x 4.5x 4.6x 5.0

The *NotesNewsletter* class is a document or collection of documents that contains information and/or document links to other documents. This method provides a vehicle to route documents to users through *NotesDocuments* or mail documents. The information passed within the newsletter document is typically shared among users in a workgroup or organization about a particular topic or topics. Therefore, this is a valuable workflow or knowledge management tool. A common usage of this class is to send newsletters to individuals or groups via e-mail as an automated agent, thus pushing valuable information to the respective recipients in an efficient and timely manner with document links to the original documents.

```
NotesSession
  └ NotesNewsletter
     └ NotesDocument
        ├ NotesEmbeddedObject
        ├ NotesItem
        │  └ NotesRichTextItem
        └ NotesRichTextItem
```

LotusScript Syntax

```
Dim nnewsNotesNewsletter As New NotesNewsletter(NotesDocumentCollection)
```

or

```
Set nnewsNotesNewsletter = New NotesNewsletter(NotesDocumentCollection)
```

In order to create a new *NotesNewsletter* object, you must first create a *NotesDocumentCollection* (▶ 149) containing the documents to include in the newsletter. LotusScript provides two ways to create a *NotesNewsletter* object. If you want to create a new *NotesNewsletter* from scratch, you can use the New keyword with the Dim or Set statements, as just shown, or you can use the CreateNewsLetter method of the *NotesSession* class (▶ 269).

LotusScript Parameters

NotesDocumentCollection   Required   O.Ref.

A collection of the *NotesDocument* objects to include in the new *NotesNewsletter*.

NotesNewsletter Properties

DoScore	R/W	T/F

DoScore
```
To get: intDoscore = nnewsNotesNewsletter.DoScore
To set: nnewsNotesNewsletter.DoScore = intDoscore
```

Indicates whether the *NotesNewsletter* should include each document's relevance score if the *NotesNewsletter* document was created using the FormatMsgWithDoclinks method. TRUE indicates that the newsletter does include each document's relevance score, and FALSE indicates that it does not. The default value for this property is TRUE.

The *NotesDocumentCollection* must be sorted for the DoScore property to have any effect. For example, to produce a *NotesDocumentCollection* that is unsorted, you could call the FTSearch method of the *NotesDatabase*. This property will have no effect if this *NotesNewsletter* was created using the FormatDocument method.

DoSubject	R/W	T/F

DoSubject
```
To get: intDosubject = nnewsNotesNewsletter.DoSubject
To set: nnewsNotesNewsletter.DoSubject = intDosubject
```

Indicates whether the *NotesNewsletter* should include a string that describes the subject of each document that was created using the FormatMsgWithDoclinks method. TRUE indicates that the newsletter does include a subject for each document. FALSE indicates that it does not. The default value for this property is FALSE.

When using the DoSubject method, you also need to set the SubjectItemName property. This property determines what item should be used as the subject line in the newsletter. If the SubjectItemName isn't specified, the DoSubject has no effect. The SubjectItemName and DoSubject must be set prior to calling the FormatMsgWithDoclinks method. In addition, this property will have no effect if this *NotesNewsletter* was created using the FormatDocument method.

SubjectItemName   R/W $

```
To get: strSubjectname = nnewsNotesNewsletter.SubjectItemName
To set: nnewsNotesNewsletter.SubjectItemName = strSubjectname
```
SubjectItem
Name

Indicates the name of the item contained in a newsletter's document that contains the text to use as the subject line for newsletters that were created using the `FormatMsgWithDoclinks` method.

When using the `DoSubject` method (setting it to `TRUE`), you also need to set the `SubjectItemName` property. If the `DoSubject` method is set to `FALSE`, the `SubjectItemName` property has no effect. The `SubjectItemName` and the `DoSubject` must be set prior to calling the `FormatMsgWithDoclinks` method. In addition, this property will have no effect if this *NotesNewsletter* was created using the `FormatDocument` method.

NotesNewsletter Methods

FormatDocument

```
Set ndocNotesDocument = nnewsNotesNewsletter.FormatDocument
➡(ndbNotesDatabase,intDocs)
```
Format
Document

NotesDatabase   *Required*   *O.Ref.*

The database to create the newsletter document in. If none is specified, the newsletter document will be created in the user's default mail database.

intDocs   *Required*   %

Indicates the number of documents to display in the newsletter document that are currently contained in the document collection. Since the document collection count begins at 1, setting this value to 1 specifies the first document from the collection, 2 specifies the second document from the collection, and so on.

This method returns a rendering of a *NotesDocument* object in the body field (item) of the document containing the newsletter. The body field must be a rich text field. The *NotesDocument* contained in the newsletter is the *n*th document (specified when calling the method) of the *NotesDocumentCollection* from within the specified *NotesDatabase*.

In order to save the newsletter document containing the rendering of the document presented in the newsletter, the `Save` method of the *NotesDocument* must be called. The new *NotesDocument* is then saved to the *NotesDatabase* specified when the method was called.

In order to mail the newsletter document containing the rendering of the document presented in the newsletter, the `Send` method of the *NotesDocument* must be called.

FormatMsgWithDoclinks

```
Set ndocNotesDocument = nnewsNotesNewsletter.FormatMsgWithDoclinks
➡(ndbNotesDatabase)
```
FormatMsg
WithDoclinks

NotesDatabase   *Required*   *O.Ref.*

The database to create the newsletter document in. If none is specified, the newsletter document will be created in the user's default mail database.

This method returns a document containing the links to each document in the newsletter's collection. In addition, this document will also contain the name of the *NotesDatabase* and the text of the original query that created the collection.

The body of the *NotesDocument* that is returned by the `FormatMsgWithDoclinks` method contains the following:

- The filename of the database containing the *NotesDocuments* in the *NotesNewsletter* collection
- A doclink to each document in the *NotesNewsletter* collection
- The relevant score of each document if the collection is sorted and the `DoScore` property is set to `TRUE`
- The title of each document if the `DoSubject` property is set to `TRUE` and the `SubjectItemName` property has a value
- The query that created the newsletter collection

In order to save the newsletter document containing the rendering of the document presented in the newsletter, the `Save` method of the *NotesDocument* must be called. The new *NotesDocument* is then saved to the *NotesDatabase* specified when the method was called.

In order to mail the newsletter document containing the rendering of the document presented in the newsletter, the `Send` method of the *NotesDocument* must be called.

New

New   Used to create a new *NotesNewsletter* object (▶ 197).

Remarks

The *NotesNewsletter* object is typically used in conjunction with sending e-mail memos regarding a particular topic or topics. This method is similar to forwarding *NotesDocuments* in Notes mail, except that the *NotesNewsletter* is a much more powerful knowledge management tool in regards to its formatting capabilities and the supplementary information it can send along with the documents. In addition, using the *NotesNewsletter* object can easily send doclinks back to the original documents from which the newsletter was generated.

Example

The following example prompts the user to enter keywords to perform a search against in the current *NotesDatabase*. The user can select as many words as desired. A full-text search is performed against each keyword, and the results are added to a common document collection. The final *NotesDocumentCollection* is then e-mailed to a recipient, determined via an input box, as a *NotesNewsletter*. With some minor modifications, this code could be used to create automatic notifications for specific users based on specific keywords.

```
Dim ns As New NotesSession
Dim ndb As NotesDatabase
Dim ndcFinal As NotesDocumentCollection
Dim ndc As NotesDocumentCollection
Dim nnews As NotesNewsletter
Dim ndoc As NotesDocument
Dim ndocProfile As NotesDocument
Dim ndocCurrent As NotesDocument
Dim intLoop As Integer
Dim intDocloop As Integer
Dim strItemname As String
Dim strRecipient As String
Set ndb = ns.CurrentDatabase
Set ndocProfile = ndb.GetProfileDocument( "NewsLetterDoc", ns.UserName)
strItemname = Inputbox$("Enter the search keyword value.")
Dim nitem As New NotesItem(ndocProfile, "Keyword", strItemname)
Do While strItemname <> ""
    strItemname = Inputbox$("Enter next keyword value (enter when done)")
    If strItemname <> "" Then
        Call nitem.AppendToTextList( strItemname )
    End If
Loop
'Loop through all keywords stored in user's profile document
If nitem.Values(0) <> "" Then
    For intLoop = 0 To Ubound(nitem.Values)
    'Build current collection for current keyword
        If intLoop = 0 Then
            'Build initial collection for first iteration
            Set ndcFinal = ndb.FTSearch( nitem.Values(intLoop), 0,
            ➥FT_DATE_DES )
        Else
            'Build additional interation
            Set ndc = ndb.FTSearch( nitem.Values(intLoop), 0, FT_DATE_DES )
            'Check for successful hits
            If ( ndc.Count > 0 ) Then
            'Loop through all documents in current collection
                Set ndocCurrent  = ndc.GetFirstDocument
                Do While Not (ndocCurrent Is Nothing)
               'Add new collection to final collection
                    Call ndcFinal.AddDocument(ndocCurrent)
                    Set ndocCurrent = ndc.GetNextDocument(ndocCurrent)
                Loop
            End If
        End If
    Next
    'Set newsletter settings and mail summary document
    Set nnews = New NotesNewsletter( ndcFinal )
    nnewsDoScore = True
    nnews.DoSubject = True
    nnews.SubjectItemname = "ChapterTitle"
    Set ndoc = nnews.FormatMsgWithDoclinks( ndb )
    ndoc.Form = "Memo"
    ndoc.Subject = Str(Today) & ": Newsletter Notification"
    strRecipient = Inputbox$("Enter the recipient for this NewsLetter.")
    Call ndoc.Send( False, strRecipient )
End If
```

5.0 NotesOutline

The *NotesOutline* class is new in Notes 5.0. It allows you to manipulate *NotesOutline* and *NotesOutlineEntry* (▶ 209) objects. The best way to think of an outline is like a map of your application. Each entry in the map represents one of the elements of your application and provides a convenient way to navigate around the application. After you have created an outline, you can embed it on a page or form, and users can click an entry to open that element.

```
...
  └ NotesDatabase
      └ NotesOutline
          └ NotesOutlineEntry
```

LotusScript Syntax

```
Set NotesOutline = NotesDatabase.CreateOutline(strName, intDefault)
```

Alternatively, you can use the GetOutline method of *NotesDatabase* (▶ 103):

```
Set noutOutline = ndbDatabase.GetOutline(strName)
```

LotusScript Parameters

strName	Required	$
A string containing the name of the outline you want to access.

intDefault	Optional	T/F
A boolean value that indicates if the outline should be created with default entries.

NotesOutline Properties

Alias	R/W	$

Alias
```
To set: noutNotesOutline.Alias = strAlias
To get: strAlias = noutNotesOutline.Alias
```

This property returns any aliases the outline might have.

Comment	R/W	$

Comment
```
To set: noutNotesOutline.Comment = strComment
To get: strComment = noutNotesOutline.Comment
```

This property provides a way to read or set a comment from an outline.

Name	R	$

Name
```
To get: strName = noutNotesOutline.Name
```

This property returns the name of the outline.

NotesOutline Methods

AddEntry

AddEntry
```
Call noutNotesOutline.AddEntry(nouteNewEntry,noutereferenceEntry,
➥intMoveAfter,intAsChild)
```

nouteNewEntry	Required	O.Ref.
A *NotesOutlineEntry* object representing the entry you want to add to the outline.

nouteReferenceEntry	Optional	O.Ref.
A *NotesOutlineEntry* object before or after which you want to add the new entry.

intMoveAfter	Optional	T/F
Set this parameter to TRUE to move the entry after the reference or FALSE to move the entry before the reference entry.

intAsChild   Optional   %

Set this parameter to TRUE to make the new entry a child of the reference entry or FALSE (the default) to make the new entry a sibling of the reference entry. This parameter has no effect if the intMoveAfter parameter is FALSE.

This method allows you to programmatically insert a new *NotesOutlineEntry* object into an existing *NotesOutline*. By using the nouteAfterEntry parameter, you can dictate the position in which to place the new entry.

CreateEntry

```
Set nouteEntry = CreateEntry(strName)
```

CreateEntry

strName   Required $

A string containing the name you want to give the new entry.

This method creates a free-floating entry. Use AddEntry to position it in the outline.

GetFirst

```
Set nouteEntry = noOutline.GetFirst()
```

GetFirst

This method returns the first *NotesOutlineEntry* object in the current *NotesOutline* object.

GetLast

```
Set nouteEntry = noOutline.GetLast()
```

GetLast

This method returns the last *NotesOutlineEntry* object in the current *NotesOutline* object.

GetNext

```
Set nouteEntry = noOutline.GetNext(nouteEntry)
```

GetNext

nouteEntry   Required   O.Ref.

A *NotesOutlineEntry* object representing the current entry.

This method takes the current *NotesOutlineEntry* as a parameter and attempts to navigate to the next *NotesOutlineEntry* in the outline. If this method is executed against the last entry in the outline, it returns Nothing.

GetNextSibling

```
Set nouteEntry = noOutline.GetNextSibling(nouteEntry)
```

GetNextSibling

nouteEntry   Required   O.Ref.

A *NotesOutlineEntry* object representing the current entry.

This method takes the current *NotesOutlineEntry* as a parameter and attempts to navigate to the next *NotesOutlineEntry* at the same level in the outline. If this method can't find a sibling for the current entry, it returns Nothing.

GetParent

```
Set nouteEntry = noOutline.GetParent(nouteEntry)
```

GetParent

nouteEntry   Required   O.Ref.

A *NotesOutlineEntry* object representing the current entry.

This method takes the current *NotesOutlineEntry* as a parameter and attempts to navigate the current entry's parent. If this method can't find a parent for the current entry (it is at level 0), it returns Nothing.

GetPrev

```
Set nouteEntry = noOutline.GetPrev(nouteEntry)
```

nouteEntry	Required	O.Ref.

A *NotesOutlineEntry* object representing the current entry.

This method takes the current *NotesOutlineEntry* as a parameter and attempts to navigate to the previous *NotesOutlineEntry* in the outline. If this method is executed against the first entry in the outline, it returns `Nothing`.

GetPrevSibling

```
Set nouteEntry = noOutline.GetPrevSibling(nouteEntry)
```

nouteEntry	Required	O.Ref.

A *NotesOutlineEntry* object representing the current entry.

This method takes the current *NotesOutlineEntry* as a parameter and attempts to navigate to the previous sibling entry in the outline. If this method can't find a sibling entry in the outline (an entry at the same level), it returns `Nothing`.

MoveEntry

```
Call noutOutline.MoveEntry(nouteEntrytomove,nouteRefEntry,intMoveAfter,
➥intAsChild)
```

nouteEntrytoMove	Required	O.Ref.

A *NotesOutlineEntry* object representing the entry to move.

nouteReferenceEntry	Optional	O.Ref.

A *NotesOutlineEntry* object before or after which you want to add the new entry.

intMoveAfter	Optional	T/F

Set this parameter to `TRUE` to move the entry after the reference or `FALSE` to move the entry before the reference entry.

intAsChild	Optional	%

Set this parameter to `TRUE` to make the new entry a child of the reference entry or `FALSE` (the default) to make the new entry a sibling of the reference entry. This parameter has no effect if the `intMoveAfter` parameter is `FALSE`.

RemoveEntry

```
Call noutOutline.RemoveEntry(nouteEntry)
```

nouteEntry	Required	O.Ref.

A *NotesOutlineEntry* object representing the entry to remove.

This method removes the specified *NotesOutlineEntry* and all subentries.

Save

```
Call noutOutline.Save()
```

You must call this method to save any changes you have made programmatically to the current *NotesOutline* object.

Example

```
Dim nsS As New NotesSession
Dim noutOutline As NotesOutline
Dim nouteCurEntry As NotesOutlineEntry
Set noutOutline=nsS.CurrentDatabase.GetOutline("MailOutline")
Set nouteCurEntry=noutOutline.GetFirst
Do While Not nouteCurEntry Is Nothing
    Print "Level= " & Trim$(Str$(noutOutline.GetLevel(nouteCurEntry)))
    Set nouteCurEntry=noOutline.GetNext(nouteCurEntry)
Loop
```

5.0 NotesOutlineEntry

The *NotesOutlineEntry* class is new in Notes 5.0. It represents an entry within an outline.

```
...
L NotesDatabase
   L NotesOutline
      L NotesOutlineEntry
```

LotusScript Syntax

```
Dim noeEntry As NotesOutlineEntry
```

To create a new *NotesOutlineEntry* object, you can call the `CreateEntry` method of *NotesOutline*.

```
Set noeEntry = noutOutline.CreateEntry(strName)
```

NotesOutlineEntry Properties

Alias   R/W $

Alias

```
To get: strAlias = noeNotesOutlineentry.Alias
To set: noenotesOutlineentry.Alias = strAlias
```

This property returns the alias of a *NotesOutlineEntry* object if it has one.

Database   R   O.Ref.

Database

```
To get: Set ndbNotesDatabase = noenotesoutlineEntry.Database
```

Returns a *NotesDatabase* object representing the database that is the resource link for the outline entry. This property returns a *NotesDatabase* object only if the *OutlineEntry* Type property is `OUTLINE_TYPE_NOTELINK` or `OUTLINE_TYPE_NAMEDELEMENT` and the `EntryClass` property is `OUTLINE_CLASS_DATABASE`, `OUTLINE_CLASS_DOCUMENT`, or `OUTLINE_CLASS_VIEW`.

Document   R   O.Ref.

Document

```
To get: Set ndbNotesDocument = noenotesOutlineEntry.Document
```

This property returns a *NotesDocument* object representing the resource link for an entry. This property returns a document only if the *OutlineEntry* Type property is `OUTLINE_TYPE_NOTELINK` and the `EntryClass` property is `OUTLINE_CLASS_DOCUMENT`.

EntryClass   R   %

EntryClass

```
To Get: intClass = noeNotesOutlineEntry.EntryClass
```

This property returns an integer constant representing an entry's class. Valid values are `OUTLINE_CLASS_DATABASE`, `OUTLINE_CLASS_DOCUMENT`, `OUTLINE_CLASS_FORM`, `OUTLINE_CLASS_FOLDER`, `OUTLINE_CLASS_FRAMESET`, `OUTLINE_CLASS_NAVIGATOR`, `OUTLINE_CLASS_PAGE`, `OUTLINE_CLASS_UNKNOWN`, and `OUTLINE_CLASS_VIEW`.

Formula   R $

Formula

```
To get: strFormula = noenotesOutlineEntry.Formula
```

Returns a string containing the formula of an action outline if the *OutlineEntry* Type property is `OUTLINE_TYPE_ACTION`.

FrameText   R/W $

FrameText

```
To get: strFrameText = noeNotesOutlineEntry.FrameText
To set: noeNotesOutlineEntry.FrameText = strFrameText
```

Contains the name of the target frame where you want the entry to appear.

HasChildren   R   %

HasChildren

```
To get: intHasChildren = noeNotesOutlineEntry.HasChildren
```

Returns `TRUE` if the current entry has children and `FALSE` if it doesn't.

ImagesText	R/W	$	

```
To get: strImageText = noeNotesOutlineEntry.ImagesText
To set: noeNotesOutlineEntry.ImagesText=strImageText
```
ImagesText

This property contains the text entered for the image value of a *NotesOutlineEntry*.

IsHidden	R	%	

```
To get: intIsHidden = noeNotesOutlineEntry.IsHidden
```
IsHidden

Returns TRUE if the current entry is hidden. Returns FALSE if the current entry is visible.

IsInThisDb	R	%	

```
To get: intIsInThisDb = noeNotesOutlineEntry.IsInThisDb
```
IsInThisDb

Returns TRUE if the current entry is in the current database, and FALSE if the current entry is not in the current database.

IsPrivate	R	%	

```
To get: intPrivate = noeNotesOutlineEntry.IsPrivate
```
IsPrivate

Returns TRUE if the current entry is private. Returns FALSE if the current entry is not specific to an individual.

Label	R/W	$	

```
To get: strLabel= noenotesOutlineEntry.label
To set: noenotesOutlineEntry.label = strLabel
```
Label

Contains the label for an entry.

Level	R	%	

```
To get: intlevel = noenotesOutlineEntry.Level
```
Level

Returns a number representing the level of the current entry in the *NotesOutline* object. For example, parent entries return 0.

NamedElement	R	$	

```
To get: strNamedElement = noeNotesOutlineEntry.NamedElement
```
NamedElement

Contains the named element referenced by an entry if the *OutlineEntry* Type property is OUTLINE_TYPE_NAMEDELEMENT.

Type	R/W	&	

```
To get: lngType = noeNotesOutlineEntry.Type
To set: noeNotesOutlineEntry.Type = lngtype
```
Type

Returns the type of the current entry. Valid values are OUTLINE_OTHER_FOLDERS_TYPE, OUTLINE_OTHER_UNKNOWN_TYPE, OUTLINE_OTHER_VIEWS_TYPE, OUTLINE_TYPE_ACTION, OUTLINE_TYPE_NAMEDELEMENT, OUTLINE_TYPE_NOTELINK, and OUTLINE_TYPE_URL.

URL	R	$	

```
To get strURL = noenotesOutlineEntry.URL
```
URL

Returns the URL of an entry if the *OutlineEntry* Type property is OUTLINE_TYPE_URL.

View	R	O.Ref.	

```
To get: Set nvwnotesView = noenotesOutlineEntry.View
```
View

Returns a *NotesView* object representing the view that is the resource link for an entry if the *OutlineEntry* Type property is OUTLINE_TYPE_NOTELINK and the EntryClass property is OUTLINE_CLASS_DOCUMENT or OUTLINE_CLASS_VIEW.

NotesOutlineEntry Methods

SetAction

`intflag = noenotesOutlineEntry.`**`SetAction`**`(strformula)`

Specifies a formula for an action outline entry. Returns TRUE if the action is set successfully and FALSE otherwise. Calling this method sets the *OutlineEntry* Type property to OUTLINE_TYPE_ACTION.

SetNamedElement

`intflag = noenotesOutlineEntry.`**`SetNamedElement`**`(ndbDatabase, strElementName,`
➥`intEntryClass)`

ndbDatabase	Required	O.Ref.

A database object representing the database containing the entry.

strElementName	Required	$

A sting value containing the name.

intEntryClass	Required	%

An integer specifying the entry's class.

Specifies a named element for an outline entry. This is TRUE if the named element is set successfully, and FALSE otherwise.

Calling this method sets the outline entry Type property to OUTLINE_TYPE_NAMEDELEMENT and the EntryClass property depending on the named element. See the description of the EntryClass property (▶ *210*).

SetNoteLink

`intflag = noenotesOutlineEntry.`**`SetNoteLink`**`(ndbnotesDatabase, nvwnotesView,`
➥`ndocnotesDocument)`

Specifies a resource link. This is TRUE if the resource link is set successfully, and FALSE otherwise. Only one object should be specified: *NotesDatabase, NotesView,* or *NotesDocument.* Bear in mind that calling this method sets the *OutlineEntry* Type property to OUTLINE_TYPE_NOTELINK and the EntryClass property to OUTLINE_CLASS_DATABASE, OUTLINE_CLASS_DOCUMENT, or OUTLINE_CLASS_VIEW, depending on the type of object passed to the method.

SetURL

`intflag = noenotesOutlineEntry.`**`SetURL`**`(strURL)`

Specifies a URL as the resource link. This is TRUE if the URL is set successfully, and FALSE otherwise. Calling this method sets the *OutlineEntry* Type property to OUTLINE_TYPE_URL.

Example

```
' This simple example loops through all of the
' Outline entries in a database and for entries that are
' Noteslinks and not private, changes them to URLs
Dim nsS As New NotesSession
Dim noutCurOutline As NotesOutline
Dim noeCurEntry As NotesOutlineEntry
Set noutCurOutline=nsS.CurrentDatabase.GetOutline("Main")
Set noeCurEntry=noutCurOutline.GetFirst()
Do While Not noeCurEntry Is Nothing
  If noeCurEntry.Type=OUTLINE_TYPE_NOTELINK Then
    If Not noeCurEntry.IsPrivate Then
      noeCurEntry.Type=OUTLINE_TYPE_URL
      intresult=noeCurEntry.SetURL("http://www.definiti.com")
    End If
  End If
  Set noeCurEntry=noutCurOutline.Getnext(noeCurEntry)
Loop
```

4.6x 5.0 NotesRegistration

The *NotesRegistration* class allows for the programmatic creation or administration of ID files. ID files contain information regarding the user's name, Notes license type, password, mail, registration, encryption keys, certificates, and so on. ID files are the basic building blocks that define the robust, distributed security model of Domino/Lotus Notes.

NotesSession
   └ NotesRegistration

Contents

LotusScript Syntax

The *NotesRegistration* object is created using the New keyword with the Dim or Set statements, as shown in the following examples:

```
Dim NotesRegistration As New NotesRegistration
```

or

```
Set NotesRegistration = New NotesRegistration
```

NotesRegistration Properties

CertifierIdFile   R/W $

CertifierId
File
```
To set: nregNotesRegistration.CertifierIdFile = strCertIDFile
To get: strCertIFFile = nregNotesRegistration.CertifierIdFile
```

This property returns orsets the file path location of the certifier ID file. You use the certifier ID file (Cert.ID) when creating user IDs and cross-certifying with other Domino Servers. When setting this property, be sure to use the complete file path to the certifier ID, starting with the drive—such as C:\notes\data\cert.id. When you're working with LotusScript, the default directory path (for example, C:\notes\data) is usually ignored with most properties, methods, and functions. The entire file path is required.

CreateMailDb   R/W   T/F

CreateMailDb
```
To set: nregNotesRegistration.CreateMailDb = intCreateMailDb
To get: intCreateMailDb = nregNotesRegistration.CreateMailDb
```

This property indicates whether a new mail database should be created immediately when generating new Notes ID files using the RegisterNewUser method (also a method of the *NotesRegistration* class) or whether the mail file should be created when the user completes the setup process. (TRUE immediately creates a new mail database. FALSE creates the ID file without also creating a new mail database. When FALSE is specified, the mail database will be created when the specific user completes the setup process.

Expiration   R/W   O.Ref.

Expiration
```
To set: nregNotesRegistration.Expiration = NotesDateTime
To get: ndtNotesDateTime = nregNotesRegistration.Expiration
```

This property returns or sets the expiration date to use when ID files are being created. This is typically set to only two years, which is often too short a time period to be practical. Consider extending this value to avoid frequently administering the expiration of the ID files.

IDType   R/W   %

IDType
```
To set: nregNotesRegistration.IDType = intIDType
To get: intIDType = nregNotesRegistration.IDType
```

This property returns or sets the type of ID file to create when registering a new user, server, or certifier. This property is used when calling the `RegisterNewUser`, `RegisterNewServer`, or `RegisterNewCertifier` methods. The value returned or used to set this property is a constant of type Integer. The allowed values are listed in the following table.

IDType Values

Values	Description
ID_FLAT	The ID created is flat.
ID_HIERARCHICAL	The ID created is hierarchical.
ID_CERTIFIER	The ID created uses the certifier ID to determine whether it is flat or hierarchical.

IsNorthAmerican   R/W   T/F

```
To set: nregNotesRegistration.IsNorthAmerican = intIsNorthAmer
To get: intIsNorthAmer = nregNotesRegistration.IsNorthAmerican
```
IsNorth
American

This property indicates whether the ID file is North American or International. If TRUE, the ID is North American. FALSE indicates that the ID file is International. (This is the only other option if the ID file is not North American.)

MinPasswordLength   R/W   %

```
To set: nregNotesRegistration.MinPasswordLength = intMinlength
To get: intMinlength = nregNotesRegistration.MinPasswordLength
```
MinPassword
Length

This property sets or returns the minimum number of characters required when creating an ID file. This property is relevant when calling the `RegisterNewUser`, `RegisterNewServer`, or `RegisterNewCertifier` methods.

OrgUnit   R/W $

```
To set: nregNotesRegistration.OrgUnit = strOrgUnit
To get: strOrgUnit = nregNotesRegistration.OrgUnit
```
OrgUnit

This property sets or returns the organizational unit to use when creating ID files. The organizational unit, referred to as "OU", is used when calling the `RegisterNewUser` method. A maximum of four organizational units can be used in an organization.

RegistrationLog   R/W $

```
To set: nregNotesRegistration.RegistrationLog = strRegLog
To get: strRegLog = nregNotesRegistration.RegistrationLog
```
RegistrationLog

This property sets or returns the name of the log file (such as `reg.nsf`) to use when creating IDs. Notes automatically determines this value by reading the `Log=` parameter located in the Notes .ini file. Therefore, be sure to consider setting the Notes .ini file when modifying this property.

RegistrationServer   R/W $

```
To set: nregNotesRegistration.RegistrationServer = strRegServer
To get: strRegServer = nregNotesRegistration.RegistrationServer
```
Registration
Server

This property sets or returns the name of the Domino server to use when creating ID files. This property is used only when the ID file is being stored in the server's address book (directory) or when the mail database is being created for the new user.

StoreIDInAddressBook   R/W   T/F

```
To set: nregNotesRegistration.StoreIDInAddressBook = intStoreID
To get: intStoreID = nregNotesRegistration. StoreIDInAddressBook
```
StoreIDIn
AddressBook

This property indicates whether the ID file being created should be stored in the Name and Address Book (directory) in the server. TRUE indicates that the ID should be stored in the Name and Address Book. FALSE indicates that it should not.

UpdateAddressBook	R/W	T/F

UpdateAddress
Book

```
To set: nregNotesRegistration.UpdateAddressBook = intUpdateAddBook
To get: intUpdateAddBook = nregNotesRegistration. UpdateAddressBook
```

This property indicates whether the ID file being created should update the server entry in the Name and Address Book (directory) in the server. This property is relevant when the `RegisterNewUser`, `RegisterNewServer`, or `RegisterNewCertifier` methods are called. TRUE indicates that the Name and Address Book should be updated. FALSE indicates that it should not.

NotesRegistration Methods

AddCertifierToAddressBook

AddCertifierTo
AddressBook

```
Call nregNotesRegistration.AddCertifierToAddressBook(strIdfile,
➥strCertpassword, strLocation, strComment)
```

strIdfile	Required	$

The certifier ID file to be added to the Name and Address Book (directory).

strCertpassword	Optional	$

The password for the certifier file.

strLocation	Optional	$

The value stored for the Location item in the address book document.

strComment	Optional	$

The value stored for the comment item in the address book document.

As when accessing the `CertifierIdFile` property, specify the complete file path, beginning at the drive specification.

AddServerToAddressBook

AddServerTo
AddressBook

```
Call nregNotesRegistration.AddServerToAddressBook(strIdfile, strServer,
➥strDomain, strUserpassword, strNetwork, strAdminname, strTitle,
➥strLocation, strComment)
```

strIdfile	Required	$

The ID file of the server to be added to the Name and Address Book (directory). Specify the entire file path, including the drive specification.

strServer	Required	$

The name of the server to be added to the Name and Address Book.

strDomain	Required	$

The domain of the server being added to the Name and Address Book.

strUserpassword	Optional	$

The server's password for the ID file.

strNetwork	Optional	$

The name of the Notes Names Network (NNN) for the server.

strAdminname	Optional	$

The full name of the server administrator.

strTitle	Optional	$

The value stored in the title item in the Name and Address Book document.

strLocation	Optional	$

The value stored in the location item in the Name and Address Book document.

strComment	Optional	$

The value stored in the comment item in the Name and Address Book document.

When calling this method, note that the `StoreIDInAddressBook` method can affect how this method executes.

AddUserProfile

```
Call nregNotesRegistration.AddUserProfile(strUsername, strProfilename)
```
AddUserProfile

strUsername	Required	$

The string representation of the username of the person whose person document will be modified to store the name of the setup profile.

strProfilename	Required	$

The name of the setup profile to be stored in the person document.

The `RegistrationServer` property must be set prior to calling this method, or an error will be returned.

AddUserToAddressBook

```
Call nregNotesRegistration.AddUserToAddressBook(strIdfile, strFullname,
➥strLastname, strUserpassword, strFirstname, strMiddleinit, strMailserver,
➥strMailidpath, strFwdaddress, strLocation, strComment)
```
AddUserTo
AddressBook

strIdfile	Required	$

The ID file of the user to add to the address book (directory). Specify the entire file path, including the drive.

strFullname	Required	$

The user's full name.

strLastname	Required	$

The user's last name.

strUserpassword	Optional	$

The password associated with the specified ID file.

strFirstname	Optional	$

The user's first name.

strMiddleinit	Optional	$

The user's middle initial.

strMailserver	Optional	$

The full name of the mail server for the current user.

strMailidpath	Optional	$	

The full file path for the specified ID file. Specify the entire file path, including the drive.

strFwdaddress	Optional	$	

The user's forwarding address.

strLocation	Optional	$	

The value stored in the location item in the Name and Address Book document.

strComment	Optional	$	

The value stored in the comment item in the Name and Address Book document.

When calling this method, note that the `StoreIDInAddressBook` method can affect how this method executes.

CrossCertify

`Call nregNotesRegistration.`**`CrossCertify`**`(strIdfile, strCertpassword,`
➥`strComment)`

strIdfile	Required	$	

The ID file of the user to be cross-certified. Specify the entire file path, including the drive.

strCertpassword	Optional	$	

The password for the certifier ID file.

strComment	Optional	$	

The value stored in the comment item in the Name and Address Book document.

This method cross-certifies a Notes ID file. Despite the fact that the *NotesRegistration* class is a back-end class, the `CrossCertify` method is available only when being run from within the user interface in a front-end. Even though the certifier password is passed as a parameter when this method is run, the user ID password must be entered during the cross-certification process as well. In addition, if the full file path is not properly entered, this method will return an error message telling you that the path was not supplied.

When calling this method, note that the `Expiration` property can be used to set the ID file's expiration date.

DeleteIdOnServer

`Call nregNotesRegistration.`**`DeleteIdOnServer`**`(strUsername, intIsserverid)`

strUsername	Required	$	

The username for the current ID file.

intIsserverid	Required	T/F	

Indicates whether the name is a server ID. `TRUE` indicates that the name represents a server, and `FALSE` indicates that the name represents a person.

This method permanently deletes an ID file from the server.

Note that the `RegistrationServer` property must be set prior to calling this method. Otherwise, you will receive the `Required registration argument not provided` error message.

GetIdFromServer

```
Call nregNotesRegistration.GetIdFromServer(strUsername, strFilepath,
➡intIsserverid)
```

strUsername	Required	$

The username for the current ID file.

strFilepath	Required	$

The full file path for the specified ID file. Specify the entire file path, including the drive.

intIsserverid	Required	T/F

Indicates whether the name is a server ID. TRUE indicates that the name represents a server. FALSE indicates that this name represents a person.

This method gets an ID file from the server.

When calling this method, note that the RegistrationServer property must be set prior to calling this method. Otherwise, you will receive the Required registration argument not provided error message.

GetUserInfo

```
Call nregNotesRegistration.GetUserInfo(strUsername, strRetmailserver,
➡strRetmailfile, strRetmaildomain, strRetmailsystem, strRetprofile)
```

strUsername	Required	$

The username for the current ID file.

strRetmailserver	Optional	$

Returns the mail server name for this user.

strRetmailfile	Optional	$

Returns the mail file for this user.

strRetmaildomain	Optional	$

Returns the mail domain for this user.

strRetmailsystem	Optional	$

Returns the mail system for this user.

strRetprofile	Optional	$

Returns the profile document for this user.

This method returns information about the specified user from the server. Any parameters used require the string ($) designation.

Note that the RegistrationServer property must be set prior to calling this method. Otherwise, you will receive the Required registration argument not provided error message.

New

```
nregNotesRegistration = New()
```

This method creates a new *NotesRegistration* object. The description and syntax of this method are described in the "LotusScript Syntax" section near the beginning of this chapter (▶ 216).

ReCertify

```
Call nregNotesRegistration.ReCertify(strIdfile, strCertpassword,
➥strComment)
```

| strIdfile | Required | $ |

The ID file of the user to be recertified. Specify the entire file path, including the drive.

| strCertpassword | Optional | $ |

The password for the certifier ID file.

| strComment | Optional | $ |

The value stored in the comment item in the Name and Address Book document.

This method recertifies a Notes ID file. Despite the fact that *NotesRegistration* class is a back-end class, the `ReCertify` method is available only when being run from within the user interface in a front-end. Even though the certifier password is passed as a parameter when this method is run, the user's ID password must be entered during the cross-certification process as well. In addition, if the full file path is not entered properly, this method will return an error message stating that the path has not been supplied.

When calling this method, note that the `Expiration` property can be used to set the ID file's expiration date.

RegisterNewCertifier

```
Call nregNotesRegistration.RegisterNewCertifier(strOrganization, strIdfile,
➥strCertpassword, strCountry)
```

| strOrganization | Required | $ |

The organization that the new certifier ID belongs to.

| strIdfile | Required | $ |

The ID file to be registered. Specify the entire file path, including the drive.

| strCertpassword | Required | $ |

The password for the certifier ID file.

| strCountry | Optional | $ |

The country code for the certifier.

This method registers a new Notes certifier ID file. Before this method can be called, all the required properties must be set. The required properties (as well as the optional ones) are described in the "Remarks" section (▶ 224) near the end of this chapter.

RegisterNewServer

```
Call nregNotesRegistration.RegisterNewServer(strServer, strIdfile,
➥strDomain, strServerpassword, strCertpassword, strLocation, strComment,
➥strNetwork, strAdminname, strTitle)
```

| strServer | Required | $ |

The name of the server that the server ID belongs to.

| strIdfile | Required | $ |

The ID file to be registered. Specify the entire file path, including the drive.

| strDomain | Required | $ |

The server's domain.

strServerpassword   Required $
The server's password for the ID file.

strCertpassword   Optional $
The password for the certifier ID file.

strLocation   Optional $
The value stored in the location item in the Name and Address Book document.

strComment   Optional $
The value stored in the comment item in the Name and Address Book document.

strNetwork   Optional $
The name of the Notes Names Network (NNN) for the server.

strAdminname   Optional $
The full name of the server administrator.

strTitle   Optional $
The value stored in the title item in the Name and Address Book document.

This method registers a new server ID file. When calling this method, note that the `CertifierIdFile` property must be set prior to calling this method. Otherwise, you will receive the `Certifier ID path not supplied` error message.

Before this method can be called, all the required properties must be set. The required properties (as well as the optional ones) are described in the "Remarks" section (▶ 224) near the end of this chapter.

RegisterNewUser

```
Call nregNotesRegistration.RegisterNewUser(strLastname, strIdfile,
➥strFirstname, strMiddleinit, strCertpassword, strLocation, strComment,
➥strMaildbpath, strFwddomain, strUserpassword, intUsertype)
```

RegisterNew
User

strLastname   Required $
The last name of the user being registered.

strIdfile   Required $
The ID file to be registered. Specify the entire file path, including the drive.

strFirstname   Optional $
The user's first name.

strMiddleinit   Optional $
The user's middle initial.

strCertpassword   Optional $
The password for the certifier ID file.

strLocation   Optional $
The value stored in the location item in the Name and Address Book document.

strComment   Optional $
The value stored in the comment item in the Name and Address Book document.

strMaildbpath   Optional $
The file path of the user's mail directory. You don't have to specify the entire file path—just the path of the mail database in the Notes Data directory.

strFwddomain   Optional $

The forwarded domain for the current user's mail file.

strUserpassword   Optional $

The current user's password.

5.0   intUsertype   Optional   %

This integer value represents a constant value indicating the type of client to create.
Here are the allowable values for the `intUsertype` property:

`intUsertype` Values

Constant Value	Description
NOTES_DESKTOP_CLIENT	The desktop client
NOTES_FULL_CLIENT	The full client (default)
NOTES_LIMITED_CLIENT	The mail client

This method registers a new user ID file. Note that the `CertifierIdFile` property
must be set prior to calling this method. Otherwise, you will receive the `Certifier ID
path not supplied` error message.

Before this method can be called, all the required properties must be set. The required
properties (as well as the optional ones) are described in the "Remarks" section.

SwitchToID

Call nregNotesRegistration.**SwitchToID**(strIdfile, strUserpassword)

SwitchToID

strIdfile   Required $

The ID file to switch to. Specify the entire file path, including the drive.

strUserpassword   Optional $

The password of the user ID that is being switched to.

This method switches to another ID file on a Notes client. (It won't work on the
Domino server.)

Remarks

The *NotesRegistration* class was introduced in Notes Release 4.6 and was modified
only slightly for Release 5.0. This class lets you programmatically perform some of
the often tedious and repetitive tasks of Domino/Lotus Notes administration.

However, because of Domino/Lotus Notes' secure and robust security model,
there are some things to watch out for when you're working with the
NotesRegistration class. For example, when calling the `RegisterNewCertifier`,
`RegisterNewServer`, and `RegisterNewUser` methods, all of the properties listed next,
must be set before you call the methods. If all of them are not set, none of the
changes will be saved, and you will receive the `Missing Registration Argument` or
`Required registration argument not provided` error message. Here are the required
properties:

```
RegistrationLog = certlog.nsf
IDType = ID_HIERARCHICAL
Expiration = CertExpireDate
MinPasswordLength = length%
IsNorthAmerican = TRUE
CertifierIDFile = certidfile
RegistrationServer = session.currentdatabase.server
OrgUnit = org
CreateMailDb = TRUE
StoreIdInAddressbook = TRUE
UpdateAddressbook = FALSE
```

Also keep in mind that many of these properties and methods do not work in a manner in which they are mutually exclusive of one another. They often affect one another in that certain properties must be set in order for other properties to be significant or for other methods to work. For example, `RegisterNewUser` works much like the `AddUserToAddressBook` method, `RegisterNewServer` works much like the `AddServertoAddressBook` method, and `RegisterNewCertifier` works much like the `AddCertifiertoAddressBook` method. What this means is that if you called both `RegisterNewUser` and `AddUserToAddressBook` (and the `UpdateAddressBook` property were set to `TRUE`), two entries would be created in the Name and Address Book (directory) rather than just one. You would certainly not want to have two entries for a particular user in the Name and Address Book (directory). In order to avoid having double entries in the Name and Address Book when generating new IDs, you can set the `UpdateAddressBook` property to `FALSE` and use `AddCertifierToAddressBook`, `AddServerToAddressbook`, or `AddUserToAddressBook` to make the actual additions (updates) to the Name and Address Book.

Example

The following LotusScript could be contained in an agent set to run on all documents in a particular view. This agent will run against all unprocessed documents and register the names of the people listed in these documents as Notes clients. This script assumes that the documents contained in the view have certain items that are used to populate required fields when creating the Name and Address Book (directory) entries. This type of agent, with modification, could be used to automate the creation of new IDs based on a predetermined view (for example, a view of a user list newly imported into Domino/Lotus Notes).

```
Dim ns As New NotesSession
Dim ndb As NotesDatabase
Dim nv As NotesView
Dim ndc As NotesDocumentCollection
Dim ndoc As NotesDocument
Dim nreg As NotesRegistration
Dim strIdpath As String
Dim strMailpath As String
Set ndb = ns.CurrentDatabase
Set nv = ndb.Getview("New Imports")
Set ndc  = ndb.UnprocessedDocuments
Set ndoc = ndc.GetFirstDocument
```

continued >>

continued >>

```
Do While Not(ndoc Is Nothing)
    strIdpath="c:\lotus\notes\"&Left$(ndoc.FName(0),1)&ndoc.LName(0)&".ID"
    strMailpath ="mail\" & Left$(ndoc.FName(0),1) & ndoc.LName(0) & ".nsf"
    Call nreg.RegisterNewUser( ndoc.LName(0), strIdpath, _
    "ACME Mail Server",ndoc.FName(0),ndoc.MI(0),"certpass","ACME Office",
    "Added with agent...",strMailpath,"ACME","password",NOTES_FULL_CLIENT)
    Set ndoc = ndc.GetNextDocument(ndoc)
Loop
Msgbox "Finished processing. "
```

5.0 NotesReplication

The *NotesReplication* object represents the replication settings for each *NotesDatabase* object. Replication is a fundamental feature of Domino/Lotus Notes that facilitates data synchronization among disparate users and servers. It allows the user to work in a disconnected state and still have full database functionality and information availability. Every *NotesDatabase* has one *NotesReplication* object that is automatically created as a property of the *NotesDatabase* when the *NotesDatabase* is created.

```
...
 └ NotesDatabase
     └ NotesReplication
```

LotusScript Syntax

```
Dim repinfo as NotesReplication
Set repinfo = session.currentdatabase.ReplicationInfo
```

The *NotesReplication* object is automatically created for each *NotesDatabase* (▶ 89) when the database is first created. There can be only one *NotesReplication* object per database.

NotesReplication Properties

Abstract   R/W   T/F

Abstract

```
To get: intAbstract = nrepNotesReplication.Abstract
To set: nrepNotesReplication.Abstract = intAbstract
```

This property controls whether large documents are truncated and attachments are removed. TRUE enables document truncation and removes all attachments. FALSE disables truncation. The property defaults to FALSE. From the native Notes user interface, this option is available as a replicator option to receive full documents or to receive a summary and 40KB of rich text. This reduces replication time and the size of the local replica by not pulling down large attachments and rich text fields. However, this setting affects only the documents being pulled to the local replica database. It leaves the full document (not truncated) on the source server.

CutoffDate   R   Variant

CutoffDate

```
To get: vatTimedate = nrepNotesReplication.CutoffDate
```

This property returns the date and time value that is being used by the Domino server's replicator task to determine whether it should automatically purge previously deleted document identifiers (deleted document stubs) that are older than the date specified. This property has no effect unless the CutoffDelete property (also a property of the *NotesReplication* object, (▶ 228) is turned on (set to TRUE). You calculate the value of this property by subtracting the value of the CutoffInterval property (also a property of the *NotesReplication* object, (▶ 229) from the current system date. Essentially, when *NotesDocuments* are deleted, identifier information is still stored with the database as document deletion stubs to ensure that the deletion is propagated to other replica database copies of the current database. After a predetermined period of time, it is assumed that all the replicas are in synch with one another and it is safe to fully remove any trace of the deleted *NotesDocument,* thus purging the deletion stub.

CutoffDelete   R/W   T/F

CutoffDelete

```
To get: intCutoffDelete = nrepNotesReplication.CutoffDelete
To set: nrepNotesReplication.CutoffDelete = intCutoffDelete
```

This property determines whether the Domino server's replicator task should automatically delete documents that haven't been modified by the CutoffDate (also a property of *NotesReplication,* (▶ 228). Essentially, *NotesDocuments* that haven't been modified after the date/time specified are deleted from the *NotesDatabase* since they are determined to be older than the cutoff date. The actual deletion occurs while the replicator task is running. Setting this property to TRUE enables the deletion of documents older than the cutoff date; FALSE disables this feature. This property defaults to FALSE.

This property is helpful in certain databases where older documents become meaningless and there is no need for a historical audit trail of the activity and content of the database—such as a discussion database.

CutoffInterval   R/W   &

CutoffInterval

```
To get: lngCutoffInterval = nrepNotesReplication.CutoffInterval
To set: nrepNotesReplication.CutoffInterval = lngCutoffInterval
```

This property sets the interval (in days) that is used to determine whether document identifiers from deleted documents should be purged from the *NotesDatabase* by the Domino server's replicator task. This property works in tandem with the `CutoffDate` property (also a property of *NotesReplication,* (▶ 228) and helps conserve space in the *NotesDatabase*. Although this property stores the purge interval in days, the actual date used to determine whether deletion stubs should be purged is automatically calculated and stored in the `CutoffDate` property. This property has no effect unless the `CutoffDelete` property (also a property of the *NotesReplication* object, (▶ 228) is turned on (set to `TRUE`). This property defaults to 90, stored as a long data type.

When the following code is placed in the click event of a button, it will display the current setting for the `CutoffDelete` value (whether or not it is enabled) and then prompt the user to enable this setting. If the user enables this setting, he is prompted to set the `CutoffInterval` value. If you are using a Notes client, you can test to see if this code was successful by checking the replication settings for the current database.

```
Dim session As New NotesSession
Dim ws As New NotesUIWorkspace
Dim db As NotesDatabase
Dim rep As NotesReplication
Dim existingflag As String
Set db = session.CurrentDatabase
Set repinfo = db.ReplicationInfo
existingflag$ = repinfo.CutoffDelete
    Msgbox "Currently, the 'CutoffDelete' value is set to: " &
    ➡existingflag$, 32, "CutoffDelete..."
    If Msgbox("Enable the 'CutoffDelete' value?", 36, "Enable
    ➡'CutoffDelete'...") = 6 Then
  repinfo.CutoffDelete = True
    repinfo.CutoffInterval = Clng(Inputbox$("Enter the CutoffInterval
    ➡in days.", "CutoffInterval..."))
  repinfo.Save
    Msgbox "Documents not modified in the last " &
    ➡repinfo.CutoffInterval & " days will be removed."
Else
  repinfo.CutoffDelete = False
  repinfo.Save
End If
```

Disabled   R/W   T/F

Disabled

```
To get: intDisabled = nrepNotesReplication.Disabled
To set: nrepNotesReplication.Disabled = intDisabled
```

This property temporarily enables or disables replication for this database. If set to `FALSE`, this database will not be replicated when the Domino server task runs. `TRUE` enables database replication. This property defaults to `FALSE`.

DoNotBrowse   R/W   T/F

DoNotBrowse

```
To get: intDoNotBrowse = nrepNotesReplication.DoNotBrowse
To set: nrepNotesReplication.DoNotBrowse = intDoNotBrowse
```

This property determines whether the database should appear in the Open Database dialog box. This property is meaningful only when the client is using a Notes client—it has no meaning on the Web. Setting this property to `TRUE` allows the database to appear in the Open Database dialog box. `FALSE` keeps the database filenames from appearing. However, even if this property is set to `TRUE`, the user can still open the database by typing the database's filename in the filename editable field. Therefore, this property should not be used as a security feature. This property defaults to `FALSE`.

DoNotCatalog	R/W	T/F

DoNotCatalog
```
To get: intDoNotCatalog = nrepNotesReplication.DoNotCatalog
To set: nrepNotesReplication.DoNotCatalog = intDoNotCatalog
```

This property determines whether the current *NotesDatabase* should be added to the `CATALOG.NSF` database when the Domino server Catalog task runs. Setting this property to `TRUE` lets the database be cataloged; `FALSE` disables it. `CATALOG.NSF` provides summary information about the *NotesDatabases* on the current server and other servers with replica copies of the databases. The information stored in the catalog includes server names, filenames, replica IDs, the name of the database manager, and any information saved in the database's About document. Users can browse the catalog and directly open databases. This property defaults to `FALSE`.

HideDesign	R/W	T/F

HideDesign
```
To get: intHideDesign = nrepNotesReplication.HideDesign
To set: nrepNotesReplication.HideDesign = intHideDesign
```

This property determines whether the design of the database should be hidden. Setting this property to `TRUE` causes the design to be hidden. Setting this property to `FALSE` disables the hide design feature. This property defaults to `FALSE`.

IgnoreDeletes	R/W	T/F

IgnoreDeletes
```
To get: intIgnoreDel = nrepNotesReplication.IgnoreDeletes
To set: nrepNotesReplication.IgnoreDeletes = intIgnoreDel
```

This property determines whether the deletion stubs created when *NotesDocuments* are deleted should be replicated to the database's other replica copies. Setting this property to `TRUE` keeps the deletion stubs from propagating during replication. Setting this property to `FALSE` enables the propagation of deletion stubs during replication. This property defaults to `FALSE`. This feature allows a user to delete unwanted documents from his local replica copy without affecting the documents on other replica copies. The ability to delete documents and allow the deletion to propagate to other replica copies is controlled by the current user's access control to the database. This feature shouldn't be used as a security feature. It is not meant to replace the inherent security features of Domino/Lotus Notes.

IgnoreDestDeletes	R/W	T/F

IgnoreDest
Deletes
```
To get: intIgnoreDestDel = nrepNotesReplication.IgnoreDestDeletes
To set: nrepNotesReplication.IgnoreDestDeletes = intIgnoreDestDel
```

This property determines whether the deletion stubs created when *NotesDocuments* are deleted in the current database should be replicated into the destination database. Setting this property to `TRUE` keeps the deletion stubs from propagating to the destination database during replication. Setting this property to `FALSE` enables the propagation of the deletion stubs during replication. This property defaults to `FALSE`.

MultiDbIndex	R/W	T/F

MultiDbIndex
```
To get: intMultiDbIndex = nrepNotesReplication.MultiDbIndex
To set: nrepNotesReplication.MultiDbIndex = intMultiDbIndex
```

This property determines whether current *NotesDatabases* should be included in the Multi-Database index. TRUE causes this database to be included. FALSE keeps the database from being included. This property defaults to FALSE.

NeverReplicate   R/W   T/F

```
To get: intNeverRepl = nrepNotesReplication.NeverReplicate
To set: nrepNotesReplication.NeverReplicate = intNeverRepl
```

This property determines whether the current *NotesDatabase* should be replicated when the Domino server Replicator task runs. Setting this property to TRUE causes the Replicator task to ignore this database. Setting this property to FALSE reenables replication. Unlike most *NotesReplicator* properties, this property isn't available from the Notes client interface and can be modified only programatically. This property defaults to FALSE.

NoChronos   R/W   T/F

```
To get: intNoChronos = nrepNotesReplication.NoChronos
To set: nrepNotesReplication.NoChronos = intNoChronos
```

This property determines whether background agents (sometimes called macros) are enabled. Setting this property to TRUE disables background agents. Setting this property to FALSE reenables background agents. This property defaults to FALSE.

Priority   R/W   &

```
To get: lngPriority = nrepNotesReplication.Priority
To set: nrepNotesReplication.Priority = lngPriority
```

This property determines the current *NotesDatabase* replicator priority. The replicator priority determines the order in which databases are replicated. It can be used to filter which databases are replicated. The value returned by this property and used to set this property is a constant; the available values are listed in the following table. The default value for this property is 1548, stored as a long data type signifying the constant value of Db_REPLICATION_PRIORITY_MED.

Priority Constants

Constant	Integer Value
Db_REPLICATION_PRIORITY_LOW	1547
Db_REPLICATION_PRIORITY_MED	1548
Db_REPLICATION_PRIORITY_HIGH	1549
Db_REPLICATION_PRIORITY_NOTSET	1565

NotesReplication Methods

ClearHistory

```
Call nrepNotesReplication.ClearHistory()
```

This method clears the replication history for the current *NotesDatabase* object. When a *NotesDatabase* is replicated, an entry is logged, recording the event. Typically, each replication event triggers an incremental replication, updating only the documents in the database that have been modified since the previous replication. Clearing the replication history causes the Replicator tasks to replicate all the documents, as if this replication were the initial database replication. This is often useful if there is concern that not all of the documents are being replicated as they should, or the system date has recently been changed on the client or server systems.

Reset

Reset

```
Call nrepNotesReplication.Reset
```

This method resets the replication values for the current *NotesDatabase* object to the values on the last-saved date. Therefore, if changes have been made, they can be reversed and put back to their prior setting configuration.

Save

Save

```
Call nrepNotesReplication.Save
```

This method saves the replication values for the current *NotesDatabase*. None of the values being manipulated by modifying the properties of the *NotesReplication* are activated until the `Save` method is called.

Remarks

Multiple properties of the *NotesReplication* object can be modified and then saved and written to disk at one time. Therefore, if you are programmatically manipulating the replication settings for the current database, a replication session will never occur while your code is modifying the database replication settings, because they are saved to disk at one time (rather than incrementally).

Example

The following example reads all the local databases stored in the *NotesDbDirectory* and builds a list of those databases, displaying some of their *NotesReplication* properties. The database list and the respective properties are saved in the `Body` field on a new *NotesDocument* in report format.

```
Dim ns As New NotesSession
Dim dbdirectory As NotesDbDirectory
Dim currentdb As NotesDatabase
Dim reportdoc As New NotesDocument( ns.CurrentDatabase )
Dim rtitem As New NotesRichTextItem( reportdoc, "Body")
Dim tabstr As String
Set dbdirectory = New NotesDbDirectory( "" )
Set currentdb = dbdirectory.GetFirstDatabase( DATABASE )
Set currentDb = dbdirectory.GetNextDatabase
tabstr$ = Chr$(9) + Chr$(9)
reportdoc.Form = "Report"
reportdoc.Author = session.CommonUserName
reportdoc.DateCreated = Today
Call rtitem.AppendText("Database Name")
Call rtitem.AddNewLine(1)
Call rtitem.AppendText(tabstr$ & "Abstract" & Chr$(9) & "CutoffDelete")
Call rtitem.AppendText(Chr$(9) & "Disabled" & Chr$(9) & "Browse" &
➥Chr$(9) & Chr$(9) & "Catalog")
```

```
Call rtitem.AppendText(Chr$(9) & Chr$(9) & "MultiDbIndex" & Chr$(9) &
➥"Never Repl")
Call rtitem.AddNewLine(3)
Do While Not (currentdb Is Nothing)
  Call currentDb.Open("","")
  Set repinfo = currentdb.ReplicationInfo
  Call rtitem.AppendText(currentdb.Title)
  Call rtitem.AddNewLine(1)
  Call rtitem.AppendText(tabstr$ & repinfo.Abstract & tabstr$ &
  ➥repinfo.CutoffDelete)
  Call rtitem.AppendText(tabstr$ & repinfo.Disabled & tabstr$ &
  ➥repinfo.Donotbrowse & tabstr$ & repinfo.Donotcatalog)
  Call rtitem.AppendText(tabstr$ & repinfo.Multidbindex & tabstr$ &
  ➥repinfo.Neverreplicate)
  Call rtitem.AddNewLine(1)
  Set currentDb = dbdirectory.GetNextDatabase
Loop
reportdoc.Save True, False
```

NotesRichTextItem

4.0 4.1x 4.5x 4.6x 5.0

The *NotesRichTextItem* object is a type of *NotesItem* that contains rich text. Therefore, not only can the *NotesRichTextItem* object contain text, but it can also be formatted with various styles, fonts, and types. In addition, it can contain graphics, tables, buttons, attachments, and virtually any other type of compound data. Similar to the *NotesItem* object, the *NotesRichTextItem* is contained in a *NotesDocument*. In other words, it is synonymous with a field contained in a record in a relational database. The *NotesRichTextItem* is derived from the *NotesItem* base class, so it inherits the properties and methods of the existing *NotesItem* class.

```
. . .
└ NotesDocument
    └ NotesRichTextItem

OR

. . .
└ NotesDocument
    └ NotesItem
        └ NotesRichTextItem
```

LotusScript Syntax

```
Dim nrtiRichtextitem As New NotesRichTextItem(NotesDocument,
➥strNewrichtextitemname)
```

or

```
Set nrtiRichtextitem = New NotesRichTextItem(NotesDocument,
➥strNewrichtextitemname)
```

LotusScript provides several ways to create a *NotesRichTextItem* object. If you want to create a new *NotesRichTextItem* object from scratch, you can use the New keyword with either the Dim or Set statements, as just shown. This Dim statement declares the *NotesRichTextItem* object in memory, and the Set statement then assigns the *NotesRichTextItem* a reference to the existing parent *NotesDocument* object. In other words, it derives its value from the existing *NotesDocument* class. In the first example, the *NotesRichTextItem* object is created in memory and is assigned a reference to the *NotesDocument* in a single line of code. In the second example, the *NotesRichTextItem* object is first declared and then is assigned in a separate statement.

Two alternative ways to get access the *NotesRichTextItem* object are through the CreateRichTextItem of the *NotesDocument* class (▶ 138) or through the GetFirstItem of the *NotesDocument* class (▶ 139).

Another way to access the *NotesRichTextItem* object is to exploit the methods of the existing *NotesDocument* object. For example, you can use the CreateRichTextItem method of the *NotesDocument* class (▶ 138) to create a new *NotesRichTextItem* object in the *NotesDocument* object.

Once you have created a *NotesRichTextItem* object in a *NotesDocument*, you must call the Save method of the parent *NotesDocument* to save the data to disk.

In addition, rather than creating a new *NotesRichTextItem,* you can access an existing *NotesRichTextItem* object created previously by using the GetFirstItem method of the *NotesDocument* class.

LotusScript Parameters

NotesDocument	Required	O.Ref.

A *NotesDocument* object that represents the underlying Notes document in which to create the new *NotesRichTextItem* object.

strNewRichTextItemName	Required	$

A string value that contains the name you want to give the new *NotesRichTextItem* or the name of the item(s) you want to replace.

NotesRichTextItem Properties

EmbeddedObjects	R	O.Ref.

Embedded
Objects   To get: notesEmbeddedObjectArray = nrtiNotesRichTextItem.**EmbeddedObjects**

Returns an array of all the OLE/1 and OLE/2 embedded objects, file attachments, and links to other objects that are contained in the *NotesRichTextItem*. At the time this chapter was written, this property wasn't supported for OS/2 and Macintosh clients.

The following example illustrates how the `type` property of the *EmbeddedObjects* object can be used to compare against the constant values in order to determine the type of object(s) that are embedded in the rich text field.

```
Sub Click(Source As Button)
Dim nws As New NotesUIWorkspace
Dim ndoc As NotesDocument
Dim nrti As Variant
Dim intAttachcount As Integer
Dim intObjectcount As Integer
Dim intObjectLinkcount As Integer
Set ndoc = nws.CurrentDocument.Document
Set nrti = ndoc.GetFirstItem( "Body" )
    If ( nrti.Type = RICHTEXT ) Then
    Forall objects In nrti.EmbeddedObjects
        Print Format$(objects.Type)
        Select Case objects.Type
        Case EMBED_ATTACHMENT
            intAttachcount = intAttchcount + 1
        Case EMBED_OBJECT
            intObjectcount = intObjectcount + 1
        Case EMBED_OBJECTLINK
            intObjectLinkcount = intObjectLinkcount + 1
        End Select
    End Forall
    Msgbox "Attachment count = " & Str$(intAttachcount)
    Msgbox "Object count = " & Str$(intObjectcount)
    Msgbox "ObjectLink count = " & Str$(intObjectLinkcount)
Else
    Msgbox "No Rich Text Item was located.", 32, "SriptError..."
End If
End Sub
```

NotesRichTextItem Methods

AddNewLine

```
Call nrtiNotesRichTextItem.AddNewLine(intLines, intForceparagraph)
```
AddNewLine

intLines   Required   %

The number of lines to append to the body of the rich text item.

intForceparagraph   Optional   T/F

Indicates whether the new line should create a new paragraph as well. TRUE creates a new paragraph; FALSE adds a new line in the same paragraph. This parameter is TRUE by default.

This method appends carriage returns (new lines or Chr$(13)) to the end of the *NotesRichTextItem*. By specifying the value of the intLines parameter, you can add multiple lines at one time.

5.0 AddPageBreak

```
Call nrtiNotesRichTextItem.AddPageBreak(NotesRichTextParagraphStyle)
```
AddPageBreak

NotesRichTextParagraphStyle   Optional   O.Ref.

The paragraph style and attributes determined by the *RichTextParagraphStyle* object to use in the beginning of the new page of the *NotesRichTextItem*.

This method appends a hard page break to the end of the *NotesRichTextItem*.

AddTab

AddTab

```
Call nrtinotesRichTextItem.AddTab( intTabs )
```

intTabs   Required   %

The number of tabs to append to the body of the rich text item.

This method appends tabs to the end of the *NotesRichTextItem*. By specifying the value of the `intTabs` parameter, you can add multiple tabs at one time.

AppendDocLink

AppendDocLink

```
Call nrtinotesRichTextItem.AppendDocLink(linkto, strComment,
➡strHotspottextstring)
```

linkto   Required   O.Ref.

The object to create the link to. This is either a *NotesDatabase, NotesView,* or *NotesDocument*.

strComment   Required $

The text displayed when the user clicks the link or moves the mouse over the link icon.

5.0   strHotspottextstring   Optional $

The text appears as boxed text that when clicked will open the object link.

This method adds a database, view, or document link to the end of a rich text item. This link is actually a handle to the *NotesDatabase, NotesView,* or *NotesDocument* object that will open the respective object in the user interface when the user clicks it.

```
Dim ns As New NotesSession
Dim nws As New NotesUIWorkspace
Dim ndoc As NotesDocument
Dim ndocNew As NotesDocument
Dim nrti As Variant
Dim nrtiNew As Variant
Dim strRecipient As String
Set ndoc = nws.CurrentDocument.Document
Set ndocNew = New NotesDocument( ns.CurrentDatabase )
Set nrti = ndoc.GetFirstItem( "Body" )
Set nrtiNew = New NotesRichTextItem(ndocNew, "Body")
strRecipient = Inputbox$( "Recipient of this doclink.", "Doclink...")
If strRecipient <>"" Then
    Call nrtiNew.AppendDocLink( ndoc, "Please review...")
    Call ndocNew.Save( False, True )
    Call ndocNew.Send( False, strRecipient)
    Msgbox "The E-Mail with doclink has been sent.", 32, "Complete..."
Else
    Msgbox "You must enter a recipient!",16, "Unable to E-Mail doclink."
End If
```

5.0 AppendParagraphStyle

Append
ParagraphStyle

```
Call nrtiNotesRichTextItem.AppendParagraphStyle(RichTextParagraphStyle)
```

RichTextParagraphStyle   Required   O.Ref.

The paragraph style and attributes determined by the *RichTextParagraphStyle* object to be appended to the *NotesRichTextItem*.

This method appends a paragraph style to the end of the *NotesRichTextItem*. All subsequent text (or objects, if applicable) that is appended to the rich text item in this paragraph will adhere to the same attributes of the paragraph style.

AppendRTItem

```
Call nrtiNotesRichTextItem.AppendRTItem(NotesRichTextItem)
```
AppendRTItem

notesRichTextItem   Required   O.Ref.

The rich text item to be appended to the first rich text item.

This method appends the contents of *NotesRichTextItem* to the end of another *NotesRichTextItem*.

The following example illustrates how to use **AppendRTItem** to attach the contents of the current *NotesRichTextItem* (contained in the current *NotesDocument* displayed in the current user interface) to a newly created *NotesDocument* that is mailed to the specified recipient.

```
Sub Click(Source As Button)
Dim ns As New NotesSession
Dim nws As New NotesUIWorkspace
Dim ndoc As NotesDocument
Dim ndocNew As NotesDocument
Dim nrti As Variant
Dim nrtiNew As Variant
Dim strRecipient As String
Set ndoc = nws.CurrentDocument.Document
Set ndocNew = New NotesDocument( ns.CurrentDatabase )
Set nrti = ndoc.GetFirstItem( "Body" )
Set nrtiNew = New NotesRichTextItem(ndocNew, "Body")
strRecipient = Inputbox$( "Recipient of this E-Mail.", "Rich text.")
If strRecipient <>"" Then
    If (nrti.Type=RICHTEXT And nrtiNew.Type=RICHTEXT) Then
        If Msgbox("Copy Rich Text to mail doc?",36,"Copy...") = 6 Then
            Call nrtiNew.AppendRTItem( nrti )
        End If
        Call ndocNew.Save( False, True )
        Call ndocNew.Send( False, strRecipient)
        Msgbox "The E-Mail has been sent.", 32, "E-Mail complete..."
    End If
Else
    Msgbox "You must enter a recipient!", 16, "Unable to E-Mail..."
End If
End Sub
```

.6, 5.0 AppendStyle

```
Call nrtiNotesRichTextItem.AppendStyle(NotesRichTextStyle)
```
AppendStyle

notesRichTextStyle   Required   O.Ref.

The rich text style to be appended to the rich text item.

This method appends a style to the end of a *NotesRichTextItem*. This style is created using the **CreateRichTextStyle** method of this class. All text appended to the *NotesRichTextItem* after the style has been applied reflects the attributes of that style. You can subsequently modify the style by appending another style to the *NotesRichTextItem*. Doing so won't affect any subsequent text (or objects) appended to the *NotesRichTextItem* using the `AppendRTItem` method (which preserves its respective attributes).

The following code snippet creates a new document and populates the *NotesRichTextItem* with text rendered with two different styles applied to them. Notice how the `AppendStyle` method is called after each *NotesRichTextStyle* modification. However, if you're making changes to a currently open *NotesDocument,* keep in mind that changes made to the *NotesRichTextItem* are not immediately visible via the user interface until the document is saved to disk, closed, and reopened in the user interface. In this example, the modifications were made to the back-end *NotesDocument,* so this limitation was not an issue.

```
Sub Click(Source As Button)
Dim ns As New NotesSession
Dim nws As New NotesUIWorkspace
Dim ndocNew As NotesDocument
Dim nrtiNew As Variant
Dim nrts As NotesRichTextStyle
Set ndoc = New NotesDocument(ns.CurrentDatabase)
Set  nrtiNew = New NotesRichTextItem(ndoc, "Body")
Set nrts = ns.CreateRichTextStyle
nrts.NotesFont = FONT_ARIAL
nrts.FontSize = 36
nrts.NotesColor = COLOR_RED
Dim nrti As New NotesRichTextItem(ndoc, "Body")
Call nrti.AppendStyle(nrts)
Call nrti.AppendText("This is important so pay attention!")
Call nrti.AddNewLine(2)
nrts.NotesFont = FONT_ARIAL
nrts.FontSize = 8
nrts.NotesColor = COLOR_BLANK
Call nrti.AppendStyle(nrts)
Call nrti.AppendText("I am not as worthy of your attention.")
ndoc.Form = "test"
ndoc.Save True, False
End Sub
```

AppendText

AppendText   `Call nrtiNotesRichTextItem.`**`AppendText`**`(strText)`

---

strText   Required $

The text to append to the end of the *NotesRichTextItem.*

This method appends text to the end of the *NotesRichTextItem.* The text appended assumes the existing style attributes of the *NotesRichTextItem.*

EmbedObject

EmbedObject   `Set nembNotesEmbeddedObject = nrtiNotesRichTextItem.`**`EmbedObject`**`(intType,`
     ➥`strClass, strSource, strName)`

---

intType   Required   %

An integer constant value that determines the type of constant to embed. More details follow.

---

strClass   Required $

The application name of the OLE object being created if `EMBED_OBJECT` was used as the parameter for `intType` and an empty object is being created. This parameter is case-sensitive. More details follow.

strSource   Required $

The filename specifying the location of the OLE object being created if `EMBED_OBJECT`   strSource
was used as the parameter for `intType`, or the name of the file to attach or link if
`EMBED_ATTACHMENT` or `EMBED_OBJECTLINK` was used as the parameter for `intType`.
More details follow.

strName   Optional $

The name to assign to the *NotesEmbeddedObject* so that it can be referenced later by script.

This method returns a handle to the newly created embedded object, attached file, or
linked object, depending on the parameters selected in the method. This method can
attach a specified file to the *NotesRichTextItem,* embed (append) a created object (specified using the application or filename) to the *NotesRichTextItem,* or place a link to a
specified file object in the *NotesRichTextItem.* At the time this chapter was written, this
method wasn't supported by OS/2 or Macintosh clients. The constant values allowed
for `intType` are listed in the following table.

`intType` **Constants**

Constant	Description
EMBED_ATTACHMENT	Creates an attachment
EMBED_OBJECT	Creates an embedded object
EMBED_OBJECTLINK	Creates an object link (to a database, view, or document)

You need to specify a value for `strClass` only when you're using `EMBED_OBJECT` for
`intType` and creating an empty embedded object from an application. In this case, this
parameter defines the application's name. When specifying the name of the application,
you can enter an empty string (`""`) for `strSource`. This parameter is case-sensitive. If
you are specifying `EMBED_OBJECTLINK` or `EMBED_ATTACHMENT` for `intType`, enter an
empty string (`""`) for this parameter.

You need to specify a value for `strSource` when using `EMBED_OBJECT` for `intType` and
creating an embedded object from a file. In this case, this parameter defines the file's
name. When specifying the name of the file, you can enter an empty string (`""`) for
`strClass`. If you are specifying `EMBED_OBJECTLINK` or `EMBED_ATTACHMENT` for `intType`,
this parameter specifies the name of the file to attach or link.

While files can be attached on all platforms that support Domino/Lotus Notes, objects
and object links can only be created on platforms and clients that support OLE.

GetEmbeddedObject

```
Set nembNotesEmbeddedObject = nrtiNotesRichTextItem.GetEmbeddedObject
➥(strName)
```
GetEmbedded
Object

strName   Required $

The name of the *NotesEmbeddedObject* to return.

This method returns a handle on the *NotesEmbeddedObject* that is referenced as the
name specified by `strName`. The `strName` is the name of a file attachment, embedded
object, or object link located in the *NotesRichTextItem* object. This method is not supported by the OS/2, UNIX, or Macintosh platforms. When attempting to locate a file
attachment, specify the filename for `strName`. When attempting to locate an embedded
object, specify the name of the object (as it reads in the info box when you're designing using the Notes Designer) that might have been assigned by the `EmbedObject`
method. Modifications made to the object with script will be saved, but the object
won't render the results until it is activated.

The following example attempts to locate an embedded Microsoft Word object and, if found, activates the Word document object and displays it in the user interface.

```
Sub Click(Source As Button)
Dim nws As New NotesUIWorkspace
Dim ndoc As NotesDocument
Dim nrti As NotesRichTextItem
Set ndoc = nws.CurrentDocument.Document
Set nrti = ndoc.GetFirstItem( "Body" )
If ( nrti.Type = RICHTEXT ) Then
    Set oleobject=nrti.GetEmbeddedObject("Microsoft Word Document")
    If ( oleobject Is Nothing ) Then
        Print "Unable to find MS Word Doc.  Please report this error."
    Else
        Print "Loading Microsoft Word Document into memory..."
        oleobject.Activate(True)
    End If
End If
End Sub
```

GetFormattedText

GetFormatted
Text

```
strPlaintext = nrtiNotesRichTextItem.GetFormattedText(intTabstrip,
➥intLinelength)
```

intTabstrip   Required   T/F

Indicates whether tabs should be stripped out of the plain text string that is returned by this method. TRUE indicates that they should be stripped out. FALSE indicates that they should not.

intLinelength   Optional   %

Indicates the character count at which to wrap the text and begin a new line. The default is 0.

This method returns the string value of a *NotesRichTextItem* as plain text. All other contents of the *NotesRichTextItem* are ignored.

The following simple example displays the plain textual contents of the *NotesRichTextItem*.

```
Sub Click(Source As Button)
Dim ns As New NotesSession
Dim nws As New NotesUIWorkspace
Dim ndoc As NotesDocument
Dim nrti As NotesRichTextItem
Dim strMessage As String
Set ndoc = nws.CurrentDocument.Document
Set nrti = ndoc.GetFirstItem( "Body" )
strMessage = nrti.GetFormattedText( False, 40 )
Msgbox strMessage, 32, "Text contents of the rich text field are..."
End Sub
```

New

New

Used to create a new *NotesRichTextItem* object and assign it to a reference variable (▶ 235).

Remarks

Once you have created a *NotesRichTextItem* object in a *NotesDocument* object, you must call the Save method of the parent *NotesDocument* to save the data to disk.

Since the *NotesRichTextItem* inherits from the *NotesItem* base class, all the properties and methods of the *NotesItem* are available to the *NotesRichTextItem* as well. In addition, the properties and methods of the *NotesRichTextItem* are extended to incorporate rich text capabilities. However, unlike the *NotesItem,* which has a physical size limit of 64KB, the *NotesRichTextItem* can hold information as large as 1 gigabyte in size. Although common sense would discourage you from storing this much data in a single item (or field) in a *NotesDocument,* the robust capability of the *NotesRichTextItem* object makes it a powerful LotusScript class.

The *NotesRichTextItem* won't be saved when the document is saved if content is not added to the *NotesRichTextItem* object. In addition, because of *NotesRichTextItem*'s dynamic capabilities, modifications made to it are not visible to the user interface until the document is saved to disk and reopened in the user interface.

Example

The following example builds a list of doclinks linking to all documents that match the criteria selected by the user. Each line item built by this agent and stored in the rich text field also contains some text describing the nature of the doclink. This simulates the *NotesNewsletter* functionality but lets you specify the formatting using the capabilities of the *NotesRichTextItem* object. This code could be modified to create an agent that "pushes" information to certain users based on creation date, topics, or keywords. This script could also be modified to incorporate other routing functions inherent to workflow and process automation applications.

Typically, this code would be written in a more modular manner and would consequently be more efficient. However, for the purposes of this example, all the functionality necessary to facilitate this example has been included in one routine. Nevertheless, the following code is complete and could be run "as is" from within an agent or by using a button. In addition, some properties and methods from other Notes classes have been used to show off the potential of *NotesRichTextItem.*

```
Dim ns As New NotesSession
Dim nws As New NotesUIWorkspace
Dim ndb As NotesDatabase
Dim ndc As NotesDocumentCollection
Dim ndoc As NotesDocument
Dim rtiNew As Variant
Dim nrts As NotesRichTextStyle
Dim intDocloop As Integer
Dim strCriteria As String
Dim strMsg As String
Dim ndocNew As New NotesDocument(ns.CurrentDatabase)
```

continued >>

continued >>

```
Set ndb = ns.CurrentDatabase
strCriteria = Inputbox$("Please enter the search criteria.", "Searching")
If strCriteria <> "" Then
    Set ndc = ndb.FTSearch( strCriteria, 0 , FT_DATE_DES)
    Set rtiNew = New NotesRichTextItem(ndocNew, "Body")
    Set nrts = ns.CreateRichTextStyle
    nrts.NotesFont = FONT_ARIAL
    nrts.FontSize = 18
    nrts.NotesColor = COLOR_BLUE
    Call rtiNew.AppendStyle(nrts)
    strMsg = "Here are all the documents that match: " & strCriteria
    Call rtiNew.AppendText(strMsg)
    Call rtiNew.AddNewLine(2)
    nrts.NotesFont = FONT_ARIAL
    nrts.FontSize = 8
    nrts.NotesColor = COLOR_BLANK
    Call rtiNew.AppendStyle(nrts)
    For intDocloop = 1 To ndc.Count
        Call rtiNew.AppendText(Str$(intDocloop)& " - ")
        Set ndoc = ndc.GetnthDocument(intDocloop)
        Call rtiNew.AppendText( Str$(ndoc.Created))
        Call rtiNew.AddTab( 1 )
        Call rtiNew.AppendText( ndoc.Form(0))
        Call rtiNew.AddTab( 1 )
        strMsg = "Created by " & ndoc.Authors(0)
        Call rtiNew.AppendDocLink( ndoc, strMsg)
        Call rtiNew.AddNewLine(1)
    Next
    ndocNew.Form = "Memo"
        ndocNew.Save True, False
        Call ndocNew.Send( False, ns.UserName)
        Msgbox "E-Mail sent, please check your inbox!", 32, "Complete..."
End If
```

NotesRichText ParagraphStyle

5.0

The *NotesRichTextParagraphStyle* object contains the rich text attributes of the current paragraph in a *NotesRichTextItem* object. These attributes allow you to further define the style associated with the text contained in the *NotesRichTextItem* by exposing the paragraph attributes, such as alignment, spacing, and tabs stops.

NotesSession
└ NotesRichTextParagraphStyle
　└ RichTextTab

LotusScript Syntax

The only way to create a new *NotesRichTextParagraphStyle* object is to use the `CreateRichTextParagraphStyle` method of the *NotesSession* object (▶ 269).

LotusScript Parameters

There are no parameters for this object since it must be created using the `CreateRichTextParagraphStyle` method of the *NotesSession* object (▶ 269).

NotesRichTextParagraphStyle Properties

Alignment   R/W   %

Alignment

To get: `intAlignment = nrtpNotesRichTextParagraphStyle.`**`Alignment`**
To set: `nrtpNotesRichTextParagraphStyle.`**`Alignment`**` = intAlignment`

This property allows you to get or set the alignment and justification of the text or objects located in the current paragraph. The value contained in `Alignment` is a constant (or integer) whose available values are listed in the following table. The default value for this property is `0`, which sets the paragraph style to left-justified. At the time this chapter was written, the `ALIGN_NOWRAP` constant was not recognized by the Lotus compiler as a constant.

Alignment Constants

Constant Value	Integer Value	Description
ALIGN_CENTER	3	Center justification
ALIGN_FULL	2	Full justification
ALIGN_NOWRAP	N/A	The text will not wrap; it continues to scroll to the right
ALIGN_RIGHT	1	Right justification
ALIGN_LEFT	0	Left justification

FirstLineLeftMargin   R/W   &

FirstLineLeft
Margin

To get: `lngMargin = nrtpNotesRichTextParagraphStyle.`**`FirstLineLeftMargin`**
To set: `nrtpNotesRichTextParagraphStyle.`**`FirstLineLeftMargin`**` = lngMargin`

This property allows you to get or set the left margin for the first line of text contained in the current paragraph. Lotus Notes uses the left margin setting for displaying the document but automatically sets the right margin setting depending on the size of the window in which Lotus Notes is currently contained. This is why the longer lines of text automatically span the width of the screen and wrap when the size of the window is adjusted. However, when printing, Lotus Notes uses both the left margin setting and the right margin setting. When setting the margins for either the left or right margin, enter the value for this property specified as twips (an extremely small unit of measurement). The default value for this property is 1,440, or one inch. The conversion scale when using twips is 1,400 twips = one inch, 567 twips = one centimeter. In addition, rather than specify the twips value for this property, you can also use the constant values of `RULER_ONE_INCH` (one inch or 1,440 twips) or `RULER_ONE_CENTIMETER` (one centimeter or 567 twips).

InterlineSpacing   R/W   %

```
To get: intSpacing = nrtpNotesRichTextParagraphStyle.InterlineSpacing
To set: nrtpNotesRichTextParagraphStyle.InterlineSpacing = intSpacing
```

This property allows you to get or set the spacing setting between selected lines of the current paragraph. The value contained in the `InterlineSpacing` variable is a constant (or integer) whose available values are listed in the following table. The default value for this property is 0, which indicates that the paragraph will be single-spaced.

InterlineSpacing Constants

Constant Value	Integer Value	Description
SPACING_DOUBLE	2	Double spacing
SPACING_ONE_POINT_50	1	1½ line spacing
SPACING_SINGLE	0	Single spacing

LeftMargin   R/W   &

```
To get: lngMargin = nrtpNotesRichTextParagraphStyle.LeftMargin
To set: nrtpNotesRichTextParagraphStyle.LeftMargin = lngMargin
```

This property lets you get or set the left margin for the current paragraph. Lotus Notes uses the left margin setting for displaying the document but automatically sets the right margin setting depending on the size of the window in which Lotus Notes is currently contained. This is why the longer lines of text automatically span the width of the screen and wrap when the size of the window is adjusted). However, when printing, Lotus Notes uses both the left margin setting and the right margin setting. When setting the margins for either the left or right margin, enter the value for this property specified as twips (an extremely small unit of measurement). The default value for this property is 1,440, or one inch. The conversion scale when using twips is 1,400 twips = one inch, 567 twips = one centimeter. In addition, rather than specify the twips value for this property, you can also use the constant values of `RULER_ONE_INCH` (one inch or 1,440 twips) or `RULER_ONE_CENTIMETER` (one centimeter or 567 twips).

Pagination   R/W   %

```
To get: intPagination = nrtpNotesRichTextParagraphStyle.Pagination
To set: nrtpNotesRichTextParagraphStyle.Pagination = intPagination
```

This property lets you get or set the pagination setting for the current paragraph. The value contained in the `Pagination` variable is a constant (or integer) whose available values are listed in the following table. The default value for this property is **0**, which indicates that the pagination will be single-spaced.

Pagination Constants

Constant Value	Integer Value	Description
PAGINATE_BEFORE	1	Page break before paragraph
PAGINATE_DEFAULT	0	Break paragraph using default settings
PAGINATE_KEEP TOGETHER	4	Keep paragraph on one page
PAGINATE_KEEP WITH NEXT	2	Keep paragraph with next paragraph

RightMargin   R/W   &

```
To get: lngMargin = nrtpNotesRichTextParagraphStyle.RightMargin
To set: nrtpNotesRichTextParagraphStyle.RightMargin = lngMargin
```

This property allows you to get or set the right margin for the current paragraph. Lotus Notes uses the left margin setting for displaying the document but automatically sets the right margin setting depending on the size of the window in which Lotus Notes is currently contained. This is why the longer lines of text automatically span the width of the screen and wrap when the size of the window is adjusted. However, when printing, Lotus Notes uses both the left margin setting and the right margin setting. When setting the margins for either the left or right margin, enter the value for this property specified as twips (an extremely small unit of measurement). The default value for this property is 0. The conversion scale when using twips is 1,400 twips = one inch, 567 twips = one centimeter. In addition, rather than specify the twips value for this property, you can also use the constant values of RULER_ONE_INCH (one inch or 1,440 twips) or RULER_ONE_CENTIMETER (one centimeter or 567 twips).

Spacingabove   R/W   %

Spacingabove

```
To get: intSpacing = nrtpNotesRichTextParagraphStyle.Spacingabove
To set: nrtpNotesRichTextParagraphStyle.Spacingabove = intSpacing
```

This property lets you get or set the spacing setting above the selected lines of the current paragraph. The value contained in the Spacingabove variable is a constant (or integer) whose available values are listed in the following table. The default value for this property is 0, which indicates that the spacing above the line of text (or other objects) is single-spaced.

Spacingabove Constants

Constant Value	Integer Value	Description
SPACING_DOUBLE	2	Double spacing
SPACING_ONE_POINT_50	1	1½ line spacing
SPACING_SINGLE	0	Single spacing

Spacingbelow   R/W   %

Spacingbelow

```
To get: intSpacing = nrtpNotesRichTextParagraphStyle.Spacingbelow
To set: nrtpNotesRichTextParagraphStyle.Spacingbelow = intSpacing
```

This property allows you to get or set the spacing setting below the selected lines of the current paragraph. The value contained in the Spacingbelow variable is a constant (or integer) whose available values are listed in the following table. The default value for this property is 0, which indicates that the spacing below the line of text (or other objects) is single-spaced.

Spacingbelow Constants

Constant Value	Integer Value	Description
SPACING_DOUBLE	2	Double spacing
SPACING_ONE_POINT_50	1	1½ line spacing
SPACING_SINGLE	0	Single spacing

Tabs   R   ()

Tabs

```
To get: lngTabs = nrtpNotesRichTextParagraphStyle.Tabs
```

This property returns an array of all the tabs that have been created for the current paragraph, in order from left to right. Each element of the array represents a specific tab stop that has been placed in the current paragraph. Regardless of whether tabs are evenly spaced or individually set, this property returns an element for each tab stop that spans the paragraph. Each element in the array of tabs contains two the position of the tab as a long value, and the type of tab as an integer.

The type value contains a constant that represents the alignment of the text in regards to the specific tab. Specifically, when the cursor reaches the tab stop, the constant specifies how the text is aligned as it is entered. The allowable constant values are listed in the following table.

Tabs Constants

Constant Value	Integer Value	Description
TAB_CENTER	3	Text is centered around the tab stop.
TAB_DECIMAL	2	Text is right-justified to the left of the tab stop and left-justified to the right of the tab stop.
TAB_LEFT	0	Text is left-justified, beginning at the tab stop.
TAB_RIGHT	1	Text is right-justified, ending at the tab stop.

NotesRichTextParagraphStyle Methods

ClearAllTabs

`Call nrtpNotesRichTextParagraphStyle.ClearAllTabs`   ClearAllTabs

This method clears all the tab stops that have been set for the current paragraph. The tabs are a property of the *NotesRichTextParagraphStyle* that are stored as an array of integers.

Settab

`Call nrtpnotesrichtextparagraphstyle.Settab( lngPosition, intType )`   Settab

Position   Required   &

The position of the tab specified in twips (an extremely small unit of measurement). The conversion scale when using twips is 1,400 twips = one inch, 567 twips = one centimeter. In addition, rather than specify the twips value for this property, you can also use the constant values of `RULER_ONE_INCH` (one inch or 1,440 twips) or `RULER_ONE_CENTIMETER` (one centimeter or 567 twips).

Type   Required   %

The type of text justification to use with this tab.

The following table lists the constants that can be used with the `Type` parameter, which determines how the text located at the respective tab stop is justified.

Settab Constants for `intType`

Constant Value	Integer Value	Description
TAB_CENTER	3	Text is centered around the tab stop.
TAB_DECIMAL	2	Text is right-justified to the left of the tab stop and left-justified to the right of the tab stop.
TAB_LEFT	0	Text is left-justified, beginning at the tab stop.
TAB_RIGHT	1	Text is right-justified, ending at the tab stop.

Settabs

`Call nrtpnotesrichtextparagraphstyle.Settabs( intNumber, lngStart,`   Settabs
`➡lngInterval, intType )`

Number   Required   %

The number of tab stops to create for this paragraph.

Start   Required   &

The position of the first tab stop specified in twips (an extremely small unit of measurement). The conversion scale when using twips is 1,400 twips = one inch, 567 twips = one centimeter. In addition, rather than specify the twips value for this property, you can also use the constant values of RULER_ONE_INCH (one inch or 1,440 twips) or RULER_ONE_CENTIMETER (one centimeter or 567 twips).

Interval   Required   &

The interval space between tab stops if more than one is specified in the Number parameter specified in twips. In addition, rather than specify the twips value for this property, you can also use the constant values of RULER_ONE_INCH (one inch or 1,440 twips) or RULER_ONE_CENTIMETER (one centimeter or 567 twips).

Type   Optional   %

The type of text justification to use.

When specifying the number of tab stops, pass a numeric value that is one less than the actual number of tab stops requested. For example, if four tab stops are required for the current paragraph, set this value to 3. The following table lists the available constants to use with the Type parameter, which determines how the text located at the respective tab stop is justified.

Settabs Constants for intType

Constant Value	Integer Value	Description
TAB_CENTER	3	Text is centered around the tab stop.
TAB_DECIMAL	2	Text is right-justified to the left of the tab stop and left-justified to the right of the tab stop.
TAB_LEFT	0	Text is left-justified, beginning at the tab stop.
TAB_RIGHT	1	Text is right-justified, ending at the tab stop.

Remarks

When using properties and methods that allow you to set or read the position of the tab, the unit of measurement is set or returned as either inches (Imperial) or centimeters (Metric). You modify this setting from the native Lotus Notes client interface in the User Preferences, in the International section.

Example

The following example demonstrates some of the formatting features available with the *NotesRichTextParagraphStyle* object. It also shows you how manipulating these properties can allow you to create professionally formatted paragraphs that are more meaningful and easier to read. This example creates a new *NotesDocument*, reads the contents of a view, and then populates the Body field of the document with information loaded from the view. The paragraph that contains this information is a rich text field that uses several different formatting techniques, justification, and tab stops. Finally, the document is saved with the form type as "Summation Form".

```
Sub Click(Source As Button)
    Dim ns As New NotesSession
    Dim nws As New NotesUIWorkspace
    Dim nv As NotesView
    Dim nrtp As NotesRichTextParagraphStyle
    Dim ndocNew As New NotesDocument( ns.CurrentDatabase )
    Dim ndocCurrent As NotesDocument
    Dim nrti As New NotesRichTextItem( ndocNew, "Body" )
    Dim intDoccount As Integer
    Set nv  = ns.CurrentDatabase.GetView( "All" )
    Set nrtp = ns.CreateRichTextParagraphStyle
    nrtp.Spacingbelow = SPACING_SINGLE
    Call nrtp.Settab( 720, TAB_RIGHT)
    Call nrtp.Settab( 1440, TAB_CENTER)
    Call nrtp.Settab( 2880, TAB_CENTER)
    Call nrtp.Settab( 4320, TAB_LEFT)
    Call nrti.AppendParagraphStyle( nrtp )
    Call nrti.AddTab(1)
    Call nrti.AppendText("Count")
    Call nrti.AddTab(1)
    Call nrti.AppendText("Date Created")
    Call nrti.AddTab(1)
    Call nrti.AppendText("Doclink")
    Call nrti.AddTab(1)
    Call nrti.AppendText("Summary Information")
    Call nrti.AddNewLine( 1 )
    Call nrti.AppendParagraphStyle( nrtp )
    Set ndocCurrent = nv.GetFirstDocument
    intDoccount = 1
    While Not ( ndocCurrent Is Nothing )
        Call nrti.AppendParagraphStyle( nrtp )
        Call nrti.AddTab(1)
        Call nrti.AppendText(Str$(intDoccount))
        Call nrti.AddTab(1)
        Call nrti.AppendText(Format$(ndocCurrent.Created, "Medium Date"))
        Call nrti.AddTab(1)
        Call nrti.AppendDocLink(ndocCurrent, "Click to open original doc.")
        Call nrti.AddTab(1)
        Call nrti.AppendText(ndocCurrent.subject(0))
        Call nrti.AddNewLine(1)
        intDoccount = intDoccount + 1
        Set ndocCurrent = nv.GetNextDocument( ndocCurrent )
    Wend
    ndocNew.Form = "Summation Form"
    ndocNew.Save True, False
End Sub
```

NotesRichTextStyle

4.6x 5.0

The *NotesRichTextStyle* object contains the rich text attributes of the *NotesRichTextItem* object or *NotesSession* object. These attributes go beyond the standard attributes associated with the static text fields used with *NotesItem* objects, which are formatted with a single font type, font size, color, and so on. This is because the style associated with the text contained in the *NotesRichTextItem* is dynamic and can change for each paragraph, line, or character. Prior to Notes version 4.6, there was no way to programmatically modify the style attributes of rich text fields. When you created *NotesRichTextItems* or modified its contents, all text automatically defaulted to 10-point Helvetica.

NotesSession
 └ NotesRichTextStyle

LotusScript Syntax

The only way to create a new *NotesRichTextStyle* object is to use the CreateRichTextStyle method of the *NotesSession* object (▶ 269).

LotusScript Parameters

There are no parameters for this object because it must be created using the CreateRichTextStyle method of the *NotesSession* object (▶ 269).

NotesRichTextStyle Properties

Bold	R/W	T/F

Bold
```
To get: intBold = nrtsNotesRichTextStyle.Bold
To set: nrtsNotesRichTextStyle.Bold = intBold
```

This property indicates whether the font characteristic of the *NotesRichTextItem* is bold. TRUE indicates that it is. FALSE indicates that it is not. STYLE_NO_CHANGE (with an integer value of 255) indicates that the style has maintained its previous state.

Effects	R/W	%

Effects
```
To get: intEffects = nrtsNotesRichTextStyle.Effects
To set: nrtsNotesRichTextStyle.Effects = intEffects
```

This property represents the font characteristics/text effects of the *NotesRichTextItem* that are covered by the other properties of the *NotesRichTextItem* object. The possible constants that are returned are listed in the following table.

Effects Constants

Constant Value	Integer Value	Description
EFFECTS_EMBOSS	4	The text appears embossed.
EFFECTS_EXTRUDE	5	The text appears extruded.
EFFECTS_NONE	0	The text has no special effects other than those represented by the other properties of the *NotesRichTextStyle* object.
EFFECTS_SHADOW	3	The text appears with a shadow.
EFFECTS_SUBSCRIPT	2	The text appears as subscript.
EFFECTS_SUPERSCRIPT	1	The text appears as superscript.
STYLE_NO_CHANGE	255	The *NotesRichTextStyle* has not been modified by any script and is currently recognizing the defaults.

Fontsize	R/W	%

Fontsize
```
To get: intFontSize = nrtsNotesRichTextStyle.FontSize
To set: nrtsNotesRichTextStyle.FontSize = intFontsize
```

This property returns an integer representing the font size (in points) or a constant value of STYLE_NO_CHANGE of the current *NotesRichTextItem*.

Italic   R/W   %

```
To get: intItalic = nrtsNotesRichTextStyle.Italic
To set: nrtsNotesRichTextStyle.Italic = intItalic
```
Italic

This property indicates whether the font characteristic of the *NotesRichTextItem* is italic. TRUE indicates that it is. FALSE indicates that it is not. STYLE_NO_CHANGE (with an integer value of 255) indicates that the style has maintained its previous state.

NotesColor   R/W   %

```
To get: intColor = nrtsNotesRichTextStyle.NotesColor
TO set: nrtsNotesRichTextStyle.NotesColor = intColor
```
NotesColor

This property indicates the color of the *NotesRichTextItem*. The possible constants that are returned are listed in the following table.

NotesColor Constants

Constant Values	Integer Value
COLOR_BLACK	0
COLOR_BLUE	4
COLOR_CYAN	7
COLOR_DARK_BLUE	10
COLOR_DARK_CYAN	13
COLOR_DARK_GREEN	9
COLOR_DARK_MAGENTA	11
COLOR_DARK_RED	8
COLOR_DARK_YELLOW	12
COLOR_GRAY	14
COLOR_GREEN	3
COLOR_LIGHT_GRAY	15
COLOR_MAGENTA	5
COLOR_RED	2
COLOR_WHITE	1
COLOR_YELLOW	6
STYLE_NO_CHANGE	255

NotesFont   R/W   %

```
To get: intFont = nrtsNotesRichTextStyle.NotesFont
To set: nrtsNotesRichTextStyle.NotesFont = intFont
```
NotesFont

This property indicates the font type of the *NotesRichTextItem*. The possible constants that are returned are listed in the following table.

NotesFont Constants

Constant Values	Integer Value
FONT_COURIER	4
FONT_HELV	1
FONT_ROMAN	0
STYLE_NO_CHANGE	255

5.0 Passthruhtml   R/W   %

Passthruhtml   To get: intPasshtml = nrtsNotesRichTextStyle.**Passthruhtml**
                To set: nrtsNotesRichTextStyle.**Passthruhtml** = intPasshtml

Indicates whether the text contained in the *NotesRichTextItem* is to be treated as Pass-Thru HTML when served by the Domino server to a Web client. TRUE indicates that it is. FALSE indicates that it is not. STYLE_NO_CHANGE (with an integer value of 255) indicates that the style has maintained its previous state.

Strikethrough   R/W   %

Strikethrough   To get: intStrike = nrtsNotesRichTextStyle.**Strikethrough**
                 To set: nrtsNotesRichTextStyle.**Strikethrough** = intStrike

This property indicates whether the font characteristic of the *NotesRichTextItem* is strikethrough. TRUE indicates that it is. FALSE indicates that it is not. STYLE_NO_CHANGE (with an integer value of 255) indicates that the style has maintained its previous state.

Underline   R/W   %

Underline   To get: intUnderline = nrtsNotesRichTextStyle.**Underline**
             To set: nrtsNotesRichTextStyle.**Underline** = intUnderline

This indicates whether the font characteristic of the *NotesRichTextItem* is underline. TRUE indicates that it is. FALSE indicates that it is not. STYLE_NO_CHANGE (with an integer value of 255) indicates that the style has maintained its previous state.

Remarks

When you're developing applications using either LotusScript or Java, the *NotesRichTextStyle* object is used by the *NotesRichTextItem* object with the AppendStyle method (▶ 239). When a new *NotesRichTextStyle* object is created, all the properties of *NotesRichTextStyle* default to STYLE_NO_CHANGE (with an integer value of 255).

Example

The following example modifies the *NotesRichTextStyle* for the text being written to the Body field of a memo. The body of the memo, though brief, uses several properties of the *NotesRichTextStyle* class to help convey the meaning of the message.

```
Dim ns As New NotesSession
Dim nws As New NotesUIWorkspace
Dim ndb As NotesDatabase
Dim nrts As NotesRichTextStyle
Set ndb = ns.CurrentDatabase
Dim ndoc As New NotesDocument(ndb)
Set nrts = ns.CreateRichTextStyle
Dim nrti As New NotesRichTextItem(ndoc, "Body")
ntri.Notescolor = COLOR_BLACK
ntri.Effects = EFFECTS_EMBOSS
ntri.FontSize = 8
```

```
Call ntri.AppendStyle(nrts)
Call ntri.AppendText("Sorry Tim, you have been ")
nrts.Notescolor = COLOR_RED
nrts.Bold = True
nrts.Underline = True
nrts.FontSize = 36
Call nrti.AppendStyle(nrts)
Call nrti.AppendText(" FIRED!")
ndoc.Form = "Memo"
ndoc.Subject = "Congratulations!"
Call ndoc.Send( False, "Tim Bankes/Definiti")
```

5.0 NotesRichTextTab

The *NotesRichTextTab* object exposes the tab attributes of the *NotesRichTextParagraphStyle*. The tabs contained in *NotesRichTextParagraph* are just one of the attributes that can be used to add rich formatting to the text and objects contained in a *NotesRichTextItem*.

NotesSession
└ NotesRichTextParagraphStyle
　└ NotesRichTextTab

LotusScript Syntax

The only way to create a new *NotesRichTextTab* object is to use the `SetTab` and `Settabs` methods of the *NotesRichTextParagraphStyle* object (▶ 249).

LotusScript Parameters

There are no parameters for this object because it must be created using the `Settabs` method of the *NotesRichTextParagraphStyle* object (▶ 249).

NotesRichTextTab Properties

Position   R   &

Position   `To get: lngPosition = nrttNotesRichTextTab.Position`

This property allows you to get or set the position of this tab specified in twips (an extremely small unit of measurement). The conversion scale when using twips is 1400 twips = one inch, 567 twips = one centimeter. In addition, rather than specify the twips value for this property, you can also use the constant values of `RULER_ONE_INCH` (one inch or 1,440 twips) or `RULER_ONE_CENTIMETER` (one centimeter or 567 twips).

Type   R   %

Type   `To get: intType = nrttNotesRichTextTab.Type`

This property allows you to get or set the type of paragraph justification for the current text or objects contained in this *NotesRichTextParagraphStyle*. The following table lists the available constants to use with the `Type` property, which determine how the text located at the respective tab stop is justified.

Type Constants

Constant Value	Integer Value	Description
TAB_CENTER	3	The text is centered around the tab stop.
TAB_DECIMAL	2	The text is right-justified to the left of the tab stop and left-justified to the right of the tab stop.
TAB_LEFT	0	The text is left-justified, beginning at the tab stop.
TAB_RIGHT	1	The text is right-justified, ending at the tab stop.

NotesRichTextTab Methods

Clear

Clear   `Call nrttNotesRichTextTab.Clear`

This method clears the current tab from the current paragraph. The tabs are a property of the *NotesRichTextParagraphStyle* that are stored as an array of integers.

Remarks

When using properties and methods that allow you to set or read the position of the tab, the unit of measurement is set or returned as either inches (Imperial) or centimeters (Metric). This setting is modified from the native Lotus Notes client interface in the Measurements field in the User Preferences, under the International section.

Example

The following example prompts the user to enter a keyword to search for in the current *NotesDatabase*. The results of the search are saved in a new memo *NotesDocument* that is created and mailed to the current user. The contents of the mail document are modified using several Notes objects—namely, *NotesItem, NotesRichTextItem, NotesRichTextParagraph, NotesRichTextParagraphStyle,* and *NotesRichTextTab.* This code could be modified to run as a scheduled agent that automatically sends information to a particular user based on new document content.

```
Dim ns As New NotesSession
Dim ndb As NotesDatabase
Dim ndc As NotesDocumentCollection
Dim ndoc As NotesDocument
Dim rtiNew As Variant
Dim nrts As NotesRichTextStyle
Dim nrtps As NotesRichTextParagraphStyle
Dim nrtt As NotesRichTextTab
Dim intDocloop As Integer
Dim strCriteria As String
Dim strMsg As String
Dim ndocNew As New NotesDocument(ns.CurrentDatabase)
Set ndb = ns.CurrentDatabase
Set nrtps = ns.CreateRichTextParagraphStyle( )
Call nrtps.ClearAllTabs()
Call nrtps.SetTab( 1440, TAB_LEFT)
Call nrtps.SetTab( 2880, TAB_CENTER)
Call nrtps.SetTab( 4320, TAB_CENTER)
strCriteria = Inputbox$("Please enter the search criteria.", "Searching")
If strCriteria <> "" Then
    Set ndc = ndb.FTSearch( strCriteria, 0 , FT_DATE_DES)
    Set rtiNew = New NotesRichTextItem(ndocNew, "Body")
    strMsg = "Here are all the documents that match: " & strCriteria
    Call rtiNew.AppendText(strMsg)
    Call rtiNew.AddNewLine(2)
    Set nrts = ns.CreateRichTextStyle
    nrts.NotesFont = FONT_ARIAL
    nrts.FontSize = 8
    nrts.NotesColor = COLOR_BLANK
    Call rtiNew.AppendStyle(nrts)
    Call rtiNew.AppendParagraphStyle( nrtps )
    For intDocloop = 1 To ndc.Count
        Call rtiNew.AppendText(Str$(intDocloop)& " - ")
```

continued >>

continued >>

```
            Set ndoc = ndc.GetnthDocument(intDocloop)
            Call rtiNew.AppendText( Str$(ndoc.Created))
            Call rtiNew.AddTab( 1 )
            Call rtiNew.AppendText( ndoc.Form(0))
            Call rtiNew.AddTab( 1 )
            strMsg = "Created by " & ndoc.Authors(0)
            Call rtiNew.AppendDocLink( ndoc, strMsg)
            Call rtiNew.AddNewLine(1)
        Next
        ndocNew.Form = "Memo"
        ndocNew.Save True, False
        Call ndocNew.Send( False, ns.UserName)
        strMsg = "[Tab one] Position: " & nrtps.Tabs(0).Position & _
        "- Tab Type:" & nrtps.Tabs(0).Type & Chr$(13) & _
        "[Tab two] Position: " & nrtps.Tabs(1).Position & "- Tab Type:" & _
        nrtps.Tabs(1).Type & Chr$(13) & "[Tab three] Position: " & _
        nrtps.Tabs(2).Position & "- Tab Type:" & nrtps.Tabs(2).Type
        Msgbox strMsg, 32, "Complete..."
    End If
```

NotesSession

The *NotesSession* class is at the top of the hierarchy of back-end classes. It can be used as the starting point to access any of the back-end classes. It also provides the following: access to address books, access to the environment of the current script, access to environment variables, information about the current user, and information about the current Notes platform and release number. It is a class you should come to know and love.

NotesSession
— NotesAgent
— NotesDatabase
— NotesDateRange
— NotesDateTime
— NotesDbDirectory
— NotesDocumentCollection
— NotesInternational
— NotesLog
— NotesName
— NotesNewsletter
— NotesNotesRegistration
— NotesRichTextParagraphStyle
— NotesRichTextStyle
— NotesTimer

LotusScript Syntax

You can create a new *NotesSession* object by using the `New` keyword with either the `Dim` or `Set` keywords:

```
Dim NotesSession As New NotesSession
```

or

```
Set NotesSession = New NotesSession
```

NotesSession Properties

AddressBooks   R   ?

AddressBooks

To get: `varDatabaseArray = nsNotesSession.AddressBooks`

This property returns an array of *NotesDatabase* objects, each representing a Notes Name and Address Book (NAB) available to the currently executing script (the NABs defined in the `NAMES=` entry in the `Notes.ini` file). If the script executes on a server, this property returns only public NABs. Otherwise, it will return both public and private NABs.

```
Dim nsS As New NotesSession
Dim varAddressBooks As Variant
Dim strPrtString
varAddressBooks=nsS.AddressBooks
Forall db In varAddressBooks
  If db.IsPublicAddressBook Then
    strPrtString = strPrtString & db.Title & ": " & db.Name & Chr(13)
  End If
End Forall
If strPrtString="" Then
  Msgbox "There are no public address books available to you.", 48,
➥"Public Address Books"
Else
  Msgbox "Public Address Books available to you:" & Chr(13) & _
strPrtString, 64, "Public Address Books"
End If
```

CommonUserName   R $

CommonUser
Name

To get: `strCommonName = nsNotesSession.CommonUserName`

This property returns the common user name of the Notes ID file in use when the script executes. When executing on a server, the server's common user name is returned. On a workstation, the current user's common name is returned.

CurrentAgent   R   O.Ref.

CurrentAgent

To get: `setnagtAgent = nsNotesSession.CurrentAgent`

This method returns a *NotesAgent* object (▶ 83) that represents the agent that is currently executing. If no agents are executing, this agent returns `Nothing`.

CurrentDatabase   R   O.Ref.

To get: setndbCurrentDb = nsNotesSession.**CurrentDatabase**

Returns a *NotesDatabase* object (▶ 89) representing the database in which the current script is running.

```
' The following example demonstrates creating a function
' that you could use dynamically to resolve the path
' of a database so that you can make applications more portable
Dim nsS As New NotesSession
Dim ndbSystem As NotesDatabase
Dim strDbName As String
strDbName="contacts" ' this is the filename of the database to open
Set ndbSystem=nsS.GetDatabase(nsS.CurrentDatabase.Server, ResolvePath
➥(nsS.CurrentDatabase) & strDbName &
➥Right$(nsS.CurrentDatabase.FileName, 4))
Function ResolvePath(ndbCurDatabase As NotesDatabase) As String
 ResolvePath=Left$(ndbCurDatabase.FilePath,
 ➥(Len(ndbCurDatabase.FilePath)-Len(ndbCurDatabase.FileName)))
End Function
```

DocumentContext   R   O.Ref.

To get: setndocCurDoc = nsNotesSession.**DocumentContext**

Returns a *NotesDocument* object representing the current document for documents accessed using the API or when you're using Web run agents. This property can be used by agents run through the WebQueryOpen and WebQuerySave events and/or when you're directly calling an agent using a Domino URL such as http://www.testing.com/ test.nsf/Test/?OpenAgent to get a handle to the current *NotesDocument*.

Additionally, when used with Web applications, this document object contains items representing the Common Gateway Interface (CGI) variable supported by Domino. Note that you can't call the Encrypt or Remove methods on documents accessed in this fashion.

```
' The following example demonstrates using the DocumentContext property
' of NotesSession to send a page to the browser that conains all of the
' CGI variables supported by Domino.
' Note: no opening <BODY> and <HTML> tags are needed, as Domino will
' automatically supply these.
Dim nsS As New NotesSession
Print ¦Authentication Type = ¦ & nsS.DocumentContext.Auth_Type(0)
Print ¦<BR>¦
Print ¦Content Length = ¦ & nsS.DocumentContext.Content_Length(0)
Print ¦<BR>¦
Print ¦Content Type = ¦ & nsS.DocumentContext.Content_Type(0)
Print ¦<BR>¦
Print ¦Gateway Interface = ¦ & nsS.DocumentContext.Gateway_Interface(0)
Print ¦<BR>¦
Print ¦HTTP Accept = ¦ & nsS.DocumentContext.HTTP_Accept(0)
Print ¦<BR>¦
Print ¦HTTP Referer = ¦ & nsS.DocumentContext.HTTP_Referer(0)
Print ¦<BR>¦
Print ¦HTTPS = ¦ & nsS.DocumentContext.HTTPS(0)
Print ¦<BR>¦
Print ¦User Agent = ¦ & nsS.DocumentContext.HTTP_User_Agent(0)
Print ¦<BR>¦
Print ¦Path Info = ¦ & nsS.DocumentContext.Path_Info(0)
Print ¦<BR>¦
```
continued >>

continued >>

```
Print ¦Path Translated = ¦ & nsS.DocumentContext.Path_Translated(0)
Print ¦<BR>¦
Print ¦Query String = ¦ & nsS.DocumentContext.Query_String(0)
Print ¦<BR>¦
Print ¦Remote Address = ¦ & nsS.DocumentContext.Remote_Addr(0)
Print ¦<BR>¦
Print ¦Remote Host = ¦ & nsS.DocumentContext.Remote_Host(0)
Print ¦<BR>¦
Print ¦Remote Indentification = ¦ & nsS.DocumentContext.Remote_Ident(0)
Print ¦<BR>¦
Print ¦Remote User = ¦ & nsS.DocumentContext.Remote_User(0)
Print ¦<BR>¦
Print ¦Request Method = ¦ & nsS.DocumentContext.Request_Method(0)
Print ¦<BR>¦
Print ¦Script Name = ¦ & nsS.DocumentContext.Script_Name(0)
Print ¦<BR>¦
Print ¦Server Name = ¦ & nsS.DocumentContext.Server_Name(0)
Print ¦<BR>¦
Print ¦Server Protocol = ¦ & nsS.DocumentContext.Server_Protocol(0)
Print ¦<BR>¦
Print ¦Server Port = ¦ & nsS.DocumentContext.Server_Port(0)
Print ¦<BR>¦
Print ¦Server Software = ¦ & nsS.DocumentContext.Server_Software(0)
Print ¦<BR>¦
Print ¦Gateway Interface = ¦ & nsS.DocumentContext.Server_URL_Gateway_
 ➥Interface(0)
```

EffectiveUserName   R $

EffectiveUser
Name

To get: strEffName = nsNotesSession.**EffectiveUserName**

This property returns different values depending on where the script reading it is run. If the script runs on a server, the distinguished name of the script owner (the person who last saved the script) is returned. If the script runs on a workstation, the current user's distinguished name is returned. If your organization doesn't use hierarchical certificates, this property returns the same value as the CommonUserName property.

International   R   O.Ref.

International

To get: setnintInternational = nsNotesSession.**International**

Returns a *NotesInternational* object (▶ 171) containing the international settings for the machine on which it's run.

IsOnServer   R   T/F

IsOnServer

To get: intOnServer = nsNotesSession.**IsOnServer**

This property returns TRUE if the executing script is "running on the server" and FALSE otherwise. Any agent in a database residing on a Domino server (and that uses one of the following trigger types: When new mail arrives; When documents have been pasted; On schedule hourly, daily, weekly, or monthly; or When documents have been created or modified) causes this property to return TRUE. Any other script "runs on the workstation," no matter whether the database itself resides on a server or a workstation.

LastExitStatus   R   &

LastExitStatus

To get: lngExitStatus = nsNotesSession.**LastExitStatus**

Returns a status code returned by the Agent Manager from the last execution of the current agent. For an agent that completed without any errors, this property returns 0.

LastRun	R	?

To get: varLastRun = nsNotesSession.**LastRun**   LastRun

Returns the date that the current agent was last run. If a script has never executed, this property returns 12:00:00 AM.

5.0 NotesBuildVersion	R	&

To get: lngVersion = nsNotesSession.**NotesBuildVersion**   NotesBuild Version

Returns a long representing the version (release) of Notes under which the current script is executing. If the script is running on a server, this property returns the server's release information; on a workstation, it will contain the workstation's release information. For example, Notes Release 5.0 Beta 2 returns 163.

NotesVersion	R	$

To get: strVersion = nsNotesSession.**NotesVersion**   NotesVersion

Returns the version (release) of Notes under which the current script is executing. If the script is running on a server, this property returns the server's release information. On a workstation, it will contain the workstation's release information. For example, Notes Release 5.0 Beta 2 returns Build 163.1 (Beta 2) ¦November 18, 1998.

Platform	R	$

To get: strPlatform = nsNotesSession.**Platform**   Platform

Returns the name of the platform (operating system) on which Notes is running. If the script runs on a server, the server's platform is returned. Otherwise, the workstation's platform is returned. Valid platform return values are "MacIntosh", "MSDos", "Netware", "OS/2v1", "OS/2v2", "Windows/16", "Windows/32", and "UNIX".

SavedData	R	O.Ref.

To get: setndocSaveDataDoc = nsNotesSession.**SavedData**   SavedData

This property returns a *NotesDocument* object that an agent can use to store information between runs. Data stored in this document can be accessed the next time the agent runs. A SavedData document is created when a script agent is saved. Each time a script agent is edited and saved, its SavedData document is deleted and a new, blank one takes its place. When you delete an agent, its SavedData document is deleted. SavedData documents replicate but are not displayed in views. You should note that this property is valid only for scripts in agents.

UserName	R	$

To get: strUserName = nsNotesSession.**UserName**   UserName

On a server, this property returns the fully distinguished name of the server. On a workstation, this property returns the fully distinguished name of the current user.

5.0 UserNameList	R	Var

To get: varNamesList = nsNotesSession.**UserNameList**   UserNameList

This new property returns an array of *NotesName* objects (▶) representing all the names in use in a session. This array includes primary and alternative user names. If no alternative names are being used, this property returns an array with a single *NotesName* element.

NotesSession Methods

CreateDateRange

```
SetndrDateRange = nsNotesSession.CreateDateRange
```

The CreateDateRange method takes no parameters and returns a *NotesDateRange* object (▶ 113). Consider the following example.

```
Dim nsS As New NotesSession
Dim ndrDateRange As NotesDateRange
Dim ndtStartTime As NotesDateTime
Dim ndtEndTime As NotesDateTime
Dim lngTimeDiff As Long, intDays As Integer
Set ndtStartTime =nsS.CreateDateTime("Today")
Set ndtEndTime =nsS.CreateDateTime("01/01/2000")
Set ndrDateRange = nsS.CreateDateRange()
Set ndrDateRange.StartDateTime = ndtStartTime
Set ndrDateRange.EndDateTime = ndtEndTime
lngTimeDiff=ndrDateRange.EndDateTime.TimeDifference
➥(ndrDateRange.StartDateTime)
intDays=(lngTimeDiff/60/60/24)
Msgbox "Y2K bug bites in " & Trim$(Str$(intDays)) & " days", 48,
➥"Countdown..."
```

CreateDateTime

```
Set ndtDateTime = nsNotesSession.CreateDateTime(strDateTime)
```

strDateTime	Required	$

A string value representing the date and/or time value you want to use.

Returns a *NotesDateTime* object (▶ 115) representing the date and/or time used as a parameter. The Notes date-time expressions "Yesterday" and "Today" can be used to initialize the object. If an empty string ("") is used, the new *NotesDateTime* object is set to a wildcard date. Use this method with OLE automation to eliminate the need to use the New method.

CreateLog

```
Set nlogNotesLog = nsNotesSession.CreateLog(strScriptName)
```

strScriptName	Required	$

A name that identifies the agent being logged.

This method returns a *NotesLog* object (▶ 185) with the name specified by the strScriptName parameter. You can use this method with OLE to create a new *NotesLog* object without using the New method.

CreateName

```
SetnnameNotesName = nsNotesSession.CreateName(strName, strLanguage)
```

strName	Required	$

A server or user name.

strLanguage	Optional	$

Specifies the language code associated with the user name.

Returns a *NotesName* object (▶ 191). If the name is not formatted as a canonical or hierarchical name, it will be considered a flat name. Use this method with OLE to avoid using the **New** method of the *NotesName* class.

CreateNewsLetter

```
setnnewsNewsLetter = nsNotesSession.CreateNewsLetter(ndcCollection)
```
CreateNews Letter

ndcCollection   **Required**   **O.Ref.**

A collection of documents to send to a newsletter.

Returns a *NotesNewsLetter* object based on the documents contained in the ndcCollection parameter. When using OLE, use this method to avoid using the **New** method of *NotesNewsLetter*.

5.0 CreateRichTextParagraphStyle

```
Set nrtpsStyle = nsNotesSession.CreateRichTextParagraphStyle()
```
CreateRichText ParagraphStyle

Call this method to create a new *NotesRichTextParagraphStyle* object (▶ 245). It takes no parameters.

4.6 CreateRichTextStyle

```
Set nrtsStyle = nsNotesSession.CreateRichTextStyle()
```
CreateRichText Style

Call this method to create a new *NotesRichTextStyle* object (▶ 253). It takes no parameters.

CreateTimer

```
Set ntmrTimer = nsNotesSession.CreateTimer()
```
CreateTimer

Call this method to create a new *NotesTimer* object (▶ 275). It takes no parameters. When using OLE, use this method to avoid using the **New** method of *NotesTimer*.

FreeTimeSearch

```
Set ndrDateRange = nsnotesSession.FreeTimeSearch(ndrWindow, intDuration,
➥strNames , intFirstFit)
```
FreeTimeSearch

ndrWindow   **Required**   **?**

A *NotesDateRange* object containing a start time and end time to search for.

intDuration   **Required**   **%**

The length of time to schedule in minutes.

strNames   **Required**   **$**

A string or array of strings containing the names of people to schedule.

intFirstFit   **Optional**   **T/F**

Pass **TRUE** to return only the first matching time or **FALSE** to return all matching times. The default is **FALSE**.

Calling this method searches the free ime of the people specified in the strNames parameter and returns an array of *NotesDateRange* objects for all available time ranges. If none are found, this method returns **NULL**.

GetDatabase

```
Set ndbNotesDatabase = nsNotesSession.GetDatabase(strServer, strDbName,
➥intCreateOnFail)
```
GetDatabase

---

strServer   Required $

The name of the server where the database resides. Use an empty string (" ") to indicate the current machine.

strDbName   Required $

The path to and name of the database.

intCreateOnFail   Optional   T/F

Specify TRUE for this parameter to create the database if it doesn't exist. Otherwise, omit this parameter to raise an error if the database doesn't exist.

Returns a *NotesDatabase* object for the database specified by the strServer and strDbName parameters and opens the database if possible. Use this method with OLE automation to create a *NotesDatabase* object without using New. GetDatabase won't create a new database on disk. To create a new database, use the Create method of *NotesDatabase*.

GetDbDirectory

GetDb
Directory

```
Set ndirDirectory = nsNotesSession.GetDbDirectory(strServerName)
```

---

strServerName   Required $

The name of the server that houses the directories you want to navigate. Enter an empty string (" ") to indicate the current machine.

Returns a *NotesDbDirectory* object for the Notes server specified in the strServerName. Use this method with OLE automation to create a *NotesDbDirectory* object without using New. Consider the following example.

```
'This example sends an e-mail to the administrator containing
'a summary of all the templates on a specified server
 Dim nsS As New NotesSession
 Dim ndirDirectory As NotesDbDirectory
 Dim ndbCDatabase As NotesDatabase
 Dim ndocMail As NotesDocument
 Dim intCount As Integer
' Load recipient's array with application administrators
 Dim aRecipients(2)
 aRecipients(0)="Samuel Hatter"
 aRecipients(1)="Wyatt Hatter"
 aRecipients(2)="Leslee Hatter"
' Prepare Memo document
 Set ndocMail=nsS.CurrentDatabase.CreateDocument
 ndocMail.Subject="Template Check Agent Summary " & Date$ & " @ " & Time$
 Set nrtfMailItem = New NotesRichTextItem(ndocMail,"Body")
' Get Directory object on current server
 Set ndirDirectory = nsS.GetDbDirectory( nsS.CurrentDatabase.Server )
 Set ndbCDatabase = ndirDirectory.GetFirstDatabase( TEMPLATE )
 If ndbCDatabase Is Nothing Then
   Call nrtfMailItem.AppendText("No Templates were found on " &
   ↪nsS.CurrentDatabase.Server)
   Call ndocMail.Send(False, aRecipients)
   Exit Sub
 End If
 Call nrtfMailItem.AppendText("The following templates were found on " &
 ↪nsS.CurrentDatabase.Server & " :")
 Call nrtfMailItem.Addnewline(2)
 Do While Not ndbCDatabase Is Nothing
```

```
 intCount=intCount+1
 Call nrtfMailItem.AddNewLine(1)
 Call nrtfMailItem.AppendText(ndbCDatabase.Title &
➥" (" & ndbCdatabase.FilePath & ")")
 Set ndbCDatabase = ndirDirectory.GetNextDatabase
Loop
Call nrtfMailItem.Addnewline(2)
Call nrtfMailItem.AppendText(Trim$(Str$(intCount)) &
➥" templates were found.")
Call ndocMail.Send(False,aRecipients)
```

GetEnvironmentString

```
valueV = nsNotesSession.GetEnvironmentString(strName, intSystem)
```

GetEnvironment
String

strName	Required	$

The name of the environment variable to retrieve.

intSystem	Optional	%

If the environment variable is a system variable, such as NAMES, pass TRUE. Otherwise, pass FALSE (the default) to retrieve nonsystem variables. When this parameter is FALSE, the strName parameter is prepended with $, which is how user-defined environment variables are stored.

This useful method returns a variant containing the value of the specified string environment variable if it is found in the Notes initialization (notes.ini) file. If the method is called in a script executing on a workstation, the local notes.ini file is read. If the script is executed on a server, the server's notes.ini file is read if the user executing the script has the authority to read it. For more information on Notes security and running agents, see the Domino Administration Help database.

```
'The following example demonstrates installing a database
'via a button in an e-mail message
 On Error Goto Errhandler
 Dim nsS As New NotesSession
 Dim nwsWs As New NotesUiWorkspace
 Dim ndocMemo As NotesDocument
 Dim intSuccess As Integer, intCount As Integer
' Create mail memo to send to administrator to track who has successfully
' installed the application
 Set ndocMemo=nsS.CurrentDatabase.CreateDocument
 Dim nrtfBody As New NotesRichTextItem(ndocMemo, "Body")
 ndocMemo.Subject= "CMGR Install Summary " & Date$ & " @ " & Time$
 Dim varDataDir As Variant
 Dim strAppDir As String
 strAppDir="\CMGR\"
 varAppDir=nsS.GetEnvironmentString("Directory",True)
 Dim nrtfItem As NotesRichtextItem
 Dim neoFile As NotesEmbeddedObject
 Set nrtfItem=nwsWs.CurrentDocument.Document.GetFirstItem("Body")
 Call nrtfBody.AppendText("The following database(s) were installed:")
 Call nrtfBody.AddNewLine(1)
 Forall neo In nrtfItem.EmbeddedObjects
  Call neo.ExtractFile(varDataDir & strAppDir & neo.Source)
  Call nrtfBody.AddNewLine(1)
  Call nrtfBody.AppendText("-> " & neo.Source)
  intCount%=intCount%+1
 End Forall
 Call nrtfBody.AddNewLine(2)
```

continued >>

continued >>
```
Call nrtfBody.AppendText( Trim$(Str$(intCount)) & " database(s) were
➥installed.")
Call ndocMemo.Send(False,nwsWs.CurrentDocument.Document.From(0))
Exit Sub

Errhandler:
  Resume Next
```

GetEnvironmentValue

GetEnvironment
Value
```
valueV = nsNotesSession.GetEnvironmentValue(strName, intSystem)
```

strName	Required	$

The name of the environment variable to retrieve.

intSystem	Optional	%

If the environment variable is a system variable, such as NAMES, pass TRUE. Otherwise, pass FALSE (the default) to retrieve nonsystem variables. When this parameter is FALSE, the strName parameter is prepended with $, which is how user-defined environment variables are stored.

This method returns a variant containing the value of the specified numeric environment variable if it is found in the Notes initialization (notes.ini) file. If the method is called in script executing on a workstation, the local notes.ini file is read. If the script is executed on a server, the server's notes.ini file is read if the user executing the script has the authority to read it. For more information Notes security and running agents, see the Domino Administration Help database.

New

New
Used to instantiate a new *NotesSession* object.

SetEnvironmentVar

SetEnvironment
Var
```
Call nsnotesSession.SetEnvironmentVar(strName, varValue, intIsSystem)
```

strName	Required	$

The name of the environment variable to set. If the variable doesn't exist in notes.ini, it will be created.

varValue	Required	?

The value to write to the environment variable.

intIsSystem	Optional	%

If the environment variable being updated is a user-defined variable (prepended with $), set this parameter to TRUE. If it's a system variable, set this parameter to FALSE or omit it.

This method allows you to update existing environment variables or add new ones to the notes.ini file (the preferences file on a Mac). This gives you a way to persistently store data. On a server, calling this method results in an attempt to write to the notes.ini file on the server. (The ability to do this is dictated by the Agent Manager and the OS.) On a workstation, this method writes to the local notes.ini file. For more information on security as it pertains to writing to notes.ini files, see the Domino Administration Help database.

```
' The following example demonstrates setting a default
' address city, state and ZIP
On Error Goto Errhandler
```

```
Dim nsS As New NotesSession
Dim strTemp As String
strTemp=Inputbox("Enter the default address", "Default Address","")
Call nsS.SetEnvironmentVar("DefaultAddress",strTemp)
strTemp=Inputbox("Enter the default city", "Default City","")
Call nsS.SetEnvironmentVar("DefaultCity",strTemp)
strTemp=Inputbox("Enter the default state", "Default State","")
Call nsS.SetEnvironmentVar("DefaultState",strTemp)
strTemp=Inputbox("Enter the default zip", "Default Zip","")
Call nsS.SetEnvironmentVar("DefaultZip",strTemp)
Exit Sub

Errhandler:
Resume Next
```

UpdateProcessedDoc

```
Call nsNotesSession.UpdateProcessedDoc(ndocDocument)
```

Update
ProcessedDoc

ndocDocument   Required   O.Ref.

The document to mark as processed by the agent.

This method was designed to be used with agents that use the "If Documents Have
Been Created or Modified" trigger and either the UnprocessedDocuments,
UnprocessedFTSearch, or UnprocessedSearch collections (all in *NotesDatabase*) to get
the newly-created and newly-modified documents. Calling this method on each document that is a member of one of the aforementioned collections ensures that the next
time the agent runs, marked documents will be ignored. If this method isn't used to
mark documents that haven't been processed, these three properties will return all documents matching that criteria—even the previously processed documents. On a final
note, UpdateProcessedDoc marks documents as processed only for the specific agent
that called it. Because this method is agent-specific, using UpdateProcessedDoc in one
agent has no effect on the documents processed by another agent.

Example

```
'This simple example demonstrates using several
' properties of the session class
 Dim nsS As New NotesSession
 Dim nwsUIWorkspace As New notesUiWorkspace
 Dim ndbLookupDb As NotesDatabase
 Dim intAuth As Integer
 intAuth=False
 Forall elem In nwsUIWorkspace.CurrentDocument.Document.AuthUsers
   If elem = nsS.CommonUserName Then
     intAuth=True
     Exit Forall
   End If
 End Forall
 If intAuth Then
   Set ndbLookupDb=nsS.GetDatabase(nsS.CurrentDatabase.Server,"Sales.nsf")
   ' insert other meaningful code here
 Else
   MsgBox("You are not authorized to use this agent", 16,
   ➥"Authorization Error")
 End If
```

4.5x 4.6x 5.0 NotesTimer

The *NotesTimer* class is new as of Notes release 4.5. It lets you trigger an event every *n* seconds (where *n* is an integer value) that can be scripted.

NotesSession
  └ NotesTimer

LotusScript Syntax

To declare a new *NotesTimer* object, you use the `New` method.

```
Dim ntmrTimer as New NotesTimer(intInterval strComment)
```

or

```
Set ntmrTimer  = New NotesTimer(intInterval, strComment)
```

LotusScript Parameters

intInterval	Required	%

This parameter sets the `Interval` property and represents the number of seconds that can elapse before the event handler for the `timer` object is called.

strComment	Optional	$

`strComment` allows you to enter information that describes the purpose of the timer. If a comment is entered, it sets the `Comment` property of the *NotesTimer* object.

NotesTimer Properties

Comment	R/W	$

Comment
```
To Get: strComment = ntmrNotesTimer.Comment
To set: ntmrNotesTimer.Comment=strComment
```

If a comment was entered as a parameter, this property returns the comment as a string.

Enabled	R/W	T/F

Enabled
```
To get: intEnabled = ntmrNotesTimer.Enabled
To set: ntmrNotesTimer.Enabled = intEnabled
```

When set to `TRUE` (the default), the timer will generate an `Alarm` event based on the *NotesTimer* interval. When set to `FALSE`, the timer is disabled and will not generate an `Alarm` event.

Interval	R/W	%

Interval
```
To get: intInterval = ntmrNotesTimer.Interval
To set: ntmrNotesTimer.Interval = intInterval
```

The `Interval` property determines how many seconds must elapse before an `Alarm` event is generated.

NotesTimer Methods

NotesTimer has only one method, `New`, as discussed above in the "LotusScript Syntax" section.

NotesTimer Events

Alarm

Alarm(Source as NotesTimer)   Alarm

Source   O.Ref.

The `Alarm` event is generated when the time specified for the *NotesTimer* interval has elapsed.

Remarks

In most cases, you will want to declare the *NotesTimer* object at the global level so that the timer is not destroyed when a subroutine exits. For example, if you declare a timer object in the `PostOpen` event of a form, the *NotesTimer* object will not be available outside the `PostOpen` event. To declare the *NotesTimer* object globally, simply use the `Dim` statement without the `New` syntax at the global level. Then, use the `Set` statement in your code to initialize the object.

One you have initialized the *NotesTimer* object, you can use the `On Event` statement to create an event handler that responds to the `Alarm` event. Your event handler should be written as a user subroutine.

Also keep in mind that the interval you have set for the timer is not guaranteed. Other events involving script and other applications might cause delays in firing the event.

Example

As just noted, you should normally declare a *NotesTimer* object globally in the Declarations section of a script so that the timer is not destroyed when a subroutine ends. The following example demonstrates code in several sections of a form that is being used as a "splash screen."

```
' This code would be placed in the Declarations section of a form
Dim ntmrSplashTimer As NotesTimer
%INCLUDE "lsconst.lss"

' This code should be placed in the PostOpen event of a form
' as indicated below
Sub Postopen(Source As Notesuidocument)
  Set ntmrSplashTimer = New NotesTimer(5, "Splash screen timer")
  On Event Alarm From ntmrSplashTimer
  Call SplashTimerHandler
End Sub
```
continued >>

continued >>
```
'This code is the event handler
Sub SplashTimerHandler
  Dim nuiwsWorkspace as New NotesUIWorkspace
  Call nuiwsWorkspace.CurrentDocument.Close
End Sub
```

NotesView

The *NotesView* class represents the views or folders contained in the *NotesDatabase*. By accessing the *NotesView* objects, you can access the *NotesDocuments* contained in them. (Although this isn't the only way to establish a handle on *NotesDocument* objects, it is a frequently used method.) The *NotesView* provides a mechanism to display the *NotesDocuments* through the user interface and provides a format to programmatically query the *NotesDocuments* through the back end. Essentially, *NotesViews* provide an "on-demand" relational and tabular format to the nonrelational back-end data store of Domino/Lotus Notes.

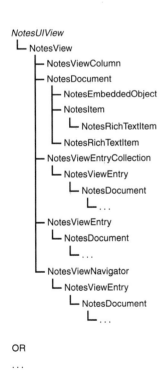

continued >>

LotusScript Syntax

To access the *NotesView* object, you can establish a handle on the parent *NotesDatabase* object that contains it and then exploit the `GetView` method (▶ 104) or the `Views` property (▶ 97). You can also use the `ParentView` property of a *NotesDocument* (▶ 135). When using the `GetView` method of the *NotesDatabase* object, you can access a particular *NotesView* using either the view name or its alias (synonym). When running on a server, the public views and folders are available. When running locally, personal views and folders are also available. To access all the views or folders contained in a database, you can use the `Views` property. This method returns an array of public views and folders and personal views and folders if running locally.

If accessing a *NotesDocument* that was retrieved from within a view or folder, you can use the `ParentView` property of the current *NotesDocument*.

NotesView Properties

Aliases   R $

`To get: strAliases = nvwNotesView.`**`Aliases`**   Aliases

This property returns all the aliases, or synonyms, for the specified view as an array of strings. Since a view can contain multiple aliases, they are all returned by this property. The displayed view name, which is the first name in the view's list of names, is not returned because by definition it isn't an alias—it's the actual view name. (It can be accessed through the `Name` property of the *NotesView* class (▶ 285).) If there are no alias names for the specified view, this property returns the constant `ISEMPTY`. However, it's a good idea to always use aliases when designing applications. This allows you to modify the view's name (which determines how it's displayed to the user) at any time and not potentially break the existing application because your code programmatically references the alias. This also provides a simpler name to reference when you're accessing the view programmatically.

5.0 AllEntries   R   O.Ref.

`To get: nvecNotesViewEntryCollection = nvwNotesView.`**`AllEntries`**   AllEntries

This property returns all the entries in the view. The ability to reference entries in *NotesView* is a new feature of Release 5.0. Prior to that release, you could access documents contained in views, but you couldn't view specific information such as categories or totals. *NotesViewEntryCollection* allows you to navigate through the documents contained in the current view and the currently selected document's respective siblings, children, and parent. In addition, you can access document information to determine the document category and category total, as well as whether a document is unread or has a conflict.

The following example builds a collection of all the entries in the All view and then builds some reporting information on the entry types contained in the view.

```
Dim ns As New NotesSession
Dim nvw As NotesView
Dim nvec As NotesViewEntryCollection
```

continued >>

continued >>

```
Dim lngCount As Long
Dim intCatCount As Integer
Dim intDocCount As Integer
Set nvw = ns.currentdatabase.Getview("All")
Set nvec = nvw.AllEntries
For lngCount = 1 To nvec.count
  Set nve = nvec.GetNthEntry( lngCount )
  If nve.IsCategory Then
   intCatCount = intCatCount + 1
  End If
  If nve.IsDocument Then
   intDocCount = intDocCount + 1
  End If
Next
Msgbox "Entries: " & Str$(nvec.Count), 32, nvw.Name & " contains:"
Msgbox "Categories: " & Str$(intCatCount), 32, nvw.Name & " contains:"
Msgbox "Documents: " & Str$(intDocCount), 32, nvw.Name & " contains:"
```

AutoUpdate   R/W   T/F

AutoUpdate

```
To get: intAutoupdate = nvwNotesView.AutoUpdate
To set: nvwNotesView.AutoUpdate = intAutoupdate
```

This property controls whether the order and pointers for the view being rendered to the user in the front end are automatically updated whenever a change occurs to the documents contained in the view through the back end. TRUE indicates that the view is automatically updated, and FALSE indicates that the view is not automatically updated. This property defaults to FALSE. This doesn't represent the actual refresh of the screen that the user can see (simulated by pressing F9 or calling the Refresh method of the *NotesView* (▶ 293)). It only updates the order of the documents as they are stored in the back-end view. It's important that the order be current (and thus any pointers to *NotesDocuments*) when acting against the documents programmatically via the back end. However, enabling this property negatively affects performance since the server or client must refresh the index and pointers whenever a document is modified. Therefore, it's generally better to set this property to FALSE (the default), especially for larger views, unless you're interactively acting against and modifying the *NotesDocuments* and their order is imperative for the code to run successfully.

5.0 BackgroundColor   R   %

Background
Color

```
To get: intBackcolor = nvwNotesView.BackgroundColor
```

This property returns an integer constant representing the background color of the specified view. The constant values returned are available to the FontColor property of the *NotesViewColumn* class (▶ 300) and the NotesColor property of the *NotesRichTextStyle* class (▶ 255). Here are the allowable values for this property:

Constant Value	Integer Value	RGB Color
COLOR_BLACK	0	0, 0, 0
COLOR_BLUE	4	0, 0, 255
COLOR_CYAN	5	0, 255, 255
COLOR_DARK_BLUE	10	0, 0, 128
COLOR_DARK_CYAN	11	0, 128, 128
COLOR_DARK_GREEN	9	0, 128, 0
COLOR_DARK_MAGENTA	13	128, 0, 128
COLOR_DARK_RED	8	128, 0, 0

Constant Value	Integer Value	RGB Color
COLOR_DARK_YELLOW	12	128, 128, 0
COLOR_GRAY	14	128, 128, 128
COLOR_GREEN	3	0, 255, 0
COLOR_LIGHT_GRAY	15	192, 192, 192
COLOR_MAGENTA	7	255, 0, 255
COLOR_RED	2	255, 0, 0
COLOR_WHITE	1	255, 255, 255
COLOR_YELLOW	6	255, 255, 0

5.0 ColumnCount   R   %

```
To get: intColcount = nvwNotesView.ColumnCount
```
ColumnCount

This property returns the number of columns in the view as an integer value.

Columns   R   O.Ref.

```
To get: nvcNotesViewColumns = nvwNotesView.Columns
```
Columns

This property returns an array of *NotesViewColums* that are contained in the specified view. The order of the columns in the *NotesView* corresponds to the numerical order of the array. Since the returned value is an array, the first element is referenced as 0 (assuming Option Base 0). Therefore, the first column is element 0, the second column is element 1, and so on. After collecting the array of columns, you can reference each *NotesViewColumn* individually (▶ 297).

The following code snippet displays the number of columns that exist in the All view and then displays their titles in a message box.

```
Dim ns As New NotesSession
Dim nvw As NotesView
Dim nvc As NotesViewColumn
Set nvw = ns.currentdatabase.Getview("All")
Dim iLoop As Integer
Msgbox "This view has " & Str$(Ubound(nvw.columns) + 1) & " columns."
For iLoop% = 0 To Ubound(nvw.columns)
  Set nvc = nvw.Columns( iLoop% )
  Msgbox "The title for column " & Str$(iLoop% + 1) & " is " & nvc.Title, _
  ➥32, "View Titles..."
Next
```

Created   R   O.Ref.

```
To get: ndtCreated = nvwNotesView.Created
```
Created

This property returns the variant date value for the date on which the view was created or saved to disk in the current database.

5.0 HeaderLines   R   %

```
To get: intHeaderlines = nvwNotesView.HeaderLines
```
HeaderLines

This property returns the number of lines as an integer in the view's header (title). The value for this property must be between 1 and **5**.

IsCalendar   R   T/F

```
To get: intIscalendar = nvwNotesView.IsCalendar
```
IsCalendar

This property returns a Boolean value indicating whether the specified view is set to display its contents in the calendar style. TRUE indicates that it has been designed to use the calendar style. FALSE indicates that it will display as the standard outline style.

5.0 IsCategorized   R   T/F

IsCategorized   To get: intIscategorized = nvwNotesView.**IsCategorized**

This property indicates whether the current view is categorized. TRUE indicates that the view is categorized. FALSE indicates that it is not. This property is more specifically determined by the columns contained in the view since the *NotesViewColumn* is where categorization is specified.

5.0 IsConflict   R   T/F

IsConflict   To get: intIsconflict = nvwNotesView.**IsConflict**

This property indicates whether conflict checking is enabled if the current view style is calendar. Conflict checking is used in Calendaring and Scheduling to warn the user of potential appointment and meeting conflicts so that multiple calendar events are not scheduled at the same time. TRUE indicates that conflict checking is enabled for the calendar view. FALSE indicates that conflict checking is disabled.

IsDefaultView   R   T/F

IsDefaultView   To get: intIsdefaultview = nvwNotesView.**IsDefaultView**

This property indicates whether the specified view is the default view for the *NotesDatabase* in which it resides. TRUE indicates that it is the default view. FALSE indicates that it is not. Every database must have a default view. Often, this is the database that is most frequently used or that contains the most common data that would be referenced by the users.

IsFolder   R   T/F

IsFolder   To get: intIsfolder = nvwNotesView.**IsFolder**

This property indicates whether the specified view is a folder. Views and folders appear to the user as significantly different design elements because of the nature of how they are used. However, except for some minor differences, they are essentially the same. Folders contain the same design elements, but documents can be added to and removed from folders on demand. Typically, these are used to categorize documents and are stored locally on individuals' file systems. An obvious example of the way folders are used is in each user's e-mail database. (In fact, the InBox is actually a folder!)

5.0 IsHierarchical   R   T/F

IsHierarchical   To get: intIshierarchical = nvwNotesView.**IsHierarchical**

This property indicates whether the documents being displayed are being shown in their respective response hierarchy. When you're designing with the view client, this property is located on the Options tab as "Show response documents in a hierarchy." TRUE indicates that the view is set to display documents in a hierarchy. FALSE indicates that they will not display in their response hierarchy.

5.0 IsModified   R   T/F

IsModified   To get: intIsmodified = nvwNotesView.**IsModified**

This property indicates whether the view has been modified. TRUE indicates that the view has been modified. FALSE indicates that it has not.

5.0 IsPrivate   R   T/F

```
To get: intIsprivate = nvwNotesView.IsPrivate
```

This property indicates whether the current *NotesView* is set as a private view. TRUE indicates that it is a private view. FALSE indicates that it is not private and is therefore public.

LastModified   R   Time/date variant

```
To get: varTimedateVar = nvwNotesView.LastModified
```

This property returns the date that the view was last modified as a time/date variant.

Name   R $

```
To get: strName = nvwNotesView.Name
```

This property returns the first name of the specified view as a string. The value returned is always the displayed string name or the first name if the view has synonyms or aliases.

Parent   R   O.Ref.

```
To get: ndbNotesDatabase = nvwNotesView.Parent
```

This property returns a handle on the *NotesDatabase* object that contains the *NotesView*.

ProtectReaders   R/W   T/F

```
To set: nvwNotesView.ProtectReaders = intProtectreaders
To get: intProtectreaders = nvwNotesView.ProtectReaders
```

This property sets or returns the property that protects the $READERS field items from being overwritten when the database is replicated. TRUE indicates that the items are protected during replication. FALSE indicates that the items are not protected during replication.

Readers   R/W $

```
To set: nvwNotesView.Readers = strReadersarray
To get: strReadersarray = nvwNotesView.Readers
```

This property sets or returns the values contained in the $Readers field for the specified view. If this value is set to Nothing (""), there is no reader restriction, so all users can view the contents of the view. Likewise, setting this value to a single value or multiple values restricts all users, groups, and servers from accessing the contents of the view unless they are specifically contained in the value of this property. When setting the value of this property, note that the new values replace the existing values; they are not appended. Therefore, be sure to read the existing values and include them in the new string array if you want to append new values to the Readers property.

5.0 RowLines   R   %

```
To get: intRowlines = nvwNotesView.RowLines
```

This property returns the number of lines in each row in the specified view. The range allowed for this property is 1 to 9. The default value is 1.

5.0 Spacing   R   %

```
To get: intSpacing = nvwNotesView.Spacing
```

This property returns an integer constant that represents the spacing between the rows in the view. Here are the possible values returned for this property:

Constant Value	Integer Value	Description
SPACING_SINGLE	0	Single-spaced
SPACING_ONE_POINT_25	1	1 1/4-spaced
SPACING_ONE_POINT_50	2	1 1/2-spaced
SPACING_ONE_POINT_75	3	1 3/4-spaced
SPACING_DOUBLE	4	Double-spaced

5.0 TopLevelEntryCount   R   %

TopLevel
EntryCount

To get: `intEntries = nvwNotesView.`**`TopLevelEntryCount`**

This property returns the integer number of top-level entries contained in the view. This property is useful when the documents contained in the view are set to show response documents in a hierarchy.

UniversalID   R $

UniversalID

To get: `strUnid = nvwNotesView.`**`UniversalID`**

This property returns the view's Universal ID. The Universal ID is the unique identifier prevalent throughout Domino/LotusNotes that denotes design elements and documents. The Universal ID is a 32-character combination of letters and numbers stored as a special type of text and is consistent among all replicas of the database.

NotesView Methods

Clear

Clear

`Call nvwNotesView.`**`Clear`**

This method clears full-text search filtering for the specific view. When you perform searches, subsequent searches continue to refine previous searches. Calling this method resets the search filter so you can start a new search.

5.0 CreateViewNav

CreateViewNav

`Set nvnNotesViewNavigator = nvwNotesView.`**`CreateViewNav`**

The method creates a new *NotesViewNavigator* (▶ 11) for all the entries contained in the view. The entries contained in the *NotesViewNavigator* include information such as category, totals, view and position. Even if the documents displayed in the view have been filtered by the full-text engine, this method still returns all the entries contained in the view.

5.0 CreateViewNavFrom

CreateView
NavFrom

`Set nvnNotesViewNavigator = nvwNotesView.`**`CreateViewNavFrom`**
➥`(navigatorobject)`

navigatorobject   Required   O.Ref.

The *NotesDocument* or *NotesViewEntry* that signifies the first entry in the *NotesViewNavigator*.

This method returns a handle to the *NotesViewNavigator*, beginning with the first entry specified as the parameter when calling this method. Even if the documents displayed in the view have been filtered by the full-text engine, this method still returns all the entries.

5.0 CreateViewNavFromCategory

```
Set nvnNotesViewNavigator = nvwNotesView.CreateViewNavFromCategory
➥(category)
```

category	Required	O.Ref.

The name of the category contained in the view.

This method returns a handle to a new *NotesViewNavigator,* beginning with the first entry contained in the specified category. Even if the documents displayed in the view have been filtered by the full-text engine, this method still returns all the entries.

5.0 CreateViewNavFromChildren

```
Set nvnNotesViewNavigator = nvwNotesView.CreateViewNavFromChildren
➥(navigatorobject)
```

navigatorobject	Required	O.Ref.

The *NotesDocument* or *NotesViewEntry* that represents the parent entry.

This method returns a handle to a new *NotesViewNavigator* for all the immediate child documents of the entry passed as the parameter. Even if the documents displayed in the view have been filtered by the full-text engine, this method still returns all the entries.

5.0 CreateViewNavFromDescendants

```
Set nvnNotesViewNavigator = nvwNotesView.CreateViewNavFromDescendants
➥(navigatorobject)
```

navigatorobject	Required	O.Ref.

The *NotesDocument* or *NotesViewEntry* that represents the parent entry.

This method returns a handle to the *NotesViewNavigator* for all the descendent documents of the entry passed as the parameter. Even if the documents displayed in the view have been filtered by the full-text engine, this method still returns all the entries.

FTSearch

```
lngDocs = nvwNotesView.FTSearch(strQuery, intMaxdocs)
```

strQuery	Required	$

A string representing the rules for the full-text query. These rules are outlined next.

intMaxdocs	Required	%

The maximum number of *NotesDocuments* to return from the query. Set this parameter to 0 to return all matching documents.

This method performs a full-text search of all the documents contained in the view. Only the documents that match the rules specified in the full-text search query are displayed in the view. This method returns a long value that represents the number of documents that matched the query string.

You can test to see whether the database is full-text indexed prior to performing this method by testing the IsFTIndexed property of the *NotesDatabase* object (▶ 94). You can create an index for the Notes database by calling the UpdateFTIndex method of the *NotesDatabase* object (▶ 111). However, the database doesn't need to be full-text indexed in order for you to perform a search against the database. Nevertheless, the search is much more slow and inefficient if the database isn't indexed.

The result of the full-text search is a collection of documents that are sorted in descending order of relevance. In other words, the document with the most hits (highest relevance) is first, and the document with the fewest hits (lowest relevance) is last. You can access the relevance score using the `FTSearchScore` property of the *NotesDocument* (▶ 132).

When searches are performed against the documents in the view, each subsequent search refines the result set from the previous search, thereby searching against the previous search. You can reset the search so that the view displays all the documents by calling the `Clear` method of the *NotesView* (▶ 286).

Although this method works on *NotesDocuments* located in the *NotesView*, you can also apply this method to the *NotesDatabase* and *NotesDocumentCollection*.

As you would expect when using a legitimate search engine, the rules for defining the search allow for building search criteria using Boolean values and specific operators. Here are the rules for using these operators:

Plain text. For simple searches, you can enter the word or phrase to search for. You don't need to include quotation marks, except when you're searching for specific keywords or reserved operators. Placing quotes around the words or phrases ensures that they are treated as literal search criteria and not as operators. These rules are similar to typical searching standards. You can always put the text in quotes regardless to ensure that it won't be treated as an operator. When programmatically defining the search criteria in LotusScript, use double quotes so that the quotes are passed as part of the literal search criteria.

Wildcards. Wildcards are supported when you perform searches. Typical to most search engines, they are represented by the ? or * characters. Use ? to allow for any single character in its respective position and * to match multiple (or no) characters in their respective position in the word.

Hyphenated words. These are used to find pairs of words that are hyphenated together as a single word or separated by a space.

Logical operators. These enable you to build more-complex searches (often referred to as Boolean searches) by using logical operators to further restrict or expand the search algorithm. The allowed operator keywords and their respective symbols (listed in order of precedence) are `not` or `!`, `and` or `&`, `accrue` or `,`, and `or` or `¦`.

Proximity operators. Proximity operators enable you to search for words that are close to one another. That is, you can see if the words are located in proximity to each other by using the operators `near`, `sentence`, and `paragraph`.

Exactcase operators. The exactcase operator enables you to restrict the search to match a specified case.

Termweight operators. The termweight *n* operator enables you to modify the relevance scores of the search by defining the relevance ranking. This is done by specifying a value for *n* between `0` and `100` representing the relevance score.

Field operators. This is a powerful capability of the Domino/Lotus Notes search engine. This feature lets you perform a search based on a specific field. The syntax for this search is `FIELD` *fieldname operator*. *fieldname* is the name of the *NotesItem* that you are performing the operation against. The allowed operators are `contains`, `=`, `>`, and `<`. Using `contains` is helpful when you're searching rich text fields. You can't combine operators as in normal programming (such as `>=`). Therefore, you must build a more-complex search algorithm using the `or` operator for multiple criteria. You may also need to help define the search's precedence order using parentheses.

GetAllDocumentsByKey

```
Set ndcNotesDocumentCollection = nvwNotesView.GetAllDocumentsByKey
➥(keyarray, intExact)
```

keyarray   Required $, %, &, #, !

A value or array in which each element corresponds to a sorted column in the view. (The first element corresponds to the first sorted column, the second element corresponds to the second sorted column, and so on.)

intExact   Optional   T/F

Indicates whether the key and value stored in the view column must be an exact match. TRUE indicates an exact match. FALSE indicates that a partial match is allowed.

This method locates documents based on the value(s) stored in the sorted column(s) in the *NotesView*. This method returns a *NotesDocumentCollection* of all the documents whose column values match those specified in the keyarray. If no documents match the keyarray, the collection is empty.

The lookup can be based on a single value. In this case, only one element is specified in the keyarray, and its value is compared against the first sorted column in the view. The lookup can also be based on multiple values specified in the keyarray, in which case the elements must correspond to each sorted column in the view.

Obviously, when you're using the GetAllDocumentsByKey method, at least one column in the view must be sorted. Since this method returns all the documents that match the keyarray criteria, you can then navigate through the documents by using the GetFirstDocument, GetNextDocument, and GetLastDocument methods of the *NotesDocumentCollection* (▶ 154).

If you need to return only a single document instead of all the documents that match the search criteria, you can call the GetDocumentByKey method of the *NotesView* (▶ 290).

5.0 GetAllEntriesByKey

```
Set nvecNotesViewEntryCollection = nvwNotesView.GetAllEntriesByKey
➥(keyarray, intExact)
```

keyarray   Required $, %, $, #, !

A value or array in which each element corresponds to a sorted column in the view. (The first element corresponds to the first sorted column, the second element corresponds to the second sorted column, and so on.)

intExact   Optional   T/F

Indicates whether the key and value stored in the view column must be an exact match. TRUE indicates an exact match. FALSE indicates that a partial match is allowed.

This method locates entries based on the value(s) stored in the sorted column(s) in the *NotesView*. This method returns a *NotesViewEntryCollection* of all the entries whose column values match those specified in the keyarray. If no documents match the keyarray, the collection is empty.

The lookup can be based on a single value. In this case, only one element is specified in the keyarray, and its value is compared against the first sorted column in the view. The lookup can also be based on multiple values specified in the keyarray, in which case the elements must correspond to each sorted column in the view.

Obviously, when you're using the GetAllEntriesByKey method, at least one column in the view must be sorted. In order to locate just one entry or the first entry in the *NotesView* that matches the criteria, use the GetEntryByKey method of the *NotesView* (▶ 290).

GetChild

`Set ndocNotesDocument = nvwNotesView.`**`GetChild`**`(NotesDocument)`

NotesDocument   Required   O.Ref.

A *NotesDocument* displayed in the view that has at least one response document.

This method returns a handle on the first response document of the parent *NotesDocument* passed as a parameter when calling the method. Once you have established a handle on the first response document, you can navigate through the remaining response documents as they appear in the view by using the `GetNextSibling` or `GetChild` methods of the *NotesView* (▶ 290). In addition, you can access a document's response documents using the `Responses` property of the *NotesDocument* (▶ 135).

If the view has already been filtered by calling the `FTSearch` method, the `GetChild` method simply returns the next document as displayed in the view.

GetDocumentByKey

`Set ndocNotesDocument = nvwNotesView.`**`GetDocumentByKey`**`(keyarray, intExact)`

---

keyarray   Required $,%, &, #,!

A value or array in which each element corresponds to a sorted column in the view. (The first element corresponds to the first sorted column, the second element corresponds to the second sorted column, and so on.)

intExact   Optional   T/F

Indicates whether the key and value stored in the view column must be an exact match. `TRUE` indicates an exact match. `FALSE` indicates that a partial match is allowed.

This method locates the *NotesDocument* based on the value(s) stored in the sorted column(s) in the *NotesView*. This method returns a handle to the *NotesDocument* whose column values match those specified in the `keyarray`. If no document matches the `keyarray`, the *NotesDocument* is `Nothing`.

The lookup can be based on a single value. In this case, only one element is specified in the `keyarray`, and its value is compared against the first sorted column in the view. The lookup can also be based on multiple values specified in the `keyarray`, in which case the elements must correspond to each sorted column in the view.

Obviously, when you're using `GetDocumentByKey` method, at least one column in the view must be sorted. Since this method returns a document that matches the `keyarray` criteria, you can then navigate through the other documents contained in the *NotesView* by using the `GetNextDocument` method of the *NotesView* (▶ 291).

If you need to return all the documents that match the search criteria, you can call the `GetAllDocumentsByKey` method of the *NotesView* (▶ 289).

5.0 GetEntryByKey

`Set nveNotesViewEntry = nvwNotesView.`**`GetEntryByKey`**`(keyarray, intExact)`

---

keyarray   Required $, %, $, #, !

A value or array in which each element corresponds to a sorted column in the view. (The first element corresponds to the first sorted column, the second element corresponds to the second sorted column, and so on.)

intExact   Optional   T/F

Indicates whether the key and value stored in the view column must be an exact match. `TRUE` indicates an exact match. `FALSE` indicates that a partial match is allowed.

This method locates the view entry based on the value(s) stored in the sorted column(s) in the *NotesView*. This method returns a *NotesViewEntry* whose column value matches those specified in the keyarray. If no document matches the keyarray, the collection is empty.

The lookup can be based on a single value. In this case, only one element is specified in the keyarray, and its value is compared against the first sorted column in the view. The lookup can also be based on multiple values specified in the keyarray, in which case the elements must correspond to each sorted column in the view.

Obviously, when using the GetEntryByKey method, at least one column in the view must be sorted. In order to locate all the entries in the *NotesView* that match the criteria, use the GetAllEntriesByKey method of the *NotesView* (▶ 289).

GetFirstDocument

```
Set ndocNotesDocument = nvwNotesView.GetFirstDocument
```
GetFirst
Document

This method sets the *NotesDocument* to the first document in the *NotesView*. If no documents are contained in the *NotesView*, this method returns Nothing. The first document is the document that appears at the top of the view when the view is displayed through the user interface.

After establishing a handle on the first document in the view, you can navigate through the view by using the GetNextDocument and GetPrevDocument methods of the *NotesView* (▶ 279).

GetLastDocument

```
Set ndocNotesDocument = nvwNotesView.GetLastDocument
```
GetLast
Document

This method sets the *NotesDocument* to the last document in the *NotesView*. If no documents are contained in the *NotesView*, this method returns Nothing. The last document is the document that appears at the bottom of the view when the view is displayed through the user interface.

After establishing a handle on the first document in the view, you can navigate through the view by using the GetNextDocument and GetPrevDocument methods of the *NotesView* (▶ 279).

GetNextDocument

```
Set ndocNotesDocument = nvwNotesView.GetNextDocument (NotesDocument)
```
GetNext
Document

NotesDocument	Required	O.Ref.

A *NotesDocument* in the current view.

This method sets the *NotesDocument* to the next document in the *NotesView* immediately following the document passed as the parameter when calling the method. The next document in the view is determined regardless of whether the document is a parent, sibling, or response document. If there are no documents following the current document in the *NotesView*, this method returns Nothing.

Prior to calling the GetNextDocument method, you must establish a handle on an existing document in the view by using the GetFirstDocument, GetLastDocument, or GetDocumentByKey methods of the *NotesView* (▶ 279).

GetNextSibling

```
Set ndocNotesDocument = nvwNotesView.GetNextSibling (NotesDocument)
```
GetNextSibling

NotesDocument	Required	O.Ref.

A *NotesDocument* in the current view.

This method sets the *NotesDocument* to the document at the same hierarchy level in the *NotesView* immediately following the document passed as the parameter when calling this method. The next sibling returned is a main document if the parameter passed was a main document or a response document if the parameter passed was a response document. If the *NotesView* is categorized in addition to being sorted, the next sibling must share the same category as the original document passed when calling this method. If there are no more siblings following the current document in the *NotesView*, this method returns `Nothing`. Similarly, this method returns `Nothing` if the current document is the last main document in the view, the last main document of the current category, or the last response or response-to-response document of the parent document.

Prior to calling the `GetNextDocument` method, you must establish a handle on an existing document in the view by using the `GetFirstDocument` method, `GetLastDocument` method, or `GetDocumentByKey` method of the *NotesView* (▶ 279).

This method is useful when you're navigating through the main documents in a view that contains response documents and that is set to display response documents in a hierarchy. It's also useful when you're navigating through a parent document's response or response-to-response documents.

If the view has already been filtered by calling the `FTSearch` method, the `GetNextSibling` method simply returns the next document as displayed in the view, regardless of whether it is a parent document, response document, or response-to-response document.

GetNthDocument

GetNth
Document

`Set ndocNotesDocument = nvwNotesView.`**`GetNthDocument`**` (lngIndex)`

lngIndex	Required	&

The position of the *NotesDocument* in the *NotesView* to return. 1 indicates the first document, 2 indicates the second, and so on.

This method establishes a handle to the *NotesDocument* in the *NotesView* by its relative position specified by the `index` parameter. Only main documents (top-level parent documents) can be located by this method. If no documents are specified in the location of the *NotesView*, this method returns `Nothing`.

GetParentDocument

GetParent
Document

`Set ndocNotesDocument = nvwNotesView.`**`GetParentDocument`**` (NotesDocument)`

NotesDocument	Required	O.Ref.

NotesDocument in the current view.

This method sets the *NotesDocument* to the parent document of the *NotesDocument* passed as the parameter when calling the method. The *NotesDocument* returned could be a main document, response document, or response-to-response document. If there is no parent document to the current document the *NotesView*, this method returns `Nothing`.

You can also establish a handle on a document's parent document by using the `ParentDocumentUNID` property of the *NotesDocument* (▶ 134).

This method is useful when you're navigating through the main documents in a view that contains response documents and that is set to display response documents in a hierarchy. It's also useful when you're navigating through a parent document's response or response-to-response documents.

If the view has already been filtered by calling the `FTSearch` method, the `GetParentDocument` method simply returns the previous document as displayed in the view, regardless of whether it is a parent document, response document, or response-to-response document.

GetPrevDocument

```
Set ndocNotesDocument = nvwNotesView.GetPrevDocument (NotesDocument)
```

NotesDocument   **Required**   **O.Ref.**

A *NotesDocument* in the current view.

This method sets the *NotesDocument* to the previous document in the *NotesView* immediately preceding the document passed as the parameter when calling the method. The preceding document in the view is determined regardless of whether the document is a parent, sibling, or response document. If there are no documents preceding the current document in the *NotesView,* this method returns `Nothing`.

Prior to calling the `GetPrevDocument` method, you must establish a handle on an existing document in the view by using the `GetFirstDocument`, `GetLastDocument`, or `GetDocumentByKey` methods of the *NotesView* (▶ 279).

GetPrevSibling

```
Set ndocNotesDocument = nvwNotesView.GetPrevSibling (NotesDocument)
```

NotesDocument   **Required**   **O.Ref.**

A *NotesDocument* in the current view.

This method sets the *NotesDocument* to the document at the same hierarchy level in the *NotesView* immediately preceding the document passed as the parameter when calling the method. The previous sibling returned is a main document if the parameter passed was a main document or a response document if the parameter passed was a response document. If the *NotesView* is categorized in addition to being sorted, the previous sibling must share the same category as the original document passed when calling this method. If there are no more siblings preceding the current document in the *NotesView,* this method returns `Nothing`. Similarly, this method returns `Nothing` if the current document is the first main document in the view, the first main document of the current category, or the first response or response-to-response document of the parent document.

Prior to calling the `GetPrevSibling` method, you must establish a handle on an existing document in the view by using the `GetFirstDocument`, `GetLastDocument`, or `GetDocumentByKey` methods of the *NotesView* (▶ 279).

This method is useful when you're navigating through the main documents in a view that contains response documents and that is set to display response documents in a hierarchy. It's also useful when you're navigating through a parent document's response or response-to-response documents.

If the view has already been filtered by calling the `FTSearch` method, the `GetPrevSibling` method simply returns the previous document as displayed in the view, regardless of whether it is a parent document, response document, or response-to-response document.

Refresh

```
Call nvwNotesView.Refresh
```

This method refreshes (updates) the contents of the view with any changes that have occurred to the documents contained in this view because a handle on the *NotesView* was established or because the view was previously refreshed. Because the information displayed in the view is not always a real-time view of the documents contained in the database, calling the `Refresh` method ensures that the information displayed is current.

Remove

Remove   `Call nvwNotesView.Remove`

This method permanently deletes a view from the database. When calling this method, the user can delete views only if he or she has sufficient database access rights (ACL).

Remarks

The *NotesView* is one method that can be used to provide access to *NotesDocuments* contained in the *NotesDatabase*. There are several benefits to accessing documents from within a *NotesView*. First, the documents are already indexed, so this method is more efficient when accessing documents stored in the database. Of course, anytime you can optimize performance, especially when working with Domino/Lotus Notes, you should take advantage of it. Because the view is indexed, a particular document or multiple documents can be located by using a specific key. This ability to locate documents based on specific keys is important because you're working with nonrelational data. Also, the view can already contain the subset of documents you want to retrieve or act against (because of the view selection formula). In addition, the documents can already be sorted, and you can navigate through them in their response hierarchy. Finally, some of the *NotesItems* contained in the documents have already been formatted in the view and can be retrieved while respecting this predetermined format.

When accessing documents in a view, use the following methods to establish a handle on the required documents:

Method	Description
GetFirstDocument	Locates the first document in the view (determined by the view sort order).
GetNextDocument, GetNthDocument, or GetDocumentByKey	Locates a document based on the location of another document or by using a specific key.
GetLastDocument	Locates the last document in the view (determined by the view sort order).

Example

The following LotusScript example uses the Notes mail database to gather a list of all the tasks that the current user has scheduled. This example builds a document collection of all the documents in the view and then displays them to the user in a meaningful message box. This example shows the user a quick task list without making him open the mail database and navigate to the tasks in order to view the task information. The message box displays the current date and the number of tasks and then lists the tasks by status, date due, priority, and subject.

```
Dim ns As New NotesSession
Dim ndbMail As NotesDatabase
Dim nvwTask As NotesView
```

```
Dim ndocTask As NotesDocument
Dim intOverdue As Integer
Dim intCurrent As Integer
Dim intFuture As Integer
Dim strOverdue As String
Dim strCurrent As String
Dim strFuture As String
Dim strHead1 As String
Dim strHead2 As String
Dim strTask As String
Dim strPriority As String
'Build Task Information
Set ndbMail = ns.GetDatabase(ns.CurrentDatabase.Server,
➥"mail\bankesmail.nsf")
Set nvwTask = ndbMail.GetView("Tasks")
Set ndocTask=nvwTask.GetFirstDocument
If Not ndocTask Is Nothing Then
'Loop against all documents in task view
  Set ndocTask = nvwTask.GetFirstDocument
  While Not ( ndocTask Is Nothing )
  'Build array for each due state type
  'Due States: 0=Overdue, 1=Current, 2=Future, 8=Rejected, 9=Complete
  'Check for no importance value
   If ndocTask.Importance(0)="99" Then
     strPriority =" 4 "
   Else
     strPriority =" " & ndocTask.Importance(0) & " "
   End If
   'Build task lists for each status type
   Select Case Trim$(ndocTask.DueState(0))
   Case "0"
     Redim Preserve sOverdueList(intOverdue) As String
     If intOverdue = 0 Then strOverdue = "-OverDue-"
     strOverdue=strOverdue + Chr(10) & Chr(9) & _
     Format$(ndocTask.DueDateTime(0), "mm/dd/yy") & Chr(9) & _
     "    " & strPriority & Chr(9) & ndocTask.Subject(0)
     intOverdue = intOverdue + 1
   Case "1"
     Redim Preserve sCurrentList(intCurrent) As String
     If intCurrent = 0 Then strCurrent = "-Current-"
     strCurrent=strCurrent + Chr(10) & Chr(9) & _
     Format$(ndocTask.DueDateTime(0), "mm/dd/yy") & Chr(9) & _
     "    " & strPriority & Chr(9) & ndocTask.Subject(0)
     intCurrent = intCurrent + 1
   Case "2"
     Redim Preserve sFutureList(intFuture) As String
     If intFuture = 0 Then strFuture = "-Future-"
     strFuture=strFuture + Chr(10) & Chr(9) & _
     Format$(ndocTask.DueDateTime(0), "mm/dd/yy") & Chr(9) & _
     "    " & strPriority & Chr(9) & ndocTask.Subject(0)
     intFuture = intFuture + 1
   End Select
   Set ndocTask = nvwTask.GetNextDocument( ndocTask )
  Wend
  'Set output for message box
  strHead1="Status" & Chr(9) & "Date Due" & Chr(9) & " Priority" & _
  Chr(9) & "Subject" & Chr(10) & "--------------" & Chr(9) & _
  "--------------" & Chr(9) & " ----------" & Chr(9) & _
  String$(91, "-") & Chr(10)
```
continued >>

continued >>

```
strHead2="You have " & Trim$(Str$(intOverdue+intCurrent+intFuture)) &_
" tasks as of today: " & Format(Date$, "Long Date") &"."& Chr(10)
strTask=strHead2 & Chr(10) & strHead1 & strOverdue & Chr(10) & _
strCurrent & Chr(10) & strFuture
Else
strTask="You have no tasks as of " & Format(Date$, "Long Date") &"."
Exit Sub
End If
'Display standard message box
Msgbox strTask, 64, "Day-At-A-Glance for " & ns.CommonUserName & "..."
```

NotesViewColumn

4.6x 5.0

The *NotesViewColumn* class represents a column design element contained in a *NotesView* (which can be a standard view or a folder). The *NotesViewColumn* determines how the data contained in the *NotesDocument* is displayed to the user, both aesthetically and in regards to sort order. In addition, the *NotesViewColumn* can contain formulas using the Notes macro language, simple functions, and various format settings.

```
...
 └ NotesView
    └ NotesViewColumn
```

Page *Contents*

Syntax

Properties

continued >>

LotusScript Syntax

To access the *NotesViewColumn* object, you must establish a handle on the parent *NotesView* object that contains it and then use the `Columns` property (▶ 283) to instantiate a *NotesViewColumn* object.

NotesViewColumn Properties

5.0 Alignment   R   %

```
To get: intAlignment = NotesViewColumn.Alignment
```
                                                                              Alignment

This property returns the alignment, or justification, of the data displayed in the current column as an integer constant value. The default alignment for views is `VC_ALIGN_LEFT`. Here are the possible values returned for this property:

Constant Value	Integer Value	Description
VC_ALIGN_CENTER	2	Center justification
VC_ALIGN_RIGHT	1	Right justification
VC_ALIGN_LEFT	0	Left justification

The following code snippet displays the number of columns contained in the "All" view and then displays their respective alignments.

```
Dim ns As New NotesSession
Dim nvw As NotesView
Dim nvc As NotesViewColumn
Set nvw = ns.currentdatabase.Getview("All")
Dim strAlign As String
Dim intLoop As Integer
Msgbox "This view has " & Str$(Ubound(nvw.columns) + 1) & " columns."
For intLoop = 0 To Ubound(nvw.columns)
  Set nvc = nvw.Columns(intLoop)
  Select Case nvc.Alignment
  Case 0
   strAlign = "left"
  Case 1
   strAlign = "right"
  Case 2
   strAlign = "center"
  End Select
  Msgbox "The alignment for column " & Str$(intLoop + 1) & " is " &
  ➥strAlign, 32, "Alignment..."
Next
```

5.0 DateFmt   R   %

```
To get: intDatefmt = NotesViewColumn.DateFmt
```
                                                                              DateFmt

This property returns the format of the date being displayed in the current column as an integer constant. The default for this property is `0`. Two new settings in Release 5.0 display the year in a Year 2000-compliant manner. Prior to Release 5.0, the year was always suppressed to a two-digit format (although the underlying value stored has always been Year 2000-compliant). You can now select the format to display either 12/25/1998 or 12/1998. Here are the possible values returned for this property:

Constant Value	Integer Value	Description
VC_FMT_MD	2	Displays the month and day of the date. December 25, 1998 would display as 12/25.
VC_FMT_YM	3	Displays the month and year of the date. December 25, 1998 would display as 12/98.
VC_FMT_YMD	0	Displays the month, day, and year of the date. December 25, 1998 would display as 12/25/98.
VC_FMT_Y4M	4	Displays the month, day, and four-digit year of the date. December 25, 1998 would display as 12/25/1998.

5.0 FontColor   R   %

FontColor   To get: `intFontcolor = NotesViewColumn.`**`FontColor`**

This property returns an integer constant that represents the color of the text displayed in the view column. Here are the possible values returned for this property (these also apply to the font color used with the `NotesColor` for *NotesRichTextItems* and the `BackgroundColor` for *Notes Views*):

Constant Value	Integer Value	RGB Color
COLOR_BLACK	0	0, 0, 0
COLOR_BLUE	4	0, 0, 255
COLOR_CYAN	5	0, 255, 255
COLOR_DARK_BLUE	10	0, 0, 128
COLOR_DARK_CYAN	11	0, 128, 128
COLOR_DARK_GREEN	9	0, 128, 0
COLOR_DARK_MAGENTA	13	128, 0, 128
COLOR_DARK_RED	8	128, 0, 0
COLOR_DARK_YELLOW	12	128, 128, 0
COLOR_GRAY	14	128, 128, 128
COLOR_GREEN	3	0, 255, 0
COLOR_LIGHT_GRAY	15	192, 192, 192
COLOR_MAGENTA	7	255, 0, 255
COLOR_RED	2	255, 0, 0
COLOR_WHITE	1	255, 255, 255
COLOR_YELLOW	6	255, 255, 0

5.0 FontFace   R $

FontFace   To get: `strFontFace = NotesViewColumn.`**`FontFace`**

This property returns the name of the font type being displayed in the column. The default value for this property is `Helvetica`.

5.0 FontPointSize   R   %

FontPointSize   To get: `intFontpointsize = NotesViewColumn.`**`FontPointSize`**

This property returns the point size as an integer of the font being displayed in the column. The default value for this property is `10`.

5.0 FontStyle   R   %

```
To get: intFontstyle = NotesViewColumn.FontStyle
```

This property returns the integer constant value of the style being used to display the text in the column. The default value for this property is 0. The options for the style are FONT_BOLD, FONT_ITALIC, FONT_UNDERLINE, and FONT_STRIKEOUT. You can select one style or a combination of styles. Therefore, the possible values returned become more complicated but are easily distinguishable when checking for the integer value returned. Here are the possible values returned for this property:

Constant Value	Integer Value	Description
VC_FONT_BOLD	1	The text is bold.
VC_FONT_ITALIC	2	The text is italic.
VC_FONT_STRIKEOUT	8	The text is strikeout.

Formula   R $

```
To get: strFormula = NotesViewColumn.Formula
```

This property returns the @Function, if used, in the particular column. When designing column formulas, you are restricted to using either simple functions, fields, or formulas (using the @Function macro language available in Domino/Lotus Notes). If the value used in the column formula is equivalent to a single field value, this property will return NULL, even if the designer specifies the formula and enters the name of the field. This is still interpreted by Domino as a single field value reference and not as an actual formula. If the simple function is used, Domino will return the formula that will return the same, equivalent value. Otherwise, the entire formula is returned. You can test whether the column contains a formula value by using the IsFormula property, also contained by *NotesViewColumn* (▶ 302).

5.0 HeaderAlignment   R   %

```
To get: intHeaderalign = NotesViewColumn.HeaderAlignment
```

This property returns a constant integer value representing the alignment, or justification, of the header, or title, in a column.

The default alignment for views is VC_ALIGN_LEFT. Here are the possible values returned for this property:

Constant Value	Integer Value	Description
VC_ALIGN_CENTER	2	Center justification
VC_ALIGN_RIGHT	1	Right justification
VC_ALIGN_LEFT	0	Left justification

The following code displays several of the *NotesViewColumn* properties described earlier for all the columns in the All view in a message box. Although this example wouldn't be all that useful in the real world, it does demonstrate how to access the view column properties.

```
Dim ns As New NotesSession
Dim nvw As NotesView
Dim nvc As NotesViewColumn
Set nvw = ns.currentdatabase.Getview("All")
Dim strMessage As String
Dim intLoop As Integer
For intLoop = 0 To Ubound(nvw.Columns)
  Set nvc = nvw.Columns(intLoop)
```

continued >>

continued >>

```
strMessage = "The view attributes are:" & Chr$(13) & Chr$(13) & _
"Column Number: " & Chr$(9) & Trim$(Str$(intLoop + 1)) & Chr$(13) & _
"Alignment: " & Chr$(9) & nvc.Alignment & Chr$(13) & _
"Date Format: " & Chr$(9) & nvc.Datefmt & Chr$(13) & _
"Font Color: " & Chr$(9) & nvc.Fontcolor & Chr$(13) & _
"Font Face: " & Chr$(9) & nvc.Fontface & Chr$(13) & _
"Font Point Size: " & Chr$(9) & nvc.Fontpointsize & Chr$(13) & _
"Font Style: " & Chr$(9) & nvc.Fontstyle & Chr$(13) & _
"Header Alignment: " & Chr$(9) & nvc.Headeralignment
Msgbox strMessage, 32, "View attributes..."
Next
```

| 5.0 IsAccentSensitiveSort | R | T/F |

IsAccent
SensitiveSort

To get: intIsaccsensitive = NotesViewColumn.**IsAccentSensitiveSort**

This property returns a Boolean value that indicates whether the column-sorting property for accent sorting is enabled or disabled. TRUE indicates that the sort should respect accents. FALSE indicates that the sort should ignore accents.

| 5.0 IsCaseSensitiveSort | R | T/F |

IsCase
SensitiveSort

To get: intIsCaseSensitive = NotesViewColumn.**IsCaseSensitiveSort**

This property returns a Boolean value that indicates whether the column-sorting property for case sorting is enabled or disabled. TRUE indicates that the sort should respect case sensitivity. FALSE indicates that the sort should ignore case sensitivity.

| IsCategory | R | T/F |

IsCategory

To get: intIsCategory = NotesViewColumn.**IsCategory**

This property indicates whether the column is categorized (as well as sorted, since a column must be sorted in order to be categorized). (Refer to the IsSorted property of the *NotesViewColumn* (▶ 304).) TRUE indicates that the column is categorized. FALSE indicates that the column is not categorized (although it still may be sorted).

| 5.0 IsField | R | T/F |

IsField

To get: intIsField = NotesViewColumn.**IsField**

This property indicates whether the values displayed in the columns are based on field values or formulas. TRUE indicates that the column values are based on field values. FALSE indicates that they are based on formulas.

| 5.0 IsFormula | R | T/F |

IsFormula

To get: intIsFormula = NotesViewColumn.**IsFormula**

This property indicates whether the values displayed in the columns are based on a Notes formula. TRUE indicates that the column values are based on a Notes formula. FALSE indicates that they are not. When designing column formulas, you are restricted to using either simple functions, fields, or formulas (using the @Function macro language available in Domino/Lotus Notes). If the value used in the column formula is equivalent to a single field value, this property returns FALSE, even if the designer specifies the formula and enters the name of the field. This is still interpreted by Domino as a single field value reference and not as an actual formula. Refer to the Formula property of *NotesViewColumn* (▶ 301).

| IsHidden | R | T/F |

IsHidden

To get: intIsHidden = NotesViewColumn.**IsHidden**

This property indicates whether the column is hidden. Hidden columns aren't visible in a view but are still functional as far as sorting, and being used in @DbLookup and @DbColumn formulas and by script (GetDocumentByKey, GetAllDocumentsByKey, and so on). TRUE indicates that the column is hidden. FALSE indicates that it is not.

5.0 **IsHideDetail**   R   T/F

To get: intIsHideDetail = NotesViewColumn.**IsHideDetail**   IsHideDetail

This property indicates whether the details (individual line items) for total columns in categorized/sorted columns should be displayed or hidden. If this property is TRUE, the details (individual line items) are hidden. FALSE indicates that they are displayed along with the totals.

5.0 **IsIcon**   R   T/F

To get: intIsIcon = NotesViewColumn.**IsIcon**   IsIcon

This property indicates whether the column property to "Display values as icons" is enabled. If this property is TRUE, the numeric value stored in the column results in the display of an icon (from a predetermined set) in the column. If this property is FALSE, this setting is ignored, and the column values are treated as normal, displaying the contents based on a simple function, formula, or field.

5.0 **IsResize**   R   T/F

To get: intIsResize = NotesViewColumn.**IsResize**   IsResize

This property indicates whether the column can be resized through the native Notes client. This property has no effect when the view is published by the Domino server. If this property is TRUE, when using a native Notes client, the user can resize the column width by placing the cursor at the vertical edge of the column and dragging the vertical crosshair to the desired width. If it's FALSE, the column width can't be adjusted.

5.0 **IsResortAscending**   R   T/F

To get: intIsResortAscending = NotesViewColumn.**IsResortAscending**   IsResort
Ascending

This property indicates whether the column can be re-sorted in ascending order. The column must have already been designed to allow for dynamic sorting (it must be re-sortable). If this property is TRUE, you can re-sort the column by clicking the arrow icon to the right of the column title. If it's FALSE, the arrow won't be displayed to the user, so the column can't be re-sorted.

5.0 **IsResortDescending**   R   T/F

To get: intIsResortDescending = NotesViewColumn.**IsResortDescending**   IsResort
Descending

This property indicates whether the column can be re-sorted in descending order. The column must have already been designed to allow for dynamic sorting (it must be re-sortable). If this property is TRUE, you can re-sort the column by clicking the arrow icon to the right of the column title. If it's FALSE, the arrow won't be displayed to the user, so the column can't be re-sorted.

5.0 **IsResortToView**   R   T/F

To get: intIsResortToView = NotesViewColumn.**IsResortToView**   IsResortToView

This property indicates whether you can re-sort the column by clicking the column title, or header. The column must have already been designed to allow for sorting (it must be re-sortable). If this property is TRUE, you can re-sort the column by clicking the arrow icon to the right of the column title. If it's FALSE, the arrow isn't displayed to the user, so the column can't be re-sorted.

IsResponse R T/F

IsResponse

`To get: intIsResponse = NotesViewColumn.`**`IsResponse`**

This property indicates whether the column contains response documents only. This is equivalent to the "Show responses only" setting of the column design. This property must be set to display response documents in their response hierarchy in views. An example is discussion threads commonly used in both native Notes and Web applications. If this property is TRUE, this column will display only response documents. If it's FALSE, this column will display any type of document.

5.0 IsSecondaryResort R T/F

IsSecondary
Resort

`To get: intIsSecondaryResort = NotesViewColumn.`**`IsSecondaryResort`**

This property indicates whether the current column is a secondary column that can be re-sorted. TRUE indicates that the current column is a secondary re-sortable column. FALSE indicates that it is not.

5.0 IsSecondaryResortDescending R T/F

IsSecondary
ResortDescending

`To get: intSecondaryResortDescending = NotesViewColumn.`
➡**`IsSecondaryResortDescending`**

This property indicates whether the current column is a secondary re-sortable column whose sort order is descending. TRUE indicates that the current column is a secondary re-sortable column in descending order. FALSE indicates that it is a secondary re-sortable column in ascending order.

5.0 IsShowTwistie R T/F

IsShowTwistie

`To get: intIsShoeTwistie = NotesViewColumn.`**`IsShowTwistie`**

If the column is expandable, this property indicates whether a twistie should be displayed to the immediate left of the column values. A twistie indicates that the current entry is a category. The category can be expanded and collapsed when you click the twistie icon. If this property is TRUE, the column will display a twistie. It's FALSE, the column won't display a twistie, even if the entry is an expandable category. This property is equivalent to the "Show twistie when row is expandable" property of the column design.

5.0 IsSortDescending R T/F

IsSort
Descending

`To get: intIsSortdescending = NotesViewColumn.`**`IsSortDescending`**

If the column is sorted, this property indicates whether the column is sorted in descending order. If it's TRUE, the column is sorted in descending order. If it's FALSE, the column is sorted in ascending order. You can also determine whether the column is sorted by using the IsSorted property as follows, also contained by the *NotesViewColumn*.

IsSorted R T/F

IsSorted

`To get: intIsSorted = NotesViewColumn.`**`IsSorted`**

This property indicates whether the column is sorted. TRUE indicates that the column is sorted. FALSE indicates that it is not sorted. You can determine the specific sort order by using the IsSortDescending property as shown above, also a property of the *NotesViewColumn*.

ItemName R $

ItemName

`To get: strItemName = NotesViewColumn.`**`ItemName`**

This property returns the name of the *NotesItem* whose value is being displayed in the column. Often, a column is set to display the contents of a *NotesItem* or field value.

If the item being displayed in the view was generated using a simple function in the column design, the internal Notes representation is displayed.

5.0 ListSep   R   %   ListSep

To get: intListSep = NotesViewColumn.**ListSep**

This property returns theseparator character being used to deliminate multiple values for display in the column contained in the multivalue *NotesItem* used as the column formula. A constant integer value is returned that represents the allowable values for deliminating multivalue *NotesItems*. Here are the allowable constant values:

Constant Value	Description
VC_SEP_COMMA	The values are separated by the comma character.
VC_SEP_NEWLINE	The values are separated by the newline character.
VC_SEP_SEMICOLON	The values are separated by the semicolon character.
VC_SEP_SPACE	The values are separated by spaces.

5.0 NumberAttrib   R   %   NumberAttrib

To get: intNumberAttrib = NotesViewColumn.**NumberAttrib**

This property returns a constant integer value representing the attributes for the numeric column values. Here are the possible values returned:

Constant Value	Description
VC_ATTR_PARENS	The numeric value should be surrounded by parentheses when it is a negative number.
VC_ATTR_PUNCTUATED	The numeric value is punctuated at thousands.
VC_ATTR_PERCENT	The numeric value is a percentage (value ★ 100).

5.0 NumberDigits   R   %   NumberDigit

To get: intNumberDigits = NotesViewColumn.**NumberDigits**

This property indicates the number of decimal places for the numeric value in the column.

5.0 NumberFormat   R   %   NumberFormat

To get: intNumberFormat = NotesViewColumn.**NumberFormat**

This property returns a constant of type integer representing the format of the numeric values in the column. Here are the possible values returned:

Constant Value	Description
VC_FMT_CURRENCY	The numeric value is currency.
VC_FMT_FIXED	The numeric value is fixed.
VC_FMT_GENERAL	The numeric value is general.
VC_FMT_SCIENTIFIC	The numeric value is scientific.

Position   R   %   Position

To get: intPosition = NotesViewColumn.**Position**

This property returns the position of the column in the view, starting at 1 and counting from left to right. Unlike the *NotesViewColumn* objects contained in the *NotesView*, which is an array with the index starting at 0 (Option Base 0), the position properties start at 1. Therefore, when you're using the position property with the array of columns returned from the columns property of the *NotesView*, be sure to add 1 to the value of the columns array.

5.0 TimeDateFmt   R   %

TimeDateFmt   `To get: intTimeDateFmt = NotesViewColumn.`**`TimeDateFmt`**

This property returns the format of the time-date value being stored in the column. Here are the possible values returned for this property:

Constant Value	Description
VC_FMT_DATE	Date only
VC_FMT_DATETIME	Date and time
VC_FMT_TIME	Time only
VC_FMT_TODAYTIME	"Today" and time

5.0 **TimeFmt**   R   %

TimeFmt   `To get: intTimeFmt = NotesViewColumn.`**`TimeFmt`**

This property returns the time format of the time value displayed in the column as an integer constant. Here are the possible values returned for this property:

Constant Value	Description
VC_FMT_HMS	The time format is month, hours, and seconds.
VC_FMT_HM	The time format is hours and month.

5.0 **TimeZoneFmt**   R   %

TimeZoneFmt   `To get: intTimeZoneFmt = NotesViewColumn.`**`TimeZoneFmt`**

This property returns a constant integer representing the format of the time zone of the column's time value. Here are the possible values returned:

Constant Value	Description
VC_FMT_ALWAYS	The time zone should always be shown.
VC_FMT_NEVER	The time should be adjusted to the local zone, so the original time zone should never be shown.
VC_FMT_SOMETIMES	The time should be shown only if the original time zone isn't local.

Title   R $

Title   `To get: strTitle = NotesViewColumn.`**`Title`**

This property returns the column's title. If the column doesn't have a title defined, this property returns `""`.

5.0 **Width**   R   %

Width   `To get: intWidth = NotesViewColumn.`**`Width`**

This property returns the width of the column in characters.

Remarks

The *NotesViewColumn* class was exposed in Notes Release 4.6 and has been dramatically improved in Release 5.0. Practically every property of the *NotesViewColumn* is exposed. Unfortunately, most of these properties are read-only.

Therefore, the design of the *NotesView* can't be programmatically modified by your script. Although the need to perform such functions is unlikely, this would be helpful in reducing the number of views to build into the database design since they could be modified on-the-fly based on the current criteria.

Example

The following LotusScript snippet prints the sorting attributes of all the columns in the All view.

```
Dim ns As New NotesSession
Dim nvw As NotesView
Dim nvc As NotesViewColumn
Set nvw = ns.currentdatabase.Getview("All")
Dim strMessage As String
Dim intLoop As Integer
For intLoop = 0 To Ubound(nvw.Columns)
  Set nvc = nvw.Columns(intLoop)
  Print "The view column design attributes are:" & Chr$(13) & Chr$(13)
  Print "Column Number: " & nvc.Position & Chr$(13)
  Print "Accent sorting: " & nvc.Isaccentsensitivesort & Chr$(13)
  Print "Case sorting: " & nvc.IsCasesensitivesort & Chr$(13)
  Print "Case Ascending: " & nvc.Isresortascending & Chr$(13)
  Print "Case Descending: " & nvc.IsresortDescending & Chr$(13)
  Print "Case Resortable: " & nvc.IsResorttoview & Chr$(13)
  Print "Case Secondary sort: " & nvc.Issecondaryresort & Chr$(13)
  Print "Is Secondary sort descending: " nvc.Issecondaryresortdescending
➥& Chr$(13)
  Print "Is Sort descending: " & nvc.Issortdescending
Next
```

5.0 NotesViewEntry

The *NotesViewEntry* class is new in Notes 5.0, and is a very welcome addition. It provides the long-awaited capability to access a row in a view. A row can be one of three things: a category, a total, or a document.

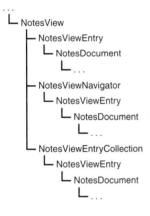

LotusScript Syntax

```
Dim nveEntry As NotesViewEntry
```

There are several ways to get a handle on a *NotesViewEntry* object. The first is to use the GetEntryByKey method of *NotesView* (▶ 290):

```
Set nveEntry = nvView.getentrybykey(aKeyarray, intexactmatch)
```

Alternatively, you can use any of the various "get" methods of either the *NotesViewNavigator* (▶ 323) or *NotesViewEntryCollection* (▶ 315) classes, several of which are shown here:

```
Set nventry = vnNavigator.GetChild(veCurrentEntry)
```

or

```
Set nveEntry=vecCollection.GetFirstEntry
```

or

```
Set nveEntry=vecCollection.GetNth(intPostoGet)
```

or

```
Set nventry = vnNavigator.GetNextSibling(veCurrentEntry)
```

NotesViewEntry Properties

ChildCount	R	%

ChildCount

```
To get: intCount = nveNotesViewEntry.ChildCount
```

Returns the number of child entries (if any) that the current view entry has.

ColumnIndentLevel		

ColumnIndent
Level

```
To get: intLevel = nvenotesviewentry.ColumnIndentLevel
```

Returns the level of indentation as an integer.

ColumnValues	R	()

ColumnValues

```
To get: aColvalues = nveNotesViewEntry.ColumnValues
```

Returns an array of variants that contains the values displayed in each of the columns of the current entry.

DescendantCount	R	%

Descendant
Count

```
To get: intDescCount = nveNotesViewEntry.DescendentCount
```

Returns the number of descendents that the current entry has. This differs from the ChildCount property because this property accounts for all of an entry's descendents, not just the immediate ones. For example, if you had a parent document that had a response, and the response had an associated response to a response, the ChildCount property would return 1 for the parent, while this property would return 2.

Document	R	O.Ref.

Document

```
To get: ndocCurDocument = nveNotesViewEntry.Document
```

Returns a handle to the underlying *NotesDocument* from which the entry is derived. This property returns nothing if the entry is not a document (category or total) or if the underlying document has been deleted since the entry object was created.

```
' This code deletes conflict documents
Dim nsS as New NotesSession
Dim nvwView as NotesView
Dim lngI as Long
Dim intCount as Integer
Dim nvecCollection as NotesViewEntryCollection
Dim nveEntry as NotesViewEntry
Set nvwView=nsS.CurrentDatabase.Getview("Testing")
Set nvecCollection=nvwView.GetAllEntries
For lngI = 1 to nvecCollection.Count
  Set nveEntry=nvecCollection.GetNthEntry(lngI)
  If nveEntry.IsConflict Then
     Call nveEntry.Document.Remove(TRUE)
     IntCount=intCount+1
  End If
Next
Print CStr(intCount) & "conflict documents were deleted."
```

FTSearchScore   R   %

`To get: intFTScore = nveNotesViewEntry.`**`FTSearchScore`**   FTSearchScore

For entries not retrieved as part of a full-text search, this property always returns 0. If a full-text search was conducted, this property returns the search score, which is calculated based on several factors, including the number of search terms found in the entry, the term weights assigned to the search words, and any proximity operators in the search query. If a full-text search is conducted on a database that hasn't been indexed, this property will yield "unpredictable" return values (according to the Lotus Help Database).

IndentLevel   R   %

`To get: intIndentLvl= nveNotesViewEntry.`**`IndentLevel`**   IndentLevel

Returns the number of levels that the current entry is indented in the view.

IsCategory   R   T/F

`To get: intCategory = nveNotesViewEntry.`**`IsCategory`**   IsCategory

Returns TRUE if the current entry is a category, and FALSE if the current view is not a category.

IsConflict   R   T/F

`To get: intConflict = nveNotesViewEntry.`**`IsConflict`**   IsConflict

Returns TRUE if the current entry represents a conflict document. Otherwise, this property returns FALSE.

IsDocument   R   T/F

`To get: intDocument = nveNotesViewEntry.`**`IsDocument`**   IsDocument

Returns TRUE if the current entry represents a document. Otherwise, this property returns FALSE.

IsTotal   R   T/F

`To get: intTotal = nveNotesViewEntry.`**`IsTotal`**   IsTotal

Returns TRUE if the current entry represents a total. Otherwise, this property returns FALSE.

IsValid   R   T/F

IsValid   `To get: intValid = nveNotesViewEntry.IsValid`

Returns TRUE if the current entry is a valid entry—meaning a document, category, or total. If the entry represents a deletion stub, this property returns FALSE.

NoteID   R $

NoteID   `To get: strNoteID = nveNotesViewEntry.NoteID`

Returns the note ID of the underlying document, prepended with the string NT.

Parent   R   O.Ref.

Parent   `To get: nvWParentView= nveNotesViewEntry.Parent`

Returns a *NotesView* object representing the parent view.

SiblingCount   R   %

SiblingCount   `To get: intSibCount = nveNotesViewEntry.SiblingCount`

Returns the number of siblings an entry has. If the current entry is a total or category, this will return 0 due to the fact that totals and categories are not documents and are really not part of the view hierarchy.

UniversalID   R $

UniversalID   `To get: strUNID = nveNotesViewEntry.UniversalID`

Returns the universal ID of the entry's underlying document. For totals and categories, this property returns an empty string (" ").

NotesViewEntry Methods

GetPosition

GetPosition   `strPosition = nveNotesViewEntry.GetPosition(strSeparator)`

StrSeparator   Required $

The separator used in the return value.

This method returns a text string that represents the entry's position in the view. For example, a position of 4.7 would indicate that you have the seventh entry under the fourth category.

Example

```
' This code checks for unread issues and, if found,
' sends a summary to the managers
  Dim nsSession As New NotesSession
  Dim ndocMail As NotesDocument
  Set ndocMail=nsSession.CurrentDatabase.CreateDocument
  Dim nrtiBody As New NotesRichTExtItem(ndocMail, "Body")
  Dim nvwIssuesView As NotesView
```

```
Dim nvecIssues As NotesViewEntryCollection
Dim nveIssue As NotesViewEntry
Dim intCount As Integer
Set nvwIssuesView=nsSession.CurrentDatabase.GetView("New Topics")
Set nvecIssues=nvwIssues.AllEntries
Set nveIssue=nvecIssues.GetFirstEntry
If nveIssue Is Nothing Then
  Exit Sub
Else
  nrtiBody.AppendText("The following issues are currently unread.
  ➥Please click the doc link to open an issue")
  nrtiBody.AddNewLine(2)
  nrtiBody.AppendText("Subject"&Chr$(9)&Chr$(9)&Chr$(9)&"Date"&
  ➥Chr$(9) & Chr$(9) &"From")
  intCount=1
End If
While Not nveIssue Is Nothing
  If nveIssue.IsUnread Then
    nrtiBody.AppendText(nveIssue.Document.Subject(0) &Chr$(9) & Chr$(9) &
    ➥nveIssue.Document.date(0) & Chr$(9) & Chr$(9) &
    ➥nveIssue.Document.From(0) )
    Call nrtiBody.AppendDocLink(nveIssue.Document, "Click Me")
    nrtiBody.AddNewLine(1)
    intCount=intCount+1
  End If
  Set nveIssue=nvecIssues.GetNextEntry(nveIssue)
Wend
ndocMail.Subject=Cstr(intCount) & " unread issues remain in Customer
➥Service database"
Call ndocMail.Send(False,"CS_Managers")
```

NotesViewEntry Collection

5.0

The *NotesViewEntryCollection* class is new in Notes 5.0. It is both much anticipated and appreciated! It represents a collection of *NotesViewEntry* objects (also new to Notes 5.0, ▸ 309) that are sorted in the order they appear in the underlying view. For the first time, developers can access documents sorted in the order of a view's index, without the need to "walk the view" (access each document sequentially). Additionally, you can use this class to access the values stored in a view's columns, to access the categories in a view, and to store the result sets from multiple full-text searches (*FTSearch,* ▸ 317).

```
 . . .
  └ NotesView
     └ NotesViewEntryCollection
        └ NotesViewEntry
           └ NotesDocument
              └ . . .
```

LotusScript Syntax

```
Dim nvecCollection As NotesViewEntryCollection
```

There are two basic ways to access a *NotesViewEntryCollection*. Both rely on the *NotesView* object (▶ 279). The first way is to use the AllEntries property of *NotesView*:

```
Set nvecCollection = nvwView.AllEntries
```

The second option is to use the GetAllEntriesByKey method of *NotesView* to return only those entries that match the value supplied as a key:

```
Set nvecCollection = nvwView.GetAllEntriesByKey("Samuel Hatter")
```

NotesViewEntryCollection Properties

Count   R   &

Count   To get: lngCount = nvecNotesViewEntryCollection.**Count**

Returns the number of entries contained in the collection.

Parent   R   O.Ref.

Parent   To get: nvwView = nvecNotesViewEntryCollection.**Parent**

Returns the *NotesView* from which the collection was built.

Query   R $

Query   To get: strQuery = nvecNotesViewEntryCollection.**Query**

Contains the query string that was used if the collection is the result of a full-text query.

NotesViewEntryCollection Methods

AddEntry

AddEntry   Call nvecNotesViewEntryCollection.**AddEntry**(nveEntrytoAdd)

| nveEntrytoAdd | Required | O.Ref. |
The *NotesViewEntry* to add to the collection.

This method allows you to insert additional entries into a view entry collection. If the collection is sorted, the entry is appended; if the collection is unsorted, the entry is inserted based on an internal algorithm. If the entry added is a duplicate, an error will be generated. When using this method, you can navigate from the new entry to determine its position in the collection.

DeleteEntry

DeleteEntry   Call nvecNotesViewEntryCollection.**DeleteEntry**(nveEntrytoDelete)

| nveEntrytoDelete | Required | O.Ref. |
The *NotesViewEntry* to delete from the collection.

Using this method allows you to remove a *NotesViewEntry* from a *NotesViewEntryCollection*. In order for this method to work, the entry being deleted must have originated in this collection. It is important to note that this method won't delete the underlying document. It deletes only the entry from the collection. If the specified entry doesn't exist, an error will be generated.

FTSearch

```
Call nvecNotesViewEntryCollection.FTSearch(strQuery,intMaxDocs)
```
FTSearch

strQuery	Required	$

The query that should be used to search the collection.

intMaxDocs	Optional	%

An integer that specifies the maximum number of entries to return.

This method uses the Notes full-text search engine to provide a fast and easy way to further filter a *NotesViewEntryCollection*.

GetEntry

```
Set nveEntry = nvecNotesViewEntryCollection.GetEntry(varEntry)
```
GetEntry

varEntry	Required	O.Ref.

A *NotesViewEntry* or *NotesDocument* object containing the entry to retrieve.

This method returns the specified entry if it is found in the collection. Otherwise, this method returns `Nothing`.

GetFirstEntry

```
Set nveEntry = nvecNotesViewEntryCollection.GetFirstEntry()
```
GetFirstEntry

This method needs no parameters since it returns the first entry in *NotesViewEntryCollection*. If the collection is empty, this method returns `Nothing`.

GetLastEntry

```
Set nveEntry = nvecNotesViewEntryCollection.GetLastEntry()
```
GetLastEntry

As you might expect, this method is the opposite of `GetFirstEntry`. It returns the last entry in a *NotesViewEntryCollection* object. If there is no last entry—for example, if no entries exist in a specific view—this method returns `Nothing`.

GetNextEntry

```
Set nveEntry = nvecNotesViewEntryCollection.GetNextEntry(nveCurrent)
```
GetNextEntry

nveCurrent	Required	O.Ref.

The current view entry.

This method works with `GetFirstEntry`, `GetLastEntry`, `GetnthEntry`, and `GetPrevEntry` to provide a comprehensive set of navigational tools that allow you to navigate through a *NotesViewEntryCollection*. When given the current view entry, this method returns the next *NotesViewEntry* in the collection.

GetnthEntry

```
Set nveEntry = nvecNotesViewEntryCollection.GetnthEntry(lngIndex)
```
GetnthEntry

intLong	Required	&

A number that represents the entry's position in the collection.

This is a very useful method that allows you to jump to a specific entry in a collection when you know its position. This is most commonly used for looping through all of the entries in a collection, as shown in the following example.

```
Sub Initialize
    Dim nsS As NotesSession
    Dim nvwReports As NotesView
    Dim nvecReports As NotesViewEntryCollection
    Dim nveEntry As NotesViewEntry
    Dim ndocReport As NotesDocument
    Dim ndocMail As NotesDocument
    Dim intI As Integer, intHigh As Integer, intMedium As Integer,
    ➥intLow As Integer
    Set nvwReports=nsS.CurrentDatabase.GetView("(AllReports)")
    Set nvecReports=nvwReports.GetAllEntries
    If nvecReports.Count>0 Then
        Set ndocMail=nsS.CurrentDatabase.CreateDocument
        ndocMail.Subject="Status Report Summary for " & Date$
        Dim nrtiBody As New NotesRichTextItem(ndocMail, "Body")
        For intI=1 To nvecReports.Count
            Set nveEntry=vecReport.getnthEntry(intI)
            Set ndocReport=nveEntry.Document
            Select Case ndocReport.Status(0)
              Case "High"
                 intHigh=intHigh+1
              Case "Medium"
                 intMedium=intMedium+1
              Case "Low"
                 intLow=intLow+1
            End Select
        Next
        Call nrtiBody.AppendText("Status Report Summary:")
        Call nrtiBody.AddnewLine(2)
        Call nrtiBody.AppendText("High Priority: " & Trim$(Str$(intHigh)))
        Call nrtiBody.AddnewLine(1)
        Call nrtiBody.AppendText("Medium Priority: " &Trim$(Str$(intMedium)))
        Call nrtiBody.AddnewLine(1)
        Call nrtiBody.AppendText("Low Priority: " & Trim$(Str$(intLow)))
        Call nrtiBody.AddnewLine(2)
        Call nrtiBody.AppendText("Total Reports: " & Trim$(Str$((intLow+
        ➥intMedium+intHigh))))
        Call ndocMail.Send(False,"SupportManagers")
    Else
        Msgbox ¦No status reports were found¦, 64, "No Hot Leads"
    End If
End Sub
```

GetPrevEntry

GetPrevEntry

```
Set nveEntry = nvecNotesViewEntryCollection.GetPrevEntry(nveCurrent)
```

nveCurrent	Required	O.Ref.

The current view entry.

Given the current view entry, this method returns the previous *NotesViewEntry* in the collection.

PutAllInFolder

PutAllInFolder

```
Call nvecNotesViewEntryCollection.PutAllInFolder(strFolderName,
➥intCreateOnFail)
```

strFolderName   Required $

The name of the folder in which to place the documents.

IntCreateOnFail   Optional   T/F

Specify TRUE to create a folder if the specified folder doesn't exist.

This method moves all the underlying documents contained in the
NotesViewEntryCollection to the specified folder. If the specified folder doesn't exist, it
will be created. For example:

```
Sub Initialize
  Dim nsS As NotesSession
  Dim nvwView As NotesView
  Dim nvecCollection As NotesViewEntryCollection
  Dim nveEntry As NotesViewEntry
  Set nvwView=nsS.CurrentDatabase.GetView("(By Customer")
  Set nvecCollection=nvwView.GetAllEntriesByKey("Wyatt Hatter")
  If nvecCollection.Count>0 Then
    Call nvecCollection.PutAllInFolder("Wyatt Hatter")
  Else
    Msgbox ¦No documents were found.¦, 64, "No Leads found..."
  End If
End Sub
```

RemoveAll

```
Call nvecNotesViewEntryCollection.RemoveAll(intForce)
```

intForce   Required   T/F

Indicates whether deleted documents should be removed from the collection.

When the intForce parameter is set to TRUE, the underlying documents are removed
from the *NotesViewEntryCollection* and are deleted from the database as well. If
intForce is FALSE, some of the documents might be left in the collection, even if they
were deleted.

RemoveAllFromFolder

```
Call nvecNotesViewEntryCollection.RemoveAllFromFolder(strFolderName)
```
RemoveAll
FromFolder

strFolderName   Required $

The name of the folder from which to remove the documents.

This method removes the underlying documents of a *NotesViewEntryCollection* from
the specified folder.

StampAll

```
Call nvecNotesViewEntryCollection.StampAll(strItemName, varValue)
```
StampAll

strItemName   Required $

The name of the item in the underlying document that you want to update.

varValue   Required   ?

The actual value to write into the specified item (field). The data type of this parameter
should match the data type of the field.

StampAll is a powerful and useful method that allows you to update a single field in every underlying document contained in a *NotesViewEntryCollection* without writing a loop and without calling the **Save** method of *NotesDocument*. When **StampAll** is used, every document in the collection has the specified item set to the value specified in varValue. If the item doesn't exist, it is created. Any changes made to the underlying documents are immediately written to disk. Consider the following example:

```
Sub Initialize
  Dim nsS As NotesSession
  Dim nvwView As NotesView
  Dim nvecCollection As NotesViewEntryCollection
  Set nvecCollection=nvwView.GetAllEntriesByKey("Definiti")
  If nvecCollection.Count>0 Then
    Call nvecCollection.StampAll("Processed",S.UserName)
  Else
    Msgbox ¦No documents were found.¦, 64, "Nothing to do..."
  End If
End Sub
```

UpdateAll

UpdateAll   `Call nvecNotesViewEntryCollection.UpdateAll()`

This method marks all the underlying documents in a collection as processed by the agent in which this method is called. For more information on updating processed documents, see the **UpdateProcessedDoc** method of the *NotesSession* class (▶ 273).

Remarks

The *NotesViewEntryCollection* class is very similar to the *NotesDocumentCollection* class, with one major difference. *NotesViewEntryCollection* returns *NotesViewEntry* objects in the order in which they are sorted in the underlying view, while documents in a *NotesDocumentCollection* are sorted by the **DocumentUNID**. The only exception to this rule is when the **FTSearch** method of *NotesDatabase, NotesView,* or *NotesDocumentCollection* is used to build the collection. In this case, the collection is sorted by the sort options specified in the **FTSearch** method.

You should keep in mind that *NotesViewEntryCollections* will not contain categories or column totals. They will contain only entries that correspond to the underlying *NotesDocuments*.

Example

```
Dim nsS As NotesSession
Dim intI As Integer
Dim ndocMail As NotesDocument
Dim nvwView As NotesView
Dim nvecCollection As NotesViewEntryCollection
Dim nveEntry As NotesViewEntry
Set nvwView=nsS.CurrentDatabase.GetView(¦(By Customer)¦)
```

```
Set nvecCollection=nvwView.AllEntries
If nvecCollection.Count>0 Then
   Call nvecCollection.FTSearch("Samuel Hatter",0)
      If nvecCollection.Count>0 Then
          Set ndocMail=nsS.CurrentDatabase.CreateDocument
          Dim nrtiBody As New NotesRichTextItem(ndocMail, "Body")
          Call nrtiBody.AppendText("The following " & Trim$(Str$
          ➥(nvecCollection.Count)) & " documents were found:")
          Call nrtiBody.AddNewLine(2)
          For intI=1 To nvecCollection.Count
             Set nveEntry=nvecCollection.GetnthEntry(intI)
             Call nrtiBody.AppendText(nveEntry.Document.Description(0) &
             ➥" =>")
             Call nrtifBody.AppendDoclink(nveEntry.Document,"Click Me")
             Call nrtiBody.AddNewLine(1)
          Next
          NdocMail.Subject="New Leads"
          Call ndocMail.Send("False","Sales_Managers")
      End If
   Else
      Msgbox ¦No documents were found.¦, 64, "No Hot Leads"
   End If
```

NotesViewNavigator

5.0

The *NotesViewNavigator* object represents a new object for Notes Release 5.0—the view navigator. A view navigator represents all document entries, categories, and category totals in a *NotesView*. This method allows you to navigate through the documents contained in the current view and the currently selected document's respective siblings, children, and parent. In addition, *NotesViewNavigator* allows you to access document information to determine the document category and the category total, as well as whether a document is unread or is a document conflict.

```
. . .
└ NotesView
    └ NotesViewNavigator
        └ NotesViewEntry
            └ NotesDocument
                └ . . .
```

LotusScript Syntax

There are several ways to create the *NotesViewNavigator* from an existing *NotesView*. A *NotesViewNavigator* can be created from scratch, or it can be created from an existing *NotesViewNavigator,* from children or descendants of an existing *NotesViewNavigator,* or from an existing category. The following list contains the methods of the *NotesView* (▶ 279) that can be used to create a *NotesViewNavigator*: `CreateViewNav`, `CreateViewNavFrom`, `CreateViewNavFromCategory`, `CreateViewNavFromChildren`, and `CreateViewNavFromDescendants`.

NotesViewNavigator Properties

MaxLevel	R/W	&

MaxLevel
```
To get: lngMaxlevel = nvnavNotesViewNavigator.MaxLevel
To set: nvnavNotesViewNavigator.MaxLevel = lngMaxlevel
```

Represents the maximum levels of navigation for the current *NotesView*. The allowed values for this property range from `0` (the top level of categorization) to `31` (the default `MaxLevel` setting).

ParentView	R	O.Ref.

ParentView
```
To get: nvwNotesView = nvnavNotesViewNavigator.ParentView
```

Returns a handle to the *NotesView* object that contains the *NotesViewNavigator*.

NotesViewNavigator Methods

GetChild

GetChild
```
Set nveNotesViewEntry = nvnavNotesViewNavigator.GetChild(NotesViewEntry)
```

NotesViewEntry	Required	O.Ref.

An entry in the *NotesView* (the default is the current entry).

This method returns a handle on the first child (*NotesDocument*) of either the current entry or a specified entry in the current view navigator. The child document is synonymous with a response document. If there are no children (responses), this method returns `NULL`. If this method successfully returns a handle on a view entry, that respective entry establishes user interface focus, and the cursor is automatically placed on that entry.

GetEntry

GetEntry
```
Set nveNotesViewEntry = nvnavNotesViewNavigator.Get Entry(NotesViewEntry)
```

NotesViewEntry	Required	O.Ref.

An entry in the *NotesView* (the default is the current entry).

This method returns a handle on an entry in the current view navigator. If there is no current entry, this method returns `NULL`.

GetFirst

```
Set nveNotesViewEntry = nvnavNotesViewNavigator.GetFirst
```

This method returns a handle on the first entry in the current view navigator. If there is no current entry, this method returns NULL. The entry establishes user interface focus, and the cursor is automatically placed on that entry.

The following example uses several of the methods available for the *NotesViewNavigator* class. This example steps through all the entries contained in the current view and builds a list of all the categories. This functionality could also be duplicated using other LotusScript calls or by using the Lotus Notes macro language, but this example demonstrates some of the new functionality of Release 5.

```
On Error Resume Next
Dim ns As New NotesSession
Dim nv As NotesView
Dim nvn As NotesViewNavigator
Dim nve As NotesViewEntry
Dim aCategory() As String
Dim intCount As Integer
Set nv = ns.CurrentDatabase.GetView("All")
Set nvn = nv.CreateViewNav(  )
Set nve = nvn.GetFirst
Do While Not (nve Is Nothing)
    If nve.IsCategory Then
        Redim Preserve aCategory(intCount) As String
        If nve.ColumnValues(0) <> Null Then
            aCategory(intCount) = nve.ColumnValues(0)
            intCount = intCount + 1
        End If
        Set nve = nvn.GetNextCategory( nve )
    Else
        Set nve = nvn.GetNextDocument( nve )
    End If
Loop
If intCount <> 0 Then
    For intLoop = 0 To Ubound(aCategory)
        Print aCategory(intLoop)
    Next
Else
    Print "This view does not contain any categories!"
End If
```

GetFirstDocument

```
Set nveNotesViewEntry = nvnavNotesViewNavigator.GetFirstDocument
```

This method returns a handle on the first document in the current view navigator. If there is no document, this method returns NULL. The document establishes user interface focus, and the cursor is automatically placed on the document.

GetLast

```
Set nveNotesViewEntry = nvnavNotesViewNavigator.GetLast
```

This method returns a handle on the last entry in the current view navigator. If there is no entry, this method returns NULL. The entry establishes user interface focus, and the cursor is automatically placed on the entry.

GetLastDocument

GetLast
Document

```
Set nveNotesViewEntry = nvnavNotesViewNavigator.GetLastDocument
```

This method returns a handle on the last document in the current view navigator. If there is no document, this method returns NULL. The document establishes user interface focus, and the cursor is automatically placed on the document. This method ignores any category or total entry that might exist in the current view.

GetNext

GetNext

```
Set nveNotesViewEntry = nvnavNotesViewNavigator.GetNext(NotesViewEntry)
```

NotesViewEntry　　　　**Required**　　　　**O.Ref.**
An entry in the *NotesView* (the default is the current entry).

This method returns a handle on the next entry in the current view navigator. If there is no current entry, this method returns NULL. The entry establishes user interface focus, and the cursor is automatically placed on that entry. For an example using this method, refer to the `GetFirst` method (▶ 325).

GetNextCategory

GetNext
Category

```
Set nveNotesViewEntry = nvnavNotesViewNavigator.GetNextCategory
➥(NotesViewEntry)
```

NotesViewEntry　　　　**Required**　　　　**O.Ref.**
An entry in the *NotesView* (the default is the current entry).

This method returns a handle on the next category in the current view navigator. If there is no current category, this method returns NULL. The category establishes user interface focus, and the cursor is automatically placed on that category. For an example using this method, refer to the `GetFirst` method (▶ 325).

GetNextDocument

GetNext
Document

```
Set nveNotesViewEntry = nvnavNotesViewNavigator.GetNextDocument
➥(NotesViewEntry)
```

NotesViewEntry　　　　**Required**　　　　**O.Ref.**
An entry in the *NotesView* (the default is the current entry).

This method returns a handle on the next document in the current view navigator. If there is no current document, this method returns NULL. The document establishes user interface focus, and the cursor is automatically placed on that document. For an example using this method, refer to the `GetFirst` method (▶ 325).

GetNextSibling

GetNextSibling

```
Set nveNotesViewEntry = nvnavNotesViewNavigator.GetNextSibling
➥(NotesViewEntry)
```

NotesViewEntry　　　　**Required**　　　　**O.Ref.**
An entry in the *NotesView* (the default is the current entry).

This method returns a handle on the next document sibling in the current view navigator. If there is no current document, this method returns NULL. The sibling document establishes user interface focus, and the cursor is automatically placed on that document.

GetNth

GetNth

```
Set nveNotesViewEntry = nvnavNotesViewNavigator.GetNth(lngIndex)
```

lngIndex   Required   &

The position of the entry in the view.

This method returns a handle on a particular entry in the current view navigator. The exact entry is determined by its position relative to the other entry contained in the *NotesViewNavigator*. The value passed as lngIndex indicates which entry to return (1 is the first entry returned). The order of the entries is the same as the sorted order of the entries in the current view. If there is no entry located in the position indicated by lngIndex, this method returns NULL. The entry establishes user interface focus, and the cursor is automatically placed on that entry.

GetParent

```
Set nveNotesViewEntry = nvnavNotesViewNavigator.GetParent(NotesViewEntry)   GetParent
```

NotesViewEntry   Required   O.Ref.

An entry in the *NotesView* (the default is the current entry).

This method returns a handle on the parent entry to the current entry in the current view navigator. If there is no parent entry, this method returns NULL. The parent entry establishes user interface focus, and the cursor is automatically placed on that entry.

GetPos

```
Set nveNotesViewEntry = nvnavNotesViewNavigator.GetPos(strPosition,   GetPos
➥strSeparator)
```

strPosition   Required $

The position of the entry in decimal delimited format.

strSeparator   Required $

The separator string used to delineate between the position levels.

This method returns a handle on a specific entry in the current view navigator based on its position. The position is determined by a string value, with each level delimited by a decimal. For example, if the value of strPosition were 1.1.1, the entry would be located at the first child (response) of the first child (response) of the first entry. If there is no entry at the specified position, this method returns NULL. The entry establishes user interface focus, and the cursor is automatically placed on that entry.

GetPrev

```
Set nveNotesViewEntry = nvnavNotesViewNavigator.GetPrev(NotesViewEntry)   GetPrev
```

NotesViewEntry   Required   O.Ref.

An entry in the *NotesView* (the default is the current entry).

This method returns a handle on the previous entry in the current view navigator. If there is no previous entry, this method returns NULL. The entry establishes user interface focus, and the cursor is automatically placed on the entry.

GetPrevCategory

```
Set nveNotesViewEntry = nvnavNotesViewNavigator.GetPrevCategory   GetPrev
➥(NotesViewEntry)                                                  Category
```

NotesViewEntry   Required   O.Ref.

An entry in the *NotesView* (the default is the current entry).

This method returns a handle on the previous category in the current view navigator. If there is no previous category, this method returns NULL. The category establishes user interface focus, and the cursor is automatically placed on the category.

GetPrevDocument

```
Set nveNotesViewEntry = nvnavNotesViewNavigator.GetPrevDocument
➥(NotesViewEntry)
```

NotesViewEntry   Required   O.Ref.

An entry in the *NotesView* (the default is the current entry).

This method returns a handle on the previous document in the current view navigator. If there is no previous document, this method returns NULL. The document establishes user interface focus, and the cursor is automatically placed on the document.

GetPrevSibling

```
Set nveNotesViewEntry = nvnavNotesViewNavigator.GetPrevSibling
➥(NotesViewEntry)
```

NotesViewEntry   Required   O.Ref.

An entry in the *NotesView* (the default is the current entry).

This method returns a handle on the previous sibling document in the current view navigator. If there is no previous sibling document, this method returns NULL. The sibling document establishes user interface focus, and the cursor is automatically placed on the sibling document.

Remarks

The *NotesViewNavigator* object can represent all the entries in a view or only a subset of the documents. Because *NotesViewNavigator* is contained by *NotesView*, if the parent *NotesView* is refreshed, the *NotesViewNavigator* is affected as well.

Depending on the design of the *NotesView*, a document can exist and be displayed under multiple categories. Nevertheless, you can still navigate to and from these documents as separate entries in the *EntryNotesViewEntry*. However, the GetNth method will return the first instance of the document as it is sorted in the *NotesView*. In addition, *NotesViewNavigators* created from an object that doesn't exist in the current *NotesView* will also return the first instance of the document as it is sorted in the *NotesView*.

Example

Contact managers, personal information managers (PIMs), and enterprise phone book applications have emerged as popular information-sharing applications and as early implementations of knowledge-management tools for Domino/Lotus Notes. The following example could be used as such a tool. Because of the nature of these (and many other) applications, the ability to synch related *NotesDocuments* often exists. However, Lotus Notes is a nonrelational data store.

Therefore, relational integrity must be maintained programmatically. This example demonstrates how this task might be accomplished. The code reads the value stored for the company name in the current document and then checks all the sibling and child (response) documents to see if their respective company name stores that same value. If the company name doesn't match, it is updated to the new value, and the sibling or child document is saved. This code would likely exist in an agent and/or in the QuerySave of the company form used to create and modify the company document.

```
Dim ns As New NotesSession
Dim ndoc As NotesDocument
Dim ndc As NotesDocumentCollection
Dim ndcContact As NotesDocumentCollection
Dim ndcCompany As NotesDocumentCollection
Dim ndocCompany As NotesDocument
Dim ndocContact As NotesDocument
Dim strUnique As String
Dim nvCompany As NotesView
Dim nvContact As NotesView
Set nvCompany = ns.CurrentDatabase.getView("Companies")
Set nvContact = ns.CurrentDatabase.GetView("Contacts")
Set ndc = ns.CurrentDatabase.AllDocuments
Set ndoc=ndc.GetFirstDocument
Print "One moment, processing documents..."
Do While Not ndoc Is Nothing
    If ndoc.Form(0) = "Company" Then
        If ndoc.tDocUNId(0) = "" Then
            strUnique = Evaluate("@Unique")
            ndoc.tDocUniqueId = strUnique & "*001"
            ndoc.Save True, False
        Else
            Set ndcCompany = nvCompany.GetalldocumentsByKey
            ➥(ndoc.tDocUNId(0),True)
            If ndcCompany.count <> 0 Then
                Set ndocCompany=ndcCompany.GetFirstDocument
                key$ = ndocCompany.TDocUNID(0)
            End If
            Set ndcContact=nvContact.GetAllDocumentsByKey(key$, True)
            For i%=1 To ndcContact.Count
                Set ndocContact=ndcContact.getnthDocument(i%)
                If ndocContact.tCompanyName(0)<>ndocCompany.tCompanyName(0)
                ➥Then
                    ndocContact.tCompanyName = ndocCompany.tCompanyName(0)
                    Call ndocContact.Save(True,False)
                End If
            Next
        End If
    End If
    Set ndoc = ndc.GetNextDocument( ndoc)
Loop
```

II

Java Classes

The *lotus.domino.ACL* object represents the Access Control List (ACL) of the parent *lotus.domino.Database* object. The ACL is one of the layers of security (at the database level) provided by Domino/Lotus Notes. The ACL contains lists of users, servers, and groups of users and servers that grant or restrict access to the database.

```
...
└ Database
    └ ACL
        └ ACLEntry
            └ Name
```

Java Syntax

By default, each *lotus.domino.Database* object contains a *lotus.domino.ACL* object. To access that object, use the `getACL` method of the *lotus.domino.Database* class (▶ 380).

You can also access and modify the *lotus.domino.ACL* object without having to declare it by using the methods available from the *lotus.domino.Database* class. Using this class, you can query (`queryAccess`), grant (`grantAccess`), or revoke (`revokeAccess`) access to a person, group, or server. However, in order to use these methods of the *lotus.domino.Database* object, you must know the name of the person, group, or server.

```
public class lotus.domino.ACL extends NotesBase
```

Once you have created or modified a *lotus.domino.ACL* object in a *lotus.domino.Database,* you must call the `save` method of the *lotus.domino.ACL* to save changes before closing the *lotus.domino.Database* object.

ACL Methods

addRole

addRole   naclACL.**addRole**(strName)

strName	Required	O.Ref.

The name of the new role.

This method adds a new role to the ACL entry of the respective *lotus.domino.ACL* object. The value passed for `strName` should never include parentheses or brackets since they are automatically added to the string value. Changes made with this method are not permanent until the `save` method of the *lotus.domino.ACL* class is called.

The following example displays the existing roles for the current database to the Java Console. A new role is then added to the *lotus.domino.ACL* using the value contained in the `tNewRole` field located on the current *lotus.domino.Document*.

```
import lotus.domino.*;
import java.util.Vector;

public class JavaAgent extends AgentBase {

    public void NotesMain() {

        try {
            Session ns = getSession();
            AgentContext agentContext = ns.getAgentContext();
            Agent nagt = agentContext.getCurrentAgent();
            Database ndb = agentContext.getCurrentDatabase();
            Document ndoc = agentContext.getDocumentContext();
            ACL nacl = ndb.getACL();
            Vector vecACLroles = nacl.getRoles();
            Vector vecFieldValue = ndoc.getItemValue("tNewRole");
            for (int intLoop=0; intLoop<vecACLroles.size(); intLoop++)
                System.out.println(vecACLroles.elementAt(intLoop));
```

```
            nacl.addRole(vecFieldValue.toString());
            nacl.save();
            System.out.println(vecFieldValue.toString() + " has been added
            ➥to the roles");

    } catch(Exception e) {
        e.printStackTrace();
    }
  }
}
```

createACLEntry

```
naclACLEntry = naclACL.createACLEntry(strName, intLevel)
```
createACLEntry

strName   Required   O.Ref.
The name of the person, group, or server for the new ACL entry.

intLevel   Required   %
The access level to assign to the person, group, or server defined in the strName. The
following table lists the constants for this parameter.

intLevel Constants

Constant Value	Access Level
ACL.LEVEL_NOACCESS	No access
ACL.LEVEL_DEPOSITOR	Depositor access
ACL.LEVEL_READER	Reader access
ACL.LEVEL_AUTHOR	Author access
ACL.LEVEL_EDITOR	Editor access
ACL.LEVEL_DESIGNER	Designer access
ACL.LEVEL_MANAGER	Manager access

The value returned from this method is the newly created *lotus.domino.ACLEntry*
(▶ 343). Any newly created *lotus.domino.ACLEntry* must be saved to disk by calling the
save method of *lotus.domino.ACL*, or it will be discarded. The value passes in strName,
which is not case-sensitive. The value must be a complete name (hierarchical names
can be passed in the abbreviated format).

deleteRole

```
naclACL.deleteRole(strName)
```
deleteRole

strName   Required   O.Ref.
The name of the role you want to remove.

This method deletes a role from the currently selected database *lotus.domino.ACL* entry.
Any newly deleted roles are not permanently removed from the *lotus.domino.ACL* until
the **save** method of the *lotus.domino.ACL* is called. If the role specified does not exist
in the selected *lotus.domino.ACL*, Notes returns the Role name not found error.

The following example displays the existing roles of the current database to the Java
Console. An existing role is then removed from the *lotus.domino.ACL* using the value
contained in the tNewRole field located on the current *lotus.domino.Document*.

```
import lotus.domino.*;
import java.util.Vector;

public class JavaAgent extends AgentBase {
```
continued >>

continued >>
```
public void NotesMain() {

    try {
        Session ns = getSession();
        AgentContext agentContext = ns.getAgentContext();
        Agent nagt = agentContext.getCurrentAgent();
        Database ndb = agentContext.getCurrentDatabase();
        Document ndoc = agentContext.getDocumentContext();
        ACL nacl = ndb.getACL();
        Vector vecACLroles = nacl.getRoles();
        Vector vecFieldValue = ndoc.getItemValue("tNewRole");
        for (int intLoop=0; intLoop<vecACLroles.size(); intLoop++)
        System.out.println(vecACLroles.elementAt(intLoop));
        nacl.deleteRole(vecFieldValue.toString());
        nacl.save();
        System.out.println(vecFieldValue.toString() + " role has been
        ➥deleted");

    } catch(Exception e) {
        e.printStackTrace();
    }
  }
}
```

---

getEntry	R.	O.Ref.

getEntry   `nacleACLEntry = naclACL.`**`getEntry`**`(strName)`

strName	Required	O.Ref.

The string name of the *lotus.domino.ACL* entry that you are looking for.

This method returns a handle to the *lotus.domino.ACLEntry* object (▶ 343) that matches the value passed in strName. The type of ACL entry can be a person, group, or server. However, this method only looks for names explicitly defined in the database ACL. It doesn't search within groups (whose values are defined in the Name and Address Book) for a particular name specified in strName. The value must be a complete name (hierarchical names can be passed in the abbreviated format). If this functionality is required, use the queryAccess method specified in the *lotus.domino.Database* class. This value is not case-sensitive. If the *lotus.domino.ACLEntry* is not found, this method returns null.

---

getFirstEntry	R.	O.Ref.

getFirstEntry   `nacleACLEntry = naclACL.`**`getFirstEntry`**`()`

The method returns a handle on the *lotus.domino.ACLEntry* (▶ 343) that is listed first in the Database ACL. For an example using this method, refer to the getNextEntry method of the *lotus.domino.ACL* class.

5.0 getInternetLevel	R	%

getInternet
Level   `intLevel = naclACL.`**`getInternetLevel`**`()`

Indicates the maximum access allowed to Web users who have authenticated with the Domino server using their respective Internet name and password. Therefore, you can limit the access allowed to a particular database for Web users who have equal or higher access when using a native Notes client. When you're working with Notes databases from a Notes client in the Notes user interface, you modify this method by selecting File | Database | Access Control. In the Advanced section, go to the drop-down list titled Maximum Internet name & password access. The integer values associated with each ACL level are listed in the following table.

Constant	Description
ACL.LEVEL_NOACCESS	No access. Can't access the database.
ACL.LEVEL_DEPOSITOR	Depositor. Can only create documents. Can't edit, delete, or read documents (even documents created by the depositor).
ACL.LEVEL_READER	Reader. Can read documents but can't create, edit, or delete them.
ACL.LEVEL_AUTHOR	Author. Can create and read documents. The author can edit and delete (optional) his own documents.
ACL.LEVEL_EDITOR	Editor. Can create, edit, read, and delete (optional) all documents.
ACL.LEVEL_DESIGNER	Designer. Has the same document access as an editor but can also create, edit, and delete design elements.
ACL.LEVEL_MANAGER	Manager. Has complete access to documents (deleting is optional), access to the database design, and access to modify the database Access Control.

The following example determines the internetLevel setting for the current database and displays the interpreted level to the Java Console.

```java
import lotus.domino.*;

public class JavaAgent extends AgentBase {

  public void NotesMain() {

    try {
      Session ns = getSession();
      AgentContext agentContext = ns.getAgentContext();
      Database ndb = agentContext.getCurrentDatabase();
      ACL nacl = ndb.getACL();
      String strLev = null;
      switch(nacl.getInternetLevel()) {
        case ACL.LEVEL_NOACCESS:
          strLev = "no"; break;
        case ACL.LEVEL_DEPOSITOR:
          strLev = "depositor"; break;
        case ACL.LEVEL_READER:
          strLev = "reader"; break;
        case ACL.LEVEL_AUTHOR:
          strLev = "author"; break;
        case ACL.LEVEL_EDITOR:
          strLev = "editor"; break;
        case ACL.LEVEL_DESIGNER:
          strLev = "designer"; break;
        case ACL.LEVEL_MANAGER:
          strLev = "manager"; break; }
      System.out.println("The internet level is " + strLev);

    } catch(Exception e) {
      e.printStackTrace();
    }
  }
}
```

getNextEntry

```
nacleACLEntry = naclACL.getNextEntry()

nacleACLEntry = naclACL.getNextEntry(nacleACLEntry)
```

getNextEntry

nacleACLEntry   Required   O.Ref.

The current *lotus.domino.ACLEntry* for the respective database. This parameter can't be `null`.

This method returns a handle on the next *lotus.domino.ACLEntry* (▶ 343) listed in the Database ACL. If there are no more entries in the *NotesACL,* this method will return `null`.

If the first signature is used (without parameters), this method will return the next entry following the previously returned entry.

The following example displays all the *lotus.domino.ACLEntries* for the current *lotus.domino.Database* to the Java Console.

```
import lotus.domino.*;

public class JavaAgent extends AgentBase {

  public void NotesMain() {

    try {
      Session ns = getSession();
      AgentContext agentContext = ns.getAgentContext();
      Agent nagt = agentContext.getCurrentAgent();
        Database ndb = agentContext.getCurrentDatabase();
        ACL nacl = ndb.getACL();
        ACLEntry nacle = nacl.getFirstEntry();
        do {
            System.out.println(nacle.getNameObject()); }
        while ((nacle = nacl.getNextEntry(nacle)) != null);

    } catch(Exception e) {
      e.printStackTrace();
    }
  }
}
```

getParent   R.   O.Ref.

getParent   `ndbDatabase = naclACL.getParent`

Returns a handle on the *lotus.domino.Database* object (▶ 373) of the database to which this ACL entry pertains.

getRoles   R   ()

getRoles   `vecRoles = naclACL.getRoles()`

Returns a string array of all the roles that are defined in the respective Access Control List. Each element in the array represents the name of a role. If only one role is defined for this ACL entry, an array is still returned with only one element. The role name returned is surrounded by square brackets (such as [Admin]).

The following example displays all the roles for the current *lotus.domino.Database* to the Java Console.

```
import lotus.domino.*;
import java.util.Vector;

public class JavaAgent extends AgentBase {

  public void NotesMain() {

    try {
      Session ns = getSession();
```

```
        AgentContext agentContext = ns.getAgentContext();
        Agent nagt = agentContext.getCurrentAgent();
        Database ndb = agentContext.getCurrentDatabase();
        ACL nacl = ndb.getACL();
        Vector vecACLroles = nacl.getRoles();
        System.out.println("The available roles are:");
        for (int intLoop=0; intLoop<vecACLroles.size(); intLoop++)
        System.out.println(vecACLroles.elementAt(intLoop));

    } catch(Exception e) {
        e.printStackTrace();
    }
  }
}
```

---

isUniformAccess   R   T/F

```
bolUniform = naclACL.isUniformAccess()
```

Indicates whether uniform access has been set for the respective *lotus.domino.Database*.
true means that uniform access is set. false means that uniform access is not set. If this
method is set to true, all replica copies that are created from this database and that replicate with this database must use a consistent ACL among one another. In other words,
they must have identical entries for all their ACL entries, or when the databases authenti-
cate with one another, replication will not be allowed. When working with Notes databases from a client in the Notes user interface, you enable or disable this method by
selecting File | Database | Access Control. In the Advanced section, go to the checkbox
titled Enforce a consistent Access Control List across all replicas of this database. Be careful when using this method. If this method has been enabled, be sure that any changes
made to the database access control are made only on the Administration Server for this
database. Otherwise, if changes are made on the nonadministration server or on a local
copy, replication for this database will be permanently disabled with other replica copies.
This is a powerful, but potentially hazardous, security feature.

---

removeACLEntry

```
naclACL.removeACLEntry(strName)
```

strName   Required   O.Ref.
The name of the person, group, or server entry to remove.

This method removes the name of a role defined in the *lotus.domino.ACL*. The value
specified in strName must be a complete name, but it can be abbreviated if it's the
hierarchical name. You must explicitly call the save method of the *lotus.domino.ACL*
object for the modifications to be permanently saved to disk.

---

renameRole

```
naclACL.renameRole(strOldname, strNewname)
```

strOldname   Required   O.Ref.
The current name of the role without brackets.

strNewname   Required   O.Ref.
The new name to assign the current role without brackets.

This method changes the name of a role defined in the *lotus.domino.ACL*. All entries
located in the ACL that had the old role defined in them will get the new role
assigned to them instead. You must explicitly call the save method of the
lotus.domino.ACL object for the modifications to be permanently saved to disk.

save

```
naclACL.save()
```

This method saves any changes that have been made to the database ACL. You must save any changes you have made to the database before you close it, or they will be discarded.

5.0 setInternetLevel

```
naclACL.setInternetLevel = (intLevel)
```

intLevel   Required   %.
The internet access level for this database.

Sets the maximum access allowed to Web users who have authenticated with the Domino server using their respective Internet name and password. Therefore, you can limit the access allowed to a particular database for Web users who have equal or higher access when using a native Notes client. When you're working with Notes databases from a Notes client in the Notes user interface, you modify this method by selecting File | Database | Access Control. In the Advanced section, go to the drop-down list titled Maximum Internet name & password access. The following table lists the integer values associated with each ACL level.

Constant	Description
ACL.LEVEL_NOACCESS	No access. Can't access the database.
ACL.LEVEL_DEPOSITOR	Depositor. Can only create documents. Can't edit, delete, or read documents (even documents created by the depositor).
ACL.LEVEL_READER	Reader. Can read documents but can't create, edit, or delete them.
ACL.LEVEL_AUTHOR	Author. Can create and read documents. The author can edit and delete (optional) his own documents.
ACL.LEVEL_EDITOR	Editor. Can create, edit, read, and delete (optional) all documents.
ACL.LEVEL_DESIGNER	Designer. Has the same document access as an editor but can also create, edit, and delete design elements.
ACL.LEVEL_MANAGER	Manager. Has complete access to documents (deleting is optional), access to the database design, and access to modify the database Access Control.

setUniformAccess

```
naclACL.setUniformAccess(bolUniform)
```

Sets the uniform access for the respective *lotus.domino.Database*. true means that uniform access is set. false means that uniform access is not set. If this method is set to true, all replica copies that are created from this database and that replicate with this database must use a consistent ACL among one another. In other words, they must have identical entries for all their ACL entries, or when the databases authenticate with one another, replication will not be allowed. When you're working with Notes databases from a client in the Notes user interface, you would enable and disable this method by selecting File | Database | Access Control. In the Advanced section, go to the checkbox titled Enforce a consistent Access Control List across all replicas of this database. Be careful when using this method. If this method has been enabled, be sure that any changes made to the database access control are made only on the Administration Server for this database. Otherwise, if changes are made on the nonadministration server or a local copy, replication for this database will be permanently disabled with other replica copies. This is a powerful but potentially hazardous security feature.

Remarks

Keep in mind that the script performing these operations (whether developed in LotusScript or Java) must still adhere to the Notes security model. Therefore, the program or user who is running the script must have manager access to the database in order to modify the ACL. If this script is being run on the server by an agent, the script might be using the access control level of the person who last modified the agent, since the person who last modifies the agent signs that agent and thus becomes its owner. When the agent is designed, it is an option to have the agent run as the current user or as the user who last saved the agent.

Example

The following script tests to see whether isUniformAccess is set. It reads all the *lotus.domino.ACLEntries* and roles for the current database and displays their values using a message box.

```
import lotus.domino.*;
import java.util.Vector;

public class JavaAgent extends AgentBase {

  public void NotesMain() {

    try {
      Session ns = getSession();
      AgentContext agentContext = ns.getAgentContext();
      Agent nagt = agentContext.getCurrentAgent();
      Database ndb = agentContext.getCurrentDatabase();
      ACL nacl = ndb.getACL();
      if (nacl.isUniformAccess()) {
          System.out.println("Uniform access is " +
          ➥nacl.isUniformAccess() + ", don't modify the ACL");
          return;
      }
      Vector vecACLroles = nacl.getRoles();
      System.out.println("The available roles are:");
      for (int intLoop=0; intLoop<vecACLroles.size(); intLoop++)
      System.out.println(vecACLroles.elementAt(intLoop));
      System.out.println("The available ACL Entries are:");
      ACLEntry nacle = nacl.getFirstEntry();
      do {
          System.out.println(nacle.getNameObject()); }
      while ((nacle = nacl.getNextEntry(nacle)) != null); }

      catch(Exception e) {
      e.printStackTrace();
    }
  }
}
```

This object represents an entry in the Domino/Lotus Notes Access Control List (ACL). The user type for this entry can be either a person, server, or a group of people of a certain type or server, or mixed. The ACL is one of the layers of security (at the database level) provided by Domino/Lotus Notes.

```
...
└ Database
   └ ACL
      └ ACLEntry
         └ Name
```

continued >>

Java Syntax

Public class **ACLEntry** extends Base

A *lotus.domino.ACLEntry* object can be created in Java through the use of the createACLEntry method of the *lotus.domino.ACL* object (▶ 335).

You can also access an existing *lotus.domino.ACLEntry* object by using the getEntry method of the *lotus.domino.ACL* class (▶ 336) if you know the name of the specific *lotus.domino.ACLEntry*. In addition, you can use the getFirstEntry and getNextEntry methods of the *lotus.domino.ACL* class (▶ 337) to locate and step through the entries.

After you have created a *lotus.domino.ACLEntry* object in a *lotus.domino.ACL,* you must call the save method of the *lotus.domino.ACL* to save to disk the changes made to the ACL.

ACLEntry Methods

disableRole

nacleACLEntry.**disableRole**(strName)   disableRole

strName	Required	O.Ref.

The name of the role to disable.

This method disables the specified role for the current *lotus.domino.ACLEntry.* If the specified role has already been disabled for the current *lotus.domino.ACLEntry,* this method will do nothing. If the specified role doesn't exist for the current *lotus.domino.ACLEntry,* this method will return a Role name not found error. Refer to the isRoleEnabled method of the *lotus.domino.ACLEntry* class for an example that uses this method (▶ 351).

You must call the save method of the *lotus.domino.ACL* object to save the changes to disk and make the modifications take effect. Otherwise, the modifications are lost when the script is complete.

enableRole

nacleACLEntry.**enableRole**(strName)   enableRole

strName	Required	O.Ref.

The name of the role to enable.

This method enables the specified role for the current *lotus.domino.ACLEntry.* If the specified role has already been enabled for the current *lotus.domino.ACLEntry,* this method will do nothing. If the specified role does not exist for the current *lotus.domino.ACLEntry,* this method will return a Role name not found error. Refer to the isRoleEnabled method of the *lotus.domino.ACLEntry* class for an example that uses this method (▶ 351).

You must call the save method of the *lotus.domino.ACL* object to save the changes to disk and make the modifications take effect. Otherwise, the modifications are lost when the script is complete.

getLevel
getLevel   R   %

```
intLevel = nacleACLEntry.getLevel()
```

This method indicates the access level of the current entry.

The value returned for this method is a constant of type integer. Here are the values that can be returned:

Constant Value	Assigned Access
ACL.LEVEL_NOACCESS	No access
ACL.LEVEL_DEPOSITOR	Depositor
ACL.LEVEL_READER	Reader
ACL.LEVEL_AUTHOR	Author
ACL.LEVEL_EDITOR	Editor
ACL.LEVEL_DESIGNER	Designer
ACL.LEVEL_MANAGER	Manager

For an example that uses this method, refer to the `isGroup` method of the *lotus.domino.ACLEntry* class (▶ 349).

getName
getName   R   O.Ref.

```
strName = nacleACLEntry.getName()
```

The string value representing the name of the current ACL entry.

Changing the name of the entry does not affect the other attributes of the *lotus.domino.ACLEntry,* such as the ACL level and whether the entry is a person, server, and so on. For an example that uses this method, refer to the `getRoles` method of the *lotus.domino.ACLEntry* class (▶ 346).

getName
Object
getNameObject   R   O.Ref.

```
strName = nacleACLEntry.getNameObject()
```

The string value representing the name of the current entry.

getParent
getParent   R   O.Ref.

```
naclACL = nacleACLEntry.getParent()
```

This method returns a handle to the *lotus.domino.ACL* object that contains the current *lotus.domino.ACLEntry.*

getRoles
getRoles   R   ()

```
vecRoles = nacleACLEntry.getRoles()
```

This method returns a string array of the roles that are enabled for a specified entry. Each element contained in this array represents the role name surrounded by brackets.

The following code snippet steps through all the entries in the current database's *lotus.domino.ACLEntry.* For each entry, a list of all the roles enabled for that entry is built and displayed to the user of the Java Console.

```java
import lotus.domino.*;
import java.util.Vector;

public class JavaAgent extends AgentBase {

  public void NotesMain() {

    try {
```

```
            Session ns = getSession();
            AgentContext agentContext = ns.getAgentContext();
            Agent nagt = agentContext.getCurrentAgent();
            Database ndb = agentContext.getCurrentDatabase();
            ACL nacl = ndb.getACL();
            ACLEntry nacle = nacl.getFirstEntry();
            do {
                Vector vecACLroles = nacl.getRoles();
                if (vecACLroles.size() == 0)
                    System.out.println(nacle.getName() + " has no roles");
                else {
                    System.out.println("ACL Entry: " + nacle.getNameObject());
                    for (int intLoop=0; intLoop<vecACLroles.size(); intLoop++)
                    System.out.println(vecACLroles.elementAt(intLoop)); } }
            while ((nacle = nacl.getNextEntry(nacle)) != null);

        } catch(Exception e) {
            e.printStackTrace();
        }
    }
}
```

5.0 getUserType   R   %

```
intUserType = nacleACLEntry.getUserType()
```
getUserType

This method returns the user type for the current entry.

The value returned for this method is a constant of type integer. The values that can be returned are ACLEntry.TYPE_MIXED_GROUP, ACLEntry.TYPE_PERSON, ACLEntry.TYPE_PERSON_GROUP, ACLEntry.TYPE_SERVER, ACLEntry.TYPE_SERVER_GROUP, and ACLEntry.TYPE_UNSPECIFIED.

5.0 isAdminReaderAuthor   R   T/F

```
bolIsAdminReadAuth = nacleACLEntry.isAdminReaderAuthor()
```
isAdminReader
Author

This method indicates whether the current entry is designated as the administration server for the current *lotus.domino.Database* object with rights to modify reader/author fields. true indicates that the entry member(s) is/are designated as the administrator reader/author. false indicates that the entry member(s) is/are not.

5.0 isAdminServer   R   T/F

```
bolIsAdminServer = nacleACLEntry.isAdminServer()
```
isAdminServer

This method indicates whether the current entry is designated as the administration server for the current *lotus.domino.Database* object. true indicates that the entry member(s) can delete documents. false indicates that they can't. When you're working in the user interface of the Domino/Lotus Notes client, you can find this entry by first selecting File | Database | Access Control...Go to the Advanced section. This setting is located under the administration server. However, be careful! This method can be set to any *lotus.domino.ACLEntry,* even if the entry isn't a server user type and doesn't have manager access! In other words, you could assign an entry that has an access level of No Access with an unspecified user type as the administration server! This method is false by default.

---

isCanCreateDocuments   R   T/F

```
bolCanCreateDocs = nacleACLEntry.isCanCreateDocuments()
```
isCanCreate
Documents

This method indicates whether the current entry has access to create new documents in the database. `true` indicates that the entry member(s) can create new documents. `false` indicates that they can't. This method affects only entries that are set at Author access to the database. It has no effect on all other entry levels because their ability to create documents is already determined by their respective ACL entry. Specifically, this setting is automatically set to `true` for entries that are Manager, Designer, Editor, or Depositor and that can't be revoked. Similarly, this setting is automatically set to `false` for entries that are Reader, Depositor, or No Access and that can't be modified. For entries that are set to Author access, this method defaults to `true`.

5.0 **isCanCreateLSOrJavaAgent**   R   T/F

isCanCreateLSOr
JavaAgent

`bolCanCreateAgent = nacleACLEntry.`**`isCanCreateLSOrJavaAgent`**`()`

This method indicates whether the current entry has access to create LotusScript/Java agents in the database. `true` indicates that the entry member(s) can create LotusScript/Java agents. `false` indicates that they can't. This method doesn't affect Manager entry levels because their ability to create documents is already determined by their respective ACLs. In other words, Managers are automatically allowed to create LotusScript and Java agents, and this access can't be revoked. ACL entries that are set to Designer, Editor, Author, or Reader can be modified by this method (for these entries, the default value for this method is `false`). Entries set to Depositor or No Access are automatically set to `false` and can't be modified.

---

isCanCreatePersonalAgent   R   T/F

isCanCreate
PersonalAgent

`bolCanCreatePersAgent = nacleACLEntry.`**`isCanCreatePersonalAgent`**`()`

This method indicates whether the current entry has access to create personal agents in the database. `true` indicates that the entry member(s) can create personal agents. `false` indicates that they can't. This method doesn't affect Manager and Designer entry levels because their ability to create personal agents is already determined by their respective ACLs. In other words, they are automatically allowed to create personal agents, and this access can't be revoked. ACL entries that are set to Editor, Author, or Reader can be modified by this method (for these entries, the default value for this method is `false`). Entries set to Depositor or No Access are automatically set to `false` and can't be modified.

---

isCanCreatePersonalFolder   R   T/F

isCanCreate
PersonalFolder

`bolCanCreateFolder = nacleACLEntry.`**`isCanCreatePersonalFolder`**`()`

This method indicates whether the current entry has access to create personal folders in the database. `true` indicates that the entry member(s) can create personal folders. `false` indicates that they can't. This method doesn't affect Manager and Designer entry levels because their ability to create personal folders is already determined by their respective ACLs. In other words, they are automatically allowed to create personal folders, and this access can't be revoked. ACL entries that are set to Editor, Author, or Reader can be modified by this method (for these entries, the default value for this method is `false`). Entries set to Depositor or No Access are automatically set to `false` and can't be modified.

The following example tests to see if the current user has rights to create a personal folder in the current database. If the user has sufficient rights to create personal folders, he can proceed with the current script. If he doesn't have sufficient access, a message is written to the Java Console, saying that the user isn't allowed to perform this request, and the script is abandoned. Keep in mind that although this method can be modified to enable or retract the rights for the current ACL entry, some *lotus.domino.ACLEntry* rights are predetermined as a result of their respective *lotus.domino.ACL* access level.

For example, this method for a user with Depositor access defaults to `false` and can't be modified with this method. Likewise, a user with Manager access will automatically be granted rights to create personal folders, and this right can't be revoked. In these cases, the method becomes read-only.

```java
import lotus.domino.*;

public class JavaAgent extends AgentBase {

    public void NotesMain() {

    try {
        Session ns = getSession();
        AgentContext agentContext = ns.getAgentContext();
        Agent nagt = agentContext.getCurrentAgent();
        Database ndb = agentContext.getCurrentDatabase();
        ACL nacl = ndb.getACL();
        ACLEntry nacle = nacl.getEntry(ns.getUserName());
        if (nacle.isCanCreatePersonalFolder())
            System.out.println("Continue with code since user has sufficient
            ➥access!");
        else
            System.out.println("You are not allowed to create personal
            ➥folders");
            return;

        } catch(Exception e) {
            e.printStackTrace();
        }
    }
}
```

5.0 isCanCreateSharedFolder   R   T/F

`bolCanCreateShared = nacleACLEntry.isCanCreateSharedFolder()`   isCanCreate
SharedFolder

This method indicates whether the current entry has access to create shared folders in the database. `true` indicates that the entry member(s) can create shared folders. `false` indicates that they can't. This method doesn't affect Manager and Designer entry levels because their ability to create shared folders is already determined by their respective ACLs. In other words, they are automatically allowed to create personal folders, and this access can't be revoked. ACL entries that are set to Editor can be modified by this method (for these entries, the default value for this method is `false`). Entries set to Author, Reader, Depositor, or No Access are automatically set to `false` and can't be modified.

---

isCanDeleteDocuments   R   T/F

`bolCanDeleteDocs = nacleACLEntry.isCanDeleteDocuments()`   isCanDelete
Documents

This method indicates whether the current entry has access to delete documents in the database. `true` indicates that the entry member(s) can delete documents. `false` indicates that they can't. This method doesn't affect Reader, Depositor, or No Access entry levels because their ability to delete documents is already determined by their respective ACLs. In other words, they are automatically set to `false` and therefore aren't allowed to delete documents, and this access can't be modified. All other ACL entries that are set to Author access or higher can be modified by this method. For entries that are set to Author access, this method defaults to `true`.

5.0 isGroup   R   T/F

`bolIsGroup = nacleACLEntry.isGroup()`   isGroup

This method indicates whether the current entry is designated as group user type. true indicates that the entry member(s) is/are a group user type. false indicates that they are not. Setting this method to false results in the user type being set to Unspecified. This method works in tandem with the isServer and isPerson methods. By default, setting isGroup to true will cause the user type of the current entry to be set to Mixed Group. However, if the isServer method is set to true, this setting will be set to Server Group. Similarly, if the isPerson setting is set to true, this method will be set to Person Group. This method is false by default.

The following example steps through all the ACL entries for the current database and displays whether they are a person, server, or group to the Java Console.

```java
import lotus.domino.*;

public class JavaAgent extends AgentBase {

  public void NotesMain() {

    try {
      Session ns = getSession();
      AgentContext agentContext = ns.getAgentContext();
      Agent nagt = agentContext.getCurrentAgent();
      Database ndb = agentContext.getCurrentDatabase();
      ACL nacl = ndb.getACL();
      ACLEntry nacle = nacl.getFirstEntry();
      do {
        if (nacle.isPerson())
          System.out.println("The " + nacle.getNameObject() +
          " is a person" + " with access set to " +
          ➥nacle.getLevel());
        if (nacle.isServer())
          System.out.println("The " + nacle.getNameObject() +
          " is a server" + " with access set to " + nacle.getLevel() +
          " and IsAdminserver set to: " + nacle.isAdminServer());
        if (nacle.isGroup())
          System.out.println("The " + nacle.getNameObject() +
          " is a group" + " with access set to " + nacle.getLevel()); }
      while ((nacle = nacl.getNextEntry(nacle)) != null);

    } catch(Exception e) {
      e.printStackTrace();
    }
  }
}
```

5.0 isPerson   R   T/F

isPerson   bolIsPerson = nacleACLEntry.**isPerson**()

This method indicates whether the current entry is designated as person user type. true indicates that the entry member(s) is/are a person user type. false indicates that they are not. Setting this method to false results in the user type being set to Unspecified. This method works in conjunction with the isGroup method. By default, setting isPerson to true will cause the user type of the current entry to be set to Person. However, if the isGroup method is set to true, this setting will be set to Person Group. This method is false by default.

isPublicReader   R   T/F

```
bolIsPublicReader = nacleACLEntry.isPublicReader()
```

This method indicates whether the current entry is a public reader of the database.
true indicates that the entry member(s) is/are public reader(s). false indicates that
they aren't. This method is false by default.

isPublicWriter   R   T/F

```
bolisPublicWriter = nacleACLEntry.isPublicWriter()
```

This method indicates whether the current entry is a public writer of the database.
true indicates that the entry member(s) is/are public writer(s). false indicates that
they aren't. This method is false by default.

isRoleEnabled

```
bolIsRolEnabled = nacleACLEntry.isRoleEnabled(strName)
```

strName   Required   T/F
The name of the role.

This method indicates whether the specified role is enabled for the current
lotus.domino.ACLEntry object. true indicates that the role is enabled for the entry.
false indicates that it is not.

The following example toggles all the *lotus.domino.ACLEntries* for the NewsEditor role.
If the role is enabled, the script disables it. If the role is disabled, the script enables it.

```
import lotus.domino.*;

public class JavaAgent extends AgentBase {

  public void NotesMain() {

    try {
      Session ns = getSession();
      AgentContext agentContext = ns.getAgentContext();
      Agent nagt = agentContext.getCurrentAgent();
      Database ndb = agentContext.getCurrentDatabase();
      ACL nacl = ndb.getACL();
      ACLEntry nacle = nacl.getFirstEntry();
      do {
        if (nacle.isRoleEnabled("NewsEditor")) {
          nacle.disableRole("NewsEditor");
          System.out.println("The " + nacle.getNameObject() +
          ➥"role was disabled"); }
        else  {
          nacle.enableRole("NewsEditor");   }
          System.out.println("The " + nacle.getNameObject() +
          ➥"role was enabled");   }
      while ((nacle = nacl.getNextEntry(nacle)) != null);
      nacl.save();

    } catch(Exception e) {
      e.printStackTrace();
    }
  }
}
```

5.0 isServer   R   T/F

isServer   `bolisServer = nacleACLEntry.isServer()`

This method indicates whether the current entry is designated as server user type. true indicates that the entry member(s) is/are a server user type. false indicates that they aren't. Setting this method to false results in the user type being set to Unspecified. This method works in conjunction with the isGroup method. By default, setting isServer to true will cause the user type of the current entry to be set to Server. However, if the isGroup method is set to true, this setting will be set to Server Group. This method is false by default.

---

remove

remove   `nacleACLEntry.remove()`

This method removes an entry from the access control list.

You must call the save method of the *lotus.domino.ACL* object to save the changes to disk and make the modifications take effect. Otherwise, the modifications are lost when the script is complete.

5.0 setAdminReaderAuthor   W   T/F

setAdmin   `nacleACLEntry.setAdminReaderAuthor(bolisAdminreadauth)`
ReaderAuthor

This method indicates whether the current entry is designated as the administration server for the current *lotus.domino.Database* object with rights to modify reader/author fields. true indicates that the entry member(s) is/are designated as the administrator reader/author. false indicates that they are not.

You must call the save method of the *lotus.domino.ACL* object to save the changes to disk and make the modifications take effect. Otherwise, the modifications are lost when the script is complete.

5.0 setAdminServer   W   T/F

setAdminServer   `nacleACLEntry.setAdminServer(bolisAdminServer)`

This method determines whether the current entry is designated as the administration server for the current *lotus.domino.Database* object. true indicates that the entry member(s) can delete documents. false indicates that they can't. When you're working in the user interface of the Domino/Lotus Notes client, you can find this entry by first selecting File | Database | Access Control...Go to the Advanced section. This setting is located under the administration server. However, be careful! This method can be set to any *lotus.domino.ACLEntry,* even if the entry isn't a server user type and doesn't have manager access! In other words, you could assign an entry that has an access level of No Access with an unspecified user type as the administration server! This method is false by default.

You must call the save method of the *lotus.domino.ACL* object to save the changes to disk and make the modifications take effect. Otherwise, the modifications are lost when the script is complete.

---

setCanCreateDocuments   W   T/F

setCanCreate   `nacleACLEntry.setCanCreateDocuments(bolCanCreateDocs)`
Documents

This method determines whether the current entry has access to create new documents in the database. true indicates that the entry member(s) can create new documents. false indicates that they can't. This method affects only entries that are set to Author access to the database. It has no effect on all other entry levels because their ability to create documents is already determined by their respective ACL entries.

Specifically, this setting is automatically set to true for entries that are Manager, Designer, Editor, or Depositor and that can't be revoked. Similarly, this setting is automatically set to false for entries that are Reader, Depositor, or No Access and that can't be modified. For entries that are set to Author access, this method defaults to true.

You must call the save method of the *lotus.domino.ACL* object to save the changes to disk and make the modifications take effect. Otherwise, the modifications are lost when the script is complete.

5.0 setCanCreateLSOrJavaAgent   W   T/F

`nacleACLEntry.setCanCreateLSOrJavaAgent(bolCanCreateAgent)`   setCanCreate
LSOrJavaAgent

This method determines whether the current entry has access to create LotusScript/Java agents in the database. true indicates that the entry member(s) can create LotusScript/Java agents. false indicates that they can't. This method doesn't affect Manager entry levels because their ability to create documents is already determined by their respective ACLs. In other words, Managers are automatically allowed to create LotusScript and Java agents, and this access can't be revoked. ACL entries that are set to Designer, Editor, Author, or Reader can be modified by this method (for these entries, the default value for this method is false). Entries set to Depositor or No Access are automatically set to false and can't be modified.

You must call the save method of the *lotus.domino.ACL* object to save the changes to disk and make the modifications take effect. Otherwise, the modifications are lost when the script is complete.

---

setCanCreatePersonalAgent   W   T/F

`nacleACLEntry.setCanCreatePersonalAgent(bolCanCreatePersAgent)`   setCanCreate
PersonalAgent

This method determines whether the current entry has access to create personal agents in the database. true indicates that the entry member(s) can create personal agents. false indicates that they can't. This method doesn't affect Manager and Designer entry levels because their ability to create personal agents is already determined by their respective ACLs. In other words, they are automatically allowed to create personal agents, and this access can't be revoked. ACL entries that are set to Editor, Author, or Reader can be modified by this method (for these entries, the default value for this method is false). Entries set to Depositor or No Access are automatically set to false and can't be modified.

You must call the save method of the *lotus.domino.ACL* object to save the changes to disk and make the modifications take effect. Otherwise, the modifications are lost when the script is complete.

---

setCanCreatePersonalFolder   W   T/F

`nacleACLEntry.setCanCreatePersonalFolder(bolCanCreateFolder)`   setCanCreate
PersonalFolder

This method determines whether the current entry has access to create personal folders in the database. (true indicates that the entry member(s) can create personal folders. false indicates that they can't. This method doesn't affect Manager and Designer entry levels because their ability to create personal folders is already determined by their respective ACLs. In other words, they are automatically allowed to create personal folders, and this access can't be revoked. ACL entries that are set to Editor, Author, or Reader can be modified by this method (for these entries, the default value for this method is false). Entries set to Depositor or No Access are automatically set to false and can't be modified.

You must call the save method of the *lotus.domino.ACL* object to save the changes to disk and make the modifications take effect. Otherwise, the modifications are lost when the script is complete.

5.0 setCanCreateSharedFolder   W   T/F

setCanCreate
SharedFolder

`nacleACLEntry.`**`setCanCreateSharedFolder`**`(bolCanCreateSharedFolder)`

This method determines whether the current entry has access to create shared folders in the database. `true` indicates that the entry member(s) can create shared folders. `false` indicates that they can't. This method doesn't affect Manager and Designer entry levels because their ability to create shared folders is already determined by their respective ACLs. In other words, they are automatically allowed to create personal folders, and this access can't be revoked. ACL entries that are set to Editor can be modified by this method (for these entries, the default value for this method is `false`). Entries set to Author, Reader, Depositor, or No Access are automatically set to `false` and can't be modified.

You must call the `save` method of the *lotus.domino.ACL* object to save the changes to disk and make the modifications take effect. Otherwise, the modifications are lost when the script is complete.

---

setCanDeleteDocuments   W   T/F

setCanDelete
Documents

`nacleACLEntry.`**`setCanDeleteDocuments`**`(bolCanDeleteDocs)`

This method determines whether the current entry has access to delete documents in the database. `true` indicates that the entry member(s) can delete documents. `false` indicates that they can't. This method doesn't affect Reader, Depositor, or No Access entry levels because their ability to delete documents is already determined by their respective ACLs. In other words, they are automatically set to `false` and therefore aren't allowed to delete documents, and this access can't be modified. All other ACL entries that are set to Author access or higher can be modified by this method. For entries that are set to Author access, this method defaults to `true`.

You must call the `save` method of the *lotus.domino.ACL* object to save the changes to disk and make the modifications take effect. Otherwise, the modifications are lost when the script is complete.

5.0 setGroup   W   T/F

setGroup

`nacleACLEntry.`**`setGroup`**`(bolisGroup)`

This method determines whether the current entry is designated as group user type. `true` indicates that the entry member(s) is/are group user type. `false` indicates that they aren't. Setting this method to `false` results in the user type being set to Unspecified. This method works in tandem with the `isServer` and `isPerson` methods. By default, setting `isGroup` to `true` will cause the user type of the current entry to be set to Mixed Group. However, if the `isServer` method is set to `true`, this setting will be set to Server Group. Similarly, if the `isPerson` setting is set to `true`, this method will be set to Person Group. This method is `false` by default.

You must call the `save` method of the *lotus.domino.ACL* object to save the changes to disk and make the modifications take effect. Otherwise, the modifications are lost when the script is complete.

---

setLevel   W   %

setLevel

`nacleACLEntry.`**`setLevel`**`(intLevel)`

This method determines the access level of the current entry.

The value returned for this method is a constant of type integer. Here are the values that can be returned:

Constant Value	Assigned Access
ACL.LEVEL_NOACCESS	No access
ACL.LEVEL_DEPOSITOR	Depositor
ACL.LEVEL_READER	Reader
ACL.LEVEL_AUTHOR	Author
ACL.LEVEL_EDITOR	Editor
ACL.LEVEL_DESIGNER	Designer
ACL.LEVEL_MANAGER	Manager

For an example that uses this method, refer to the `isGroup` method of the
lotus.notes.ACLEntry class (▶ 349).

---

setName   W   O.Ref.

`nacleACLEntry.`**`setName`**`(strName)`   setName

`nacleACLEntry.`**`setName`**`(nnName)`

Sets the *lotus.domino.Name* or string value representing the name of the current entry.
When calling this method, you can either pass a reference to a *lotus.domino.Name* object
or pass a string representing the *lotus.domino.Name*. When passing a string value, use the
canonical or abbreviated format of the hierarchical name. The parameter passed when
calling this method (as either *lotus.domino.Name* or `strName`) can not be NULL.

Changing the name of the entry doesn't affect the other attributes of the
lotus.domino.ACLEntry, such as the ACL level and whether the entry is a person, server,
and so on. For an example that uses this method, refer to the `getRoles` method of the
lotus.domino.ACLEntry class (▶ 346).

5.0 setPerson   W   T/F

`nacleACLEntry.`**`setPerson`**`(bolisPerson)`   setPerson

This method determines whether the current entry is designated as person user type.
`true` indicates that the entry member(s) is/are person user type. `false` indicates that
they aren't. Setting this method to `false` results in the user type being set to
Unspecified. This method works in conjunction with the `isGroup` method. By default,
setting `isPerson` to `true` causes the user type of the current entry to be set to Person.
However, if the `isGroup` method is set to `true`, this setting will be set to Person
Group. This method is `false` by default.

You must call the `save` method of the *lotus.domino.ACL* object to save the changes to
disk and make the modifications take effect. Otherwise, the modifications are lost
when the script is complete.

---

setPublicReader   W   T/F

`nacleACLEntry.`**`setPublicReader`**`(bolIsPublicReader)`   setPublic
Reader

This method determines whether the current entry is a public reader of the database.
`true` indicates that the entry member(s) is/are public reader(s). `false` indicates that
they aren't. This method is `false` by default.

---

setPublicWriter   W   T/F

`nacleACLEntry.`**`setPublicWriter`**`(bolisPublicWriter)`   setPublic
Writer

This method determines whether the current entry is a public writer of the database.
`true` indicates that the entry member(s) is/are public writer(s). `false` indicates that
they aren't. This method is `false` by default.

5.0 setServer   W   T/F

setServer   `nacleACLEntry.setServer(bolisServer)`

This method determines whether the current entry is designated as server user type. `true` indicates that the entry member(s) is/are server user type. `false` indicates that they aren't. Setting this method to `false` results in the user type being set to Unspecified. This method works in conjunction with the isGroup method. By default, setting isServer to `true` causes the user type of the current entry to be set to Server. However, if the isGroup method is set to `true`, this setting will be set to Server Group. This method is `false` by default.

You must call the `save` method of the *lotus.domino.ACL* object to save the changes to disk and make the modifications take effect. Otherwise, the modifications are lost when the script is complete.

5.0 setUserType   R   %

setUserType   `nacleACLEntry.setUserType(intUserType)`

This method sets the user type for the current entry.

The value returned for this method is a constant of type integer. The values that can be returned are `ACLEntry.TYPE_MIXED_GROUP`, `ACLEntry.TYPE_PERSON`, `ACLEntry.TYPE_PERSON_GROUP`, `ACLEntry.TYPE_SERVER`, `ACLEntry.TYPE_SERVER_GROUP`, and `ACLEntry.TYPE_UNSPECIFIED`.

Remarks

Using the parent class *lotus.domino.ACL,* you can access an existing *lotus.domino.ACLEntry* in one of three ways. If you know the name of the *lotus.domino.ACLEntry,* you can use the getEntry method of the *lotus.domino.ACL* object. Similarly, you can use the getFirstEntry or getNextEntry methods of *lotus.domino.ACL* to step through the entries of the *lotus.domino.ACLEntry* object. Be careful when manipulating databases' Access Control Lists not to accidentally remove yourself, any manager or designer groups, or the servers when manipulating the *lotus.domino.ACLEntry* and *lotus.domino.ACL* objects, especially when testing and debugging your code.

Example

The following example shows a practical use of the *lotus.domino.ACLEntry* class. This code, which could be saved in an agent and then run against all new or existing databases, updates the access control of the specified database to a standard format. After tweaking this example, you could use this code to make maintaining the access control settings simpler. "ACME" represents the name of the organization or company for this specific server. When working with databases that reside on servers that might be accessible by other servers, domains, and companies, it's good practice not to use generic ACL entry names, such as "LocalDomainServers" and "Designers," because they will have different meanings with other servers or organizations. It's almost always more efficient and secure to be as specific as possible when naming groups, especially with issues related to security. The following example adds the following groups to the ACL of the currently selected database object with the following settings:

ACLEntry Name	Entry Type	Access Level
ACMEServers	Server Group	Manager access
ACMEAdminServer	Server	Manager access as Admin server
OtherServers	Server Group	Editor access
ACMEManagers	Person Group	Manager access
ACMEAdmin	Person Group	Editor access
ACMEDesigners	Person Group	Designer access
ACMEUsers	Person Group	Author access
Terminations	Mixed Group	No access

In addition, this example removes the default database access control entries for "LocalDomainServers" and "OtherDomainServers" if they exist.

```java
import lotus.domino.*;

public class JavaAgent extends AgentBase {

  public void NotesMain() {

    try {
      Session ns = getSession();
      AgentContext agentContext = ns.getAgentContext();
      Agent nagt = agentContext.getCurrentAgent();
      Database ndb = agentContext.getCurrentDatabase();
      ACL nacl = ndb.getACL();
      nacl.createACLEntry("ACMEServers", ACL.LEVEL_MANAGER);
      ACLEntry nacleServer = nacl.getEntry("ACMEServers");
      nacleServer.setGroup(true);
      nacleServer.setServer(true);
      System.out.println("The " + nacleServer.getNameObject() +
      ➥" is complete");
      nacl.createACLEntry("AdminServers", ACL.LEVEL_MANAGER);
      ACLEntry nacleAdminServer = nacl.getEntry("AdminServers");
      nacleAdminServer.setServer(true);
      nacleAdminServer.setAdminServer(true);
      System.out.println("The " + nacleAdminServer.getNameObject() +
      ➥" is complete");
      nacl.createACLEntry("OtherServers", ACL.LEVEL_EDITOR);
      ACLEntry nacleOtherServers = nacl.getEntry("OtherServers");
      nacleOtherServers.setGroup(true);
      nacleOtherServers.setServer(true);
      System.out.println("The " + nacleOtherServers.getNameObject() +
      ➥" is complete");
      nacl.createACLEntry("ACMEManagers", ACL.LEVEL_MANAGER);
      ACLEntry nacleManagers = nacl.getEntry("ACMEManagers");
      nacleManagers.setGroup(true);
      nacleManagers.setPerson(true);
      System.out.println("The " + nacleManagers.getNameObject() +
      ➥" is complete");
```

continued >>

continued >>

```
nacl.createACLEntry("ACMEAdmin", ACL.LEVEL_EDITOR);
ACLEntry nacleAdmin = nacl.getEntry("ACMEAdmin");
nacleAdmin.setGroup(true);
nacleAdmin.setPerson(true);
nacleAdmin.setCanCreatePersonalAgent(true);
nacleAdmin.setCanCreatePersonalFolder(true);
nacleAdmin.setCanCreateSharedFolder(true);
System.out.println("The " + nacleAdmin.getNameObject() +
➥" is complete");
nacl.createACLEntry("ACMEDesigners", ACL.LEVEL_DESIGNER);
ACLEntry nacleDesigners = nacl.getEntry("ACMEDesigners");
nacleDesigners.setGroup(true);
nacleDesigners.setPerson(true);
nacleDesigners.setCanCreateLSOrJavaAgent(true);
System.out.println("The " + nacleDesigners.getNameObject() +
➥" is complete");
nacl.createACLEntry("ACMEUsers", ACL.LEVEL_AUTHOR);
ACLEntry nacleUsers = nacl.getEntry("ACMEUsers");
nacleUsers.setGroup(true);
nacleUsers.setPerson(true);
nacleUsers.setCanCreatePersonalAgent(true);
nacleUsers.setCanCreatePersonalFolder(true);
System.out.println("The " + nacleUsers.getNameObject() +
➥" is complete");
nacl.createACLEntry("Terminations", ACL.LEVEL_NOACCESS);
ACLEntry nacleTerminations = nacl.getEntry("Terminations");
nacleTerminations.setGroup(true);
System.out.println("The " + nacleTerminations.getNameObject() +
➥" is complete");
ACLEntry nacleOtherDomainServers =
➥nacl.getEntry("OtherDomainServers");
if (nacleOtherDomainServers != null)
➥nacleOtherDomainServers.remove();
    System.out.println("The OtherDomainServers is complete");
ACLEntry nacleLocalDomainServers =
➥nacl.getEntry("LocalDomainServers");
    if (nacleLocalDomainServers != null)
    ➥nacleLocalDomainServers.remove();
System.out.println("The LocalDomainServers is complete");
nacl.save();

} catch(Exception e) {
    e.printStackTrace();
}
    }
}
```

The *lotus.domino.Agent* class allows you to access existing public and personal agents in a *lotus.domino.Database*. You can't create new agents with this class.

Session
— AgentContext
  └─ Agent
     └─ DateTime
— Database
  └─ Agent
     └─ DateTime

Java Syntax

```
public class lotus.notes.Agent extends Base
```

To access an agent object, you have two basic choices: You can either use the getCurrentAgent method of *lotus.domino.AgentContext* to access the currently running agent (if there is one), or you can use the getAgents method of *lotus.domino.NotesDatabase* to iterate through a collection of all the agents in a database. Unfortunately, there is no method that allows you to access an agent directly by name.

Agent Methods

getComment	R	O.Ref.

getComment

```
strComment=nagtagent.getComment()
```

Returns an object of type *java.lang.String* containing a comment describing the agent as entered by the agent's programmer.

getCommonOwner	R	O.Ref.

getCommon
Owner

```
strComment=nagtagent.getCommonOwner()
```

Returns an object of type *java.lang.String* containing the common name of the last person to edit and save the agent.

getLastRun	R	O.Ref.

getLastRun

```
ndtLastRun=nagtagent.getLastRun()
```

This method returns a *lotus.domino.DateTime* object containing the time and date the agent was last executed. If a particular agent has never been run, getLastrun will return the infamous 12/30/1899.

getName	R	O.Ref.

getName

```
strName=nagtagent.getName()
```

This method returns an object of type *java.lang.String* containing the name of the agent as a string value. Consider the following example:

```
import lotus.domino.*;
import java.util.Vector;
public class JavaAgent extends AgentBase {
  public void NotesMain() {
    try {
      Session nssession = getSession();
      AgentContext nacContext = nssession.getAgentContext();
      String strTestAgentName="Empty Trash";
      String strAgentName;
      Database ndbCurrent = nacContext.getCurrentDatabase();
      Vector agents=ndbCurrent.getAgents();
      // loop through all agents in the current database
      for (int i=0; i<agents.size(); i++)
        {
          Agent nagtCurrent = (Agent)agents.elementAt(i);
```

```
              String strname = nagtCurrent.getName();
              If (strTestAgentName == strname)
                If (nagtCurrent.getLastRun() < ndbCurrent.getLastModified())
                  {
                    nagtCurrent.setEnabled(true);
                    nagtCurrent.Save(0);
                  }
              }
        } catch(Exception e) {
          e.printStackTrace();
          }
        }
      }
```

---

getOwner   R   O.Ref.

```
  nnamOwner=nagtagent.getOwner()
```

Returns a *lotus.domino.Name* object containing the hierarchical name of the person
who last saved the agent.

---

getParent   R   O.Ref.

```
  ndbParent=nagtagent.getParent()
```

Returns a *lotus.domino.Database* object representing the database that contains the
agent.

```
import lotus.domino.*;
public class JavaAgent extends AgentBase {
  public void NotesMain() {
    try {
      Session nssession = getSession();
      AgentContext nacContext = nssession.getAgentContext();
      Agent nagtCurrent=nacContext.getCurrentAgent();
      Database ndbCDb=nagtCurrent.getParent();
      System.out.println
      ("The parent database of this agent is: " + ndbCDb.getFileName() +"
      ➥(" + ndbCDb.getTitle() + " )" );
    } catch(Exception e) {
    e.printStackTrace();
    }
  }
}
```

---

getQuery   R   O.Ref.

```
  strQuery=nagtagent.getQuery()
```

Returns an object of type *java.lang.String* containing the query string used by the agent
to select documents if the Add Search button is used to add a query. If this feature isn't
used, this method will return an empty string (" ").

---

getServerName   R   O.Ref.

```
  strServer=nagtagent.getServerName()
```

This method returns the name of the server on which the agent runs. The exact value
returned varies, depending on whether the agent is scheduled or not. If the agent is scheduled, ServerName returns the name of the server on which the agent runs. For unscheduled
agents in a database on a server, ServerName returns the name of the parent database.

If in a local database, it returns the common user name. If you want the agent to run on any server, set this method to `"*"`. Consider the following example:

```
import lotus.domino.*;
public class JavaAgent extends AgentBase {
  public void NotesMain() {
    try {
      Session session = getSession();
      AgentContext nacContext = session.getAgentContext();
      Agent nagtAgent=nacContext.getCurrentAgent();
      nagtAgent.setServerName("*");
      nagtAgent.save();
    } catch(Exception e) {
      e.printStackTrace();
    }
  }
}
```

5.0 getTarget   R   %

getTarget   intTarget=nagtagent.**getTarget**()

This method (which is roughly equivalent to the "Which document(s) should it act on" field in the agent builder) returns an integer that represents which documents the agent will run on. The valid values returned by this method are constants, as follows: `Agent.TARGET_ALL_DOCS`, `Agent.TARGET_NEW_DOCS`, `Agent.TARGET_NEW_OR_MODIFIED_DOCS`, `Agent.TARGET_SELECTED_DOCS`, `Agent.TARGET_ALL_DOCS_IN_VIEW`, `Agent.TARGET_UNREAD_DOCS_IN_VIEW`, `Agent.TARGET_NONE`.

5.0 getTrigger   R   %

getTrigger   intTrigger=nagtagent.**getTrigger**()

This method (which is roughly equivalent to the "When should this agent run" field in the agent builder) returns an integer indicating when the agent should run. The valid values for this method are `Agent.TRIGGER_NONE`, `Agent.TRIGGER_SCHEDULED`, `Agent.TRIGGER_AFTER_MAIL_DELIVERY`, `Agent.TRIGGER_DOC_PASTED`, `Agent.TRIGGER_MANUAL`, `Agent.TRIGGER_DOC_UPDATE`, `Agent.TRIGGER_BEFORE_MAIL_DELIVERY`, and `Agent.TARGET_NONE`.

---

isEnabled   R   T/F

isEnabled   bolenabled=nagtagent.**isEnabled**()

Indicates whether the agent is enabled. This is `true` if the agent is enabled and `false` if it is not. Because this method is designed for scheduled agents, setting it for agents that are hidden or run from the menu will have no effect. If you make a change to this method, you must call the **save** method of *lotus.domino.Agent*.

5.0 isNotesAgent   R   T/F

isNotesAgent   bolNotes=nagtagent.**isNotesAgent**()

Indicates whether the agent can run in a Notes client. This method will return `true` if the agent can run in a Notes client. Otherwise, it will return `false`.

---

isPublic   R   T/F

isPublic   bolPublic=nagtagent.**isPublic**()

Indicates whether the agent is public (stored in the database and accessible to all the database's users) or personal (stored in the owner's desktop.dsk file). This method returns `true` if the agent is a public agent and `false` otherwise.

5.0 isWebAgent	R	T/F

`bolWeb=nagtagent.`**`isWebAgent`**`()`   isWebAgent

Indicates whether the agent can run be run from a Web browser. It returns `true` if the agent can run in a Web client. Otherwise, it returns `false`.

remove

`nagtagent.`**`remove`**   remove

This method takes no parameters and is used to permanently delete an agent from the database.

run

`nagtagent.`**`run`**   run

This method takes no parameters and is used to execute an agent. There are a few caveats to note when using the `run` method to execute an agent. First, agents can't be run from themselves (recursively). Additionally, no user interaction is possible, including the debugger.

4.6 runOnServer

`nagtagent.`**`runOnServer`**   runOnServer

This method takes no parameters and causes an agent to run on the remote server where the parent database resides.

4.6 save

`nagtagent.`**`save`**   save

This method was introduced in Release 4.6 and is used to save the agent when the `setEnabled` or `setServerName` methods are called to update the agent.

setEnabled

`nagtagent.`**`setEnabled`**`(bolEnabled)`   setEnabled

bolEnabled	R	T/F

A Boolean value that determines whether the agent is enabled or not.

This method accepts a Boolean value that can either enable or disable the agent. `true` enables the agent and `false` disables it. Remember that you must call the `save` method to make the changes take effect.

setServerName

`nagtagent.`**`setServerName`**`(strServer)`   setServerName

strServer	R	O.Ref.

A string value naming the server on which to run.

This method accepts a *java.lang.String* object that is used to set the name of the server on which the agent will run. You can use `"*"` to indicate any server or an empty string (`""`) to indicate local.

Remarks

It's very important to remember to call the `save` method whenever you make changes to an agent using its properties. Otherwise, the changes won't be written to disk.

Example

```
import lotus.domino.*;
import java.util.Vector;
public class JavaAgent extends AgentBase {
  public void NotesMain() {
    try {
      Session nssession = getSession();
      AgentContext nacContext = nssession.getAgentContext();
      Database ndbMailDb;
      Database ndbCur=nacContext.getCurrentDatabase();
      DateTime ndtLastRunThreshold=nssession.createDateTime("Today");
      DateTime ndtLastRunDate=nssession.createDateTime("Today");
      View nvwPeopleView=nacContext.getCurrentDatabase().getView("People");
      Document ndocPerson = nvwPeopleView.getFirstDocument();
      int intDiff;
      String strAgentName;
      ndtLastRunThreshold.adjustMonth(-1);
      strAgentName="Periodic Archive";
      while (ndocPerson !=null)
        {
         String strServer=ndbCur.getServer();
          //Vector vecMailFile=ndocPerson.getItemValue("mailfile");
          Item nitmMailFile=ndocPerson.getFirstItem("mailfile");
          //String strDb=vecMailFile.elementAt(0);
          String strDb=nitmMailFile.getValueString();
          ndbMailDb=session.getDatabase(strServer, strDb);
          if (ndbMailDb !=null && ndbMailDb.isOpen())
            {
              Vector vecAgents = ndbMailDb.getAgents();
              for (int i=0; i <vecAgents.size(); i++)
                {
                  Agent nagtCurAgent = (Agent)vecAgents.elementAt(i);
                    if (nagtCurAgent.getName()==strAgentName)
                      {
                          ndtLastRunDate=nagtCurAgent.getLastRun();
                          intDiff=ndtLastRunDate.timeDifference
                          ➡(ndtLastRunThreshold);
                          if (2592000/ intDiff >1) // # of seconds in 30
                            {
                              // days/by time difference
                              nagtCurAgent.setEnabled(true);
                              nagtCurAgent.save();
                            }
                      }
                }
            }
          else
            {
            System.out.println("Could not open " +
            ➡ndbMailDb.getTitle());
            ndocPerson=nvwPeopleView.getNextDocument(ndocPerson);
            }
        }
      } catch(Exception e) {
      e.printStackTrace();
    }
  }
}
```

AgentContext

The *lotus.domino.AgentContext* class represents the environment in which the current agent is running. It is new as of Notes 4.6 and has no LotusScript counterpart. It provides a number of very useful methods that make it easy to interact with the agent's environment.

Session
└─ AgentContext
   ├─ Agent
   │ └─ DateTime
   ├─ Database
   └─ Document
      └─ ...

Java Syntax

```
public class AgentContext extends Base
```

This class allows your agents to access the environment in which they are executing.

AgentContext Methods

---

getCurrentAgent   R   O.Ref.

getCurrentAgent

```
nagtCurrent = nacAgentContext.getCurrentAgent()
```

Returns a *lotus.domino.Agent* object representing the currently executing agent.

---

getCurrentDatabase   R   O.Ref.

getCurrent
Database

```
ndbCurrent = nacAgentContext.getCurrentDatabase()
```

Returns an object of type *lotus.domino.Database* representing the current database in which the agent is executing.

---

getDocumentContext   R   O.Ref.

getDocument
Context

```
ndocContext = nacAgentContext.getDocumentContext()
```

Returns a *lotus.domino.Document* object representing either the document that is currently highlighted in a view if the agent is activated through a view, the document that is currently open in a Web browser, or an in-memory document created by a C/C++ program.

---

getEffectiveUserName   R   O.Ref.

getEffective
UserName

```
strEffective = nacAgentContext.getEffectiveUserName()
```

Returns a *java.lang.String* object containing the name of the user (if the agent is running on a workstation) or the name of the server (if the agent is running on a server).

---

getLastExitStatus   R   %

getLast
ExitStatus

```
intExitStatus = nacAgentContext.getLastExitStatus()
```

Returns a status code returned by the Agent Manager from the last execution of the current agent. For an agent that completed without any errors, this method returns 0.

---

getLastRun   R   O.Ref.

getLastRun

```
ndtLastRun = nacAgentContext.getLastRun()
```

Returns the date that the current agent was last run as a *lotus.domino.DateTime* object. If a script has never executed, this method will contain 11/30/1899.

---

getSavedData   R   O.Ref.

getSavedData

```
ndocSaveData = nacAgentContext.getSavedData()
```

This method returns a *lotus.domino.Document* object representing a document that an agent can use to store information between runs, so that data stored in this document can be accessed the next time the agent runs. A SavedData document is created when a script agent is saved. Each time a script agent is edited and saved, its SavedData document is deleted and a new, blank one takes its place. When you delete an agent, its `SavedData` document is deleted. `SavedData` documents replicate but are not displayed in views. You should note that this method is valid only for scripts in agents.

getUnprocessedDocuments R   O.Ref.

```
ndcUnprocessed = nacAgentContext.getUnprocessedDocuments()
```

getUnprocessed
Documents

This method is valid only when called from an agent. It returns a *lotus.domino.DocumentCollection* object containing the documents in a database that the current agent considers "unprocessed." Keep in mind that if you're using agents that run on new and modified documents, you must call the `updateProcessedDoc` method of *lotus.domino.AgentContext* to mark each document in the collection as "processed." This prevents each document in the collection from being processed more than once, unless it's modified again. By not calling this method for each document, the agent will process the same documents each time it runs. You should note that `updateProcessedDoc` marks a document as "processed" only for the specific agent in which it is called.

The following table illustrates exactly what to expect when using this method.

What the Agent Runs On	Documents Returned
All documents in database	Documents that match the search criteria specified in the Agent Builder.
All new documents and those modified since the last run	Documents that weren't previously processed by this agent with the `UpdateProcessedDoc` method, newly created or modified documents, and documents that match the criteria specified in theAgent Builder.
All unread documents in view	Unread in-view documents and those that match criteria specified in the Agent Builder.
All documents in view	Documents that are in-view and that match criteria specified in the Agent Builder.
Selected documents	Selected in-view documents and those that match criteria specified in the Agent Builder.
Run once	The current document.

unprocessedFTSearch

```
ndcUnprocessedFT = nacAgentContext.unprocessedFTSearch(strQuery,
➡intMaxDocs)
```

unprocessedFT
Search

```
ndcUnprocessedFT = nacAgentContext.unprocessedFTSearch(strQuery,
➡intMaxDocs, intSortOptions, intOtherOptions)
```

strQuery   Required   O.Ref.

A *java.lang.String* object containing the query you want to execute.

intMaxDocs   Required   %

Indicates the maximum number of documents you want returned when the query is executed. You can set this parameter to `0` to return all the documents that match the query.

intSortOptions   Required   %

Indicates which of three sorting options you want to use. You should use one of the following constants:

Constant	Result
`Database.FT_SCORES`	Sorts results by relevance score. This is the default.
`Database.FT_DATE_DES`	Sorts results by document creation date in descending order.
`Database.FT_DATE_ASC`	Sorts results by document creation date in ascending order.

intOtherOptions   Required   %

Indicates additional search options. You can use one of the following constants:

Constant	Result
Database.FT_DATABASE	Includes Notes databases in the search scope.
Database.FT_FILESYSTEM	Includes file types other than Notes databases in the search scope.
Database.FT_FUZZY	Indicates that a "fuzzy" search should be performed.
Database.FT_STEMS	Uses stem words to search.

If you would like to use more than one of the OtherOptions parameters, you can pass them as database.FT_STEMS + database.FT_FUZZY.

This method is valid only for agents. It returns a *lotus.domino.DocumentCollection* object containing the documents in a database that the current agent considers to be "unprocessed." Keep in mind that if you're using agents that run on new and modified documents since the last run, you must call the updateProcessedDoc method to mark each document in the collection as "processed." This prevents each document in the collection from being processed more than once, unless it's modified, mailed, or pasted again. By not calling this method for each document, the agent will process the same documents each time it runs. Note that updateProcessedDoc marks a document as "processed" only for the specific agent in which it is called.

The following table illustrates exactly what to expect when using this method:

What the Agent Runs On	Documents Returned
All documents in database	Documents matching the search criteria specified in the Agent Builder and the search criteria specified for this method.
All new documents and those modified since the last run	Documents that weren't previously processed by this agent with the updateProcessedDoc method, documents that meet the search criteria specified in the Agent Builder, documents that meet the search criteria specified for this method, and newly created or modified documents.
All unread documents in view	In-view and unread documents, those that meet the search criteria specified in the Agent Builder, and those that meet the search criteria specified for this method.
All documents in view	In-view documents, those that meet the search criteria specified in the Agent Builder, and those that meet the search criteria specified for this method.
Selected documents	Selected in-view documents, those that meet the search criteria specified in the Agent Builder, and those that meet the search criteria specified for this method.
Run once	The current document.

If these conditions are met, this method performs a full-text search against the documents that are considered by the agent to be unprocessed and returns the results as a sorted document collection.

unprocessedSearch

unprocessed
Search

```
ndcUnprocessed = nacAgentContext.unprocessedSearch(strFormula,
➥ndtDateTime, intMaxDocs)
```

strFormula	Required	O.Ref.

This *java.lang.String* parameter is used to pass an @function formula defining the selection criteria.

ndtDateTime	Required	O.Ref.

This parameter is a *lotus.domino.DateTime* object to be used as a cutoff date so that only documents created or modified after the cutoff date are searched.

intMaxDocs	Required	%

This parameter specifies the number of documents that should be returned in the collection. You can pass **0** to indicate that you want all matching documents.

This method is valid only for agents. It returns a *lotus.document.DocumentCollection* object containing the documents in a database that the current agent considers to be "unprocessed" and that match the search criteria specified. This method is always substantially slower than performing a full-text search, so you should avoid it when you can perform a full-text search instead.

Keep in mind that if you're using agents that run on new or modified documents, you must use the `updateProcessedDoc` method of *lotus.domino.AgentContext* to mark each document in the collection as "processed." This prevents each document in the collection from being processed more than once, unless it's modified, mailed, or pasted again. By not calling this method for each document, the agent will process the same documents each time it runs. You should note that `updateProcessedDoc` marks a document as "processed" only for the specific agent in which it is called.

The following table illustrates how unprocessed documents are determined.

What the Agent Runs On	Documents Returned
All documents in database	Documents matching the search criteria specified in the Agent Builder, the criteria specified in the search formula, and the specified cutoff date.
All new documents and those modified since the last run	Documents that weren't previously processed by this agent with the `updateProcessedDoc` method, those that meet the search criteria specified in the Agent Builder, those that meet the search criteria specified in the search formula, and those that are newly created or modified and that meet the specified cutoff date.
All unread documents in view	Documents that are in-view and unread, those that meet the search criteria specified in the Agent Builder, those that meet the search criteria specified in the search formula, and those that meet the specified cutoff date.
All documents in view	In-view documents, those that meet the search criteria specified in the Agent Builder, those that meet the search criteria specified in the search formula, and those that meet the specified cutoff date.
Selected documents	Selected in-view documents, those that meet the search criteria specified in the Agent Builder, those that meet the search criteria specified in the search formula, and those that meet the specified cutoff date.
Run once	The current document.

If these conditions are met, this method performs a search against the documents that are considered by the agent to be unprocessed and returns the results as a sorted document collection.

updateProcessedDoc

nacAgentContext.**updateProcessedDoc**(ndocDocument)

ndocDocument	Required	O.Ref.

The document to mark as processed by the agent.

This method was designed to be used with agents that use the "If Documents Have Been Created or Modified" trigger and either the unprocessedDocuments, unprocessedFTSearch, or unprocessedSearch methods (all of which are in *lotus.domino.AgentContext*) to get the newly-created and newly-modified documents. Calling updateProcessedDoc on each document that is a member of a collection generated by one of these three methods ensures that the next time the agent runs, marked documents will be ignored. If this technique is not used to mark documents that have not been processed, these three methods will return all documents matching that criteria—even the previously processed documents. On a final note, updateProcessedDoc marks documents as "processed" only for the specific agent that called it. Because this method is agent-specific, using updateProcessedDoc in one agent has no effect on the documents processed by another agent.

Example

```
import lotus.domino.*;
import java.util.Vector;
public class JavaAgent extends AgentBase {
  public void NotesMain() {
    try {
        Session nssession = getSession();
        AgentContext nacContext = nssession.getAgentContext();
        Database ndbCurr=nacContext.getCurrentDatabase();
        View nvwPeopleView=ndbCurr.getView("People");
        Document ndocPerson = nvwPeopleView.getFirstDocument();
        DateTime ndtLastRunThreshold =nssession.createDateTime("Today");
        DateTime ndtLastRunDate;
        ndtLastRunThreshold.adjustMonth(-1);
        String strAgentName="Periodic Archive";
        while(ndocPerson != null)
          {
            Vector vecMailFile=ndocPerson.getItemValue("MailFile");
            Database ndbMailDb=nssession.getDatabase(ndbCurr.getServer(),
            ➡vecMailFile.firstElement());
            if(ndbMailDb !=null-& ndbMailDb.isOpen())
                {
                  Vector vecAgents=ndbMailDb.getAgents();
                  for(int i=0;i<=vecAgents.size(); i++)
                    {
                      Agent agtCurr=(Agent)vecAgents.elementAt(i);
                      if(agtCurr.getName()StrAgentName)
                        {
                          ndtLastRunDate.setLocalTime(agtCurr.getLastRun());
                          long lngDiff=ndtLastRunDate.timeDifference
                          ➡(ndtLastRunThreshold);
                          if(2592000/lngDiff > 1) // number of seconds in
                                                  // 30 days divided by
                                                  ➡time
```

```
                                              // difference
                    {
                      agtCurr.setEnabled(true);
                      agtCurr.save();
                    }
                  }
                }
              }
          ndocPerson=nvwPeopleView.getNextDocument(ndocPerson);
        }
      } catch(Exception e) {
      e.printStackTrace();
    }
  }
}
```

The *lotus.domino.Database* class is one of the most powerful and fundamental of all the Notes classes, because the database (Notes Storage Facility) is the primary means of storing data in Notes/Domino. Mastering its many methods is essential to becoming a proficient Notes/Domino developer.

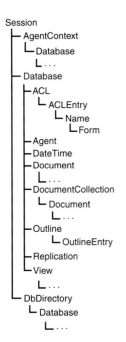

continued >>

Java Syntax

You have a plethora of choices when it comes to accessing a *lotus.domino.Database* object. Any of the following options will work:

The createDatabase method of *lotus.domino.DbDirectory* (▶ 408) can be used to create a new database from scratch.

If you want to create a new database based on an existing database, try the createCopy, createFromTemplate, or createReplica methods of *lotus.domino.Database*.

To access an existing database when its server and filename are known, use the getDatabase method of *lotus.domino.Session* (▶ 581).

To access the database in which an agent is currently running, without indicating a server or filename, use the getCurrentDatabase method of *lotus.domino.AgentContext* (▶ 366).

To open an existing database when the server and ReplicaID are known, use the openDatabaseByReplicaID method of *lotus.domino.DbDirectory* (▶ 410).

If you know the name of the server on which a database resides, but you don't know its filename, you can use either the openDatabase (▶ 410) or openDatabaseIfModified (▶ 410) methods of the *lotus.domino.DbDirectory* class to iterate through all the databases on a server and open the ones you want.

To determine which databases are Domino Directories and Personal Address Books, and open them, use the getAddressBooks method of *lotus.domino.Session* (▶ 580).

If you want to open the current user's mail database, use the openMailDatabase method of *lotus.domino.DbDirectory* (▶ 411).

If you already have any of the following objects—*lotus.domino.View, lotus.domino.Document, lotus.domino.DocumentCollection, lotus.domino.ACL, lotus.domino.ViewEntry,* or *lotus.domino.ViewEntryCollection*—try the getParent or getParentDatabase methods.

Database Methods

compact

```
intsizediff = ndbDatabase.compact()
```
compact

This method returns an integer of the amount of space freed up after compacting. Keep in mind that an agent can't compact the current database (it's open) and will throw an error when used on a database that isn't local.

createCopy

```
ndbDatabase = createCopy(strServer, strFileName)
```
createCopy

strServer   Required   O.Ref.

A *java.lang.String* object containing the name of the server where the new copy of the database will reside. Pass an empty string ("") to create a new copy on the current machine.

strFileName   Required   O.Ref.

A *java.lang.String* object containing the filename you want to assign to the new copy.

This method creates a new copy (not a replica) of the current database, which is returned as a *lotus.domino.Database* object. Keep in mind that if there is a database on the server specified in `strServer` that has the same name as that specified in `strFileName`, an error will be reported. Also, the current ACL will be copied to the new database.

---

createDocument

createDocument

```
ndocDocument = ndbDatabase.createDocument()
```

This method returns a new *lotus.domino.Document* (▶ 413) object. Remember to call the save method of *lotus.domino.Document* to write the new document to disk. Consider the following example.

```
import lotus.domino.*;
public class JavaAgent extends AgentBase {
  public void NotesMain() {
    try {
            Session nssession = getSession();
            AgentContext nacContext = nssession.getAgentContext();
            Database ndbCurr=nacContext.getCurrentDatabase();
            Document ndocCurrentDoc=ndbCurr.createDocument();
            ndocCurrentDoc.replaceItemValue("Form","Contact");
            ndocCurrentDoc.replaceItemValue("tLastName","Hatter");
            ndocCurrentDoc.replaceItemValue("tFirstName","Wyatt");
            ndocCurrentDoc.save(true,false);
        } catch(Exception e) {
        e.printStackTrace();
    }
  }
}
```

---

createFromTemplate

createFrom
Template

```
ndbDatabase = ndbDatabase.createFromTemplate(strServer,strFileName,
  ➥bolInherit)
```

---

strServer   Required   O.Ref.

A *java.lang.String* object containing the name of the server where the new copy of the database will reside. Pass an empty string (`""`) to create the new copy on the current machine.

---

strFileName   Required   O.Ref.

A *java.lang.String* object containing the filename you want to assign to the new copy.

---

bolInherit   Required   T/F

If you want the new database to inherit its design from the current database, set this parameter to `true`. Otherwise, set it to `false`.

Use this method to create a new database from an existing database. The new database will contain all the design elements and documents of the source database. It returns a *lotus.domino.Database* object representing the new database. If a database with the same name already exists, an error will be generated. Consider the following example.

```
import lotus.domino.*;
public class JavaAgent extends AgentBase {
  public void NotesMain() {
    try {
            Session nssession = getSession();
```

```
            AgentContext nacContext = nssession.getAgentContext();
            Database ndbCurr=nacContext.getCurrentDatabase();
            Document ndocCurrentDoc=ndbCurr.createDocument();
            Database ndbNewDatabase;
            String strFilePath=ndbCurr.getFilePath();
            String strFileName=ndbCurr.getFileName();
            String strPathOnly;
            int intFilePathLen=strFilePath.length();
            int intFileNameLen=strFileName.length();
            strPathOnly=strFilePath.substring(1, (intFilePathLen
            ➥-intFileNameLen));
            ndbNewDatabase=ndbCurr.createFromTemplate(ndbCurr.getServer(),
            ➥strPathOnly, true);
            ndbNewDatabase.setTitle(ndbCurr.getTitle() + "(New) ");
            System.out.println("New Database has been created");
        } catch(Exception e) {
        e.printStackTrace();
    }
  }
}
```

---

createOutline

noutOutline = ndbDatabase.**createOutline**(strName)   createOutline

createOutline(strName, bolDefault)

strName	Required	O.Ref.

A *java.lang.String* object containing the name you want to assign to the outline.

bolDefault	Required	O.Ref.

A Boolean value that indicates whether a blank outline should be created. Pass `false`
(the default) to create a blank outline.

This method allows you to create a new *lotus.domino.Outline* object in the current
database.

---

createReplica

ndbDatabase = ndbDatabase.**createReplica**(strServer, strFileName)   createReplica

strServer	Required	O.Ref.

A *java.lang.String* object containing the name of the server where the new copy of the
database will reside. Pass an empty string (" ") to create a new copy on the current
machine.

strFileName	Required	O.Ref.

A *java.lang.String* object containing the filename you want to assign to the new copy.

This method returns a *lotus.domino.Database* object representing a new replica copy of
the current database. The ACL of the current database is copied to the new replica. As
with the `CreateCopy` method, if there is a database on the server specified in `strServer`
that has the same name as that specified in `strFileName`, an error will be reported. Also,
the ACL will be copied to the new database.

---

enableFolder

ndbDatabase.**enableFolder**(strFolder)   enableFolder

strFolder	Required	O.Ref.

A *java.util.String* object containing the name of the folder to enable.

This method checks to see whether the named folder exists. If the folder doesn't exist, it is created. Otherwise, this method does nothing.

5.0 FTDomainSearch

FTDomain Search

```
ndcDocument = ndbDatabase.FTDomainSearch(strQuery, intMaxDocs,
➥intSortOptions, intOtherOptions, intStart, intCount, strEntryform)
```

strQuery   Required   O.Ref.
A *java.lang.String* object containing the query you want to execute.

intMaxDocs   Required   %
Indicates the maximum number of documents you want returned when the query is executed. You can set this parameter to 0 to get all documents matching the query.

intSortOptions   Optional   %
Indicates which of three sorting options you want to use. Use one of the following constants:

Constant	Description
Database.FT_SCORES	Sorts results by relevance score. This is the default.
Database.FT_DATE_DES	Sorts results by document creation date in descending order.
Database.FT_DATE_ASC	Sorts results by document creation date in ascending order.

intOtherOptions   Optional   %
Indicates additional search options. You can use one of the following constants:

Constant	Description
Database.FT_DATABASE	Includes Domino databases in the search scope.
Database.FT_FILESYSTEM	Includes file types other than Notes databases in the search scope.
Database.FT_FUZZY	Specifies that a fuzzy search should be performed.
Database.FT_STEMS	Uses stem words to search.

If you would like to use more than one of the intOtherOptions parameters, you can pass this parameter as FT_STEMS + FT_FUZZY.

intStart   Optional   %
The first page to return.

intCount   Optional   %
The number of pages to return.

strEntryForm   Required   O.Ref.
The name of the domain search form as listed in the domain catalog. An example might be "Domain Search Form".

This very powerful method executes a full-text search of all the documents in a domain and returns a *lotus.domino.Document* containing a list of formatted documents that match the query. In order to use this method, you must first configure a Domain Catalog.

FTSearch

FTSearch

```
DocumentCollection = ndbDatabase.FTSearch(strQuery)

DocumentCollection = ndbDatabase.FTSearch(strQuery, intMaxDocs)

DocumentCollection, ndcCollection = ndbDatabase.FTSearch(strQuery,
➥intMaxDocs, intSortOptions, intOtherOptions)
```

strQuery   Required   O.Ref.

A *java.lang.String* object containing the query you want to execute.

intMaxDocs   Required   %

Indicates the maximum number of documents you want returned when the query is executed. You can set this parameter to 0 to get all documents matching the query.

intSortOptions   Required   %

Indicates which of three sorting options you want to use. Use one of the following constants:

Constant	Description
Database.FT_SCORES	Sorts results by relevance score. This is the default.
Database.FT_DATE_DES	Sorts results by document creation date in descending order.
Database.FT_DATE_ASC	Sorts results by document creation date in ascending order.

intOtherOptions   Optional   %

Indicates additional search options. You can use one of the following constants:

Constant	Description
Database.FT_DATABASE	Includes Domino databases in the search scope.
Database.FT_FILESYSTEM	Includes file types other than Domino databases in the search scope.
Database.FT_FUZZY	Specifies a fuzzy search.
Database.FT_STEMS	Uses stem words to search.

If you would like to use more than one of the intOtherOptions parameters, you can pass them as FT_STEMS + FT_FUZZY.

This method searches against all the documents in a database and returns a *lotus.domino.DocumentCollection* containing all the documents that match the full-text query. The documents are sorted based on the intSortOptions parameter. If no sort options are specified, the documents are returned sorted by their relevance score. If the results are sorted by date, no relevance scores will be returned. It is important to note that although this method will work if the database isn't full-text indexed, it will work much more slowly.

If you don't want to search against all the documents in the database, you can use the FTSearch method of *lotus.domino.View* (▶ 591) to search only the documents contained in a particular view, or you can use the FTSearch method of *lotus.domino.DocumentCollection* (▶ 437). Consider the following example.

```
import lotus.domino.*;
public class JavaAgent extends AgentBase {
  public void NotesMain() {
    try {
            Session nssession = getSession();
            AgentContext nacContext = nssession.getAgentContext();
            Database ndbCurr=nacContext.getCurrentDatabase();
            Document ndocNewsletter;
            Newsletter nnltrNewsletter;
            DocumentCollection ndcCollection;
            String strQuery="FIELD tLastName contains 'Hatter'";
            if(! ndbCurr.isFTIndexed())
```
continued >>

continued >>

```
                            {
                              if(ndbCurr.getServer()=="")
                                {
                                  ndbCurr.updateFTIndex(true);
                                }
                              ndcCollection=ndbCurr.FTSearch(strQuery,0);
                              nnltrNewsletter = session.createNewsletter
                              ➥(ndcCollection);
                              nnltrNewsletter.setSubjectItemName("Subject");
                              nnltrNewsletter.setDoSubject(true);
                              ndocNewsletter= nnltrNewsletter.formatMsgWithDoclinks
                              ➥(ndbCurr);
                              ndocNewsletter.replaceItemValue("SubjectItemName",
                              ➥"Full text query (" + strQuery + ") results.");
                              ndocNewsletter.send(false, session.getCommonUserName());
                            }
                          else
                          {
                            System.out.println("You cannot full-text index a database on
                            ➥the server. Please see your administrator.");
                          }
                          } catch(Exception e) {
                          e.printStackTrace();
                    }
                  }
                }
```

getACL   R   O.Ref.

getACL   `nacl=ndbDatabase.getACL()`

Returns a *lotus.domino.ACL* (▶ 333) object containing the database's Access Control List.

getAgent

getAgent   `nagtAgent = ndbDatabase.getAgent(strAgentName)`

strAgentName   Required   O.Ref.

A *java.lang.String* object containing the name of the agent you want to retrieve.

This method returns a *lotus.domino.Agent* object (▶ 359) representing the named agent.

getAgents   R   O.Ref.

getAgents   `vecAgents = ndbDatabase.getAgents()`

Returns a *java.util.Vector* object containing elements of type *lotus.domino.Agent* (▶ 359). If this method is accessed on a workstation, the vector will contain both public agents and personal agents that belong to the current user. If this method is called on a server, the vector will contain only public agents.

getAllDocuments   R   O.Ref.

getAll
Documents   `ndcCollection = ndbDatabase.getAllDocuments()`

This method returns an unsorted *lotus.domino.DocumentCollection* (▶ 435) that contains all the documents in the database. Use this method only if you really want to access all the documents in a database, because this method might return a huge collection. If you're interested in accessing a subset of documents in the database, explore the getAllDocumentsByKey method of *lotus.domino.View* (▶ 593), the FTSearch method of *lotus.domino.Database* (▶ 378), or the getAllEntriesByKey method of *lotus.domino.View* (▶ 594).

---

getCategories   R   O.Ref.

```
strCategories = ndbCategories.getCategories()
```
getCategories

Contains a list of categories in which a database appears in the Database Library. If the database is listed under multiple categories, they will be separated by commas or semicolons.

---

getCreated   R   O.Ref.

```
ndtCreated = ndbDatabase.getCreated()
```
getCreated

This method returns a *lotus.domino.DateTime* object indicating the time and date the database was created.

---

getCurrentAccessLevel   R   %

```
intCurrent = ndbDatabase.getCurrentAccessLevel()
```
getCurrent
AccessLevel

Returns the current user's access level as an integer between 0 (no access) and 6 (manager access). Keep in mind that this method returns the access level of the current user on a workstation or if it is running remote, but it returns the access level of the agent owner (the person who last saved the agent) on a server. Each of the integers can be represented as one of the following constants:

Constant	Description
ACL.LEVEL_NOACCESS	No access
ACL.LEVEL_DEPOSITOR	Depositor access
ACL.LEVEL_READER	Reader access
ACL.LEVEL_AUTHOR	Author access
ACL.LEVEL_EDITOR	Editor access
ACL.LEVEL_DESIGNER	Designer access
ACL.LEVEL_MANAGER	Manager access

---

getDesignTemplateName   R   O.Ref.

```
strTempName = ndbDatabase.getDesignTemplateName()
```
getDesign
TemplateName

If a database inherits its design from a template, this method returns the template's name. Otherwise, this method returns an empty string (""). If a database inherits only certain design elements (such as a view or a navigator) rather than the entire design, this method returns an empty string.

---

getDocumentByID

```
ndocDocument = ndbDatabase.getDocumentByID(strNoteID)
```
getDocument
ByID

strNoteID   Required   O.Ref.
The NoteID of a document.

This method returns a *lotus.domino.Document* object (▶ 413) representing the document whose NoteID matches the value specified in **strNoteID**. Consider the following example.

```
import lotus.domino.*;
public class JavaAgent extends AgentBase {
  public void NotesMain() {
    try {
            Session nssession = getSession();
            AgentContext nacContext = nssession.getAgentContext();
```
continued >>

continued >>
```
                          Database ndbCurr=nacContext.getCurrentDatabase();
                          Document ndocCurrentDoc;
                          ndocCurrentDoc=ndbCurr.getDocumentByID("18FA");
                    } catch(Exception e) {
                    e.printStackTrace();
              }
          }
      }
```

---

getDocumentByUNID

getDocument
ByUNID

ndocDocument = ndbDatabase.**getDocumentByUNID**(strUNID)

---

strUNID   Required   O.Ref.

A *java.lang.String* object containing a document's Universal ID.

This method returns a *lotus.domino.Document* object (▶ 413) representing the document whose Universal ID matches the value specified in strUNID. Consider the following example:

```
import lotus.domino.*;
public class JavaAgent extends AgentBase {
  public void NotesMain() {
     try {
            Session nssession = getSession();
            AgentContext nacContext = nssession.getAgentContext();
            Database ndbCurr=nacContext.getCurrentDatabase();
            Document ndocCurrentDoc;
            ndocCurrentDoc=ndbCurr.getDocumentByUNID
            ➥("7DDFA878DbDbC909852566FE0032C5B8 ");
        } catch(Exception e) {
        e.printStackTrace();
      }
    }
}
```

---

getDocumentByURL

getDocument
ByURL

ndocDocument = ndbDatabase.**getDocumentByURL**(strURL, bolReload)

ndocDocument = ndbDatabase.**getDocumentByURL**(strURL, bolReload,
➥bolRelifmod, bolUrllist, strCharset, strUsername, strPassword,
➥strProxyuser, strProxypassword, bolNowait)

---

strURL   Required   O.Ref.

A *java.lang.String* object containing the URL of the page you want to retrieve. You can enter up to 15KB.

bolReload   Optional   T/F

This parameter determines how the how the page should be retrieved. Set this parameter to 0 (the default) to load the page from its host only if it doesn't already exist in the Web Navigator. Specify 1 to reload the page from its host and 2 to reload the page only if the version on the host has been modified.

bolRelifmod   Required   T/F

Pass true to reload the page only if it has been modified. Pass false (the default) to load the page only if it doesn't exist in the Web navigator database.

bolUrllist   Required   T/F

This parameter allows you to specify whether you want to save links in the retrieved page into a field called URLLinksn in the Notes document. (The Web Navigator creates a new URLLinksn field each time the field size reaches 64KB.) Specify true if you want to save the URLs in the URLLinksn field(s) or false if you don't want to save the URLs in the URLLinksn field(s).

strCharset   Required   O.Ref.

Specify the MIME character set (such as ISO-8859-1 for the U.S.) that you want to use when the Web Navigator processes the Web page. This parameter should be specified only when the Web Navigator is unable to determine the page's correct MIME character set.

strUsername   Required   O.Ref.

If a host requires authentication, you can use this parameter to pass a username to the host as a *java.lang.String* object.

strPassword   Required   O.Ref.

If a host requires authentication, you can use this parameter to pass a password to the host as a *java.lang.String* object.

strProxyuser   Required   O.Ref.

Use this parameter, a *java.lang.String* object, to specify a username to proxy servers that require authentication.

strProxypassword   Required   O.Ref.

Use this parameter, a *java.lang.String* object, to specify a password to proxy servers that require authentication.

bolNowait   Required   T/F

This parameter indicates whether the script should continue without waiting for the retrieval process to complete. Specify true for immediate return or false (the default) to wait. Remember that if you specify true, this method will not return the *lotus.domino.Document* object representing the page referenced by the supplied URL.

This method creates a document in the Web Navigator database and returns a *lotus.domino.Document* object for it (unless the intReturnImmediately parameter is specified as false). It works with both the Server Web Navigator and Personal Web Navigator databases.

```
import lotus.domino.*;
public class JavaAgent extends AgentBase {
  public void NotesMain() {
    try {
        Session nssession = getSession();
        AgentContext nacContext = nssession.getAgentContext();
        Database ndbCurr=nacContext.getCurrentDatabase();
        Document ndocCurrentDoc;
        ndocCurrentDoc=ndbCurr.getDocumentByURL
        ➥("http://www.definiti.com", true,true,false,"",
        ➥"Wyatt Hatter", "GoGOP","","",true);
    } catch(Exception e) {
        e.printStackTrace();
    }
  }
}
```

getFileName	R	O.Ref.

getFileName

`strFileName = ndbDatabase.getFileName()`

Returns a *java.lang.String* object containing the actual filename and extension of a database without the path.

getFilePath

getFilePath	R	O.Ref.

`strFilePath = ndbDatabase.getFilePath()`

Returns a *java.lang.String* object containing the actual filename and extension of a database as well as its path. Databases on a workstation will return the complete path (such as C:\Notes\data\definiti\cmgr.nsf), while databases on a server will return a path relative to the Notes data directory (such as definiti\cmgr.nsf).

5.0

getFolder
ReferencesEnabled

getFolderReferencesEnabled	R	T/F

`bolFldrRefs = ndbDatabase.getFolderReferencesEnabled()`

This method returns `true` if folder references are enabled. Before attempting to use a document's folder references, be sure to test this method. Additionally, each database that uses folder references must have the `FolderRef` hidden view. Keep in mind that maintaining folder references in a database adds some performance overhead.

getForm		

getForm

`nfrmForm = ndbDatabase.getForm(strName)`

strName	Required	O.Ref.

A *java.lang.String* object containing the name or alias of the form you want to access.

This method returns a *lotus.domino.Form* object (▶ 453) representing the form specified in the `strName` parameter.

getForms	R	O.Ref.

getForms

`vecAllForms = ndbDatabase.getForms()`

This method returns a *java.util.Vector* of all the *lotus.domino.Form* objects (▶ 453) in the database.

getLastFTIndexed	R	O.Ref.

getLastFT
Indexed

`ndtlastindex = ndbDatabase.getLastFTIndexed()`

Returns a *lotus.domino.DateTime* object containing the date and time the database was last full-text indexed. If the database has no index, this method returns the ever-popular `12/30/1899`.

getLastModified	R	O.Ref.

getLast
Modified

`ndtlastindex = ndbDatabase.getLastModified()`

Returns a *lotus.domino.DateTime* object containing the date and time the database was last modified.

getManagers	R	O.Ref.

getManagers

`vecManagers = ndbDatabase.getManagers()`

This method returns a *java.util.Vector* object containing elements of type *java.lang.String* representing the names of people, servers, and groups who have been granted manager access to a database. Consider the following example.

```
import lotus.domino.*;
public class JavaAgent extends AgentBase {
  public void NotesMain() {
    try {
        Session nssession = getSession();
        AgentContext nacContext = nssession.getAgentContext();
        Database ndbCurr = nacContext.getCurrentDatabase();
        Document ndocMail;
        double dblSize=0;
        int intSize=0;
        int intQuota=0;
        String strLocation;
        String strServer;
        strServer=ndbCurr.getServer();
        dblSize=ndbCurr.getSize();
        intSize=(int)dblSize;
        intQuota=ndbCurr.getSizeQuota();
        if(intSize>=intQuota)
            {
            if(strServer =="")
              {
                 strLocation="Local";
              }
            else
              {
                strLocation=strServer;
              }
            ndocMail=ndbCurr.createDocument();
            ndocMail.replaceItemValue("subject","Size Quota has
            ➥been reached on " + ndbCurr.getTitle());
            ndocMail.replaceItemValue("Body","The size quota ("+
            ➥ndbCurr.getSizeQuota() + ") has been reached in " +
            ➥ndbCurr.getTitle() + " (" + ndbCurr.getFileName() +
            ➥") on " + strLocation +".");
            ndocMail.send(false, ndbCurr.getManagers());
            }
        } catch(Exception e) {
          e.printStackTrace();
        }
    }
  }
}
```

5.0 getMaxSize   R   &   getMaxSize

```
lngMaxSize = ndbDatabase.getMaxSize()
```

This method returns the maximum allowable size of a database as set when the database
was created. This can be set only when you're creating a database.

---

getOutline

```
noutOutline = ndbDatabase.getOutline(strName)
```
                                                                                         getOutline

strName	Required	O.Ref.

A *java.lang.String* object containing the name of the outline to retrieve.

This method allows you to retrieve the *lotus.domino.Outline* named in the strName
parameter.

---

getParent	R	O.Ref.

```
nssession = ndbDatabase.getParent()
```

This method returns a *lotus.domino.Session* (▶ 577) object representing the current session.

---

getPercentUsed	R	#

```
dblUsed = ndbDatabase.getPercentUsed()
```

This method returns a double representing the amount of space utilized in a database to store data. When this value drops below 90 percent, you should consider compacting the database. Consider the following example.

```
import lotus.domino.*;
public class JavaAgent extends AgentBase {
  public void NotesMain() {
    try {
        Session nssession = getSession();
        AgentContext nacContext = nssession.getAgentContext();
        Database ndbCurr=nacContext.getCurrentDatabase();
        if (ndbCurr.getPercentUsed() =< 89)
          {
             int intSaved = ndbCurr.compact();
          }
    } catch(Exception e) {
    e.printStackTrace();
    }
  }
}
```

---

getProfileDocCollection

```
ndcCollection = ndbDatabase.getProfileDocCollection(strProfileName)
```

strProfileName	Required	O.Ref.

A *java.lang.String* containing the name or alias of the form used to create the profile documents you want to retrieve.

This method retrieves all the profile documents that were created with the form named in strProfileName and returns them as a *lotus.domino.DocumentCollection* (▶ 435).

---

getProfileDocument

```
ndocDocument = ndbDatabase.getProfileDocument(strProfilename,
➥strUsername)
```

strProfilename	Required	O.Ref.

A *java.lang.String* object containing the name or alias of the profile document you want to create or access.

strUsername	Optional	O.Ref.

A *java.lang.String* object containing the user name or key of the profile document you want to retrieve or create.

If no profile document matches the specified parameters, this method will create a new profile document with the name and user name specified by strProfileName and strUserName. Otherwise, a *lotus.domino.Document* (▶ 413) object representing the matching profile document will be returned.

getReplicaID   R   O.Ref.

```
strRepID = ndbDatabase.getReplicaID()
```

This method returns a *java.lang.String* containing the current database's replica ID (which is a 16-digit alphanumeric string) of a database.

5.0 getReplicationInfo   R   O.Ref.

```
nRepInfo = ndbDatabase.getReplicationInfo()
```

Each *lotus.domino.Database* contains one *lotus.domino.Replication* object (▶ 533), and you can use this method to access it for the current database.

getServer   R   O.Ref.

```
strServer = ndbDatabase.getServer()
```

This method returns the name of the server on which the database resides as a *java.lang.String*. If the database is on a workstation, this method returns an empty string (" ").

getSize   R

```
dblSize = ndbDatabase.getSize()
```

Returns the size of the database in bytes as a double.

getSizeQuota   R   %

```
int lngQuota = ndbDatabase.getSizeQuota()
```

This method returns the size quota for a database (in kilobytes). Not all databases have a quota, and this method returns 0 for such databases.

getTemplateName   R   O.Ref.

```
strTplName = ndbDatabase.getTemplateName()
```

This method returns a *java.lang.String* containing an empty string (" ") if the database is not a template. Otherwise, it eturns the value entered for the template name.

getTitle   R   O.Ref.

```
strTitle = ndbDatabase.getTitle()
```

This method returns the title of the database (as displayed on the database icon) as a *java.lang.String*.

getURLHeaderInfo

```
strHeader = ndbDatabase.getURLHeaderInfo(strURL, strHeader, strUsername,
➥strPassword, strProxyUsername, strProxyPassword)
```

strURL   Required   O.Ref.
A *java.lang.String* object containing the URL of the page you want to retrieve. You can enter up to 15KB.

strHeader   Required   O.Ref.
A *java.lang.String* object containing the header string for the URL header you want to retrieve. For more information on acceptable header strings, check the HTTP specification (http://www.w3.org/).

strUsername   Required   O.Ref.
If a host requires authentication, you can use this parameter, a *java.lang.String* object, to pass a username to the host. If this parameter isn't needed, specify null.

strPassword   Required   O.Ref.

If a host requires authentication, you can use this parameter, a *java.lang.String* object, to pass a password to the host. If this parameter isn't needed, specify `null`.

strProxyUsername   Required   O.Ref.

Use this parameter, a *java.lang.String* object, to specify a username to proxy servers that require authentication. If this parameter isn't needed, specify `null`.

strProxyPassword   Required   O.Ref.

Use this parameter, a *java.lang.String* object, to specify a password to proxy servers that require authentication. If this parameter isn't needed, specify `null`.

This method returns the requested header value as a string. If an empty string (`""`) is returned, either the requested header value wasn't found in the header of the specified URL, or the specified URL wasn't found.

getView

getView   `nvwView = ndbDatabase.getView(strViewName)`

strViewName   Required   O.Ref.

This parameter, a *java.lang.String* object, specifies the name or alias of a view or folder that you want to access. Be sure to use either the entire name of the view or folder (including backslashes for cascading views and folders), or an alias, but not both.

This method returns a *lotus.domino.View* (▶ 587) object representing the view or folder specified by the `strViewName` parameter.

If you call this method on a local database, it returns public and personal views and folders. For server-based databases, it returns only public views and folders.

getViews   R   O.Ref.

getViews   `vecViews = ndbDatabase.getViews()`

This method returns a *java.util.Vector* containing all the views in the database. The elements in the vector are of type *lotus.domino.View* (▶ 587).

grantAccess

grantAccess   `ndbDatabase.grantAccess(strName, intLevel)`

strName   Required   O.Ref.

Use this parameter, a *java.lang.String* object, to indicate the name of the server, person, or group whose access level you want to set.

intLevel   Required   %

Indicates the level of access you want to grant. The following table lists the acceptable constants for this parameter:

Constant	Description
ACL.LEVEL_NOACCESS	No access
ACL.LEVEL_DEPOSITOR	Depositor access
ACL.LEVEL_READER	Reader access
ACL.LEVEL_AUTHOR	Author access
ACL.LEVEL_EDITOR	Editor access
ACL.LEVEL_DESIGNER	Designer access
ACL.LEVEL_MANAGER	Manager access

This method allows you to set the appropriate access level for any server, person, or group in the database ACL. If the server, person, or group specified in `strName` exists in the ACL, it is updated with the access level specified by `intLevel`. Otherwise, the name is added to the ACL with the specified level. When this method is called, it sets ACL roles to their default values. The following example shows a simple agent that could add a new group to the ACL of every database in a directory.

```java
import lotus.domino.*;
public class JavaAgent extends AgentBase {
  public void NotesMain() {
    try {
            Session nssession = getSession();
            AgentContext nacContext = nssession.getAgentContext();
            Database ndbCurr;
            Document ndocCurrDoc;
            DbDirectory nDirCurrDir = nssession.getDbDirectory(null);
            ndbCurr=nDirCurrDir.getFirstDatabase(DbDirectory.DATABASE);
            while(ndbCurr!=null)
              {
                ndbCurr.grantAccess("WP_Application_Admin",
                ➡ACL.LEVEL_EDITOR);
                ndbCurr=nDirCurrDir.getNextDatabase();
              }
        } catch(Exception e) {
        e.printStackTrace();
    }
  }
}
```

isDelayUpdates   R   T/F

```java
bolDelayUpdates = ndbDatabase.isDelayUpdates()
```

This method returns `true` if writes to the database are being batched (which increases performance) and `false` otherwise. Bear in mind that although using this method increases performance, you stand a chance of losing data if the server crashes before the changes are committed. Delayed updates are applied to both save and delete operations.

isFTIndexed   R   T/F

```java
bolIsFTIndexed = ndbDatabase.isFTIndexed()
```

This method indicates whether a database has a full-text index. It returns `true` if an index exists and `false` otherwise.

isMultiDbSearch   R   T/F

```java
bolMultiSearch = ndbDatabase.isMultiDbSearch()
```

This method returns `true` if a database is part of a multidatabase search index and `false` otherwise.

isOpen   R   T/F

```java
bolIsOpen = ndbDatabase.isOpen()
```

Indicates whether a database has been opened. If the database is open, this method returns `true`. Otherwise, it returns `false`.

isPrivateAddressBook   R   T/F

```java
bolPrivNAB = ndbDatabase.isPrivateAddressBook()
```

For any database accessed through the `getAddressBooks` method of *lotus.domino.Session* (▶ 580) that is a Personal Address Book, this method returns `true`. For any other database, including Personal Address Books *not* accessed through the `getAddressBooks` method of *lotus.domino.Session,* this method returns `false`.

isPublicAddressBook   R   T/F

isPublicAddress
Book

`bolPrivNAB = ndbDatabase.isPublicAddressBook()`

For any database accessed through the `getAddressBooks` method of *lotus.domino.Session* (▶ 580) that is a Domino Directory (formerly called a Public Address Book), this method returns `true`. For any other database, including Public Address Books *not* accessed through the `getAddressBooks` method of *lotus.domino.Session,* this method returns `false`.

open

open

`intflag = ndbDatabase.open()`

This method allows you to open a database so that an agent can access its methods. This method returns `true` if the specified database was found and opened successfully and `false` if the specified database couldn't be opened. In order for you to use this method, the calling script must have at least reader access to the database.

There are two basic ways to use this method. The first is to open a database that has already been instantiated. In this case, simply pass an empty string (`" "`) for both parameters. The second way is to open an existing database that hasn't been instantiated, in which case you must specify a server name and filename.

queryAccess

queryAccess

`intLevel = ndbDatabase.queryAccess(strName)`

strName   Required   O.Ref.

This parameter, a *java.lang.String* object, specifies the name of the person, group, or server for which you want to know the access level.

This method searches a database's ACL for the value specified in the `strName` parameter and returns a constant that represents the access level for that name, as shown in the following table:

Constant	Description
ACL.LEVEL_NOACCESS	No access
ACL.LEVEL_DEPOSITOR	Depositor access
ACL.LEVEL_READER	Reader access
ACL.LEVEL_AUTHOR	Author access
ACL.LEVEL_EDITOR	Editor access
ACL.LEVEL_DESIGNER	Designer access
ACL.LEVEL_MANAGER	Manager access

The following paragraphs define how this method derives the access level.

If the specified name is explicitly listed in the ACL and is also a member of group(s) listed in the ACL, the highest access level is returned.

If the specified name is a group member, the group's access level is returned.

If the specified name is a member of several groups in the ACL, the highest access level granted to any of the groups is returned.

If the specified name is not a member of any group, the default access level is returned. It is important to remember that this method uses the Primary Address Book on the machine where the script is being executed. On a workstation, it uses the Personal Address Book. On a server, the Public Address Book on that server is used.

remove

```
ndbDatabase.remove()
```
remove

This method permanently deletes a database from the disk drive.

replicate

```
intFlag = ndbDatabase.replicate(strServerName)
```
replicate

strServerName   Required   O.Ref.
Specifies, as a *java.lang.String* object, the name of the server to replicate with. If there is more than one replica of the database on the specified server, they will all replicate.

This method provides the ability to automate the replication process. It returns `true` if the replication completes successfully and `false` if any errors are generated.

revokeAccess

```
ndbDatabase.revokeAccess(strName)
```
revokeAccess

strName   Required   O.Ref.
This parameter, a *java.lang.String* object, is used to specify the name of the server, person, or group whose access you are revoking.

This method allows you to remove a server, person, or group from a database's ACL, effectively granting the revoke default access to the database. Bear in mind that this is not the same as assigning No Access with the `GrantAccess` method, which totally locks a server, person, or group out of the database. If this method can't find the server, person, or group specified in `strName`, an error will be generated.

search

```
ndcDocumentCollection = ndbDatabase.search(strFormula)
```
search

```
ndcDocumentCollection = ndbDatabase.search(strFormula, ndtNotesDate)
```

```
ndcDocumentCollection = ndbDatabase.search(strFormula, ndtNotesDate,
➥intMaxDocs)
```

strFormula   Required   O.Ref.
A *java.lang.String* object containing the @function formula defining the selection criteria.

ndtNotesDate   Required   O.Ref.
This parameter is a *lotus.domino.DateTime* object (▶ 399) to be used as a cutoff date so that only documents created or modified after the cutoff date are searched.

intMaxDocs   Required   %
This parameter specifies the number of documents that should be returned in the collection. You can pass `0` to indicate that you want all matching documents.

This method returns an unsorted *lotus.domino.DocumentCollection* containing all the documents that match the selection criteria. This method is always substantially slower than performing a full-text search. It should be avoided when a full-text search can be performed.

setCategories

setCategories

ndbDatabase.**setCategories**(strCategories)

strCategories	Required	O.Ref.

A *java.util.String* object containing the categories in which you want the database to appear in the Database Library.

This method allows you to add categories under which the database will be displayed in the Database Library. Enter multiple values as a comma-separated list.

setDelayUpdates

setDelay Updates

ndbDatabase.**setDelayUpdates**(bolDelayUpdates)

bolDelayUpdates	Required	T/F

A Boolean value that indicates whether updates should be delayed.

Use this method to specify whether updates to the database should immediately be written to the database. Specify `true` to delay writes and `false` to have writes take place immediately. Keep in mind that delaying updates increases performance but also increases the possibility of data loss in the event of a server crash.

5.0 setFolderReferencesEnabled

setFolder References Enabled

ndbDatabase.**setFolderReferencesEnabled**(bolEnabled)

bolEnabled	Required	T/F

If set to `true`, this method determines which folders contain a document. Before attempting to use a document's folder references, be sure to test this method. Additionally, each database that uses folder references must have the `FolderRef` hidden view.

setSizeQuota

setSizeQuota

ndbDatabase.**setSizeQuota**(intQuota)

intQuota	Required	%

This method sets the size quota for a database (in kilobytes).

setTitle

setTitle

ndbDatabase.**setTitle**(strTitle)

strTitle	Required	O.Ref.

This method, when passed a *java.lang.String* containing a title, changes a database's title. The title of the current database can't be changed.

updateFTIndex

updateFTIndex

ndbDatabase.**updateFTIndex**(bolCreateFlag)

bolCreateFlag	Required	T/F

If no index exists, specifying `true` will create a new index (this is valid only with local databases). Otherwise, an existing index will be updated. If the database is not local, specify `false`.

This method allows you to programmatically create (local databases only) or update full-text indexes.

Remarks

In most cases, you must explicitly open a database before most of its methods can be accessed with Java.

The isOpen method can be called to determine whether the database is open. If it isn't, you can open it by calling the open method.

In order to open a database, you or your agent (agent owner) must have a minimum of reader access.

Any script running on a server can't access databases on another server. This will generate an error if it is attempted. Likewise, if a script doesn't have the appropriate access to perform a function, it will be denied.

If a *lotus.domino.Database* object is accessed through a *lotus.domino.DbDirectory* object, it is not considered open. *NotesDatabase* objects accessed through the AddressBooks property in *NotesSession* are not open. However, the following methods are available on the closed database: getFileName, getFilePath, isOpen, isPrivateAddressBook, isPublicAddressBook, getParent, and getServer.

Example

The following example demonstrates reading the contents of a field on a Web page and conducting a domain search based on the field's value.

```java
import lotus.domino.*;
public class JavaAgent extends AgentBase {
  public void NotesMain() {
    try {
            Session nssession = getSession();
            AgentContext nacContext = nssession.getAgentContext();
            Database ndbCurr=nacContext.getCurrentDatabase();
            Document ndocResultsDoc = ndbCurr.createDocument();
            Document ndocCurr=nacContext.getDocumentContext();
            Item nitem=ndocCurr.getFirstItem("query");
            String strQuery=nitem.getValueString();
            if(strQuery != "")
             {
            ndocResultsDoc = ndbCurr.FTDomainSearch(strQuery, 0,
            ➡Database.FT_SCORES,Database.FT_DATABASE,1,0,
            ➡"Domain Search" );
                ndocResultsDoc.replaceItemValue("Subject",
                ➡"The following results were found");
                ndocResultsDoc.send(false,nssession.getCommonUserName());
            }
        } catch(Exception e) {
        e.printStackTrace();
    }
  }
}
```

4.5x 4.6x 5.0 DateRange

When you're developing Notes/
Domino applications using Java, the
lotus.domino.DateRange class provides a
mechanism to work with a range of dates
and times.

Session
  └ DateRange
      └ DateTime

Java Syntax

```
public class DateRange extends Base
```

To create a new *lotus.domino.DateRange* object, you must use the `createDateTime` method of *lotus.domino.Session* (▶ 578), which will return the new *lotus.domino.DateRange* object. The `createDateTime` method can be used in one of three ways:

```
ndrRange = nsSession.createDateRange()
```

or

```
ndrRange = nsSession.createDateRange(DateTime ndtstart, DateTime ndtend)
```

or

```
ndrRange = nsSession.createDateRange(java.util.Date startt,
➥java.util.Date endt)
```

Java Parameters

DateTime ndtstart   Optional   O.Ref.
A *DateTime* object representing the range's starting time.

DateTime ndtend   Optional   O.Ref.
A *DateTime* object representing the range's ending time.

Date start
A *java.util.Date* object representing the starting time of the *lotus.domino.DateRange*.

Date end
A *java.util.Date* object representing the ending time of the *lotus.domino.DateRange*.

DateRange Methods

getEndDateTime   R   O.Ref.

getEndDateTime

```
ndtTime = ndrDateRange.getEndDateTime()
```

This method returns a *lotus.domino.DateTime* object (▶ 399) that contains the ending date and time of the *lotus.domino.DateRange*.

getParent   R   O.Ref.

getParent

```
nsSession = ndrDateRange.getParent()
```

This method indicates the name of the *lotus.domino.Session* (▶ 577) that contains the *lotus.domino.DateRange*.

getStartDateTime   R   O. Ref.

getStart
DateTime

```
ndtTime = ndrDateRange.getStartDateTime()
```

This method returns a *lotus.domino.DateTime* object (▶ 399) that represents the starting date and time of the *lotus.domino.DateRange*.

---

getText   R   O.Ref.

```
strRangeText = ndrDateRange.getText()
```
getText

This method returns an object of type *java.lang.String* containing a textual representation of the *lotus.domino.DateRange*.

---

setEndDateTime

```
ndrdaterange.setEndDateTime(ndtEndTime)
```
setEndDateTime

---

ndtEndTime   Required   O.Ref.

A *lotus.domino.DateTime* object representing the date time range.

This method accepts a *lotus.domino.DateTime* object (▶ 399) used to set the ending date and time of the *lotus.domino.DateRange*.

---

setStartDateTime

```
ndrdaterange.setStartDateTime(ndtEndTime)
```
setStart
DateTime

---

ndtStartTime   Required   O.Ref.

A *lotus.domino.DateTime* object representing the date time range.

This method accepts a *lotus.domino.DateTime* object (▶ 399) representing the starting date and time of the *lotus.domino.DateRange*.

---

setText

```
ndrdaterange.setText(strTimeRange)
```
setText

---

strTimeRange   Required   O.Ref.

A string object representing the date time range.

This method accepts an object of type *java.lang.String* that can be used to set the range of the *lotus.domino.DateRange*.

Example

```
import lotus.domino.*;
public class JavaAgent extends AgentBase {
  public void NotesMain() {
    try {
      Session ns = getSession();
      AgentContext nac = ns.getAgentContext();
      Database ndb = nac.getCurrentDatabase();
      DateTime ndtstart = ns.createDateTime("");
      DateTime ndtend = ns.createDateTime("");
      ndtstart.setNow();
      ndtstart.adjustHour(-12, true);
      ndtend.setNow();
      DateRange ndr = ns.createDateRange(ndtstart, ndtend);
      System.out.println ("Date Range:" + ndr.getText());
      } catch(Exception e) {
      e.printStackTrace();
    }
  }
}
```

The *lotus.domino.DateTime* object allows you to easily manipulate time and date values in Java applications.

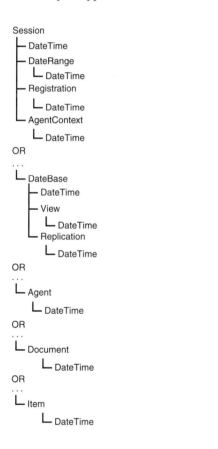

```
Session
 ├─ DateTime
 ├─ DateRange
 │   └─ DateTime
 ├─ Registration
 │   └─ DateTime
 └─ AgentContext
     └─ DateTime
OR
. . .
 └─ DateBase
     ├─ DateTime
     ├─ View
     │   └─ DateTime
     └─ Replication
         └─ DateTime
OR
. . .
 └─ Agent
     └─ DateTime
OR
. . .
 └─ Document
         └─ DateTime
OR
. . .
 └─ Item
         └─ DateTime
```

Java Syntax

```
public class lotus.notes.DateTime extends Base
```

To create a new *lotus.domino.DateTime* object, call the `createDateTime` method in the *lotus.domino.Session* class (► 578).

```
DateTime ndtDateTime = Session.createDateTime(strDatetimetoset)
```

Java Parameters

strDatetimetoset	Optional	$

A *java.lang.String* value that represents the time and date with which to initialize the object.

DateTime Methods

adjustDay

```
Datetime.adjustDay(intadjustdays, bolpreservelocalzone)
```

intadjustdays	Required	%

An integer representing the number of days to increment or decrement the *lotus.domino.DateTime* object.

bolpreservelocalzone	Optional	T/F

If the adjustment to the date-time crosses the boundary for daylight saving time purposes, you can set this parameter to `true`. Setting this method to `false` or omitting this parameter will not adjust for daylight saving time.

This method provides a way to increment or decrement a date-time object by *n* days, where *n* is an integer representing the number of days.

```
import lotus.domino.*;
public class JavaAgent extends AgentBase {
  public void NotesMain() {
    try {
    Session session = getSession();
    AgentContext nac = session.getAgentContext();
    Document ndocWebPage = nac.getDocumentContext();
    Vector vecRsvDate= ndocWebPage.getItemValue("dReservationDate");
    DateTime ndtRsvDate = session.createDateTime
    ➥(vecRsvDate.firstElement());
    if (getWeekday(ndtRsvDate.getLocalTime())=1)
       ndtRsvDate.AdjustDay(1); // Push reservation forward to Monday
    elseif (getWeekday(ndtRsvDate.getLocalTime())=7)
       ndtRsvDate.AdjustDay(2); // Push reservation forward to Monday
    } catch(Exception e) {
      e.printStackTrace();
    }
  }
}
```

adjustHour

```
datetime.adjustHour(intadjusthours, bolpreservelocalzone)
```

intadjusthours   Required   %

An integer representing the number of days by which to increment or decrement the *lotus.domino.DateTime* object.

bolpreservelocalzone   Optional   T/F

If the adjustment to the date-time crosses the boundary for daylight saving time purposes, you can set this parameter to `true`. Setting this method to `false` or omitting this parameter will not adjust for daylight saving time.

This method provides a way to increment or decrement a date-time object by *n* hours, where *n* is an integer representing the number of hours. A *lotus.domino.DateTime* object that contains only a date component will not be changed by this method. If you increment (or decrement) the *lotus.domino.DateTime* object by enough hours to move into a new day, the date component will be adjusted accordingly.

adjustMinute

```
datetime.adjustMinute(intadjustminutes, bolpreservelocalzone)
```

intadjustminutes   Required   %

An integer representing the number of minutes by which to increment or decrement the *lotus.domino.DateTime* object.

bolpreservelocalzone   Optional   T/F

If the adjustment to the date-time crosses the boundary for daylight saving time purposes, you can set this parameter to `true`. Setting this method to `false` or omitting this parameter will not adjust for daylight saving time.

This method provides a way to increment or decrement a date-time object by *n* minutes, where *n* is an integer representing the number of minutes. A *lotus.domino.DateTime* object, which contains only a date component, will not be changed by this method. If you increment (or decrement) the *lotus.domino.DateTime* object by enough minutes to move into a new day, the date component will be adjusted accordingly.

adjustMonth

```
datetime.adjustMonth(intadjustmonths, bolpreservelocalzone)
```

intadjustmonths   Required   %

An integer representing the number of months by which to increment or decrement the *lotus.domino.DateTime* object.

bolpreservelocalzone   Optional   T/F

If the adjustment to the date-time crosses the boundary for daylight saving time purposes, you can set this parameter to `true`. Setting this method to `false` or omitting this parameter will not adjust for daylight saving time.

This method provides a way to increment or decrement a date-time object by *n* months, where *n* is an integer representing the number of months.

adjustSecond

```
datetime.adjustSecond(intadjustseconds, bolpreservelocalzone)
```

intadjustseconds   Required   %

An integer representing the number of seconds by which to increment or decrement the *lotus.domino.DateTime* object.

bolpreservelocalzone   Optional   T/F

If the adjustment to the date-time crosses the boundary for daylight saving time purposes, you can set this parameter to `true`. Setting this method to `false` or omitting this parameter will not adjust for daylight saving time.

This method provides a way to increment or decrement a date-time object by *n* seconds, where *n* is an integer representing the number of seconds. A *lotus.domino.DateTime* object that contains only a date component will not be changed by this method. If you increment (or decrement) the *lotus.domino.DateTime* object by enough seconds to move into a new day, the date component will be adjusted accordingly.

adjustYear

adjustYear

```
datetime.adjustYear(intadjustyears, bolpreservelocalzone)
```

intadjustyears   Required   %

An integer representing the number of years by which to increment or decrement the *lotus.domino.DateTime* object.

bolpreservelocalzone   Optional   T/F

If the adjustment to the date-time crosses the boundary for daylight saving time purposes, you can set this parameter to `true`. Setting this method to `false` or omitting this parameter will not adjust for daylight saving time.

This method provides a way to increment or decrement a date-time object by *n* years, where *n* is an integer representing the number of years. A *lotus.domino.DateTime* object that contains only a date component will not be changed by this method. If you increment (or decrement) the *lotus.domino.DateTime* object by enough days to move into a new year, the date component will be adjusted accordingly.

```
import lotus.domino.*;
public class JavaAgent extends AgentBase {
  public void NotesMain() {
    try {
      // A simple Y2K compliance test
      Session session = getSession();
      AgentContext agentContext = session.getAgentContext();
      DateTime ndtY2K=session.createDateTime("Today");
      ndtY2K.adjustYear(1);
      System.out.println(ndtY2K.getLocalTime());
    } catch(Exception e) {
    e.printStackTrace();
    }
  }
}
```

convertToZone

```
datetime.convertToZone(intnewzone, boldst)
```

convertToZone

intnewzone   Required   %

An integer containing a valid time zone, which ranges from **0** to **15**.

boldst   Required   T/F

A Boolean value that determines whether daylight saving time is in effect or not.

This method changes the `TimeZone` and `isDST` methods of this class as specified by the `intnewzone` and `boldst` parameters.

---

getDateOnly   R   O.Ref.

    strDate = datetime.**getDateOnly**()   getDateOnly

This method returns a *java.lang.String* object containing the date portion of a *lotus.domino.DateTime* in the local time zone.

---

getGMTTime   R   O.Ref.

    strgmttime = datetime.**getGMTTime**()   getGMTTime

This method returns a *java.lang.String* object containing the date-time converted to Greenwich Mean Time, which is time zone 0. This value is dependent on the `isDST` and `TimeZone` values of the object.

---

getLocalTime   R $

    strlocaltime = datetime.**getLocalTime**()   getLocalTime

This method returns a *java.lang.String* object containing the date-time in the local time zone.

---

getParent

    Session ns = DateTime.**getParent**()   getParent

This method returns the *lotus.domino.Session* object that contains the current *lotus.domino.DateTime* object.

---

getTimeOnly   R   O.Ref.

    strTime = datetime.**getTimeOnly**()   getTimeOnly

This method returns a *java.lang.String* object containing the time portion of a date-time in the local time zone.

---

getTimeZone   R   %

    intTimeZone = datetime.**getTimeZone**()   getTimeZone

Returns an integer representing the time zone of a date-time. The integer may be positive or negative.

---

getZoneTime   R   O.Ref.

    strZoneTime = datetime.**getZoneTime**()   getZoneTime

A string representation of the time, adjusted based on the `TimeZone` and `isDST` values. When a *lotus.domino.DateTime* object is created, the `ZoneTime` value is the same as `LocalTime`. Once the `ConvertToZone` method is called, changes to the `TimeZone` and `isDST` values are reflected in `ZoneTime`, but `LocalTime` stays the same.

---

isDST   R   T/F

    boldst = datetime.**isDST**()   isDST

This method indicates whether the date-time is adhering to daylight saving time (`true` if it is, `false` if it isn't).

---

setAnyDate

    datetime.**setAnyDate**()   setAnyDate

This method takes no parameters. It sets the date portion of a *lotus.domino.DateTime* object to a wildcard date.

---

setAnyTime

datetime.**setAnyTime**()

This method takes no parameters. It sets the time portion of a *lotus.domino.DateTime* object to a wildcard time.

---

setLocalDate

datetime.**setLocalDate**(intyeartoset, intmonthtoset, intdaytoset)

datetime.**setLocalDate**(intyeartoset, intmonthtoset, intdaytoset,
➥bolpreservelocaltime)

intyeartoset	Required	%

An integer containing a valid time representing the year component of a time.

intmonthtoset	Required	%

An integer containing a valid time representing the month component of a time.

intdaytoset	Required	%

An integer containing a valid time representing the day component of a time.

bolpreservelocaltime	Required	T/F

A Boolean value used to determine whether daylight saving time should be used.

This method can be used with a series of integer values to manipulate the `LocalTime` value of a *lotus.domino.DateTime*.

---

setLocalTime

datetime.**setLocalTime**(strsetdatetime)

datetime.**setLocalTime**(inthourtoset, intminutetoset, intsecondtoset,
➥inthundredthstoset)

datetime.**setLocalTime**(dtdatetoset)

strsetdatetime	Required	O.Ref.

A *java.lang.String* object containing the date and time value you want to set.

inthourtoset	Required	%

An integer containing a valid time representing the hour component of a time.

intminutetoset	Required	%

An integer containing a valid time representing the minute component of a time.

intsecondstoset	Required	%

An integer containing a valid time representing the second component of a time.

inthundredthstoset	Required	%

An integer containing a valid time representing the hundredths of a second component of a time.

dtdatetoset	Required	O.Ref.

A *java.util.Date* object containing a valid time representing the date you want to set.

This method can be used with either a *java.lang.String* object or with a series of integer values to manipulate the `LocalTime` value of a *lotus.domino.DateTime*.

setNow

```
datetime.setNow()
```
setNow

This method takes no parameters and sets a *lotus.domino.DateTime* to the current system date and time.

timeDifference

```
intTimeDiff = ndtDateTime.timeDifference(ndtDateTime)
```
timeDifference

ndtDateTime   Required   O.Ref.

A *lotus.domino.DateTime* object from which you want to determine the difference.

This method calculates the difference between two *lotus.domino.DateTime* objects and returns the value in seconds as an integer.

timeDifferenceDouble

```
dblTimeDiff = ndtDateTime.timeDifferenceDouble(ndtDateTime)
```
timeDifference
Double

ndtDateTime   Required   O.Ref.

A *lotus.domino.DateTime* object from which you want to determine the difference.

This method calculates the difference between two *lotus.domino.DateTime* objects and returns the value in seconds as a double.

toJavaDate

```
java.util.Date Date = DateTime.toJavaDate()
```
toJavaDate

This method returns a *java.util.Date* object containing the *lotus.domino.DateTime* in Java format.

Remarks

Keep in mind that *lotus.domino.DateTime* objects contain both a time zone and hundredths.

Example

The following agent demonstrates using the *lotus.domino.DateTime* class to test the "age" of documents and to archive documents that have "expired."

```
import lotus.domino.*;
import java.util.Vector;
import java.lang.Integer;
public class JavaAgent extends AgentBase {
  public void NotesMain() {
    try {
    Session session =getSession();
    AgentContext nac=session.getAgentContext();
    Database ndbCurr=nac.getCurrentDatabase();
    double dblDiff;
```

continued >>

continued >>

```
                    double dblResult;
                    double dblMonths;
                    //Get handle on archive database
                    Database ndbADb=session.getDatabase(ndbCurr.getServer(),
                  ➥"archive.nsf");
                    //Get handle on system database
                    Database ndbLDb=session.getDatabase(ndbCurr.getServer(),
                  ➥"control.nsf");
                    View nvwLView=ndbLDb.getView("KeyLookup");
                    //Get doc in system db that contains the expiration date
                    Document ndocLDoc=nvwLView.getDocumentByKey("ExpirationDate");
                    DateTime ndtArchiveThreshold = session.createDateTime("Today");
                    DateTime ndtLastRunDate = session.createDateTime("Today");
                    //Set archive date by adjusting month by threshold
                    ndtArchiveThreshold.adjustMonth(1);
                    //Get first document in Unprocessed documents collection
                    DocumentCollection ndcAllDocs=ndbCurr.getAllDocuments();
                    Document ndocCurrDoc=ndcAllDocs.getFirstDocument();
                    //Loop through all documents in Unprocessed collection
                    for (int i = 1; i<=ndcAllDocs.getCount(); i++)
                      {
                        // Calculate the time difference in seconds
                        dblDiff = ndtLastRunDate.timeDifferenceDouble
                      ➥(ndtArchiveThreshold);
                        dblMonths=(2592000*1);
                        //See if the threshold in the control database has been reached
                        // or surpassed.
                        if (dblDiff/dblMonths >=1)
                          {
                            Document ndocADoc=ndbADb.createDocument(); // create
                                                                        // document in
                                                                        // archive
                                                                        // database
                            ndocCurrDoc.copyAllItems(ndocADoc, true);
                            Document ndocTDoc=ndocCurrDoc;
                            ndocCurrDoc=ndcAllDocs.getNthDocument(i);
                            ndocTDoc.remove(true);
                          }
                        else
                          ndocCurrDoc=ndcAllDocs.getNthDocument(i);
                      }
                    } catch(Exception e) {
                    e.printStackTrace();
                  }
                }
              }
```

4.6x 5.0 DbDirectory

The *lotus.domino.DbDirectory* class represents the directories storing *lotus.domino.Databases* on a specified server or the local computer. Using this method, you can navigate through all the databases stored locally or on a particular server, as well as open and create new *lotus.domino.Database* objects.

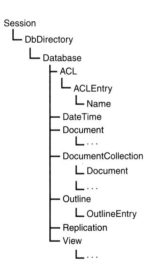

Java Syntax

Public class **DbDirectory** extends Base

Because *lotus.domino.objects* can't be created with the new modifier, they must be created with methods emanating from the root *lotus.domino.Session* object. Therefore, a new *lotus.domino.DbDirectory* object can be created in Java using the getDbDirectory method contained in *lotus.domino.Session.*

Java Parameters

There are no parameters for initializing this object. However, you can use the getDbDirectory of the *lotus.domino.Session* (▶ 581) to create a new *lotus.domino.DbDirectory* object.

DbDirectory Methods

createDatabase

createDatabase

```
ndbDatabase = ndbdirDbDirectory.createDatabase(strDbfile)

ndbDatabase = ndbdirDbDirectory.createDatabase(bolOpen)
```

strDbfile   Required   O.Ref.
The filename for the new database.

bolOpen   Required   T/F
Indicates whether you want to open the database. true opens the database. false does not.

In order for you to access the methods of the *lotus.domino.Database,* a database must be open (using bolopen). If the bolOpen parameter is set to false, the database must be opened using the openDatabase or openDatabaseIfModified methods of the *lotus.domino.DbDirectory* object.

getFirstDatabase

getFirstDatabase

```
ndbDatabase = ndbdirDbDirectory.getFirstDatabase(intType)
```

intType   Required   %
The constant type of database file to search.

Database File Type Constants

File Type Integer	Indicated File Type
DbDirectory.DATABASE	All Notes databases with an .nsf, .nsg, nsh, or .nst extension
DbDirectory.TEMPLATE	All Notes database templates with an .ntf extension
DbDirectory.REPLICA_CANDIDATE	All Notes databases or templates where replication has not been disabled
DbDirectory.TEMPLATE_CANDIDATE	All Notes databases and templates

This method returns a text string that contains the first database located in the *lotus.domino.DbDirectory* on the server or local computer of the specified file type. This method doesn't open the specified database. Instead, it gets a handle on the back-end *lotus.domino.Database* object. Therefore, not all of the methods of *lotus.domino.Database* are available.

Every time the method is called, a new search is conducted in the *lotus.domino.DbDirectory*. In other words, the handle to the existing *lotus.domino.DbDirectory* is discarded in memory and reinitialized. This feature is necessary as you might not want the new search to be conducted on the same file type as the previous search.

The following example of a Java agent displays the file path of the first *lotus.domino.Database* object found in the local directory to the Java Console.

```
import lotus.domino.*;

public class JavaAgent extends AgentBase {

  public void NotesMain() {

    try {
      Session ns = getSession();
      AgentContext agentContext = ns.getAgentContext();
      DbDirectory ndbdir = ns.getDbDirectory(null);
      Database ndb = ndbdir.getFirstDatabase(DbDirectory.DATABASE);
      ndb.open();
      System.out.println("First Db Filepath: " +
      ndb.getFilePath());

    } catch(Exception e) {
      e.printStackTrace();
    }
  }
}
```

---

getName   R   O.Ref.

```
StrName = ndbdirDbDirectory.getName()
```
getName

Returns the string value of the name of the server you are currently searching. This method returns `null` when searching the local computer.

---

getNextDatabase

```
ndbDatabase = ndbdirDbDirectory.getNextDatabase()
```
getNext
Database

This method returns a handle to a *lotus.domino.Database* object located on the server or local machine specified in the *lotus.domino.DbDirectory*. If no more databases remain in the *lotus.domino.DbDirectory*, a `null` value is returned. Similar to the `getFirstDatabase` method, this method doesn't open the specified database. Instead, it gets a handle on the back-end *lotus.domino.Database* object. Therefore, not all of the methods of *lotus.domino.Database* are available.

The following example of a Java agent displays the database title of all the first *lotus.domino.Database* objects found in the local directory to the Java Console.

```
import lotus.domino.*;

public class JavaAgent extends AgentBase {

  public void NotesMain() {
```

continued >>

continued >>

```
try {
    Session ns = getSession();
    AgentContext agentContext = ns.getAgentContext();
    DbDirectory ndbdir = ns.getDbDirectory(null);
    Database ndb = ndbdir.getFirstDatabase(DbDirectory.DATABASE);
    while (ndb != null) {
        ndb.open();
        System.out.println("Current Db Name: " +
        ndb.getTitle());
        ndb = ndbdir.getNextDatabase(); }

    } catch(Exception e) {
    e.printStackTrace();
    }
  }
}
```

getParent

getParent   nsSession = ndbdirDbDirectory.**getParent**()

Indicates the *lotus.domino.Session* that contains the *lotus.domino.DbDirectory* object.

openDatabase

openDatabase   ndbDatabase = ndbdirDbDirectory.**openDatabase**(strDbfile)

ndbDatabase = ndbdirDbDirectory.**openDatabase**(strDbfile, bolFailOver)

strDbfile	Required	O.Ref.

The filename of the database to open.

bolFailOver	Required	T/F

Indicates whether the script should search for another server in the cluster.

If the database can't be found on the current server and this is set to **true**, the script attempts to open the database on another server in the cluster if one exists. For remote access (IIOP), this parameter is always **false**.

Calling this method will return a handle on the open *lotus.domino.Database* object (▶ 373). The program running this script must have at least reader access to the database in order to use the openDatabase method. Otherwise, an **error** is returned.

openDatabaseByReplicaID

openDatabase
ByReplicaID   ndbDatabase = ndbdirDbDirectory.**openDatabaseByReplicaID**(strRid)

strRid	Required	O.Ref.

The replica ID of the database to open.

Calling this method will return a handle to the open *lotus.domino.Database* object if a database with the specified replica ID is located. The program running this script must have at least reader access to the database in order to use the openDatabaseByReplicaID method. Otherwise, an **error** is returned.

openDatabaseIfModified

openDatabase
IfModified   ndbDatabase = ndbdirDbDirectory.**OpenDatabaseIfModified** (strDbfile,
➥ndtDateTime)

strDbfile	Required	O.Ref

The filename of the database to open.

ndtDateTime   Required   Date/Time
The date to compare the last modified date against.

Using the date specified when calling this method, this will open the specified database if the actual date modified is more recent than the date passed as a parameter.
Calling this method will return a handle on the open *lotus.domino.Database* object. The
program running this script must have at least Reader access to the database in order
to use the `openDatabaseIfModified` method. Otherwise, an `error` is returned.

openMailDatabase

```
ndbDatabase = ndbdirDbDirectory.openMailDatabase()
```
openMail
Database

This method will return the opened mail database or `null` if the mail database is not
opened. If this script is running on a workstation, this method will find the current
user's mail server and mail database by referencing the settings specified in the user's
notes.ini or Notes Preferences file. If this script is run on the server, the script attempts
to open the mail database of the person who last modified the agent. Since the last person to modify an agent becomes the owner of that agent, the script opens that person's
mail database on his or her specified mail server as specified in the Domino directory
on the server. If the script is making remote calls to a server (IIOP), the current user is
the user who created the session. Therefore, the script opens that user's mail database on
his or her specified mail server as specified in the Domino directory on the server.

Remarks

When working with the *lotus.domino.DbDirectory* class, keep in mind that the
directory structure assumes that you are working in the Notes directory structure
and the virtual file system maintained by Notes. Therefore, the root directory is
the directory specified in the notes.ini file for the respective server or the local
computer—such as the line in the .ini file that reads `Directory=C:\notes5\data`.
This is important, because the actual file location on the file server is not important. Notes, along with the script that is searching the directory structure using
the *lotus.domino.DbDirectory* methods, is only searching for Notes database files in
the notes\data directory or directories that may be mapped using .dir files on the
server. Therefore, you don't need to be concerned about the actual file path.

Example

The following script evaluates the *lotus.domino.DbDirectory* and creates two arrays.
The first string array will contain all the filenames of all the Notes databases, and
the second string array will contain all the Notes templates. Each dynamic array is
built as the script reads the Notes directory. Both arrays are then written to fields
stored in a new *lotus.domino.Document* created in the current *lotus.domino.Database*.

```
import lotus.domino.*;
import java.util.Vector;

public class JavaAgent extends AgentBase {

    public void NotesMain() {
```

continued >>

continued >>

```
try {
  Session ns = getSession();
  AgentContext agentContext = ns.getAgentContext();
  DbDirectory ndbdir = ns.getDbDirectory(null);
  Database ndb = ndbdir.getFirstDatabase(DbDirectory.DATABASE);
  Database ndbCurrent = agentContext.getCurrentDatabase();
  Document ndoc = ndbCurrent.createDocument();
  int intDbcount=0;
  int intTemplatecount=0;
  Vector vecDatabases = new Vector();
  Vector vecTemplates = new Vector();
  ndoc.appendItemValue("Form", "Test Document");
    while (ndb != null) {
    ndb.open();
    vecDatabases.addElement(ndb.getFileName());
    intDbcount++;
    ndb = ndbdir.getNextDatabase(); }
    ndoc.appendItemValue("slDatabaseList", vecDatabases);
    Database ndbTemp = ndbdir.getFirstDatabase(DbDirectory.TEMPLATE);
    while (ndbTemp != null) {
    ndbTemp.open();
    vecTemplates.addElement(ndbTemp.getFileName());
    intTemplatecount++;
    ndbTemp = ndbdir.getNextDatabase(); }
    ndoc.appendItemValue("slTemplateList", vecTemplates);
     if (ndoc.save())
    System.out.println("Java agent completed and doc was saved");
  else
    System.out.println("Java agent did not complete, doc was not
    ➥saved");
    } catch(Exception e) {
  e.printStackTrace();
  }
 }
}
```

Document

The *lotus. domino. Document* object represents a collection or subset of *lotus. domino. Documents*. *lotus. domino. Documents* are the common data storage mechanism used throughout Domino/Lotus Notes that contains the *lotus. domino. Items, lotus. domino. RichTextItems,* and any *lotus. domino. EmbeddedObjects*.

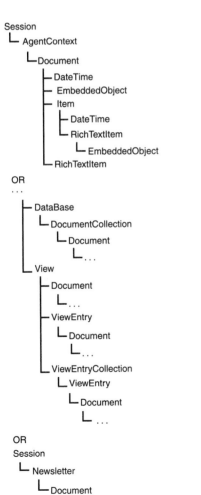

```
Session
  └ AgentContext
      └ Document
          ├ DateTime
          ├ EmbeddedObject
          ├ Item
          │   ├ DateTime
          │   └ RichTextItem
          │         └ EmbeddedObject
          └ RichTextItem
  OR
  ...
          ├ DataBase
          │   └ DocumentCollection
          │        └ Document
          │             └ ...
          └ View
              ├ Document
              │    └ ...
              ├ ViewEntry
              │    └ Document
              │         └ ...
              └ ViewEntryCollection
                   └ ViewEntry
                        └ Document
                             └ ...
  OR
Session
  └ Newsletter
      └ Document
           └ ...
```

Page	Contents
	Syntax
	Methods
416	appendItemValue
417	computeWithForm
417	copyAllItems
417	copyItem
418	copyToDatabase
418	createReplyMessage
418	createRichTextItem
418	encrypt
419	getAttachment
419	getAuthors
419	getColumnValues
420	getCreated
420	getEmbeddedObjects
420	getEncryptionKeys
421	getFirstItem
421	getFolderReferences
421	getFTSearchScore
421	getItems
421	getItemValue
422	getItemValueDouble
422	getItemValueInteger
422	getItemValueString
422	getKey
423	getLastAccessed
423	getLastModified
423	getNameOfProfile
423	getNoteID
423	getParentDatabase
423	getParentDocument UNID
423	getParentView
423	getResponses

continued >>

Java Syntax

```
public class Document extends Base
```

Various methods can be used to establish a handle on an existing *lotus.domino.Document* object. Which method you use depends on what action you want to perform on the *lotus.domino.Document* object. The following paragraphs explain the various methods you can use to access existing *lotus.domino.Documents* and why you would use each one.

lotus.domino.View. Establish a handle based on the document's position in a *lotus.domino.View* object (▶ 587). Based on the document's relative position in a response hierarchy.

Use the `FTSearch` method to locate all documents that match the search query criteria (▶ 591).

lotus.domino.Database. Establish a handle based on the document's UNID or `noteID` using `getDocumentByID` (▶ 381) or `getDocumentByUNID` (▶ 382) methods.

Establish a handle on all the documents contained in the *lotus.domino.Database* using the `getAllDocuments` method (▶ 380).

Use the `FTSearch` method to locate all documents that match the search query criteria (▶ 378).

Use the `search` method to locate all documents that match the search criteria determined using the formula language (▶ 391).

Establish a handle on all the documents that haven't been processed by a *lotus.domino.Agent* using the `getUnproccessedDocuments` (▶ 367), `unprocessedFTSearch` (▶ 367), or `unprocessedSearch` (▶ 368) methods of the *lotus.domino.AgentContext* class.

lotus.domino.Document. Establish a handle on all the response documents of the current *lotus.domino.Document* using the `getResponses` method (▶ 423).

Establish a handle on the parent document using the `getParentDocumentUNID` method of the current *lotus.domino.Document* (▶ 423).

In order to create a new *lotus.domino.Document* object, use the `createDocument` method of the *lotus.domino.Database* object (▶ 376). After a new *lotus.domino.Document* is created, modified, or deleted, the `save` method must be explicitly called before the changes are permanently saved to disk. Otherwise, the modifications are lost when the script completes. Also, if a new *lotus.domino.Document* is created but no *lotus.domino.Items* are created, the document will not be saved, even if the `save` method is explicitly called.

Document Methods

appendItemValue

```
niItem = ndocDocument.appendItemValue(strItemname)

niItem = ndocDocument.appendItemValue(strItemname, intValue)

niItem = ndocDocument.appendItemValue(strItemname, dblvalue)

niItem = ndocDocument.appendItemValue(strItemname, value)
```

strItemname	Required	O.Ref.

The name of the new *lotus.domino.Item*.

intValue	Required	%

The value of the new *lotus.domino.Item* as an integer type.

dblvalue	Required	#

The value of the new *lotus.domino.Item* as a double type.

value	Required	O.Ref.

The value of the new *lotus.domino.Item* as the same data type as the object.

This method creates and returns a handle on a new *lotus.domino.Item* in the *lotus.domino.Document* and sets the item's value. The data type of the new *lotus.domino.Item* depends on the data type of the value passed in the method call. Here are the possible resulting data types:

Data Type of value	Data Type of New Item
java.lang.String	Text item
java.util.Vector	Text item array containing *java.lang.String* elements
java.util.Vector	Number array containing integer elements
java.util.Vector	Number array containing double elements
Integer	Number item
Double	Number item
java.util.Vector	Date-time item array containing *lotus.domino.DateTime* elements
lotus.domino.DateTime	Date-time item
lotus.domino.Item	*lotus.domino.Item* data type matching the *lotus.domino.Item* data type

The new *lotus.domino.Item* isn't permanently saved to disk until the save method of the *lotus.domino.Document* is called. Also, if an item already exists in the *lotus.domino.Document* that has the same name as the strItemName specified when this method is called, a new *lotus.domino.Item* is created in the document. In other words, both *lotus.domino.Items* are preserved in the document even though they share the same item name.

lotus.domino.Items can also be created for the *lotus.domino.Document* by using extended syntax, which enables you to add and modify *lotus.domino.Items* as if they were methods of the *lotus.domino.Document*. This technique is described in the "Remarks" section near the end of this chapter (▶ 432).

computeWithForm

```
bolComputewithform = ndocDocument.computeWithForm (bolDoDataTypes,
➥bolRaiseError)
```

bolDoDataTypes   Required   T/F

This method is currently ignored.

bolRaiseError   Required   T/F

Indicates whether an error should be raised if validation fails.

This method validates the *lotus.domino.Document* by executing all the default field values (if they don't already exist), the translation formulas, and the validation formulas of the field design elements stored in the specified form. This is similar to refreshing the document when it is opened in the user interface. This method returns true if the validation was successful and no errors were returned, and false if there are errors on the document. The form design elements used for the validation are determined in the following order:

1. The form stored in the document. This is done during the document's creation.
2. The value stored in the *lotus.domino.Item* named "Form."
3. The default database form if not *lotus.domino.Item.*

Unlike creating *lotus.domino.Documents* using the native Notes client user interface, documents created using LotusScript don't use a form when they are created. Consequently, form-specific default field values, translation formulas, and validation formulas are not used when new documents are created. This method allows *lotus.domino.Documents* that are created as back-end objects to conform to the requirements of *lotus.domino.Documents* that are created as front-end objects in the user interface. Unlike when documents are created in the user interface, documents can still be saved even if not all of the field validation formulas pass.

You should always specify a *lotus.domino.Item* named "Form" when creating new *lotus.domino.Documents,* regardless of whether this method is being called. This will ensure that the documents are opened using the correct form.

copyAllItems

```
Document.copyAllItems(ndocDocument, bolReplace)
```

Document   Required   O.Ref.

The destination *lotus.domino.Document.*

bolReplace   Required   T/F

Indicates whether the *lotus.domino.Items* in the destination document should be replaced or appended. true replaces the current items. false appends them.

This method copies all the *lotus.domino.Items* in the current *lotus.domino.Document* to the destination *lotus.domino.Document.* The actual names of the *lotus.domino.Items* and their respective values are unchanged.

copyItem

```
niItem = ndocDocument.copyItem(niItem)

niItem = ndocDocument.copyItem(niItem, strNewname)
```

Item   Required   O.Ref.

The *lotus.domino.Item* to copy.

strNewname   Required   O.Ref.

The name to assign to the new *lotus.domino.Item.* Specify "" to use the existing name.

This method returns a handle on a *lotus.domino.Item* that is copied into the current *lotus.domino.Document*. It also assigns it the name specified in the `strNewName` parameter (if specified).

copyToDatabase

```
ndocDocument = ndocDocument.copyToDatabase(ndbDatabase)
```

Database	Required	O.Ref.

The *lotus.domino.Database* to copy the *lotus.domino.Document* into.

This method copies a *lotus.domino.Document* into the specified *lotus.domino.Database* and returns a handle on the new *lotus.domino.Document*.

createReplyMessage

```
ndocDocument = ndocDocument.createReplyMessage(bolAll)
```

bolAll	Required	T/F

Specifies whether the recipient list should contain all the members of the original list. `true` includes all the original recipients. `false` includes only the sender of the original memo.

This method creates a new *lotus.domino.Document* as a reply to the current *lotus.domino.Document* and returns a handle to the new reply document. Prior to sending the new document, be sure to specify a value for the "Subject" *lotus.domino.Item*. Also, the new document won't get mailed unless the `send` method is explicitly called (▶ 430).

createRichTextItem

```
nrtiRichTextItem = ndocDocument.createRichTextItem(strName)
```

strName	Required	O.Ref.

The name of the new *lotus.domino.RichTextItem*.

This method creates a new *lotus.domino.RichTextItem* for the specified *lotus.domino.Document* and returns a handle to the new rich text item. The name of the new rich text item is determined by the `strName` passed as a parameter in the method.

encrypt

```
ndocDocument.encrypt()
```

This method encrypts the *lotus.domino.Document* and all the *lotus.domino.Items* contained in the document that have the `isEncrypted` method set to `true`. This encryption doesn't take effect until you write the document to disk by calling the `save` method.

The keys used to encrypt the document can be either a single string value or an array of strings. The string value (or each element of the string array) contains the name of the encryption key. Any users who have the encryption key can decrypt the document.

The name of the specified encryption key is stored in the *lotus.domino.Document* in a *lotus.domino.RichTextItem* named `secretEncryptionKeys`. If the document is encrypted but no encryption keys are specified, the document is encrypted using the current user's public key. Therefore, the document can be decrypted by that user only.

If the script calling this method is running on a server, the server must have permission to use the `encrypt` method.

getAttachment

```
nembAttachment = ndocDocument.getAttachment(strFilename)
```

strFilename	Required	O.Ref.

The name of the file attachment to locate.

This method returns a handle to the *lotus.domino.EmbeddedObject* for the specified file attachment. This method locates any file attachments, regardless of whether they are contained in a *lotus.domino.RichTextItem*. If the file attachment specified in the strFilename isn't located, this method returns null. Also, the parent method of the *lotus.domino.EmbeddedObject* returns null as well since the file attachment wasn't accessed through the *lotus.domino.RichTextItem*.

getAuthors   R   O.Ref.

```
vecAuthors = ndocDocument.getAuthors()
```

Represents the usernames (fully distinguished if the name is hierarchical) of everyone who has previously saved the document. This method returns an object of type *java.util.Vector*. Its elements are *java.lang.String*.

The following example displays the names of all the entries in the Authors field of the current *lotus.domino.Document*.

```
import lotus.domino.*;
import java.util.Vector;

public class JavaAgent extends AgentBase {

    public void NotesMain() {

        try {
            Session ns = getSession();
            AgentContext agentContext = ns.getAgentContext();
            Document ndocCurrent = agentContext.getDocumentContext();
            Vector vecAuthors;
            vecAuthors = ndocCurrent.getAuthors();
            System.out.println("Author Names:" + vecAuthors);

        } catch(Exception e) {
            e.printStackTrace();
        }
    }
}
```

getColumnValues   R   O.Ref.

```
vecColumnValues = ndocDocument.getColumnValues()
```

If the current handle on the *lotus.domino.Document* was established from a parent *lotus.domino.View*, this method will store an array of objects, each corresponding to the column values of the current document's parent view. The order of the elements contained in the array logically corresponds to the columns in the respective parent view. In other words, the first element of the array is the value that appears in the first column of the view, the second element of the array is the value that appears in the second column of the view, and so on.

It's important to understand that the value contained in the vecColumnValues Vector array may or may not match any actual item value contained in the current document. This is because the value contained in the vecColumnValues Vector array represents the values displayed in the view, which may be altered as a result of the view's column formulas. In addition, because vecColumnValues Vector is derived from the *lotus.domino.View*, if a column value displays a null value, the respective array element will be null as well.

If the current *lotus.domino.Document* wasn't accessed using a *lotus.domino.View*, this method will return null.

If it's necessary to retrieve an item value from the document, using this method to access particular items on a *lotus.domino.Document* is more efficient than accessing the *lotus.domino.Item* value from the document directly. However, often the required item value isn't displayed in the *lotus.domino.View*.

This method ignores the "Responses Only" design feature of the *lotus.domino.View* column formulas and will return a value regardless of the document type.

The following example locates a document based on a specific key and returns the value stored in the column values of the view.

```java
import lotus.domino.*;
import java.util.Vector;

public class JavaAgent extends AgentBase {

    public void NotesMain() {

        try {
            Session ns = getSession();
            AgentContext agentContext = ns.getAgentContext();
            Database ndb = agentContext.getCurrentDatabase();
            View nvw = ndb.getView("StandardView");
            Vector vecValue;
            Document ndoc = nvw.getDocumentByKey("Acme Inc.", true);
            vecValue = ndoc.getColumnValues();
            System.out.println(vecValue);

        } catch(Exception e) {
            e.printStackTrace();
        }
    }
}
```

getCreated	R	Time/Date

varndtCreated() = ndocDocument.**getCreated**()

getCreated

Represents the date that the *lotus.domino.Document* was created. This method returns a *lotus.domino.DateTime* object.

getEmbeddedObjects	R	O.Ref.

vecEmbObjects = ndocDocument.**getEmbeddedObjects**()

getEmbedded
Objects

Represents an array of the OLE/1 and OLE/2 embedded objects that are contained in the *lotus.domino.Document*. This method doesn't contain any file attachments or OLE/1 objects that were created in Release 3. If the *lotus.domino.Form* used to create the document had an embedded object in its design, that object could be accessed using this method provided that it was activated, modified, and saved in the *lotus.domino.Document*. getEmbeddedObjects isn't currently supported under OS/2, UNIX, or Macintosh.

getEncryptionKeys	R	O.Ref.

vecEncryptionKeys = ndocDocument.**getEncryptionKeys**()

getEncryption
Keys

Represents the keys used to encrypt the document. The keys set or returned from this method are used when the `encrypt` method is called (▶ 418). When retrieving this value using the `get` syntax just shown, the value returned is an array of strings. The string value, or each element of the string array, contains the name of the encryption key. Any users who have the encryption key can decrypt the document.

The name of the specified encryption key is stored in the *lotus.domino.Document* in a *lotus.domino.RichTextItem* named `secretEncryptionKeys`. If the document is encrypted but no encryption keys are specified, the document is encrypted using the current user's public key. Therefore, the document can be decrypted by that user only.

getFirstItem

```
niItem = ndocDocument.getFirstItem(strName)
```

strName	Required	O.Ref.

The name of the *lotus.domino.Item* to locate.

This method returns a handle on the first *lotus.domino.Item* in the document with the name specified in the `strName` parameter. If no *lotus.domino.Item* named `strName` is located, this method returns `null`.

getFolderReferences   R   O.Ref.

```
vecFolderRefs = ndocDocument.getFolderReferences()
```

Indicates what folders (as an array of strings) in the current *lotus.domino.Database* have references to the *lotus.domino.Document*. In order for this method to have any effect, the *lotus.domino.Database* must support folder references and have the hidden FolderRef view design. The `getFolderReferencesEnabled` method of the *lotus.domino.Database* can be tested to ensure that the current database has folder references enabled (▶ 384).

getFTSearchScore   R   %

```
intFTSearchScore = ndocDocument.getFTSearchScore()
```

Returns the full-text search score of the documents that were retrieved as the result of a full-text search. The document's score is based on the search query and the frequency of successful hits for the document—in other words, the number of successful words that were located in the document, any term weights specified for the words, and any proximity characters specified. Because a document can be contained in multiple *lotus.domino.DocumentCollections* and *lotus.domino.ViewEntryCollections,* `FTSearchScore` will reflect the score of the most recent search. If a document is added to a collection, deleted from a view, or wasn't retrieved as part of a full-text index, `FTSearchScore` will be set to 0. If the document was retrieved using the `FTSearch` method but the *lotus.domino.Database* wasn't full-text indexed, the search will still work. However, the value assigned to `FTSearchScore` will be unreliable.

getItems   R   O.Ref.

```
vecItems = ndocDocument.getItems()
```

Represents an array of all the *lotus.domino.Items* contained in the *lotus.domino.Document*.

getItemValue

```
vecItemValue = ndocDocument.getItemValue(strItemname)
```

strItemname	Required	O.Ref.

The name of the *lotus.domino.Item*.

This method returns the value(s) of the specified *lotus.domino.Item* in the *lotus.domino.Document*. If the *lotus.domino.Item* has only one element, a vector is returned with only one element. This is because a vector is always returned for all text, number, and time–date items. If the *lotus.domino.Item* has more than one value, a vector of elements is returned, where each element corresponds to a value in the *lotus.domino.Item*. The data type of the returned value depends on the data type of the *lotus.domino.Item*. Here are the possible resulting data types:

Data Type of *Item*	Returned Value Type
Rich text	*java.util.Vector* with one element rendered in plain text
Text or text list (for Names, Authors, and Reader types)	*java.util.Vector* with *java.lang.String* elements
Number or number list	*java.util.Vector* with double elements
Date-time or range of date-time values	*java.util.Vector* with *lotus.domino.DateTime* elements

lotus.domino.Items can also be accessed from the *lotus.domino.Document* by using extended syntax, which allows you to locate *lotus.domino.Items* as if they are methods of the *lotus.domino.Document*. This technique is described in the "Remarks" section near the end of this chapter (▶ 432).

getItemValueDouble

getItemValue Double

```
dblItemvalue = ndocDocument.getItemValueDouble(strItemname)
```

strItemname   Required   O.Ref.
The name of the *lotus.domino.Item*.

This method returns the value(s) of type double for the specified *lotus.domino.Item* in the *lotus.domino.Document*. If the *lotus.domino.Item* has more than one value, the first value is returned.

getItemValueInteger

getItemValue Integer

```
intItemvalue = ndocDocument.getItemValueInteger(strItemname)
```

strItemname   Required   O.Ref.
The name of the *lotus.domino.Item*.

This method returns the value(s) of type integer for the specified *lotus.domino.Item* in the *lotus.domino.Document*. If the *lotus.domino.Item* has more than one value, the first value is returned.

getItemValueString

getItemValue String

```
strItemvalue = ndocDocument.getItemValueString(strItemname)
```

strItemname   Required   O.Ref.
The name of the *lotus.domino.Item*.

This method returns the value(s) of type string for the specified *lotus.domino.Item* in the *lotus.domino.Document*. If the *lotus.domino.Item* has more than one value, the first value is returned.

getKey   R   O.Ref.

getKey

```
strKey = ndocDocument.getKey()
```

If the *lotus.domino.Document* is a profile document, this method indicates the username used (or key) of the profile document.

---

getLastAccessed   R   Time/Date

`ndtLastaccessed = ndocDocument.getLastAccessed()`

Represents the date that the document was last accessed (this includes modifications or reading).

For an example that uses `lastAccessed`, refer to the example at the end of this chapter (▶ 433).

---

getLastModified   R   Time/Date

`ndtLastModified = ndocDocument.getLastModified()`

Represents the date that the document was ast modified.

---

getNameOfProfile   R   O.Ref.

`strProfileName = ndocDocument.getNameOfProfile()`

If the *lotus.domino.Document* is a profile document, this method indicates the name of the profile document.

For an example that uses `getNameOfProfile`, refer to example at the end of this chapter (▶ 433).

---

getNoteID   R   O.Ref.

`strNoteID = ndocDocument.getNoteID()`

Indicates the `noteID` of the *lotus.domino.Document*. The `noteID` is an eight-character combination of letters and numbers used to uniquely identify the document location in the *lotus.domino.Database*. Therefore, the `noteID` for each document is unique for each database. However, `noteIDs` are not consistent across replica copies of the *lotus.domino.Databases*. Each `noteID` is the same for the document and is unique to the document until it is deleted.

---

getParentDatabase   R   O.Ref.

`ndbParentDatabase = ndocDocument.getParentDatabase()`

Represents the parent *lotus.domino.Database* that contains the *lotus.domino.Document*.

---

getParentDocumentUNID   R   O.Ref.

`strParentUNID = ndocDocument.getParentDocumentUNID()`

If the *lotus.domino.Document* is a response document, this method represents the Universal ID of the document's parent (similar to accessing the current document's Universal ID by using the `getUniversalID` method (▶ 424)). If the document is not a response document (and thus doesn't have a parent), this method returns an empty string (`""`).

---

getParentView   R   O.Ref..

`nvParentView = ndocDocument.getParentView()`

If the *lotus.domino.Document* handle was retrieved from a *lotus.domino.View,* this method returns the name of the view from which it was retrieved. If the document handle was established from other methods (such as from a *lotus.domino.DocumentCollection* or from a *lotus.domino.Database*), this method returns `null`.

---

getResponses   R   O.Ref..

`ndcResponses = ndocDocument.getResponses()`

Returns a *lotus. domino. DocumentCollection* of the immediate response documents to the current *lotus. domino. Document*. All the entries in the collection are immediate responses (children) only. Therefore, responses-to-responses are not included in the collection. If the current *lotus. domino. Document* has no response documents, this method returns an empty collection with a count of 0.

getSigner	R	O.Ref.

getSigner

`strSigner = ndocDocument.getSigner()`

If the document is signed, this method represents the name of the person who created the signature contained in the *lotus. domino. Document*. If the document has not been signed, this method returns an empty string (" ").

getSize	R	%

getSize

`intSize = ndocDocument.getSize()`

Indicates the size in bytes of the *lotus. domino. Document*. The value represented here includes all the items and file attachments that are contained in the document.

getUniversalID	R	O.Ref.

getUniversalID

`strUniversalID = ndocDocument.getUniversalID()`

Represents the Universal ID of the *lotus. domino. Document*. The Universal ID is a 32-character combination of hexadecimal digits that uniquely identifies the document. This identification is unique across all replicas of this database (unlike the `noteID`). In fact, this method is used to determine whether documents in replica *lotus. domino. Databases* are replicas of one another. Therefore, if a document's `universalID` is modified, the document then becomes a new document. The hexadecimal digits include the numbers 0 to 9 and the letters A to F. Because each `universalID` must be unique within all replicas of the database, you can't set this value to an existing `universalID` in the *lotus. domino. Database*. Attempting to do so generates a runtime error 4000 message.

getVerifier	R	O.Ref.

getVerifier

`strVerifier = ndocDocument.getVerifier()`

If the *lotus. domino. Document* is signed, this method represents the name of the certificate that was used to verify the signature contained in the document.

hasEmbedded	R	T/F

hasEmbedded

`bolHasEmbedded = ndocDocument.hasEmbedded()`

Indicates whether the document contains one or more *lotus. domino. EmbeddedObjects* (embedded objects, database links, view links, document links, and file attachments). `true` indicates that embedded objects are contained in the document. `false` indicates that no embedded objects are recognized. This method has no effect on OS/2, UNIX, or Macintosh operating systems.

hasItem		

hasItem

`bolHasItem = ndocDocument.hasItem(strItemname)`

strItemname	Required	T/F

The name of the *lotus. domino. Item*.

This method indicates whether the *lotus. domino. Item* specified in the `strItemname` is contained in the *lotus. domino.Document*. `true` indicates that the *lotus. domino. Item* exists in the *lotus. domino. Document*. `false` indicates that it does not exist.

5.0 isDeleted   R   T/F

```
bolIsDeleted = ndocDocument.isDeleted()
```

Indicates whether the document has been deleted from the *lotus.domino.Database*. `true` indicates that it has been deleted. `false` indicates that it has not.

isEncryptOnSend   R   T/F

```
bolEncryptonsend = ndocDocument.isEncryptOnSend()
```

Indicates whether the document is to be encrypted when mailed. `true` indicates that it should be encrypted when mailed. `false` indicates that it should not be encrypted. This method defaults to `false`. When the document is mailed, the system attempts to locate the public key for each recipient in the Directory (Public Address Book). Each user whose public key can't be located will still receive the e-mail, but their messages won't be encrypted. The users whose public key *was* located will receive an encrypted document.

isNewNote   R   T/F

```
bolIsNewNote = ndocDocument.isNewNote()
```

Indicates whether the document is a new *lotus.domino.Document*—that is, you haven't yet saved it to disk by calling the `save` method. `true` indicates that it is a new document. `false` indicates that it is not new and has previously been saved to disk.

The following simple example could be used when saving a *lotus.domino.Document*. This example tests the value of the field called `kwHotClient`, which is a checkbox located on the current form (which is a company profile document). If this field has been selected, the current document is then copied to the Hot Clients folder automatically.

```
import lotus.domino.*;

public class JavaAgent extends AgentBase {

    public void NotesMain() {

        try {
            Session ns = getSession();
            AgentContext agentContext = ns.getAgentContext();
            Document ndocCurrent = agentContext.getDocumentContext();
            if (ndocCurrent.isNewNote());
                if (ndocCurrent.getItemValueString("kwHotClient") == "Yes");
                    ndocCurrent.putInFolder("Hot Clients", true);

        } catch(Exception e) {
            e.printStackTrace();
        }
    }
}
```

isProfile   R   T/F

```
bolIsProfile = ndocDocument.isProfile()
```

Indicates whether the document is a profile document—a special type of *lotus.domino.Document* Domino object that stores user-specific information.

isResponse   R   T/F

```
bolIsResponse = ndocDocument.isResponse()
```

Indicates whether the document is a response document to a parent *lotus.domino.Document*. `true` indicates that it is a response. `false` indicates that it is not. Of course, the parent *lotus.domino.Document* can also be a response or main document.

---

isSaveMessageOnSend   R   T/F

isSaveMessage
OnSend

`bolSaveMsg = ndocDocument.`**`isSaveMessageOnSend`**`()`

Indicates whether the document should be saved immediately after it is mailed (by calling the `send` method of the *lotus.domino.Document*). `true` indicates that the document is saved after being mailed. `false` indicates that it is not. This method will work only when the *lotus.domino.Document* is a new document and hasn't yet been saved. Therefore, subsequent calls to the `send` method will not resave the document.

---

isSentByAgent   R   T/F

isSentByAgent

`bolSentByAgent = ndocDocument.`**`isSentByAgent`**`()`

Indicates whether the document was mailed to the current user by LotusScript. `true` indicates that the document was mailed by script. `false` indicates that it was mailed by a person. This method uses a reserved *lotus.domino.Item* named `$AssistMail` that is set to 1 if the document is mailed by script. This *lotus.domino.Item* is automatically created and saved to the *lotus.domino.Document* when the document is mailed.

---

isSigned   R   T/F

isSigned

`bolIsSigned = ndocDocument.`**`isSigned`**`()`

Indicates whether the document is signed, therefore containing a *lotus.domino.Item* object of type `SIGNATURE`. `true` indicates that the document contains one or more signatures. `false` indicates that it does not contain any signatures.

---

isSignOnSend   R   T/F

isSignOnSend

`bolSignOnSend = ndocDocument.`**`isSignOnSend`**`()`

Indicates whether the document is signed when mailed. `true` indicates that the document is signed when mailed. `false` indicates that it is not.

---

isValid   R   T/F

isValid

`bolIsValid = ndocDocument.`**`isValid`**`()`

Indicates whether the document represents a "valid" *lotus.domino.Document* object and not a deletion stub. `true` indicates that the document is not a deletion stub. `false` indicates that the document is a deletion stub. This method differs from the `isDeleted` method because `isValid` indicates that the document was deleted before a handle to the *lotus.domino.Document* was established. After the document handle has been established, the `isDeleted` method can be examined to ensure that the document wasn't deleted while the user or script was processing the document.

---

makeResponse

makeResponse

`Document.`**`makeResponse`**`(ndocDocument)`

Document   Required   O.Ref.

The *lotus.domino.Document* that will become a response to the initial *lotus.domino.Document*.

This method makes the *lotus.domino.Document* passed as the parameter (in parentheses) a response to the initial *lotus.domino.Document*. Both *lotus.domino.Documents* must be located in the same *lotus.domino.Database*. In addition, you must explicitly call the `save` method (▶ 429) before the *lotus.domino.Document* is permanently set as a response document to the parent document.

putInFolder

putInFolder

```
ndocDocument.putInFolder(strFoldername)

ndocDocument.putInFolder(strFoldername, bolCreateonfail)
```

strFoldername   Required   O.Ref.

The name of the folder to add the document to.

bolCreateonfail   Required   T/F

Determines whether the folder should be created if it doesn't already exist. `true` creates the folder. `false` doesn't create it.

This method adds the *lotus.domino.Document* to the folder specified as `strFolderName`. If the folder doesn't exist, the `bolCreateonfail` parameter determines whether it should be created in the current *lotus.domino.Database*.

If the folder is nested in another folder, specify the complete path to the destination folder, separating the folder names with backslashes (much as you would in the file directory). If any or all of the folders specified in the path do not exist, they will be created. Therefore, if this method is called, if the `strFolderName` is Administration\Projects\Billing, if none of the folders exists, and if `bolCreateonfail` is set to `true`, the folders will all be created automatically. If the script is running locally on the user's workstation, the folder can be a personal folder.

If the document already exists in the destination folder, calling this method returns `null`. Also, if the destination folder is a "Shared, Personal on first use," a document must already be added or this method will generate an error. Once a document has already been added, this method can add documents to the folder.

remove

remove

```
bolRemove = ndocDocument.remove(bolForce)
```

bolForce   Required   T/F

Specifies whether the document should be deleted even if another user has modified the document after the current user began accessing it. `true` forces the deletion. `false` aborts the deletion.

This method permanently deletes (removes) a *lotus.domino.Document* from the current *lotus.domino.Database* and returns a Boolean value indicating whether the deletion was successful. `true` indicates that the deletion was successfully completed. `false` indicates that the document was not deleted because another user modified it.

removeFromFolder

removeFrom Folder

```
ndocDocument.removeFromFolder(strFoldername)
```

strFoldername   Required $

The name of the folder to remove the document from.

This method removes the *lotus.domino.Document* from the folder specified as `strFolderName`. If the *lotus.domino.Document* isn't contained in the folder, or the folder doesn't exist, this method returns `null`.

If the folder is nested in another folder, specify the complete path to the destination folder, separating the folder names with backslashes (much as you would in the file directory). If the script is running locally on the user's workstation, the folder can be a personal folder.

removeItem

removeItem

```
ndocDocument.removeItem(strItemname)
```

strItemname	Required	O.Ref.

The name of the *lotus.domino.Item* to remove from the *lotus.domino.Document*.

This method deletes the *lotus.domino.Item* specified in the `strItemName` parameter from the *lotus.domino.Document*. If more than one *lotus.domino.Item* in the form has the same name, they are all removed. If `strItemName` is not contained in the *lotus.domino.Document*, this method returns `null`. You must explicitly call the `save` method (▶ 429) in order for the *lotus.domino.Item* to be permanently removed from the document. Also, you can remove *lotus.domino.Items* from *lotus.domino.Documents* by calling the `remove` method of the *lotus.domino.Item* class (▶ 428).

renderToRTItem

renderToRTItem

```
bolRenderToRTItem = ndocDocument.renderToRTItem(nrtiRichTextItem)
```

RichTextItem	Required	O.Ref.

The *lotus.domino.RichTextItem* in which to store the image.

This method creates an image of the specified *lotus.domino.Document* and places it into a *lotus.domino.RichTextItem*. A Boolean value is returned, indicating whether the method call was successful. `true` indicates that it was successful. `false` indicates that it was not. The image is rendered as a capture of the current *lotus.domino.Document* and *lotus.domino.Form,* so all field formulas (default, translation, and validation) and hide-when formulas are executed.

replaceItemValue

replaceItem
Value

```
niItem = ndocDocument.replaceItemValue(strItemname, value)
```

strItemname	Required	O.Ref.

The *lotus.domino.Document* to be replaced.

value	Required	O.Ref.

The value of the new *lotus.domino.Item.*

This method replaces all the *lotus.domino.Items* of the name specified in `strItemName` with the specified `value` and returns a handle on a new *lotus.domino.Item* in the *lotus.domino.Document.* The data type of the modified *lotus.domino.Item* depends on the data type of the `value` passed in the method call. Here are the possible resulting data types:

Data Type of value	Data Type of New Item
java.lang.String	Text item
java.util.Vector	Text item array containing *java.lang.String* elements
java.util.Vector	Number array containing integer elements
java.util.Vector	Number array containing double elements
Integer	Number item
Double	Number item
java.util.Vector	Date-time item array containing DateTime elements
lotus.domino.DateTime	Date-time item
lotus.domino.Item	*lotus.domino.Item* data type matching the *lotus.domino.Item* data type

The modified value of the *lotus.domino.Item* doesn't need to be the same type as the previous *lotus.domino.Item* value. When using this method to modify the contents of the *lotus.domino.Item,* the `isSummary` method of the *lotus.domino.Item* is set to `true`, so the new item value won't display in a view or folder. You must set this method to `false` if you want this item to be able to be displayed in views and folders.

The new *lotus.domino.Item* is not permanently saved to disk until the `save` method of the *lotus.domino.Document* is called.

save

```
bolSave = ndocDocument.save()

bolSave = ndocDocument.save(bolForce)

bolSave = ndocDocument.save(bolForce, bolCreateResponse)

bolSave = ndocDocument.save(bolForce, bolCreateResponse, bolMarkRead)
```

bolForce	Required	T/F

Indicates whether the document should be saved even if another user has modified and saved it since it was opened by the current user. `true` forces the latest version to overwrite the previous version. `false` causes the method to use the `bolCreateResponse` setting.

bolCreateResponse	Required	T/F

If `bolForce` is `false`, setting this parameter to `true` forces the current document to become a response document. If `false`, the save is canceled.

bolMarkRead	Required	T/F

Indicates whether the document should be marked as read. `true` marks the document as read. `false` does not.

This method saves any changes made to the current *lotus.domino.Document* to disk and returns a Boolean variable indicating whether the save was successful. `true` indicates that the save was successful. `false` indicates that the save failed. If `bolForce` is set to `false`, the `bolCreateResponse` parameter has no effect.

The following example creates a *lotus.domino.Document* in the back end and populates the items on the new *lotus.domino.Document* using values contained in the current *lotus.domino.UIDocument.* The new back-end document is then saved, and a meaningful message is printed to the Java Console.

```
import lotus.domino.*;

public class JavaAgent extends AgentBase {

    public void NotesMain() {

        try {
            Session ns = getSession();
            AgentContext agentContext = ns.getAgentContext();
            Database ndb = agentContext.getCurrentDatabase();
            Document ndocCurrent = agentContext.getDocumentContext();
            Document ndoc = ndb.createDocument();
            ndoc.replaceItemValue("Form", "Customer Profile");
            ndoc.replaceItemValue("strFormname", "Customer Profile Form");
            ndoc.replaceItemValue("strParentCompany",
            ➥ndocCurrent.getItemValue("strParentCompany"));
```

continued >>

continued >>

```
ndoc.replaceItemValue("strLocation",
↪ndocCurrent.getItemValue("strLocation"));
ndoc.replaceItemValue("strCustNumber",
↪ndocCurrent.getItemValue("strCustNumber"));
ndoc.replaceItemValue("strCustName",
↪ndocCurrent.getItemValue("strCustName"));
ndoc.replaceItemValue("strTransactionType",
↪ndocCurrent.getItemValue("strTransactionType"));
ndoc.replaceItemValue("intTransactionNumber",
↪ndocCurrent.getItemValue("intTransactionNumber"));
ndoc.replaceItemValue("dtTransactionDate",
↪ndocCurrent.getItemValue("dtTransactionDate"));
ndoc.replaceItemValue("strTransactionDescription",
↪ndocCurrent.getItemValue("strTransactionDescription"));
ndoc.replaceItemValue("strTransactionComments",
↪ndocCurrent.getItemValue("strTransactionComments"));
ndoc.save(true);
System.out.println("Document has been saved.");

        } catch(Exception e) {
            e.printStackTrace();
        }
    }
}
```

---

send

send   `ndocDocument.`**`send`**`(strRecipient)`

`ndocDocument.`**`send`**`(vecRecipients)`

`ndocDocument.`**`send`**`(bolAttachform, strRecipient)`

`ndocDocument.`**`send`**`(bolAttachform, vecRecipients)`

---

strRecipient	Optional	O.Ref.

Specifies the recipient of the document.

vecRecipients	Optional	O.Ref.

Specifies the recipients of the document.

bolAttachform	Required	T/F

Indicates whether the form should be stored and sent with the document. `true` stores the document. `false` does not.

This method mails the *lotus.domino.Document* to the recipients specified in the `strRecipient` or `vecRecipients` parameter. If `bolAttachform` is set to `true`, the size of the document increases, but this causes the recipient(s) to view the document in its original form design. The recipients can be people, groups, or mail-in databases. If the *lotus.domino.Document* contains a `SendTo` field, this parameter is ignored. If the document doesn't contain a `SendTo` field, this parameter is required. Also, if the document contains additional `CopyTo` or `BlindCopy` fields, they will be sent the document as well. Other mail-routing-specific *lotus.domino.Items* are used as well. For example, Delivery Priority, DeliveryReport, and ReturnReceipt will also be used when the document is mailed.

Set the `saveMessageOnSend` method of the *lotus.domino.Document* to `true` and `bolAttachForm` to `true` if you want the document to be saved when it is mailed.

When the document is mailed, Notes will automatically create a *lotus.domino.Item* called $AssistMail in the document, which allows the sentByAgent method to determine whether the document was mailed by script. If the script calling this method is running locally on a user's workstation, the user's name will automatically be assigned to the From *lotus.domino.Item*. If the script is running as a scheduled agent, the From item will contain the name of the person who last signed the agent.

sign

`ndocDocument.`**`sign`**`()`   sign

This method signs the document with the current user's signature. You must explicitly call the save method to permanently save the signature to disk, or the signature will be discarded when the script completes. If this method is called and the script is running on the server, this method has no effect.

setEncryptionKeys   W   O.Ref.

`ndocDocument.`**`setEncryptionKeys`**`(vecKeys)`   setEncryption
                                                                                              Keys
Represents the keys used to encrypt the document. The keys set or returned from this method are used when the encrypt method is called. When setting this method, either a single string value or an array of strings can be used. The string value (or each element of the string array) contains the name of the encryption key. Any users who also have the encryption key can decrypt the document.

The name of the specified encryption key is stored in the *lotus.domino.Document* in a *lotus.domino.RichTextItem* named secretEncryptionKeys. If the document is encrypted but no encryption keys are specified, the document is encrypted using the current user's public key. Therefore, the document can be decrypted by that user only.

As when modifying other methods of the *lotus.domino.Document,* you must explicitly call the save method after setting the encryption keys in order to encrypt the document.

setEncryptOnSend   W   T/F

`ndocDocument.`**`setEncryptOnSend`**`(bolEncryptonsend)`   setEncrypt
                                                                                              OnSend
Indicates whether the document is to be encrypted when mailed. true indicates that it should be encrypted when mailed. false indicates that it should not be encrypted. This method defaults to false. When the document is mailed, the system attempts to locate the public key for each recipient in the Directory (Public Address Book). Each user whose public key can't be located will still receive the e-mail, but their messages will not be encrypted. The users whose public key was located will receive an encrypted document.

setSaveMessageOnSend   W   T/F

`ndocDocument.`**`setSaveMessageOnSend`**`(bolSaveMsg)`   setSaveMessage
                                                                                              OnSend
Indicates whether the document should be saved immediately after it is mailed (by calling the send method of the *lotus.domino.Document*). true indicates that the document is saved after being mailed. false indicates that it is not. This method works only when the *lotus.domino.Document* is a new document and hasn't yet been saved. Therefore, subsequent calls to the send method will not resave the document.

setSignOnSend   W   T/F

`ndocDocument.`**`setSignOnSend`**`(bolSignOnSend)`   setSignOnSend

Indicates whether the document is signed when mailed. true indicates that the document is signed when mailed. false indicates that it is not.

setUniversalID	W	O.Ref.

`ndocDocument.`**`setUniversalID`**`(strUniversalID)`

Represents the Universal ID of the *lotus.domino.Document*. The Universal ID is a 32-character combination of hexadecimal digits that uniquely identifies the document. This identification is unique across all replicas of this database (unlike the `noteID`). In fact, this method is used to determine whether documents in replica *lotus.domino.Databases* are replicas of one another. Therefore, if a document's `universalID` is modified, the document then becomes a new document. The hexadecimal digits include the numbers 0 to 9 and the letters A to F. Because each `universalID` must be unique within all replicas of the database, you can't set this value to an existing `universalID` in the *lotus.domino.Database*. Attempting to do so generates a runtime error 4000 message.

Remarks

When working with the *lotus.domino.Document* object, it is important to remember that you must explicitly call the `save` method before any of the changes are permanently saved and written to disk. This is true when existing documents are modified, when new documents are created, or when existing documents are deleted from the *lotus.domino.Database*. Failing to call the `save` method will cause all the modifications to be ignored when the current script completes. When the `save` method is called, the document is resaved, even if it was not previously modified in the script.

You can use the *lotus.domino.DocumentCollection* to access all *lotus.domino.Documents* or a subset of *lotus.domino.Documents* contained in a *lotus.domino.Database*. In addition, the *lotus.domino.View* can also be used to access *lotus.domino.Documents* based on specific criteria. Accessing *lotus.domino.Documents* using the *lotus.domino.View* class can be much more efficient and easier to program, because these documents are already indexed based on the design specifications of the *lotus.domino.View*. Often, when performing actions on multiple *lotus.domino.Documents*, performance can become a major consideration, especially when you're working with non-relational data. However, when using *lotus.domino.Views* to locate specific *lotus.domino.DocumentCollections*, the content of the view must be predetermined and can't be built on-the-fly. Often, *lotus.domino.DocumentCollections* can be created using a *lotus.domino.View* to retrieve a subset of the documents based on specific criteria (such as the form used to create the document) and then refined programmatically.

Under the hood, a *lotus.domino.Document* can reside in several *lotus.domino.DocumentCollections* simultaneously. These collections essentially contain pointers to the actual *lotus.domino.Documents*. The *lotus.domino.Document* is a single object, but it can have multiple parent indexes and be located in multiple collections. Therefore, consider this when working with multiple collections or when deleting or modifying *lotus.domino.Documents* that might be referenced by other collections.

The methods of the *lotus.domino.Document* can be extended to allow for a more efficient way to create *lotus.domino.Items* for the current document. Once you have determined the name of the item value (and its value if you're creating or modifying), you can use the extended class syntax to manipulate item values or one of the following methods of the *lotus.domino.Document* class:

lotus.domino.Document **Method**	**Result/Action**
getItemValue	Gets an item's value
replaceItemValue	Sets an item's value
appendItemValue	Creates a new item
hasItem	Checks to see whether the item exists in the document
removeItem	Deletes the item from the document

When using the extended class syntax to create or modify the *lotus.domino.Item,* you are essentially treating the *lotus.domino.Document* as an extended class and using the item name as a method of the *lotus.domino.Document* object. When using extended class syntax, the values assigned can be any LotusScript data type—namely, a scalar data type, an array, or a reference to another *lotus.domino.Item* object, *lotus.domino.DateTime* object, or *lotus.domino.DateRange* object. Unlike the appendItemValue method, when a new *lotus.domino.Item* is created using the extended syntax and a *lotus.domino.Item* of the same name already exists in the *lotus.domino.Document,* the item is replaced with the new value. (When you're using the appendItemValue method, another *lotus.domino.Item* is created using the same name.) Also, the appendItemValue method returns a handle on the *lotus.domino.Item* object so that its methods can be modified and its method called is desired. These are not available when using extended syntax.

The extended class syntax is not available for Java. Therefore, the *lotus.notes.Document* and *lotus.notes.Item* methods must be used to reference item values.

Using the extended class syntax reduces the amount of code that must be written and thus can make the code easier to read. In addition, it can preserve memory since the need to dimension additional *lotus.domino.Items* is eliminated. However, using the extended class syntax doesn't let you manipulate the value data type or use the intSpecialType. For example, if the new *lotus.domino.Item* must be an authors field type, you can't use the extended syntax to create the field (this is a common mistake made by inexperienced developers).

If the current *lotus.domino.Document* is encrypted, the script will attempt to decrypt the *lotus.domino.Document* after it attempts to access or call one of the document's methods.

Example

The following code example is an administrative function that removes all the profile documents in the current database that have not been modified during the current day. This function is helpful if the information stored in the profile document is relevant only for the current day.

```
import lotus.domino.*;

public class JavaAgent extends AgentBase {

    public void NotesMain() {

        try {
            Session ns = getSession();
            AgentContext agentContext = ns.getAgentContext();
            Database ndb = agentContext.getCurrentDatabase();
            DocumentCollection ndc = ndb.getAllDocuments();
                Document ndocCollection = ndc.getFirstDocument();
                while (ndocCollection != null) {
                    if (ndocCollection.isProfile()) {
                        DateTime ndtNow = ns.createDateTime("Today");
                        ndtNow.setNow();
                        DateTime ndtCurrentdate = ndtNow;
                        DateTime ndtAccesseddate =
                        ➥ndocCollection.getLastAccessed();
                        int intDifference = ndtCurrentdate.timeDifference
                        ➥(ndtAccesseddate) / 86400;
                        System.out.println("Diff: " + intDifference);
                        if (intDifference !=0)  {
                            ndocCollection.remove(true);
                            System.out.println("Profile Document named " +
                            ndocCollection.getNameOfProfile() +
                            " was removed...");  }   }
                        ndocCollection = ndc.getNextDocument();    }
                    System.out.println("Agent complete.");

        } catch(Exception e) {
            e.printStackTrace();
        }
    }
}
```

DocumentCollection

4.6x 5.0

The *lotus.domino.DocumentCollection* object represents a collection or subset of *lotus.domino.Document.* The collection of documents can be derived from the front end and back end of a *lotus.domino.Database* class, the *lotus.domino.View* class, or the current *lotus.domino.Session* class. *lotus.domino.DocumentCollection* lets you modify, perform specific actions on, search, or navigate through particular documents based on document content, specific keys, optional sorted order, and so on.

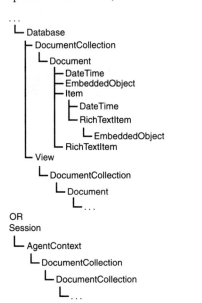

```
...
 └ Database
   ├ DocumentCollection
   │ └ Document
   │   ├ DateTime
   │   ├ EmbeddedObject
   │   ├ Item
   │   │ ├ DateTime
   │   │ └ RichTextItem
   │   │     └ EmbeddedObject
   │   └ RichTextItem
   └ View
     └ DocumentCollection
       └ Document
           └ ...
OR
Session
 └ AgentContext
   └ DocumentCollection
     └ DocumentCollection
         └ ...
```

Java Syntax

Public class **DocumentCollection** extends Base

There are various methods to establish a handle on a *lotus.domino.DocumentCollection* object. Which method you use depends on the action you want to perform on the *lotus.domino.DocumentCollection* and how the database is searched.

The following methods of the *lotus.domino.Database* and *lotus.domino.AgentContext* classes create a *lotus.domino.DocumentCollection* object. Refer to *lotus.domino.Database* (▶ 373) and *lotus.domino.AgentContext* (▶ 365) for details on how to use these methods.

The getAllDocuments method of the *lotus.domino.Database* class (▶ 380)

The getUnprocessedDocuments method of the *lotus.domino.AgentContext* class (▶ 367)

The search method of the *lotus.domino.Database* class (▶ 391)

The unprocessedSearch method of the *lotus.domino.AgentContext* class (▶ 368)

The FTSearch method of the *lotus.domino.Database* class (▶ 378)

The getResponses method of the *lotus.domino.Document* class (▶ 423)

The getProfileDocCollection method of the *lotus.notes.Database* class (▶ 386)

The getAllDocumentsByKey method of the *lotus.notes.View* class (▶ 593)

DocumentCollection Methods

5.0 addDocument

addDocument   ndcDocumentCollection.**addDocument**(ndocDocument)

ndcDocumentCollection.**addDocument**(ndocDocument, bolChkDuplicates)

Document	Required	O.Ref.

The *lotus.domino.Document* to be added.

bolChkDuplicates	Required	T/F

Determines whether a remote add should be forced immediately. true forces the add; false does not.

This method adds a *lotus.domino.Document* entry to the existing collection of documents. In the version of Domino/Lotus Notes prior to Release 5.0, if you wanted to add a document to the existing collection, you had to discard the current collection and rebuild it based on the new criteria. Of course, then you had to make sure that none of the information being located was being cached.

If the *lotus.domino.DocumentCollection* is sorted, the added document is appended to the end of the collection. When the collection is not sorted, the document is inserted into the collection, most likely based on its unique document ID. This makes it difficult to locate the document's current position in the *lotus.domino.DocumentCollection*.

In fact, the only way to determine its position is to navigate to the previous or next document in the collection and attempt to determine its location relative to the preceding or following document.

If a *lotus.domino.Document* already exists in the *lotus.domino.DocumentCollection,* a duplicate exception is thrown. `bolChkDuplicates` determines whether a remote add (IIOP) should be forced immediately as opposed to during the subsequent navigation or method call to the server. Therefore, if a duplicate *lotus.domino.Document* exists in the *lotus.domino.DocumentCollection,* a duplicate exception can be thrown immediately.

Be careful when using this method, because it can have a significant effect on performance. Because the document's position is unknown, locating the documents can also negatively affect performance. This method will throw an exception if the *lotus.domino.Document* is a duplicate of a *lotus.domino.Document* that already exists in the collection, or if the collection was built as the result of a multidatabase full-text search.

5.0 deleteDocument

ndcDocumentCollection.**deleteDocument**ndoc(Document)

delete Document

ndocDocument   **Required**   O.Ref.

The *lotus.domino.Document* to be deleted.

This method deletes (removes) a document entry from the document collection. It doesn't actually delete the *lotus.domino.Document* from the database. Instead, it simply removes the document from the current document collection. This method generates an error (throws an exception) if the *lotus.domino.Document* doesn't exist in the collection, if it has been removed (from the collection or the database), if the document collection was retrieved as a result of the multidatabase full-text search, or if the document can't be retrieved from the collection. You can use the `getDocument` method of the *lotus.domino.DocumentCollection* class to test for this (▶ 439).

FTSearch

ndcDocumentCollection.**FTSearch**(strQuery)

FTSearch

ndcDocumentCollection.**FTSearch**(strQuery, intMaxdocs)

strQuery   **Required**   O.Ref.

A string representing the rules for the full-text query. These rules are outlined next.

intMaxdocs   **Required**   %

The maximum number of documents to return from the query. Set this parameter to `0` to return all matching documents.

This method performs a full-text search of the all the *lotus.domino.Documents* contained in the *lotus.domino.DocumentCollection* or refines an existing collection and moves the cursor (pointer) to the first document in the collection. The result of the full-text search is a collection of documents that are sorted in descending order of relevance. In other words, the document with the most hits (highest relevance) is first, while the document with the fewest hits (lowest relevance) is last. You can access the actual relevance score by using the `getFTSearchScore` method of the *lotus.domino.Document* (▶ 421).

Fortunately, this method will run even if the *lotus.domino.Database* isn't full-text–indexed, although the user will encounter a performance loss. If it's likely that this method will be run more than once (which is usually the case), you can test for an existing full-text index prior to calling this method by using the `isFTIndexed` method of the *lotus.domino.Database* (▶ 389). If no full-text index exists, you can create one programmatically by using the `updateFTIndex` method of the *lotus.domino.Database* (▶ 392).

Although this method works on *lotus.domino.Documents* located in the *lotus.domino.DocumentCollection*, you can also apply it to the *lotus.domino.Database* and *lotus.domino.View*.

As you would expect when using a legitimate search engine, the rules for defining the search let you build search criteria using Boolean values and specific operators. Here are the rules for using these operators:

Operator	Rules
Plain text	For simple searches, you can enter the word or phrase for which to search. You don't need to include quotation marks, except when you're searching for specific keywords or reserved operators. Placing quotes around the words or phrases ensures that they are treated as literal search criteria and not operators. These rules are similar to typical searching standards. You can always put the text in quotes regardless to ensure that it will not be treated as an operator.
Wildcard	Wildcards are supported when you're performing searches. Typical to most search engines, they are represented by the ? or * characters. Use the ? to represent any single character in its respective position and * to match multiple (or no) characters in their respective position in the word.
Hyphenated word	This is used to find pairs of words that are hyphenated together as a single word or separated by a space.
Logical operator	This allows you to build more complex searches (often referred to as Boolean searches) by using logical operators to further restrict or expand the search algorithm. The allowed operator keywords and their respective symbols (listed in order of precedence) are not or !, and or &, accrue or ,, and or or ¦.
Proximity operator	Proximity operators allow you to search for words that are close to one another. That is, you can see if the words are located in proximity to each other by using the operators near, sentence, and paragraph.
Exactcase operator	The exactcase operator allows you to restrict the search to match a specified case.
Termweight operator	The termweight *n* operator allows you to modify the relevance scores of the search by defining the relevance ranking. This is done by specifying a value for *n* between 0 and 100 representing the relevance score.
Field operator	This is a powerful capability of the Domino/Lotus Notes search engine. This feature lets you perform a search based on a specific field. The syntax for this search is FIELD fieldname operator. fieldname is the name of the *NotesItem* that you are performing the operation against. The allowed operators are contains, =, >, and <. Using contains is helpful when searching rich-text fields. You can't combine operators as in normal programming (such as >=). Therefore, you must build a more complex search algorithm by using the or operator for multiple criteria. You may also need to help define the search's precedence order by using parentheses.

5.0 getCount   R   %

getCount   intCount = ndcDocumentCollection.**getCount**

Returns the number of documents in the current *lotus.domino.DocumentCollection*.

There are various reasons why you would want to perform an action on a collection of *lotus. domino. Documents*. However, often you need to know how many documents are contained in a collection before any action can be taken. Another common use of this method is to determine the count so that a loop statement can be run on all the documents without stepping through them one at a time. . The following code would be called from within a *lotus. domino. View*. This code gets a handle on the currently selected documents in the current view and asks the user if he or she has selected more than one document. Otherwise, the currently selected document is forwarded to the recipient list.

```java
import lotus.domino.*;

public class JavaAgent extends AgentBase {

    public void NotesMain() {

        try {
            Session ns = getSession();
            AgentContext agentContext = ns.getAgentContext();
            DocumentCollection ndc = agentContext.getUnprocessedDocuments();
                if (ndc.getCount() > 1)
                    System.out.println("You've selected more than one
                    ➡document" +
                    ndc.getCount());
                if (ndc.getCount() < 1)
                    System.out.println("There are no documents selected.");
                if (ndc.getCount() == 1)    {
                    Document ndocCollection = ndc.getFirstDocument();
                    String strRecipients =
                    ➡ndocCollection.getItemValueString("SalesRep");
                ndocCollection.send(true, strRecipients);    }
                System.out.println("Agent complete.");

        } catch(Exception e) {
            e.printStackTrace();
        }
    }
}
```

getDocument

```
ndocDocument = ndcDocumentCollection.getDocument(ndocDocument)
```
getDocument

This method returns a handle to the *lotus. document. Document* entry located in the document collection. Of course, the *lotus. document. Document* is used as a parameter when calling this method. However, this does let you check for the existence of the *lotus. document. Document* to ensure that it hasn't been removed. If it is indeed no longer present in the collection, this method returns null. Otherwise, a handle to the *lotus. document. Document* entry is again returned. If the collection was built as the result of a multidatabase full-text search, this method returns an error (throws an exception).

getFirstDocument

```
ndocDocument = ndcDocumentCollection.getFirstDocument()
```
getFirst
Document

This method sets the *lotus. document. Document* to the first document in the collection. If no documents are contained in the *lotus. document. DocumentCollection,* this method returns null.

For an example using the getFirstDocument method, refer to the getNextDocument method, also in this chapter (▶ 440).

getLastDocument

```
ndocDocument = ndcDocumentCollection.getLastDocument()
```

This method sets the *lotus.domino.Document* to the last document in the collection. If no documents are contained in the *lotus.domino.DocumentCollection,* this method returns null.

getNextDocument

```
ndocDocument = ndcDocumentCollection.getNextDocument()

ndocDocument = ndcDocumentCollection.getNextDocument(ndocDocument)
```

ndocDocument	Required	O.Ref

The current document in the *lotus.domino.DocumentCollection.*

This method sets the *lotus.domino.Document* to the next document in the collection, immediately following the current document passed as the parameter. If no more documents are contained in the *lotus.domino.DocumentCollection,* this method returns null.

The following example establishes a handle on all the documents in a particular *lotus.domino.Database* (using the unprocessedDocuments method of the *lotus.domino.Database.* This code was placed in an agent that was run manually from the Actions menu. The *lotus.domino.DocumentCollection* can contain both main documents and response documents. This code will rebuild the *lotus.domino.DocumentCollection* on-the-fly by removing any documents in the collection that are response documents. In larger databases, this would be a costly procedure if run against all the documents in the database. But if run on smaller collections or by scheduled agents, this code could be useful when acting on *lotus.domino.Documents.*

```
import lotus.domino.*;

public class JavaAgent extends AgentBase {

    public void NotesMain() {

        try {
            Session ns = getSession();
            AgentContext agentContext = ns.getAgentContext();
            DocumentCollection ndc = agentContext.getUnprocessedDocuments();
            System.out.println("Processing " + ndc.getCount() + " docs...");
            Document ndocCollection = ndc.getFirstDocument();
            int intCount = 0;
            while (ndocCollection != null) {
            if (ndocCollection.isResponse())   {
                Document ndocPrevious = ndc.getPrevDocument(ndocCollection);
                ndc.deleteDocument(ndocCollection);
                intCount++;
                ndocCollection = ndc.getNextDocument(ndocPrevious);   }
            else
                ndocCollection = ndc.getNextDocument(ndocCollection);   }
                System.out.println("Finished processing. " + intCount +
                ➥" responses removed.");
                System.out.println(ndc.getCount() + " documents left in
                ➥collection.");

        } catch(Exception e) {
            e.printStackTrace();
        }
    }
}
```

getNthDocument

```
ndocDocument = ndcDocumentCollection.getNthDocument(intCount)
```

intCount   **Required**   %

The position (count) of the *Document* in the collection to return. This value begins at 1 for the first document.

This method returns a handle on a *lotus.domino.Document* based on its relative position in the *lotus.domino.DocumentCollection*. If no document is located at the specific position in the *lotus.domino.DocumentCollection,* this method returns null. This method is commonly used when stepping through an entire *lotus.domino.DocumentCollection.* For example, you could establish a *lotus.domino.DocumentCollection* and then loop through the documents by using a `Forall` loop, setting the current *lotus.domino.Document* to the current value of the `Forall` variable. However, this is an inefficient way to traverse the *lotus.domino.DocumentCollection.* A more efficient method is to use `getFirstDocument` followed by `getNextDocument` to step through the collection.

Another consideration when you're looking for a specific document in the collection is how current the index is. Specifically, if certain entries have been deleted or modified in such a manner that modifies the *lotus.domino.DocumentCollection* index, the position of the *lotus.domino.Document* or entry is modified. Therefore, if there have been many deletions or modifications to the documents contained in the *lotus.domino.DocumentCollection,* this again could be an inefficient or inaccurate operation.

getParent   R   O.Ref.

```
ndDatabase = ndcDocumentCollection.getParent()
```

Returns a handle to the parent *lotus.domino.Database* (▶ 373) that contains the document collection. If the parent database can't be located, an error is returned (an exception is thrown).

getPrevDocument

```
ndocDocument = ndcDocumentCollection.getPrevDocument()
ndocDocument = ndcDocumentCollection.getPrevDocument(NotesDocument)
```

NotesDocument   **Required**   O.Ref.

The current document in the *NotesDocumentCollection.*

This method sets the *lotus.domino.Document* to the previous document in the collection. If no more documents are contained in the *lotus.domino.DocumentCollection,* this method returns null.

For an example using the `getPrevDocument` method, refer to the `getNextDocument` method in this chapter (▶ 440).

getQuery   R $

```
strQuery = ndcDocumentCollection.getQuery()
```

This method returns the text value representing the query that was used to build the document collection. This method applies only to document collections that are built using a search method, such as the full-text search. Therefore, collections built not using a search will return a null value (" ").

isSorted   R   T/F

```
bolIsSorted = ndcDocumentCollection.isSorted()
```

Indicates whether the documents contained in the *lotus.domino.DocumentCollection* are sorted. This is `true` if the documents are sorted and `false` if they are not. Documents can be sorted only when the collection was built using the full-text search method of a *lotus.domino.Database*. The sorting of the documents is determined by the relevance score (the number of matches found in the current document based on the search criteria). A relevance score is then assigned to each document, with the most relevant document appearing first. The remaining documents are then sorted in descending order.

putAllInFolder

ndcDocumentCollection.**putAllInFolder**(strFoldername)

ndcDocumentCollection.**putAllInFolder**(strFoldername, bolCreateonfail)

strFoldername   Required   O.Ref.
The name of the folder in which to place the *lotus.domino.Documents* contained in the *lotus.domino.DocumentCollection*.

bolCreateonfail   Required   T/F
Determines whether a new folder should be created if the specified folder doesn't exist. `true` creates the folder. `false` throws an exception.

This method moves the contents of the *lotus.domino.DocumentCollection* into the folder specified in the parameter. If the script performing this action is located in the user's local workstation, the folder can be a personal folder. You can place the documents in nested folders (folders contained in other folders) by using backslashes to specify the folder path (similar to specifying directories in the file system). If the document is already located in the specified folder, no action is taken on that document (it's already there!). If the folder doesn't exist, `bolCreateonfail` determines whether the folder should be created or an exception should be thrown. If `bolCreateonfail` is set to `true` and the specified folder doesn't already exist, it is created automatically. Similarly, if the path specified doesn't yet exist, it is created automatically as well. This method also adheres to the access control settings for the *lotus.domino.Database* (that is, the capability to create personal and shared folders and views).

removeAll

ndocDocument = ndcDocumentCollection.**removeAll**(intForce)

intForce   Required   T/F
Specifies whether this method should force the collection to become empty even if documents are modified by other users after the document was opened. `true` forces the collection to become empty. `false` allows documents to remain after this method is executed.

This method deletes the documents in the collection from the database. Unlike the `deleteDocument` method, which simply removes the *lotus.domino.Document* from the *lotus.domino.DocumentCollection*, the `removeAll` method actually removes the *lotus.domino.Document* from disk. Entries in the collection are also removed when this method is executed. In other words, the *lotus.domino.DocumentCollection* is updated to reflect the removed documents. Therefore, if all the documents were removed, the collection will be empty and will have a count of `0`.

removeAllFromFolder

ndocDocument = ndcDocumentCollection.**removeAllFromFolder**()
➡(strFoldername)

strFoldername   Required $
The name of the folder to remove the *lotus.domino.Documents* from.

This method removes the contents of the *lotus.domino.DocumentCollection* from the folder specified in the parameter. If the script performing this action is located in the user's local workstation, the folder can be a personal folder. You can remove documents in nested folders (folders contained in other folders) by using backslashes to specify the folder path (similar to specifying directories in the file system). If the document isn't located in the specified folder, no action is taken on that document. If the folder doesn't exist, this method does nothing.

stampAll

```
ndDocument = ndcDocumentCollection.stampAll(strItemname, value)
```
stampAll

strItemname   Required   O.Ref.

The name of the *lotus.domino.Item* whose value to modify.

value   Required   Varies

The value to assign to the *lotus.domino.Item*.

This method replaces all the *lotus.domino.Item* values for all the *lotus.domino.Documents* contained in the collection with the value specified. If the *lotus.domino.Item* doesn't yet exist in the *lotus.domino.Documents,* it is created automatically. Modifications made to the documents contained in the collection are automatically written to back-end documents and therefore are automatically saved to disk. Consequently, the `save` method doesn't need to be called because the changes are already written to disk. Similarly, any documents to be modified by the `stampAll` method must have already been saved to disk before this method is executed. In other words, the documents must already physically exist before this method can modify the document contents.

updateAll

```
ndcDocumentCollection.updateAll()
```
updateAll

This method marks all the *lotus.domino.Documents* contained in the collection as being processed by the current agent. This ensures that the agent runs only on documents that haven't yet been processed by this agent—namely, new or modified documents in the database. (Refer to the `updateProcessedDoc` method of the *lotus.domino.Session* for information on updating processed documents.)

Remarks

In addition to using the *lotus.domino.DocumentCollection* to access all documents or a subset of documents contained in a *lotus.domino.Database,* the *lotus.domino.View* can also be used to access documents based on specific criteria. Accessing documents using the *lotus.domino.View* class can be much more efficient and easier to program, because these documents are already indexed based on the design specifications of the *lotus.domino.View.* Often, when performing actions on multiple documents, performance can become a major consideration, especially because you're working with a nonrelational database store. However, when using *lotus.domino.Views* to locate specific document collections, the content of the view must be predetermined and can't be built on-the-fly. Often, document collections can be created by using a *lotus.domino.View* to retrieve a subset of the documents based on specific criteria (such as the form used to create the document) and then refined programmatically.

Nevertheless, the *lotus.domino.DocumentCollection* is usually best to use when the criteria for the collection is too complex to be met with a *lotus.domino.View*, when no *lotus.domino.View* contains all the documents that are needed, or when you need to navigate through the hierarchy of the documents (using a document's parents, children, siblings, and so on).

When you're creating a *lotus.domino.DocumentCollection* using the FTSearch method, the *lotus.domino.Documents* contained in the collection are sorted based on the search criteria. When collections are constructed using other methods, they are automatically sorted by the DocumentUNID—a special text item of the *lotus.domino.Document* that represents that document's unique ID. In document collections, this item is used to sort the collection alphanumerically.

Under the hood, a *lotus.domino.Document* can reside in several *lotus.domino.DocumentCollections* simultaneously. These collections essentially contain pointers to the actual *lotus.domino.Documents*. Within the lsxbe, the document is a single object, but it can have multiple parent indexes and can be located in multiple collections. Therefore, consider this when working with multiple collections or when deleting or modifying *lotus.domino.Documents* that might be referenced by other collections.

Example

The following example could be used in an application that moves or copies documents to a particular folder based on certain criteria in the document. The folder could be "Hot Prospects," "Dead Leads," "Archived," or another folder where personal categorization would be helpful. This code checks the contents of all the documents in the current *lotus.domino.DocumentCollection* and moves any documents whose form type is "Prospect" and that have been created on the same day into the "New Leads" folder. The *lotus.domino.DocumentCollection* is a collection of all the documents in the current database.

```
import lotus.domino.*;

public class JavaAgent extends AgentBase {

    public void NotesMain() {

        try {
            Session ns = getSession();
            AgentContext agentContext = ns.getAgentContext();
            Database ndb = agentContext.getCurrentDatabase();
            DocumentCollection ndc = ndb.getAllDocuments();
            DocumentCollection ndcNew = ndb.getAllDocuments();
            System.out.println("Processing " + ndc.getCount() + " docs...");
            Document ndocCollection = ndc.getFirstDocument();
            int intCount = 0;
            boolean bolFlag = false;
            while (ndocCollection != null) {
                if (ndocCollection.getItemValueString("Form") ==
                ➡"Prospect" )  {
                    DateTime ndtNow = ns.createDateTime("Today");
```

```
                ndtNow.setNow();
                DateTime ndtCurrentdate = ndtNow;
                DateTime ndtOriginaldate = ndocCollection.getCreated();
                int intDifference = ndtCurrentdate.timeDifference
                ➥(ndtOriginaldate) / 86400;
                System.out.println("Diff: " + intDifference);
                if (intDifference ==0)
                    bolFlag = true;
                else
                    bolFlag = false;  }
            else
                bolFlag = false;
            if (bolFlag != false) {
                ndcNew.deleteDocument(ndocCollection);
                intCount++;
                ndocCollection = ndc.getNextDocument();  }
            else
                ndocCollection = ndc.getNextDocument();   }
        ndcNew.putAllInFolder("New Leads", true);
        System.out.println("Agent complete.");

    } catch(Exception e) {
        e.printStackTrace();
    }
  }
}
```

4.6x 5.0 EmbeddedObject

The *lotus.domino.EmbeddedObject* object contains all the OLE/1 and OLE/2 embedded objects, file attachments, and links to other objects (database links, view links, and document links) that are contained in the *lotus.domino.RichTextItem*. At the time this book was published, this class wasn't supported for OS/2 and Macintosh clients.

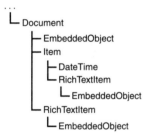

Java Syntax

`Public class **EmbeddedObject** extends Base`

In order to create a new *lotus.domino.EmbeddedObject,* you must use the `embedObject` method of the *lotus.domino.RichTextItem* class (▶ 548). This method lets you create a new object, object link, or file attachment. In order to establish a handle on an existing *lotus.domino.EmbeddedObject* contained in a rich text field stored in a document, you must use the `getEmbeddedObject` or `getEmbeddedObjects` method of the *lotus.domino.RichTextItem.* Use the `getEmbeddedObject` method to access an object, object link, or attachment when you know the name of the object and the *lotus.domino.RichTextItem* that contains it. The `getEmbeddedObjects` method lets you access all the objects, object links, or file attachments in the respective rich text item.

In order to establish a handle to an object or object link stored in a document as part of the form design used to create that document, you can use the `getEmbeddedObjects` method of the *lotus.domino.Document* class (▶ 420). The *lotus.domino.EmbeddedObject* can't be created from scratch using the `New` keyword. It must derive its value from the existing *lotus.domino.RichTextItem* or *lotus.domino.Document* class.

EmbeddedObject Methods

activate

activate

`intOLEhandle = nembEmbeddedObject.**activate**(bolshow)`

bolshow	Required	T/F

Determines whether the server application will display the object and server application to the user interface. `true` displays the object. `false` hides it.

This method causes the OLE server to load the object and return an OLE handle to the *lotus.domino.EmbeddedObject.* If the object or object link doesn't support OLE automation, this method will return `null`. This method will return an error if the *lotus.domino.EmbeddedObject* is a file attachment.

When establishing an OLE handle for object links, this method is often unable to return a handle because this functionality isn't supported by the OLE-compliant application.

doVerb

doVerb

`nembEmbeddedObject.**doVerb**(strVerb)`

strVerb	Required	O.Ref.

The string name of an object's verb.

This method executes the object verb of the *lotus.domino.EmbeddedObject.*

extractFile

extractFile

`nembEmbeddedObject.**extractFile**(strFilepath)`

strFilepath	Required	O.Ref.

The path and filename of where to store the extracted file on the file system or disk.

This method copies the file attachment to the file system or disk. This method won't work for embedded objects and object links and will raise an error when invoked (throw an exception).

---

getClassName   R   O.Ref.

```
strClassName = nembEmbeddedObject.getClassName()
```

This method returns the name of the application that was used to create the embedded object. All objects created and stored with a *lotus.domino.RichTextField* or *lotus.domino.Document* have a default object name assigned to them. When the *lotus.domino.EmbeddedObject* is a file attachment, this method returns null (an empty string— " "). Some default object names and their respective applications are listed in the following table.

Application	Class Name
Lotus WordPro	`WordPro.Application.9`
Microsoft Word 97	`Word.Document.8`
Microsoft Excel 97	`Excel.Application.8`
Lotus Notes	`Notes.NotesSession`
Visio	`Visio.Application.5`

---

getFileSize   R   %

```
intSize = nembEmbeddedObject.getFileSize()
```

This method returns the size in bytes of the file attachment. If the *lotus.domino.EmbeddedObjects* is an embedded object or object link, this method returns 0.

---

getName   R   O.Ref.

```
strName = nembEmbeddedObject.getName()
```

The name used to reference the embedded object or object link. When the *lotus.domino.EmbeddedObject* is a file attachment, this method returns a null value (an empty string—" "). In addition, it is possible for the embedded object or object link not to have a name associated with it. Therefore, it will also return a null value.

If the embedded object or object link was created using the embedObject of the *lotus.domino.RichTextItem* object, this method will return the name that was used when the object was created.

Despite the fact that this method is read-only when you're accessing the object with script, this method of the object is actually editable when you're accessing the object through the user interface. The value returned by this method is displayed in the infobox of the Object Properties as Object Name: when you view the object properties.

---

getObject   R   %

```
intObject = nembEmbeddedObject.getObject()
```

Once the *lotus.domino.EmbeddedObject* has been successfully loaded into memory, this method returns an OLE handle to the embedded object (an IUnknown or IDispatch handle). If the object supports OLE automation, you can programmatically access the object's methods via the established handle.

Because this method accesses other objects created with foreign applications, there is always a possibility that some functionality might be lost or inaccessible. For example, when establishing a handle on an object link, this method is often unable to return a handle on the embedded object link because this functionality isn't supported by the OLE-compliant application.

---

getParent   R   O.Ref.

getParent   `nrtiParent = nembEmbeddedObject.getParent()`

The name of the *lotus.domino.RichTextItem* that contains the
lotus.domino.EmbeddedObject.

---

getSource   R   O.Ref.

getSource   `strSource = nrmbEmbeddedObject.getSource()`

This method returns a different value depending on the type of the
lotus.domino.EmbeddedObject. If the embedded object is an object or object link, this
method will return a string name representing the internal name that Domino/Notes uses
to refer to the source document. If the embedded object is a file attachment, this method
returns the attachment's filename. Furthermore, if the `embedObject` method was used to
embed the object in a *lotus.domino.RichTextItem,* this method will return the attachment's
full path and filename. Otherwise, this method returns only the attachment's filename.

---

getType   R   %

getType   `intType = nembEmbeddedObject.getType()`

This method indicates the type of the *lotus.domino.EmbeddedObject*—namely, whether it
is an embedded object, object link, or file attachment.

Here are the constant values allowed for `intType`:

Constant	Description
EmbeddedObject.EMBED_ATTACHMENT	The object is a file attachment.
EmbeddedObject.EMBED_OBJECT	The object is an embedded object.
EmbeddedObject.EMBED_OBJECTLINK	The object is an object link.

---

getVerbs   R   ()

getVerbs   `vecVerbs = nembEmbeddedObject.getVerbs()`

If the *lotus.domino.EmbeddedObject* is an OLE/2 embedded object, this method returns
the verbs that an object supports. The supported verbs are returned as an array of
strings. In order to invoke a verb on the object, use the `doVerb` method (▶ 448).

---

remove

remove   `nembEmbeddedObject.remove()`

This method removes (deletes) the object from the *lotus.domino.RichTextItem*. This
method doesn't take effect until you save the parent *lotus.domino.Document* object to
disk by calling the `save` method of the *lotus.domino.Document*.

Remarks

In addition to using the `embeddedObjects` method of the *lotus.domino.RichTextItem*
to locate embedded objects, you can use the `hasEmbedded` method of the
lotus.domino.Document object to determine whether the document has any
embedded objects. This method not only detects embedded objects in
lotus.domino.RichTextItem fields but also detects embedded objects that were
stored in a document at the time of its creation. This feature is limited to native
Lotus Notes and can be activated only from the Lotus Notes form design
(however, this will not detect file attachments).

Also, some of the methods available for both embedded and linked objects are not available for file attachments. This was noted in these methods' descriptions.

Example

The following example locates the *lotus.domino.EmbeddedObjects* stored in the Body field of the current document. If the *lotus.domino.EmbeddedObject* is a file attachment, the properties of the file attachment are displayed to the Java console, and the file is detached to the c:\\temp directory. If the *lotus.domino.EmbeddedObject* is an object control embedded in the current document or form, the object's properties are displayed to the Java console, and the object is activated and displayed to the user interface.

```java
import lotus.domino.*;
import java.util.Vector;
import java.util.Enumeration;

public class JavaAgent extends AgentBase {

    public void NotesMain() {

        try {
            Session ns = getSession();
            AgentContext agentContext = ns.getAgentContext();
            Database ndb = agentContext.getCurrentDatabase();
            Document ndoc = agentContext.getDocumentContext();
            RichTextItem nrti = (RichTextItem)ndoc.getFirstItem("Body");
            Vector nobj = nrti.getEmbeddedObjects();
            Enumeration eobj = nobj.elements();
            while (eobj.hasMoreElements()) {
                EmbeddedObject nemb = (EmbeddedObject)eobj.nextElement();
                if (nemb.getType() == EmbeddedObject.EMBED_ATTACHMENT ) {
                    System.out.println("Located File Attachment: ");
                    System.out.println("FileName:\t" + nemb.getName());
                    System.out.println("Source:\t\t" + nemb.getSource());
                    System.out.println("Size:\t\t" + nemb.getFileSize() +
                    ➥" bytes");
                    nemb.extractFile("c:\\temp\\" + nemb.getSource());  }
                else  {
                    System.out.println("Object Name:\t" + nemb.getName());
                    System.out.println("Source:\t\t" + nemb.getSource());
                    System.out.println("Verbs:\t\t" + nemb.getVerbs());
                    System.out.println("Class name:\t" +
                    ➥nemb.getClassName());
                    if (nemb.getType() == EmbeddedObject.EMBED_OBJECT ) {
                        int intActivate = nemb.activate(true); }  }
                System.out.println("\nFinished, the object is ready for
                ➥use.");  }

        } catch(Exception e) {
            e.printStackTrace();
        }
    }
}
```

The *lotus.domino.Form* object represents a form in a *lotus.domino.NotesDatabase* object (▶ 373).

```
...
└ Database
  └ Form
```

Java Syntax

```
public class lotus.domino.Form extends Base
```

Currently, there are only two ways to access a form. You must either iterate through the getForms property of *lotus.domino.Database,* or you can call the getForm method of *lotus.domino.Database.*

Form Methods

getAliases   R   O.Ref.

getAliases   `vecAliases = nfrmform.getAliases()`

This method returns an object of type *java.util.Vector* containing elements of type *java.lang.String.* This method returns everything but the first name in the list because it is accessed through the getNames method. If no aliases are found for a form, IsEmpty will be true.

getFields   R   O.Ref.

getFields   `VecFields = nfrmform.getFields()`

This method returns an object of type *java.util.Vector* containing elements of type *java.lang.String.* This method returns the name of every field on a form. This can be very useful when you need to programmatically access items in a document created with a certain form.

```
import lotus.domino.*;
import java.util.Vector;
import java.lang.String;
public class JavaAgent extends AgentBase {
  public void NotesMain() {
    try {
      // This agent builds a list of all the fields in a form ending in
      // _e for exporting
      Session ns = getSession();
      AgentContext nac = ns.getAgentContext();
      Database ndb = nac.getCurrentDatabase();
      Form nfrm = ndb.getForm("Task");
      Vector vecFields = nfrm.getFields();
      for (int i=0;  i <= vecFields.size(); i++)
        {
          String[] ExportFields = new String[vecFields.size()];
          String strFieldName=(String)vecFields.elementAt(i);
          int intPos=strFieldName.indexOf("_e");
          if (intPos>0)
            {
              int intLength= strFieldName.length();
              ExportFields[i]=strFieldName.substring(1,(intLength-2));
            }
        }
      if (ExportFields.length >0)
        {
          //Call your export routine here
```

```
            }
            } catch(Exception e) {
            e.printStackTrace();
        }
    }
}
```

---

getFormUsers   R   O.Ref.

`vecUsers = nfrmform.getFormUsers()`

This method returns an object of type *java.util.Vector* containing elements of type
java.lang.String that represent the entries in the $FormUsers item. The $FormUsers item
can be set using the "Who can create documents with this form" option on the Key
tab of the form properties info box. When it's set to "All Authors and above," anyone
with author access or above can create documents using the form. If users and groups
are explicitly named, only the named groups can create documents using the form.

---

getName   R   O.Ref.

`strName = nfrmform = getName()`

This method returns the name of a form.

---

getReaders   R   O.Ref.

`vecReaders = nfrmform.getReaders()`

This method returns an object of type *java.util.Vector* containing elements of type
java.lang.String that represent the entries in the $Readers item. The $Readers item can
be set using the "Who can create documents with this form" option on the Key tab of
the form properties info box. When it's set to "All Authors and above," anyone with
author access or above can create documents using the form. If users and groups are
explicitly named, only the named groups can create documents using the form.

---

isProtectReaders   R   T/F

`bolProtReaders = nfrmform.isProtectReaders()`

This method indicates whether or not the $Readers item can be overwritten by replica-
tion. If the method returns true, the $Readers item is protected, while false indicates
that $Readers is not protected.

---

isProtectUsers   R   T/F

`bolProtUsers = nfrmform.isProtectUsers()`

This method indicates whether or not the $FormUsers item can be overwritten by
replication. If the method returns true, the $FormUsers item is protected, while false
indicates that $FormUsers is not protected.

---

isSubForm   R   T/F

`bolSub = nfrmform.isSubForm()`

This method indicates whether a form is or is not a subform. If a form is a subform,
this method returns true. Otherwise, it returns false.

Remove

`nfrmform.Remove`

This method is used to permanently delete a form from the database.

---

setFormUsers	W	O.Ref.

`nfrmform.`**`setFormUsers`**`(vecusers)`

---

vecusers	Required	O.Ref.

Contains the users and groups that should be allowed to read documents created with this form.

This method accepts a *java.util.Vector* object containing user names and groups that should be allowed to compose documents using this form.

---

setProtectReaders	W	O.Ref.

`nfrmform.`**`setProtectReaders`**`(bolflag)`

---

bolflag	Required	T/F

Set to `true` to protect the form readers. Set to `false` to allow form readers to be overwritten.

This method, when set to `true`, prevents the `$Readers` item from being overwritten during replication.

---

setProtectUsers	W	T/F

`nfrmform.`**`setProtectUsers`**`(bolflag)`

---

bolflag	Required	T/F

Set to `true` to protect the form users. Set to `false` to allow form users to be overwritten.

When set to `true`, this method prevents the `$FormUsers` item from being overwritten during replication.

---

setReaders	W	O.Ref.

`nfrmform.`**`setReaders`**`(vecreaders)`

---

vecreaders	Required	O.Ref.

Contains the users and groups that should be allowed to read documents created with this form.

This method accepts a *java.util.Vector* object containing user names and groups that should be allowed to read documents created with this form.

Example

```java
import lotus.domino.*;
import java.util.Vector;
import java.lang.String;
public class JavaAgent extends AgentBase {
  public void NotesMain() {
    try {
      // This agent updates the $FormUsers and $Readers items and
      // changes the ProtectUser and ProtectReaders properties so that
      // replication will not be permitted to update these fields
      // for all the "Admin" forms in a database. After this agent runs,
      // all "Admin" forms can be used for reading, but only users and
      // groups named in the NewUsers array can create documents.
```

```
Session ns = getSession();
AgentContext nac = ns.getAgentContext();
Database ndb = nac.getCurrentDatabase();
Form nfrm;
Vector vecForms = ndb.getForms();
String strUpdates;
Vector NewUsers = new Vector();
// Load new users
NewUsers.addElement("Definiti Administrators");
NewUsers.addElement("CMGR Administrators");
NewUsers.addElement("CMGR Editors");
NewUsers.addElement("Samuel Hatter");
NewUsers.addElement("Wyatt Hatter");
for (int i=0; i<vecForms.size(); i++)
   {
     nfrm = (Form)vecForms.elementAt(i);
     String FormName=nfrm.getName();
     int intPos=FormName.indexOf("Admin");
     if (intPos>0)
       {
         nfrm=ndb.getForm(FormName);
         nfrm.setFormUsers(NewUsers);
         nfrm.setReaders(null);
         nfrm.setProtectReaders(true);
         nfrm.setProtectUsers(true);
       }
   }
  } catch(Exception e) {
  e.printStackTrace();
  }
  }
}
```

International

The *lotus.domino.International* class allows you to access your operating system's current international settings. If any of these settings are changed through the operating system, Domino will immediately recognize the new setting.

Session
└─ International

Java Syntax

```
public class lotus.domino.International extends Base
```

The only way to access a *lotus.domino.International* object is through the
`getInternational` method of a *lotus.domino.Session* object.

International Methods

getAMString   R   O.Ref.

getAMString

```
strAM = inatinternational.getAMString()
```

Returns an object of type *java.lang.String* containing the value used to denote an a.m.
time.

getCurrencyDigits   R   %

getCurrency
Digits

```
intDigits = inatinternational.getCurrencyDigits()
```

Returns an integer representing the number of decimal places to allow in currency
values.

getCurrencySymbol   R   O.Ref.

getCurrency
Symbol

```
strCurSymbol = inatinternational.getCurrencySymbol()
```

Returns an object of type *java.lang.String* containing the symbol used to denote that a
numeric value is currency.

getDateSep   R   O.Ref.

getDateSep

```
strDateSep = inatinternational.getDateSep()
```

Returns an object of type *java.lang.String* containing the character used as a delimiter
to separate months, days, and years.

getDecimalSep   R   O.Ref.

getDecimalSep

```
strDecimalSep = inatinternational.getDecimalSep()
```

Returns an object of type *java.lang.String* containing the character used to denote the
decimal place in a numeric value.

getParent   R   O.Ref.

getParent

```
nsSession = inatinternational.getParent()
```

Returns a *lotus.domino.Session* object containing the session in which the current
lotus.domino.international object exists.

getPMString   R   O.Ref.

getPMString

```
strPM = inatinternational.getPMString()
```

Returns an object of type *java.lang.String* containing the string value used to denote a
p.m. time.

getThousandsSep   R   O.Ref.

getThousandsSep

```
strKSep = inatinternational.getThousandsSep()
```

Returns an object of type *java.lang.String* containing the character used as a placeholder in numeric values greater than 1000. The default for English is the comma
character (,).

getTimeSep	R	O.Ref.	

`strTimeSep = inatinternational.getTimeSep()`   getTimeSep

Returns an object of type *java.lang.String* containing the character used as a placeholder in time values. The default for English is the colon character (:).

getTimeZone	R	%	

`intZone = inatinternational.getTimeZone()`   getTimeZone

Returns an integer representing the time zone.

getToday	R	O.Ref.	

`strToday = inatinternational.getToday()`   getToday

Returns an object of type *java.lang.String* containing the string used to represent the current day in the client's language. For example, this method returns Today in English.

getTomorrow	R	O.Ref.	

`strTomorrow = inatinternational.getTomorrow()`   getTomorrow

Returns an object of type *java.lang.String* containing the string used to represent tomorrow in the client's language. For example, this method returns Tomorrow in English.

getYesterday	R	O.Ref.	

`strYesterday = inatinternational.getYesterday()`   getYesterday

Returns an object of type *java.lang.String* containing the string used to represent yesterday in the client's language. For example, this method returns Yesterday in English.

isCurrencySpace	R	T/F	

`bolcurspace = inatinternational.isCurrencySpace()`   isCurrency Space

Returns true if currency values contain a space between the currency symbol and the number. Returns false if there is no embedded space.

isCurrencySuffix	R	T/F	

`bolcursuffix = inatinternational.isCurrencySuffix()`   isCurrency Suffix

Returns true if the currency symbol follows the number in currency values. Returns false if the currency symbol doesn't follow the currency value.

isCurrencyZero	R	T/F	

`bolcurzero = inatinternational.isCurrencyZero()`   isCurrencyZero

Returns true if fractions have a zero before the decimal point in number format. Otherwise, returns false.

isDateDMY	R	T/F	

`boldatedmy = inatinternational.isDateDMY()`   isDateDMY

Returns true if the date is formatted "day, month, year." Otherwise, returns false.

isDateMDY	R	T/F	

`boldatemdy = inatinternational.isDateMDY()`   isDateMDY

Returns true if the date is formatted "month, day, year." Otherwise, returns false.

isDateYMD	R	T/F	

`boldateymd = inatinternational.isDateYMD()`   isDateYMD

Returns true if the date is formatted "year, month, day." Otherwise, returns false.

isDST	R	T/F

isDST

```
boldst = inatinternational.isDST()
```

Returns true if the time format reflects daylight saving time. Otherwise, returns false.

isTime24Hour	R	T/F

isTime24Hour

```
bolmiltime = inatinternational.isTime24Hour()
```

Returns true if the time values are formatted in military time (24-hour clock). Otherwise, returns false.

Remarks

The *lotus.domino.International* class allows you to manipulate Notes date-time values in their native format. It's a powerful and necessary tool for your development efforts.

Example

```java
import lotus.domino.*;
public class JavaAgent extends AgentBase {
public void NotesMain() {
      try {
      Session ns = getSession();
      AgentContext nac = ns.getAgentContext();
          International inat = ns.getInternational();
          System.out.println("The international settings for the
          ➥locat machine are as follows:");
      System.out.println("AM String = " +
      ➥inat.getAMString());
      System.out.println("Currency Digits = " + inat.getCurrencyDigits());
      System.out.println("Currency Symbol = " + inat.getCurrencySymbol());
      System.out.println("Date Separator = " + inat.getDateSep());
      System.out.println("Decimal Separator = " + inat.getDecimalSep());
      System.out.println("PM String = " + inat.getPMString());
      System.out.println("Thousands Separator = " +
      ➥inat.getThousandsSep());
      System.out.println("Time Separator = " + inat.getTimeSep());
      System.out.println("Time Zone = " + inat.getTimeZone());
      System.out.println("Today = " + inat.getToday());
      System.out.println("Tommorrow = " + inat.getTomorrow());
      System.out.println("Yesterday = " + inat.getYesterday());
      System.out.println("Currency Space = " + inat.isCurrencySpace());
      System.out.println("Currency Suffix = " + inat.isCurrencySuffix());
      System.out.println("Currency Zero = " + inat.isCurrencyZero());
      System.out.println("Daylight Savings Time = " + inat.isDST());
      System.out.println("DMY Date = " + inat.isDateDMY());
      System.out.println("MDY Date = " + inat.isDateMDY());
      System.out.println("YMD Date = " + inat.isDateYMD());
      System.out.println("24 Hour Time = " + inat.isTime24Hour());
      } catch(Exception e) {
      e.printStackTrace();
      }
   }
}
}
```

The *lotus.domino.Item* object represents the data stored in the *lotus.domino.Document*. It is much like a field in a relational database. It holds a specific piece of data in a document and is the smallest unit of storage (atomic) in a Notes database. The values of *lotus.domino.Item* are displayed to the user through the field design elements located on the Notes form. However, they exist physically in the back-end *lotus.domino.Documents* and are accessible programmatically regardless of whether they are rendered via the field design elements.

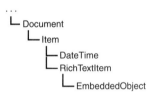

continued >>

Java Syntax

A *lotus.domino.Item* can be created in Java in one of two ways. The first way creates a new *lotus.domino.Item* using the `appendItemValue` or `replaceItemValue` method in the *lotus.domino.Document* object:

```
Item ndocDocument.replaceItemValue(strName, Object value)
```

The second way is used when you want to create a new *lotus.domino.Item* object from an existing *lotus.domino.Item* object using the `copyItemToDocument` method of *lotus.domino.Item.* In addition, you can use the `copyItem`, `copyAllItems`, or `replaceItemValue` of the *lotus.domino.Document.*

You must call the `save` method of the parent *lotus.domino.Document* to save the new or modified *lotus.domino.Item* to disk. If the `save` method isn't called, all changes are discarded when the handle on the *lotus.domino.Item* is lost or when the script completes. In addition, by default, newly created *lotus.domino.Items* are not set to display in views or folders. Therefore, you must explicitly call the `setSummary` method of the *lotus.domino.Item* and set the value to `true`. Otherwise, the values contained in the *lotus.domino.Items* will not display when the document is rendered in a Notes view. This is similar to the behavior of the *lotus.domino.RichTextItem,* which can never be displayed in a Notes view or folder.

Java Parameters

strName	Required	O.Ref.

A string value that contains the name you want to give the new *lotus.domino.Item,* or the name of the item(s) you want to replace.

Object value	Required	%, &, !, #, @, $

The value to assign to the new item. The value's data type determines the type of item that Notes creates. If you're replacing an existing *lotus.domino.Item,* the data type doesn't need to match the data type of the original *lotus.domino.Item.*

Java Item Data Type	Values
java.lang.String	Text
java.util.Vector with *java.lang.String* elements	Text list (including Names, Authors, and Readers item types)
Integer or Double	Number
java.util.Vector with Integer elements	Number list
lotus.domino.DateTime	Date/time
Java.util.Vector with *lotus.domino.DateTime* elements	Date/time range

Item Methods

abstractText

strAbbreviation = niItem.**abstractText**(intMaxlength, bolDropVowels, ⮡bolUseDictionary)

---

intMaxlength   Required   %

The maximum length of the string to return.

bolDropVowels   Required   %

Indicates whether vowels should be dropped from the abbreviation. true drops vowels, and false retains them.

bolUseDictionary   Optional   %

Indicates the table of abbreviations defined in NOTEABBR.TXT. true uses the abbreviation table. false doesn't use the table.

This method returns a text string that contains the abbreviated contents of a text item. The text value is truncated if the size of the text exceeds the allowed value for the string.

appendToTextList

niItem.**appendToTextList**(strNewvalue)

niItem.**appendToTextList**(vecNewvalue)

---

strNewvalue   Required   O.Ref.

The string value you want to add to the item.

vecNewvalue   Required   O.Ref.

The string values you want to add to the item, where the strings are elements in a vector.

This method adds a new element to the existing text list while preserving the existing item values.

The following code appends the common username of the current user to the ModifiedBy item and saves the document to disk.

```java
import lotus.domino.*;

public class JavaAgent extends AgentBase {

    public void NotesMain() {

        try {
            Session ns = getSession();
            AgentContext agentContext = ns.getAgentContext();
            Document ndoc = agentContext.getDocumentContext();
            Item niContactName = ndoc.getFirstItem("ModifiedBy");
            String strCommonName = ns.getCommonUserName();
            niContactName.appendToTextList(strCommonName);
            ndoc.save();
            System.out.println("Agent complete.");

        } catch(Exception e) {
            e.printStackTrace();
        }
    }
}
```

This very handy method allows you to add a new text element to a multivalue item while preserving the existing values.

---

containsValue

```
boolean bolContains = niItem.containsValue(strValue)
```

---

strValue   Required $

The value for which to search the method.

This method searches to see whether the strValue matches at least one of the items contained in the *lotus.domino.Item*. The method returns a Boolean value indicating whether the value was found in the item. true means that the value matches one of the values in the item. false means that the value doesn't match one of the values in the item.

This method can be used to search an item that contains multivalues (a list). The data type for this parameter should match the data type of the item you're trying to search. For example, if you want to search a date-time range to see whether a time exists in the range, you must pass it a *lotus.domino.DateTime* (▶ 395). Likewise, if you want to search a text list, you must pass it a string value. If value is a distinguished name, and if the item contains Notes user names, the distinguished name matches the common version of the hierarchical name. You should not use this method to search for a particular character, string, word, or phrase.

The following example checks the contents of the Categories field, which is a multivalue field, to see if one of the values in the field has the string value of "Competitor Products".

```java
import lotus.domino.*;

public class JavaAgent extends AgentBase {

    public void NotesMain() {

        try {
            Session ns = getSession();
            AgentContext agentContext = ns.getAgentContext();
            Document ndoc = agentContext.getDocumentContext();
            Item niContactName = ndoc.getFirstItem("Categories");
            if (niContactName.containsValue("Competitor Products"))
                System.out.println("Ready to continue...");
            else
                System.out.println("This action is not authorized...");
            System.out.println("Agent complete.");

        } catch(Exception e) {
            e.printStackTrace();
        }
    }
}
```

---

copyItemToDocument

```
nitemItem = niItem.copyItemToDocument(ndocDocument)
```
```
nitemItem = niItem.copyItemToDocument(ndocDocument, strNewname)
```

Document   Required   O.Ref.

The target *document* object.

strNewname   Required   O.Ref.

The name of the new item in the target document.

This method provides a simple way to copy an item from a source document to a target document. When you use the first signature, which passes only the *lotus.domino.Document* object, the new *lotus.domino.Item* is created with the same name as the original item. When you use the second signature, which passes the *lotus.domino.Document* object and the strNewname, the new *lotus.domino.Item* is created with the name specified in strNewname. This method returns a copy of the *lotus.domino.Item*. When you use this method for *lotus.domino.RichTextItems,* only the text is copied. All rich text objects, file attachments, and object links are ignored. The following example runs on every document currently selected in a view. It creates a new document of type "Company" in the current database and copies the values of the company name and phone number into the newly created document from the currently selected document and then saves the new document to disk.

```java
import lotus.domino.*;

public class JavaAgent extends AgentBase {

    public void NotesMain() {
        try {
            Session ns = getSession();
            AgentContext agentContext = ns.getAgentContext();
            Database ndb = agentContext.getCurrentDatabase();
            View nvw = ndb.getView("DesignerView");
            Document ndocCollection = nvw.getFirstDocument();
            while (ndocCollection != null) {
                Document ndocNew = ndb.createDocument();
                ndocNew.appendItemValue("Type", "Company");
                Item niName = ndocCollection.getFirstItem("CompanyName");
                Item niPhone = ndocCollection.getFirstItem("OfficePhone");
                niName.copyItemToDocument(ndocNew);
                niPhone.copyItemToDocument(ndocNew);
                ndocNew.save(true,false);
                ndocCollection = nvw.getNextDocument(ndocCollection);
            }
            System.out.println("Agent complete.");

        } catch(Exception e) {
            e.printStackTrace();
        }
    }
}
```

---

getDateTimeValue   R   *DateTime*

**getDateTime
Value**

```
ndtDateTime = niItem.getDateTimeValue()
```

Returns a *lotus.domino.DateTime* object containing the value of the item if the item is of type date-time. For other item types, such as text and numeric, this method returns nothing. Unlike LotusScript date-time variants, Notes date-time items and *lotus.domino.DateTime* objects store a time zone and hundredths of a second. If the value contained in the *lotus.domino.Item* is not of type *lotus.domino.DateTime,* this method returns null.

---

getLastModified   R   Variant

getLastModified

```
ndtdatetime = niItem.getLastModified()
```

Returns a variant of type date of the date and time this document was last modified and saved to disk.

getName   R $

```
strItemname = niItem.getName()
```

Returns the item's name as a string. Multiple items with the same name can exist in one document, and all file attachments have the name $FILE. You can use the `getFirstItem` and `Items` methods of *lotus.domino.Document* to access several items with the same name.

getParent   R   O.Ref.

```
ndocDocument = niItem.getParent()
```

Returns a *lotus.domino.Document* object that refers to the document in which the item exists.

getText   R $

```
String strItemtext = niItem.getText()
```

Returns a string containing the text representation of the item's value. (When this method is used with *lotus.domino.RichTextItem,* all nontext data is ignored.) If the item contains multiple values, the string value returned will have each item separated by semicolons. If the item's value is larger than 64KB, the returned string will be truncated at the 64KB mark. When this method is used with HTML items, it returns `null`.

getText   R $

```
strItemtext = niItem.getText(intMaxlength)
```

Returns a string with a maximum length of `intMaxlength` that contains the text representation of the item's value. (When this method is used with *lotus.domino.RichTextItem,* all nontext data is ignored.) If the item contains multiple values, the string value returned will have each item separated by semicolons. If the item's value is larger than 64KB, the returned string will be truncated at the 64KB mark. When this method is used with HTML items, it returns `null`.

getType   R   %

```
intItemtype = niItem.getType()
```

Indicates an item's datatype. The constants are listed in the following table.

Data Type	Description
Item.ATTACHMENT	The item contains a file attachment.
Item.AUTHORS	An Authors item that limits edit access to those explicitly named.
Item.DATETIMES	The item contains a date-time value or range of date-time values.
Item.EMBEDDEDOBJECT	The item contains an embedded object.
Item.ERRORITEM	An error occurred while accessing the type.
Item.FORMULA	The item contains a Notes formula.
Item.HTML	The item contains HTML source text.
Item.ICON	The item is an icon.
Item.NAMES	The item is of type Names.
Item.NOTELINKS	A link to a database, view, or document.
Item.NOTESREFS	The item is a reference to the parent document.

continued >>

continued >>

Data Type	Description
Item.NUMBERS	The item is a number or number list.
Item.OTHEROBJECT	Another object.
Item.READERS	A Readers item that limits read access to those explicitly named.
Item.RICHTEXT	Rich text.
Item.SIGNATURE	The item contains a digital signature.
Item.TEXT	The item is a text value or text list.
Item.UNAVAILABLE	The item's data type isn't available.
Item.UNKNOWN	The item's data type isn't known.
Item.USERDATA	User data.
Item.USERID	The item contains a user ID name.

getValueDouble   R

getValue
Double

```
dblValue = niItem.getValueDouble()
```

Represents the double value that the *lotus.domino.Item* contains.

getValueInteger   R   %

getValue
Integer

```
intValue = niItem.getValueInteger()
```

Represents the integer value that the *lotus.domino.Item* contains.

getValueLength   R   %

getValueLength

```
intValuelength = niItem.getValueLength()
```

Represents the item's size in bytes as an integer.

getValues   R   Variant

getValues

```
vecValues = niItem.getValues()
```

Returns the values that the item contains, varying data types depending on the item's type, as shown in the following table. This method returns the same value(s) for an item as the getItemValue method in *lotus.domino.Document* (▶ 421). This method always returns an array for text items, number items, date-time items, and attachments, even when there is only a single value in the item. If you know that the item contains only a single value, you should access the first element in the array at the index 0. When working with attachments, you can use this method to determine the name of the attachment. Then you can use the returned value with the getAttachment method in *lotus.domino.Document* to get a handle on the file attachment.

Item Type Value	Data Type
Rich text	String. Vector with one string element rendered into plain text. This is the same value returned by the formattedText method of *lotus.domino.RichTextItem*.
Text or text list	Vector with string elements (includes Names, Authors, and Readers item types).
Number or number list	Vector with Double elements.
Date-time or a range of date-time values	Vector with DateTime elements.
Attachment	Vector with String elements. The name of the first attachment in the first element is 0.

getValueString	R	O.Ref.

```
strValue = niItem.getValueString()
```

Represents the value that the *lotus.domino.Item* contains as a string.

isAuthors	R	T/F

```
bolAuthors = niItem.isAuthors()
```

Indicates whether the *lotus.domino.Item* is of type Authors. It's `true` if the item is of type Authors and `false` if it is not.

isEncrypted	R	T/F

```
bolEcrypted = niItem.isEncrypted()
```

Indicates whether the item is encrypted. It's `true` if the item is encrypted and `false` if it is not. Setting this method to `true` won't cause the item to be encrypted unless and until the encrypt method of the parent *lotus.domino.Document* is called.

isNames	R	T/F

```
bolNames = niItem.isNames()
```

Indicates whether the *lotus.domino.Item* is of type Names. It's `true` if the item is a Names item and `false` if it is not.

isProtected	R	T/F

```
bolProtected = niItem.isProtected()
```

Indicates whether the user needs a minimum access level of editor to edit the *lotus.domino.Item*. If this method is `true`, the current user needs at least editor access to modify the item. If this method is `false`, the current user doesn't need editor access and therefore can modify the item if he or she has author access or better.

isReaders	R	T/F

```
bolReaders = niItem.isReaders()
```

Indicates whether the *lotus.domino.Item* is of type Readers. It's `true` if the item is of type Readers and `false` if it is not.

isSaveToDisk	R	T/F

```
bolSaved = niItem.isSaveToDisk()
```

Indicates whether the *lotus.domino.Item* should be saved to disk when its parent document is saved. It's `true` if the item is saved to disk when the document is saved and `false` if the item is not saved to disk when the document is saved. This method defaults to `true`. If you mark an existing item as not to be saved, it will disappear from disk the next time you save the document.

isSigned	R	T/F

```
bolSigned = niItem.isSigned()
```

Indicates whether the *lotus.domino.Item* has been digitally signed. `true` means that the item is signed. `false` means that it is not.

isSummary	R	T/F

```
bolSummary = niItem.isSummary()
```

Indicates whether the item can be displayed in a view or folder. true means that the item is a summary. false means that it is not. When a new *lotus.domino.Item* is created using the New keyword or the replaceItemValue method in *lotus.domino.Document*, this method defaults to false. Similarly, this method always returns false for *lotus.domino.RichTextItem* because rich text can't appear in views. *lotus.domino.Items* created with the extended class syntax or created using the appendItemValue method in *lotus.domino.Document* have this method set to true by default.

remove

remove

niItem.**remove**

This method permanently deletes an item from a document. You must call the save method of the parent *lotus.domino.Document* to write your changes to disk. You can also remove an item from a *lotus.domino.Document* using the removeItem method in the *lotus.domino.Document* class.

setAuthors   W   T/F

setAuthors

niItem.**setAuthors**(boolean bolAuthors)

Indicates whether the *lotus.domino.Item* is of type Authors. It's true if the item is of type Authors and false if it isn't.

setDateTimeValue   W   *Date/Time*

setDate
TimeValue

niItem.**setDateTimeValue**(ntdDateTime)

Returns a *lotus.domino.DateTime* object containing the value of the item if the item is of type date-time. For other item types, such as text and numeric, this method returns nothing. Unlike LotusScript date-time variants, Notes date-time items and *lotus.domino.DateTime* objects store a time zone and hundredths of a second.

setEncrypted   W   T/F

setEncrypted

niItem.**setEncrypted**(bolEncrypt)

Indicates whether the item is encrypted. true means that the item is encrypted. false means that it is not. Setting this method to true won't cause the item to be encrypted unless and until the encrypt method of the parent *lotus.domino.Document* is called.

setNames   W   T/F

setNames

niItem.**setNames**(bolNames)

Indicates whether the *lotus.domino.Item* is of type Names. It's true if the item is a Names item and false if it isn't.

setProtected   W   T/F

setProtected

niItem.**setProtected**(bolProtected)

Indicates whether a user needs a minimum access level of editor to edit the *lotus.domino.Item*. If this method is true, the current user needs at least editor access to modify the item. If this method is false, the current user doesn't need editor access and therefore can modify the item if he or she has author access or better.

setReaders   W   T/F

setReaders

niItem.**setReaders**(bolReaders)

Indicates whether the *lotus.domino.Item* is of type Readers. It's true if the item is of type Readers and false if it isn't.

---

setSaveToDisk   W   T/F

niItem.**setSaveToDisk**(bolSaved)   setSaveToDisk

Indicates whether the *lotus.domino.Item* should be saved to disk when its parent document is saved. true means that the item is saved to disk when the document is saved. false means that the item is not saved to disk when the document is saved. This method defaults to true. If you mark an existing item as not to be saved, it will disappear from the disk the next time you save the document.

setSigned   W   T/F

niItem.**setSigned**(bolSigned)   setSigned

Indicates whether the *lotus.domino.Item* has been digitally signed. true means that the item is signed. false means that it isn't.

setSummary   W   T/F

niItem.**setSummary**(bolSummary)   setSummary

Indicates whether the item can be displayed in a view or folder. true means that the item is a summary. false means that it isn't. When a new *lotus.domino.Item* is created using the New keyword or the replaceItemValue method in *lotus.domino.Document,* this method defaults to false. Similarly, this method always returns false for *lotus.domino.RichTextItem* because rich text can't appear in views. *lotus.domino.Items* created with the extended class syntax or created using the appendItemValue method in *lotus.domino.Document* have this method set to true by default.

setValueDouble   W

niItem.**setValueDouble**(dblValue)   setValueDouble

Sets the double value that the *lotus.domino.Item* contains.

setValueInteger   W   %

niItem.**setValueInteger**(intValue)   setValueInteger

Sets the integer value that the *lotus.domino.Item* contains.

setValues   W   ()

niItem.**setValues**(vecValues)   setValues

Returns the values that the item contains, varying data types depending on the item's type, as shown in the following table. This method returns the same value(s) for an item as the getItemValue method in *lotus.domino.Document* (▶ 421). This method always returns an array for text items, number items, date-time items, and attachments, even when there is only a single value in the item. If you know that the item contains only a single value, you should access the first element in the array at the index 0. When working with attachments, you can use this method to determine the name of the attachment. Then you can use the returned value with the getAttachment method in *lotus.domino.Document* to get a handle on the file attachment.

Item Type Value	Data Type
Rich text	Vector with one String element rendered into plain text. This is the same value returned by the formattedText method of *lotus.domino.RichTextItem.*
Text or text list	Vector with String elements (includes Names, Authors, and Readers item types).

continued >>

continued >>

Item Type Value	Data Type
Number or number list	Vector with Double elements.
Date-time or a range of date-time values	Vector with DateTime elements.
Attachment	Vector with String elements. The name of the first attachment in the first element.

setValueString   W   O.Ref.

setValueString   niItem.**setValueString**(strValue)

Represents the value that the *lotus.domino.Item* contains as a string.

Remarks

The *lotus.domino.Document* and *lotus.domino.Item* methods must be used to reference item values. An existing *lotus.domino.Item* object can be accessed by using the getFirstItem method of the *lotus.domino.Document*. All existing *lotus.domino.Items* can be accessed using the getItems method of the *lotus.domino.Document*.

When you're developing with Java, certain methods let you access *lotus.domino.Items* without having to declare and instantiate a handle on the *lotus.domino.Item* object. The following table lists the methods you can use to directly access *lotus.domino.Items* previously created and saved to the *lotus.domino.Document*.

Java Method	Action
getItemValue	Gets an item's value
replaceItemValue	Sets an item's value
appendItemValue	Creates a new item
hasItem	Checks for the existence of an item in the *lotus.domino.Document*
removeItem	Deletes an item from the *lotus.domino.Document*

Example

To understand the power and flexibility of the *lotus.domino.Item* class, consider the following example. You need to write an agent that will search all the documents in a view and will determine whether they contain a multivalue *lotus.domino.Item* named rnReaders. The item, if it exists, will be of type Readers and will require editor access or higher to change. If the item exists, and if it hasn't been modified during the same day that the agent is being run, this code will delete it and re-create it from a vector. Additionally, because this is a Readers field, this code will get all the setReaders methods. To increase security, you don't want it to be displayed in a view or folder, so this code also calls the setProtected method.

The following code, placed in the click event of a view action, demonstrates one way to accomplish this.

```java
import lotus.domino.*;
import java.util.Vector;

public class JavaAgent extends AgentBase {

    public void NotesMain() {

        try {
            Session ns = getSession();
            AgentContext agentContext = ns.getAgentContext();
            Database ndb = agentContext.getCurrentDatabase();
            DocumentCollection ndc = ndb.getAllDocuments();
            Document ndocCollection = ndc.getFirstDocument();
            while (ndocCollection != null) {
                if (ndocCollection.hasItem("rnReaders"))
                {
                    Item niOriginalname = ndocCollection.getFirstItem
                    ➥("rnReaders");
                    DateTime ndtNow = ns.createDateTime("Today");
                    ndtNow.setNow();
                    DateTime ndtCurrentdate = ndtNow;
                    DateTime ndtOriginaldate =
                    ➥niOriginalname.getLastModified();
                    int intDifference = ndtCurrentdate.timeDifference
                    ➥(ndtOriginaldate) / 86400;
                    if (intDifference == 0)
                    {
                        niOriginalname.remove();
                        Vector strReaders = new Vector();
                        strReaders.addElement("Tim Bankes");
                        strReaders.addElement("Richard Bankes");
                        strReaders.addElement("Judy Bankes");
                        strReaders.addElement("Molly Thumann");
                        ndocCollection.replaceItemValue("rnReaders",
                        ➥strReaders);
                        Item niName = ndocCollection.getFirstItem("rnReaders");
                        niName.setReaders(true);
                        niName.setProtected(true);
                        ndocCollection.save(true,false);
                    }
                }
            ndocCollection = ndc.getNextDocument(ndocCollection);
            }
            System.out.println("Agent complete.");

        } catch(Exception e) {
            e.printStackTrace();
        }
    }
}
```

The *lotus.domino.Log* class provides extensive logging capabilities, making it easy to
record the actions and errors (hopefully
you won't have any!) that occur as an
agent executes. You can log to a Notes
database, in a mail memo, to a text file (if
the script runs locally), or to an agent's log.

Session
 └ Log

Java Syntax

```
public class Log extends Base
```

To create a new *lotus.domino.Log* object, call the `CreateLog` method of the *lotus.domino.Session* class (▶ 578).

```
Log nlog (log = nssession.createLog) (str name)
```

Java Parameters

strName	Required	O.Ref.

A *java.lang.String* object that contains the name you want to use to identify the code that is being logged. Examples include the name of an agent that is being logged and the name of a script library that is being executed.

Log Methods

close

close

```
log.close()
```

Calling the `close` method closes the *lotus.domino.Log* object. If you're logging to a mail message, it will be sent when this method is called.

getNumActions   R   %

getNumActions

```
intNumActions = nloglog.getNumActions()
```

Returns the number of actions that have been logged for the agent.

getNumErrors   R   %

getNumErrors

```
intNumErrors = nloglog.getNumErrors()
```

Returns the number of errors that have been logged for the agent.

getParent   R   O.Ref.

getParent

```
Session Parent = nagtagent.getParent()
```

Returns a *lotus.domino.Session* object representing the session that contains the *lotus.domino.Log*.

getProgramName   R   O.Ref.

getProgram
Name

```
strProgName = nloglog.getProgramName()
```

This method can be used to determine the name associated with the agent that is being logged. By default, it will return a *java.lang.String* object containing the name that was used when the *lotus.domino.Log* object was created.

isLogActions   R   T/F

isLogActions

```
bollogactions = nloglog.isLogActions()
```

This method can be called to determine whether an agent's actions should be logged. When it's set to `true` (the default), actions will be logged.

isLogErrors   R   T/F

isLogErrors

```
bollogerrors = nloglog.isLogErrors()
```

This method is used as a toggle to indicate whether an agent's errors should be logged. When it's set to `true` (the default), errors will be logged.

---

isOverwriteFile   R   T/F

```
boloverwrite = nloglog.isOverwriteFile()
```
isOverwrite File

If you're logging to a file, this method indicates that the existing log file should be overwritten or appended. To overwrite an existing log file, be sure to set this method to `true` before calling the `OpenFileLog` method. This method has no effect if you're logging to a mail message, database, or agent.

---

logAction

```
log.logAction(strDescription)
```
logAction

strDescription   Required   O.Ref.

A *java.lang.String* object containing the description of the action you want to write to the log.

This method allows you to describe the action your script has performed, but its exact functionality will vary depending on the type of log you're writing.

If you called `openNotesLog` to log to a *lotus.domino.Database*, this method will create a new document in the specified database with an `$ACTION` item containing the description you specified.

When you log to a mail memo using `openMailLog`, the description is added to a new line in the Body item of the memo, as are the current date and time.

Calling the `openFileLog` method causes the description to be written to a new line in the file, along with the value of the `ProgramName` method and the current date and time.

---

logError

```
log.logError(intCode, strDescription)
```
logError

intCode   Required   %

A numeric value representing the error that has occurred.

strDescription   Required   O.Ref.

A *java.lang.String* object containing the description of the error that has occurred.

This method can be used to log errors that occur during the execution of your script. Like the `LogAction` method, the functionality of this method varies depending on the type of log you're writing.

The `openNotesLog` method will create a new document in the specified database and will write the `intCode` and `strDescription` to the `A$ERRCODE` and `A$ERRMSG` items, respectively.

When you log to a mail memo using `openMailLog`, the error code and description are added to a new line in the Body item of the memo, as are the current date and time.

Calling the `openFileLog` method causes the error code and description to be written to a new line in the file, along with the value of the `ProgramName` method and the current date and time.

---

logEvent

```
log.logEvent(strMessage, strQuename, intType, intSeverity)
```
logEvent

strMessage   Required   O.Ref.

A *java.lang.String* object containing the message you want to send over the network.

strQuename   Required   O.Ref.

A *java.lang.String* object containing the name of the queue to use. Passing an empty string ("") allows Notes to pick the queue.

intType   Required   %

A constant specifying the type of event being logged. The constants are `Log.EV_ALARM`, `Log.EV_COMM`, `Log.EV_MAIL`, `Log.EV_MISC`, `Log.EV_REPLICA`, `Log.EV_RESOURCE`, `Log.EV_SECURITY`, `Log.EV_SERVER`, `Log.EV_UNKNOWN`, and `Log.EV_UPDATE`.

intSeverity   Required   %

Specifies the severity of the event being logged. The types are `Log.SEV_FAILURE`, `Log.SEV_FATAL`, `Log.SEV_NORMAL`, `Log.SEV_WARNING1`, `Log.SEV_WARNING2`, and `Log.SEV_UNKNOWN`.

This method can only be used with scripts running on a server. It lets you define a Notes event and severity and send it over the network. If you elect to use this event, it will have no effect on other open logs, and vice versa. For more information on Notes events and severities, see the Domino Administration Database.

openAgentLog

openAgentLog   `nloglog.`**`openAgentLog`**`()`

Calling this method directs the *lotus.domino.Log* object to store its output in the agent log for the current agent. If the method is not being called from an agent, it fails.

openFileLog

openFileLog   `nloglog.`**`openFileLog`**`(strFileName)`

strFileName   R   O.Ref.

A *java.lang.String* object containing the name and path of the file to which the output should be written.

Calling this method directs the *lotus.domino.Log* object to store its output in the specified file on the Domino server. If the file doesn't exist, it will be created. If the file already exists, it will be overwritten if the `isOverwriteFile` method is called with `true`.

openMailLog

openMailLog   `nloglog.`**`openMailLog`**`(vecRecipients, strSubject)`

vecRecipients   R   O.Ref.

A *java.util.Vector* object containing the names of people and groups who should receive the message. Each of the vector's elements is a *lotus.domino.String* object.

strSubject   R   O.Ref.

A *java.lang.String* object containing the text to use as the subject of the mail message.

Calling this method directs the *lotus.domino.Log* object to store its output in a document that will be mailed to the people and groups specified in the `vecRecipients` parameter.

openNotesLog

openNotesLog   `nloglog.`**`openNotesLog`**`(strServer, strDbName)`

strServer   R   O.Ref.

A *java.lang.String* object containing the name of the server where the *lotus.domino.Notes* log file resides.

strDbName   R   O.Ref.

A *java.lang.String* object containing the name and path of the *lotus.domino.Notes* log file. strDbName

Calling this method directs the *lotus.domino.Log* object to store its output in the *lotus.domino.Log* database. A document is created in the database for each error and/or action that is logged. Each document will contain the following items and values:

Document Values

Form	Log Entry
A$PROGNAME	The value in the `ProgramName` property
A$LOGTIME	The date and time that the error/action was logged
A$USER	The user when the error/action is logged
A$LOGTYPE	`Error` or `Action`
A$ACTION	A description of the action logged
A$ERRCODE	The error code logged
A$ERRMSG	A description of the error logged

setLogActions

`nloglog.`**`setLogActions`**`(bolFlag)`   setLogActions

bolFlag   Required   T/F

Specify `true` to enable action logging or `false` to disable action logging.

This method allows you to enable and disable action logging by passing it a Boolean parameter, `bolFlag`. Pass `true` to enable action logging.

setLogErrors

`nloglog.`**`setLogErrors`**`(bolFlag)`   setLogErrors

bolFlag   Required   T/F

Specify `true` to enable error logging or `false` to disable error logging.

This method allows you to enable and disable error logging by passing it a Boolean parameter, `bolFlag`. Pass `true` to enable error logging.

setOverwriteFile

`nloglog.`**`setOverwriteFile`**`(bolFlag)`   setOverwrite
                                                                          File

bolFlag   Required   T/F

Specify `true` to enable error logging or `false` to disable error logging.

If you're logging to a file, you can use this method to indicate that the existing log file should be overwritten. To overwrite an existing log file, be sure to set this method to `true` before calling the `openFileLog` method. This method has no effect if you're logging to a mail message, database, or agent.

setProgramName

`nlog.`**`setProgramName`**`(strName)`   setProgram
                                                                          Name

strName   Required   O.Ref.

A *java.lang.String* object containing the name to use for this *lotus.domino.Log* object. This has the same effect as the `strName` parameter used in the `createLog` method.

This method allows you to name the *lotus.domino.Log* object.

Remarks

Although *lotus.domino.Log* is a very useful way to keep track of what your scripts and agents are up to, it can be especially useful when you're working with scheduled agents and with agents run by Domino because of the lack of debugging capabilities. Scheduled agents can't provide output through the user interface, making them difficult to debug. The same can be said of agents run by Domino. You can use the *lotus.domino.Log* class to log the agent's actions and errors so that you can ensure that the agent is completing successfully. You can also use it to determine what errors are occurring, and where.

Example

```
import lotus.domino.*;
import java.util.Vector;
public class JavaAgent extends AgentBase {
  public void NotesMain() {
    try {
      // This agent uses a view that shows only response docs to check
      // for orphans
      Session session = getSession();
      AgentContext nac=session.getAgentContext();
      Agent agtCurrent = nac.getCurrentAgent();
      Database ndbCur = nac.getCurrentDatabase();
      View nvwChildren;
      Document ndocChild;
      Document ndocParent;
      Log nlog=session.createLog(agtCurrent.getName());
      int intCount=0;
      int intProc=0;
      Vector vecRecipients = new Vector();
      vecRecipients.addElement("Samuel Hatter");
      vecRecipients.addElement("Wyatt Hatter" );
      vecRecipients.addElement("Leslee Hatter");
      vecRecipients.addElement("George Young");
      vecRecipients.addElement("Rose Wezel");
      vecRecipients.addElement("Jack Hatter");
      vecRecipients.addElement("Roger Sebastian");
      nlog.openMailLog(vecRecipients, agtCurrent.getName());
      nvwChildren=ndbCur.getView("(Children)");
      ndocChild =nvwChildren.getFirstDocument();
      while (ndocChild != null)
        {
          intProc++;
          ndocParent=ndbCur.getDocumentByUNID
          ➥(ndocChild.getParentDocumentUNID());
          if (ndocParent==null)
            {
              nlog.logAction("No parent was found for child: " +
              ➥ndocChild.getNoteID());
              ndocChild.replaceItemValue("Orphan","Y");
              boolean bolflag=ndocChild.save(true);
```

```
                intCount++;
              }
          ndocChild =nvwChildren.getNextDocument(ndocChild);
        }
      String strProc=String.valueOf(intProc);
      String strCount=String.valueOf(intCount);
      nlog.logAction(strProc + " children docs processed, " +
      ➡strCount + " orphans found and marked.");
      nlog.close();
      catch(Exception e) {
       e.printStackTrace();
    }
  }
}
```

The name of the user or server for the current session.

Session
   └ Name
OR
. . .
   └ Database
      └ ALCEntry
         └ Name

Java Syntax

```
public class Name extends Base
```

In order to create a new *lotus.domino.Name* object, you must use the `createName` method of the *lotus.domino.Session* object:

```
nnameName = ns.createName (strName)

nnameName = ns.createName (strName, strLanguage)
```

Java Parameters

---

string strName   Required $

A string representing the name of the user or server. This value will be created as a flat name if the name passed is not in the format of an abbreviated or canonical hierarchical name.

string strLanguage   Required   O.Ref.

A string representing the language associated with the username.

Name Methods

---

getAbbreviated   R   O.Ref.

getAbbreviated   `strAbbreviated = nnameName.`**`getAbbreviated`**`()`

Returns a string representation of the hierarchical name in the abbreviated format. If this method is undefined or empty, it will return `null`.

The following example prints the current user's abbreviated name to the Java console:

```
import lotus.domino.*;

public class JavaAgent extends AgentBase {

    public void NotesMain() {
        try {
            Session ns = getSession();
            Name nname = ns.getUserNameObject();
            System.out.println(nname.getAbbreviated());

        } catch(Exception e) {
            e.printStackTrace();
        }
    }
}
```

---

getAddr821   R   O.Ref.

getAddr821   `strAddress = nnameName.`**`getAddr821`**`()`

Returns a string representation of the Internet address of the name for the current *lotus.domino.Name* in the format based on RFC 821 Address Format Syntax.

---

getAddr822Comment1   R   O.Ref.

getAddr822
Comment1   `strAddress = nnameName.`**`getAddr822Comment1`**`()`

Returns a string representation of the Comment1 component of the Internet address of the name for the current *lotus.domino.Name* in the format based on RFC 822 Address Format Syntax.

---

getAddr822Comment2   R   O.Ref.

`strAddress = nnameName.`**`getAddr822Comment2()`**   getAddr822
                                                                        Comment2

Returns a string representation of the Comment2 component of the Internet address
of the name for the current *lotus.domino.Name* in the format based on RFC 822
Address Format Syntax.

---

getAddr822Comment3   R   O.Ref.

`strAddress = nnameName.`**`getAddr822Comment3()`**   getAddr822
                                                                        Comment3

Returns a string representation of the Comment3 component of the Internet address
of the name for the current *lotus.domino.Name* in the format based on RFC 822
Address Format Syntax.

---

getAddr822LocalPart   R   O.Ref.

`strAddress = nnameName.`**`getAddr822LocalPart()`**   getAddr822
                                                                        LocalPart
Returns a string representation of the LocalPart component of the Internet address of
the name for the current *lotus.domino.Name* in the format based on RFC 822 Address
Format Syntax.

---

getAddr822Phrase   R   O.Ref.

`strAddress = nnameName.`**`getAddr822Phrase()`**   getAddr822
                                                                        Phrase
Returns a string representation of the Phrase component of the Internet address of the
name for the current *lotus.domino.Name* in the format based on RFC 822 Address
Format Syntax.

---

getADMD   R   O.Ref.

`strName = nnameName.`**`getADMD()`**   getADMD

Returns a string representation of the administration management domain name
associated with the current *lotus.domino.Name*.

---

getCanonical   R   O.Ref.

`strName = nnameName.`**`getCanonical()`**   getCanonical

Returns a string representation of the canonical form of the name for the current
lotus.domino.Name.

---

getCommon   R   O.Ref.

`strName = nnameName.`**`getCommon()`**   getCommon

Returns the string representation of the common-name component of a hierarchical
name. If the *lotus.domino.Name* is flat, the entire name is returned. This value is typically
denoted as "CN" by most Lotus Notes documentation and when the Lotus Notes
macro language is used for development.

---

getCountry   R   O.Ref.

`strName = nnameName.`**`getCountry()`**   getCountry

Returns the string representation of the country component of a hierarchical name.
This value is typically denoted as "C" by most Lotus Notes documentation and when
the Lotus Notes macro language is used for development.

---

getGeneration   R   O.Ref.

`strName = nnameName.`**`getGeneration()`**   getGeneration

Returns the string representation of the generation component of a *lotus.domino.Name*.
This method returns values such as Sr., Jr., and so on.

<table>
<tr><td></td><td>getGiven</td><td>R</td><td>O.Ref.</td></tr>
</table>

getGiven

```
strName = nnameName.getGiven()
```

Returns the string representation of the given part of a *lotus.domino.Name*.

<table>
<tr><td></td><td>getInitials</td><td>R</td><td>O.Ref.</td></tr>
</table>

getInitials

```
strName = nnameName.getInitials()
```

Returns the string representation of the initials part of a *lotus.domino.Name*.

<table>
<tr><td></td><td>getKeyword</td><td>R</td><td>O.Ref.</td></tr>
</table>

getKeyword

```
strName = nnameName.getKeyword()
```

Returns the string representation of the components of a hierarchical name in order, separated by backslashes—for example, country\organization\organizational unit1\ organizational unit2\etc.

<table>
<tr><td></td><td>getLanguage</td><td>R</td><td>O.Ref.</td></tr>
</table>

getLanguage

```
strLanguage = nnameName.getLanguage()
```

Returns the string representation of the language tag associated with the name. Here are the language tags that are returned by this method:

Tag	Language
ar	Arabic
ar-ae	Arabic—United Arab Emirates
ar-bh	Arabic—Bahrain
ar-dz	Arabic—Algeria
ar-iq	Arabic—Iraq
ar-jo	Arabic—Jordan
ar-kw	Arabic—Kuwait
ar-lb	Arabic—Lebanon
ar-ly	Arabic—Libyan Arab Jamahiriya
ar-ma	Arabic—Morocco
ar-om	Arabic—Oman
ar-qa	Arabic—Qatar
ar-sa	Arabic—Saudi Arabia
ar-sy	Arabic—Syrian Arab Republic
ar-tn	Arabic—Tunisia
ar-ye	Arabic—Yemen
be	Belorussian
bg	Bulgarian
ca	Catalan
cs	Czech
da	Danish
de	German
de-at	German—Austria
de-ch	German—Switzerland
de-li	German—Liechtenstein

Tag	Language
de-lu	German—Luxembourg
e3	Spain (traditional collation)
e1	Greek
en	English
en-au	English—Australia
en-ca	English—Canada
en-gb	English—United Kingdom
en-ie	English—Ireland
en-jm	English—Jamaica
en-nz	English—New Zealand
en-us	English—United States
en-za	English—South Africa
es-ar	Spanish—Argentina
es-bo	Spanish—Bolivia
es-cl	Spanish—Chile
es-co	Spanish—Columbia
es-cr	Spanish—Costa Rica
es-do	Spanish—Dominican Republic
es-ec	Spanish—Ecuador
es-gt	Spanish—Guatemala
es-mx	Spanish—Mexico
es-pa	Spanish—Panama
es-pe	Spanish—Peru
es-py	Spanish—Paraguay
es-uy	Spanish—Uruguay
es-ve	Spanish—Venezuela
et	Estonian
fi	Finnish
fr	French
fr-be	French—Belgium
fr-ca	French—Canada
fr-ch	French—Switzerland
fr-lu	French—Luxembourg
he	Hebrew
hr	Croatian
hu	Hungarian
it	Italian
it-ch	Italian—Switzerland
ja	Japanese
ko	Korean
lt	Lithuanian

continued >>

continued >>

Tag	Language
lv	Latvian
mk	Macedonian
nl	Dutch
no	Norwegian
pl	Polish
pl-pl	Polish—Poland
pt	Portuguese
pt-br	Portuguese—Brazil
ro	Romanian
ru	Russian
sk	Slovak
sl	Slovenian
sq	Albanian
sr	Serbian
sv	Swedish
th	Thai
tr	Turkish
uk	Ukranian
vi	Vietnamese
zh-cn	Chinese—China
zh-hk	Chinese—Hong Kong
zh-sg	Chinese—Singapore
zh-tw	Chinese—Taiwan

getOrganization   R   O.Ref.

getOrganization   strName = nnameName.**getOrganization**()

Returns the string representation of the organizational component of a hierarchical name. This value is typically denoted as "O" by most Lotus Notes documentation and when the Lotus Notes macro language is used for development.

getOrgUnit1   R   O.Ref.

getOrgUnit1   strName = nnameName.**getOrgUnit1**()

Returns the string representation of the first organizational unit component of a hierarchical name. This value is typically denoted as "OU" by most Lotus Notes documentation and when the Lotus Notes macro language is used for development.

getOrgUnit2   R   O.Ref.

getOrgUnit2   strName = nnameName.**getOrgUnit2**()

Returns the string representation of the second organizational unit component of a hierarchical name. This value is typically denoted as "OU" by most Lotus Notes documentation and when the Lotus Notes macro language is used for development.

getOrgUnit3   R   O.Ref.

getOrgUnit3   strName = nnameName.**getOrgUnit3**()

Returns the string representation of the third organizational unit component of a hierarchical name. This value is typically denoted as "OU" by most Lotus Notes documentation and when the Lotus Notes macro language is used for development.

getOrgUnit4	R	O.Ref.

```
strName = nnameName.getOrgUnit4()
```
getOrgUnit4

Returns the string representation of the fourth organizational unit component of a hierarchical name. This value is typically denoted as "OU" by most Lotus Notes documentation and when the Lotus Notes macro language is used for development.

getParent	R	O.Ref.

```
nsSession = nnameName.getParent()
```
getParent

Returns the *lotus.domino.Session* that contains the *lotus.domino.Name*.

getPRMD	R	O.Ref.

```
strName = nnameName.getPRMD()
```
getPRMD

Returns the string representation of the private management domain name of the *lotus.domino.Name*.

getSurname	R	O.Ref.

```
strName = nnameName.getSurname()
```
getSurname

Returns the string representation of the surname of the *lotus.domino.Name*.

isHierarchical	R	T/F

```
bolIsHierarchical = nnameName.isHierarchical()
```
IsHierarchical

Indicates whether the name is hierarchical. This method returns true if the name is hierarchical and false if it isn't.

Remarks

The methods of the *lotus.domino.Name* class are commonly used to manipulate how a username is being displayed to the screen or saved to disk within a document so that it is more meaningful. For example, a field that stores a historical audit trail of everyone who has edited a *lotus.domino.Document* might not need to be stored (or later displayed) in canonical format. It might be equally meaningful and more friendly if it were stored in abbreviated or common format. In addition, it might also be necessary to extract the method value (that is, the organizational unit or country) programmatically in order to take some action dependent on the current user's respective component value.

You can also use some of the methods available within *lotus.domino.Session* (▶ 577) to return other versions of *lotus.domino.Name*. For example, you can use getUserNameList to return the primary username of the current Domino user, getUserNameObject to return the alternative username of the current Domino user, getUserName to return the full username of the current user, and getCommonUserName to return the common user name of the current user.

Example

The following code displays most of the components described in this section
for the current username:

```
import lotus.domino.*;

public class JavaAgent extends AgentBase {

    public void NotesMain() {

        try {
            Session ns = getSession();
            Name nname = ns.getUserNameObject();
            if (nname.isHierarchical())
            {
                System.out.println("Canonical name..." +
                ➥nname.getCanonical());
                System.out.println("Abbreviated name..." +
                ➥nname.getAbbreviated());
            }
            System.out.println("Common name..." + nname.getCommon());
            if (nname.getCountry() != null)
                System.out.println("Country..." + nname.getCountry());
            if (nname.getOrganization() != null)
                System.out.println("Organization..." +
                ➥nname.getOrganization());
            if (nname.getOrgUnit1() != null)
                System.out.println("OrgUnit1..." + nname.getOrgUnit1());
            if (nname.getOrgUnit2() != null)
                System.out.println("OrgUnit2..." + nname.getOrgUnit2());
            if (nname.getOrgUnit3() != null)
                System.out.println("OrgUnit3..." + nname.getOrgUnit3());
            if (nname.getOrgUnit4() != null)
                System.out.println("OrgUnit4..." + nname.getOrgUnit4());
            if (nname.getGiven() != null)
                System.out.println("Given..." + nname.getGiven());
            if (nname.getSurname() != null)
                System.out.println("Surname..." + nname.getSurname());
            if (nname.getInitials() != null)
                System.out.println("Initials..." + nname.getInitials());
            if (nname.getGeneration() != null)
                System.out.println("Generation..." + nname.getGeneration());
            if (nname.getADMD() != null)
                System.out.println("ADMD..." + nname.getADMD());
            if (nname.getPRMD() != null)
                System.out.println("PRMD..." + nname.getPRMD());
            if (nname.getKeyword() != null)
                System.out.println("Keyword..." + nname.getKeyword());

        } catch(Exception e) {
            e.printStackTrace();
        }
    }
}
```

The *lotus.domino.Newsletter* class is a document or collection of documents that contains information and/or links to other documents. This method provides a vehicle to route documents to users through *lotus.domino.Documents* or mail documents. The information passed in the newsletter document is typically shared among users in a workgroup or organization about a particular topic or topics. Therefore, this is a valuable workflow or knowledge-management tool. A common usage of this class is to send newsletters to individuals or groups via e-mail as an automated agent, thus pushing valuable information to the respective recipients in an efficient and timely manner with document links to the original documents.

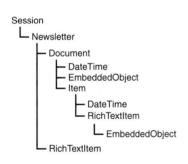

Java Syntax

```
public class Newsletter extends Base
```

Because *lotus.domino* objects can't be created with the "new" modifier, they must be created with methods emanating from the root *lotus.domino.Session* object. Therefore, a new *lotus.domino.Newsletter* object can be created in Java using the createNewsletter method in the *lotus.domino.Session* object, referencing the *lotus.domino.DocumentCollection* that contains the documents to make up the newsletter:

```
nnewsNewsletter = ns.createNewsletter (ndcDocumentCollection)
```

Java Parameters

lotus.domino.DocumentCollection	Required	O.Ref.

A collection of the documents to include in the newsletter.

This parameter returns a handle to the newly created *lotus.domino.Newsletter* object.

Newsletter Methods

formatDocument

formatDocument

```
ndocDocument = nnewsNewsletter.formatDocument(ndbDatabase, intIndex)
```

Database	Required	O.Ref.

The database to create the newsletter document in. If none is specified by setting this parameter to null, the newsletter document will be created in the user's default mail database.

intIndex	Required	%

Indicates the number of documents to display in the newsletter document that are currently contained in the document collection. Because the document collection count begins at 1, setting this value to 1 indicates the first document from the collection, 2 indicates the second document from the collection, and so on.

This method returns a rendering of a *lotus.domino.Document* object in the body field (item) of the document containing the newsletter. The body field must be a rich text field. The *lotus.domino.Document* contained in the newsletter is the *n*th document (specified when calling the method) of the *lotus.domino.DocumentCollection* from within the specified *lotus.domino.Database*.

In order to save the newsletter document containing the rendering of the document presented in the newsletter, the save method of the *lotus.domino.Document* must be called. The new *lotus.domino.Document* is then saved to the *lotus.domino.Database* specified when the method was called.

In order to mail the newsletter document containing the rendering of the document presented in the newsletter, the send method of the *lotus.domino.Document* must be called.

formatMsgWithDoclinks

```
ndocDocument = nnewsNewsletter.formatMsgWithDoclinks(ndbDatabase)
```

ndbDatabase   Required   O.Ref.

The database to create the newsletter document in. If none is specified, the newsletter document will be created in the user's default mail database.

This method returns a *lotus.domino.Document* containing the links to each document in the newsletter's collection. This document also contains the name of the *lotus.domino.Database* and the text of the original query that created the collection.

The body of the *lotus.domino.Document* that is returned by the `formatMsgWithDoclinks` method contains the following:

The filename of the database containing the *lotus.domino.Documents* in the *lotus.domino.Newsletter* collection.

A doclink to each document in the *lotus.domino.Newsletter* collection.

The relevance score of each document if the collection is sorted and the `isDoScore` method is set to `true`.

The title of each document if the `isDoSubject` method is set to `true` and the `setSubjectItemName` method has a value.

The query that created the newsletter collection.

In order to save the newsletter document containing the rendering of the document presented in the newsletter, the `save` method of the *lotus.domino.Document* must be called. The new *lotus.domino.Document* is then saved to the *lotus.domino.Database* specified when the method was called.

In order to mail the newsletter document containing the rendering of the document presented in the newsletter, the `send` method of the *lotus.domino.Document* must be called.

getParent

```
nsSession = nnewsNewsletter.getParent()
```

Indicates the name of the *lotus.domino.Session* that contains the newsletter.

getSubjectItemName

```
strItemName = nnewsNewsletter.getSubjectItemName()
```

Indicates the name of the item contained in a newsletter's document that contains the text to use as the subject line for newsletters that were created using the `formatMsgWithDoclinks` method. Consequently, if the newsletter's documents were created using the `formatDocument` method, this method has no effect. Similarly, if the `doSubject` method is set to `false`, this method has no effect. Therefore, the `doSubject` must be set to `true` before you can use this method.

isDoScore

```
intIsDoScore = nnewsNewsletter.isDoScore()
```

Indicates whether the *lotus.domino.Newsletter* should include each document's relevance score if the *lotus.domino.Newsletter* document is contained in a collection that is sorted and was created using the `formatMsgWithDoclinks` method. `true` indicates that the newsletter includes each document's relevance score. `false` indicates that it does not. If the newsletter's documents were created using the `formatDocument` method, or the document collection containing the newsletter documents is unsorted, this method has no effect. The default value for this method is `true`.

isDoSubject

`intisDoSubject = nnewsNewsletter.isDoSubject()`

Indicates whether the *lotus.domino.Newsletter* should include a string that describes the subject of each document that was created using the `formatMsgWithDoclinks` method. `true` indicates that the newsletter includes a subject for each document. `false` indicates that it does not. If the newsletter's documents were created using the `formatDocument` method, this method has no effect. Similarly, if the `getSubjectItemName` method is set to `false`, this method has no effect. The default value for this method is `false`.

setDoScore

`nnewsNewsletter.setDoScore(bolDoScore)`

bolDoScore   Required   T/F

A Boolean value that indicates whether the newsletter should include the relevance score for each document. Specify `true` (the default) to create a subject line.

This method indicates whether the *lotus.domino.Newsletter* should include each document's relevance score if the *lotus.domino.Newsletter* document was created using the `formatMsgWithDoclinks` method. `true` indicates that the newsletter includes each document's relevance score. `false` indicates that it does not. The default value for this method is `true`.

The *lotus.domino.DocumentCollection* must be sorted in order for the `setDoScore` method to have any effect. As an example of how you would produce a *lotus.domino.DocumentCollection* that is unsorted, you could call the `FTSearch` method of the *lotus.domino.Database*. This method will have no effect if this *lotus.domino.Newsletter* was created using the `formatDocument` method.

setDoSubject   W   T/F

`nnewsNewsletter.setDoSubject(bolDoSubject)`

bolDoSubject   Required   T/F

A Boolean value that indicates whether the newsletter should include a subject line for each document. Specify `true` (the default) to create a subject line.

This method indicates whether the *lotus.domino.Newsletter* should include a string that describes the subject of each document that was created using the `formatMsgWithDoclinks` method. `true` indicates that the newsletter includes a subject for each document. `false` indicates that it does not. The default value for this method is `false`.

When using the `isDoSubject` method, you also need to set the `SubjectItemName` method. This method determines what item should be used as the subject line in the newsletter. If the `setSubjectItemName` isn't specified, `isDoSubject` has no effect. `setSubjectItemName` and `isDoSubject` must be set prior to calling the `formatMsgWithDoclinks` method. This method will have no effect if this *lotus.domino.Newsletter* was created using the `formatDocument` method.

setSubjectItemName

`nnewsNewsletter.setSubjectItemName(strItemName)`

strItemName   Required   O.Ref.

A *java.lang.String* object containing the name you want to use for the item that will contain the subject.

This method indicates the name of the item contained in a newsletter's document that contains the text to use as the subject line for newsletters that were created using the `formatMsgWithDoclinks` method.

When using the `setDoSubject` method (setting it to `true`), you also need to set the `setSubjectItemName` method. If the `isDoSubject` method is set to `false`, the `setSubjectItemName` method has no effect. `SubjectItemName` and `setDoSubject` must be set prior to calling the `formatMsgWithDoclinks` method. In addition, this method will have no effect if this new *lotus.domino.Newsletter* was created using the `formatDocument` method.

Remarks

The *lotus.domino.Newsletter* object is typically used in conjunction with sending e-mail memos regarding a particular topic or topics. This method is similar to forwarding *lotus.domino.Documents* within Notes mail, except that *lotus.domino.Newsletter* is a much more powerful knowledge-management tool in regards to its formatting capabilities and the supplementary information it can send along with the documents. In addition, *lotus.domino.Newsletter* can easily send doclinks back to the original documents from which the newsletter was generated.

Example

The following example reads the `tSearchValue` from the current document to perform a search against the current *lotus.domino.Database*. A full-text search is performed against the keyword specified. The results are contained in a *lotus.domino.DocumentCollection*, which is then e-mailed to a recipient, also read from the current document, as a *lotus.domino.Newsletter*. With some minor modifications, this code could be used to create automatic notifications for specific users based on specific keywords.

```
import lotus.domino.*;

public class JavaAgent extends AgentBase {

  public void NotesMain() {

    try {
      Session ns = getSession();
      AgentContext agentContext = ns.getAgentContext();
      Database ndb = agentContext.getCurrentDatabase();
      Document ndoc = agentContext.getDocumentContext();
      String strItemname = ndoc.getItemValueString("tSearchValue");
      String strRecipient=ndoc.getItemValueString("tRecipient");
      System.out.println("Starting agent");
      ndb.updateFTIndex(true);
      DocumentCollection ndc = ndb.FTSearch(strItemname.toString(), 100,
      ➥Database.FT_DATE_ASC, 0);
      if (ndc.getCount() > 0) {
        System.out.println("Collection found, working...");
```

continued >>

continued >>

```
Newsletter nnews = ns.createNewsletter(ndc);
nnews.setDoScore(true);
nnews.setDoSubject(true);
nnews.setSubjectItemName("ChapterTitle");
Document ndocNews = nnews.formatMsgWithDoclinks(ndb);
ndoc.appendItemValue("Form", "Memo");
ndoc.appendItemValue("Subject", "Newsletter Notification");
ndoc.send(false, strRecipient);
System.out.println("Agent complete");  }
else
System.out.println("No collection of documents found.");

} catch(Exception e) {
e.printStackTrace();
}
}
}
```

The *NotesFactory* class provides your applications the ability to access the *lotus.domino.Session* object, which is the highest object in the Notes back-end object hierarchy.

```
NotesFactory
  └ Session
      ├ AgentContext
      │    └ ...
      ├ Database
      │    └ ...
      ├ DataRange
      │    └ DateTime
      ├ DataTime
      ├ DbDirectory
      │    └ Database
      │         └ ...
      ├ International
      ├ Log
      ├ Name
      ├ Newsletter
      │    └ Document
      │         └ ...
      ├ Registration
      │    └ DateTime
      ├ RichTextParagraphStyle
      │    └ RichTextTab
      └ RichTextStyle
```

Java Syntax

```
public class NotesFactory extends Object
```

NotesFactory Methods

createSession

```
Session createSession()

Session createSession(strIOR)

Session = NotesFactory.createSession(strIOR, appApplet, strUser,
➥strPassword)

Session createSession(appApplet, strUser, strPassword)

Session createSession(strIOR, appApplet, strUser, strPassword)
```

| strIOR | Required | O.Ref. |

A *java.lang.String* object containing the initial object reference.

| appApplet | Required | O.Ref. |

An object of type *java.applet.*

| strUser | Required | O.Ref. |

A *java.lang.String* object containing a valid user name found in the public Name and Address Book.

| strPassword | Required | O.Ref. |

A *java.lang.String* object containing a valid password for the specified user and found in the public Name and Address Book.

This method returns an object of type *lotus.domino.Session* that can be used to access the other objects in the Notes back-end object hierarchy. If your application is making local calls, you can call this method with no parameters. If you're making remote calls, you must specify the IOR, which is a string found in ior.txt in the Notes directory of the Domino server. If the user and password parameters are specified, they must be valid entries in the public Name and Address Book, or anonymous access must be granted for the server.

getIOR

```
IOR = NotesFactory.getIOR(strHostname)
```

| strHostname | Required | O.Ref. |

A *java.lang.String* object containing the name of the server whose IOR you want to retrieve.

You can call this method to retrieve the IOR for the named server.

Example

```
import lotus.domino.*;
public class testing
{
    public static void main(String argv[])
    {
        try
        {
            NotesThread.sinitThread();
            Session s = NotesFactory.createSession();
            String strPlatform = s.getPlatform();
            String strVersion = s.getNotesVersion();
            System.out.println("System is:" + strVersion +" on " +
            ➥strPlatform);
        }
        catch(NotesException e)
        {
            e.printStackTrace();
        }
        finally
        {
            NotesThread.stermThread();
        }
    }
}
```

The *lotus.domino.Outline* class is new in Notes 5.0. It allows you to manipulate *lotus.domino.Outline* and *lotus.domino.OutlineEntry* (▶ 509) objects. The best way to think of an outline is like a map of your application. Each entry in the map represents one of the elements of your application and provides a convenient way to navigate around the application. Once you have created an outline, you can embed it on a page or form, and users can click an entry to open that element.

...

Database
  Outline
    OutlineEntry

Java Syntax

```
public class Log extends Base
```

To access a *lotus.domino.Outline* object, you can use the getOutline method of *lotus.domino.Database* (▶ 385):

```
noutoutline = ndbDatabase.getOutline(strName)
```

Java Parameters

strName	Required	$

A string object containing the name of the outline you want to access.

Outline Methods

addEntry

addEntry

```
noutoutline.addEntry(nouteNewEntry, nouteAfterEntry)
```

```
noutoutline.addEntry(nouteNewEntry, nouteAfterEntry, bolAfter)
```

```
noutoutline.addEntry(nouteNewEntry, nouteAfterEntry, bolAfter, bolAsChild)
```

nouteNewEntry	Required	O.Ref.

A *lotus.domino.OutlineEntry* object representing the entry you want to add to the outline.

nouteAfterEntry	Required	O.Ref.

A *lotus.domino.OutlineEntry* object after which you want to add the new entry.

bolAfter	Required	T/F

Specify true to insert the entry after the entry specified in nouteAfterEntry, or false to insert it before.

bolAsChild	Required	T/F

Specify true to make the new entry a child of the entry specified in nouteAfterEntry. Specify this parameter only if bolAfter is true.

This method allows you to programmatically insert a new *lotus.domino.OutlineEntry* object into an existing outline and dictate the position in which to place the new entry.

createEntry

createEntry

```
nouteEntry = noutoutline.createEntry(strName)
```

strName	Required	O.Ref.

A *java.lang.String* object containing the name you want to give the new entry.

This method creates a free-floating entry. Use the addEntry method to position the new entry in the outline.

getAlias   R   O.Ref.

getAlias

```
strAlias = noutoutline.getAlias()
```

This method returns a *java.lang.String* object containing any aliases that an outline might have.

---

getComment   R   O.Ref.

```
strComment = noutoutline.getComment()
```

If the developer entered a comment for an outline, it can be accessed through this
method as a *java.lang.String* object.

getFirst

```
nouteEntry = noutoutline.getFirst()
```

This method returns the first *lotus.domino.OutlineEntry* object in the current
lotus.domino.Outline object.

getLast

```
nouteEntry = noutoutline.getLast()
```

This method returns the last *lotus.domino.OutlineEntry* object in the current
lotus.domino.Outline object.

getName   R   O.Ref.

```
strName = noutoutline.getName()
```

This method returns the name of the outline as a *java.lang.String* object.

getNext

```
nouteEntry = noutoutline.getNext(nouteEntry)
```

nouteEntry   Required   O.Ref.
A *lotus.domino.OutlineEntry* object representing the current entry.

This method takes the current *lotus.domino.OutlineEntry* as a parameter and attempts to
navigate to the next *lotus.domino.OutlineEntry* in the outline. If this method is executed
against the last entry in the outline, it will return `null`.

getNextSibling

```
nouteEntry = noutoutline.getNextSibling(nouteEntry)
```

nouteEntry   Required   O.Ref.
A *lotus.domino.OutlineEntry* object representing the current entry.

This method takes the current *lotus.domino.OutlineEntry* as a parameter and attempts to
navigate to the next *lotus.domino.OutlineEntry* at the same level in the outline. If this
method can't find a sibling for the current entry, it will return `null`.

getParent

```
nouteEntry = noutoutline.getParent(nouteEntry)
```

nouteEntry   Required   O.Ref.
A *lotus.domino.OutlineEntry* object representing the current entry.

This method takes the current *lotus.domino.OutlineEntry* as a parameter and attempts to
navigate the current entry's parent. If this method can't find a parent for the current
entry (it is at level `0`), it will return `null`.

getPrev

```
nouteEntry = noutoutline.getPrev(nouteEntry)
```

nouteEntry   Required   O.Ref.
A *lotus.domino.OutlineEntry* object representing the current entry.

This method takes the current *lotus.domino.OutlineEntry* as a parameter and attempts to navigate to the previous *lotus.domino.OutlineEntry* in the outline. If this method is executed against the first entry in the outline, it will return `null`.

getPrevSibling

`nouteEntry = noutoutline.`**`getPrevSibling`**`(nouteEntry)`

nouteEntry	Required	O.Ref.

A *lotus.domino.OutlineEntry* object representing the current entry.

This method takes the current *lotus.domino.OutlineEntry* as a parameter and attempts to navigate to the previous sibling entry in the outline. If this method can't find a sibling entry in the outline (an entry at the same level), it will return `null`.

moveEntry

`noutoutline.`**`moveEntry`**`(nouteEntrytoMove, nouteRefEntry)`

`noutoutline.`**`moveEntry`**`(nouteEntrytoMove, nouteRefEntry, bolAfter)`

`noutoutline.`**`moveEntry`**`(nouteEntrytoMove, nouteRefEntry, bolAfter, bolAsChild)`

nouteEntrytoMove	Required	O.Ref.

A *lotus.domino.OutlineEntry* object representing the entry to move.

nouteRefEntry	Required	O.Ref.

The *lotus.domino.OutlineEntry* object to which you want to move the entry.

bolAfter	Required	T/F

Specify `true` to insert the entry after the entry specified in `nouteRefEntry`, or `false` to insert it before.

bolAsChild	Required	T/F

Specify `true` to make the new entry a child of the entry specified in `nouteRefEntry`. Specify a parameter only if `bolAfter` is `true`.

This method allows you to move a *lotus.domino.OutlineEntry* object within an outline.

removeEntry

`noutoutline.`**`removeEntry`**`(nouteEntry)`

nouteEntry	Required	O.Ref.

A *lotus.domino.OutlineEntry* object representing the entry to remove.

This method removes the specified *lotus.domino.OutlineEntry* from the current outline.

save

`noutoutlineEntry.`**`save`**`()`

You must call this method to save any changes you have programmatically made to the current *lotus.domino.Outline* object.

setAlias

`noutoutlineEntry.`**`setAlias`**`(strAliases)`

strAliases	R	O.Ref.

This parameter expects a *java.lang.String* value containing the list of aliases.

This method allows you to create aliases for a *lotus.domino.OutlineEntry*.

setComment

`OutlineEntry.`**`setComment`**`(strComment)`

strComment   R   O.Ref.

This parameter expects a *java.lang.String* object containing the comments you'd like to add to an outline entry.

Example

```
import lotus.domino.*;
import java.util.Date;
public class JavaAgent extends AgentBase {
  public void NotesMain() {
    try {
    Session nssession = getSession();
    AgentContext nac = nssession.getAgentContext();
    Database ndbCurr=nac.getCurrentDatabase();
    Outline noutCurr=ndbCurr.getOutline("MailOutline");
    OutlineEntry nouteCurr=noutCurr.getFirst();
    while (outeCurr !=null)
      {
        if (outeCurr.getAlias()=="Testing")
          {
            OutlineEntry nouteNew=noutCurr.createEntry("Testing Child");
            outCurr.addEntry(nouteNew, nouteCurr,true, true);
            outeNew.setAlias("Testing Child");
            outeNew.setComment("Last modified by " +
            ➥nssession.getUserName());
            outCurr.save();
          }
        nouteCurr=nouteCurr.getNext(nouteCurr);
    } catch(Exception e) {
    e.printStackTrace();
    }
  }
}
```

5.0 OutlineEntry

The *lotus.domino.OutlineEntry* class is new in Notes 5.0. It lets you access and manipulate specific entries, such as a page or a frameset in a *lotus.domino.Outline* object (which is also new to Notes 5.0).

```
...
  └ Database
     └ Outline
        └ OutlineEntry
```

Java Syntax

You can use any of the various get methods of the *lotus.domino.Outline* class, a couple of which are shown here:

```
nouteOutlineEntry = nouteoutline.getFirst()

nouteOutlineEntry = nouteoutline.getNext()
```

OutlineEntry Methods

getAlias	R	O.Ref.

getAlias

```
strAlias = nouteoutlineEntry.getAlias()
```

This method returns the alias of the *lotus.domino.OutlineEntry* object, if it has one.

getDatabase	R	O.Ref.

getDatabase

```
ndbParent = nouteoutlineEntry.getDatabase()
```

This method returns the parent database of the *lotus.domino.OutlineEntry* object.

getDocument	R	O.Ref.

getDocument

```
ndocParent = nouteoutlineEntry.getDocument()
```

This method returns the document linked to by the *lotus.domino.OutlineEntry* object, if it has one.

getEntryClass	R	%

getEntryClass

```
intClass = nouteoutlineEntry.getEntryClass()
```

This method returns an integer representing the class of entry. The classes of entries are as follows: OutlineEntry.OUTLINE_CLASS_DATABASE, OutlineEntry.OUTLINE_CLASS_DOCUMENT, OutlineEntry.OUTLINE_CLASS_FORM, OutlineEntry.OUTLINE_CLASS_FOLDER, OutlineEntry.OUTLINE_CLASS_FRAMESET, OutlineEntry.OUTLINE_CLASS_NAVIGATOR, OutlineEntry.OUTLINE_CLASS_PAGE, OutlineEntry.OUTLINE_CLASS_UNKNOWN, OutlineEntry.OUTLINE_CLASS_VIEW.

getFormula	R	O.Ref.

getFormula

```
strFormula = nouteoutlineEntry.getFormula()
```

This method returns a *java.lang.String* object containing the formula, if the entry has one.

getFrameText	R	O.Ref.

getFrameText

```
strFrameText = nouteoutlineEntry.getFrameText()
```

Returns a *java.lang.String* object containing the text entered for the frame value of a *lotus.domino.OutlineEntry* object.

getImagesText	R	O.Ref.

getImagesText

```
strImageText = nouteoutlineEntry.getImagesText()
```

This method returns a string object containing the filename of the image file used to add an icon.

getLabel   R   O.Ref.

```
strLabel = nouteoutlineEntry.getLabel()
```
getLabel

This method returns a string object containing the text on the label of a
lotus.domino.OutlineEntry object.

getLevel   R   %

```
intLevel = nouteoutlineEntry.getLevel()
```
getLevel

This method returns an integer containing the level at which the entry exists in the
lotus.domino.OutlineEntry object.

getNamedElement   R   O.Ref.

```
strElement = nouteoutlineEntry.getNamedElement()
```
getNamed
Element

This method returns a *java.lang.String* object containing the named element referenced
by the entry.

getType   R   %

```
intType = nouteoutlineEntry.getType()
```
getType

This method returns an integer representing the entry's type: OutlineEntry.
OUTLINE_OTHER_FOLDERS_TYPE, OutlineEntry.OUTLINE_OTHER_UNKNOWN_TYPE,
OutlineEntry.OUTLINE_OTHER_VIEWS_TYPE, OutlineEntry.OUTLINE_TYPE_ACTION,
OutlineEntry.OUTLINE_TYPE_NAMEDELEMENT, OutlineEntry.OUTLINE_TYPE_NOTELINK,
OutlineEntry.OUTLINE_TYPE_URL.

getURL   R   O.Ref.

```
strURL = nouteoutlineEntry.getURL()
```
getURL

This method returns a *java.lang.String* object containing the URL of the entry, if
applicable.

getView   R   O.Ref.

```
strView = nouteoutlineEntry.getView()
```
getView

This method returns a *lotus.domino.View* object that the entry references.

hasChildren   R   T/F

```
bolhaschild = nouteoutlineEntry.hasChildren()
```
hasChildren

Returns true if the current entry has children and false if it doesn't.

isHidden   R   T/F

```
bolHidden = nouteoutlineEntry.isHidden()
```
isHidden

Returns true if the current entry is hidden. Returns false if the current entry is visible.

isInThisDb   R   T/F

```
bolThisDb = nouteoutlineEntry.isInThisDb()
```
IsInThisDb

Returns true if the entry is in the current database, and false if the current entry is
not in the current database.

isPrivate   R   T/F

```
bolprivate = nouteoutlineEntry.isPrivate()
```
isPrivate

Returns true if the current entry is private or false if the current entry is not private.

setAction

`bolsuccess = nouteoutlineEntry.`**`setAction`**`(strAction)`

strAction	R	O.Ref.

A *java.lang.String* object containing a formula for an action outline.

This method allows you to set an action. It returns a Boolean that indicates whether the method completed successfully.

setAlias

`nouteoutlineEntry.`**`setAlias`**`(strAlias)`

strAlias	R	O.Ref.

A *java.lang.String* object containing the aliases you want to assign to this entry.

This method accepts a *java.lang.String* object containing the aliases you want to set for a given entry.

setFrameText

`nouteoutlineEntry.`**`setFrameText`**`(strFrameText)`

strFrameText	R	O.Ref.

A *java.lang.String* object containing the text you want to assign to this entry's frame.

This method accepts a *java.lang.String* object containing the text to assign to the entry's frame.

setHidden

`nouteoutlineEntry.`**`setHidden`**`(bolHidden)`

bolHidden	R	T/F

A Boolean indicating whether the entry should be hidden or not.

This method accepts a Boolean used to determine whether the entry should be hidden. Set to `true` to hide the entry or `false` to show it.

setImagesText

`nouteoutlineEntry.`**`setImagesText`**`(strImageText)`

strImageText	R	O.Ref.

A *java.lang.String* object containing the text you want to assign to this entry's image.

This method accepts a *java.lang.String* object containing the text to assign to the entry's image.

setLabel

`nouteoutlineEntry.`**`setLabel`**`(strLabel)`

strLabel	R	O.Ref.

A *java.lang.String* object containing the text to display as a label.

This method accepts a *java.lang.String* object containing the text you'd like to use for the entry's label.

setNamedElement

`bolflag = nouteoutlineEntry.`**`setNamedElement`**`(ndbDatabase, strString,`
`➥intClass)`

ndbDatabase	R	O.Ref.

A *lotus.domino.Database* object containing the named element.

strString	R	O.Ref.

A *java.lang.String* object containing the name of a database element.

intClass	R	%

An integer containing the class of the named element.

This method allows you to set a named element. It returns a Boolean that indicates whether the method completed successfully.

---

setNoteLink

```
nouteoutlineEntry.setNoteLink(ndbDatabase)
```

```
nouteoutlineEntry.setNoteLink(ndocDocument)
```

```
nouteoutlineEntry.setNoteLink(nvwView)
```

setNoteLink

ndbDatabase	R	O.Ref.

The database object you want to link to.

ndocDocument	R	O.Ref.

The document object you want to link to.

nvwView	R	O.Ref.

The view object you want to link to.

This method sets the outline entry type to OUTLINE_TYPE_NOTELINK and the entry class to OUTLINE_CLASS_DATABASE, OUTLINE_CLASS_DOCUMENT, or OUTLINE_CLASS_VIEW, depending on how this method was called.

---

setURL

```
nouteoutlineEntry.setURL(strURL)
```

setURL

strURL	R	O.Ref.

A *java.lang.String* object containing the text you want to assign to this entry's URL.

This method accepts a *java.lang.String* object containing the text to assign to the entry's URL.

Example

```java
import lotus.domino.*;
public class JavaAgent extends AgentBase {
  public void NotesMain() {
    try {
      Session nsSession = getSession();
      AgentContext nacContext = nsSession.getAgentContext();
      Database ndbCurr = nacContext.getCurrentDatabase();
      Outline noutoutline = ndbCurr.getOutline("MainOutline");
      System.out.println("Outline Name: " + noutoutline.getName());
      System.out.println("Outline Alias: " + noutoutline.getAlias());
      System.out.println("Outline Comment: " + noutoutline.getComment());
      OutlineEntry nouteCurrent = noutoutline.getFirst();
```
continued >>

continued >>

```
String strClass = null;
String strType = null;
while (nouteCurrent != null)
  {
  System.out.println("\tEntry Label: " +nouteCurrent.getLabel());
  if (nouteCurrent.getAlias().length() > 0)
  {
    System.out.println("\tEntry Alias: " +
    ➥nouteCurrent.getAlias());
    }

  switch (nouteCurrent.getType())
    {
    case OutlineEntry.OUTLINE_OTHER_FOLDERS_TYPE:
      strType = "Other folders";
       break;
    case OutlineEntry.OUTLINE_OTHER_VIEWS_TYPE:
      strType= "Other views";
      break;
    case OutlineEntry.OUTLINE_OTHER_UNKNOWN_TYPE:
      strType = "Other unknown";
      break;
    case OutlineEntry.OUTLINE_TYPE_ACTION:
      strType = "Action";
      break;
    case OutlineEntry.OUTLINE_TYPE_NAMEDELEMENT:
      strType = "Named element";
      break;
    case OutlineEntry.OUTLINE_TYPE_NOTELINK:
      strType = "Note link";
      break;
    case OutlineEntry.OUTLINE_TYPE_URL:
      strType = "URL";
      break;
    }
  System.out.println("\tEntry Type: " + strType);

  switch (nouteCurrent.getEntryClass())
    {
    case OutlineEntry.OUTLINE_CLASS_DATABASE:
      strClass = "Database";
       break;
    case OutlineEntry.OUTLINE_CLASS_DOCUMENT:
      strClass = "Document";
      break;
    case OutlineEntry.OUTLINE_CLASS_FORM:
      strClass = "Form";
      break;
    case OutlineEntry.OUTLINE_CLASS_FOLDER:
      strClass = "Folder";
      break;
    case OutlineEntry.OUTLINE_CLASS_FRAMESET:
      strClass = "Frame set";
      break;
    case OutlineEntry.OUTLINE_CLASS_NAVIGATOR:
      strClass = "Navigator";
      break;
    case OutlineEntry.OUTLINE_CLASS_PAGE:
      strClass = "Page";
```

```
              break;
          case OutlineEntry.OUTLINE_CLASS_UNKNOWN:
            strClass = "Unknown";
             break;
          case OutlineEntry.OUTLINE_CLASS_VIEW:
            strClass = "View";
            break;
        }
      System.out.println("\tEntry class: " + strClass);
      System.out.println("\tEntry Level: " + nouteCurrent.getLevel());
      if (nouteCurrent.isInThisDB())
        System.out.println("\tEntry is an element in this database.");
      else
        System.out.println ("\tEntry is not an element in this
        ➥database.");
      if (nouteCurrent.isPrivate())
        System.out.println("\tEntry is private.");
      else
        System.out.println("\tEntry is public.");
      if (nouteCurrent.getFrameText().length() > 0)
        System.out.println("\tEntry Frame text: " +
        ➥nouteCurrent.getFrameText());
      if (nouteCurrent.getImagesText().length() > 0)
        System.out.println("\tEntry Image text: " +
        ➥nouteCurrent.getImagesText());
      nouteCurrent = noutoutline.getNext(nouteCurrent);
        }

    } catch(Exception e) {
      e.printStackTrace();
    }
  }
}
}
```

Registration

The *lotus.domino.Registration* class allows for the programmatic creation or administration of ID files. ID files contain information regarding the user's name, Notes license type, password, mail, registration, encryption keys, certificates, and so on. ID files are the basic building blocks that define the robust, distributed security model of Domino/Lotus Notes.

Session
　└ Registration
　　　└ DateTime

continued >>

Java Syntax

Use the create**Registration** method of the *lotus.domino.Session* object to establish a handle to a *lotus.domino.Registration* object.

Registration Methods

addCertifierToAddressBook

```
bolAddCertifier = nregRegistration.addCertifierToAddressBook
➥(strIdfile)
```
addCertifierTo
AddressBook

```
bolAddCertifier = nregRegistration.addCertifierToAddressBook(strIdfile,
➥strCertpassword, strLocation, strComment)
```

strIdfile	Required	O.Ref.

The certifier ID file to be added to the Name and Address Book (now called the Directory).

strCertpassword	Required	O.Ref.

The password for the certifier file.

strLocation	Required	O.Ref.

The value stored for the location item in the Name and Address Book (Directory) document.

strComment	Required	O.Ref.

The value stored for the comment item in the Name and Address Book (Directory) document.

This method adds the specified certifier ID file to the Directory. `true` is returned if the method was successful. `false` is returned if it was not. As when accessing the `getCertifierIdFile` method, specify the complete file path, beginning at the drive specification.

addServerToAddressBook

```
bolAddServer = nregRegistration.addServerToAddressBook(strIdfile,
➥strServer, strDomain)
```
addServerTo
AddressBook

```
bolAddServer = nregRegistration.addServerToAddressBook(strIdfile,
➥strServer, strDomain, strUserpassword, strNetwork, strAdminname,
➥strTitle, strLocation, strComment)
```

strIdfile	Required	O.Ref.

The ID file of the server to be added to the Name and Address Book (Directory). Specify the entire file path, including the drive.

strServer	Required	O.Ref.

The name of the server to be added to the Name and Address Book (Directory).

strDomain	Required	O.Ref.

The domain of the server being added to the Name and Address Book (Directory).

strUserpassword	Required	O.Ref.

The user's password for the ID file.

strNetwork	Required	O.Ref.

The name of the Notes Names Network (NNN) for the server.

strAdminname	Required	O.Ref.

The full name of the server administrator.

strTitle	Required	O.Ref.

The value stored in the title item in the Name and Address Book (Directory) document.

strLocation	Required	O.Ref.

The value stored in the location item in the Name and Address Book (Directory) document.

strComment	Required	O.Ref.

The value stored in the comment item in the Name and Address Book (Directory) document.

This method adds the specified server to the Directory. `true` is returned if the method was successful. `false` is returned if it was not. When calling this method, note that the `setstoreIDInAddressbook` method can affect how this method executes.

addUserProfile

addUserProfile

`nregRegistration.`**`addUserProfile`**`(strUsername, strProfilename)`

strUsername	Required	O.Ref.

The string representation of the username of the person whose person document will be modified to store the name of the setup profile.

strProfilename	Required	O.Ref.

The name of the setup profile to be stored in the person document.

The `setregistrationServer` method must be set prior to calling this method, or an error will be returned.

addUserToAddressBook

addUserTo
AddressBook

`bolAddUser = nregRegistration.`**`addUserToAddressBook`**`(strIdfile,`
`➥strFullname, strLastname)`

`bolAddUser = nregRegistration.`**`addUserToAddressBook`**`(strIdfile,`
`➥strFullname, strLastname, strUserpassword, strFirstname, strMiddleinit,`
`➥strMailserver, strMailidpath, strFwdaddress, strLocation, strComment)`

strIdfile	Required	O.Ref.

The ID file of the user to add to the Name and Address Book (Directory). Specify the entire file path, including the drive.

strFullname	Required	O.Ref.

The user's full name.

strLastname	Required	O.Ref.

The user's last name.

strUserpassword	Required	O.Ref.

The password associated with the specified ID file.

strFirstname	Required	O.Ref.

The user's first name.

strMiddleinit	Required	O.Ref.

The user's middle initial.

strMailserver	Required	O.Ref.

The full name of the mail server for the current user.

strMailidpath	Required	O.Ref.

The full file path for the specified ID file. Specify the entire file path, including the drive.

strFwdaddress	Required	O.Ref.

The user's forwarding address.

strLocation	Required	O.Ref.

The value stored in the location item in the Name and Address Book (Directory) document.

strComment	Required	O.Ref.

The value stored in the comment item in the Name and Address Book (Directory) document.

This method adds a user to the Directory. `true` is returned if the method was successful. `false` indicates that it was not.

crossCertify

```
bolCrosscertify = nregRegistration.crossCertify(strIdfile)

bolCrosscertify = nregRegistration.crossCertify(strIdfile,
➥strCertpassword, strComment)
```
crossCertify

strIdfile	Required	O.Ref.

The ID file of the user to be cross-certified. Specify the entire file path, including the drive.

strCertpassword	Required	O.Ref.

The password for the certifier ID file.

strComment	Required	O.Ref.

The value stored in the comment item in the Name and Address Book (Directory) document.

This method cross-certifies a Notes ID file. Despite the fact that the *lotus.domino.Registration* class is a back-end class, the `crossCertify` method is available only when it is run from within the user interface in a front end. Even though the certifier password is passed as a parameter when this method is run, the user ID password must be entered during the cross-certification process as well. In addition, if the full file path is not properly entered, this method will return an error message telling you that the path was not supplied.

When calling this method, note that the `expiration` method can be used to set the ID file's expiration date.

deleteIDOnServer

nregRegistration.**deleteIDOnServer**(strUsername, bolIsserverid)

| strUsername | Required | O.Ref. |

The username for the current ID file.

| bolIsserverid | Required | T/F |

Indicates whether the name is a server ID. true indicates that the name represents a server, and false indicates that the name represents a person.

This method permanently deletes an ID file from the server.

Note that the setregistrationServer method must be set prior to calling this method. Otherwise, you will receive the Required registration argument not provided error message.

getCertifierIdFile   R   O.Ref.

strCertIFFile = nregRegistration.**getCertifierIdFile**()

This method returns the file path location of the certifier ID file. You use the certifier ID file (Cert.ID) when creating user IDs and cross-certifying with other Domino servers. When setting this method, be sure to use the complete file path to the certifier ID, starting with the drive—such as C:\notes\data\cert.id.

getCreateMailDb   R   T/F

bolCreateMailDb = nregRegistration.**getCreateMailDb**()

This method indicates whether a new mail database should be created immediately when generating new Notes ID files using the registerNewUser method (also a method of the *lotus.domino.Registration* class) or whether the mail file should be created when the user completes the setup process. true immediately creates a new mail database. false creates the ID file without also creating a new mail database. When false is specified, the mail database will be created when the specific user completes the setup process.

getExpiration   R   lotus.domino.DateTime

ndtNotesDateTime = nregRegistration.**getExpiration**()

This method returns the expiration date to use when ID files are being created. This is typically set to only two years, which is often too short a time period to be practical. Consider extending this value to avoid having to frequently administer the expiration of the ID files.

getIDFromServer

nregRegistration.**getIDFromServer**(strUsername, strFilepath, bolIsserverid)

| strUsername | Required | O.Ref. |

The username for the current ID file.

| strFilepath | Required | O.Ref. |

The full file path for the specified ID file. Specify the entire file path, including the drive.

| bolIsserverid | Required | T/F |

Indicates whether the name is a server ID. true indicates that the name represents a server. false indicates that this name represents a person.

This method gets an ID file from the server.

When calling this method, note that the `setregistrationServer` method must be set prior to calling this method. Otherwise, you will receive the `Required registration argument not provided` error message.

---

getIDType   R   %

```
intIDType = nregRegistration.getIDType()
```
getIDType

This method returns or sets the type of ID file to create when registering a new user, server, or certifier. This method is used when calling the `registerNewUser`, `registerNewServer`, or `registerNewCertifier` methods. The value returned or used to set this method is a constant of type Integer. The allowed values are listed in the following table.

IDType Values

Values	Description
Registration.ID_FLAT	The ID created is flat.
Registration.ID_HIERARCHICAL	The ID created is hierarchical.
Registration.ID_CERTIFIER	The ID created uses the certifier ID to determine whether it is flat or hierarchical.

---

getMinPasswordLength   R   %

```
intMinlength = nregRegistration.getMinPasswordLength()
```
getMinPassword Length

This method returns the minimum number of characters required when creating an ID file. This method is relevant when calling the `registerNewUser`, `registerNewServer`, or `registerNewCertifier` methods.

---

getOrgUnit   R   O.Ref.

```
strOrgUnit = nregRegistration.getOrgUnit()
```
getOrgUnit

This method returns the organizational unit to use when creating ID files. The organizational unit is a string representation of the organizational unit (OU), as used when calling the `registerNewUser` method. A maximum of four OUs can be used in an organization.

---

getRegistrationLog   R   O.Ref.

```
strRegLog = nregRegistration.getRegistrationLog()
```
getRegistration Log

This method returns the name of the log file (such as reg.nsf) to use when creating IDs. Domino automatically determines this value by reading the `Log=` parameter located in the Notes .ini file. Therefore, be sure to consider setting the Notes .ini file when modifying this method.

---

getRegistrationServer   R   O.Ref.

```
strRegServer = nregRegistration.getRegistrationServer()
```
getRegistration Server

This method returns the name of the Domino server to use when creating ID files. This method is used only when the ID file is being stored in the server's Name and Address Book (Directory) or when mail database is being created for the new user.

---

getStoreIDInAddressBook   R   T/F

```
bolStoreID = nregRegistration.getStoreIDInAddressBook()
```
getStoreIDIn AddressBook

This method indicates whether the ID file being created should be stored in the Name and Address Book (Directory) in the server. `true` indicates that the ID should be stored in the Name and Address Book. `false` indicates that it should not.

---

getUpdateAddressBook   R   T/F

`bolUpdateAddBook = nregRegistration.getUpdateAddressBook()`

This method indicates whether the ID file being created should update the server entry in the Name and Address Book (Directory) in the server. This method is relevant when the `registerNewUser`, `registerNewServer`, or `registerNewCertifier` methods are called. `true` indicates that the Name and Address Book (Directory) should be updated. `false` indicates that it should not.

---

getUserInfo

`nregRegistration.getUserInfo(strUsername, strmailserver, strmailfile,`
`➥strmaildomain, strmailsystem, strprofile)`

strUsername	Required	O.Ref.

The username for the current ID file.

strmailserver	Required	O.Ref.

Returns the mail server name for this user.

strmailfile	Required	O.Ref.

Returns the mail file for this user.

strmaildomain	Required	O.Ref.

Returns the mail domain for this user.

strmailsystem	Required	O.Ref.

Returns the mail system for this user.

strprofile	Required	O.Ref.

Returns the profile document for this user.

This method returns information about the specified user from the server. Any parameters used require the string ($) designation.

Note that the `setregistrationServer` method must be set prior to calling this method. Otherwise, you will receive the `Required registration argument not provided` error message.

---

isNorthAmerican   R   T/F

`bolIsNorthAmer = nregRegistration.isNorthAmerican()`

This method indicates whether the ID file is North American or International. If it's true, the ID is North American. `false` indicates that the ID file is International. (This is the only other option if the ID file is not North American.)

---

recertify

`bolRecertify = nregRegistration.recertify(strIdfile)`

`bolRecertify = nregRegistration.recertify(strIdfile, strCertpassword,`
`➥strComment)`

strIdfile	Required	O.Ref.

The ID file of the user to be recertified. Specify the entire file path, including the drive.

strCertpassword	Required	O.Ref.

The password for the certifier ID file.

strComment	Required	O.Ref.

The value stored in the comment item in the Name and Address Book (Directory) document.

This method recertifies a Notes ID file and returns **true** if the method is successful and **false** if it is not. Despite the fact that *lotus.domino.Registration* is a back-end class, the recertify method is available only when being run from within the user interface in a front end. Even though the certifier password is passed as a parameter when this method is run, the user's ID password must be entered during the cross-certification process as well. In addition, if the full file path is not entered properly, this method will return an error message stating that the path was not supplied.

When calling this method, note that the **getexpiration** method can be used to set the ID file's expiration date.

registerNewCertifier

```
bolRegsiternewcert = nregRegistration.registerNewCertifier
➥(strOrganization, strIdfile, strUserpassword)

bolRegsiternewcert = nregRegistration.registerNewCertifier
➥(strOrganization, strIdfile, strCertpassword, strCountry,
➥strUserpassword)
```

registerNew
Certifier

strOrganization	Required	O.Ref.

The organization that the new certifier ID belongs to.

strIdfile	Required	O.Ref.

The ID file to be registered. Specify the entire file path, including the drive.

strUserpassword	Required	O.Ref.

The password for the user ID file.

strCertpassword	Required	O.Ref.

The password for the certifier ID file.

strCountry	Optional	O.Ref.

The country code for the certifier.

This method registers a new Notes certifier ID file and returns **true** if the method is successful, and **false** if it is not. Before this method can be called, all the required methods must be set. The required methods (as well as the optional ones) are described in the "Remarks" section near the end of this chapter (▶ 529).

registerNewServer

```
bolRegisternewserver = nregRegistration.registerNewServer(strServer,
➥strIdfile, strDomain, strServerpassword)

bolRegisternewserver = nregRegistration.registerNewServer(strServer,
➥strIdfile, strDomain, strServerpassword, strCertpassword, strLocation,
➥strComment, strNetwork, strAdminname, strTitle)
```

registerNew
Server

strServer	Required	O.Ref.

The name of the server that the server ID belongs to.

strIdfile	Required	O.Ref.

The ID file to be registered. Specify the entire file path, including the drive.

strDomain	Required	O.Ref.

The server's domain.

strServerpassword	Required	O.Ref.

The server's password for the ID file.

strCertpassword	Required	O.Ref.

The password for the certifier ID file.

strLocation	Required	O.Ref.

The value stored in the location item in the Name and Address Book (Directory) document.

strComment	Required	O.Ref.

The value stored in the comment item in the Name and Address Book (Directory) document.

strNetwork	Required	O.Ref.

The name of the Notes Names Network (NNN) for the server.

strAdminname	Required	O.Ref.

The full name of the server administrator.

strTitle	Required	O.Ref.

The value stored in the title item in the Name and Address Book (Directory) document.

This method registers a new server ID file and returns `true` if the method is successful and `false` if it is not. When calling this method, note that the `setcertifierIdFile` method must be set prior to calling this method. Otherwise, you will receive the `Certifier ID path not supplied` error message.

Before this method can be called, all the required methods must be set. The required methods (as well as the optional ones) are described in the "Remarks" section (▶ 529) near the end of this chapter.

---

registerNewUser

registerNewUser

```
bolRegisternewuser = nregRegistration.registerNewUser(strLastname,
strIdfile, strServer)

bolRegisternewuser = nregRegistration.registerNewUser(strLastname,
➡strIdfile, strServer, strFirstname, strMiddleinit, strCertpassword,
➡strLocation, strComment, strMaildbpath, strFwddomain, strUserpassword)
```

strLastname	Required	O.Ref.

The last name of the user being registered.

strIdfile	Required	O.Ref.

The ID file to be registered. Specify the entire file path, including the drive.

strServer	Required	O.Ref.

The name of the Domino server that contains the user's mail file.

strFirstname	Required	O.Ref.

The user's first name.

strMiddleinit   Required   O.Ref.

The user's middle initial.

strCertpassword   Required   O.Ref.

The password for the certifier ID file.

strLocation   Required   O.Ref.

The value stored in the location item in the Name and Address Book (Directory) document.

strComment   Required   O.Ref.

The value stored in the comment item in the Name and Address Book (Directory) document.

strMaildbpath   Required   O.Ref.

The file path of the user's mail directory. You don't have to specify the entire file path—just the path of the mail database in the Notes Data directory.

strFwddomain   Required   O.Ref.

The forwarded domain for the current user's mail file.

strUserpassword   Required   O.Ref.

The current user's password.

This method registers a new user ID file and returns `true` if the method is successful and `false` if it is not. Note that the `setcertifierIdFile` method must be set prior to calling this method. Otherwise, you will receive the `Certifier ID path not supplied` error message.

Before this method can be called, all the required methods must be set. The required methods (as well as the optional ones) are described in the "Remarks" section (▶ 529) near the end of this chapter.

---

setCertifierIdFile   W   O.Ref.

`nregRegistration.`**`setCertifierIdFile`**`(strCertIDFile)`   setCertifierId
File

This method sets the file path location of the certifier ID file. You use the certifier ID file (Cert.ID) when creating user IDs and cross-certifying with other Domino servers. When setting this method, be sure to use the complete file path to the certifier ID, starting with the drive—such as C:\notes\data\cert.id. The default directory path (for example, C:\notes\data) is usually ignored with most methods. The entire file path is required.

---

setCreateMailDb   W   T/F

`nregRegistration.`**`setCreateMailDb`**`(bolCreateMailDb)`   setCreateMailDb

This method indicates whether a new mail database should be created immediately when generating new Notes ID files using the `registerNewUser` method (also a method of the *lotus.domino.Registration* class) or whether the mail file should be created when the user completes the setup process. `true` immediately creates a new mail database. `false` creates the ID file without also creating a new mail database. When `false` is specified, the mail database will be created when the specific user completes the setup process.

---

setExpiration   W   *NotesDateTime*

`nregRegistration.`**`setExpiration`**`(ndDate)`   setExpiration

This method sets the expiration date to use when ID files are being created. This is typically set to only two years, which is often too short a time period to be practical. Consider extending this value to avoid having to frequently administer the expiration of the ID files.

---

setIDType   W   %

`nregRegistration.`**`setIDType`**`(intIDType)`

This method sets the type of ID file to create when registering a new user, server, or certifier. This method is used when calling the `registerNewUser`, `registerNewServer`, or `registerNewCertifier` methods. The value returned or used to set this method is a constant of type Integer. The allowed values are listed in the following table.

IDType **Values**

Values	**Description**
`Registration.ID_FLAT`	The ID created is flat.
`Registration.ID_HIERARCHICAL`	The ID created is hierarchical.
`Registration.ID_CERTIFIER`	The ID created uses the certifier ID to determine whether it is flat or hierarchical.

---

setMinPasswordLength   W   %

`nregRegistration.`**`setMinPasswordLength`**`(intMinlength)`

This method sets the minimum number of characters required when creating an ID file. This method is relevant when calling the `registerNewUser`, `registerNewServer`, or `registerNewCertifier` methods.

---

setNorthAmerican   W   T/F

`nregRegistration.`**`setNorthAmerican`**`(bolIsNorthAmer)`

This method indicates whether the ID file is North American or International. If `true`, the ID is North American. `false` indicates that the ID file is International. (This is the only other option if the ID file is not North American.)

---

setOrgUnit   W   O.Ref.

`nregRegistration.`**`setOrgUnit`**`(strOrgUnit)`

This method sets the organizational unit to use when creating ID files. The organizational unit is a string representation of the organizational unit (OU), as used when calling the `registerNewUser` method. A maximum of four OUs can be used in an organization.

---

setRegistrationLog   W   O.Ref.

`nregRegistration.`**`setRegistrationLog`**`(strRegLog)`

This method sets the name of the log file (such as `reg.nsf`) to use when creating IDs. Notes automatically determines this value by reading the `Log=` parameter located in the Notes `.ini` file. Therefore, be sure to consider setting the Notes `.ini` file when modifying this method.

---

setRegistrationServer   W   O.Ref.

`nregRegistration.`**`setRegistrationServer`**`(strRegServer)`

This method sets the name of the Domino server to use when creating ID files. This method is used only when the ID file is being stored in the server's Name and Address Book (Directory) or when the mail database is being created for the new user.

---

setStoreIDInAddressBook   W   T/F

`nregRegistration.`**`setStoreIDInAddressBook`**`(bolStoreID)`

This method indicates whether the ID file being created should be stored in the Name and Address Book (Directory). `true` indicates that the ID should be stored in the Name and Address Book. `false` indicates that it should not.

---

setUpdateAddressBook   W   T/F

`nregRegistration.`**`setUpdateAddressBook`**`(bolUpdateAddBook)`   setUpdate
AddressBook

This method indicates whether the ID file being created should update the server entry in the Name and Address Book (Directory). This method is relevant when the `registerNewUser`, `registerNewServer`, or `registerNewCertifier` methods are called. `true` indicates that the Name and Address Book (Directory) should be updated. `false` indicates that it should not.

---

switchToID

`nregRegistration.`**`switchToID`**`(strIdfile, strUserpassword)`   switchToID

---

strIdfile   Required   O.Ref.

The ID file to switch to. Specify the entire file path, including the drive.

strUserpassword   Required   O.Ref.

The password of the user ID that is being switched to.

This method switches to another ID file on a Notes client. (It won't work on the Domino server.)

Remarks

The *lotus.domino.Registration* class was introduced in Notes Release 4.6 and was modified only slightly for Release 5.0. This class lets you programmatically perform some of the often tedious and repetitive tasks of Domino/Lotus Notes administration.

However, because of Domino/Lotus Notes' secure and robust security model, there are some things to watch out for when you're working with the *lotus.domino.Registration* class. For example, when calling the `registerNewCertifier`, `registerNewServer`, and `registerNewUser` methods, all of the methods listed next must be set before you call the methods. If not all of them are set, none of the changes will be saved, and you will receive the `Missing Registration Argument` or `Required registration argument not provided` error message. Here are the required methods:

```
RegistrationLog = certlog.nsf

IDType = ID_HIERARCHICAL

Expiration = CertExpireDate

MinPasswordLength = length%

IsNorthAmerican = TRUE

CertifierIDFile = certidfile

RegistrationServer = session.currentdatabase.server
```

continued >>

continued >> `OrgUnit = org`

`CreateMailDb = TRUE`

`StoreIdInAddressbook = TRUE`

`UpdateAddressbook = FALSE`

Also keep in mind that many of these methods do not work in a manner in which they are mutually exclusive of one another. They often affect one another in that certain methods must be set in order for other methods to work or to be significant. For example, `registerNewUser` works much like the `addUserToAddressBook` method, `registerNewServer` works much like the `addServerToAddressBook` method, and `registerNewCertifier` works much like the `addCertifierToAddressBook` method. What this means is that if you called both `registerNewUser` and `addUserToAddressBook` (and if the `updateAddressBook` method were set to `true`), two entries would be created in the Name and Address Book (Directory) rather than just one. You certainly wouldn't want to have two entries for a particular user in the Name and Address Book (Directory). In order to avoid having double entries in the Name and Address Book (Directory) when generating new IDs, you can set the `updateAddressBook` method to `false` and use `addCertifierToAddressBook`, `addServerToAddressbook`, or `addUserToAddressBook` to make the actual additions (updates) to the Name and Address Book.

Example

The following code example could be contained in an agent set to run on all documents in a particular *lotus.domino.Database* or *lotus.domino.View*. This agent will run against all unprocessed documents and register the names of the people listed in these documents as Notes clients. This code assumes that the documents contained in the view have certain items that are used to populate required fields when creating the Name and Address Book (Directory) entries. This type of agent, with modification, could be used to automate the creation of new IDs based on certain document types or a predetermined view (for example, a view of a user list newly imported into Domino/Lotus Notes).

```
import lotus.domino.*;

public class JavaAgent extends AgentBase {

  public void NotesMain() {

      try {
          Session ns = getSession();
          AgentContext agentContext = ns.getAgentContext();
          Database ndb = agentContext.getCurrentDatabase();
          DocumentCollection ndc = agentContext.getUnprocessedDocuments();
          Document ndoc = ndc.getFirstDocument();
          Registration nreg = ns.createRegistration();
          int intDoccount=0;
          while (ndoc != null) {
              intDoccount++;
```

```
        String strIdpath="c:\\lotus\\notes\\" +
            ndoc.getItemValueString("FInitial") +
            ndoc.getItemValueString("LName") + ".ID";
        String strMailpath ="mail\\" +
        ndoc.getItemValueString("FInitial") +
            ndoc.getItemValueString("LName") + ".nsf";
        nreg.RegisterNewUser( ndoc.getItemValueString("LName"),
        ➥strIdpath, "ACME Mail Server",
        ➥ndoc.getItemValueString("FName"),
        ➥ndoc.getItemValueString("MI"),"certpass","ACME Office",
        ➥"Added with agent...",strMailpath,"ACME","password");
        ndoc = ndc.getNextDocument(); }
    System.out.println("Finished processing. ");

} catch(Exception e) {
   e.printStackTrace();
}
 }
}
```

5.0 Replication

The *lotus.domino.Replication* object represents the replication settings for each *lotus.domino.Database* object. Replication is a fundamental feature of Domino/Lotus Notes that facilitates data synchronization among disparate users and servers and allows the user to work in a disconnected state and still have full database functionality and information availability. Every *lotus.domino.Database* has one *lotus.domino.Replication* object, which is automatically created and is contained by the *lotus.domino.Database* object when the *lotus.domino.Database* is created.

...

└ Database
   └ Replication
      └ DateTime

Java Syntax

Use the `getReplicationInfo` method of the *lotus.domino.Database* object to establish a handle to the *lotus.domino.Replication* object. There can be only one *lotus.domino.Replication* object per database.

Replication Methods

clearHistory

clearHistory

```
intClearHistory = nrepNotesReplication.clearHistory()
```

This method clears the replication history for the current *lotus.domino.Database* object. When a *lotus.domino.Database* is replicated, an entry is logged recording the event. Typically, each replication event triggers an incremental replication, updating only the documents in the database that have been modified since the previous replication. Clearing the replication history will cause the Replicator tasks to replicate all the documents, as if this replication were the initial database replication. This is often useful if there is a concern that not all of the documents are being replicated as they should or if the system date has recently been changed on the client or server systems.

getCutOffDate   R   O.Ref.

getCutOffDate

```
ndtCutOffDate = nrepReplication.getCutOffDate()
```

This method returns the date and time value that is being used by the Domino server's Replicator task to determine whether it should automatically purge previously deleted document identifiers (deleted document stubs) that are older than the date specified. This method has no effect unless the `setCutOffDelete` method (also a method of the *lotus.domino.Replication* object, (▶ 538) is turned on (set to `true`). The value of this method is calculated by subtracting the value of the `setCutOffInterval` method (also a method of the *lotus.domino.Replication* object, (▶ 538) from the current system date. Essentially, when *lotus.domino.Documents* are deleted, identifier information is still stored with the database as document deletion stubs to ensure that the deletion is propagated to other replica database copies of the current database. After a predetermined period of time, it is assumed that all the replicas are in synch with one another and it is safe to fully remove any trace of the deleted *lotus.domino.Document,* thus purging the deletion stub.

getCutOffInterval   R   &

getCutOff
Interval

```
lngCutOffInterval = nrepReplication.getCutOffInterval()
```

This method indicates the interval (in days) that is used to determine whether deleted document identifiers should be deleted from the *lotus.domino.Database* by the Domino server's Replicator task. This method works in tandem with the `getCutOffDate` method (also a method of the *lotus.domino.Replication* object, (▶ 534) and helps conserve space in the *lotus.domino.Database.* Although this method stores the interval in days for the purge, the actual date used to determine whether deletion stubs should be purged is automatically calculated and stored in the `getCutOffDate` method. This method has no effect unless the `setCutOffDelete` method (also a method of the *lotus.domino.Replication* object, (▶ 534) is turned on (set to `true`). This method defaults to `90`, stored as a long data type.

The following code snippet, when placed within the click event of a button, displays the current setting for the `getCutOffDelete` value (whether or not it is enabled) and then prompts the user to enable this setting. If the user enables this setting, he is prompted to set the `getCutOffInterval` value. If you are using a Notes client, you can test to see if this code was successful by checking the replication settings for the current database.

```java
import lotus.domino.*;

public class JavaAgent extends AgentBase {

    public void NotesMain() {

        try {
            Session ns = getSession();
            AgentContext agentContext = ns.getAgentContext();
            Database ndb = agentContext.getCurrentDatabase();
            Replication nrep = ndb.getReplicationInfo();
            System.out.println("Cutoff date is " + nrep.getCutoffDate());
            nrep.setCutoffDelete(true);
            System.out.println("CutoffDelete has been enabled");
            nrep.save();
            long lngCutoffinterval = nrep.getCutoffInterval();
            System.out.println("Documents not modified in the last " +
            ➥String.valueOf(lngCutoffinterval) +
            ➥" days will be removed.");

        } catch(Exception e) {
            e.printStackTrace();
        }
    }
}
```

getPriority	R	%

`intPriority = nrepReplication.getPriority()`   getPriority

This method indicates the setting for the current *lotus.domino.Database* Replicator priority. The Replicator priority determines the order in which databases are replicated and can be used to filter which databases are replicated. The value returned by this method and used to set this method is a constant whose available values are listed in the following table. The default value for this method is 1548, stored as a long data type signifying the constant value of `Db_REPLICATION_PRIORITY_MED`.

Constant	Integer Value
Replication.Db_REPLICATION_PRIORITY_LOW	1547
Replication.Db_REPLICATION_PRIORITY_MED	1548
Replication.Db_REPLICATION_PRIORITY_HIGH	1549
Replication.Db_REPLICATION_PRIORITY_NOTSET	1565

isAbstract	R	T/F

`bolAbstract = nrepReplication.isAbstract()`   isAbstract

This method indicates whether large documents are truncated and attachments are removed. `true` indicates document truncation and removes all attachments. `false` indicates no truncation. The method defaults to `false`. From the native Notes user interface, this option is available as a Replicator option to receive full documents or a summary and 40KB of rich text. This reduces replication time and the size of the local replica by not pulling down large attachments and rich text fields. However, this setting affects only the documents being pulled to the local replica database and leaves the full document (not truncated) on the source server.

isCutOffDelete R T/F

`bolCutOffDelete = nrepReplication.`**`isCutOffDelete`**`()`

This method indicates whether the Domino server's Replicator task should automatically delete documents that haven't been modified by the `getCutOffDate` method (also a method of *lotus.domino.Replication,* (▶ 534). Essentially, *lotus.domino.Documents* that haven't been modified after the specified date/time are deleted from the *lotus.domino.Database* since they are determined to be "older than" the cutoff date. The actual deletion occurs while the Replicator task is running. If this method is `true`, the deletion of documents older than the cutoff date is enabled. `false` indicates that this feature is disabled. This method defaults to `false`. This method is helpful in certain databases where older documents become meaningless and there is no need for a historical audit trail of the database's activity and content—such as with a discussion database.

isDisabled R T/F

`bolDisabled = nrepReplication.`**`isDisabled`**`()`

This method indicates whether replication for this database is temporarily enabled or disabled. If it's set to `false`, this database will not be replicated when the Domino server task runs. `true` enables database replication. This method defaults to `false`. This method can also be enabled or disabled from a native Domino/Lotus Notes client user interface by modifying the replication settings of the specific database. You can also use the `isNeverReplicate` method to disable replication for the database. Unlike the `isDisabled` method, the `isNeverReplicate` method can't be modified through the Domino/Lotus Notes user interface.

isDoNotBrowse R T/F

`bolDoNotBrowse = nrepReplication.`**`isDoNotBrowse`**`()`

This method indicates whether the database should appear in the Open Database dialog box. This method is meaningful only when the client is using a Notes client. It has no meaning on the Web. `true` allows the database to appear in the Open Database dialog. `false` keeps the database filenames from appearing. However, even if this method is set to `true`, the user can still open the database by typing its filename in the `filename` editable field. Therefore, this method shouldn't be used as a security feature. This method defaults to `false`.

isDoNotCatalog R T/F

`bolDoNotCatalog = nrepReplication.`**`isDoNotCatalog`**`()`

This method indicates whether the current *lotus.domino.Database* should be added to the `CATALOG.NSF` database when the Domino server Catalog task runs. Setting this method to `true` allows the database to be cataloged. `false` disables it. `CATALOG.NSF` provides summary information about the *lotus.domino.Databases* on the current server and other servers with replica copies of the databases. The information stored in the catalog includes the server names, filenames, replica IDs, the name of the database manager, and any information saved in the database's "About" document. Users can browse the catalog and open databases directly. This method defaults to `false`.

isHideDesign R T/F

`bolHideDesign = nrepReplication.`**`isHideDesign`**`()`

This method indicates whether the design of the database should be hidden. `true` causes the design to be hidden. Setting this method to `false` disables the hide design feature. This method defaults to `false`.

isIgnoreDeletes   R   T/F

```
bolIgnoreDel = nrepReplication.isIgnoreDeletes()
```
isIgnoreDeletes

This method indicates whether the deletion stubs created when *lotus.domino.Documents* are deleted should be replicated to the database's other replica copies. If this method is set to **true**, deletion stubs don't propagate during replication. If this method is set to **false**, deletion stubs propagate during replication. This method defaults to **false**. This feature allows users to delete unwanted documents from their local replica copy without affecting the documents on other replica copies. The ability to delete documents and allow the deletion to propagate to other replica copies is also controlled by the current user's access control to the database. This method shouldn't be used as a security feature. It isn't meant to replace the inherent security features of Domino/Lotus Notes.

isIgnoreDestDeletes   R   T/F

```
bolIgnoreDestDel = nrepReplication.isIgnoreDestDeletes()
```
isIgnoreDest
Deletes

This method determines whether the deletion stubs created when *lotus.domino.Documents* are deleted in the current database should be replicated into the destination database. If this method is **true**, the deletion stubs don't propagate to the destinationdatabase during replication. **false** enables the propagation of the deletion stubs during replication. This method defaults to **false**.

isMultiDbIndex   R   T/F

```
bolMultiDbIndex = nrepReplication.isMultiDbIndex()
```
isMultiDbIndex

This method determines whether the current *lotus.domino.Database* should be included in the Multi-Database index. **true** indicates that this database is included. **false** indicates that it isn't. This method defaults to **false**.

isNeverReplicate   R   T/F

```
bolNeverRepl = nrepReplication.isNeverReplicate()
```
isNever
Replicate

This method indicates whether the current *lotus.domino.Database* should be replicated when the Domino server Replicator task runs. Setting this method to **true** causes the Replicator task to ignore this database. Setting this method to **false** reenables replication. Unlike most *lotus.domino.Replicator* methods, this method is not available from the Notes client interface and can be modified only programmatically. This method defaults to **false**.

isNoChronos   R   T/F

```
bolNoChronos = nrepReplication.isNoChronos()
```
isNoChronos

This method indicates whether background agents (sometimes referred to as macros) are enabled. If this method is **true**, background agents are disabled. If this method is set to **false**, background agents are enabled. This method defaults to **false**.

reset

```
intReset = nrepReplication.reset()
```
reset

This method resets the replication values for the current *lotus.domino.Database* object to the values on the last-saved date. Therefore, if changes have been made, they can be reversed and set back to their prior setting configuration.

save

```
intSave = nrepReplication.save()
```
save

This method saves the replication values for the current *lotus.domino.Database*. None of the values that are manipulated when you modify the methods of the *lotus.domino.Replication* are activated until the **save** method is called.

---

setAbstract   W   T/F

nrepReplication.**setAbstract**(bolAbstract)

This method controls whether large documents are truncated and attachments are removed. `true` enables document truncation and removes all attachments. `false` disables truncation. This method defaults to `false`. From the native Notes user interface, this option is available as a Replicator option to receive full documents or a summary and 40KB of rich text. This reduces replication time and the size of the local replica by not pulling down large attachments and rich text fields. However, this setting affects only the documents being pulled to the local replica database and leaves the full document (not truncated) on the source server.

---

setCutOffDelete   W   T/F

nrepReplication.**setCutOffDelete**(bolCutOffDelete)

This method determines whether the Domino server's Replicator task should automatically delete documents that haven't been modified by the `getCutOffDate` (also a method of *lotus.domino.Replication,* (▶ 534). Essentially, *lotus.domino.Documents* that haven't been modified after the specified date/time are deleted from the *lotus.domino.Database* since they are determined to be "older than" the cutoff date. The actual deletion occurs while the Replicator task is running. Setting this method to `true` enables the deletion of documents older than the cutoff date. `false` disables this feature. This method defaults to `false`. This method is helpful in certain databases where older documents become meaningless and there is no need for a historical audit trail of the database's activity and content—such as with a discussion database.

---

setCutOffInterval   W   &

nrepReplication.**setCutOffInterval**(lngCutOffInterval)

This method sets the interval (in days) that is used to determine whether deleted document identifiers should be deleted from the *lotus.domino.Database* by the Domino server's Replicator task. This method works in tandem with the `getCutOffDate` method (also a method of *lotus.domino.Replication,* (▶ 534) and helps conserve space in the *lotus.domino.Database*. Although this method stores the interval in days for the purge, the actual date used to determine whether deletion stubs should be purged is automatically calculated and stored in the `getCutOffDate` method. This method has no effect unless the `setCutOffDelete` method (▶ 538) is turned on (set to `true`). This method defaults to `90`, stored as a long data type.

---

setDisabled   W   T/F

nrepReplication.**setDisabled**(bolDisabled)

This method temporarily enables or disables the replication for this database. If it's set to `false`, this database will not be replicated when the Domino server task runs. `true` enables database replication. This method defaults to `false`.

---

setDoNotBrowse   W   T/F

nrepReplication.**setDoNotBrowse**(bolDoNotBrowse)

This method determines whether the database should appear in the Open Database dialog box. This method is meaningful only when the client is using a Notes client. It has no meaning on the Web. Setting this method to `true` allows the database to appear in the Open Database dialog. `false` keeps the database filenames from appearing. However, even if this method is set to `true`, the user can still open the database by typing its filename in the `filename` editable field. Therefore, this method shouldn't be used as a security feature. This method defaults to `false`.

setDoNotCatalog W T/F

`nrepReplication.`**`setDoNotCatalog`**`(bolDoNotCatalog)`

This method determines whether the current *lotus.domino.NotesDatabase* should be added to the `CATALOG.NSF` database when the Domino server Catalog task runs. Setting this method to `true` allows the database to be cataloged. `false` disables it. `CATALOG.NSF` provides summary information about the *lotus.domino.Databases* on the current server and other servers with replica copies of the databases. The information stored in the catalog includes the server names, filenames, replica IDs, the name of the database manager, and any information saved in the database's "About" document. Users can browse the catalog and open databases directly. This method defaults to `false`.

setHideDesign W T/F

`nrepReplication.`**`setHideDesign`**`(bolHideDesign)`

This method determines whether the design of the database should be hidden. Setting this method to `true` causes the design to be hidden. Setting it to `false` disables the hide design feature. This method defaults to `false`.

setIgnoreDeletes W T/F

`nrepReplication.`**`setIgnoreDeletes`**`(bolIgnoreDel)`

This method determines whether the deletion stubs created when *lotus.domino.Documents* are deleted should be replicated to the database's other replica copies. Setting this method to `true` causes the deletion stubs not to propagate during replication. Setting this method to `false` propagates the deletion stubs during replication. This method defaults to `false`. This feature allows users to delete unwanted documents from their local replica copy without affecting the documents on other replica copies. The ability to delete documents and allow the deletion to propagate to other replica copies is also controlled by the current user's access control to the database. This method shouldn't be used as a security feature. It isn't meant to replace the inherent security features of Domino/Lotus Notes.

setIgnoreDestDeletes W T/F

`nrepReplication.`**`setIgnoreDestDeletes`**`(bolIgnoreDestDel)`

This method determines whether the deletion stubs created when *lotus.domino.Documents* are deleted in the current database should be replicated into the destination database. Setting this method to `true` causes the deletion stubs not to propagate to the destination database during replication. Setting this method to `false` allows the propagation of the deletion stubs during replication. This method defaults to `false`.

setMultiDbIndex W T/F

`nrepReplication.`**`setMultiDbIndex`**`(bolMultiDbIndex)`

This method determines whether the current *lotus.domino.Database* should be included in the Multi-Database index. `true` causes this database to be included. `false` keeps it from being included. This method defaults to `false`.

setNeverReplicate W T/F

`nrepReplication.`**`setNeverReplicate`**`(bolNeverRepl)`

This method determines whether the current *lotus.domino.Database* should be replicated when the Domino server Replicator task runs. Setting this method to `true` causes the Replicator task to ignore this database. Setting this method to `false` reenables replication. Unlike most *lotus.domino.Replicator* methods, this method is not available from the Notes client interface and can be modified only programmatically. This method defaults to `false`.

setNoChronos	W	T/F

```
nrepReplication.setNoChronos(bolNoChronos)
```

This method determines whether background agents (sometimes referred to as macros) are enabled. Setting this method to `true` disables background agents. Setting this method to `false` reenables background agents. This method defaults to `false`.

setPriority	W	&

```
nrepReplication.setPriority(lngPriority)
```

This method determines the current *lotus.domino.Database* Replicator priority. The Replicator priority determines the order in which databases are replicated and can be used to filter which databases are replicated. The value returned by this method and used to set this method is a constant whose available values are listed in the following table. The default value for this method is `1548`, stored as a long data type signifying the constant value of `Db_REPLICATION_PRIORITY_MED`.

Constant	Integer Value
Replicate.Db_REPLICATION_PRIORITY_LOW	1547
Replicate.Db_REPLICATION_PRIORITY_MED	1548
Replicate.Db_REPLICATION_PRIORITY_HIGH	1549
Replicate.Db_REPLICATION_PRIORITY_NOTSET	1565

Remarks

Multiple methods of the *lotus.domino.Replication* object can be modified and then saved and written to disk at one time. Therefore, if you are programmatically manipulating the replication settings for the current database, there will never be a situation in which a replication session occurs while your code is modifying the database replication settings, because they are saved to disk at one time (rather than incrementally).

When you're using Java, the *lotus.domino.Replication* object applies only to the new lotus.domino package.

Example

The following example reads all the local databases stored in the *lotus.domino.DbDirectory* and builds a list of those databases, displaying some of their *lotus.domino.Replication* methods. The database list and its respective methods are saved in the Body field on a new *lotus.domino.Document* in a report format.

```
import lotus.domino.*;

public class JavaAgent extends AgentBase {
  public void NotesMain() {
    try {
      Session ns = getSession();
      AgentContext agentContext = ns.getAgentContext();
```

```
DbDirectory ndbdir = ns.getDbDirectory(null);
Database ndb = ndbdir.getFirstDatabase(DbDirectory.DATABASE);
Database ndbCurrent = agentContext.getCurrentDatabase();
Document ndoc = ndbCurrent.createDocument();
DateTime ndt = ns.createDateTime("Today");
ndoc.appendItemValue("Form", "Report");
ndoc.appendItemValue("Author", ns.getCommonUserName());
ndoc.appendItemValue("DateCreated", ndt.getLocalTime());
RichTextItem nrti = ndoc.createRichTextItem("Body");
nrti.appendText("Database Name");
nrti.addNewLine();
nrti.addTab();
nrti.appendText("Abstract");
nrti.addTab();
nrti.appendText("CutoffDelete");
nrti.addTab();
nrti.appendText("Disabled");
nrti.addTab();
nrti.appendText("Browse");
nrti.addTab(2);
nrti.appendText("Catalog");
nrti.addTab(2);
nrti.appendText("MultiDbIndex");
nrti.addTab();
nrti.appendText("Never Repl");
nrti.addNewLine(3);
while (ndb != null) {
    ndb.open();
    Replication nrep = ndb.getReplicationInfo();
    nrti.appendText(ndb.getTitle());
    nrti.addNewLine();
    nrti.addTab();
    if (nrep.isAbstract())
        nrti.appendText("True");
    else
        nrti.appendText("False");
    nrti.addTab(2);
    if (nrep.isCutoffDelete())
        nrti.appendText("True");
    else
        nrti.appendText("False");
    nrti.addTab(2);
    if (nrep.isDisabled())
        nrti.appendText("True");
    else
        nrti.appendText("False");
    nrti.addTab(2);
    if (nrep.isDoNotBrowse())
        nrti.appendText("True");
    else
        nrti.appendText("False");
    nrti.addTab(2);
    if (nrep.isDoNotCatalog())
        nrti.appendText("True");
    else
        nrti.appendText("False");
    nrti.addTab(2);
    if (nrep.isMultiDbIndex())
        nrti.appendText("True");
```

continued >>

continued >>

```
            else
                nrti.appendText("False");
            nrti.addTab(2);
             if (nrep.isNeverReplicate())
                nrti.appendText("True");
            else
                nrti.appendText("False");
            nrti.addNewLine(2);
            ndb = ndbdir.getNextDatabase(); }
        if (ndoc.save())
            System.out.println("Java agent completed and doc was saved");
        else
            System.out.println("Java agent did not complete, doc was not
            ↪saved");

          } catch(Exception e) {
        e.printStackTrace();
      }
    }
  }
```

4.6x 5.0 RichTextItem

The *lotus.domino.RichTextItem* object is a type of *lotus.domino.Item* that contains rich text. Therefore, not only can the *lotus.domino.RichTextItem* object contain text, but it can also be formatted with various styles, fonts, and types. In addition, it can contain graphics, tables, buttons, attachments, and virtually any other type of compound data. Similar to the *lotus.domino.Item* object, the *lotus.domino.RichTextItem* is contained in a *lotus.domino.Document*. In other words, it is synonymous to a field contained in a record in a relational database. The *lotus.domino.RichTextItem* is derived from the *lotus.domino.Item* base class, so it inherits the methods of the existing *lotus.domino.Item* class.

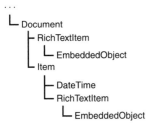

Java Syntax

```
Public class RichTextItem extends Item
```

In order to create a new *lotus.domino.RichTextItem* object with Java, you must use the createRichTextItem method of the *lotus.domino.Document* (▶ 418).

Because the *lotus.domino.RichTextItem* object inherits from the *lotus.domino.Item* class, you can use the getFirstItem method of the *lotus.domino.Item* class to access an existing *lotus.domino.RichTextItem* object. All the other methods of the *lotus.domino.Item* are available to the *lotus.domino.RichTextItem* object, although some return slightly different results.

RichTextItem Methods

addNewLine

addNewLine

```
nrtiRichTextItem.addNewLine()RichTextItem.addNewLine(intCount)
```

```
nrtiRichTextItem.addNewLine(intCount, bolforceparagraph)
```

| intCount | Required | % |

The number of lines to append to the body of the rich text item.

| bolforceparagraph | Required | T/F |

Indicates whether the new line should also create a new paragraph. true creates a new paragraph. false adds a new line in the same paragraph. This parameter is true by default.

This method appends carriage returns (new lines or Chr$(13)) to the end of the *lotus.domino.RichTextItem*. By specifying the value of the n% parameter, you can add multiple lines at one time.

5.0 addPageBreak

addPageBreak

```
nrtiRichTextItem.addPageBreak()
```

```
nrtiRichTextItem.addPageBreak(RichTextParagraphStyle)
```

| *RichTextParagraphStyle* | Required | O.Ref. |

The paragraph style and attributes determined by the *RichTextParagraphStyle* object to use in the beginning of the new page of the *lotus.domino.RichTextItem*.

This method appends a hard page break to the end of the *lotus.domino.RichTextItem* in order to start a new page.

addTab

addTab

```
nrtiRichTextItem.addTab()
```

```
nrtiRichTextItem.addTab(intCount)
```

| intCount | Required | % |

The number of tabs to append to the body of the rich text item.

This method appends multiple tabs to the end of the *lotus.domino.RichTextItem*. By specifying the value of the n% parameter, you can add multiple tabs at one time.

appendDocLink

```
nrtiRichTextItem.appendDocLink(Document)

nrtiRichTextItem.appendDocLink(View)

nrtiRichTextItem.appendDocLink(Database)

nrtiRichTextItem.appendDocLink(Document, strComment)

nrtiRichTextItem.appendDocLink(View, strComment)

nrtiRichTextItem.appendDocLink(Database, strComment)

nrtiRichTextItem.appendDocLink(Document, strComment, strHotspottext)

nrtiRichTextItem.appendDocLink(View, strComment, strHotspottext)

nrtiRichTextItem.appendDocLink(Database, strComment, strHotspottext)
```

Document	Required	O.Ref.

The *lotus.domino.Document* object to create the link to.

View	Required	O.Ref.

The *lotus.domino.View* object to create the link to.

Database	Required	O.Ref.

The *lotus.domino.Database* object to create the link to.

strComment	Required	O.Ref.

The text displayed when the user clicks the link or moves the mouse over the link icon.

strHotspottext	Required	O.Ref.

The text appears as boxed text that, when clicked, will open the object link.

This method adds a document, view, or database link to the end of a rich text item. This link is actually a handle to the *lotus.domino.Document* object, *lotus.domino.View* object, or *lotus.domino.Database* object that will open the respective object in the user interface when the user clicks it.

The following example creates a new *lotus.domino.Document* object and attaches a doclink to the current *lotus.domino.Document* object open in the user interface for a Web client or a native Notes client. The newly created document is then e-mailed to the name(s) listed in the `recipients` field on the current form.

```java
import lotus.domino.*;

public class JavaAgent extends AgentBase {

  public void NotesMain() {

    try {
      Session ns = getSession();
      AgentContext agentContext = ns.getAgentContext();
      Database ndb = agentContext.getCurrentDatabase();
      Document ndoc = ndb.createDocument();
      Document ndocCurrent = agentContext.getDocumentContext();
      RichTextItem nrti = ndoc.createRichTextItem("Body");
      nrti.appendDocLink(ndocCurrent, "Please review...");
      ndoc.appendItemValue("Form", "Memo");
      ndoc.save(true, false);
      ndoc.send(false, ndocCurrent.getItemValueString("Recipients"));
```

continued >>

continued >>

```
                System.out.println("The E-Mail with doclink has been sent.");

            } catch(Exception e) {
                e.printStackTrace();
            }
        }
    }
```

5.0 appendParagraphStyle

appendParagraph
Style

`nrtiRichTextItem.`**`appendParagraphStyle`**`(RichTextParagraphStyle)`

RichTextParagraphStyle	Required	O.Ref.

The paragraph style and attributes determined by the *RichTextParagraphStyle* object to be appended to the *lotus.domino.RichTextItem*.

This method appends a paragraph style to the end of the *lotus.domino.RichTextItem*. All subsequent text (or objects, if applicable) that is appended to the rich text item in this paragraph will adhere to the same attributes of the paragraph style.

appendRTItem

appendRTItem

`nrtiRichTextItem.`**`appendRTItem`**`(RichTextItem)`

RichTextItem	Required	O.Ref.

The rich text item to be appended to the first rich text item.

This method appends the contents of *lotus.domino.RichTextItem* to the end of another *lotus.domino.RichTextItem*.

The following example illustrates how to use `appendRTItem` to attach the contents of the current *lotus.domino.RichTextItem* (contained in the current *lotus.domino.Document* displayed in the current user interface) to a newly created *lotus.domino.Document* that is mailed to the specified recipient.

```
import lotus.domino.*;

public class JavaAgent extends AgentBase {

    public void NotesMain() {

        try {
            Session ns = getSession();
            AgentContext agentContext = ns.getAgentContext();
            Database ndb = agentContext.getCurrentDatabase();
            Document ndoc = ndb.createDocument();
            Document ndocCurrent = agentContext.getDocumentContext();
            String strRecipients = ndocCurrent.getItemValueString
            ➥("Recipients");
            RichTextItem nrtiCurrent =
            ➥(RichTextItem)ndocCurrent.getFirstItem("Body");
            if (strRecipients != null)  {
                RichTextItem nrti = ndoc.createRichTextItem("Body");
                nrti.appendRTItem(nrtiCurrent);
                ndoc.save(true, false);
                ndoc.send(false, strRecipients );
            }
            else
                System.out.println("You must enter a recipient!");
            System.out.println("The E-Mail has been sent.");

        } catch(Exception e) {
```

```
            e.printStackTrace();
        }
    }
}
```

appendStyle

nrtiRichTextItem.**appendStyle**(RichTextStyle)

RichTextStyle	Required	O.Ref.

The rich text style to be appended to the rich text item.

This method appends a style to the end of a *lotus.domino.RichTextItem*. This style is created using the `createRichTextStyle` method of this class. All text appended to the *lotus.domino.RichTextItem* after the style has been applied reflects the attributes of that style. The style can then subsequently be modified by appending another style to the *lotus.domino.RichTextItem*. However, this method will not affect any subsequent text (or objects) appended to the *lotus.domino.RichTextItem* using the `appendRTItem` method (which will preserve its respective attributes).

The following code snippet creates a new document and populates the *lotus.domino.RichTextItem* with text rendered with two different styles applied to them. Notice how the `appendStyle` method is called after each *lotus.domino.RichTextStyle* modification. However, if you're making changes to a currently open *lotus.domino.Document*, keep in mind that changes made to the *lotus.domino.RichTextItem* are not immediately visible via the user interface until the document is saved to disk, closed, and reopened in the user interface. In this example, the modifications were made to the back-end *lotus.domino.Document*, so this limitation was not an issue.

```
import lotus.domino.*;

public class JavaAgent extends AgentBase {

  public void NotesMain() {

    try {
        Session ns = getSession();
        AgentContext agentContext = ns.getAgentContext();
        Database ndb = agentContext.getCurrentDatabase();
        Document ndoc = ndb.createDocument();
        RichTextStyle nrtsMessage = ns.createRichTextStyle();
        RichTextItem nrti = ndoc.createRichTextItem("Body");
        nrtsMessage.setColor(RichTextStyle.COLOR_RED);
        nrtsMessage.setFont(RichTextStyle.FONT_HELV);
        nrtsMessage.setFontSize(16);
        nrti.appendStyle(nrtsMessage);
        nrti.appendText("This is important so pay attention!");
        nrti.addNewLine(2);
        nrtsMessage.setColor(RichTextStyle.COLOR_BLACK);
        nrtsMessage.setFont(RichTextStyle.FONT_HELV);
        nrtsMessage.setFontSize(8);
        nrti.appendStyle(nrtsMessage);
        nrti.appendText("I am not as worthy of your attention.");
        ndoc.appendItemValue("Form", "test form");
        ndoc.save(true, false);

    } catch(Exception e) {
        e.printStackTrace();
    }
  }
}
```

appendText

appendText   `nrtiRichTextItem.appendText(String strText)`

| strText | Required | O.Ref. |

The text to append to the end of the *lotus.domino.RichTextItem*.

This method appends text to the end of the *lotus.domino.RichTextItem*. The appended text assumes the existing style attributes of the *lotus.domino.RichTextItem*.

embedObject

embedObject   `EmbeddedObject = nrtiRichTextItem.embedObject(intType, strClass, strSource, ➡strName)`

| intType | Required | % |

An integer constant value that determines the type of constant to embed. Details follow.

| strClass | Required | O.Ref. |

The application name for the OLE object being created if `EMBED_OBJECT` was used as the parameter for `intType` and an empty object is being created. This parameter is case-sensitive. Details follow.

| strSource | Required | O.Ref. |

This is either the filename specifying the location of the OLE object being created if `EMBED_OBJECT` was used as the parameter for `intType`, or the name of the file to attach or link if `EMBED_ATTACHMENT` or `EMBED_OBJECTLINK` was used as the parameter for `intType`. Details follow.

| strName | Optional | O.Ref. |

The name to assign to the *lotus.domino.EmbeddedObject* so that it can be referenced later by script.

This method returns a handle to the newly created embedded object, attached file, or linked object, depending on the parameters selected in the method. This method can attach a specified file to the *lotus.domino.RichTextItem,* embed (append) a created object (specified using the application or filename) to the *lotus.domino.RichTextItem,* or place a link to a specified file object in the *lotus.domino.RichTextItem.* At the time this book was published, this method wasn't supported by OS/2 or Macintosh clients. Here are the constant values allowed for `intType`:

Constant	Description
`EmbeddedObject.EMBED_ATTACHMENT`	Indicates to create an attachment.
`EmbeddedObject.EMBED_OBJECT`	Indicates to create an embedded object.
`EmbeddedObject.EMBED_OBJECTLINK`	Indicates to create an object link to a database, view, or document.

You need to specify a value for `strClass` only when using `EMBED_OBJECT` for `intType` and creating an empty embedded object from an application. In this case, this parameter defines the name of the application. When specifying the name of the application, you can enter an empty string (`""`) for `strSource`. This parameter is case-sensitive. If you are specifying `EMBED_OBJECTLINK` or `EMBED_ATTACHMENT` for `intType`, enter an empty string (`""`) for this parameter.

You need to specify a value for `strSource` when using `EMBED_OBJECT` for `intType` and creating an embedded object from a file. In this case, this parameter defines the name of the file. When specifying the name of the file, you can enter an empty string (`""`) for `strClass`. If you are specifying `EMBED_OBJECTLINK` or `EMBED_ATTACHMENT` for `intType`, this parameter specifies the name of the file to attach or link.

Although files can be attached on all platforms that support Domino/Lotus Notes, objects and object links can be created only on platforms and clients that support OLE.

getEmbeddedObject

```
nembEmbeddedObject = nrtiRichTextItem.getEmbeddedObject(strName)
```

getEmbedded
Object

strName	Required	O.Ref.

The name of the *lotus.domino.EmbeddedObject* to return.

This method returns a handle on the *lotus.domino.EmbeddedObject* that is referenced as the name specified by strName. strName is the name of a file attachment, embedded object, or object link located in the *lotus.domino.RichTextItem* object. This method isn't supported by OS/2, UNIX, or Macintosh platforms. When attempting to locate a file attachment, specify the filename for strName. When attempting to locate an embedded object, specify the name of the object (as it reads in the infobox when you're designing using the Notes Designer) that might have been assigned by the embedObject method. Modifications made to the object with script will be saved, but the object won't render the results until it is activated.

The following example attempts to locate an embedded Microsoft Word object. If the object is found, the Word document object is activated and displayed in the user interface.

```java
import lotus.domino.*;
import java.util.Vector;
import java.util.Enumeration;

public class JavaAgent extends AgentBase {

    public void NotesMain() {

        try {
            Session ns = getSession();
            AgentContext agentContext = ns.getAgentContext();
            Database ndb = agentContext.getCurrentDatabase();
            Document ndoc = agentContext.getDocumentContext();
            RichTextItem nrti = (RichTextItem)ndoc.getFirstItem("Body");

                Vector vecEmbobj = nrti.getEmbeddedObjects();
                Enumeration eEmbObj = vecEmbobj.elements();
                while (eEmbObj.hasMoreElements()) {
                    EmbeddedObject nemb = nrti.getEmbeddedObject("Microsoft
                    ➥Word Document");
                    if (nemb != null) {
                        System.out.println("Loading Microsoft Word Document
                        ➥into memory...");
                        int intActivate = nemb.activate(true); }    }

        } catch(Exception e) {
            e.printStackTrace();
        }
    }
}
```

getEmbeddedObjects   R   O.Ref.

```
vecEmbObjects = nrtiRichTextItem.getEmbeddedObjects()
```

getEmbedded
Objects

Returns an array of all the OLE/1 and OLE/2 embedded objects, file attachments, and links to other objects that are contained in the *lotus.domino.RichTextItem*. At the time this book was published, this method wasn't supported for OS/2 and Macintosh clients.

The following example illustrates how the `getType` method of the *EmbeddedObjects* object can be used to compare against the constant values in order to determine the type of object(s) that are embedded in the rich text field.

```java
import lotus.domino.*;
import java.util.Vector;
import java.util.Enumeration;

public class JavaAgent extends AgentBase {

    public void NotesMain() {

        try {
            Session ns = getSession();
            AgentContext agentContext = ns.getAgentContext();
            Database ndb = agentContext.getCurrentDatabase();
            Document ndoc = agentContext.getDocumentContext();
            RichTextItem nrti = (RichTextItem)ndoc.getFirstItem("Body");
            Vector nobj = nrti.getEmbeddedObjects();
            Enumeration eobj = nobj.elements();
            int intAttachcount=0;
            int intObjectcount=0;
            int intObjectLinkcount=0;
            while (eobj.hasMoreElements()) {
                EmbeddedObject nemb = (EmbeddedObject)eobj.nextElement();
                switch (nemb.getType()) {
                    case EmbeddedObject.EMBED_ATTACHMENT :
                        intAttachcount++;
                    case EmbeddedObject.EMBED_OBJECT :
                        intObjectcount++;
                    case EmbeddedObject.EMBED_OBJECTLINK :
                        intObjectLinkcount++;
                }

            System.out.println("Attachment count = " + intAttachcount);
            System.out.println("Object count = " + intObjectcount);
            System.out.println("ObjectLink count = " +
            ➥intObjectLinkcount);
            System.out.println("\nFinished, the object is ready for
            ➥use.");   }

        } catch(Exception e) {
            e.printStackTrace();
        }
    }
}
```

---

getFormattedText

getFormatted Text   `strFormattedText = nrtiRichTextItem.**getFormattedText**(bolTabstrip,`
`➥intLinelen, intMaxlen)`

bolTabstrip	Required	T/F

Indicates whether tabs should be stripped out of the plain-text string that is returned by this method. `true` indicates that they should be stripped out. `false` indicates that they should not.

intLinelen	Required	%

Indicates the character count at which to wrap the text and begin a new line. The default is `0`.

intMaxlen	Required	%

Indicates the maximum number of characters to return. The default is 0.

This method returns the string value of a *lotus.domino.RichTextItem* as plain text. All other contents of the *lotus.domino.RichTextItem* are ignored.

The following simple example displays the plain-text contents of the *lotus.domino.RichTextItem*.

```java
import lotus.domino.*;

public class JavaAgent extends AgentBase {

    public void NotesMain() {

        try {
            Session ns = getSession();
            AgentContext agentContext = ns.getAgentContext();
            Database ndb = agentContext.getCurrentDatabase();
            Document ndoc = agentContext.getDocumentContext();
            String strMessage=null;
            RichTextItem nrti = (RichTextItem)ndoc.getFirstItem("Body");
            strMessage = nrti.getFormattedText(false, 0, 0);
            System.out.println("The contents of the rich text field are:");
            System.out.println(strMessage);

        } catch(Exception e) {
            e.printStackTrace();
        }
    }
}
```

Remarks

Once you have created a *lotus.domino.RichTextItem* object in a *lotus.domino.Document* object, you must call the save method of the parent *lotus.domino.Document* to save the data to disk.

Since the *lotus.domino.RichTextItem* inherits from the *lotus.domino.Item* base class, all the methods of the *lotus.domino.Item* are available to the *lotus.domino.RichTextItem* as well. In addition, the methods of the *lotus.domino.RichTextItem* are extended to incorporate rich text capabilities. However, unlike the *lotus.domino.Item,* which has a physical size limit of 64KB, the *lotus.domino.RichTextItem* can hold information as large as 1 gigabyte. While common sense would discourage you from storing this much data in a single item (or field) in a *lotus.domino.Document,* the robust capability of the *lotus.domino.RichTextItem* object makes it a powerful LotusScript class.

The *lotus.domino.RichTextItem* won't be saved when the document is saved if content isn't added to the *lotus.domino.RichTextItem* object. In addition, because of the dynamic capabilities of the *lotus.domino.RichTextItem* object, modifications made to the *lotus.domino.RichTextItem* aren't visible to the user interface until the document is saved to disk and reopened in the user interface.

Example

The following example builds a list of doclinks linking to all documents that
match the criteria selected by the user. Each line item built by this agent and
stored in the rich text field also contains some text describing the nature of the
doclink. This simulates the *lotus.domino.Newsletter* functionality but lets you specify
the formatting using the capabilities of the *lotus.domino.RichTextItem* object. This
code could be modified to create an agent that "pushes" information to certain
users based on creation date, topics, or keywords. In addition, this code could also
be modified to incorporate other routing functions inherent to workflow and
process automation applications.

Typically, this code would be written in a more modular manner and would
consequently be more efficient. However, for the purposes of this example, all
the functionality necessary to facilitate this example has been included in one
routine. Nevertheless, the following code is complete and could be run "as is"
from within an agent or by a button. In addition, some methods from other
Notes classes have been used to show off the potential of the
lotus.domino.RichTextItem.

```java
import lotus.domino.*;

public class JavaAgent extends AgentBase {

  public void NotesMain() {

    try {
        Session ns = getSession();
        AgentContext agentContext = ns.getAgentContext();
        Agent nagt = agentContext.getCurrentAgent();
        Database ndb = agentContext.getCurrentDatabase();
        View nvw = ndb.getView("All");
        Document ndoc = ndb.createDocument();
        Document ndocCurrent = agentContext.getDocumentContext();
        String strCriteria = ndocCurrent.getItemValueString
        ➥("tSearchCriteria");

        DocumentCollection ndc = ndb.FTSearch(strCriteria, 0,
        ➥Database.FT_DATE_DES, 0);
        RichTextItem nrti = ndoc.createRichTextItem("Body");
        RichTextStyle nrts = ns.createRichTextStyle();
        nrts.setColor(RichTextStyle.COLOR_BLUE);
        nrts.setFont(RichTextStyle.FONT_COURIER);
        nrts.setFontSize(18);
        nrti.appendStyle(nrts);
        nrti.appendText("Here are all the documents that match: " +
        ➥strCriteria + "\n\n");
        nrts.setColor(RichTextStyle.COLOR_BLACK);
        nrts.setFont(RichTextStyle.FONT_COURIER);
        nrts.setFontSize(8);
        nrti.appendStyle(nrts);

        Document ndocCollection = ndc.getFirstDocument();
        int intDoccount=0;
        while (ndocCollection != null) {
```

```
            intDoccount++;
            nrti.appendText(String.valueOf(intDoccount) + " - ");
            nrti.appendText(ndocCollection.getCreated().getLocalTime());
            nrti.addTab(1);
            nrti.appendText(ndocCurrent.getItemValueString("From"));
            nrti.addTab(1);
            nrti.appendText("Created By: " +
            ➥ndocCollection.getItemValueString("Authors"));
            nrti.appendDocLink(ndocCollection, "Here are all the documents
            ➥that match: " + strCriteria);
            nrti.addNewLine(1);
            ndocCollection = ndc.getNextDocument(); }

        ndoc.appendItemValue("Form", "Memo");
        ndoc.save(true, false);
        ndoc.send(false, agentContext.getEffectiveUserName());
        System.out.println("E-Mail sent, please check your inbox!");

        } catch(Exception e) {
            e.printStackTrace();
        }
    }
}
```

RichTextParagraphStyle

5.0

The *lotus.domino.RichTextParagraphStyle*
object contains the rich-text attributes of
the current paragraph contained in a
lotus.domino.RichTextItem object. These
attributes enable you to further define the
style associated with the text contained in
the *lotus.domino.RichTextItem* by exposing
paragraph attributes, such as alignment,
spacing, and tab stops.

Session
   └ RichTextParagraphStyle
      └ RichTextTab

Java Syntax

The only way to create a new *lotus.domino.RichTextParagraphStyle* object is to use the `createRichTextParagraphStyle` method of the *lotus.domino.Session* object (▶ 579).

Java Parameters

There are no parameters for this object because it must be created by using the `createRichTextParagraphStyle` method of the *lotus.domino.Session* object (▶ xxx).

RichTextParagraphStyle Methods

clearAllTabs

clearAllTabs

`nrtpRichTextParagraphStyle.clearAllTabs()`

This method clears all the tab stops that have been set for the current paragraph. The tabs are contained in the *lotus.domino.RichTextParagraphStyle* and are stored as an array of integers.

getAlignment   R   %

getAlignment

`intAlignment = nrtpRichTextParagraphStyle.getAlignment()`

This method allows you to get the alignment and justification of the text or objects located in the current paragraph. The value contained in `intAlignment` is a constant (or integer) whose available values are listed in the following table. The default value for this method is `0`, which sets the paragraph style to left-justified.

Constant Value	Integer Value	Description
`RichTextParagraphStyle.ALIGN_CENTER`	3	Center justification
`RichTextParagraphStyle.ALIGN_FULL`	2	Full justification
`RichTextParagraphStyle.ALIGN_NOWRAP`	4	The text will not wrap but will continue to scroll to the right
`RichTextParagraphStyle.ALIGN_RIGHT`	1	Right justification
`RichTextParagraphStyle.ALIGN_LEFT`	0	Left justification

getFirstLineLeftMargin   R   %

getFirstLine
LeftMargin

`intMargin = nrtpRichTextParagraphStyle.getFirstLineLeftMargin()`

This method allows you to get the left margin for the first line of text contained in the current paragraph. Domino automatically uses the left margin settings for displaying the document. However, it always uses the right margin settings for printing and automatically sets the right margin when the document is displayed based on the size of the window in which Domino is currently contained. This method returns either a constant value (`RichTextParagraphStyle.RULER_ONE_CENTIMETER`, which represents one centimeter, or `RichTextParagraphStyle.RULER_ONE_INCH`, which represents one inch) or an integer value representing the margin measured in twips. With twips, one centimeter equals 537 twips, and one inch equals 1440 twips. You can perform arithmetic using the constants. For example, `RichTextParagraphStyle.RULER_ONE_CENTIMETER *` 5 sets the margin at 5 centimeters, and `RichTextParagraphStyle.RULER_ONE_INCH *` .5 sets the margin at one-half inch. The default value for this method is 1,440 twips.

getInterlineSpacing R %

```
intSpacing = nrtpRichTextParagraphStyle.getInterlineSpacing()
```

This method allows you to get the spacing setting between selected lines of the current paragraph. The value contained in the `intSpacing` variable is a constant (or integer) whose available values are shown in the following table. The default value for this method is `0`, which indicates that the paragraph will be single-spaced.

Constant Value	Integer Value	Description
`RichTextParagraphStyle.SPACING_DOUBLE`	2	Double spacing
`RichTextParagraphStyle.SPACING_ONE_POINT_50`	1	1½ line spacing
`RichTextParagraphStyle.SPACING_SINGLE`	0	Single spacing

getLeftMargin R %

```
intMargin = nrtpRichTextParagraphStyle.getLeftMargin()
```

This method allows you to get the left margin for the current paragraph. Domino automatically uses the left margin settings for displaying the document. However, it always uses the right margin settings for printing and automatically sets the right margin when the document is displayed based on the size of the window in which Domino is currently contained. This method returns either a constant value (`RichTextParagraphStyle.RULER_ONE_CENTIMETER`, which represents one centimeter, or `RichTextParagraphStyle.RULER_ONE_INCH`, which represents one inch) or an integer value representing the margin measured in twips. With twips, one centimeter equals 537 twips, and one inch equals 1,440 twips. You can perform arithmetic using the constants. For example, `RichTextParagraphStyle.RULER_ONE_CENTIMETER * 5` sets the margin at 5 centimeters, and `RichTextParagraphStyle.RULER_ONE_INCH * .5` sets the margin at one-half inch. The default value for this method is 1,440 twips.

getPagination R %

```
intPagination = nrtpRichTextParagraphStyle.getPagination()
```

This method allows you to get the pagination for the *lotus.domino. RichTextParagraphStyle*. The allowed values returned by this method are
`RichTextParagraphStyle.PAGINATE_BEFORE`,
`RichTextParagraphStyle.PAGINATE_DEFAULT`,
`RichTextParagraphStyle.PAGINATE_KEEP_TOGETHER`, and
`RichTextParagraphStyle.PAGINATE_KEEP_WITH_NEXT`.

getRightMargin R %

```
intMargin = nrtpRichTextParagraphStyle.getRightMargin()
```

This method allows you to get the right margin for the current paragraph. Domino automatically uses the left margin settings for displaying the document. However, it always uses the right margin settings for printing and automatically sets the right margin when the document is displayed based on the size of the window in which Domino is currently contained. This method returns either a constant value (`RichTextParagraphStyle.RULER_ONE_CENTIMETER`, which represents one centimeter, or `RichTextParagraphStyle.RULER_ONE_INCH`, which represents one inch) or an integer value representing the margin measured in twips. With twips, one centimeter equals 537 twips, and one inch equals 1,440 twips. You can perform arithmetic with the constants. For example, `RichTextParagraphStyle.RULER_ONE_CENTIMETER * 5` sets the margin at 5 centimeters, and `RichTextParagraphStyle.RULER_ONE_INCH * .5` sets the margin at one-half inch. The default value for this method is 1,440 twips.

---

getSpacingAbove   R   %

intSpacingabove = nrtpRichTextParagraphStyle.**getSpacingAbove**()

This method allows you to get the spacing setting above the selected lines of the current paragraph. The value contained in the `intSpacingabove` variable is a constant (or integer) whose available values are shown in the following table. The default value for this method is `0`, which indicates that the spacing above the line of text (or other objects) is single-spaced.

Constant Value	Integer Value	Description
RichTextParagraphStyle.SPACING_DOUBLE	2	Double spacing
RichTextParagraphStyle.SPACING_ONE_POINT_50	1	1½ line spacing
RichTextParagraphStyle.SPACING_SINGLE	0	Single spacing

---

getSpacingBelow   R   %

intSpacingbelow = nrtpRichTextParagraphStyle.**getSpacingBelow**()

This method allows you to get the spacing setting below the selected lines of the current paragraph. The value contained in the `intSpacingbelow` variable is a constant (or integer) whose available values are shown in the following table. The default value for this method is `0`, which indicates that the spacing below the line of text (or other objects) is single-spaced.

Constant Value	Integer Value	Description
RichTextParagraphStyle.SPACING_DOUBLE	2	Double spacing
RichTextParagraphStyle.SPACING_ONE_POINT_50	1	1½ line spacing
RichTextParagraphStyle.SPACING_SINGLE	0	Single spacing

---

getTabs   R   ()

vecTabs= nrtpRichTextParagraphStyle.**getTabs**()

This method returns an array of all the tabs that have been created for the current paragraph, in order from left to right. Each element of the array represents a specific tab stop that has been placed in the current paragraph and returns a vector of *lotus.domino.RichTextTab* objects, one for each tab.

---

setAlignment   W   %

nrtpRichTextParagraphStyle.**setAlignment**(intAlignment)

This method allows you to set the alignment and justification of the text or objects located in the current paragraph. The value contained in `intAlignment` is a constant (or integer) whose available values are shown in the following table. The default value for this method is `0`, which sets the paragraph style to left-justified.

Constant Value	Integer Value	Description
RichTextParagraphStyle.ALIGN_CENTER	3	Center justification
RichTextParagraphStyle.ALIGN_FULL	2	Full justification
RichTextParagraphStyle.ALIGN_NOWRAP	4	The text will not wrap but will continue to scroll to the right
RichTextParagraphStyle.ALIGN_RIGHT	1	Right justification
RichTextParagraphStyle.ALIGN_LEFT	0	Left justification

setFirstLineLeftMargin   W   %

nrtpRichTextParagraphStyle.**setFirstLineLeftMargin**(intMargin)

This method allows you to set the left margin for the first line of text contained in the current paragraph. Domino automatically uses the left margin settings for displaying the document. However, it always uses the right margin settings for printing and automatically sets the right margin when the document is displayed based on the size of the window in which Domino is currently contained. When using this method, you can use either a constant value (RichTextParagraphStyle.RULER_ONE_CENTIMETER, which represents one centimeter, or RichTextParagraphStyle.RULER_ONE_INCH, which represents one inch) or an integer value representing the margin measured in twips. With twips, one centimeter equals 537 twips, and one inch equals 1,440 twips. You can perform arithmetic with the constants. For example, RichTextParagraphStyle.RULER_ONE_CENTIMETER * 5 sets the margin at 5 centimeters, and RichTextParagraphStyle.RULER_ONE_INCH * .5 sets the margin at one-half inch. The default value for this method is 1,440 twips.

setInterlineSpacing   W   %

nrtpRichTextParagraphStyle.**setInterlineSpacing**(intSpacing)

This method allows you to set the spacing setting between selected lines of the current paragraph. The value contained in the intSpacing variable is a constant (or integer) whose available values are shown in the following table. The default value for this method is 0, which indicates that the paragraph will be single-spaced.

Constant Value	Integer Value	Description
RichTextParagraphStyle.SPACING_DOUBLE	2	Double spacing
RichTextParagraphStyle.SPACING_ONE_POINT_50	1	1½ line spacing
RichTextParagraphStyle.SPACING_SINGLE	0	Single spacing

setLeftMargin   W   %

nrtpRichTextParagraphStyle.**setLeftMargin**(intMargin)

This method allows you to set the left margin for the current paragraph. Domino automatically uses the left margin settings for displaying the document. However, it always uses the right margin settings for printing and automatically sets the right margin when the document is displayed based on the size of the window in which Domino is currently contained. When using this method, you can use either a constant value (RichTextParagraphStyle.RULER_ONE_CENTIMETER, which represents one centimeter, or RichTextParagraphStyle.RULER_ONE_INCH, which represents one inch) or an integer value representing the margin measured in twips. With twips, one centimeter equals 537 twips, and one inch equals 1,440 twips. You can perform arithmetic with the constants. For example, RichTextParagraphStyle.RULER_ONE_CENTIMETER * 5 sets the margin at 5 centimeters, and RichTextParagraphStyle.RULER_ONE_INCH * .5 sets the margin at one-half inch. The default value for this method is 1,440 twips.

setPagination   W   %

nrtpRichTextParagraphStyle.**setPagination**(intPagination)

This method allows you to set the pagination for the *lotus.domino.RichTextParagraphStyle*. The allowed values when calling this method are RichTextParagraphStyle.PAGINATE_BEFORE, RichTextParagraphStyle.PAGINATE_DEFAULT, RichTextParagraphStyle.PAGINATE_KEEP_TOGETHER, and RichTextParagraphStyle.PAGINATE_KEEP_WITH_NEXT.

setRightMargin W %

setRight
Margin

nrtpRichTextParagraphStyle.**setRightMargin**(intMargin)

This method allows you to set the right margin for the current paragraph. Domino automatically uses the left margin settings for displaying the document. However, it always uses the right margin settings for printing and automatically sets the right margin when the document is displayed based on the size of the window in which Domino is currently contained. When using this method, you can use either a constant value (RichTextParagraphStyle.RULER_ONE_CENTIMETER, which represents one centimeter, or RichTextParagraphStyle.RULER_ONE_INCH, which represents one inch) or an integer value representing the margin measured in twips. With twips, one centimeter equals 537 twips, and one inch equals 1,440 twips. You can perform arithmetic with the constants. For example, RichTextParagraphStyle.RULER_ONE_CENTIMETER * 5 sets the margin at 5 centimeters, and RichTextParagraphStyle.RULER_ONE_INCH * .5 sets themargin at one-half inch. The default value for this method is 1,440 twips.

setSpacingAbove W %

setSpacing
Above

nrtpRichTextParagraphStyle.**setSpacingAbove**(intSpacingAbove)

This method allows you to set the spacing setting above the selected lines of the current paragraph. The value contained in the intSpacingabove variable is a constant (or integer) whose available values are shown in the following table. The default value for this method is 0, which indicates that the spacing above the line of text (or other objects) is single-spaced.

Constant Value	Integer Value	Description
RichTextParagraphStyle.SPACING_DOUBLE	2	Double spacing
RichTextParagraphStyle.SPACING_ONE_POINT_50	1	1½ line spacing
RichTextParagraphStyle.SPACING_SINGLE	0	Single spacing

setSpacingBelow W %

setSpacing
Below

nrtpRichTextParagraphStyle.**setSpacingBelow**(intSpacingBelow)

This method allows you to set the spacing setting below the selected lines of the current paragraph. The value contained in the intSpacingbelow variable is a constant (or integer) whose available values are shown in the following table. The default value for this method is 0, which indicates that the spacing below the line of text (or other objects) is single-spaced.

Constant Value	Integer Value	Description
RichTextParagraphStyle.SPACING_DOUBLE	2	Double spacing
RichTextParagraphStyle.SPACING_ONE_POINT_50	1	1½ line spacing
RichTextParagraphStyle.SPACING_SINGLE	0	Single spacing

setTab

setTab

nrtpRichTextParagraphStyle.**setTab**(intPosition, intType)

intPosition Required %

The position of the tab in twips, inches, or centimeters.

intType Required %

The type of text justification to use with this tab.

For the `intPosition` parameter, you can use either a constant value
(`RichTextParagraphStyle.RULER_ONE_CENTIMETER`, which represents one centimeter,
or `RichTextParagraphStyle.RULER_ONE_INCH`, which represents one inch) or an integer value representing the margin measured in twips. With twips, one centimeter
equals 537 twips, and one inch equals 1,440 twips. You can perform arithmetic with
the constants. For example, `RichTextParagraphStyle.RULER_ONE_CENTIMETER * 5`
sets the margin at 5 centimeters, and `RichTextParagraphStyle.RULER_ONE_INCH * .5`
sets the margin at one-half inch.

The following table lists the available constants to use with the `intType` parameter,
which determines how the text located at the respective tab stop is justified.

Constant Value	Integer Value	Description
`RichTextParagraphStyle.TAB_CENTER`	3	Text is centered around the tab stop
`RichTextParagraphStyle.TAB_DECIMAL`	2	Text is right-justified to the left of the tab stop and left-justified to the right of the tab stop
`RichTextParagraphStyle.TAB_LEFT`	0	Text is left-justified, beginning at the tab stop
`RichTextParagraphStyle.TAB_RIGHT`	1	Text is right-justified, ending at the tab stop

setTabs

```
nrtpRichTextParagraphStyle.setTabs(intCount, intStart, intInterval)
```
setTabs

```
nrtpRichTextParagraphStyle.setTabs(intCount, intStart, intInterval,
➥intType)
```

intCount   Required   %
The number of tab stops to create for this paragraph.

intStart   Required   %
The position of the first tab stop.

intInterval   Required   %
The interval space between tab stops if more than one is specified in the `intCount`
parameter.

intType   Required   %
The type of text justification to use with this tab.

When specifying the number of tab stops, pass a numeric value that is one less than
the actual number of tab stops requested. For example, if four tab stops are required for
the current paragraph, set this value to 3.

For both the `intStart` and `intInterval` parameters, you can use either a constant
value (`RichTextParagraphStyle.RULER_ONE_CENTIMETER`, which represents one centimeter, or `RichTextParagraphStyle.RULER_ONE_INCH`, which represents one inch) or
an integer value representing the margin measured in twips. With twips, one centimeter equals 537 twips, and one inch equals 1,440 twips. You can perform arithmetic
with the constants. For example, `RichTextParagraphStyle.RULER_ONE_CENTIMETER *`
5 sets the margin at 5 centimeters, and `RichTextParagraphStyle.RULER_ONE_INCH *`
.5 sets the margin at one-half inch.

The following table lists the available constants to use with the `intType` parameter, which determines how the text located at the respective tab stop is justified.

Constant Value	Integer Value	Description
RichTextParagraphStyle.TAB_CENTER	3	Text is centered around the tab stop
RichTextParagraphStyle.TAB_DECIMAL	2	Text is right-justified to the left of the tab stop and left-justified to the right of the tab stop
RichTextParagraphStyle.TAB_LEFT	0	Text is left-justified, beginning at the tab stop
RichTextParagraphStyle.TAB_RIGHT	1	Text is right-justified, ending at the tab stop

Remarks

When using methods that allow you to set or read the position of the tab, the unit of measurement is set or returned as either inches (Imperial) or centimeters (Metric). This setting is modified from the native Domino client interface in the User Preferences, under the International section.

Example

The following example demonstrates some of the formatting features available with the *lotus.domino.RichTextParagraphStyle* object and shows you how manipulating these methods can help you create professionally formatted paragraphs that are more meaningful and easier to read. This example creates a new *lotus.domino.Document,* reads the contents of a view, and then populates the `Body` field of the document with information loaded from the view. The paragraph that contains this information is a rich-text field that uses several different formatting techniques, justification, and tab stops. Finally, the document is saved with the form type as `"Summation Form"`.

```
import lotus.domino.*;

public class JavaAgent extends AgentBase {

  public void NotesMain() {

    try {
        Session ns = getSession();
        AgentContext agentContext = ns.getAgentContext();
        Agent nagt = agentContext.getCurrentAgent();
        Database ndb = agentContext.getCurrentDatabase();
        View nvw = ndb.getView("All");
        Document ndoc = ndb.createDocument();
        RichTextItem nrti = ndoc.createRichTextItem("Body");
        RichTextParagraphStyle nrtp = ns.createRichTextParagraphStyle();
```

```
nrtp.setSpacingAbove(RichTextParagraphStyle.SPACING_SINGLE);
nrtp.setTab(RichTextParagraphStyle.RULER_ONE_INCH * 1,
➥RichTextParagraphStyle.TAB_RIGHT);
nrtp.setTab(RichTextParagraphStyle.RULER_ONE_INCH * 2,
➥RichTextParagraphStyle.TAB_CENTER);
nrtp.setTab(RichTextParagraphStyle.RULER_ONE_INCH * 4,
➥RichTextParagraphStyle.TAB_CENTER);
nrtp.setTab(RichTextParagraphStyle.RULER_ONE_INCH * 6,
➥RichTextParagraphStyle.TAB_LEFT);
nrti.appendParagraphStyle(nrtp);
nrti.addTab(1);
nrti.appendText("Count");
nrti.addTab(1);
nrti.appendText("Date Created");
nrti.addTab(1);
nrti.appendText("DocLin");
nrti.addTab(1);
nrti.appendText("Summary Information");
nrti.addNewLine(1);
nrti.appendParagraphStyle(nrtp);
Document ndocCurrent = nvw.getFirstDocument();
int intDoccount=0;
while (ndocCurrent != null) {
    intDoccount++;
    nrti.appendParagraphStyle(nrtp);
    nrti.addTab(1);
    nrti.appendText(String.valueOf(intDoccount));
    nrti.addTab(1);
    nrti.appendText(ndocCurrent.getCreated().getLocalTime());
    nrti.addTab(1);
    nrti.appendDocLink(ndoc, ndoc.getItemValueString("Subject"),
    ➥"Click to open original doc.");
    nrti.addTab(1);
    nrti.appendText(ndocCurrent.getItemValueString("Subject"));
    nrti.addNewLine(1);
    ndocCurrent = nvw.getNextDocument(ndocCurrent); }
ndoc.appendItemValue("Form", "Summation Form");
ndoc.save(true, false);

} catch(Exception e) {
    e.printStackTrace();
}
    }
}
```

RichTextStyle

The *lotus.domino.RichTextStyle* object
contains the rich text attributes of the
lotus.domino.RichTextItem object or the
lotus.domino.Session object. These attributes
go beyond the standard attributes associated with the static text fields used with
lotus.domino.Item objects, which are formatted with a single font type, font size,
color, and so on. This is because the style
associated with the text contained in the
lotus.domino.RichTextItem is dynamic and
can change for each paragraph, line, or
character. Prior to Notes 4.6, there was
no way to programmatically modify the
style attributes of rich text fields. When
you created *lotus.domino.RichTextItem* or
modified its contents, all text automatically defaulted to 10-point Helvetica.

Session
    └ RichTextStyle

Java Syntax

```
Public class RichTextStyle extends Base
```

The only way to create a new *lotus.domino.RichTextStyle* object is to use the createRichTextStyle method of the *lotus.domino.Session* object.

Java Parameters

There are no parameters for this object since it must be created using the createRichTextStyle method of the *lotus.domino.Session* object.

RichTextStyle Methods

getBold   R   %

getBold   `intBold = nrtsRichTextStyle.getBold()`

This method indicates whether the font characteristic of the *lotus.domino.RichTextItem* is bold. Here are the values that may be returned:

Value	Description
RichTextStyle.YES	Text appears bold.
RichTextStyle.NO	Text doesn't appear bold.
RichTextStyle.STYLE_NO_CHANGE	Text doesn't change.
RichTextStyle.MAYBE	Text doesn't change.

getColor   R   %

getColor   `intcolor = nrtsRichTextStyle.getColor()`

This method indicates the color of the *lotus.domino.RichTextItem*. Here are the possible constants that are returned:

Constant Value	Integer Value
RichTextStyle.COLOR_BLACK	0
RichTextStyle.COLOR_BLUE	4
RichTextStyle.COLOR_CYAN	7
RichTextStyle.COLOR_DARK_BLUE	10
RichTextStyle.COLOR_DARK_CYAN	13
RichTextStyle.COLOR_DARK_GREEN	9
RichTextStyle.COLOR_DARK_MAGENTA	11
RichTextStyle.COLOR_DARK_RED	8
RichTextStyle.COLOR_DARK_YELLOW	12
RichTextStyle.COLOR_GRAY	14
RichTextStyle.COLOR_GREEN	3
RichTextStyle.COLOR_LIGHT_GRAY	15
RichTextStyle.COLOR_MAGENTA	5
RichTextStyle.COLOR_RED	2

Constant Value	Integer Value
RichTextStyle.COLOR_WHITE	1
RichTextStyle.COLOR_YELLOW	6
RichTextStyle.STYLE_NO_CHANGE	255
RichTextStyle.MAYBE	255

getEffects   R   %

```
intEffects = nrtsRichTextStyle.getEffects()
```

getEffects

This method represents the font characteristics and text effects of the
lotus.domino.RichTextItem that are covered by the other methods of the
lotus.domino.RichTextItem object. Here are the possible constants that are returned:

Constant Value	Integer Value	Description
RichTextStyle.EFFECTS_EMBOSS	4	Text appears embossed.
RichTextStyle.EFFECTS_EXTRUDE	5	Text appears extruded.
RichTextStyle.EFFECTS_NONE	0	Text has no special effects other than those represented by the other methods of the *lotus.domino.RichTextStyle* object.
RichTextStyle.EFFECTS_SHADOW	3	Text appears with a shadow.
RichTextStyle.EFFECTS_SUBSCRIPT	2	Text appears as subscript.
RichTextStyle.EFFECTS_SUPERSCRIPT	1	Text appears as superscript.
RichTextStyle.STYLE_NO_CHANGE	255	The *lotus.domino.RichTextStyle* hasn't been modified by any script and currently recognizes the defaults.

getFont   R   %

```
intFont = nrtsRichTextStyle.getFont()
```

getFont

This method indicates the font type of the *lotus.domino.RichTextItem*. Here are the possible constants that are returned:

Constant Value	Integer Value
RichTextStyle.FONT_COURIER	4
RichTextStyle.FONT_HELV	1
RichTextStyle.FONT_ROMAN	0
RichTextStyle.STYLE_NO_CHANGE	255
RichTextStyle.MAYBE	255

getFontSize   R   %

```
intFontSize = nrtsRichTextStyle.getFontSize()
```

getFontSize

This method returns an integer representing the font size of the current
lotus.domino.RichTextItem. The size is returned in font point size, ranging from
1 to 250. It can also be a constant value of RichTextStyle.STYLE_NO_CHANGE or
RichTextStyle.MAYBE, signifying that the font size hasn't changed from the previous
font size.

getItalic   R   T/F

```
intItalic = nrtsRichTextStyle.getItalic()
```

This method indicates whether the font characteristic of the *lotus.domino.RichTextItem* is italic. Here are the values that may be returned:

Value	Description
RichTextStyle.YES	Text appears italic.
RichTextStyle.NO	Text doesn't appear italic.
RichTextStyle.STYLE_NO_CHANGE	Text doesn't change.
RichTextStyle.MAYBE	Text doesn't change.

getParent   R   O.Ref.

```
nsSession = nrtsRichTextStyle.getParent()
```

This method returns a handle on the *lotus.domino.Session* that contains the current *lotus.domino.RichTextStyle* object.

getStrikeThrough   R   %

```
intStrike = nrtsRichTextStyle.getStrikeThrough()
```

This method indicates whether the font characteristic of the *lotus.domino.RichTextItem* is strikethrough. Here are the values that may be returned:

Value	Description
RichTextStyle.YES	Text appears strikethrough.
RichTextStyle.NO	Text doesn't appear strikethrough.
RichTextStyle.STYLE_NO_CHANGE	Text doesn't change.
RichTextStyle.MAYBE	Text doesn't change.

getUnderline   R   %

```
intUnderline = nrtsRichTextStyle.getUnderline()
```

This method indicates the underline font characteristic of the *lotus.domino.RichTextItem*. Here are the values that may be returned:

Value	Description
RichTextStyle.YES	Text appears underlined.
RichTextStyle.NO	Text doesn't appear underlined.
RichTextStyle.STYLE_NO_CHANGE	Text doesn't change.
RichTextStyle.MAYBE	Text doesn't change.

setBold   W   %

```
nrtsRichTextStyle.setBold(intBold)
```

This method sets the bold font characteristic of the *lotus.domino.RichTextItem*. Here are the values used for this method:

Value	Description
RichTextStyle.YES	Text appears bold.
RichTextStyle.NO	Text doesn't appear bold.
RichTextStyle.STYLE_NO_CHANGE	Text doesn't change.
RichTextStyle.MAYBE	Text doesn't change.

setColor   W   %

nrtsRichTextStyle.**setColor**(intColor)   setColor

This method sets the color of the *lotus.domino.RichTextItem*. Here are the possible constants that are returned:

Constant Value	Integer Value
RichTextStyle.COLOR_BLACK	0
RichTextStyle.COLOR_BLUE	4
RichTextStyle.COLOR_CYAN	7
RichTextStyle.COLOR_DARK_BLUE	10
RichTextStyle.COLOR_DARK_CYAN	13
RichTextStyle.COLOR_DARK_GREEN	9
RichTextStyle.COLOR_DARK_MAGENTA	11
RichTextStyle.COLOR_DARK_RED	8
RichTextStyle.COLOR_DARK_YELLOW	12
RichTextStyle.COLOR_GRAY	14
RichTextStyle.COLOR_GREEN	3
RichTextStyle.COLOR_LIGHT_GRAY	15
RichTextStyle.COLOR_MAGENTA	5
RichTextStyle.COLOR_RED	2
RichTextStyle.COLOR_WHITE	1
RichTextStyle.COLOR_YELLOW	6
RichTextStyle.STYLE_NO_CHANGE	255
RichTextStyle.MAYBE	255

setEffects   W   %

nrtsRichTextStyle.**setEffects**(intEffects)   setEffects

This method sets the font characteristics and text effects of the *lotus.domino.RichTextItem* that are covered by the other methods of the *lotus.domino.RichTextItem* object. Here are the possible constants that are returned:

Constant Value	Integer Value	Description
RichTextStyle.EFFECTS_EMBOSS	4	Text appears embossed.
RichTextStyle.EFFECTS_EXTRUDE	5	Text appears extruded.
RichTextStyle.EFFECTS_NONE	0	Text has no special effects other than those represented by the other methods of the *lotus.domino.RichTextStyle* object.
RichTextStyle.EFFECTS_SHADOW	3	Text appears with a shadow.
RichTextStyle.EFFECTS_SUBSCRIPT	2	Text appears as subscript.
RichTextStyle.EFFECTS_SUPERSCRIPT	1	Text appears as superscript.
RichTextStyle.STYLE_NO_CHANGE	255	The *lotus.domino.RichTextStyle* hasn't been modified by any script and currently recognizes the defaults.

setFont   W   %

setFont   `nrtsRichTextStyle.`**`setFont`**`(intFont)`

This method sets the font type of the *lotus.domino.RichTextItem*. Here are the possible constants that are returned:

Constant Value	Integer Value
RichTextStyle.FONT_COURIER	4
RichTextStyle.FONT_HELV	1
RichTextStyle.FONT_ROMAN	0
RichTextStyle.STYLE_NO_CHANGE	255
RichTextStyle.MAYBE	255

setFontSize   W   %

setFontSize   `nrtsRichTextStyle.`**`setFontSize`**`(intFontsize)`

This method sets an integer representing the font size of the current *lotus.domino.RichTextItem*. The size is set in font point size, ranging from 1 to 250. It can also be a constant value of `RichTextStyle.STYLE_NO_CHANGE` or `RichTextStyle.MAYBE`, signifying that the font size hasn't changed from the previous font size.

setItalic   W   %

setItalic   `nrtsRichTextStyle.`**`setItalic`**`(intItalic)`

This method sets the italic font characteristic of the *lotus.domino.RichTextItem*. Here are the values that may be set:

Value	Description
RichTextStyle.YES	Text appears italic.
RichTextStyle.NO	Text doesn't appear italic.
RichTextStyle.STYLE_NO_CHANGE	Text doesn't change.
RichTextStyle.MAYBE	Text doesn't change.

setStrikeThrough   W   %

setStrike Through   `nrtsRichTextStyle.`**`setStrikeThrough`**`(intStrike)`

This method sets the strikethrough font characteristic of the *lotus.domino.RichTextItem*. Here are the values that may be set:

Value	Description
RichTextStyle.YES	Text appears strikethrough.
RichTextStyle.NO	Text doesn't appear strikethrough.
RichTextStyle.STYLE_NO_CHANGE	Text doesn't change.
RichTextStyle.MAYBE	Text doesn't change.

setUnderline   W   %

setUnderline   `nrtsRichTextStyle.`**`setUnderline`**`(intUnderline)`

This sets the underline font characteristic of the *lotus.domino.RichTextItem*. Here are the values that may be set:

Value	Description
RichTextStyle.YES	Text appears underlined.
RichTextStyle.NO	Text doesn't appear underlined.
RichTextStyle.STYLE_NO_CHANGE	Text doesn't change.
RichTextStyle.MAYBE	Text doesn't change.

Remarks

When you develop applications using Java, the *lotus.domino.RichTextStyle* object is used by the *lotus.domino.RichTextItem* object with the appendStyle method. When a new *lotus.domino.RichTextStyle* object is created, all of its methods default to STYLE_NO_CHANGE (with an integer value of 255).

Example

The following example modifies the *lotus.domino.RichTextStyle* for the text being written to the Body field of a memo. The body of the memo, though brief, uses several methods of the *lotus.domino.RichTextStyle* class to help convey the meaning of the message.

```
import lotus.domino.*;

public class JavaAgent extends AgentBase {

  public void NotesMain() {

    try {
        Session ns = getSession();
        AgentContext agentContext = ns.getAgentContext();
        Agent nagt = agentContext.getCurrentAgent();
        Database ndb = agentContext.getCurrentDatabase();
        Document ndoc = ndb.createDocument();
        RichTextItem nrti = ndoc.createRichTextItem("Body");
        RichTextStyle nrtsMessage = ns.createRichTextStyle();
        nrtsMessage.setColor(RichTextStyle.COLOR_BLACK);
        nrtsMessage.setEffects(RichTextStyle.EFFECTS_EMBOSS);
        nrtsMessage.setFontSize(8);
        nrti.appendStyle(nrtsMessage);
        nrti.appendText("Sorry Tim, you have been ");
        nrti.addNewLine();
        RichTextStyle nrtsFired = ns.createRichTextStyle();
        nrtsFired.setColor(RichTextStyle.COLOR_RED);
        nrtsFired.setBold(RichTextStyle.YES);
        nrtsFired.setUnderline(RichTextStyle.YES);
        nrtsFired.setFontSize(36);
```

continued >>

continued >>

```
                nrti.appendStyle(nrtsFired);
                nrti.appendText("FIRED!");
                nrti.addNewLine();
                ndoc.appendItemValue("Form", "Memo");
                ndoc.appendItemValue("Subject", "Congratulations!");
                ndoc.send(false, "Tim Bankes/Definiti");

            } catch(Exception e) {
                e.printStackTrace();
            }
        }
    }
```

5.0 RichTextTab

The *lotus.domino.RichTextTab* object
exposes the tab attributes of the
lotus.domino.RichTextParagraphStyle.
The tabs contained in the
lotus.domino.RichTextParagraph are just one
of the attributes that can be used to add
rich formatting to the text and objects
contained in a *lotus.domino.RichTextItem*.

Session
L RichTextParagraphStyle
L RichTextTab

Java Syntax

The only way to create a new *lotus.domino.RichTextTab* object is to use the
getTabs method of the *lotus.domino.RichTextParagraphStyle* object (▶ 558). Here
are the other methods available for tabs located in *lotus.domino.RichTextItem,*
lotus.domino.RichTextTab, and *lotus.domino.RichTextParagraphStyle:*

Method	Description
addTab	Inserts a tab in a *lotus.domino.RichTextItem.*
clear	Clears tab(s) in a *lotus.domino.RichTextTab.*
clearAllTabs	Clears all tabs in a *lotus.domino.RichTextParagraphStyle.*
getPosition	Used to return the position of a tab contained in a *lotus.domino.RichTextTab.*
getTabs	Creates a *lotus.domino.RichTextTab* object within a *lotus.domino.RichTextParagraphStyle.*
getType	Used to return the type of a tab contained within a *lotus.domino.RichTextTab.*
setTab	Sets a tab in a *lotus.domino.RichTextParagraphStyle.*
setTabs	Sets multiple tabs in a *lotus.domino.RichTextParagraphStyle.*

RichTextTab Methods

clear

clear   nrttRichTextTab.**clear**()

This method clears the current tab from the current paragraph. The tabs are contained
in the *lotus.domino.RichTextParagraphStyle* as an array of integers.

getPosition   R   %

getPosition   intPosition = nrttRichTextTab.**getPosition**()

This method allows you to get the position of the tab contained in the current paragraph—in twips, inches, or centimeters. This method can return either a constant value
(RichTextParagraphStyle.RULER_ONE_CENTIMETER, representing one centimeter, or
RichTextParagraphStyle.RULER_ONE_INCH, representing one inch) or an integer value
representing the margin measured in twips. One centimeter equals 537 twips, and one
inch equals 1,440 twips. You can perform arithmetic with the constants. For example,
RichTextParagraphStyle.RULER_ONE_CENTIMETER * 5 sets the margin at five centimeters, and RichTextParagraphStyle.RULER_ONE_INCH * .5 sets the margin at one-
half inch. The default value for this method is 1,440 twips.

getType   R   %

getType   intType = nrttRichTextTab.**getType**()

This method allows you to get the type of paragraph justification for the current text
or objects contained in this *lotus.domino.RichTextParagraphStyle.* The following table lists
the available constants to use with the intType parameter that determine how the text
located at the respective tab stop is justified.

Constant Value	Integer Value	Description
RichTextParagraphStyle.TAB_CENTER	3	Text is centered around the tab stop.
RichTextParagraphStyle.TAB_DECIMAL	2	Text is right-justified to the left of the tab stop and left-justified to the right of the tab stop.
RichTextParagraphStyle.TAB_LEFT	0	Text is left-justified, beginning at the tab stop.
RichTextParagraphStyle.TAB_RIGHT	1	Text is right-justified, ending at the tab stop.

Remarks

When you use methods that allow you to set or read a tab's position, the unit of measurement can be set or returned as either inches (Imperial) or centimeters (Metric), where RichTextParagraphStyle.RULER_ONE_CENTIMETER represents one centimeter and RichTextParagraphStyle.RULER_ONE_INCH represents one inch. You modify this setting from the native Lotus Notes client interface in the Measurements field in the User Preferences, under the International section. The tab position can also be set or returned as an integer value representing the margin measured in twips. With twips, one centimeter equals 537 twips, and one inch equals 1,440 twips. You can perform arithmetic with the constants. For example, RichTextParagraphStyle.RULER_ONE_CENTIMETER * 5 sets the margin at five centimeters, and RichTextParagraphStyle.RULER_ONE_INCH * .5 sets the margin at one-half inch.

Example

The following example gets a value from the current *lotus.domino.Document* to use as the keyword to search the current *lotus.domino.Database*. The results of the search are saved in a new memo called *lotus.domino.Document* that is created and mailed to the specified user. The contents of the mail document are modified using several Notes objects—namely, *lotus.domino.Item, lotus.domino.RichTextItem, lotus.domino.RichTextParagraph, lotus.domino.RichTextParagraphStyle,* and *lotus.domino.RichTextTab*. This code could be modified to run as a scheduled agent that automatically sends information to a particular user based on new document content.

```
import lotus.domino.*;

public class JavaAgent extends AgentBase {

  public void NotesMain() {

    try {
```

continued >>

continued >>

```
                        Session ns = getSession();
                        AgentContext agentContext = ns.getAgentContext();
                        Agent nagt = agentContext.getCurrentAgent();
                        Database ndb = agentContext.getCurrentDatabase();
                        View nvw = ndb.getView("All");
                        Document ndoc = ndb.createDocument();
                        Document ndocCurrent = agentContext.getDocumentContext();
                        RichTextItem nrti = ndoc.createRichTextItem("Body");
                        RichTextParagraphStyle nrtp = ns.createRichTextParagraphStyle();
                        RichTextStyle nrts = ns.createRichTextStyle();
                        String strCriteria = ndocCurrent.getItemValueString
                        ➥("tSearchCriteria");

                        nrtp.clearAllTabs();
                        nrtp.setTab(RichTextParagraphStyle.RULER_ONE_INCH * 2,
                        ➥RichTextParagraphStyle.TAB_LEFT);
                        nrtp.setTab(RichTextParagraphStyle.RULER_ONE_INCH * 4,
                        ➥RichTextParagraphStyle.TAB_CENTER);
                        nrtp.setTab(RichTextParagraphStyle.RULER_ONE_INCH * 6,
                        ➥RichTextParagraphStyle.TAB_CENTER);

                        nrts.setColor(RichTextStyle.COLOR_BLACK);
                        nrts.setBold(RichTextStyle.YES);
                        nrts.setUnderline(RichTextStyle.YES);
                        nrts.setFont(RichTextStyle.FONT_COURIER);
                        nrts.setFontSize(8);

                        nrti.appendStyle(nrts);
                        nrti.appendParagraphStyle(nrtp);
                        nrti.appendText("Here are all the documents that match: " +
                        ➥strCriteria);
                        nrti.addNewLine(2);

                        DocumentCollection ndc = ndb.FTSearch(strCriteria, 100,
                        ➥Database.FT_DATE_DES, 0);
                        Document ndocCollection = ndc.getFirstDocument();
                        int intDoccount=0;
                        while (ndocCollection != null) {
                            intDoccount++;
                            nrti.appendText(String.valueOf(intDoccount) + " - ");
                            nrti.appendText(ndocCollection.getCreated().getLocalTime());
                            nrti.addTab(1);
                            nrti.appendText(ndocCollection.getItemValueString("Form"));
                            nrti.addTab(1);
                            nrti.appendText("Create By: " +
                            ➥ndocCollection.getItemValueString("Authors"));
                            nrti.appendDocLink(ndocCollection, "Here are all the documents
                            ➥that match: " + strCriteria);
                            ndocCollection = ndc.getNextDocument(); }

                        ndoc.appendItemValue("Form", "Memo");
                        ndoc.save(true, false);
                        ndoc.send(false, "Tim Bankes/Definiti");
                        System.out.println("RichTextTab agent complete");

                    } catch(Exception e) {
                        e.printStackTrace();
                    }
                }
            }
```

The *lotus.domino.Session* class is at the top of the hierarchy of Domino classes. It can be used as the starting point when using Java to access any of the subclasses. It also specifically provides access to address books and information about the current user, environment variables, and the current Notes platform and release number. It is a class you should come to know and love.

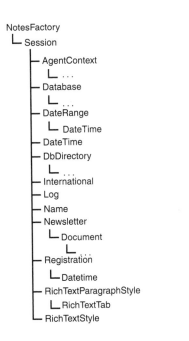

NotesFactory
└ Session
   ├ AgentContext
     └ ...
   ├ Database
     └ ...
   ├ DateRange
     └ DateTime
   ├ DateTime
   ├ DbDirectory
     └ ...
   ├ International
   ├ Log
   ├ Name
   ├ Newsletter
     └ Document
       └ ...
   ├ Registration
     └ Datetime
   ├ RichTextParagraphStyle
     └ RichTextTab
   └ RichTextStyle

Java Syntax

```
public class Session extends Base
```

To access the *lotus.domino.Session* object, you have three basic choices that depend on what you're trying to do. If you're building stand-alone Java applications, you should call one of the createSession methods of the *lotus.domino.NotesFactory* class. If you're building Java agents, you can call the getSession method of *lotus.domino.AgentContext*. If you want to access the current session from running code, you can call the getParent method of the *lotus.domino.Database* object.

Session Methods

createDateRange

createDate
Range

```
ndrDateRange = nssession.createDateRange()

ndrDateRange createDateRange(ndtStart, ndtEnd)

ndrDateRange createDateRange(strStartTime, strEndTime)
```

ndtStart	Required	O.Ref.

A *lotus.domino.DateTime* object used as the range's starting date.

ndtEnd	Required	O.Ref.

A *lotus.domino.DateTime* object used as the range's ending date.

strStartTime	Required	O.Ref.

A *java.util.Date* object used as the range's starting date.

strEndTime	Required	O.Ref.

A *java.util.Date* object used as the range's ending date.

The createDateRange method allows you to create new *lotus.domino.DateRange* objects (▶ 395).

createDateTime

createDate
Time

```
ndtDateTime = nssession.createDateTime(strDateTime)

ndtDateTime = nssession.createDateTime(strDatetoSet)
```

strDateTime	Required	O.Ref.

A string value representing the date and/or time value you want to use.

strDatetoSet	Required	O.Ref.

A *java.util.Date* value representing the date and/or time value you want to use.

This method returns a *lotus.domino.DateTime* object (▶ 399) representing the date and/or time used as a parameter. The Notes date-time expressions "Yesterday" and "Today" can be used to initialize the object.

createLog

createLog

```
nlogLog = nssession.createLog(strName)
```

strName	Required	O.Ref.

A *java.lang.String* object containing a name that identifies the agent being logged.

This method returns a *lotus.domino.Log* object (▶ 477) with the name specified in the strName parameter.

createName

```
nnamName = nssession.createName(strName)

nnamName = nssession.createName(strName, strLang)
```

createName

strName	Required	O.Ref.

A *java.lang.String* containing the server or user name.

strLang	Required	O.Ref.

A *java.lang.String* containing the language to associate with the user name, if there is one.

This method returns a *lotus.domino.Name* (▶ 485) object. If the name is not formatted as a canonical or hierarchical name, it will be considered a flat name.

createNewsLetter

```
nnewsNewsLetter = nssession.createNewsLetter(ndcCollection)
```

createNews
Letter

ndcCollection	Required	O.Ref.

A *lotus.domino.DocumentCollection* object containing the documents to send a newsletter.

This method returns a *lotus.domino.NewsLetter* object based on the documents contained in the ndcCollection parameter.

createRegistration

```
nregRegistration = nssession.createRegistration()
```

create
Registration

Call this method to create a new *lotus.domino.Registration* (▶ 517) object. It takes no parameters.

5.0 createRichTextParagraphStyle

```
nrtpstyParaStyle = nssession.createRichTextParagraphStyle()
```

createRichText
ParagraphStyle

Call this method to create a new *lotus.domino.RichTextParagraphStyle* (▶ 555) object. It takes no parameters.

4.6 createRichTextStyle

```
Richtextsytle nrtstylStyle = nssession.createRichTextStyle()
```

createRichText
Style

Call this method to create a new *lotus.domino.RichTextStyle* (▶ 565) object. It takes no parameters.

evaluate	R	O.Ref.

```
vecResult = nssession.evaluate(strFormula)

vecResult = nssession.evaluate(strFormula, ndocDocwithField)
```

evaluate

strFormula	Required	O.Ref.

A *java.util.String* object containing the Notes formula to evaluate.

ndocDocwithField	Required	O.Ref.

A *lotus.domino.Document* object containing a field or fields used in the formula being executed.

This method allows you to execute Notes formulas and access their results. The result is returned in the first element of the *java.util.Vector*. Keep in mind that if you're using the value of a field in the formula, you must call this method using both parameters.

freeTimeSearch

```
vecfreetime = freeTimeSearch(ndrWindow, intDuration, vecNames,
➥bolFirstfit)
```

ndrWindow	Required	O.Ref.

A *lotus.domino.DateRange* object containing start and end times within which to search for free time.

intDuration	Required	%

The length in minutes of the free-time interval.

vecNames	Required	O.Ref.

A string or vector of strings containing names of the people or groups whose free time to search.

bolFirstfit	Required	T/F

`true` uses the first matching date range. `false` uses all the matching times.

This method returns a *java.util.Vector* containing the elements of type *lotus.domino.DateRange* representing the time ranges that are available. If no matching times were found, the vector is `null`.

getAddressBooks   R   O.Ref.

```
vecaddressbooks = nssession.getAddressBooks()
```

This method returns an object of type *java.util.Vector* where the elements are `NotesDatabases` representing the Notes Name and Address Book (NAB) available to the currently executing agent (the NABs defined in the `NAMES=` entry in the Notes.ini file). If the agent executes on a server, this method will return only public NABs. Otherwise, it will return both public and private NABs. Consider the following example.

```
import lotus.domino.*;
import java.util.*;

public class JavaAgent extends AgentBase {
  public void NotesMain() {
    try {
            Session nssession = getSession();
            AgentContext nacContext = nssession.getAgentContext();
            Vector vecAddressBooks=nssession.getAddressBooks();
            Enumeration enum=vecAddressBooks.elements();
            String strPrtString="";
            while (enum.hasMoreElements())
              {
                Database dbCurr=(Database)enum.nextElement();
                System.out.println("The following public address books are
                ➥available: " + "\n" + strPrtString);
                if (dbCurr.isPublicAddressBook())
                  strPrtString=strPrtString + dbCurr.getTitle() + ": " +
                  ➥dbCurr.getFileName()+"\n";
              }
          catch(Exception e) {
          e.printStackTrace();
      }
    }
  }
}
```

getAgentContext	R	O.Ref.	

`nacContext = nssession.`**`getAgentContext`**`()`

getAgent
Context

This method returns an object of type *lotus.domino.AgentContext* representing an agent's current environment. If an agent is not running, this method will return `null`.

getCommonUserName	R	O.Ref.	

`strCommonName = nssession.`**`getCommonUserName`**

getCommon
UserName

This method returns a string object containing the common user name of the Notes ID file in use. When executing on a server, the server's common user name is returned. On a workstation, the current user's common name is returned.

getDatabase	R	O.Ref.	

`ndbCurrentDb = nssession.`**`getDatabase`**`(strServer, strDb)`

getDatabase

`ndbCurrentDb = nssession.`**`getDatabase`**`(strServer, strDb, bolCreateonfail)`

strServer	Required	O.Ref.

Passes the name of the server where the database resides. Pass `null` to access a local database.

strDb	Required	O.Ref.

The path and filename of the database.

bolCreateonfail	Required	T/F

When set to `true`, returns a *lotus.domino.Database* object even if the specified database can't be opened. If `false` (the default), returns `null` if the database can't be opened.

This method returns a *lotus.domino.Database* object representing the database in which the current agent is running.

getDbDirectory	R	O.Ref	

`ndirDirectory = nssession.`**`getDbDirectory`**`(strServer)`

getDbDirectory

strServer	Required	O.Ref.

Passes the name of the server whose directories you want to search. Passes `null` to access a local database.

This method returns a *lotus.domino.DbDirectory* object representing the server's file system. Consider the following example.

```
import lotus.domino.*;
import java.util.Vector;

public class JavaAgent extends AgentBase {
  public void NotesMain() {
    try {
        Session nssession = getSession();
        AgentContext nacContext = nssession.getAgentContext();
        // Load recipient's array with application administrators
        Vector vecRecipients= new Vector();
        vecRecipients.addElement("Samuel Hatter");
        vecRecipients.addElement("Wyatt Hatter");
        vecRecipients.addElement("Leslee Hatter");
        Database dbCurr=nacContext.getCurrentDatabase();
        // Prepare Memo document
```
continued >>

continued >>

```
Document ndocMail=dbCurr.createDocument();
ndocMail.appendItemValve("Subject", "Template Check Agent
➥Summary")
RichTextItem rtiBody = ndocMail.createRichTextItem("Body");
int intCount=0;
//Get Directory object on current server
DbDirectory ndirDirectory=nssession.getDbDirectory
➥(dbCurr.getServer());
Database ndbCDatabase = ndirDirectory.getFirstDatabase
➥(DbDirectory.TEMPLATE);
rtiBody.appendText("The following templates were found on " +
➥dbCurr.getServer() + " :");
rtiBody.addNewLine(2);
while(ndbCDatabase != null)
  {
    intCount++;
    rtiBody.addNewLine(1);
    rtiBody.appendText(ndbCDatabase.getTitle() + " (" +
    ➥ndbCDatabase.getFilePath() + ")");
    ndbCDatabase = ndirDirectory.getNextDatabase();
  }
rtiBody.addNewLine(2);
rtiBody.appendText(intCount + " templates were found.");
ndocMail.send(false,vecRecipients) ;
} catch(Exception e) {
  e.printStackTrace();
      }
    }
  }
```

---

getEnvironment
String

getEnvironmentString

```
strVar = nssession.getEnvironmentString(strName)
```

```
strVar = nssession.getEnvironmentString(strName, bolSystem)
```

strName	Required	O.Ref.

The name of the environment variable to retrieve.

bolSystem	Required	T/F

If the environment variable is a system variable, such as NAMES, pass true. Otherwise, pass false (the default) to retrieve nonsystem variables. When this parameter is false, the strName parameter is prepended with $, which is how user-defined environment variables are stored.

This useful method returns a string containing the value of the specified string environment variable, if it is found in the Notes initialization (notes.ini) file. If the method is called in a script executing on a workstation, the local notes.ini file is read. If the script is executed on a server, the server's notes.ini file will be read if the user executing the script has the authority to read the notes.ini file. For more information on Notes security and running agents, see the Domino Administration Help database.

---

getEnvironment
Value

getEnvironmentValue

```
objVar = nssession.getEnvironmentValue(strName)
```

```
objVar = nssession.getEnvironmentValue(strName, bolSystem)
```

strName	Required	O.Ref.

The name of the environment variable to retrieve.

bolSystem	Required	T/F

If the environment variable is a system variable, such as `NAMES`, pass `true`. Otherwise, pass `false` (the default) to retrieve nonsystem variables. When this parameter is `false`, the `strName` parameter is prepended with `$`, which is how user-defined environment variables are stored.

This method returns an object containing the value of the specified numeric environment variable, if it is found in the Notes initialization (notes.ini) file. If the method is called in script executing on a workstation, the local notes.ini file is read. If the script is executed on a server, the server's notes.ini file will be read if the user executing the script has the authority to read the notes.ini file. For more information on Notes security and running agents, see the Domino Administration Help database.

getInternational   R   O.Ref.

`nintInternation = nssession.`**`getInternational()`**   getInternational

This method returns an object of type *lotus.domino.International* (▶ 459), which contains all the international settings for the current machine.

getNotesVersion   R   O.Ref.

`strVersion = nssession.`**`getNotesVersion()`**   getNotesVersion

Returns a string representing the version (release) of Notes/Domino under which the current agent is executing.

getPlatform   R   O.Ref.

`strPlatform = nssession.`**`getPlatform()`**   getPlatform

Returns the name of the platform (operating system) on which Notes is running. If the agent runs on a server, the server's platform is returned. Otherwise, the workstation's platform is returned. Valid platform return values are `"MacIntosh"`, `"MSDos"`, `"Netware"`, `"OS/2v1"`, `"OS/2v2"`, `"Windows/16"`, `"Windows/32"`, and `"UNIX"`.

getServerName   R   O.Ref.

`strServer = nssession.`**`getServerName()`**   getServerName

This method returns a string object containing the name of the current server, or `null` if the agent is running locally.

getUserName   R   O.Ref.

`strUserName = nssession.`**`getUserName()`**   getUserName

On a server, this method returns the fully distinguished name of the server. On a workstation, this method returns the fully distinguished name of the current user.

5.0 getUserNameList   R   O.Ref.

`vecNamesList = nssession.`**`getUserNameList()`**   getUserName List

This new method returns a *java.util.Vector* of *lotus.domino.Name* objects (▶ 485) representing all the names in use in a session.

5.0 getUserNameObject   R   O.Ref.

`nnamUserName = nssession.`**`getUserNameObject()`**   getUserName Object

This new method returns a *lotus.domino.Name* (▶ 485) object containing the name of the current user.

---

isOnServer	R	T/F

```
bolOnServer = nssession.isOnServer()
```

This method returns `true` if the executing agent is "running on the server" and `false` otherwise. Any agent in a database residing on a Domino server (and that uses one of the following trigger types: When new mail arrives; When documents have been pasted; On schedule hourly, daily, weekly, or monthly; or When documents have been created or modified) will cause this method to return `true`. Any other script "runs on the workstation," no matter whether the database itself resides on a server or workstation.

---

resolve

```
Base resolve = nssession.resolve(strURL)
```

strURL	Required	O.Ref.

A valid URL that you want to resolve to its source object.

This method returns a *lotus.domino.Database, lotus.domino.View, lotus.domino.Form, lotus.domino.Document,* or *lotus.domino.Agent* object representing the object referred to in the `strURL` parameter. Remember to cast the return value to the expected type.

---

setEnvionmentVar

```
nssession.setEnvironmentVar(strName, objvalue)
```
```
nssession.setEnvironmentVar(strName, objvalue, bolSystem)
```

strName	Required	O.Ref.

The name of the environment variable to set. If the variable doesn't exist in Notes.ini, it will be created.

objvalue	Required	O.Ref.

The value to write to the environment variable. Date values are converted to strings.

bolSystem	Required	T/F

If the environment variable being updated is a user-defined variable (prepended with $), set this parameter to `true`. If it's a system variable, set this parameter to `false`, or use the first signature.

This method allows you to update existing environment variables or add new environment variables to the Notes.ini file (the preferences file on a Mac). This gives you a way to persistently store data. On a server, calling this method results in an attempt to write to the Notes.ini file on the server. (The ability to do this is dictated by the Agent Manager and the OS.) On a workstation, this method writes to the local Notes.ini file. For more information on security as it pertains to writing to Notes.ini files, see the Domino Administration Help database.

Example

```
import lotus.domino.*;
import java.util.*;
public class JavaAgent extends AgentBase {
  public void NotesMain() {
    try {
            nssession session = getSession();
            AgentContext nacContext = nssession.getAgentContext();
```

```
// This simple example demonstrates using several properties
// of the session class
Database ndbLookupDb;
Database dbCurr=nacContext.getCurrentDatabase();
boolean intAuth=false;
DocumentCollection ndcCollection=
➥nacContext.getUnprocessedDocuments();
Document ndocCurr=ndcCollection.getFirstDocument();
Vector vecAuthUsers=ndocCurr.getItemValue("AuthUsers");
Enumeration enum=vecAuthUsers.elements();
while (enum.hasMoreElements())
  {
     String uname=(String)enum.nextElement();
     int intindex=uname.indexOf(nssession.getCommonUserName());
     if (intindex>0)
        {
        intAuth=true;
        break;
        }
  }
  if(intAuth=true)
    ndbLookupDb=nssession.getDatabase(dbCurr.getServer(),
    ➥"Sales.nsf");
    // insert other meaningful code here
    System.out.println("You are not authorized to use this
    ➥agent"");
catch(Exception e) {
e.printStackTrace();
}
}
}
```

The *lotus.domino.View* class represents the views or folders contained in the *lotus.domino.Database*. By accessing the *lotus.domino.View* objects, you can access the *lotus.domino.Documents* contained in them. (Although this isn't the only method of establishing a handle on *lotus.domino.Document* objects, it is a frequently used method.) *lotus.domino.View* provides a mechanism to display the *lotus.domino.Documents* through the user interface and provides a format to programmatically query the *lotus.domino.Documents* through the back end. Essentially, *lotus.domino.View* provides an "on-demand" relational and tabular format to the nonrelational back-end data store of Domino/Lotus Notes.

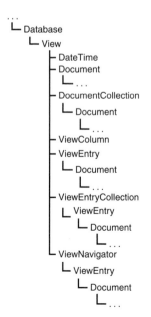

Page	Contents
	Syntax
	Methods

continued>>

Java Syntax

```
public class View extends Base
```

There are two ways to access the *lotus.domino.View* object. You can establish a handle on the parent *lotus.domino.Database* object that contains it and then exploit the getView or getViews method (▶ 388), or you can use the getParentView method of the *lotus.domino.Document* (▶ 423). When using the getView method of the *lotus.domino.Database* object, you can access a particular *lotus.domino.View* using either the view name or its alias (synonym). When running on a server, the public views and folders are available. When running locally, personal views and folders are available. To access all the views or folders contained in a database, you can use the getViews method. This method returns a vector of public views and folders and personal views and folders if running locally.

If accessing a *lotus.domino.Document* that was retrieved from within a view or folder, you can use the getParentView method of the current *lotus.domino.Document*.

View Methods

clear

```
nvwView.clear()
```
clear

This method clears the full-text search filtering for the specific view. When you're performing searches, subsequent searches continue to refine previous searches. Calling this method resets the search filter so that you can start a new search.

5.0 createViewNav

```
nvnViewNavigator = nvwView.createViewNav()
```
createViewNav

```
nvnViewNavigator = nvwView.createViewNav(intCachesize)
```

intCachesize	Required	%

The size of the navigator cache in view entries from 0 (no cache) through 128 (the default). This is available only for remote calls.

The method creates a new *lotus.domino.ViewNavigator* (▶ 637) for all the entries contained in the view. The entries contained in the *lotus.domino.ViewNavigator* include information such as category, totals, and view position. Even if the documents displayed in the view have been filtered by the full-text engine, this method still returns all the entries contained in the view.

5.0 createViewNavFrom

```
nvnViewNavigator = nvwView.createViewNavFrom (navigatorobject)
```
createViewNav
From

```
nvnViewNavigator = nvwView.createViewNavFrom (navigatorobject,
➥intCachesize)
```

navigatorobject	Required	O.Ref.

The *lotus.domino.Document* or *lotus.domino.ViewEntry* that signifies the first entry in the *lotus.domino.ViewNavigator*.

intCachesize   Required   %

The size of the navigator cache in view entries from 0 (no cache) through 128 (the default). This is available only for remote calls.

This method returns a handle to the *lotus.domino.ViewNavigator,* beginning with the first entry specified as the parameter when calling this method. Even if the documents displayed in the view have been filtered by the full-text engine, this method still returns all the entries.

5.0 createViewNavFromCategory

createViewNav
FromCategory

```
nvnViewNavigator = nvwView.createViewNavFromCategory (strCategoryname)

nvnViewNavigator = nvwView.createViewNavFromCategory (strCategoryname,
➥intCachesize)
```

strCategoryname   Required   O.Ref.

The name of the category contained in the view.

intCachesize   Required   %

The size of the navigator cache in view entries from 0 (no cache) through 128 (the default). This is available only for remote calls.

This method returns a handle to a new *lotus.domino.ViewNavigator,* beginning with the first entry contained in the specified category. Even if the documents displayed in the view have been filtered by the full-text engine, this method still returns all the entries.

5.0 createViewNavFromChildren

createViewNav
FromChildren

```
nvnViewNavigator = nvwView.createViewNavFromChildren (navigatorobject)

nvnViewNavigator = nvwView.createViewNavFromChildren (navigatorobject,
➥intCachesize)
```

navigatorobject   Required   O.Ref.

The *lotus.document.Document* or *lotus.document.ViewEntry* that represents the parent entry.

intCachesize   Required   %

The size of the navigator cache in view entries from 0 (no cache) through 128 (the default). This is available only for remote calls.

This method returns a handle to a new *lotus.domino.ViewNavigator* for all the immediate child documents of the entry passed as the parameter. Even if the documents displayed in the view have been filtered by the full-text engine, this method still returns all the entries.

5.0 createViewNavFromDescendants

createViewNav
FromDescendants

```
nvnViewNavigator = nvwView.createViewNavFromDescendants (navigatorobject)

nvnViewNavigator = nvwView.createViewNavFromDescendants (navigatorobject,
➥intCachesize)
```

navigatorobject   Required   O.Ref.

The *lotus.domino.Document* or *lotus.domino.ViewEntry* that represents the parent entry.

intCachesize   Required   %

The size of the navigator cache in view entries from 0 (no cache) through 128 (the default). This is available only for remote calls.

This method returns a handle to the *lotus.domino.ViewNavigator* for all the descendant documents of the entry passed as the parameter. Even if the documents displayed in the view have been filtered by the full-text engine, this method still returns all the entries.

5.0 createViewNavMaxLevel

```
nvnViewNavigator = nvwView.createViewNavMaxLevel (intLevel)
nvnViewNavigator = nvwView.createViewNavMaxLevel (intLevel, intCachesize)
```

createViewNav
MaxLevel

intLevel   Required   %

The maximum level of navigation, ranging from 0 (top level) to 32 (the default).

intCachesize   Required   %

The size of the navigator cache in view entries from 0 (no cache) through 128 (the default). This is available only for remote calls.

This method returns a handle to the *lotus.domino.ViewNavigator* for all entries in the view down to a specific level. Even if the documents displayed in the view have been filtered by the full-text engine, this method still returns all the entries.

FTSearch

```
intDocs = nvwView.FTSearch(strquery)
intDocs = nvwView.FTSearch(strquery, intmaxdocs)
```

FTSearch

strquery   Required $

A string representing the rules for the full-text query. These rules are outlined next.

intmaxdocs   Required   %

The maximum number of *lotus.domino.Documents* to return from the query. Set this parameter to 0 to return all matching documents.

This method performs a full-text search of all the documents contained in the view and returns the number of documents that matched the query (which are the only documents displayed in the view). Only the documents that match the rules specified in the full-text search query are displayed in the view. This method returns a long value that represents the number of documents that matched the query string.

You can test to see if the database is full-text indexed prior to performing this method by testing the isFTIndexed method of the *lotus.domino.Database* object (▶ 389). You can create an index for the Notes database by calling the updateFTIndex method of the *lotus.domino.Database* object (▶ 392). It isn't necessary for the database to be full-text indexed to perform a search against the database. However, the search is much more slow and inefficient if the database isn't indexed.

The result of the full-text search is a collection of documents that are sorted in descending order of relevance. In other words, the document with the most hits (highest relevance) is first, and the document with the fewest hits (lowest relevance) is last. You can access the relevance score by using the getFTSearchScore method of the *lotus.domino.Document* (▶ 421).

When performing searches against the documents in the view, each subsequent search refines the result set from the previous search, thereby searching against the previous search. You can reset the search so that the view displays all the documents by calling the `clear` method of the *lotus.domino.View* (▶ 589).

Although this method works on *lotus.domino.Documents* located in the *lotus.domino.View*, you can also apply this method to the *lotus.domino.Database* and *lotus.domino.DocumentCollection*.

As you would expect when using a legitimate search engine, the rules for defining the search allow for building search criteria using Boolean values and specific operators. Here are the rules for using these operators:

Rule	Description
Plain text	For simple searches, you can enter the word or phrase for which to search. You don't need to include quotation marks, except when you're searching for specific keywords or reserved operators. Placing quotes around the words or phrases ensures that they are treated as literal search criteria and not as operators. These rules are similar to typical searching standards. You can always put the text in quotes regardless to ensure that it will not be treated as an operator. When programmatically defining the search criteria in LotusScript, use double quotes so that the quotes are passed as part of the literal search criteria.
Wildcards	Wildcards are supported when you perform searches. Typical to most search engines, they are represented by the ? and * characters. Use ? to represent any single character in its respective position and * to match multiple (or no) characters in their respective position in the word.
Hyphenated words	These are used to find pairs of words that are hyphenated together as a single word or separated by a space.
Logical operators	These allow you to build more-complex searches (often referred to as Boolean searches) by using logical operators to further restrict or expand the search algorithm. The allowed operator keywords and their respective symbols (listed in order of precedence) are not or !, and or &, accrue or ,, and or or !.
Proximity operators	Proximity operators enable you to search for words that are close to one another. That is, you can see if the words are located in proximity to each other by using the operators `near`, `sentence`, and `paragraph`.
Exactcase operators	The exactcase operator enables you to restrict the search to match a specified case.
Termweight operators	The termweight *n* operators enables you to modify the relevance scores of the search by defining the relevance ranking. This is done by specifying a value for *n* between 0 and 100 representing the relevance score.
Field operators	This is a powerful capability of the Domino/Lotus Notes search engine. This feature enables you to perform a search based on a specific field. The syntax for this search is `FIELD fieldname operator`. `fieldname` is the name of the *NotesItem* that you are performing the operation against. The allowed operators are `contains`, `=`, `>`, and `<`. Using `contains` is helpful when searching rich-text fields. You can't combine operators as in normal programming (such as `>=`). Therefore, you must build a more-complex search algorithm by using the `or` operator for multiple criteria. You may also need to help define the search's precedence order by using parentheses.

getAliases   R   O.Ref.

getAliases

vecAliases = View.**getAliases**()

This method returns all the aliases, or synonyms, for the specified view as an array of strings. Because a view can contain multiple aliases, they are all returned by this method. The displayed view name, which is the first name in the view's list of names, isn't returned because by definition it isn't an alias but is the actual view name. (It can be located by using the getname method of the *lotus.domino.View* class (▶ 599).) It's a good idea to always use aliases when designing applications. This enables you to modify the name of the view (which determines how it's displayed to the user) at any time and not potentially break the existing application, because your code programmatically references the alias. This also provides a simpler name to reference when programmatically accessing the view.

getAllDocumentsByKey

ndcAllDocuments = nvwView.**getAllDocumentsByKey** (vecKeys)

ndcAllDocuments = nvwView.**getAllDocumentsByKey** (Key)

ndcAllDocuments = nvwView.**getAllDocumentsByKey** (vecKeys, bolExact)

ndcAllDocuments = nvwView.**getAllDocumentsByKey** (Key, bolExact)

getAllDocuments ByKey

vecKeys   Required $, %, &, #, !
A *java.util.Vector* or array in which each element corresponds to a sorted column in the view. (The first element corresponds to the first sorted column, the second element corresponds to the second sorted column, and so on.)

Key   Required $, %, &, #, !
A value that corresponds to the first sorted column in the view.

bolExact   Required   T/F
Indicates whether the key and value stored in the view column must be an exact match. true indicates an exact match. false indicates that a partial match is allowed.

This method locates documents based on the value(s) stored in the sorted column(s) in the *lotus.domino.View*. This method returns a *lotus.domino.DocumentCollection* of all documents whose column values match those specified in vecKeys or Key. If no documents match vecKeys or Key, the collection is empty.

The lookup can be based on a single value. In this case, only one element is specified in Key, and its value is compared against the first sorted column in the view. The lookup can also be based on multiple values specified in vecKeys, in which case the elements must correspond to each sorted column in the view.

Obviously, when you use getAllDocumentsByKey, at least one column in the view must be sorted. Because this method returns all the documents that match the vecKeys or Key criteria, you can then navigate through the documents by using the getFirstDocument (▶ 439), getNextDocument, or getLastDocument methods of the *lotus.domino.DocumentCollection* (▶ 440).

If you need to return only a single document and not all the documents that match the search criteria, you can call the getDocumentByKey method of the *lotus.domino.View* (▶ 597).

5.0 getAllEntries   R   O.Ref.

getAllEntries   `nvecAllEntries = nvwView.`**`getAllEntries`**`()`

This method returns all the entries in the view in the order they appear in the view. The capability to reference entries in *lotus.domino.Views* is a new feature in Release 5.0. Prior to that release, you could access only documents contained in views. You couldn't view specific information, such as categories or totals. *lotus.domino.ViewEntryCollections* enables you to navigate through the documents contained in the current view and the currently selected document's respective siblings, children, and parent. In addition, you can access document information to determine the document category, the category total, whether a document is unread, or if there is a document conflict. The following example builds a collection of all the entries in the All view and then builds some reporting information on the entry types contained in the view.

```
import lotus.domino.*;

public class JavaAgent extends AgentBase {

    public void NotesMain() {

        try {
            Session ns = getSession();
            AgentContext agentContext = ns.getAgentContext();
            Database ndb = agentContext.getCurrentDatabase();
            View nvw = ndb.getView("All");
            ViewNavigator nvn = nvw.createViewNav();
            ViewEntryCollection nvec = nvw.getAllEntries();
            System.out.println("Located " + nvec.getCount() + " entries");
            ViewEntry nve = nvec.getFirstEntry();
            int intCategoryCount = 0;
            int intDocumentCount = 0;
            while (nve != null) {
                if (nve.isCategory())
                    intCategoryCount++;
                    if (nve.isDocument())
                        intDocumentCount++;
                nve = nvec.getNextEntry();   }
            System.out.println("The view [" + nvw.getName() + "]
            ➥contains:");
            System.out.println(intCategoryCount + " categories");
            System.out.println(intDocumentCount + " documents");
        } catch(Exception e) {
            e.printStackTrace();
        }
    }
}
```

5.0 getAllEntriesByKey

getAllEntries   `nvecAllViewEntries = nvwView.`**`getAllEntriesByKey`**` (vecKeys)`
ByKey
`nvecAllViewEntries = nvwView.`**`getAllEntriesByKey`**` (Key)`

`nvecAllViewEntries = nvwView.`**`getAllEntriesByKey`**` (vecKeys, bolExact)`

`nvecAllViewEntries = nvwView.`**`getAllEntriesByKey`**` (Key, bolExact)`

vecKeys	Required	O.Ref.

A *java.util.Vector* or array in which each element corresponds to a sorted column in the view. (The first element corresponds to the first sorted column, the second element corresponds to the second sorted column, and so on.)

Key	Required	O.Ref.

A value that corresponds to the first sorted column in the view.

bolExact	Required	T/F

Indicates whether the key and value stored in the view column must be an exact match. `true` indicates an exact match. `false` indicates that a partial match is allowed.

This method locates entries based on the value(s) stored in the sorted column(s) in the *lotus.domino.View*. This method returns a *lotus.domino.ViewEntryCollection* of all entries whose column values match those specified in `vecKeys` or `Key`. If no documents match `vecKeys` or `Key`, the collection is empty.

The lookup can be based on a single value. In this case, only one element is specified in `Key`, and its value is compared against the first sorted column in the view. The lookup can also be based on multiple values specified in `vecKeys`, in which case the elements must correspond to each sorted column in the view.

Obviously, when you use `getAllEntriesByKey`, at least one column in the view must be sorted. To locate just one entry, or the first entry in the *lotus.domino.View* that matches the criteria, use the `getEntryByKey` method of the *lotus.domino.View* (▶ 598).

---

getBackgroundColor   R   %

```
intBackgroundcolor = nvwView.getBackgroundColor()
```

getBackground
Color

This method returns an integer constant representing the background color of the specified view. The constant values returned are available to the `getFontColor` method of the *lotus.domino.ViewColumn* class (▶ 612) and the `getColor` method of the *lotus.domino.RichTextStyle* class (▶ 566). Here are the allowable values for this method:

Constant Value	Integer Value	RGB Color
RichTextStyle.COLOR_BLACK	0	0, 0, 0
RichTextStyle.COLOR_BLUE	4	0, 0, 255
RichTextStyle.COLOR_CYAN	5	0, 255, 255
RichTextStyle.COLOR_DARK_BLUE	10	0, 0, 128
RichTextStyle.COLOR_DARK_CYAN	11	0, 128, 128
RichTextStyle.COLOR_DARK_GREEN	9	0, 128, 0
RichTextStyle.COLOR_DARK_MAGENTA	13	128, 0, 128
RichTextStyle.COLOR_DARK_RED	8	128, 0, 0
RichTextStyle.COLOR_DARK_YELLOW	12	128, 128, 0
RichTextStyle.COLOR_GRAY	14	128, 128, 128
RichTextStyle.COLOR_GREEN	3	0, 255, 0
RichTextStyle.COLOR_LIGHT_GRAY	15	192, 192, 192
RichTextStyle.COLOR_MAGENTA	7	255, 0, 255
RichTextStyle.COLOR_RED	2	255, 0, 0
RichTextStyle.COLOR_WHITE	1	255, 255, 255
RichTextStyle.COLOR_YELLOW	6	255, 255, 0

---

getChild

```
ndocChild = nvwView.getChild(NotesDocument)
```

NotesDocument	Required	O.Ref.

A *lotus.domino.Document* displayed in the view that has at least one response document.

This method returns a handle on the first response document of the parent *lotus.domino.Document* passed as a parameter when calling the method. After you have established a handle on the first response document, you can navigate through the remaining response documents as they appear in the view by using the `getNextSibling` or `getChild` methods of the *lotus.domino.View* (▶ 599). In addition, you can access a document's response documents by using the `getResponses` method of the *lotus.domino.Document* (▶ 423).

If the view has already been filtered by calling the `FTSearch` method, the `getChild` method returns the next document as displayed in the view.

---

getColumn	R	ViewColumn

```
nvcolumn = nvwView.getColumn(intColumnnumber)
```

This method returns a handle on the specified *lotus.domino.ViewColumn*. When setting the value for `intColumnnumber`, use 1 for the first column, 2 for the second column, and so on.

5.0 getColumnCount	R	%

```
intColumnCount = nvwView.getColumnCount()
```

This method returns the number of columns in the view as an integer value.

5.0 getColumnNames	R	O.Ref.

```
vecColumnnames = nvwView.getColumnNames()
```

This method returns the column names of all the columns in the view in the order that they appear from left to right.

---

getColumns	R	O.Ref.

```
nvcColumns = nvwView.getColumns()
```

This method returns a *java.util.Vector* with *lotus.domino.ViewColumn* elements that are contained in the specified view. The order of the columns in the *lotus.domino.View* corresponds to the numerical order of the array. Because the returned value is an array, the first element is referenced as 0 (assuming Option Base 0). Therefore, the first column is element 0, the second column is element 1, and so on. After collecting the array of columns, you can reference each *lotus.domino.ViewColumn* individually (▶ 609).

The following code snippet displays the number of columns that exist in the All view and then displays their titles in a message box.

```java
import lotus.domino.*;
import java.util.Vector;

public class JavaAgent extends AgentBase {

    public void NotesMain() {

        try {
            Session ns = getSession();
            AgentContext agentContext = ns.getAgentContext();
            Database ndb = agentContext.getCurrentDatabase();
            View nvw = ndb.getView("ManagerView");
```

```
        int intCount = 0;
        Vector nvc = nvw.getColumns();
        System.out.println("This view has " + nvc.size() +
        ➥" columns.");
        System.out.println("Their titles are:");
        for (intCount=0; intCount<nvc.size(); intCount++) {
            ViewColumn nvColumn = (ViewColumn)nvc.elementAt(intCount);
                if (nvColumn.getTitle() == "")
                    System.out.println("No title");
                else
                    System.out.println(nvColumn.getTitle()); }
        System.out.println("Agent complete.");
    } catch(Exception e) {
        e.printStackTrace();
    }
  }
}
```

---

getCreated   R   Time/Date

```
ndtTimeDate = nvwView.getCreated()
```
getCreated

This method returns the variant date value for the date on which the view was created or saved to disk in the current database.

getDocumentByKey

```
ndocDocument = nvwView.getDocumentByKey(vecKeys)
```
getDocument
ByKey
```
ndocDocument = nvwView.getDocumentByKey(Key)
```

```
ndocDocument = nvwView.getDocumentByKey(vecKeys, bolExact)
```

```
ndocDocument = nvwView.getDocumentByKey(Key, bolExact)
```

vecKeys   Required   O.Ref.

A *java.util.Vector* or array in which each element corresponds to a sorted column in the view. (The first element corresponds to the first sorted column, the second element corresponds to the second sorted column, and so on.)

Key   Required   O.Ref.

A value that corresponds to the first sorted column in the view.

bolExact   Required   T/F

Indicates whether the key and value stored in the view column must be an exact match. `true` indicates an exact match. `false` indicates that a partial match is allowed.

This method locates the *lotus.domino.Document* based on the value(s) stored in the sorted column(s) in the *lotus.domino.View*. This method returns a handle to the *lotus.domino.Document* whose column values match those specified in vecKeys or Key. If no document matches vecKeys or Key, the *lotus.domino.Document* is null.

The lookup can be based on a single value. In this case, only one element is specified in Key, and its value is compared against the first sorted column in the view. The lookup can also be based on multiple values specified in vecKeys, in which case the elements must correspond to each sorted column in the view.

Obviously, when you use getDocumentByKey, at least one column in the view must be sorted. Because this method returns a document that matches the vecKeys or Key criteria, you can then navigate through the other documents contained in the *lotus.domino.View* by using the getNextDocument method of the *lotus.domino.View* (▶ 599).

If you need to return all the documents that match the search criteria, you can call the getAllDocumentsByKey method of the *lotus.domino.View* (▶ 593).

5.0 getEntryByKey

```
nveEntry = nvwView.getEntryByKey(vecKeys)

nveEntry = nvwView.getEntryByKey(Key)

nveEntry = nvwView.getEntryByKey(vecKeys, bolExact)

nveEntry = nvwView.getEntryByKey(Key,bolExact)
```

---

vecKeys	Required	O.Ref.

A *java.util.Vector* or array in which each element corresponds to a sorted column in the view. (The first element corresponds to the first sorted column, the second element corresponds to the second sorted column, and so on.)

Key	Required	O.Ref.

A value that corresponds to the first sorted column in the view.

bolExact	Required	T/F

Indicates whether the key and value stored in the view column must be an exact match. true indicates an exact match. false indicates that a partial match is allowed.

This method locates the view entry based on the value(s) stored in the sorted column(s) in the *lotus.domino.View*. This method returns a *lotus.domino.ViewEntry* whose column value matches those specified in vecKeys or Key. If no document matches vecKeys or Key, the collection is empty.

The lookup can be based on a single value. In this case, only one element is specified in Key, and its value is compared against the first sorted column in the view. The lookup can also be based on multiple values specified in vecKeys, in which case the elements must correspond to each sorted column in the view.

Obviously, when you use getEntryByKey, at least one column in the view must be sorted. To locate all the entries in the *lotus.domino.View* that match the criteria, use the getAllEntriesByKey method of the *lotus.domino.View* (▶ 594).

---

getFirstDocument

```
ndocFirstDocument = nvwView.getFirstDocument()
```

This method sets the *lotus.domino.Document* to the first document in the *lotus.domino.View*. If no documents are contained in the *lotus.domino.View,* this method returns null. The first document is the document that appears at the top of the view when the view is displayed through the user interface.

After establishing a handle on the first document in the view, you can navigate through the view by using the getNextDocument (▶ 599) and getPrevDocument (▶ 600) methods of the *lotus.domino.View*.

5.0 getHeaderLines   R   %

```
intHeaderLines = nvwView.getHeaderLines()
```

This method returns the number of lines as an integer in the view's header (title). The value for this method must be between 1 and 5.

---

getLastDocument

```
ndocLastDocument = nvwView.getLastDocument()
```

This method sets the *lotus.domino.Document* to the last document in the *lotus.domino.View*. If no documents are contained in the *lotus.domino.View,* this method returns null. The last document is the document that appears at the bottom of the view when the view is displayed through the user interface.

After establishing a handle on the first document in the view, you can navigate through the view by using the getNextDocument (▶ 599) and getPrevDocument (▶ 600) methods of the *lotus.domino.View.*

---

getLastModified   R   Time/date ?

```
ndtDateTime = nvwView.getLastModified()
```

getLast
Modified

This method returns a *lotus.domino.DateTime* object that indicates when the view was last modified as a time/date variant.

---

getName   R $

```
strName = nvwView.getName()
```

getName

This method returns the first name of the specified view as a string. The value returned is always the displayed string name or the first name if the view has synonyms or aliases. To find the view's alias names, use the getAliases method of the *lotus.notes.View* class (▶ 593).

---

getNextDocument

```
ndocNextDocument = ncwView.getNextDocument (ndocnotesdocument)
```

getNext
Document

NotesDocument   Required   O.Ref.
A *lotus.domino.Document* in the current view.

This method sets the *lotus.domino.Document* to the next document in the *lotus.domino.View* immediately following the document passed as the parameter when calling this method. The next document in the view is determined regardless of whether the document is a parent, sibling, or response document. If no documents follow the current document in the *lotus.domino.View,* this method returns null.

Before you call the getNextDocument method, you must establish a handle on an existing document in the view by using the getFirstDocument, getLastDocument, or getDocumentByKey methods of the *lotus.domino.View* (▶ 587).

---

getNextSibling

```
ndocNextSibling = nvwView.getNextSibling (ndocnotesdocument)
```

getNextSibling

NotesDocument   Required   O.Ref.
A *lotus.domino.Document* in the current view.

This method sets the *lotus.domino.Document* to the document at the same hierarchy level in the *lotus.domino.View* immediately following the document passed as the parameter when calling this method. The next sibling returned is a main document if the parameter passed was a main document or a response document if the parameter passed was a response document. If the *lotus.domino.View* is categorized in addition to being sorted, the next sibling must share the same category as the original document passed when calling this method. If no more siblings follow the current document in the *lotus.domino.View,* this method returns null. Similarly, this method returns null if the current document is the last main document in the view, the last main document of the current category, or the last response or response-to-response document of the parent document.

Before you call the `getNextDocument` method, you must establish a handle on an existing document in the view by using the `getFirstDocument`, `getLastDocument`, or `getDocumentByKey` methods of the *lotus.domino.View* (▶ 587).

This method is useful when you're navigating through the main documents in a view that contains response documents and that is set to display response documents in a hierarchy. It's also useful when you're navigating through a parent document's response or response-to-response documents.

If the view has already been filtered by calling the `FTSearch` method, the `getNextSibling` method returns the next document as displayed in the view, regardless of whether it is a parent document, response document, or response-to-response document.

getNthDocument

getNth
Document

`ndocNthDocument = nvwView.`**`getNthDocument`**` (intIndex)`

intIndex	Required	&

The *lotus.domino.Document*'s position in the *lotus.domino.View*. `1` indicates the first document, `2` indicates the second, and so on.

This method establishes a handle to the *lotus.domino.Document* in the *lotus.domino.View* by its relative position specified by the `intIndex` parameter. Only main documents (top-level parent documents) can be located by this method. If no documents are specified in the location of the *lotus.domino.View*, this method returns `null`.

getParent   R   NotesDatabase

getParent

`ndbParent = nvwView.`**`getParent`**`()`

This method returns a handle on the *lotus.domino.Database* object that contains the *lotus.domino.View*.

getParentDocument

getParent
Document

`ndocParentDocument = nvwView.`**`getParentDocument`**` (ndocnotesdocument)`

NotesDocument	Required	O.Ref.

A *lotus.domino.Document* in the current view.

This method sets the *lotus.domino.Document* to the parent document of the *lotus.domino.Document* passed as the parameter when calling the method. The *lotus.domino.Document* returned could be a main document, response document, or response-to-response document. If there is no parent document to the current document the *lotus.domino.View*, this method returns `null`.

You can also establish a handle on a document's parent document by using the `getParentDocumentUNID` method of the *lotus.domino.Document* (▶ 423).

This method is useful when you're navigating through the main documents in a view that contains response documents and that is set to display response documents in a hierarchy. It's also useful when you're navigating through a parent document's response or response-to-response documents.

If the view has already been filtered by calling the `FTSearch` method, the `getParentDocument` method returns the previous document as displayed in the view, regardless of whether it is a parent document, response document, or response-to-response document.

getPrevDocument

getPrev
Document

`ndocPrevDocument = nvwView.`**`getPrevDocument`**` (ndocnotesdocument)`

NotesDocument	Required	O.Ref.

A *lotus.domino.Document* in the current view.

This method sets the *lotus.domino.Document* to the previous document in the *lotus.domino.View* immediately preceding the document passed as the parameter when calling this method. The preceding document in the view is determined regardless of whether the document is a parent, sibling, or response document. If no documents precede the current document in the *lotus.domino.View,* this method returns `null`.

Before you call the `getPrevDocument` method, you must establish a handle on an existing document in the view by using the `getFirstDocument`, `getLastDocument`, or `getDocumentByKey` methods of the *lotus.domino.View* (▶ 587).

getPrevSibling

```
ndocPrevSibling = nvwView.getPrevSibling (ndocnotesdocument)
```
getPrevSibling

NotesDocument	Required	O.Ref.

A *lotus.domino.Document* in the current view.

This method sets the *lotus.domino.Document* to the document at the same hierarchy level in the *lotus.domino.View* immediately preceding the document passed as the parameter when calling this method. The previous sibling returned is a main document if the parameter passed was a main document or a response document if the parameter passed was a response document. If the *lotus.domino.View* is categorized in addition to being sorted, the previous sibling must share the same category as the original document passed when calling this method. If no more siblings precede the current document in the *lotus.domino.View,* this method returns `null`. Similarly, this method returns `null` if the current document is the first main document in the view, the first main document of the current category, or the first response or response-to-response document of the parent document.

Before you call the `getPrevSibling` method, you must establish a handle on an existing document in the view by using the `getFirstDocument`, `getLastDocument`, or `getDocumentByKey` methods of the *lotus.domino.View* (▶ 587).

This method is useful when you're navigating through the main documents in a view that contains response documents and that is set to display response documents in a hierarchy. It's also useful when you're navigating through a parent document's response or response-to-response documents.

If the view has already been filtered by calling the `FTSearch` method, the `getPrevSibling` method returns the previous document as displayed in the view, regardless of whether it is a parent document, response document, or response-to-response document.

getReaders   R   O.Ref.

```
vecReaders = nvwView.getReaders()
```
getReaders

This method returns the values contained in the `$Readers` field for the specified view. If this value is set to `null` (`" "`), there is no reader restriction, so all users can view the contents of the view. Likewise, setting this value to a single value or multiple values restricts all users, groups, and servers from accessing the contents of the view unless they are specifically contained in the value of this method. When setting the value of this method, note that the new values replace the existing values; they are not appended. Therefore, be sure to read the existing values and include them in the new string array if you want to append new values to the `getReaders` method.

5.0 getRowLines   R   %

getRowLines   `intRowlines = nvwView.`**`getRowLines()`**

This method returns the number of lines in each row in the specified view. The range allowed for this method is 1 to 9. The default value is 1.

5.0 getSpacing   R   %

getSpacing   `intSpacing = nvwView.`**`getSpacing()`**

This method returns an integer constant that represents the spacing between the rows in the view. This method is available only when you're using LotusScript. Here are the possible values returned for this method:

Constant Value	Integer Value	Description
`View.SPACING_SINGLE`	0	Single-spaced
`View.SPACING_ONE_POINT_25`	1	1 1/4-spaced
`View.SPACING_ONE_POINT_50`	2	1 1/2-spaced
`View.SPACING_ONE_POINT_75`	3	1 3/4-spaced
`View.SPACING_DOUBLE`	4	Double-spaced

5.0 getTopLevelEntryCount   R   %

getTopLevel   `intToplevelentrycount = nvwView.`**`getTopLevelEntryCount()`**
EntryCount
This method returns the integer number of top-level entries contained in the view. This method is useful when the documents contained in the view are set to show response documents in a hierarchy.

---

getUniversalID   R $

getUniversalID   `strUniversalID = nvwView.`**`getUniversalID()`**

This method returns the view's Universal ID. The Universal ID is the unique identifier prevalent throughout Domino/Lotus Notes that denotes design elements and documents. The Universal ID is a 32-character combination of letters and numbers stored as a special type of text, as is consistent among all replicas of the database.

---

isAutoUpdate   R   T/F

isAutoUpdate   `bolIsAutoUpdate = nvwView.`**`isAutoUpdate()`**

This method controls whether the order and pointers for the view being rendered to the user in the front end are automatically updated whenever a change occurs to the documents contained in the view through the back end. `true` indicates that the view is automatically updated, and `false` indicates that the view is not automatically updated. This method defaults to `false`. This doesn't represent the actual refresh of the screen that the user can see (simulated by pressing F9 or calling the `refresh` method of the *lotus.domino.View* (▶ 604)). It only updates the order of the documents as they are stored in the back-end view. It's important that the order be current, as well as any pointers to *lotus.domino.Documents,* when acting against the documents programmatically via the back end. However, enabling this method will affect performance because the server or client must refresh the index and pointers. Therefore, it's generally better to set this method to `false` (the default), especially for larger views, unless you're interactively acting against and modifying the *lotus.domino.Documents* and their order is imperative for the code to run successfully.

isCalendar	R	T/F

```
bolIscalendar = nvwView.isCalendar()
```

This method returns a Boolean value indicating whether the specified view is set to display its contents in the calendar style. true indicates that it has been designed to use the calendar style. false indicates that it will display as the standard outline style.

5.0 isCategorized	R	T/F

```
bolIscategorized = nvwView.isCategorized()
```

This method indicates whether the current view is categorized. true indicates that the view is categorized. false indicates that it is not. This method is more specifically determined by the columns contained in the view because the *lotus.domino.ViewColumn* is where categorization is specified.

5.0 isConflict	R	T/F

```
bolIsconflict = nvwView.isConflict()
```

This method indicates whether conflict checking is enabled if the current view style is calendar. Conflict checking is used in Calendaring and Scheduling to warn the user of potential appointment and meeting conflicts so that multiple calendar events are not scheduled at the same time. true indicates that conflict checking is enabled for the calendar view. false indicates that conflict checking is disabled.

5.0 isDefaultView	R	T/F

```
bolIsdefaultview = nvwView.isDefaultView()
```

This method indicates whether the specified view is the default view for the *lotus.domino.Database* in which it resides. true indicates that it is the default view. false indicates that it is not. Every database must have a default view. Often, this is the database that is most frequently used or that contains the most common data that would be referenced by the users.

isFolder	R	T/F

```
bolIsfolder = nvwView.isFolder()
```

This method indicates whether the specified view is a folder. Although views and folders appear to the user as different design elements because of the nature of how they are used, except for some minor differences, they are essentially the same. Folders contain the same design elements, but documents can be added to and removed from folders on demand. Typically, these folders are used to categorize documents and are stored locally on individuals' file systems. An obvious example of the way folders are used is in each user's e-mail database. (In fact, the InBox is actually a folder!)

5.0 isHierarchical	R	T/F

```
bolIshierarchical = nvwView.isHierarchical()
```

This method indicates whether the documents being displayed are being shown in their respective response hierarchy. When you're designing with the view client, this method is located on the Options tab as "Show response documents in a hierarchy." true indicates that the view is set to display documents in a hierarchy. false indicates that they will not display in their response hierarchy.

5.0 isModified	R	T/F

```
bolIsmodified = nvwView.isModified()
```

This method indicates whether the view has been modified. true indicates that it has been modified. false indicates that it has not.

---

isProtectReaders   R   T/F

isProtect
Readers

```
bolIsprotectreaders = nvwView.isProtectReaders()
```

This method returns the method that protects the $READERS *lotus.domino.Items* from being overwritten when the database is replicated. `true` indicates that the items are protected during replication. `false` indicates that the items are not protected during replication.

---

refresh

refresh   nvwView.**refresh**

This method refreshes (updates) the contents of the view with any changes that have occurred to the documents contained in this view since a handle on the *lotus.domino.View* was established or since the view was previously refreshed. Because the information displayed in the view is not always a real-time view of the documents contained in the database, calling the `refresh` method ensures that the information displayed is current. You can test to see whether the *lotus.domino.View* has been modified by using the `isModified` method of the *lotus.domino.View* class (▶ 603).

---

remove

remove   nvwView.**remove**

This method permanently deletes a view from the database. When calling this method, the user can delete views only if he or she has sufficient database access rights (ACL). The user interface will not be modified until the *lotus.domino.Database* object is closed and reopened.

---

setAutoUpdate   W   T/F

setAuto
Update

```
nvwView.setAutoUpdate(bolAutoupdate)
```

This method controls whether the order and pointers for the view being rendered to the user in the front end are automatically updated whenever a change occurs to the documents contained in the view through the back end. `true` indicates that the view is automatically updated, and `false` indicates that the view is not automatically updated. This method defaults to `false`. This doesn't represent the actual refresh of the screen that the user can see (simulated by pressing F9 or calling the `refresh` method of the *lotus.domino.View* (▶ 604)), it only updates the order of the documents as they are stored in the back-end view. It's important that the order be current, as well as any pointers to *lotus.domino.Documents,* when acting against the documents programmatically via the back end. However, enabling this method affects performance because the server or client must refresh the index and pointers. Therefore, it's generally better to set this method to `false` (the default), especially for larger views, unless you're interactively acting against and modifying the *lotus.domino.Documents* and their order is imperative for the code to run successfully.

---

setProtectReaders   W   T/F

setProtect
Readers

```
nvwView.setProtectReaders(bolProtectreaders)
```

This method sets the method that protects the $READERS *lotus.domino.Items* from being overwritten when the database is replicated. `true` indicates that the items are protected during replication. `false` indicates that the items are not protected during replication.

---

setReaders   W $

setReaders   nvwView.**setReaders**(vecReadersarray)

This method sets the values contained in the $Readers field for the specified view. If this value is set to null (""), there is no reader restriction, so all users can view the contents of the view. Likewise, setting this value to a single value or multiple values restricts all users, groups, and servers from accessing the contents of the view unless they are specifically contained in the value of this method. When setting the value of this method, note that the new values replace the existing values; they are not appended. Therefore, be sure to read the existing values and include them in the new string array if you want to append new values to the readers method.

Remarks

The *lotus.domino.View* is one method that can be used to provide access to *lotus.domino.Documents* contained in the *lotus.domino.Database*. There are several benefits to accessing documents from within a *lotus.domino.View*. First, the documents are already indexed, so this method is more efficient when accessing documents stored in the database. Of course, anytime you can optimize performance, especially when working with Domino/Lotus Notes, you should take advantage of it. Because the view is indexed, a particular document or multiple documents can be located by using a specific key. This capability to locate documents based on specific keys is important because you're working with nonrelational data. Also, the view can already contain the subset of documents you want to retrieve or act against (because of the view selection formula). In addition, the documents can already be sorted, and you can navigate through them in their response hierarchy. Finally, some of the *lotus.domino.Items* contained in the documents have already been formatted in the view and can be retrieved while respecting this predetermined format.

When accessing documents in a view, use the following methods to establish a handle on the required documents:

Method	Description
getFirstDocument	Locates the first document in the view (determined by the view sort order).
getNextDocument getNthDocument getDocumentByKey	Locates a document based on the location of another document or by using a specific key.
getLastDocument	Locates the last document in the view (determined by the view sort order).

Example

The following example uses the Notes mail database to gather a list of all the tasks that the current user has scheduled. This example builds a document collection of all the documents in the view and then displays them to the user in the Java Console. This example shows the user a quick task list without making him open the mail database and navigate to the tasks to view the task information. The Console displays the current date and the number of tasks and then lists the tasks by status, date due, priority, and subject.

```
import lotus.domino.*;
import java.util.Vector;

public class JavaAgent extends AgentBase {

    public void NotesMain() {

        try {
            Session ns = getSession();
            AgentContext agentContext = ns.getAgentContext();
            Database ndb = agentContext.getCurrentDatabase();
            View nvw = ndb.getView("TodoByStatus");
            int intOverdue = 0;
            int intCurrent = 0;
            int intFuture = 0;
            String strOD = "";
            String strCR = "";
            String strFT = "";
            String strCHead = "";
            String strTask = "";
            String strTemp = "";
            String strPriority = "";
            String strType = "";
            DateTime ndToday= ns.createDateTime("Today");
            System.out.println("Loading Day at a glance...\n");
            Document ndocTask = nvw.getFirstDocument();
            while (ndocTask != null) {
                // Loop against all documents in task view
                // Due States: 0 = Overdue, 1 = Current, 2 = Future,
                // 8 = Rejected, 9 = Complete
                if (ndocTask.getItemValueString("Importance") == "99")
                    strPriority = "   4   ";
                else
                    strPriority = "   " + ndocTask.getItemValueString
                    ➥("Importance") + "   ";
                if (ndocTask.getItemValueInteger("DueState") == 0)   {
                    intOverdue++;
                    strOD = strOD + "Overdue\t" + ndocTask.getItemValue
                    ➥("DueDateTime").toString() +
                    "\t" + strPriority + "\t" + ndocTask.getItemValueString
                    ➥("Subject") + "\n";   }
                else
                    if (ndocTask.getItemValueInteger("DueState") == 1)   {
                        intCurrent++;
                        strCR = strCR + "Current\t" +
                        ndocTask.getItemValue("DueDateTime").toString() + "\t"
                        ➥+ strPriority + "\t" + ndocTask.getItemValueString
                        ➥("Subject") + "\n";   }
                else   {
                    intFuture++;
                    strFT = strFT + "Future\t" + ndocTask.getItemValue
                    ➥("DueDateTime").toString() + "\t" + strPriority +
                    ➥"\t" + ndocTask.getItemValueString("Subject") +
                    ➥"\n";   }
                ndocTask = nvw.getNextDocument(ndocTask);   }
                System.out.println("You have " + (intOverdue +
                ➥intCurrent +  intFuture) +
                ➥" total tasks as of today: " +
                ➥ndToday.getDateOnly());
```

```
            System.out.println("Current: " + intCurrent +
            ➥", Future: " + intFuture + ", Overdue: " +
            ➥intOverdue + "\n");
            System.out.println("Status\tDate Due\t\t\tPriority\
            ➥tSubject");
            System.out.println(strOD);
            System.out.println(strCR);
            System.out.println(strFT);

        } catch(Exception e) {
        e.printStackTrace();
    }
  }
}
```

The *lotus.domino.ViewColumn* class represents a column design element contained in a *lotus.domino.View* (which can be a standard view or a folder). The *lotus.domino.ViewColumn* determines how the data contained in the *lotus.domino.Document* is displayed to the user, both aesthetically and in regards to sort order. In addition, the *lotus.domino.ViewColumn* can contain formulas using the Notes macro language, simple functions, and various format settings.

. . .

continued >>

Java Syntax

```
public class ViewColumn extends Base
```

To access the *lotus.domino.ViewColumn* object, you must establish a handle on the *lotus.domino.View* object that contains it and then use the getColumns or getColumn method (▶ 596) to instantiate a *lotus.domino.ViewColumn* object.

ViewColumn Methods

5.0 getAlignment   R   %

```
intAlignment = nvcViewColumn.getAlignment()
```
getAlignment

This method returns the alignment, or justification, of the data displayed in the current column as an integer constant value. The default alignment for views is ViewColumn.ALIGN LEFT. Here are the possible values returned for this method:

Constant Value	Integer Value	Description
ViewColumn.ALIGN_CENTER	2	Center justification
ViewColumn.ALIGN_RIGHT	1	Right justification
ViewColumn.ALIGN_LEFT	0	Left justification

The following code snippet displays the number of columns contained in the "All" view and then displays their respective alignments.

```
import lotus.domino.*;
import java.util.Vector;

public class JavaAgent extends AgentBase {

    public void NotesMain() {

        try {
            Session ns = getSession();
            AgentContext agentContext = ns.getAgentContext();
            Database ndb= agentContext.getCurrentDatabase();
            View nvw = ndb.getView("All");
            Vector columns = nvw.getColumns();
            ViewColumn nvc = null;
            String strAlign = null;
            System.out.println("This view has " + columns.size() +
            ➥" columns.");
            if (columns.size() != 0) {
                for (int i=0; i<columns.size(); i++) {
                    nvc = (ViewColumn)columns.elementAt(i);
                switch (nvc.getAlignment()) {
                    case ViewColumn.ALIGN_CENTER : strAlign = "center"; break;
                    case ViewColumn.ALIGN_LEFT : strAlign = "left";break;
                    case ViewColumn.ALIGN_RIGHT : strAlign = "right"; break; }
                System.out.println("The alignment for column " +
                ➥nvc.getPosition() +
                " is " + strAlign);   }
```
continued >>

continued >>
```
                    }
               }
           catch(Exception e) {
               e.printStackTrace();
           }
        }
     }
```

5.0 getDateFmt   R   %

getDateFmt   `intFormat = nvcViewColumn.getDateFmt()`

This method returns the format of the date being displayed in the current column as an integer constant. The default for this method is 0. There are two new settings in Release 5 to display the year in a Year 2000-compliant manner. Prior to Release 5, the year was always suppressed to a two-digit format (although the underlying value stored has always been Year 2000-compliant). You can now select the format to display either 12/25/1998 or 12/1998. Here are the possible values returned for this method:

Constant Value	Description
`ViewColumn.DT_MD`	Displays the month and day of the date. December 25, 1998 would display as 12/25.
`ViewColumn.DT_YM`	Displays the month and year of the date. December 25, 1998 would display as 12/98.
`ViewColumn.DT_Y4M`	Displays the month and year of the date. December 25, 1998 would display as 12/1998.
`ViewColumn.DT_YMD`	Displays the month, day, and year of the date. December 25, 1998 would display as 12/25/98.

5.0 getFontColor   R   %

getFontColor   `intFontcolor = nvcViewColumn.getFontColor()`

This method returns an integer constant that represents the color of the text displayed in the View column. Here are the possible values returned for this method (they also apply to the font color used with the `notesColor` for *lotus.domino.RichTextItem* and the `backgroundcolor` for *lotus.domino.View*):

Constant Value	Integer Value	RGB Color
`RichTextStyle.COLOR_BLACK`	0	0, 0, 0
`RichTextStyle.COLOR_BLUE`	4	0, 0, 255
`RichTextStyle.COLOR_CYAN`	5	0, 255, 255
`RichTextStyle.COLOR_DARK_BLUE`	10	0, 0, 128
`RichTextStyle.COLOR_DARK_CYAN`	11	0, 128, 128
`RichTextStyle.COLOR_DARK_GREEN`	9	0, 128, 0
`RichTextStyle.COLOR_DARK_MAGENTA`	13	128, 0, 128
`RichTextStyle.COLOR_DARK_RED`	8	128, 0, 0
`RichTextStyle.COLOR_DARK_YELLOW`	12	128, 128, 0
`RichTextStyle.COLOR_GRAY`	14	128, 128, 128
`RichTextStyle.COLOR_GREEN`	3	0, 255, 0
`RichTextStyle.COLOR_LIGHT_GRAY`	15	192, 192, 192

Constant Value	Integer Value	RGB Color
RichTextStyle.COLOR_MAGENTA	7	255, 0, 255
RichTextStyle.COLOR_RED	2	255, 0, 0
RichTextStyle.COLOR_WHITE	1	255, 255, 255
RichTextStyle.COLOR_YELLOW	6	255, 255, 0

5.0 getFontFace R O.Ref.

getFontFace

```
strFontface = nvcViewColumn.getFontFace()
```

This method returns the name of the font type being displayed in the column. The default value for this method is Helvetica.

5.0 getFontPointSize R %

getFont
PointSize

```
intFontpointsize = nvcViewColumn.getFontPointSize()
```

This method returns the point size as an integer of the font being displayed in the column. The default value for this method is 10.

5.0 getFontStyle R %

getFontStyle

```
intFontstyle = nvcViewColumn.getFontStyle()
```

This method returns the integer constant value of the style being used to display the text in the column. The default value for this method is 0. The options for the style are FONT_BOLD, FONT_ITALIC, FONT_UNDERLINE, and FONT_STRIKEOUT, and you can select one of them or a combination. Therefore, the possible values returned become more complicated but are easily distinguishable when you're checking for the integer value returned. Here are the possible values returned for this method:

Constant Value(s)	Integer Value	Description
ViewColumn.FONT_BOLD	1	The text is bold.
ViewColumn.FONT_ITALIC	2	The text is italic.
ViewColumn.FONT_BOLD and ViewColumn.FONT_ITALIC	3	The text is bold and italic.
ViewColumn.FONT_UNDERLINE	4	The text is underlined.
ViewColumn.FONT_BOLD and ViewColumn.FONT_UNDERLINE	5	The text is bold and underlined.
ViewColumn.FONT_ITALIC and ViewColumn.FONT_UNDERLINE	6	The text is italic and underlined.
ViewColumn.FONT_BOLD, ViewColumn.FONT_ITALIC, and ViewColumn.FONT_UNDERLINE	7	The text is bold, italic, and underlined.
ViewColumn.FONT_STRIKEOUT	8	The text is strikeout.
ViewColumn.FONT_BOLD and ViewColumn.FONT_STRIKEOUT	9	The text is bold and strikeout.
ViewColumn.FONT_ITALIC and ViewColumn.FONT_STRIKEOUT	10	The text is italic and strikeout.
ViewColumn.FONT_BOLD, ViewColumn.FONT_ITALIC, and ViewColumn.FONT_STRIKEOUT	11	The text is bold, italic, and strikeout.

continued >>

continued >>

Constant Value(s)	Integer Value	Description
ViewColumn.FONT_UNDERLINE and ViewColumn.FONT_STRIKEOUT	12	The text is strikeout and underlined.
ViewColumn.FONT_BOLD, ViewColumn.FONT_UNDERLINE, and ViewColumn.FONT_STRIKEOUT	13	The text is bold, strikeout, and underlined.
ViewColumn.FONT_ITALIC, ViewColumn.FONT_UNDERLINE, and ViewColumn.FONT_STRIKEOUT	14	The text is italic, strikeout, and underlined.
ViewColumn.FONT_BOLD, ViewColumn.FONT_ITALIC, ViewColumn.FONT_UNDERLINE, and ViewColumn.FONT_STRIKEOUT	15	The text is bold, italic, strikeout, and underlined.

getFormula   R   O.Ref.

getFormula   `strFormula = nvcViewColumn.getFormula()`

This method returns the @Function, if used, in the particular column. When designing column formulas, you are restricted to using either simple functions, fields, or formulas (using the @Function macro language available in Domino/Lotus Notes). If the value used in the column formula is equivalent to a single field value, this method will return `null`, even if the designer specifies the formula and enters the name of the field. (Use the `getItemValue` method of the *lotus.domino.Document* to retrieve the field value (▶ 421).) This is still interpreted by Domino as a single field value reference and not an actual @formula. If the simple function is used, Domino will return the @formula that will return the same, equivalent value. Otherwise, the entire @formula is returned. You can test whether the column contains a @formula value by using the `isFormula` method, also contained by *lotus.domino.ViewColumn* (▶ 619).

5.0 getHeaderAlignment   R   %

getHeader Alignment   `intHeaderalignment = nvcViewColumn.getHeaderAlignment()`

This method returns a constant integer value representing the alignment, or justification, of the header, or title, in a column.

The default alignment for views is `ALIGN_LEFT`. Here are the possible values returned for this method:

Constant Value	Integer Value	Description
ViewColumn.ALIGN_CENTER	2	Center justification
ViewColumn.ALIGN_RIGHT	1	Right justification
ViewColumn.ALIGN_LEFT	0	Left justification

The following code displays several of the *lotus.domino.ViewColumn* methods described earlier for all the columns in the "All" view in a message box. Although this example wouldn't be especially useful in the real world, it does demonstrate how to access the view column methods.

```
import lotus.domino.*;
import java.util.Vector;

public class JavaAgent extends AgentBase {

    public void NotesMain() {
```

```
try {
    Session ns = getSession();
    AgentContext agentContext = ns.getAgentContext();
    Database ndb= agentContext.getCurrentDatabase();
    View nvw = ndb.getView("All");
    Vector columns = nvw.getColumns();
    ViewColumn nvc = null;
    String strAlign = null;
    String strDateformat = null;
    String strFontcolor = null;
    String strFontstyle = null;
    System.out.println("The view attributes are:");
    if (columns.size() != 0) {
        for (int i=0; i<columns.size(); i++) {
            nvc = (ViewColumn)columns.elementAt(i);
        System.out.println("Column Number: " + nvc.getPosition());
        switch (nvc.getAlignment()) {
            case ViewColumn.ALIGN_CENTER : strAlign = "center"; break;
            case ViewColumn.ALIGN_LEFT : strAlign = "left";break;
            case ViewColumn.ALIGN_RIGHT : strAlign = "right"; break; }
        System.out.println("Alignment: "  + strAlign);
        switch (nvc.getTimeDateFmt()) {
            case ViewColumn.FMT_DATE : strDateformat = "date only";
            ➥break;
            case ViewColumn.FMT_DATETIME : strDateformat =
            ➥"date and time"; break;
            case ViewColumn.FMT_TIME : strDateformat = "time only";
            ➥break;
            case ViewColumn.FMT_TODAYTIME : strDateformat =
            ➥"today and time"; break; }
        System.out.println("Date Format: "  + strDateformat);
                switch (nvc.getFontColor()) {
            case RichTextStyle.COLOR_BLACK :
                strFontcolor = "black"; break;
            case RichTextStyle.COLOR_WHITE :
                strFontcolor = "white"; break;
            case RichTextStyle.COLOR_RED :
                strFontcolor = "red"; break;
            case RichTextStyle.COLOR_GREEN :
                strFontcolor = "green"; break;
            case RichTextStyle.COLOR_BLUE :
                strFontcolor = "blue"; break;
            case RichTextStyle.COLOR_MAGENTA :
                strFontcolor = "magenta"; break;
            case RichTextStyle.COLOR_YELLOW :
                strFontcolor = "yellow"; break;
            case RichTextStyle.COLOR_CYAN :
                strFontcolor = "cyan"; break;
            case RichTextStyle.COLOR_DARK_RED :
                strFontcolor = "dark red"; break;
            case RichTextStyle.COLOR_DARK_GREEN :
                strFontcolor = "dark green"; break;
            case RichTextStyle.COLOR_DARK_BLUE :
                strFontcolor = "dark blue"; break;
            case RichTextStyle.COLOR_DARK_MAGENTA :
                strFontcolor = "dark magenta"; break;
            case RichTextStyle.COLOR_DARK_YELLOW :
                strFontcolor = "dark yellow"; break;
            case RichTextStyle.COLOR_DARK_CYAN :
```

continued >>

continued >>

```
                              strFontcolor = "dark cyan"; break;
                      case RichTextStyle.COLOR_GRAY :
                          strFontcolor = "gray"; break;
                      case RichTextStyle.COLOR_LIGHT_GRAY :
                          strFontcolor = "light gray"; break;
                      default :
                          strFontcolor = "no color"; }
                      System.out.println("Font Color: "  + strFontcolor);
                      System.out.println("Font Face: "  + nvc.getFontFace());
                      System.out.println("Font Point Size: "  +
                      nvc.getFontPointSize());

                      if ((nvc.getFontStyle() & ViewColumn.FONT_BOLD) ==
                      ViewColumn.FONT_BOLD)
                          strFontstyle = "bold";
                      else strFontstyle = "plain";
                      if ((nvc.getFontStyle() &
                      ViewColumn.FONT_ITALIC) ==
                      ViewColumn.FONT_ITALIC)
                          strFontstyle = strFontstyle + " italic";
                      if ((nvc.getFontStyle() &
                      ViewColumn.FONT_UNDERLINE) ==
                      ViewColumn.FONT_UNDERLINE)
                          strFontstyle = strFontstyle + " underline";
                      if ((nvc.getFontStyle() &
                      ViewColumn.FONT_STRIKEOUT) ==
                      ViewColumn.FONT_STRIKEOUT)
                          strFontstyle = strFontstyle + " strikeout";
                      System.out.println("Font Style: "  + strFontstyle);
                        switch (nvc.getHeaderAlignment()) {
                        case ViewColumn.ALIGN_CENTER : strAlign = "center"; break;
                        case ViewColumn.ALIGN_LEFT : strAlign = "left";break;
                        case ViewColumn.ALIGN_RIGHT : strAlign = "right"; break; }
                      System.out.println("Alignment: "  + strAlign);
                      System.out.println("Header Alignment: "  + strAlign);
                      }
                    }
                  }
                catch(Exception e) {
                   e.printStackTrace();
                }
              }
            }
```

getItemName	R	O.Ref.

getItemName   `strItemName = nvcViewColumn.getItemName()`

This method returns the name of the *lotus.domino.Item* whose value is being displayed in the column. Often, a column is set to display the contents of a *lotus.domino.Item* or field value. If the item being displayed in the view was generated using a simple function in the column design, the internal Notes representation will be displayed.

5.0 getListSep	R	%

getListSep   `intListSep = nvcViewColumn.getListSep()`

This method returns the separator character being used to deliminate multiple values for display in the column contained in the multivalue *lotus.domino.Item* used as the column formula. A constant integer value is returned that represents the allowable values for deliminating multivalue *lotus.domino.Items*. Here are the allowable constant values:

Constant Value	Description
ViewColumn.SEP_COMMA	The values are separated by the comma character.
ViewColumn.SEP_NEWLINE	The values are separated by the newline character.
ViewColumn.SEP_SEMICOLON	The values are separated by the semicolon character.
ViewColumn.SEP_SPACE	The values are separated by spaces.

5.0 getNumberAttrib   R   %

```
intNumberAttrib = nvcViewColumn.getNumberAttrib()
```

This method returns a constant integer value representing the attributes for the numeric column values. Here are the possible values returned:

Constant Value	Description
ViewColumn.ATTR_PARENS	The numeric value should be parenthesized on negative numbers.
ViewColumn.ATTR_PUNCTUATED	The numeric value is punctuated at thousands.
ViewColumn.ATTR_PERCENT	The numeric value is a percentage (value ⋆ 100).

5.0 getNumberDigits   R   %

```
intNumberdigits = nvcViewColumn.getNumberDigits()
```

This method indicates the number of decimal places for the numeric value in the column.

5.0 getNumberFormat   R   %

```
intNumberformat = nvcViewColumn.getNumberFormat()
```

This method returns a constant of type integer representing the format of the numeric values in the column. Here are the possible constants returned for this method:

Constant Value	Description
ViewColumn.FMT_CURRENCY	The numeric value is currency.
ViewColumn.FMT_FIXED	The numeric value is fixed.
ViewColumn.FMT_GENERAL	The numeric value is general.
ViewColumn.FMT_SCIENTIFIC	The numeric value is scientific.

getParent   R   O.Ref.

```
nvView = nvcViewColumn.getParent()
```

This method returns a handle on the *lotus.domino.View* that contains the *lotus.domino.ViewColumn*.

getPosition   R   %

```
intPosition = nvcViewColumn.getPosition()
```

This method returns the position of the column in the view, starting at 1 and counting from left to right. Unlike the *lotus.domino.ViewColumn* objects contained in the *lotus.domino.View*, which is an array with the index starting at 0 (Option Base 0), the position value starts at 1. Therefore, when using the position method with the array of columns returned from the `columns` method of the *lotus.domino.NotesView*, be sure to add 1 to the value of the `columns` array.

5.0 getTimeDateFmt   R   %

```
intTimedatefmt = nvcViewColumn.getTimeDateFmt()
```

This method returns the format of the time-date value being stored in the column. Here are the possible values returned for this method:

Constant Value	Description
ViewColumn.FMT_DATE	Date only
ViewColumn.FMT_DATETIME	Date and time
ViewColumn.FMT_TIME	Time only
ViewColumn.FMT_TODAYTIME	Format is "today"
ViewColumn.FMT_TODAYTIME	Format is "today" and time

5.0 **getTimeFmt**   R   %

getTimeFmt   `intTimefmt = nvcViewColumn.getTimeFmt()`

This method returns the time format of the time value displayed in the column as an integer constant. Here are the possible values returned for this method:

Constant Value	Description
FMT HMS	The time format is month, hours, and seconds.
FMT HM	The time format is hours and month.

5.0 **getTimeZoneFmt**   R   %

getTimeZone
Fmt   `intTimezonefmt = nvcViewColumn.getTimeZoneFmt()`

This method returns a constant integer representing the format of the time zone of the time value in the column. Here are the possible values returned:

Constant Value	Description
ViewColumn.FMT ALWAYS	The time zone should always be shown.
ViewColumn.FMT NEVER	The time should be adjusted to the local zone. Therefore, the original time zone will never be shown.
ViewColumn.FMT SOMETIMES	The time should be shown only if the original time zone isn't local.

---

getTitle   R   O.Ref.

getTitle   `strTitle = nvcViewColumn.getTitle()`

This method returns the title of the column. If the column doesn't have a title defined, this method returns `""`.

5.0 **getWidth**   R/W   O.Ref.

getWidth   `intWidth = nvcViewColumn.getWidth()`

This method returns the width of the column in characters.

5.0 **isAccentSensitiveSort**   R   T/F

isAccentSensitive
Sort   `bolIsaccentinsenssort = nvcViewColumn.isAccentSensitiveSort()`

This method indicates whether the column-sorting method for accent sorting is enabled or disabled. `true` indicates that the sort should respect accents. `false` indicates that the sort should ignore accents.

5.0 **isCaseSensitiveSort**   R   T/F

isCaseSensitive
Sort   `bolIscaseinsenssort = nvcViewColumn.isCaseSensitiveSort()`

This method indicates whether the column-sorting method for case sorting is enabled or disabled. `true` indicates that the sort should respect case sensitivity. `false` indicates that the sort should ignore case sensitivity.

---

isCategory R T/F

```
bolIscategory = nvcViewColumn.isCategory()
```

This method indicates whether the column is categorized (as well as sorted, since a column must be sorted in order to be categorized). Refer to the `isSorted` method of the *lotus.domino.ViewColumn* (▶ 621). `true` indicates that the column is categorized. `false` indicates that the column is not categorized (although it still may be sorted).

5.0 isField R T/F

```
bolIsfield = nvcViewColumn.isField()
```

This method indicates whether the values displayed in the columns are based on field values or formulas. `true` indicates that the column values are based on field values. `false` indicates that they are based on formulas.

5.0 isFormula R T/F

```
bolIfformula = nvcViewColumn.isFormula()
```

This method indicates whether the values displayed in the columns are based on a Notes formula. `true` indicates that the column values are based on a Notes formula. `false` indicates that they are not. When designing column formulas, you are restricted to using either simple functions, fields, or formulas (using the @Function macro language available in Domino/Lotus Notes). If the value used in the column formula is equivalent to a single field value, this method returns `false`, even if the designer specifies formula and enters the name of the field. This is still interpreted by Domino as a single field value reference and not an actual @formula. Refer to the `getformula` method of *lotus.domino.ViewColumn* (▶ 614).

---

isHidden R T/F

```
bolIshidden = nvcViewColumn.isHidden()
```

This method indicates whether the column is hidden. Hidden columns aren't visible in a view but are still functional as far as sorting and being used in @DbLookup and @DbColumn formulas and by script (`getDocumentByKey`, `getAllDocumentsByKey`, and so on). `true` indicates that the column is hidden. `false` indicates that it is not hidden.

---

isHideDetail R T/F

```
bolIshidedetail = nvcViewColumn.isHideDetail()
```

This method indicates whether the details (individual line items) for total columns in categorized/sorted columns should be displayed or hidden. If this method is `true`, the details are hidden. If this method is `false`, they are displayed along with the totals.

---

isIcon R T/F

```
bolIsflag = nvcViewColumn.isIcon()
```

This method indicates whether the column method to "Display values as icons" is enabled. If it's `true`, the numeric value stored in the column will result in the display of an icon (from a predetermined set) in the column. If it's `false`, this setting is ignored, and the column values are treated as normal, displaying the contents based on a simple function, formula, or field.

5.0 isResize	R	T/F

isResize

```
bolIsResize = nvcViewColumn.isResize()
```

This method indicates whether the column can be resized through the native Notes client. This method has no effect when the view is published by the Domino server. If it's **true**, when using a native Notes client, the user can resize the column width by placing the cursor at the vertical edge of the column and dragging the vertical crosshair to the desired width. If it's **false**, the column width can't be adjusted.

5.0 isResortAscending	R	T/F

isResort
Ascending

```
bolIsresortasc = nvcViewColumn.isResortAscending()
```

This method indicates whether the column can be re-sorted in ascending order. The column must have already been designed to allow for dynamic sorting (it must be re-sortable). If this method is **true**, you can re-sort the column by clicking the arrow icon to the right of the column title. If this method is **false**, the arrow won't be displayed to the user and therefore can't be re-sorted. This method isn't available on the Web.

5.0 isResortDescending	R	T/F

isResort
Descending

```
bolIsresortdesc = nvcViewColumn.isResortDescending()
```

This method indicates whether the column can be re-sorted in descending order. The column must have already been designed to allow for dynamic sorting (it must be re-sortable). If this method is **true**, you can re-sort the column by clicking the arrow icon to the right of the column title. If this method is **false**, the arrow won't be displayed to the user and therefore can't be re-sorted. This method isn't available on the Web.

5.0 isResortToView	R	T/F

isResortToView

```
bolIsresorttoview = nvcViewColumn.isResortToView()
```

This method indicates whether the column can be re-sorted by clicking the column title, or header. The column must have already been designed to allow for sorting (it must be re-sortable). If this method is **true**, you can re-sort the column by clicking the arrow icon to the right of the column title. If this method is **false**, the arrow won't be displayed to the user and therefore can't be re-sorted. This method isn't available on the Web.

isResponse	R	T/F

isResponse

```
bolIsresponse = nvcViewColumn.isResponse()
```

This method indicates whether the column contains response documents only. This is equivalent to the "Show responses only" setting of the column design. This method must be set to display response documents in their response hierarchy in views. An example is discussion threads commonly used in both native Notes and Web applications. If this method is **true**, this column will display only response documents. If this method is **false**, this column will display any type of document.

5.0 isSecondaryResort	R	T/F

isSecondary
Resort

```
bolIssecondaryresort = nvcViewColumn.isSecondaryResort()
```

This method indicates whether the current column is a secondary column that is re-sortable. **true** indicates that the current column is a secondary re-sortable column. **false** indicates that it is not.

5.0 isSecondaryResortDescending   R   T/F

```
bolIssecresortdesc = nvcViewColumn.isSecondaryResortDescending()
```
isSecondary
Resort
Descending

This method indicates whether the current column is a secondary re-sortable column whose sort order is descending. true indicates that the current column is a secondary re-sortable column in descending order. false indicates that it is a secondary re-sortable column in ascending order.

5.0 isShowTwistie   R   T/F

```
bolIsshowtwistie = nvcViewColumn.isShowTwistie()
```
isShowTwistie

If the column is expandable, this method indicates whether a twistie should be displayed to the immediate left of the column values. A twistie visually indicates that the current entry is a category. The category can be expanded and collapsed when you click the twistie icon. If this method is true, the column will display a twistie. If this method is false, the column will not display the twistie, even if the entry is an expandable category. This method is equivalent to the "Show twistie when row is expandable" method of the column design.

5.0 isSortDescending   R   T/F

```
bolIssortdescending = nvcViewColumn.isSortDescending()
```
isSort
Descending

If the column is sorted, this method indicates whether it is sorted in descending order. If this method is true, the column is sorted in descending order. If this method is false, the column is sorted in ascending order. You can also determined if the column is sorted by using the isSorted method, as shown below, also contained by *lotus.domino.ViewColumn*.

isSorted   R   T/F

```
bolIssorted = nvcViewColumn.isSorted()
```
isSorted

This method indicates whether the column is sorted. true indicates that the column is sorted. false indicates that it is not sorted. The specific sort order can be determined by using the isSortDescending method, as shown above, also a method of the *lotus.domino.ViewColumn*.

Remarks

The *lotus.domino.ViewColumn* class was exposed in Notes Release 4.6 and has been dramatically improved in Release 5.0. Practically every method of the *lotus.domino.ViewColumn* is exposed. Unfortunately, most of these are read-only methods. Therefore, the design of *lotus.domino.View* can't be programmatically modified by your script. Although the need to perform such functions is unlikely, this would be helpful in reducing the number of views to build into the database design because they could be modified on-the-fly based on the current criteria.

Example

The following LotusScript snippet prints the sorting attributes of all the columns in the "All" view.

```
import lotus.domino.*;
import java.util.Vector;

public class JavaAgent extends AgentBase {

    public void NotesMain() {

        try {
            Session ns = getSession();
            AgentContext agentContext = ns.getAgentContext();
            Database ndb= agentContext.getCurrentDatabase();
            View nvw = ndb.getView("All");
            Vector columns = nvw.getColumns();
            ViewColumn nvc = null;
            System.out.println("The view column design attributes are:");
            if (columns.size() != 0) {
                for (int i=0; i<columns.size(); i++) {
                    nvc = (ViewColumn)columns.elementAt(i);
                    System.out.println("Column Number: " +
                    ➥nvc.getPosition());
                    System.out.println("Accent sorting: " +
                    ➥nvc.isAccentSensitiveSort());
                    System.out.println("Case sorting: " +
                    ➥nvc.isCaseSensitiveSort());
                    System.out.println("Case Ascending: " +
                    ➥nvc.isResortAscending());
                    System.out.println("Case Descending: " +
                    ➥nvc.isResortDescending());
                    System.out.println("Case Secondary sort: " +
                    ➥nvc.isSecondaryResort());
                    System.out.println("Is Secondary sort descending: " +
                    ➥nvc.isSecondaryResortDescending());
                    System.out.println("Is Sort descending: " +
                    ➥nvc.isSortDescending());
                }
            }
        }
        catch(Exception e) {
            e.printStackTrace();
        }
    }
}
```

The *lotus.domino.ViewEntry* class is new in Notes 5.0—and it's a very welcome addition. It provides the long-awaited capability to access a row in a view. A row can be one of three things: a category, a total, or a document.

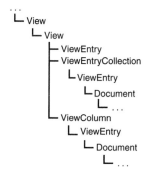

Java Syntax

```
public class ViewEntry extends Base
```

There are several ways to get a handle on a *lotus.domino.ViewEntry* object. The first method is to use the getEntryByKey method of *lotus.domino.View* (▶ 598):

```
ViewEntry nveentry = view.getEntryByKey(vecKeys)
```

or

```
Viewentry nveentry = view.getEntryByKey(strKey)
```

Alternatively, you can use any of the various get methods of either the *lotus.domino.ViewNavigator* (▶ 637) or *lotus.domino.ViewEntryCollection* (▶ 629) classes, several of which are shown here:

```
ViewEntry nveentry = viewnavigator.getFirstEntry()
```

or

```
ViewEntry nveentry = viewentrycollection.getNthEntry(int n)
```

or

```
ViewEntry nveentry = viewentrycollection.getNextSibling()
```

ViewEntry Methods

getChildCount   R   %

getChildCount

```
intCount = nveviewentry.getChildCount()
```

This method returns, as an integer, the number of child entries (if any) that the current view entry has.

getColumnIndentLevel   R   %

getColumn
IndentLevel

```
intLevel = nveviewentry.getColumnIndentLevel()
```

This method returns, as an integer, the number of levels the entry is indented in a column.

getColumnValues   R   O.Ref.

getColumn
Values

```
vecColvalues = nveviewentry.getColumnValues()
```

Returns an object of type *java.util.Vector* that contains elements of type string, int, or double that represent the values displayed in each of the columns of the current entry.

getDescendantCount   R   %

getDescendant
Count

```
intDescCount = nveviewentry.getDescendantCount()
```

Returns the number of descendants that the current entry has as an integer. This differs from the getChildCount method in that this method accounts for all of an entry's descendants—not just the immediate ones. For example, if you had a parent document that had a response, and the response had an associated response to response, the getChildCount method would return 1 for the parent, and getDescendantCount would return 2.

getDocument   R   O.Ref.

getDocument

```
ndocCurDoc = viewentry.getDocument()
```

This method returns a handle to the underlying *lotus.domino.Document* (▶ 413) from which the entry is derived. This method will return `null` if the entry is not a document (category or total) or if the underlying document has been deleted since the entry object was created. Consider the following example:

```
import lotus.domino.*;
public class JavaAgent extends AgentBase {
  public void NotesMain() {
    try {
    // Last mods 990119.034401 - dhatter@definiti.com
    // This code deletes conflict documents
    Session session = getSession();
    AgentContext nac= session.getAgentContext();
    Database ndbCurr=nac.getCurrentDatabase();
    View nvwView=ndbCurr.getView("Testing");
    ViewEntryCollection nvecCollection=nvwView.getAllEntries();
    int intCount=0;
    for (int i=0; i <= nvecCollection.getCount(); i++)
      {
        ViewEntry nveEntry=nvecCollection.getNthEntry(i);
        if (nveEntry.isConflict())
          {
            Document ndocCurr=nveEntry.getDocument();
            ndocCurr.remove(true);
            intCount++;
          }
      }
    System.out.println(intCount + "conflict documents were deleted.");
    } catch(Exception e) {
    e.printStackTrace();
    }
  }
}
```

getFTSearchScore   R   %.

getFtSearch
Score

```
intFTScore = nveviewentry.getFTSearchScore()
```

This method returns an integer representing a document's search score. For entries not retrieved as part of a full-text search, this method always returns 0. The search score is based on several factors, including the number of search terms found in the entry, the term weights assigned to the search words, and any proximity operators in the search query. If a full-text search is conducted on a database that hasn't been indexed, this method will yield "unpredictable" return values (according to the Lotus Help Database).

getIndentLevel   R   %

getIndentLevel

```
intindent = nveviewentry.getIndentLevel()
```

Returns, as an integer, the number of levels the current entry is indented in the view.

getNoteID   R   O.Ref.

getNoteID

```
strNoteID = nveviewentry.getNoteID()
```

Returns a *java.lang.String* object containing the Note ID of the underlying document. Remember that the actual Note ID is prepended with the string "NT".

getParent	R	O.Ref.

getParent

```
object = nveviewentry.getParent()
```

This method returns an object of type *lotus.domino.View, lotus.domino.ViewNavigator*, or *lotus.domino.ViewEntryCollection* representing the parent object.

getPosition

getPosition

```
strPos = nveviewEntry.getPosition(charPos)
```

charPos	Required	O.Ref.

The separator character used in the return value. Normally this will be a period.

This method returns a char containing the entry's position in the view. For example, a position of 4.7 would indicate that you have the seventh entry under the fourth category.

getSiblingCount	R	%

getSibling
Count

```
intSibcount = nveviewentry.getSiblingCount()
```

Returns, as an integer, the number of siblings an entry has. If the current entry is a total or category, this method returns 0 due to the fact that totals and categories are not documents and aren't really part of the view hierarchy.

getUniversalID	R	O.Ref.

getUniversalID

```
strUNID = nveviewentry.getUniversalID()
```

Returns the Universal ID of the entry's underlying document. For totals and categories, this method returns an empty string (""). Remember that the Universal ID is a 32-character string comprised of hexadecimal digits that uniquely identifies a document across all copies of a database.

isCategory	R	T/F

isCategory

```
boliscat = nveviewentry.isCategory()
```

Returns true if the current entry is a category and false if it isn't.

isConflict	R	T/F

isConflict

```
bolisconf = nveviewentry.isConflict()
```

Returns true if the current entry represents a conflict document. Otherwise, this method returns false.

isDocument	R	T/F

isDocument

```
bolisdoc = nveviewentry.isDocument()
```

Returns true if the current entry represents a document. Otherwise, this method returns false.

isTotal	R	T/F

isTotal

```
bolistot = nveviewentry.isTotal()
```

Returns true if the current entry represents a total. Otherwise, this method returns false.

isValid	R	T/F

isValid

```
bolIscat = nveviewentry.isValid()
```

Returns true if the current entry represents a valid entry—meaning a document, category, or total. If the entry represents a deletion stub, this method returns false.

Example

```java
import lotus.domino.*;
import java.util.Vector;
public class JavaAgent extends AgentBase {
  public void NotesMain() {
    try {
      // Last mods 990119.034401 - dhatter@definiti.com
      // This code checks for new issues and, if found, sends a summary
      // to the managers
      Session session = getSession();
      AgentContext nac= session.getAgentContext();
      Database ndbCurr =nac.getCurrentDatabase();
      Document ndocMail=ndbCurr.createDocument();
      RichTextItem nrtiBody= ndocMail.createRichTextItem("Body");
      int intCount=0;
      View nvwIssues=ndbCurr.getView("New Topics");
      ViewEntryCollection nvecIssues=nvwIssues.getAllEntries();
      ViewEntry nveIssue=nvecIssues.getFirstEntry();
      nrtiBody.appendText("The following issues are currently unread.
      ➥Please click the doc link to open an issue");
      nrtiBody.addNewLine(2);
      nrtiBody.appendText("Subject"+"\t\t\t"+"Date"+"\t\t\t"+"From");
      while(nveIssue !=null)
      {
            Document ndocCurr=nveIssue.getDocument();
            Vector vecSubject=ndocCurr.getItemValue("Subject");
            Vector vecDate=ndocCurr.getItemValue("Date");
            Vector vecFrom=ndocCurr.getItemValue("From");
            nrtiBody.appendText(vecSubject.firstElement()+"\t\t"+
            ➥vecDate.firstElement()+"\t\t"+vecFrom.firstElement());
            nrtiBody.appendDocLink(ndocCurr, "Click Me");
            nrtiBody.addNewLine(1);
            intCount++;
            nveIssue=nvecIssues.getNextEntry(nveIssue);
      }
      ndocMail.replaceItemValue("Subject",intCount + " unread issues
      ➥remain in Customer Service database");
      ndocMail.send(false,"CS_Managers");
    } catch(Exception e) {
    e.printStackTrace();
    }
  }
}
```

ViewEntryCollection

5.0

The *lotus.domino.ViewEntryCollection* class is new in Notes 5.0. It is both much anticipated and appreciated! It represents a collection of *lotus.domino.ViewEntry* objects (also new to Notes 5.0, ▶ 623) that are sorted in the order they appear in the underlying view. For the first time, developers can access documents sorted in the order of a view's index, without the need to "walk the view" (access each document sequentially). Additionally, you can use this class to access the values stored in a view's columns, to access the categories in a view, and to store the result sets from multiple full-text searches (FTSearch, ▶ 630).

```
...
 L View
    L ViewEntryCollection
        L ViewEntry
            L Document
                L ...
```

Java Syntax

```
public class ViewEntryCollection extends Base
```

There are two basic ways to access a *lotus.domino.ViewEntryCollection*. Both rely on the *lotus.domino.View* object (▶ 587). The first approach is to use the getAllEntries method of *lotus.domino.View:*

```
nveccollection = view.getAllEntries()
```

The second option is to use the getAllEntriesByKey method of *lotus.domino.View* to return only those entries that match the value supplied as a key:

```
nvecCollection = nvwView.getAllEntriesByKey ("Samuel Hatter")
```

ViewEntryCollection Methods

addEntry

addEntry
```
nveEntry = nvecviewEntryCollection.addEntry(nveEntrytoAdd)

nveEntry = nvecviewEntryCollection.addEntry(nveEntrytoAdd, bolCheckDupes)
```

nveEntrytoAdd	Required	O.Ref.

The *lotus.domino.ViewEntry* to add to the collection.

bolCheckDupes	Required	T/F

Specify true to check for duplicate entries.

This method allows you to insert additional entries into a view entry collection. If the collection is sorted, the entry is appended. For unsorted collections, the entry is inserted based on an internal algorithm. If the entry being added is a duplicate, an error is generated. When using this method, you can navigate from the new entry to determine its position in the collection.

deleteEntry

deleteEntry
```
nvecviewEntryCollection.deleteEntry(nveEntrytoDelete)
```

nveEntrytoDelete	Required	O.Ref.

The *lotus.domino.ViewEntry* to delete from the collection.

This method allows you to remove a *lotus.domino.ViewEntry* from a *lotus.domino.ViewEntryCollection*. For this method to work, the entry being deleted must have originated in this collection. It is important to note that this method will not delete the underlying document. It deletes only the entry from the collection. If the specified entry doesn't exist, an error is generated.

FTSearch

FTSearch
```
nvecviewEntryCollection.FTSearch(strQuery)

nvecviewEntryCollection.FTSearch(strQuery, intMaxDocs)
```

strQuery	Required	$

The query that should be used to search the collection.

intMaxDocs   Optional   %

An integer that specifies the maximum number of entries to return.

This method uses the Notes full-text search engine to provide a fast and easy way to further filter a *lotus.domino.ViewEntryCollection*.

---

getCount   R   %

```
intcount = nvecviewentrycollection.getCount()
```
<code>getCount</code>

Returns an integer containing the number of entries in the collection. Consider the following example:

```java
import lotus.domino.*;
import java.io.PrintWriter;
import java.util.Vector;
public class JavaAgent extends AgentBase {
  public void NotesMain() {
    try {
        Session nssession = getSession();
        AgentContext nac = session.getAgentContext();
        Database ndbCurr=nac.getCurrentDatabase();
        View nvwAllleads=ndbCurr.getView("By  Status");
        ViewEntryCollection nvecHot=nvwAllleads.getAllEntriesByKey
        ➥("Hot");
        PrintWriter pw=getAgentOutput();
        int intCount=nvecHot.getCount();
        if (intCount>0)
          {
            ViewEntry nveCurr=nvecHot.getFirstEntry();
            Document ndocCurr=nveCurr.getDocument();
            pw.println("<H2><FONT color=red>Hot Leads</FONT></H2>
            ➥<BR>");
            pw.println("<TABLE border=0 cellspacing=0 cellpadding=0
            ➥width=0>");
            for (int i=1; i<=intCount; i++)
              {
                Vector vecKey=ndocCurr.getItemValue("CustomerKey");
                Vector vecCompany=ndocCurr.getItemValue
                ➥("CompanyName");
                pw.println("<TR>");
                pw.println("<TD><A href=/"+ndbCurr.getFileName()+
                ➥"/Hotleads/"+vecKey.firstElement()+"?OpenDocument>"+
                ➥vecCompany.firstElement()+"</A>");
                pw.println("</TR>");
                nveCurr=nvecHot.getNextEntry(nveCurr);
                ndocCurr=nveCurr.getDocument();
              }
            pw.println("</TABLE>");
          }
      else
        pw.println("<H2><FONT color=red>No Hot Leads Were Found</FONT>
        ➥</H2><BR>");
    } catch(Exception e) {
    e.printStackTrace();
  }
 }
}
```

---

getEntry

```
nveEntry = nvecviewEntryCollection.getEntry(varEntry)
```
<code>getEntry</code>

varEntry	Required	O.Ref.

A *lotus.domino.ViewEntry* or *lotus.domino.Document* object containing the entry to retrieve.

This method returns the specified entry if it is found in the collection. Otherwise, this method returns `null`.

getFirstEntry

getFirstEntry

```
nveFirstEntry = nvecviewEntryCollection.getFirstEntry()
```

This method needs no parameters because it returns the first entry in the *lotus.domino.ViewEntryCollection*. If the collection is empty, this method returns `null`.

getLastEntry

getLastEntry

```
nveLastEntry = nvecviewEntryCollection.getLastEntry()
```

As you might expect, this method is the opposite of `getFirstEntry`. It returns the last entry in a *lotus.domino.ViewEntryCollection* object. If there is no last entry—for example, if no entries exist in a specific view—this method returns `null`.

getNextEntry

getNextEntry

```
nveNextEntry = nvecviewEntryCollection.getNextEntry()

nveNextEntry = nvecviewEntryCollection.getNextEntry(nveCurrent)
```

nveCurrent	Optional	O.Ref.

The current view entry.

This method works with `getFirstEntry`, `getLastEntry`, `getNthEntry`, and `getPrevEntry` to provide a comprehensive set of navigational tools that allow you to navigate through a *lotus.domino.ViewEntryCollection*. When given the current *lotus.domino.ViewEntry*, this method returns the next *lotus.domino.ViewEntry* in the collection. If no parameter is specified, the next entry after the current entry is returned.

getNthEntry

getNthEntry

```
nveEntry = nvecviewEntryCollection.getNthEntry(intIndex)
```

intIndex	Required	%

A number that represents the entry's position in the collection.

This is a very useful method that allows you to jump to a specific entry in a collection when you know its position. This is most commonly used for looping through all the entries in a collection, as shown in the following example.

```
import lotus.domino.*;
import java.util.Vector;
public class JavaAgent extends AgentBase {
  public void NotesMain() {
    try { //Last mods 990228.110606 - dhatter@definiti.com
        Session session = getSession();
        AgentContext nac = session.getAgentContext();
        Database ndbCurr=nac.getCurrentDatabase();
        View nvwReports=ndbCurr.getView("(AllReports)");
        ViewEntryCollection nvecReports=nvwReports.getAllEntries();
        int intHigh=0;
        int intMed=0;
        int intLow=0;
```

```
if (nvecReports.getCount()>0)
  {
    Document ndocMailDoc=ndbCurr.createDocument();
    ndocMailDoc.replaceItemValue("Subject","Status Report
    ➥Summary ");
    RichTextItem nrtfiBody = ndocMailDoc.createRichTextItem
    ➥("Body");
    for(int i=1; i<=nvecReports.getCount();i++)
      {
        ViewEntry nveEntry=nvecReports.getNthEntry(i);
        Document ndocReport=nveEntry.getDocument();
        Vector vecStatus=ndocReport.getItemValue("Status");
        if (vecStatus.firstElement()=="Hot")
            intHigh++;
        else if (vecStatus.firstElement()=="Medium")
            intMed++;
        else
            intLow++;
      }
    nrtfiBody.appendText("Status Report Summary:");
    nrtfiBody.addNewLine(2);
    nrtfiBody.appendText("High Priority: " + intHigh);
    nrtfiBody.addNewLine(1);
    nrtfiBody.appendText("Medium Priority: " + intMed);
    nrtfiBody.addNewLine(1);
    nrtfiBody.appendText("Low Priority: " + intLow);
    nrtfiBody.addNewLine(2);
    nrtfiBody.appendText("Total Reports: " + intHigh+intMed+
    ➥intLow);
    ndocMailDoc.send(false,"SupportManagers");
  }
else
    System.out.println("No status reports found.");
} catch(Exception e) {
e.printStackTrace();
    }
  }
}
```

---

getParent   R   O.Ref.

```
nvwParent = nvecviewentrycollection.getParent()
```
getParent

Returns a *lotus.domino.View* object containing the view from which the collection was built.

---

getPrevEntry

```
nveEntry = nvecviewEntryCollection.getPrevEntry()
```
getPrevEntry

```
nveEntry = nvecviewEntryCollection.getPrevEntry(nveCurrent)
```

nveCurrent   Required   O.Ref.
The current view entry.

Given the current *lotus.domino.ViewEntry*, this method returns the previous *lotus.domino.ViewEntry* in the collection.

---

getQuery   R $

```
strquery = nvecviewentrycollection.getQuery()
```
getQuery

Contains the query string that was used if the collection is the result of a full-text query.

putAllInFolder

`nvecviewEntryCollection.`**`putAllInFolder`**`(strFolderName)`

`nvecviewEntryCollection.`**`putAllInFolder`**`(strFolderName, bolCreateonfail)`

| strFolderName | Required | O.Ref. |

The name of the folder in which to place the documents.

| bolCreateonfail | Optional | T/F |

Specify `true` to create the folder if it doesn't already exist. Otherwise, an error will be thrown.

This method moves all the underlying documents contained in the *lotus.domino.ViewEntryCollection* to the specified folder. If the specified folder doesn't exist, it will be created. Consider the following example:

```
import lotus.domino.*;
public class JavaAgent extends AgentBase {
  public void NotesMain() {
    try {
            Session session = getSession();
            AgentContext nac = session.getAgentContext();
            Database ndbCurr=nac.getCurrentDatabase();
            View nvwView=ndbCurr.getView("(By Customer)");
            ViewEntryCollection nvecCollection=nvwView.getAllEntriesByKey
        ➥("Wyatt Hatter");
            if (nvecCollection.getCount()>0)
               nvecCollection.putAllInFolder("Wyatt Hatter");
            else
               System.out.println("No matching documents were found.");
        } catch(Exception e) {
        e.printStackTrace();
      }
    }
  }
```

removeAll

`nvecviewEntryCollection.`**`removeAll`**`(bolForce)`

| bolForce | Required | T/F |

Indicates whether deleted documents should be removed from the collection.

When the `bolForce` parameter is set to `true`, the underlying documents are removed from the *lotus.domino.ViewEntryCollection* and are deleted from the database as well. If `bolForce` is `false`, some of the documents might be left in the collection, even if they were deleted.

removeAllFromFolder

`nvecviewEntryCollection.`**`removeAllFromFolder`**`(strFolderName)`

| strFolderName | Required | $ |

The name of the folder from which to remove the documents.

This method removes the underlying documents of a *lotus.domino.ViewEntryCollection* from the specified folder.

stampAll

`nvecviewEntryCollection.`**`stampAll`**`(strItemName, value)`

strItemName	Required	$

The name of the item in the underlying document that you want to update.

value	Required	O.Ref.

The actual value to write into the specified item (field). The data type of this parameter should match the data type of the field.

stampAll is a powerful and useful method that allows you to update a single field in every underlying document contained in a *lotus. domino. ViewEntryCollection* without writing a loop and without calling the **save** method of *lotus.domino.Document.* When stampAll is used, every document in the collection has the specified item set to the value specified in **value**. If the item doesn't exist, it is created. Any changes made to the underlying documents are immediately written to disk. Consider the following example:

```
import lotus.domino.*;
public class JavaAgent extends AgentBase {
  public void NotesMain() {
    try {
        Session session = getSession();
        AgentContext nac = session.getAgentContext();
        Database ndbCurr=nac.getCurrentDatabase();
        View nvwView = ndbCurr.getView("People");
        ViewEntryCollection nvecCollection=nvwView.getAllEntriesByKey
        ➥("Samuel Hatter");
        if (nvecCollection.getCount()>0)
            nvecCollection.stampAll("Processed",session.getUserName());
        else
            System.out.println("No documents were found.");
    } catch(Exception e) {
    e.printStackTrace();
    }
  }
}
```

updateAll

```
nvecviewEntryCollection.updateAll()
```
updateAll

This method marks all entries on thecollection, as updated by the agent.

Remarks

The *lotus.domino.ViewEntryCollection* class is very similar to the *lotus.domino.DocumentCollection* class, with one major difference. *lotus.domino.ViewEntryCollection* returns *lotus.domino.ViewEntry* objects in the order in which they are sorted in the underlying view, while documents in a *lotus.domino.DocumentCollection* are sorted by the DocumentUNID. The only exception to this rule is when the FTSearch method of *lotus.domino.Database, lotus.domino.View,* or *lotus.domino.DocumentCollection* is used to build the collection. In this case, the collection is sorted by the sort options specified in the FTSearch method.

You should keep in mind that a *lotus.domino.ViewEntryCollection* will not contain categories or column totals. Rather, it will contain only entries that correspond to the underlying documents.

Example

```java
import lotus.domino.*;
import java.util.Vector;
public class JavaAgent extends AgentBase {
  public void NotesMain() {
    try {
        Session session = getSession();
        AgentContext nac = session.getAgentContext();
        Database ndbCurr=nac.getCurrentDatabase();
        View nvwView=ndbCurr.getView("(By Customer)");
        ViewEntryCollection nvecCollection=nvwView.getAllEntries();
        if (nvecCollection.getCount()>0)
          {
            nvecCollection.FTSearch("Samuel Hatter",0);
            if (nvecCollection.getCount()>0)
              {
                Document ndocMail=ndbCurr.createDocument();
                RichTextItem nrtfiBody = ndocMail.createRichTextItem
                ➡("Body");
                nrtfiBody.appendText("The following " +
                ➡nvecCollection.getCount() + " documents were
                ➡found:");
                nrtfiBody.addNewLine(2);
                for(int i=1; i<=nvecCollection.getCount();i++)
                  {
                    ViewEntry nveEntry=nvecCollection.getNthEntry(i);
                    Document ndocLink = nveEntry.getDocument();
                    Vector vecDesc=ndocLink.getItemValue
                    ➡("Description");
                    nrtfiBody.appendText(vecDesc.firstElement() +
                    ➡" =>");
                    nrtfiBody.appendDocLink(ndocLink,"Click Me");
                    nrtfiBody.addNewLine(1);
                  }
                ndocMail.replaceItemValue("Subject","New Leads");
                ndocMail.send(false,"Sales_Managers");
              }
        else
            System.out.println("No documents were found.");
        }
    } catch(Exception e) {
    e.printStackTrace();
    }
  }
}
```

The *lotus.domino.ViewNavigator* object represents a new object for Notes Release 5.0. A view navigator represents all document entries (including *lotus.domino.Documents,* categories, and category totals) in a *lotus.domino.View.* This method enables you to navigate through the documents contained in the current view and the currently selected document's respective siblings, children, and parent. In addition, *lotus.domino.ViewNavigator* enables you to access document information to determine the document category, the category total, and whether a document is unread or is a document conflict.

```
...
L View
   L ViewNavigator
      L ViewEntry
         L Document
            L ...
```

continued >>

Java Syntax

```
public class ViewNavigator extends Base
```

There are several ways to create the *lotus.domino.ViewNavigator* from an existing *lotus.domino.View*. A *lotus.domino.ViewNavigator* can be created from scratch. It can also be created from an existing *lotus.domino.ViewNavigator*, from children or descendants of an existing *lotus.domino.ViewNavigator*, or from an existing category. Here are the methods of *lotus.domino.View* (▶ 587) that can be used to create and return an object handle on a *lotus.domino.ViewNavigator:* createViewNav, createViewNavFrom, createViewNavFromCategory, createViewNavFromChildren, createViewNavFromDescendants, createViewNavMaxLevel.

ViewNavigator Methods

getCacheSize   R   %

```
intCachesize = nvnavViewNavigator.getCacheSize()
```
getCacheSize

When you're making calls to the Domino server (remote IIOP operations), this method indicates the size of the navigator cache for view entries. When you're making local calls, this method returns 0 (similarly, setCacheSize will also have no effect). The minimum setting for this value is 0 (for no cache), and the maximum setting is 128 (the default setting).

getChild

```
nveViewEntry = nvnavViewNavigator.getChild()
```
getChild

```
nveViewEntry = nvnavViewNavigator.getChild(ViewEntry)
```

ViewEntry   Required   O.Ref.

An entry in the *lotus.domino.View* (the current entry is the default).

This method returns a handle on the first child (*lotus.domino.Document*) of either the current entry or a specified entry in the current view navigator. The child document is synonymous to a response document. If there are no children (responses), this method will return null. If this method successfully returns a handle on a view entry, that respective entry establishes user interface focus, and the cursor (pointer) is automatically placed on that entry. If the parent entry is a category, the child can be either another category or a *lotus.domino.Document*.

getCurrent

```
nveViewEntry = nvnavViewNavigator.getCurrent()
```
getCurrent

This method returns a handle on the current entry in the current view navigator. If there is no current entry, this method returns null.

getFirst

```
nveViewEntry = nvnavViewNavigator.getFirst()
```
getFirst

This method returns a handle on the first entry in the current view navigator. If there is no current entry, this method returns null. The entry establishes user interface focus, and the cursor (pointer) is automatically placed on that entry.

The following example uses several of the methods available for the *lotus.domino.ViewNavigator* class. This example steps through all the entries contained in the current view and builds a list of all the categories.

```
import lotus.domino.*;
import java.util.Vector;

public class JavaAgent extends AgentBase {

    public void NotesMain() {

        try {
            Session ns = getSession();
            AgentContext agentContext = ns.getAgentContext();
            Database ndb = agentContext.getCurrentDatabase();
            View nvw = ndb.getView("All");
            ViewNavigator nvn = nvw.createViewNav();
                ViewEntry nve = nvn.getFirst();
                    while (nve != null) {
                        if (nve.isCategory())   {
                            Vector vecColumnValue = nve.getColumnValues();
                            if (vecColumnValue.elementAt(0) != null) {
                            vecColumnValue.elementAt(0).getClass().getName();
                                System.out.println
                                 ⮕(vecColumnValue.elementAt(0)); }   }
                        nve = nvn.getNext();   }
                    System.out.println("Agent complete.");

        } catch(Exception e) {
            e.printStackTrace();
        }
    }
}
```

getFirstDocument

getFirst
Document

`nveViewEntry = nvnavViewNavigator.`**`getFirstDocument`**`()`

This method returns a handle on the first document in the current view navigator. If there is no document, this method returns null. The document establishes user interface focus, and the cursor (pointer) is automatically placed on the document.

getLast

getLast

`nveViewEntry = nvnavViewNavigator.`**`getLast`**`()`

This method returns a handle on the last entry in the current view navigator. If there is no entry, this method returns null. The entry establishes user interface focus, and the cursor (pointer) is automatically placed on the entry. If the *lotus.domino.View* was set up to display totals for one or more of the columns, this method will return the totals in the current entry.

getLastDocument

getLast
Document

`nveViewEntry = nvnavViewNavigator.`**`getLastDocument`**`()`

This method returns a handle on the last document in the current view navigator. If there is no document, this method returns null. The document establishes user interface focus, and the cursor (pointer) is automatically placed on the document. The method ignores any category or total entry that may exist in the current view.

getMaxLevel   R   %

```
intMaxlevel = nvnavViewNavigator.getMaxLevel()
```
getMaxLevel

Represents the maximum levels of navigation for the current *lotus.domino.View*. The allowed values for this method range from **0** (the top level of categorization) to **30** (the default `getmaxLevel` setting).

getNext

```
nveViewEntry = nvnavViewNavigator.getNext()
```
getNext

```
nveViewEntry = nvnavViewNavigator.getNext(nveViewEntry)
```

ViewEntry   Required   O.Ref.

An entry in the *lotus.domino.View* (the current entry is the default).

This method returns a handle on the next entry in the current view navigator. If there is no current entry, this method returns `null`. The entry establishes user interface focus, and the cursor (pointer) is automatically placed on that entry. For an example using this method, refer to the `getFirst` method (▶ 639).

getNextCategory

```
nveViewEntry = nvnavViewNavigator.getNextCategory()
```
getNext
Category

This method returns a handle on the next category in the current view navigator. If there is no current category, this method returns `null`. The category establishes user interface focus, and the cursor (pointer) is automatically placed on that category. When you're using this method, if the *lotus.domino.View* has been designed to display totals for one or more of the columns, the column's entry is considered a category entry. For an example using this method, refer to the `getFirst` method (▶ 639).

getNextDocument

```
nveViewEntry = nvnavViewNavigator.getNextDocument()
```
getNext
Document

This method returns a handle on the next document in the current view navigator. If there is no current document, this method returns `null`. The document establishes user interface focus, and the cursor (pointer) is automatically placed on that document. For an example using this method, refer to the `getFirst` method (▶ 639).

getNextSibling

```
nveViewEntry = nvnavViewNavigator.getNextSibling()
```
getNextSibling

```
nveViewEntry = nvnavViewNavigator.getNextSibling(nveViewEntry)
```

ViewEntry   Required   O.Ref.

An entry in the *lotus.domino.View* (the current entry is the default).

This method returns a handle on the next document sibling in the current view navigator. If there is no current document, this method returns `null`. The sibling document establishes user interface focus, and the cursor (pointer) is automatically placed on that document.

getNth

```
nveViewEntry = nvnavViewNavigator.getNth(intIndex)
```
getNth

intIndex   Required   O.Ref.

The position of the entry in the view.

This method returns a handle on a particular entry in the current view navigator. The exact entry is determined by its position relative to the other entry contained in the *lotus.domino.ViewNavigator*. The value passed as `intIndex` indicates which entry to return (1 is the first entry returned). The order of the entries is the same as the sorted order of the entries in the current view. If no entry is located in the position indicated by `intIndex`, this method returns `null`. The entry establishes user interface focus, and the cursor (pointer) is automatically placed on that entry.

getParent

getParent

```
nveViewEntry = nvnavViewNavigator.getParent()

nveViewEntry = nvnavViewNavigator.getParent(nveViewEntry)
```

ViewEntry	Required	O.Ref.

An entry in the *lotus.domino.View* (the current entry is the default).

This method returns a handle on the parent entry to the current entry in the current view navigator. If there is no parent entry, this method returns `null`. The parent entry establishes user interface focus, and the cursor (pointer) is automatically placed on that entry.

getParentView

getParentView

```
nveParentView = nvnavViewNavigator.getParentView()
```

This method returns a handle on the parent *lotus.domino.View* that contains the current view navigator.

getPos

getPos

```
nveViewEntry = nvnavViewNavigator.getPos(strPosition,
➥strSeparator)
```

strPosition	Required	O.Ref.

The position of the entry in decimal delimited format.

strSeparator	Required	O.Ref.

The separator string used to delimit the position levels.

This method returns a handle on a specific entry in the current view navigator based on its position. The position is determined by a string value, and each level is delimited by a decimal. For example, if the value of `strPosition` is `"1.1.1"`, the entry would be located at the first child (response) of the first entry. If there is no entry at the specified position, this method returns `null`. The entry establishes user interface focus, and the cursor (pointer) is automatically placed on that entry.

getPrev

getPrev

```
nveViewEntry = nvnavViewNavigator.getPrev()

nveViewEntry = nvnavViewNavigator.getPrev(nveViewEntry)
```

ViewEntry	Required	O.Ref.

An entry in the *lotus.domino.View* (the current entry is the default).

This method returns a handle on the previous entry in the current view navigator. If there is no previous entry, this method returns `null`. The entry establishes user interface focus, and the cursor (pointer) is automatically placed on the entry.

getPrevCategory

getPrev
Category

```
nveViewEntry = nvnavViewNavigator.getPrevCategory()
```

This method returns a handle on the previous category in the current view navigator. If there is no previous category, this method returns null. The category establishes user interface focus, and the cursor (pointer) is automatically placed on the category.

getPrevDocument

```
nveViewEntry = nvnavViewNavigator.getPrevDocument()
```
getPrev
Document

This method returns a handle on the previous document in the current view navigator. If there is no previous document, this method returns null. The document establishes user interface focus, and the cursor (pointer) is automatically placed on the document.

getPrevSibling

```
nveViewEntry = nvnavViewNavigator.getPrevSibling()
```
getPrevSibling

```
nveViewEntry = nvnavViewNavigator.getPrevSibling(nveViewEntry)
```

ViewEntry   **Required**   **O.Ref.**

An entry in the *lotus.domino.View* (the current entry is the default).

This method returns a handle on the previous sibling document in the current view navigator. If there is no previous sibling document, this method returns null. The sibling document establishes user interface focus, and the cursor (pointer) is automatically placed on the sibling document.

gotoChild

```
bolChild = nvnavViewNavigator.gotoChild(nveViewEntry)
```
gotoChild

ViewEntry   **Required**   **O.Ref.**

An entry in the *lotus.domino.View* (the current entry is the default).

This method moves the pointer to a child (response document, main document, or category) entry for a specific *lotus.domino.ViewNavigator*. A Boolean value is returned. It's true if the entry was successfully located and selected, and false if no child entry exists.

gotoEntry

```
bolEntry = nvnavViewNavigator.gotoEntry(Entry)
```
gotoEntry

Entry   **Required**   **O.Ref.**

An entry in the *lotus.domino.View* (the current entry is the default).

This method moves the pointer to a particular entry for a specific *lotus.domino.Document* or *lotus.domino.ViewEntry* object in the specified *lotus.domino.ViewNavigator*. The handle on the *lotus.domino.Document* or *lotus.domino.ViewEntry* object doesn't have to originate from the current *lotus.domino.ViewNavigator*. This method will still search for the respective entry in the current *lotus.domino.View*. When this method is called, a Boolean value is returned. It's true if the entry was successfully located and selected, and false if the entry doesn't exist.

gotoFirst

```
bolFirst = ViewNavigator.gotoFirst()
```
gotoFirst

This method moves the pointer to the first entry for a specific *lotus.domino.ViewNavigator*. A Boolean value is returned. It's true if the entry was successfully located and selected, and false if the entry doesn't exist.

gotoFirstDocument

```
bolFirstdoc = nvnavViewNavigator.gotoFirstDocument()
```

This method moves the pointer to the first document in a specific *lotus.domino.ViewNavigator*. A Boolean value is returned. It's `true` if the document was successfully located and selected, and `false` if no document exists.

gotoLast

```
bolLast = nvnavViewNavigator.gotoLast()
```

This method moves the pointer to the last entry in a specific *lotus.domino.ViewNavigator*. A Boolean value is returned. It's `true` if the entry was successfully located and selected, and `false` if no entry exists.

gotoLastDocument

```
bolLastdoc = nvnavViewNavigator.gotoLastDocument()
```

This method moves the pointer to the last document in a specific *lotus.domino.ViewNavigator*. A Boolean value is returned. It's `true` if the document was successfully located and selected, and `false` if no document exists.

gotoNext

```
bolNext = nvnavViewNavigator.gotoNext()
```

```
bolNext = nvnavViewNavigator.gotoNext(nveViewEntry)
```

ViewEntry	Required	O.Ref.

An entry in the *lotus.domino.View* (the current entry is the default).

This method moves the pointer to the next entry in a specific *lotus.domino.ViewNavigator*. A Boolean value is returned. It's `true` if the entry was successfully located and selected, and `false` if no entry exists.

gotoNextCategory

```
bolNextcat = nvnavViewNavigator.gotoNextCategory()
```

```
bolNextcat = nvnavViewNavigator.gotoNextCategory(nveViewEntry)
```

ViewEntry	Required	O.Ref.

An entry in the *lotus.domino.View* (the current entry is the default).

This method moves the pointer to the next category in a specific *lotus.domino.ViewNavigator*. A Boolean value is returned. It's `true` if the category was successfully located and selected, and `false` if no category exists.

gotoNextDocument

```
bolNextdoc = nvnavViewNavigator.gotoNextDocument()
```

```
bolNextdoc = nvnavViewNavigator.gotoNextDocument(nveViewEntry)
```

ViewEntry	Required	O.Ref.

An entry in the *lotus.domino.View* (the current entry is the default).

This method moves the pointer to the next document in a specific *lotus.domino.ViewNavigator*. A Boolean value is returned. It's `true` if the document was successfully located and selected, and `false` if no document exists.

gotoNextSibling

```
bolNextsibling = nvnavViewNavigator.gotoNextSibling()
bolNextsibling = nvnavViewNavigator.gotoNextSibling(nveViewEntry)
```

ViewEntry   Required   O.Ref.

An entry in the *lotus.domino.View* (the current entry is the default).

This method moves the pointer to the next sibling document in a specific
lotus.domino.ViewNavigator. A Boolean value is returned. It's true if the sibling document was successfully located and selected, and false if no sibling document exists.

gotoParent

```
bolParent = nvnavViewNavigator.gotoParent()
```

```
bolParent = nvnavViewNavigator.gotoParent(nveViewEntry)
```

ViewEntry   Required   O.Ref.

An entry in the *lotus.domino.View* (the current entry is the default).

This method moves the pointer to the parent entry for a specific
lotus.domino.ViewNavigator. A Boolean value is returned. It's true if the parent entry was
successfully located and selected, and false if the parent entry was not located.

gotoPos

```
bolPos = nvnavViewNavigator.gotoPos (strPosition, chrSeparator)
```

strPosition   Required   O.Ref.

The position of the entry in decimal delimited format.

chrSeparator   Required   O.Ref.

The separator character used between the position levels.

This method moves the pointer to a specific entry for the current
lotus.domino.ViewNavigator. A Boolean value is returned. It's true if the specified entry
was successfully located and selected, and false if the entry was not located. The position is determined by a string value, and each level is delimited by a decimal. For
example, if the value of strPosition is "1.1.1", the entry would be located at the
first child (response) of the first entry.

gotoPrev

```
bolPrev = nvnavViewNavigator.gotoPrev()
```

```
bolPrev = nvnavViewNavigator.gotoPrev(nveViewEntry)
```

ViewEntry   Required   O.Ref.

An entry in the *lotus.domino.View* (the current entry is the default.)

This method moves the pointer to the previous entry in a specific
lotus.domino.ViewNavigator. A Boolean value is returned. It's true if the entry was
successfully located and selected, and false if no entry exists.

gotoPrevCategory

```
bolPrevcat = nvnavViewNavigator.gotoPrevCategory()
```

This method moves the pointer to the previous entry in a specific
lotus.domino.ViewNavigator. A Boolean value is returned. It's true if the entry
was successfully located and selected, and false if no entry exists.

gotoPrevDocument

```
bolPrevdoc = nvnavViewNavigator.gotoPrevDocument()
```

This method moves the pointer to the previous document in a specific *lotus.domino.ViewNavigator*. A Boolean value is returned. It's `true` if the document was successfully located and selected, and `false` if no document exists.

gotoPrevSibling

```
bolPrevsibling = nvnavViewNavigator.gotoPrevSibling()
```

```
bolPrevsibling = nvnavViewNavigator.gotoPrevSibling (nveViewEntry)
```

ViewEntry	Required	O.Ref.

An entry in the *lotus.domino.View* (the current entry is the default).

This method moves the pointer to the previous sibling document in a specific *lotus.domino.ViewNavigator*. A Boolean value is returned. It's `true` if the sibling document was successfully located and selected, and `false` if no sibling document exists.

setCacheSize   W   %

```
nvnavViewNavigator.setCacheSize(intCachesize)
```

When you're making calls to the Domino server, this method sets the size of the navigator cache for view entries. When you're making local calls, this method returns `0`. The minimum setting for this value is `0` (for no cache), and the maximum setting is `128` (the default setting).

setMaxLevel   W   %

```
nvnavViewNavigator.setMaxLevel(intMaxlevel)
```

Represents the maximum levels of navigation for the current *lotus.domino.View*. The allowed values for this method range from `0` (the top level of categorization) to `31` (the default `maxLevel` setting).

Remarks

The *lotus.domino.ViewNavigator* object can represent all the entries in a view, or only a subset of the documents. Because *lotus.domino.ViewNavigator* is contained by *lotus.domino.View,* if the parent *lotus.domino.View* is refreshed, the *lotus.domino.ViewNavigator* is affected as well.

Depending on the design of the *lotus.domino.View,* a document can exist and be displayed under multiple categories. Nevertheless, you can still navigate to and from these documents as separate entries in the *lotus.domino.ViewEntry*. However, the getNth method will return the first instance of the document as it is sorted in the *lotus.domino.View*. In addition, *lotus.domino.ViewNavigators* created from an object that doesn't exist in the current *lotus.domino.View* will also return the first instance of the document as it is sorted in the *lotus.domino.View*.

Example

This example prints many of the methods available for the current
lotus.domino.ViewNavigator.

```java
import lotus.domino.*;

public class JavaAgent extends AgentBase {

    public void NotesMain() {

        try {
            Session ns = getSession();
            AgentContext agentContext = ns.getAgentContext();
            Database ndb = agentContext.getCurrentDatabase();
            View nvw = ndb.getView("All");
            ViewNavigator nvn = nvw.createViewNav();
                ViewEntry nve = nvn.getFirst();
                int intDocCount = 0;
                int intCategoryCount = 0;
                int intTotalCount = 0;
                while (nve != null) {
                    if (nve.isDocument())
                        intDocCount++;
                    if (nve.isCategory())
                        intCategoryCount++;
                    if (nve.isTotal())
                        intTotalCount++;
                    nve = nvn.getNext();   }
                System.out.println("Total documents = " + intDocCount);
                System.out.println("Total categories = " +
                ➥intCategoryCount);
                System.out.println("Total total entries = " +
                ➥intTotalCount);
                System.out.println("Parent view = " +
                ➥nvn.getParentView().getName());
                System.out.println("Cache size = " + nvn.getCacheSize());
                System.out.println("Maximum level = " + nvn.getMaxLevel());
                System.out.println("Agent complete.");

        } catch(Exception e) {
            e.printStackTrace();
        }
    }
}
```

III

Object Hierarchies

Appendix A: LotusScript Object Hierarchy

Appendix B: Java Object Hierarchy

Appendix A

LotusScript Object Hierarchy

The following is the LotusScript object
hierarchy. References in parentheses are
the page numbers where the specific class
can be found. Single lines denote a normal relationship. Double lines indicate that
the class is inherited. Front-end classes
appear in italic.

Front-End Classes

Button (►3)

Navigator (► 11)

Field (► 7)

NotesUIWorkspace (► 47)
   NotesUIDocument (► 21)
     └─ NotesDocument (► 127)
       ├─ NotesEmbeddedObject (► 159)
       ├─ NotesItem (► 175)
         ╙─ NotesRichTextItem (► 235)
       └─ NotesRichTextItem (► 235)

NotesUIView (► 41)
  ├─NotesDocumentCollection (► 149)
  │   └─ NotesDocument (► 127)
  │   ├─ NotesEmbeddedObject (► 159)
  │   ├─ NotesItem (► 175)
  │   ╙─ NotesRichTextItem (► 235)
  │   └─ NotesRichTextItem (► 235)
  └─NotesView (► 279)
    ├─ NotesDocument (► 127)
    │ ├─ NotesEmbeddedObject (► 159)
    │ ├─ NotesItem (► 175)
    │   ╙─ NotesRichTextItem (► 235)
    │ └─ NotesRichTextItem (► 235)
    ├─ NotesViewColumn (► 297)
    ├─ NotesViewEntry (► 309)
    │ └─ NotesDocument (► 127)
    │   ├─ NotesEmbeddedObject (► 159)
    │   ├─ NotesItem (► 175)
    │   ╙─ NotesRichTextItem (► 235)
    │   └─ NotesRichTextItem (► 235)
    └─ NotesViewEntryCollection (► 315)
      └─ NotesViewEntry (► 309)
        └─ NotesDocument (► 127)
          ├─ NotesEmbeddedObject (► 159)
          ├─ NotesItem (► 175)
            ╙─ NotesRichTextItem (► 235)
          ⋮
          ⋮

```
.      .
.      .
.      .
│     └─ NotesRichTextItem (▶ 235)
└─ NotesViewNavigator (▶ 323)
   └─ NotesViewEntry (▶ 309)
      └─ NotesDocument (▶ 127)
         ├─ NotesEmbeddedObject (▶ 159)
         ├─ NotesItem (▶ 175)
         │  └─ NotesRichTextItem (▶ 235)
         └─ NotesRichTextItem (▶ 235)

NotesUIDatabase (▶ 13)
├─ NotesDatabase (▶ 89)
│  ├─ NotesACL (▶ 63)
│  │  └─ NotesACLEntry (▶ 71)
│  ├─ NotesAgent (▶ 83)
│  ├─ NotesDocument (▶ 127)
│  │  ├─ NotesEmbeddedObject (▶ 159)
│  │  ├─ NotesItem (▶ 175)
│  │  │  └─ NotesRichTextItem (▶ 235)
│  │  └─ NotesRichTextItem (▶ 235)
│  ├─ NotesDocumentCollection (▶ 149)
│  │  └─ NotesDocument (▶ 127)
│  │     ├─ NotesEmbeddedObject (▶ 159)
│  │     ├─ NotesItem (▶ 175)
│  │     │  └─ NotesRichTextItem (▶ 235)
│  │     └─ NotesRichTextItem (▶ 235)
│  ├─ NotesForm (▶ 167)
│  ├─ NotesOutline (▶ 215)
│  │  └─ NotesOutlineEntry (▶ 221)
│  ├─ NotesReplication (▶ 227)
│  └─ NotesView (▶ 279)
│     ├─ NotesDocument (▶ 127)
│     │  ├─ NotesEmbeddedObject (▶ 159)
│     │  ├─ NotesItem (▶ 175)
│     │  │  └─ NotesRichTextItem (▶ 235)
│     │  └─ NotesRichTextItem (▶ 235)
│     ├─ NotesViewColumn (▶ 297)
│     ├─ NotesViewEntry (▶ 309)
│     │  └─ NotesDocument (▶ 127)
│     │     ├─ NotesEmbeddedObject (▶ 159)
│     │     ├─ NotesItem (▶ 175)
│     │     │  └─ NotesRichTextItem (▶ 235)
│     │     └─ NotesRichTextItem (▶ 235)
│     ├─ NotesViewEntryCollection (▶ 315)
│     │  └─ NotesViewEntry (▶ 309)
│     │     └─ NotesDocument (▶ 127)
│     │        ├─ NotesEmbeddedObject (▶ 159)
│     │        ├─ NotesItem (▶ 175)
│     │        │  └─ NotesRichTextItem (▶ 235)
│     │        └─ NotesRichTextItem (▶ 235)
│     └─ NotesViewNavigator (▶ 323)
│        └─ NotesViewEntry (▶ 309)
│           └─ NotesDocument (▶ 127)
│              ├─ NotesEmbeddedObject (▶ 159)
.           .
.           .
.           .
```

```
    .                 .
    .                 .
    .                 .
    │              ┌─NotesItem (▶ 175)
    │              │  └─NotesRichTextItem (▶ 235)
    │              └─NotesRichTextItem (▶ 235)
    └─NotesDocumentCollection (▶ 149)
       └─ NotesDocument (▶ 127)
          ├─NotesEmbeddedObject (▶ 159)
          ├─NotesItem (▶ 175)
          │  └─NotesRichTextItem (▶ 235)
          └─NotesRichTextItem (▶ 235)
```

Back-End Classes

```
NotesSession (▶ 263)
 ├─NotesAgent (▶ 83)
 ├─NotesDatabase (▶ 89)
 │  ├─NotesACL (▶ 63)
 │  │  └─NotesACLEntry (▶ 71)
 │  ├─NotesAgent (▶ 83)
 │  ├─NotesDocument (▶ 127)
 │  │  ├─NotesEmbeddedObject (▶ 159)
 │  │  ├─NotesItem (▶ 175)
 │  │  │  └─NotesRichTextItem (▶ 235)
 │  │  └─NotesRichTextItem (▶ 235)
 │  ├─NotesDocumentCollection (▶ 149)
 │  │  └─NotesDocument (▶ 127)
 │  │     ├─NotesEmbeddedObject (▶ 159)
 │  │     ├─NotesItem (▶ 175)
 │  │     │  └─ NotesRichTextItem (▶ 235)
 │  │     └─NotesRichTextItem (▶ 235)
 │  ├─ NotesForm (▶ 167)
 │  ├─ NotesOutline (▶ 215)
 │  │  └─NotesOutlineEntry (▶ 221)
 │  ├─ NotesReplication (▶ 227)
 │  ├─ NotesView (▶ 279)
 │  │  ├─NotesDocument (▶ 127)
 │  │  │  ├─NotesEmbeddedObject (▶ 159)
 │  │  │  ├─NotesItem (▶ 175)
 │  │  │  │  └─ NotesRichTextItem (▶ 235)
 │  │  │  └─NotesRichTextItem (▶ 235)
 │  │  ├─NotesViewColumn (▶ 297)
 │  │  ├─NotesViewEntry (▶ 309)
 │  │  │  └─NotesDocument (▶ 127)
 │  │  │     ├─ NotesEmbeddedObject (▶ 159)
 │  │  │     ├─ NotesItem (▶ 175)
 │  │  │     │  └─NotesRichTextItem (▶ 235)
 │  │  │     └─NotesRichTextItem (▶ 235)
 │  │  └─NotesViewEntryCollection (▶ 315)
 │  │     ├─NotesViewEntry (▶ 309)
 │  │     │  └─ NotesDocument (▶ 127)
 │  │     │     ├─NotesEmbeddedObject (▶ 159)
 │  │     │     └─NotesItem (▶ 175)
 │  │     │        └─ NotesRichTextItem (▶ 235)
 │  │     └─NotesRichTextItem (▶ 235)
 │  .  .
 │  .  .
 │  .  .
```

```
└── NotesViewNavigator (▶ 323)
    └── NotesViewEntry (▶ 309)
        └── NotesDocument (▶ 127)
            ├── NotesEmbeddedObject (▶ 159)
            ├── NotesItem (▶ 175)
            │   └── NotesRichTextItem (▶ 235)
            └── NotesRichTextItem (▶ 235)
─ NotesDateRange (▶ 113)
  └── NotesDateTime (▶ 115)
─ NotesDateTime (▶ 115)
─ NotesDbDirectory (▶ 123)
  └── NotesDatabase (▶ 89)
      ├── NotesACL (▶ 63)
      │   └── NotesACLEntry (▶ 71)
      ├── NotesAgent (▶ 83)
      ├── NotesDocument (▶ 127)
      │   ├── NotesEmbeddedObject (▶ 159)
      │   ├── NotesItem (▶ 175)
      │   │   └── NotesRichTextItem (▶ 235)
      │   └── NotesRichTextItem (▶ 235)
      ├── NotesDocumentCollection (▶ 149)
      │   └── NotesDocument (▶ 127)
      │       ├── NotesEmbeddedObject (▶ 159)
      │       ├── NotesItem (▶ 175)
      │       │   └── NotesRichTextItem (▶ 235)
      │       └── NotesRichTextItem (▶ 235)
      ├── NotesForm (▶ 167)
      ├── NotesOutline (▶ 215)
      │   └── NotesOutlineEntry (▶ 221)
      ├── NotesReplication (▶ 227)
      ├── NotesView (▶ 279)
      │   NotesDocument (▶ 127)
      │       ├── NotesEmbeddedObject (▶ 159)
      │       ├── NotesItem (▶ 175)
      │       │   └── NotesRichTextItem (▶ 235)
      │       └── NotesRichTextItem (▶ 235)
      │   ├── NotesViewColumn (▶ 297)
      │   ├── NotesViewEntry (▶ 309)
      │   │   └── NotesDocument (▶ 127)
      │   │       ├── NotesEmbeddedObject (▶ 159)
      │   │       ├── NotesItem (▶ 175)
      │   │       │   └── NotesRichTextItem (▶ 235)
      │   │       └── NotesRichTextItem (▶ 235)
      │   ├── NotesViewEntryCollection (▶ 315)
      │   │   └── NotesViewEntry (▶ 309)
      │   │       └── NotesDocument (▶ 127)
      │   │           ├── NotesEmbeddedObject (▶ 159)
      │   │           ├── NotesItem (▶ 175)
      │   │           │   └── NotesRichTextItem (▶ 235)
      │   │           └── NotesRichTextItem (▶ 235)
      │   └── NotesViewNavigator (▶ 323)
      │       └── NotesViewEntry (▶ 309)
      │           └── NotesDocument (▶ 127)
```

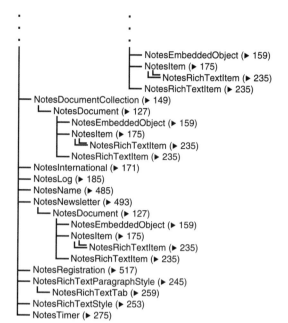

Appendix B

Java Object Hierarchy

The following is the Java object hierarchy. References in parentheses are the page numbers where the specific class can be found. Single lines denote a normal relationship. Double lines indicate that the class is inherited.

JAVA Object Hierarchy

```
NotesFactory (▶ 499)
└─ Session (▶ 577)
    ├─ AgentContext (▶ 365)
    │   ├─ Agent (▶ 359)
    │   │   └─ DateTime (▶ 399)
    │   ├─ Database (▶ 373)
    │   │   ├─ ACL (▶ 333)
    │   │   │   └─ ACLEntry (▶ 343)
    │   │   │       └─ Name (▶ 485)
    │   │   ├─ Agent (▶ 359)
    │   │   │   └─ DateTime (▶ 399)
    │   │   ├─ DateTime (▶ 399)
    │   │   ├─ Document (▶ 413)
    │   │   │   ├─ DateTime (▶ 399)
    │   │   │   ├─ EmbeddedObject (▶ 447)
    │   │   │   ├─ Item (▶ 463)
    │   │   │   │   ╠═ DateTime (▶ 399)
    │   │   │   │   ╚═ RichTextItem (▶ 543)
    │   │   │   │       └─ EmbeddedObject (▶ 447)
    │   │   │   └─ RichTextItem (▶ 543)
    │   │   │       └─ EmbeddedObject (▶ 447)
    │   │   ├─ DocumentCollection (▶ 435)
    │   │   │   └─ Document (▶ 413)
    │   │   │       ├─ DateTime (▶ 399)
    │   │   │       ├─ EmbeddedObject (▶ 447)
    │   │   │       ├─ Item (▶ 463)
    │   │   │       │   ╠═ DateTime (▶ 399)
    │   │   │       │   ╚═ RichTextItem (▶ 543)
    │   │   │       │       └─ EmbeddedObject (▶ 447)
    │   │   │       └─ RichTextItem (▶ 543)
    │   │   │           └─ EmbeddedObject (▶ 447)
    │   │   ├─ Form (▶ 453)
    │   │   ├─ Outline (▶ 503)
    │   │   │   └─ OutlineEntry (▶ 509)
    │   │   ├─ Replication (▶ 533)
    │   │   │   └─ DateTime (▶ 399)
    │   │   └─ View (▶ 587)
    │   │       ├─ DateTime (▶ 399)
    │   │       ├─ Document (▶ 413)
    │   │       │   ├─ DateTime (▶ 399)
```

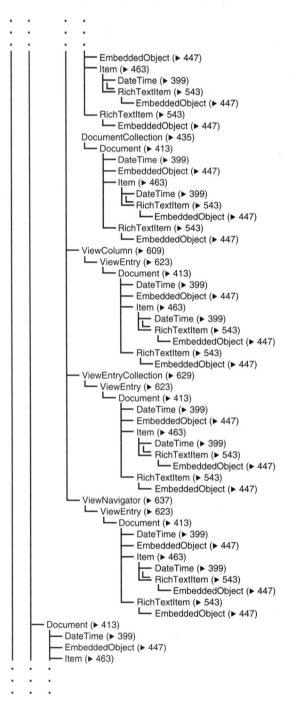

EmbeddedObject (▶ 447)
Item (▶ 463)
— DateTime (▶ 399)
— RichTextItem (▶ 543)
  — EmbeddedObject (▶ 447)
RichTextItem (▶ 543)
— EmbeddedObject (▶ 447)
DocumentCollection (▶ 435)
— Document (▶ 413)
  — DateTime (▶ 399)
  — EmbeddedObject (▶ 447)
  — Item (▶ 463)
    — DateTime (▶ 399)
    — RichTextItem (▶ 543)
      — EmbeddedObject (▶ 447)
  — RichTextItem (▶ 543)
    — EmbeddedObject (▶ 447)
ViewColumn (▶ 609)
— ViewEntry (▶ 623)
  — Document (▶ 413)
    — DateTime (▶ 399)
    — EmbeddedObject (▶ 447)
    — Item (▶ 463)
      — DateTime (▶ 399)
      — RichTextItem (▶ 543)
        — EmbeddedObject (▶ 447)
    — RichTextItem (▶ 543)
      — EmbeddedObject (▶ 447)
ViewEntryCollection (▶ 629)
— ViewEntry (▶ 623)
  — Document (▶ 413)
    — DateTime (▶ 399)
    — EmbeddedObject (▶ 447)
    — Item (▶ 463)
      — DateTime (▶ 399)
      — RichTextItem (▶ 543)
        — EmbeddedObject (▶ 447)
    — RichTextItem (▶ 543)
      — EmbeddedObject (▶ 447)
ViewNavigator (▶ 637)
— ViewEntry (▶ 623)
  — Document (▶ 413)
    — DateTime (▶ 399)
    — EmbeddedObject (▶ 447)
    — Item (▶ 463)
      — DateTime (▶ 399)
      — RichTextItem (▶ 543)
        — EmbeddedObject (▶ 447)
    — RichTextItem (▶ 543)
      — EmbeddedObject (▶ 447)
Document (▶ 413)
— DateTime (▶ 399)
— EmbeddedObject (▶ 447)
— Item (▶ 463)

```
.   .   .   .   .
.   .   .   .   .
.   .   .   .   .
                  ┌─ DateTime (▶ 399)
                  └─ RichTextItem (▶ 543)
              └─ EmbeddedObject (▶ 447)
                  └─ RichTextItem (▶ 543)
                      └─ EmbeddedObject (▶ 447)
          ── DocumentCollection (▶ 435)
              └─ Document (▶ 413)
                  ├─ DateTime (▶ 399)
                  ├─ EmbeddedObject (▶ 447)
                  ├─ Item (▶ 463)
                  │   ┌─ DateTime (▶ 399)
                  │   └─ RichTextItem (▶ 543)
                  └─ EmbeddedObject (▶ 447)
                      └─ RichTextItem (▶ 543)
                          └─ EmbeddedObject (▶ 447)
  ── Database (▶ 373)
      ├─ ACL (▶ 333)
      │   └─ ACLEntry (▶ 343)
      │       └─ Name (▶ 485)
      ├─ Agent (▶ 359)
      │   └─ DateTime (▶ 399)
      ├─ DateTime (▶ 399)
      ├─ Document (▶ 413)
      │   ├─ DateTime (▶ 399)
      │   ├─ EmbeddedObject (▶ 447)
      │   ├─ Item (▶ 463)
      │   │   ┌─ DateTime (▶ 399)
      │   │   └─ RichTextItem (▶ 543)
      │   │       └─ EmbeddedObject (▶ 447)
      │   └─ RichTextItem (▶ 543)
      │           EmbeddedObject (▶ 447)
      ├─ DocumentCollection (▶ 435)
      │   └─ Document (▶ 413)
      │       ├─ DateTime (▶ 399)
      │       ├─ EmbeddedObject (▶ 447)
      │       ├─ Item (▶ 463)
      │       │   ┌─ DateTime (▶ 399)
      │       │   └─ RichTextItem (▶ 543)
      │       │       └─ EmbeddedObject (▶ 447)
      │       └─ RichTextItem (▶ 543)
      │           └─ EmbeddedObject (▶ 447)
      ├─ Form (▶ 453)
      ├─ Outline (▶ 503)
      │   └─ OutlineEntry (▶ 509)
      ├─ Replication (▶ 533)
      │   └─ DateTime (▶ 399)
      └─ View (▶ 587)
          ├─ DateTime (▶ 399)
          ├─ Document (▶ 413)
          │   ├─ DateTime (▶ 399)
          │   ├─ EmbeddedObject (▶ 447)
          │   ├─ Item (▶ 463)
          │   │   ┌─ DateTime (▶ 399)
          │   │   └─ RichTextItem (▶ 543)
.   .   .   .
.   .   .   .
.   .   .   .
```

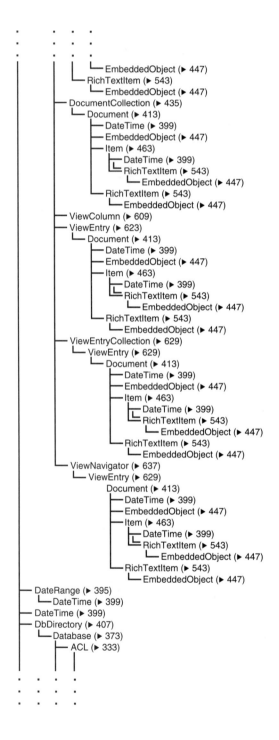

```
                         └─ EmbeddedObject (▶ 447)
                   └─ RichTextItem (▶ 543)
                      └─ EmbeddedObject (▶ 447)
              ├─ DocumentCollection (▶ 435)
              │  └─ Document (▶ 413)
              │     ├─ DateTime (▶ 399)
              │     ├─ EmbeddedObject (▶ 447)
              │     ├─ Item (▶ 463)
              │     │  ├─ DateTime (▶ 399)
              │     │  └─ RichTextItem (▶ 543)
              │     │     └─ EmbeddedObject (▶ 447)
              │     └─ RichTextItem (▶ 543)
              │        └─ EmbeddedObject (▶ 447)
              ├─ ViewColumn (▶ 609)
              ├─ ViewEntry (▶ 623)
              │  └─ Document (▶ 413)
              │     ├─ DateTime (▶ 399)
              │     ├─ EmbeddedObject (▶ 447)
              │     ├─ Item (▶ 463)
              │     │  ├─ DateTime (▶ 399)
              │     │  └─ RichTextItem (▶ 543)
              │     │     └─ EmbeddedObject (▶ 447)
              │     └─ RichTextItem (▶ 543)
              │        └─ EmbeddedObject (▶ 447)
              ├─ ViewEntryCollection (▶ 629)
              │  └─ ViewEntry (▶ 629)
              │     └─ Document (▶ 413)
              │        ├─ DateTime (▶ 399)
              │        ├─ EmbeddedObject (▶ 447)
              │        ├─ Item (▶ 463)
              │        │  ├─ DateTime (▶ 399)
              │        │  └─ RichTextItem (▶ 543)
              │        │     └─ EmbeddedObject (▶ 447)
              │        └─ RichTextItem (▶ 543)
              │           └─ EmbeddedObject (▶ 447)
              └─ ViewNavigator (▶ 637)
                 └─ ViewEntry (▶ 629)
                    └─ Document (▶ 413)
                       ├─ DateTime (▶ 399)
                       ├─ EmbeddedObject (▶ 447)
                       ├─ Item (▶ 463)
                       │  ├─ DateTime (▶ 399)
                       │  └─ RichTextItem (▶ 543)
                       │     └─ EmbeddedObject (▶ 447)
                       └─ RichTextItem (▶ 543)
                          └─ EmbeddedObject (▶ 447)
├─ DateRange (▶ 395)
│  └─ DateTime (▶ 399)
├─ DateTime (▶ 399)
├─ DbDirectory (▶ 407)
│  └─ Database (▶ 373)
│     ├─ ACL (▶ 333)
```

```
.        .   .   .
.        .   .   .
.        .   .   .
              └─ACLEntry (▶ 343)
                 └─Name (▶ 485)
              Agent (▶ 359)
              └─DateTime (▶ 399)
        ─DateTime (▶ 399)
        ─Document (▶ 413)
            ├─DateTime (▶ 399)
            ├─EmbeddedObject (▶ 447)
            ├─Item (▶ 463)
            │  ┌─DateTime (▶ 399)
            │  └─RichTextItem (▶ 543)
            │     └─EmbeddedObject (▶ 447)
            └─RichTextItem (▶ 543)
               └─EmbeddedObject (▶ 447)
        ─DocumentCollection (▶ 435)
           └─Document (▶ 413)
               ├─DateTime (▶ 399)
               ├─EmbeddedObject (▶ 447)
               ├─Item (▶ 463)
               │  ┌─DateTime (▶ 399)
               │  └─RichTextItem (▶ 543)
               │     └─EmbeddedObject (▶ 447)
               └─RichTextItem (▶ 543)
                  └─EmbeddedObject (▶ 447)
        ─Form (▶ 453)
        ─Outline (▶ 503)
        │  └─OutlineEntry (▶ 509)
        ─Replication (▶ 533)
        │  └─DateTime (▶ 399)
        └─View (▶ 587)
            ├─DateTime (▶ 399)
            ├─Document (▶ 413)
            │   ├─DateTime (▶ 399)
            │   ├─EmbeddedObject (▶ 447)
            │   ├─Item (▶ 463)
            │   │  ┌─DateTime (▶ 399)
            │   │  └─RichTextItem (▶ 543)
            │   │     └─EmbeddedObject (▶ 447)
            │   └─RichTextItem (▶ 543)
            │      └─EmbeddedObject (▶ 447)
            ├─DocumentCollection (▶ 435)
            │   └─Document (▶ 413)
            │       ├─DateTime (▶ 399)
            │       ├─EmbeddedObject (▶ 447)
            │       ├─Item (▶ 463)
            │       │  ┌─DateTime (▶ 399)
            │       │  └─RichTextItem (▶ 543)
            │       │     └─EmbeddedObject ▶ 447)
            │       └─RichTextItem (▶ 543)
            │          └─EmbeddedObject (▶ 447)
            ├─ViewColumn (▶ 609)
            ├─ViewEntry (▶ 623)
            │  └─Document (▶ 413)
            │      └─DateTime (▶ 399)
.        .   .
.        .   .
.        .   .
```

```
:        :        :
:        :        :
:        :        :
│        │        ├─ EmbeddedObject (▶ 447)
│        │        ├─ Item (▶ 463)
│        │        │    ├─ DateTime (▶ 399)
│        │        │    └─ RichTextItem (▶ 543)
│        │        │         └─ EmbeddedObject (▶ 447)
│        │        └─ RichTextItem (▶ 543)
│        │             └─ EmbeddedObject (▶ 447)
│        ├─ ViewEntryCollection ([xb] 629)
│        │    └─ ViewEntry (▶ 623)
│        │         └─ Document (▶ 413)
│        │              ├─ DateTime (▶ 399)
│        │              ├─ EmbeddedObject (▶ 447)
│        │              ├─ Item (▶ 463)
│        │              │    ├─ DateTime (▶ 399)
│        │              │    └─ RichTextItem (▶ 543)
│        │              │         └─ EmbeddedObject (▶ 447)
│        │              └─ RichTextItem (▶ 543)
│        │                   └─ EmbeddedObject (▶ 447)
│        └─ ViewNavigator (▶ 637)
│             └─ ViewEntry (▶ 623)
│                  └─ Document (▶ 413)
│                       ├─ DateTime (▶ 399)
│                       ├─ EmbeddedObject (▶ 447)
│                       ├─ Item (▶ 463)
│                       │    ├─ DateTime (▶ 399)
│                       │    └─ RichTextItem (▶ 543)
│                       │         └─ EmbeddedObject (▶ 447)
│                       └─ RichTextItem (▶ 543)
│                            └─ EmbeddedObject (▶ 447)
├─ International (▶ 459)
├─ Log (▶ 477)
├─ Name (▶ 485)
├─ Newsletter (▶ 493)
│    └─ Document (▶ 413)
│         ├─ DateTime (▶ 399)
│         ├─ EmbeddedObject (▶ 447)
│         ├─ Item (▶ 463)
│         │    ├─ DateTime (▶ 399)
│         │    └─ RichTextItem (▶ 543)
│         │         └─ EmbeddedObject (▶ 447)
│         └─ RichTextItem (▶ 543)
│              └─ EmbeddedObject (▶ 447)
├─ Registration (▶ 517)
│    └─ Newsletter (▶ 493)
│         └─ Document (▶ 413)
│              ├─ DateTime (▶ 399)
│              ├─ EmbeddedObject (▶ 447)
│              ├─ Item (▶ 463)
│              │    ├─ DateTime (▶ 399)
│              │    └─ RichTextItem (▶ 543)
│              │         └─ EmbeddedObject (▶ 447)
│              └─ RichTextItem (▶ 543)
│                   └─ EmbeddedObject (▶ 447)
├─ RichTextParagraphStyle (▶ 555)
│       RichTextTab (▶ 573)
└─ RichTextStyle (▶ 565)
```

Index

Q-R

S

Books for Networking Professionals

New Riders

Windows NT Titles

Windows NT TCP/IP

By Karanjit Siyan

1st Edition

480 pages, $29.99

ISBN: 1-56205-887-8

If you're still looking for good documentation on Microsoft TCP/IP, then look no further—this is your book. *Windows NT TCP/IP* cuts through the complexities and provides the most informative and complete reference book on Windows-based TCP/IP. Concepts essential to TCP/IP administration are explained thoroughly, then related to the practical use of Microsoft TCP/IP in a real-world networking environment. The book begins by covering TCP/IP architecture, advanced installation, and configuration issues, then moves on to routing with TCP/IP, DHCP Management, and WINS/DNS Name Resolution.

Windows NT DNS

By Michael Masterson, Herman L. Knief, Scott Vinick, and Eric Roul

1st Edition

340 pages, $29.99

ISBN: 1-56205-943-2

Have you ever opened a Windows NT book looking for detailed information about DNS only to discover that it doesn't even begin to scratch the surface? DNS is probably one of the most complicated subjects for NT administrators, and there are few books on the market that really address it in detail. This book answers your most complex DNS questions, focusing on the implementation of the Domain Name Service within Windows NT, treating it thoroughly from the viewpoint of an experienced Windows NT professional. Many detailed, real-world examples illustrate further the understanding of the material throughout. The book covers the details of how DNS functions within NT, then explores specific interactions with critical network components. Finally, proven procedures to design and set up DNS are demonstrated. You'll also find coverage of related topics, such as maintenance, security, and troubleshooting.

Windows NT Registry

By Sandra Osborne

1st Edition

564 pages, $29.99

ISBN: 1-56205-941-6

The NT Registry can be a very powerful tool for those capable of using it wisely. Unfortunately, there is very little information regarding the NT Registry, due to Microsoft's insistence that their source code be kept secret. If you're looking to optimize your use of the Registry, you're usually forced to search the Web for bits of information. This book is your resource. It covers critical issues and settings used for configuring network protocols, including NWLink, PTP, TCP/IP, and DHCP. This book approaches the material from a unique point of view, discussing the problems related to a particular component, and then discussing settings, which are the actual changes necessary for implementing robust solutions. There is also a comprehensive reference of Registry settings and commands, making this the perfect addition to your technical bookshelf.

Windows NT Performance

By Mark Edmead and Paul Hinsberg
1st Edition
288 pages, $29.99
ISBN: 1-56205-942-4

Performance monitoring is a little like preventative medicine for the administrator: No one enjoys a checkup, but it's a good thing to do on a regular basis. This book helps you focus on the critical aspects of improving the performance of your NT system, showing you how to monitor the system, implement benchmarking, and tune your network. The book is organized by resource components, which makes it easy to use as a reference tool.

Windows NT Terminal Server

By Ted Harwood
1st Edition
416 pages, $29.99
ISBN: 1-56205-944-0

It's no surprise that most administration headaches revolve around integration with other networks and clients. This book addresses these types of real-world issues on a case-by-case basis, giving tools and advice for solving each problem. The author also offers the real nuts and bolts of thin client administration on multiple systems, covering such relevant issues as installation, configuration, network connection, management, and application distribution.

Windows NT Security

By Richard Puckett
1st Edition Fall 1999
600 pages, $29.99
ISBN: 1-56205-945-9

Swiss cheese. That's what some people say Windows NT security is like. And they may be right, because they only know what the NT documentation says about implementing security. Who has the time to research alternatives; play around with the features, service packs, hot fixes, and add-on tools; and figure out what makes NT rock solid? Well, Richard Puckett does. He's been researching Windows NT security for the University of Virginia for a while now, and he's got pretty good news. He's going to show you how to make NT secure in your environment, and we mean really secure.

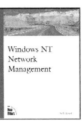

Windows NT Network Management

By Anil Desai
1st Edition Spring 1999
400 pages, $34.99
ISBN: 1-56205-946-7

Administering a Windows NT network is kind of like trying to herd cats—an impossible task characterized by constant motion, exhausting labor, and lots of hairballs. Author Anil Desai knows all about it—he's a Consulting Engineer for Sprint Paranet, and specializes in Windows NT implementation, integration, and management. So we asked him to put together a concise manual of best practices, a book of tools and ideas that other administrators can turn to again and again in managing their own NT networks. His experience shines through as he shares his secrets for reducing your organization's Total Cost of Ownership.

Planning for Windows 2000

By Eric K. Cone
1st Edition Spring 1999
400 pages, $29.99
ISBN: 0-7357-0048-6

Windows 2000 is poised to be one of the largest and most important software releases of the next decade, and you are charged with planning, testing, and deploying it in your enterprise.

Are you ready? With this book, you will be. *Planning for Windows 2000* lets you know what the upgrade hurdles will be, informs you how to clear them, guides you through effective Active Directory design, and presents you with detailed roll-out procedures. Eric K. Cone gives you the benefit of his extensive experience as a Windows 2000 Rapid Deployment Program member, sharing problems and solutions he's encountered on the job.

MCSE Core NT Exams Essential Reference

By Matthew Shepker
1st Edition
256 pages, $19.99
ISBN: 0-7357-0006-0

You're sitting in the first session of your Networking Essentials class and the instructor starts talking about RAS and you have no idea what that means. You think about raising your hand to ask about RAS, but you reconsider—you'd feel pretty foolish asking a question in front of all these people. You turn to your handy *MCSE Core NT Exams Essential Reference* and find a quick summary on Remote Access Services. Question answered. It's a couple months later and you're taking your Networking Essentials exam the next day. You're reviewing practice tests and you keep forgetting the maximum lengths for the various commonly used cable types. Once again, you turn to the *MCSE Core NT Exams Essential Reference* and find a table on cables, including all of the characteristics you need to memorize in order to pass the test.

BackOffice Titles

Implementing Exchange Server

By Doug Hauger, Marywynne Leon, and William C. Wade III
1st Edition
400 pages, $29.99
ISBN: 1-56205-931-9

If you're interested in connectivity and maintenance issues for Exchange Server, then this book is for you. Exchange's power lies in its ability to be connected to multiple email subsystems to create a "universal email backbone." It's not unusual to have several different and complex systems all connected via email gateways, including Lotus Notes or cc:Mail, Microsoft Mail, legacy mainframe systems, and Internet mail. This book covers all of the problems and issues associated with getting an integrated system running smoothly and addresses troubleshooting and diagnosis of email problems with an eye towards prevention and best practices.

Exchange Server Administration

By Janice K. Howd
1st Edition Spring 1999
350 pages, $34.99
ISBN: 0-7357-0081-8

OK, you've got your Exchange Server installed and connected, now what? Email administration is one of the most critical networking jobs, and Exchange can be particularly troublesome in large, heterogenous environments. So Janice Howd, a noted consultant and teacher with over a decade of email administration experience, has put together this advanced, concise handbook for daily, periodic, and emergency administration. With in-depth coverage of topics like managing disk resources, replication, and disaster recovery, this is the one reference book every Exchange administrator needs.

SQL Server System Administration

By Sean Baird, Chris Miller, et al.

1st Edition
352 pages, $29.99
ISBN: 1-56205-955-6

How often does your SQL Server go down during the day when everyone wants to access the data? Do you spend most of your time being a "report monkey" for your co-workers and bosses? *SQL Server System Administration* helps you keep data consistently available to your users. This book omits the introductory information. The authors don't spend time explaining queries and how they work. Instead they focus on the information that you can't get anywhere else, like how to choose the correct replication topology and achieve high availability of information.

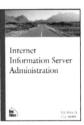

Internet Information Server Administration

By Kelli Adam, et. al.

1st Edition Fall 1999
300 pages, $29.99
ISBN: 0-7357-0022-2

Are the new Internet technologies in Internet Information Server giving you headaches? Does protecting security on the Web take up all of your time? Then this is the book for you. With hands-on configuration training, advanced study of the new protocols in IIS, and detailed instructions on authenticating users with the new Certificate Server and implementing and managing the new e-commerce features, *Internet Information Server Administration* gives you the real-life solutions you need. This definitive resource also prepares you for the release of Windows 2000 by giving you detailed advice on working with Microsoft Management Console, which was first used by IIS.

SMS Administration

By Wayne Koop and Brian Steck

1st Edition Fall 1999
350 pages, $29.99
ISBN: 0-7357-0082-6

Microsoft's new version of its Systems Management Server (SMS) is starting to turn heads. While complex, it's allowing administrators to lower their total cost of ownership and more efficiently manage clients, applications and support operations. So if your organization is using or implementing SMS, you'll need some expert advice. Wayne Koop and Brian Steck can help you get the most bang for your buck, with insight, expert tips, and real-world examples. Brian and Wayne are consultants specializing in SMS, having worked with Microsoft on one of the most complex SMS rollouts in the world, involving 32 countries, 15 languages, and thousands of clients.

Unix/Linux Titles

Solaris Essential Reference

By John P. Mulligan

1st Edition
350 pages, $24.95
ISBN: 0-7357-0023-0

Looking for the fastest, easiest way to find the Solaris command you need? Need a few pointers on shell scripting? How about advanced administration tips and sound, practical expertise on security issues? Are you looking for trustworthy information about available third-party software packages that will enhance your operating system? Author John Mulligan—creator of the popular Unofficial Guide to Solaris Web site (sun.icsnet.com)—delivers all that and more in one attractive, easy-to-use reference book. With clear and concise instructions on how to perform important administration and management tasks and key information on powerful commands and advanced topics, *Solaris Essential Reference* is the reference you need when you know what you want to do and you just need to know how.

Linux System Administration

By M Carling and James T. Dennis

1st Edition Summer 1999
450 pages, $29.99
ISBN: 1-56205-934-3

As an administrator, you probably feel that most of your time and energy is spent in endless firefighting. If your network has become a fragile quilt of temporary patches and workarounds, then this book is for you. For example, have you had trouble sending or receiving your email lately? Are you looking for a way to keep your network running smoothly with enhanced performance? Are your users always hankering for more storage, more services, and more speed? *Linux System Administration* advises you on the many intricacies of maintaining a secure, stable system. In this definitive work, the author addresses all the issues related to system administration, from adding users and managing files permission to Internet services and Web hosting to recovery planning and security. This book fulfills the need for expert advice that will ensure a trouble-free Linux environment.

Linux Enterprise Security

By John S. Flowers

1st Edition Fall 1999
400 pages, $39.99
ISBN: 0-7357-0035-4

New Riders is proud to offer the first book aimed specifically at Linux security issues. While there are a host of general UNIX security books, we thought it was time to address the practical needs of the Linux network. In this definitive work, author John Flowers takes a balanced approach to system security, from discussing topics like planning a secure environment to firewalls to utilizing security scripts. With comprehensive information on specific system compromises, and advice on how to prevent and repair them, this is one book that every Linux administrator should have on the shelf.

Developing Linux Applications

By Eric Harlow

1st Edition
400 pages, $34.99
ISBN: 0-7357-0021-4

We all know that Linux is one of the most powerful and solid operating systems in existence. And as the success of Linux grows, there is an increasing interest in developing applications with graphical user interfaces that really take advantage of the power of Linux. In this book, software developer Eric Harlow gives you an indispensable development handbook focusing on the GTK+ toolkit. More than an overview on the elements of application or GUI design, this is a hands-on book that delves deeply into the technology. With in-depth material on the various GUI programming tools and loads of examples, this book's unique focus will give you the information you need to design and launch professional-quality applications.

Linux Firewalls
By Robert Ziegler

Fall 1999
400 pages, $29.99
ISBN: 0-7357-0900-9

New Riders is proud to offer the first book aimed specifically at Linux security issues. While there are a host of general UNIX security books, we think it is time to address the practical needs of the Linux network. Author Robert Ziegler takes a balanced approach to system security, discussing topics like planning a secure environment, firewalls, and utilizing securtiy scripts. With comprehensive information on specific system compromises, and advice on how to prevent and repair them, this is one book that every Linux administrator should have on their shelf.

Development Titles

GTK+/Gnome Development
By Havoc Pennington

Summer 1999
400 pages, $29.99
ISBN: 0-7357-0078-8

GTK+ /Gnome Develpment provides the experienced programmer the knowledge to develop X Window applications with the powerful GTK+ toolkit. The author provides the reader with a checklist of features every application should have, advanced GUI techniques, and the ability to create custom widgets. The title also contains reference information for more experienced users already familiar with usage, but require knowledge of function prototypes and detailed descriptions. These tools let the reader write powerful applications in record time.

Python Essential Reference
By David Beazley
Fall 1999
270 pages, $19.99
ISBN: 0-7357-0901-7

This book describes the Python programming language and its library of standard modules. Python is an informal language that has become a highly valuable software development tool for many computing professionals. This language reference covers Python's lexical conventions, built-in datatypes, control flow, functions, statements, classes, and execution model. This book also covers the contents of the Python library as bundled in the standard Python distribution.

Lotus Notes and Domino Titles

Domino System Administration

By Rob Kirkland
1st Edition Fall 1999
500 pages, $29.99
ISBN: 1-56205-948-3

Your boss has just announced that you will be upgrading to the newest version of Notes and Domino when it ships. As a Premium Lotus Business Partner, Lotus has offered a substantial price break to keep your company away from Microsoft's Exchange Server. How are you supposed to get this new system installed, configured, and rolled out to all of your end users? You understand how Lotus Notes works—you've been administering it for years. What you need is a concise, practical explanation about the new features, and how to make some of the advanced stuff really work. You need answers and solutions from someone like you, who has worked with the product for years, and understands what it is you need to know. *Domino System Administration* is the answer—the first book on Domino that attacks the technology at the professional level, with practical, hands-on assistance to get Domino running in your organization.

Lotus Notes and Domino Essential Reference

By Dave Hatter & Tim Bankes
1st Edition
700 pages, $45.00
ISBN: 0-7357-0007-9

You're in a bind because you've been asked to design and program a new database in Notes for an important client that will keep track of and itemize a myriad of inventory and shipping data. The client wants a user-friendly interface, without sacrificing speed or functionality. You are experienced (and could develop this app in your sleep), but feel that you need to take your talents to the next level. You need something to facilitate your creative and technical abilities, something to perfect your programming skills. Your answer is waiting for you: *Lotus Notes and Domino Essential Reference*. It's compact and simply designed. It's loaded with information. All of the objects, classes, functions, and methods are listed. It shows you the object hierarchy and the overlaying relationship between each one. It's perfect for you. Problem solved.

Networking Titles

Cisco Router Configuration and Troubleshooting

By Mark Tripod
1st Edition
300 pages, $34.99
ISBN: 0-7357-0024-9

Want the real story on making your Cisco routers run like a dream? Why not pick up a copy of *Cisco Router Configuration and Troubleshooting* and see what Mark Tripod has to say? His company is the one responsible for making some of the largest sites on the Net scream, like Amazon.com, Hotmail, USAToday, Geocities, and Sony. In this book, he provides advanced configuration issues, sprinkled with advice and preferred practices. You won't see a general overview on TCP/IP—we talk about more meaty issues like security, monitoring, traffic management, and more. In the troubleshooting section, Mark provides a unique methodology and lots of sample problems to illustrate. By providing real-world insight and examples instead of rehashing Cisco's documentation, Mark gives network administrators information they can start using today.

Implementing Virtual Private Networks

By Tina Bird and Ted Stockwell
1st Edition Fall 1999
300 pages, $32.99
ISBN: 0-7357-0047-8

Tired of looking for decent, practical, up-to-date information on virtual private networks? *Implementing Virtual Private Networks*, by noted authorities Dr. Tina Bird and Ted Stockwell, finally gives you what you need—an authoritative guide on the design, implementation, and main-tenance of Internet-based access to private networks. This book focuses on real-world solutions, demonstrating how the choice of VPN architecture should align with an organization's business and technological requirements. Tina and Ted give you the information you need to determine whether a VPN is right for your organiza-tion, select the VPN that suits your needs, and design and implement the VPN you have chosen.

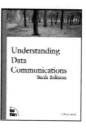

Understanding Data Communications, Sixth Edition

By Gilbert Held
6th Edition Summer 1999
550 pages, $34.99
ISBN: 0-7357-0036-2

Updated from the highly successful fifth edition, this book explains how data communications systems and their various hardware and software components work. Not an entry-level book, it approaches the material in a textbook format, addressing the complex issues involved in internetworking today. A great reference book for the experienced networking professional, written by noted networking authority, Gilbert Held.

We Want to Know What You Think

New Riders

To better serve you, we would like your opinion on the content and quality of this book. Please complete this card and mail it to us or fax it to 317-581-4663.

Name_____

Address _____

City _____State _____Zip _____

Phone _____

Email Address _____

Occupation _____

Operating System(s) that you use _____

What influenced your purchase of this book?

❑ Recommendation ❑ Cover Design
❑ Table of Contents ❑ Index
❑ Magazine Review ❑ Advertisement
❑ New Riders' Reputation ❑ Author Name

How would you rate the contents of this book?

❑ Excellent ❑ Very Good
❑ Good ❑ Fair
❑ Below Average ❑ Poor

How do you plan to use this book?

❑ Quick reference ❑ Self-training
❑ Classroom ❑ Other

What do you like most about this book?
Check all that apply.

❑ Content ❑ Writing Style
❑ Accuracy ❑ Examples
❑ Listings ❑ Design
❑ Index ❑ Page Count
❑ Price ❑ Illustrations

What do you like least about this book?
Check all that apply.

❑ Content ❑ Writing Style
❑ Accuracy ❑ Examples
❑ Listings ❑ Design
❑ Index ❑ Page Count
❑ Price ❑ Illustrations

What would be a useful follow-up book to this one for you? _____

Where did you purchase this book? _____

_____

Can you name a similar book that you like better than this one, or one that is as good? Why?

_____

_____

How many New Riders books do you own? _____

What are your favorite computer books? _____

_____

What other titles would you like to see us develop? _____

_____

Any comments for us? _____

_____

_____

_____

LotusNotes & Domino Essential Reference, 0-7357-0007-9

Fold here and tape to mail

Place
Stamp
Here

New Riders Publishing
201 W. 103rd St.
Indianapolis, IN 46290

New Riders | How to Contact Us

Visit Our Web Site

www.newriders.com

On our Web site, you'll find information about our other books, authors, tables of contents, indexes, and book errata. You can also place orders for books through our Web site.

Email Us

Contact us at this address:
newriders@mcp.com

- If you have comments or questions about this book
- To report errors that you have found in this book
- If you have a book proposal to submit or are interested in writing for New Riders
- If you would like to have an author kit sent to you
- If you are an expert in a computer topic or technology and are interested in being a technical editor who reviews manuscripts for technical accuracy

newriders-sales@mcp.com

- To find a distributor in your area, please contact our international department at the address above.

newriders-pr@mcp.com

- For instructors from educational institutions who wish to preview New Riders books for classroom use. Email should include your name, title, school, department, address, phone number, office days/hours, text in use, and enrollment in the body of your text along with your request for desk/examination copies and/or additional information.

Write to Us

New Riders Publishing
201 W. 103rd St.
Indianapolis, IN 46290-1097

Call Us

Toll-free (800) 571-5840 + 9 + 7494
If outside U.S. (317) 581-3500. Ask for New Riders.

Fax Us

(317) 581-4663